동아출판이 만든 진짜 기출예상문제집

특급기출

중간고사

중학 영어 **3-2**

How to Study

이 책의 구성과 특징

STEP A 영역별로 교과서 핵심 내용을 학습하고, 연습 문제로 실력을 다집니다. 실전 TEST로 학교 시험에 대비합니다.

Words 만점 노트
교과서 흐름대로 핵심 어휘와 표현을 학습합니다.
Words Plus 만점 노트
대표 어휘의 영영풀이 및 다의어, 반의어 등을
학습하며 어휘를 완벽히 이해합니다.

Words 연습 문제 &
Words Plus 연습 문제
다양한 유형의 연습 문제를 통해 어휘 실력을
다집니다.

Words 실전 TEST
학교 시험 유형의 어휘 문제를 풀며
실전에 대비합니다.

Listen and Talk 핵심 노트
교과서 속 핵심 의사소통 기능을
학습하고, 시험 포인트를 확인합니다.
Listen and Talk 만점 노트
교과서 속 모든 대화문의 심층 분석을
통해 대화문을 철저히 학습합니다.

Listen and Talk 연습 문제
빈칸 채우기와 대화 순서 배열하기를
통해 교과서 속 모든 대화문을 완벽히
이해합니다.

Listen and Talk 실전 TEST
학교 시험 유형의 Listen and Talk 문제를
풀며 실전에 대비합니다. 서술형 실전 문항으로
서술형 문제까지 대비합니다.

Grammar 핵심 노트
교과서 속 핵심 문법을 명쾌한 설명과
시험 포인트로 이해하고, Quick Check로
명확히 이해했는지 점검합니다.

Grammar 연습 문제
핵심 문법별로 연습 문제를 풀며
문법의 기본을 다집니다.

Grammar 실전 TEST
학교 시험 유형의 문법 문제를 풀며
실전에 대비합니다. 서술형 실전 문항으로
서술형 문제까지 대비합니다.

Reading 만점 노트
교과서 속 읽기 지문을
심층 분석하여 시험에
나올 내용을 완벽히
이해하도록 합니다.

Reading 연습 문제
빈칸 채우기, 바른 어휘·어법 고르기, 틀린 문장
고치기, 배열로 문장 완성하기 등 다양한 형태의
연습 문제를 풀며 읽기 지문을 완벽히 이해하고,
시험에 나올 내용에 완벽히 대비합니다.

Reading 실전 TEST
학교 시험 유형의 읽기 문제를
풀며 실전에 대비합니다. 서술형
실전 문항으로 서술형 문제까지
대비합니다.

기타 지문 만점 노트 &
기타 지문 실전 TEST
학교 시험에 나올 만한 각 영역의
기타 지문들까지 학습하고 실전
문항까지 풀어 보면 빈틈없는 내신
대비가 가능합니다.

STEP B 내신 만점을 위한 고득점 TEST 구간으로, 다양한 유형과 난이도의 학교 시험에 완벽히 대비합니다.

고득점을 위한 연습 문제
● Listen and Talk 영작하기
● Reading 영작하기

영작 완성 연습 문제를 통해, 대화문과
읽기 지문을 완벽히 이해하면서 암기합니다.

고득점 맞기 TEST
● Words 고득점 맞기   ● Listen and Talk 고득점 맞기
● Grammar 고득점 맞기   ● Reading 고득점 맞기

고난도 문제를 각 영역별로 풀며 실전에 대비합니다.
수준 높은 서술형 실전 문항으로 서·논술형 문제까지
영역별로 완벽 대비합니다.

서술형 100% TEST
다양한 유형의 서술형 문제를
통해 학교 시험에서 비중이
확대되고 있는 서술형 평가에
철저히 대비합니다.

내신 적중 모의고사 학교 시험과 유사한 모의고사로 실전 감각을 기르며, 내신에 최종적으로 대비합니다.

[1~3회] 대표 기출로 내신 적중 모의고사
학교 시험에 자주 출제되는 대표적인 기출 유형의
모의고사를 풀며 실전에 최종적으로 대비합니다.

[4회] 고난도로 내신 적중 모의고사
학교 시험에서 변별력을 높이기 위해 출제되는
고난도 문제 유형의 모의고사를 풀며 실전에
최종적으로 대비합니다.

오답 공략
모의고사에서 틀린 문제를 표시한 후, 부족한
영역과 학습 내용을 점검하여 내신 대비를
완벽히 마무리합니다.

Contents 차례

Lesson 05 The Team Behind the Team

STEP A

Words 만점 노트 ~ 실전 TEST 8

Listen and Talk 핵심 노트 ~ 실전 TEST 13

Grammar 핵심 노트 ~ 실전 TEST 22

Reading 만점 노트 ~ 실전 TEST 30

기타 지문 만점 노트 ~ 실전 TEST 44

STEP B

Words 고득점 맞기 46

Listen and Talk 영작하기 ~ 고득점 맞기 48

Grammar 고득점 맞기 52

Reading 영작하기 ~ 고득점 맞기 55

서술형 100% TEST 60

내신 적중 모의고사

제1회 대표 기출로 내신 적중 모의고사 64

제2회 대표 기출로 내신 적중 모의고사 68

제3회 대표 기출로 내신 적중 모의고사 72

제4회 고난도로 내신 적중 모의고사 76

Lesson 06 Stories for All Time

STEP A

Words 만점 노트 ~ 실전 TEST 82

Listen and Talk 핵심 노트 ~ 실전 TEST 87

Grammar 핵심 노트 ~ 실전 TEST 96

Reading 만점 노트 ~ 실전 TEST 104

기타 지문 만점 노트 ~ 실전 TEST 120

STEP B

Words 고득점 맞기 122

Listen and Talk 영작하기 ~ 고득점 맞기 124

Grammar 고득점 맞기 128

Reading 영작하기 ~ 고득점 맞기 131

서술형 100% TEST 136

내신 적중 모의고사	제1회 대표 기출로 내신 적중 모의고사	140
	제2회 대표 기출로 내신 적중 모의고사	144
	제3회 대표 기출로 내신 적중 모의고사	148
	제4회 고난도로 내신 적중 모의고사	152

Lesson 07 Technology in Our Lives

STEP A	Words 만점 노트 ~ 실전 TEST	158
	Listen and Talk 핵심 노트 ~ 실전 TEST	163
	Grammar 핵심 노트 ~ 실전 TEST	172
	Reading 만점 노트 ~ 실전 TEST	180
	기타 지문 만점 노트 ~ 실전 TEST	194
STEP B	Words 고득점 맞기	196
	Listen and Talk 영작하기 ~ 고득점 맞기	198
	Grammar 고득점 맞기	202
	Reading 영작하기 ~ 고득점 맞기	205
	서술형 100% TEST	210
내신 적중 모의고사	제1회 대표 기출로 내신 적중 모의고사	214
	제2회 대표 기출로 내신 적중 모의고사	218
	제3회 대표 기출로 내신 적중 모의고사	222
	제4회 고난도로 내신 적중 모의고사	226

정답 및 해설

If you can dream it, you can do it.

- Walt Disney -

Lesson 5

The Team Behind the Team

Let's Go!

Victory Is Ours

Way to Go!

주요 학습 내용			
의사소통 기능	빈도 묻고 말하기	**A:** How often do you exercise? (너는 얼마나 자주 운동을 하니?) **B:** I exercise once a week. (나는 일주일에 한 번 운동을 해.)	
	제안이나 권유하기	I suggest you exercise more often. (네가 더 자주 운동할 것을 제안해.)	
언어 형식	현재분사	Pacers usually have flags or balloons **showing** their finish time. (페이서들은 보통 자신들의 완주 시간을 나타내는 깃발이나 풍선을 가지고 있다.)	
	as ~ as	They are **as** important **as** the players. (그들은 선수들만큼 중요하다.)	

학습 단계 PREVIEW

STEP A	Words	Listen and Talk	Grammar	Reading	기타 지문
STEP B	Words	Listen and Talk	Grammar	Reading	서술형 100% Test
내신 적중 모의고사	제 1 회	제 2 회	제 3 회	제 4 회	

Words

만점 노트

Listen and Talk

* 완벽히 외운 단어는 □ 안에 √표 해 봅시다.

□□ join	통 가입하다, 함께하다	□□ suggest☆	통 제안하다, 추천하다
□□ light	형 가벼운	□□ twice☆	부 두 번
□□ limit	명 제한, 한도	□□ weekday	명 평일 (cf. weekend 주말)
□□ often☆	부 자주; 흔히, 보통	□□ do stretching exercises	스트레칭을 하다
□□ once☆	부 한 번; (과거) 언젠가	□□ sign up	(강좌에) 등록하다
□□ register	통 등록하다	□□ take lessons	수업을 받다, 강습을 받다

Reading

□□ achieve	통 달성하다, 성취하다	□□ perfect	형 완벽한
□□ attention☆	명 주목, 관심	□□ pit	명 (자동차 경주의) 피트
□□ breathe	통 숨 쉬다 (명 breath)	□□ race	명 경주, 달리기 (시합)
□□ crew	명 (함께 일하는) 팀, 조	□□ several	형 몇몇의
□□ eastern	형 동쪽의	□□ support☆	통 지원하다; 지지하다
□□ especially	부 특히	□□ target	명 목표, 목표로 하는 대상
□□ experienced	형 경험이 풍부한, 능숙한	□□ therefore	부 그러므로
□□ flag	명 기, 깃발	□□ tribe	명 종족, 부족
□□ harmony	명 조화, 화합	□□ trophy	명 트로피
□□ hide	통 숨기다, 감추다 (-hid-hidden)	□□ depending on	~에 따라
□□ hidden☆	형 숨겨진	□□ in short	요컨대, 요약하면
□□ hire	통 고용하다	□□ keep track of☆	(계속해서) ~을 파악하다
□□ invisible☆	형 보이지 않는, 볼 수 없는 (↔ visible)	□□ lead *A* to *B*	A를 B로 이끌다
□□ pacer	명 페이서, 보조를 맞춰 걷는 사람	□□ on one's own☆	혼자서, 혼자 힘으로
□□ particular	형 특정한	□□ wear out☆	(낡아서) 닳다, 해지다

Language in Use

□□ direct	형 직접적인 (↔ indirect)	□□ possible	형 가능한 (↔ impossible)
□□ formal	형 격식을 차린 (↔ informal)	□□ stool	명 (팔걸이 · 등받이 없는) 의자
□□ patient	형 참을성 있는 (↔ impatient)	□□ suit	명 정장
□□ polite	형 정중한 (↔ impolite)	□□ give a speech	연설하다

Think and Write & Team Project

□□ cheer	통 응원하다, 힘을 북돋우다	□□ spirit	명 정신
□□ fit	형 건강한	□□ most of all	무엇보다도
□□ recommend	통 추천하다 (명 recommendation)	□□ play a role	역할을 맡다, 한몫을 하다

Review

| □□ allow | 통 허락하다 | □□ hold | 통 잡고 있다, 들고 있다 (-held-held) |

Words

연습 문제

A 다음 단어의 우리말 뜻을 쓰시오.

01 suggest

02 invisible

03 eastern

04 hire

05 achieve

06 attention

07 formal

08 breathe

09 several

10 crew

11 support

12 polite

13 pacer

14 allow

15 particular

16 therefore

17 tribe

18 experienced

19 especially

20 hide

B 다음 우리말 뜻에 알맞은 영어 단어를 쓰시오.

01 두 번

02 평일

03 직접적인

04 기, 깃발

05 가능한

06 조화, 화합

07 한 번; (과거) 언젠가

08 완벽한

09 참을성 있는

10 응원하다, 힘을 북돋우다

11 등록하다

12 경주, 달리기 (시합)

13 목표(로 하는 대상)

14 (자동차 경주의) 피트

15 정신

16 제한, 한도

17 트로피

18 가입하다, 함께하다

19 추천하다

20 숨겨진

C 다음 영어 표현의 우리말 뜻을 쓰시오.

01 in short

02 sign up

03 wear out

04 on one's own

05 keep track of

06 give a speech

07 take lessons

08 most of all

09 play a role

10 depending on

D 다음 우리말 뜻에 알맞은 영어 표현을 쓰시오.

01 (낡아서) 닳다, 해지다

02 무엇보다도

03 A를 B로 이끌다

04 ~에 따라

05 스트레칭을 하다

06 요컨대, 요약하면

07 혼자서, 혼자 힘으로

08 (강좌에) 등록하다

09 연설하다

10 (계속해서) ~을 파악하다

Words Plus
만점 노트

영영풀이

☐☐ achieve	달성하다, 성취하다	to succeed in doing or getting something you want
☐☐ attention	주목, 관심	the act of watching or listening to something carefully
☐☐ breathe	숨 쉬다	to take air into your body and let it out again
☐☐ crew	(함께 일하는) 팀, 조	a group of people with particular skills who work together
☐☐ hide	숨기다	to put something in a place where no one can see it
☐☐ hire	고용하다	to employ or pay someone to do a particular job
☐☐ invisible	(눈에) 보이지 않는, 볼 수 없는	not able to be seen
☐☐ pacer	페이서, 보조를 맞춰 걷는 사람	a runner who sets the pace for others in a race
☐☐ particular	특정한	relating to a specific person, thing, or place
☐☐ pit	(자동차 경주의) 피트	the area beside a race track where cars are repaired or get more gas during a race
☐☐ register	등록하다	to put someone's or something's name on an official list
☐☐ several	몇몇의	some, but not many
☐☐ support	돕다, 지원하다	to help someone, often when they are having problems
☐☐ target	목표	the aim or result that you try to achieve
☐☐ tribe	종족, 부족	a group of people who have their own language and ways of living
☐☐ trophy	트로피	a metal cup or other object that someone gets for winning a game or race
☐☐ depending on	~에 따라	determined by conditions or circumstances that follow
☐☐ keep track of	(계속해서) ~을 파악하다	to pay attention to someone or something so that you know where they are or what is happening to them
☐☐ on one's own	혼자서, 혼자 힘으로	for oneself or by oneself

단어의 의미 관계

● 유의어
  particular (특정한) = specific
  target (목표) = goal

● 반의어
  direct (직접적인) ↔ indirect (간접적인)
  patient (참을성 있는) ↔ impatient (못 견디는)
  polite (정중한) ↔ impolite (무례한)
  visible ((눈에) 보이는) ↔ invisible (보이지 않는)

● 동사 – 명사
  breathe (숨 쉬다) – breath (입김, 숨)
  recommend (추천하다) – recommendation (추천)
  register (등록하다) – registration (등록)
  suggest (제안(추천)하다) – suggestion (제안, 추천)

다의어

● target 1. 몡 목표 2. 몡 과녁
  1. You have to set your **target** first. (너는 먼저 목표를 설정해야 해.)
  2. The player missed the **target**. (그 선수는 과녁을 못 맞혔다.)

● support 1. 동 지원하다; 지지하다 2. 몡 지원; 지지
  1. They **support** marathon runners.
     (그들은 마라톤 선수들을 돕는다.)
  2. He asked us for **support**. (그는 우리에게 지원을 요청했다.)

● once 1. 뷔 한 번 2. 뷔 (과거) 언젠가, 한때
        3. 젭 ~하자마자, 일단 ~하면
  1. We eat out **once** a week. (우리는 일주일에 한 번 외식한다.)
  2. Did you know that Dan was **once** a police officer?
     (Dan이 한때 경찰이었던 것 알았니?)
  3. **Once** you get there, you'll love it.
     (그곳에 도착하자마자 너는 그곳을 좋아하게 될 거야.)

Words Plus

연습 문제

A 다음 영영풀이에 해당하는 단어를 [보기]에서 찾아 쓴 후, 우리말 뜻을 쓰시오.

[보기]	tribe	several	hire	breathe	target	support	invisible	particular

1 _____ : not able to be seen : _____

2 _____ : some, but not many : _____

3 _____ : the aim or result that you try to achieve : _____

4 _____ : relating to a specific person, thing, or place : _____

5 _____ : to take air into your body and let it out again : _____

6 _____ : to employ or pay someone to do a particular job : _____

7 _____ : to help someone, often when they are having problems : _____

8 _____ : a group of people who have their own language and ways of living : _____

B 다음 빈칸에 알맞은 단어를 [보기]에서 찾아 쓰시오.

[보기]	hide	attention	register	harmony	suggest

1 I'd like to _____ for a cooking class.

2 He pretended to be sick to get _____.

3 The dog was digging a hole to _____ a bone.

4 The students worked together in perfect _____.

5 Ms. Kim _____(e)d that we should read books every day.

C 우리말과 의미가 같도록 빈칸에 알맞은 말을 쓰시오.

1 내 장화가 닳기 시작하고 있다. → My boots are beginning to _____ _____.

2 할아버지께서 그 집을 혼자 힘으로 지으셨다. → Grandpa built the house _____ _____ _____.

3 그녀는 요가 수업에 등록하기로 결정했다. → She has decided to _____ _____ for a yoga class.

4 요리 시간은 오븐에 따라 약간 달라질 수 있다.

→ Cooking time may vary slightly, _____ _____ your oven.

5 요컨대, 대다수의 학생들이 자신들이 돈에 관해 현명하지 않다고 생각한다.

→ _____ _____, the majority of students think they are not smart with their money.

D 다음 짝지어진 두 단어의 관계가 같도록 빈칸에 알맞은 단어를 쓰시오.

1 target : goal = specific : _____

2 direct : indirect = polite : _____

3 patient : impatient = visible : _____

4 suggest : suggestion = _____ : registration

5 recommend : recommendation = _____ : breath

실전 TEST

01 다음 짝지어진 두 단어의 관계가 나머지와 <u>다른</u> 하나는?

① true – false ② visible – invisible

③ polite – impolite ④ particular – specific

⑤ patient – impatient

[02~03] 짝지어진 두 단어의 관계가 같도록 빈칸에 알맞은 단어를 쓰시오.

02
suggest : suggestion = breathe : _____

03
one : once = two : _____

04 다음 중 단어의 영영풀이가 알맞지 <u>않은</u> 것은?

① **hire**: to employ or pay someone to do a particular job

② **target**: the aim or result that you try to achieve

③ **attention**: the act of watching or listening to something carefully

④ **register**: to help someone, often when they are having problems

⑤ **crew**: a group of people with particular skills who work together

05 다음 문장의 밑줄 친 부분과 바꿔 쓸 수 있는 것은?

Angela solved the problem <u>on her own</u>.

① easily ② by herself

③ together ④ one by one

⑤ on the spot

06 다음 빈칸에 들어갈 말이 순서대로 바르게 짝지어진 것은?

• Depending _____ the weather, we may go camping or not.

• _____ short, we're living in a world full of information.

① on – In ② on – For ③ to – In

④ to – On ⑤ in – On

07 다음 빈칸 ⓐ~ⓔ에 들어갈 단어로 알맞지 <u>않은</u> 것은?

• They go to New York ___ⓐ___ a year.

• Are there any ___ⓑ___ guides to help us?

• I always ___ⓒ___ my diary in a secret place.

• The winner of the game will get a ___ⓓ___ or medal.

• She tried hard to ___ⓔ___ her dream of becoming a singer.

① ⓐ: twice ② ⓑ: experienced

③ ⓒ: hire ④ ⓓ: trophy

⑤ ⓔ: achieve

08 주어진 우리말과 의미가 같도록 빈칸에 알맞은 말을 쓰시오.

우리가 매달 돈을 얼마나 쓰는지 파악하는 것은 매우 어렵다.

→ It's very hard to keep _____ _____ how much money we spend every month.

Listen and Talk
핵심 노트

1 빈도 묻고 말하기

A: **How often** do you exercise?

B: I exercise **once a week**.

너는 얼마나 자주 운동을 하니?

나는 일주일에 한 번 운동을 해.

상대방에게 무언가를 얼마나 자주 하는지 물을 때 How often do you ~?라고 말한다. How many times a week do you ~?와 같이 좀 더 구체적으로 물을 수도 있다. 이에 답해 빈도를 말할 때는 「횟수+a day/week/month/year」로 표현한다. 횟수는 「숫자+times」로 나타내는데, 보통 '한 번'은 once로, '두 번'은 twice로 쓴다.

point

시험 포인트

빈도나 횟수를 말하는 대답을 보고 질문을 유추하는 문제가 자주 출제되므로 어떤 일을 얼마나 자주 하는지를 물어보는 표현을 잘 익혀 둔다. 또한 일정표 등 주어진 정보를 보고 빈도나 횟수를 답하는 서술형 문제도 자주 출제되므로 빈도나 횟수를 말하는 다양한 표현을 정확히 사용하여 답할 수 있도록 한다.

· A: How often do you eat out? (너는 얼마나 자주 외식을 하니?)
  B: I eat out twice a month. (나는 한 달에 두 번 외식을 해.)

· A: How often do you practice the piano? (너는 얼마나 자주 피아노 연습을 하니?)
  B: I practice the piano every day. (나는 피아노 연습을 매일 해.)

· A: How often do you go to the movies? (너는 얼마나 자주 영화를 보러 가니?)
  B: Once a month. (한 달에 한 번.)

· A: How many times a week do you play computer games?
    (너는 일주일에 몇 번 컴퓨터 게임을 하니?)
  B: I play three times a week. (일주일에 세 번 해.)

2 제안이나 권유하기

A: **I suggest you exercise** more often.

B: OK. I'll try.

네가 더 자주 운동할 것을 제안해.

알겠어. 해 볼게.

상대방에게 어떤 일을 하도록 제안하거나 권유할 때 「I suggest (that) you (should)+동사원형 ~.」으로 표현한다. 이외에도 「(I think) You should+동사원형 ~.」, 「(I think) You need to+동사원형 ~.」 등으로도 제안하거나 권유하는 말을 할 수 있다.

point

시험 포인트

제안이나 권유의 내용이 무엇인지, 또는 상대방의 문제에 대한 적절한 제안이 무엇인지 답하는 문제가 출제되므로, I suggest 다음에 이어지는 내용을 파악하는 데 주력한다. 또한, I suggest you 다음에 조동사 should가 주로 생략되어 동사원형이 쓰이는 것에 유의한다.

· A: I suggest you get up at a regular time. (네가 규칙적인 시간에 일어나기를 권해.)
  B: OK. I'll try. (알겠어. 해 볼게.)

· A: I suggest that you visit one of the museums there.
    (네가 그곳에서 박물관 중 한 곳을 방문하기를 제안해.)
  B: That sounds good. (좋아.)

· A: I think you should go see a doctor. (너는 진찰을 받아야 할 것 같아.)
  B: OK, I will. (알겠어, 그럴게.)

· A: I suggest we go on a vacation. (우리가 휴가를 가는 것을 제안해.)
  B: That's a good idea. (좋은 생각이야.)

만점 노트

STEP A

Listen and Talk A-1

교과서 84쪽

B: ❶How often do you play basketball?

G: ❷I play once a week, but I want to play ❸more often.

B: ❹I suggest you join my basketball club. We play ❺three times a week.

G: That sounds good! It'll be fun to play with you.

❶ How often do you ~?는 상대방이 어떤 일을 얼마나 자주 하는지 빈도를 묻는 표현이다.

❷ once는 '한 번'이라는 뜻의 횟수를 나타내는 표현이며, 빈도는 주로 「횟수+a day/week/month/year」로 나타낸다.

❸ 더 자주

❹ 상대방에게 어떤 일을 제안하거나 권유할 때 「I suggest (that) you (should)+동사원형 ~.」으로 표현한다.

❺ 횟수는 「숫자+times」로 나타낸다.

Q1 소년의 농구 동아리에서는 얼마나 자주 농구를 하나요? ( )

ⓐ 일주일에 한 번 ⓑ 일주일에 세 번

Listen and Talk A-2

교과서 84쪽

B: I don't swim often. ❶How about you, Kate? How often do you swim?

G: I swim four times a week.

B: ❷That often? ❸Anyway, it'll be fun swimming together today.

G: Yes, but before we swim, ❹I suggest we do stretching exercises.

B: That's a good idea.

❶ How about you?는 앞에 언급된 내용에 대해 상대방은 어떤지 물을 때 사용하는 말이다.

❷ 일주일에 네 번 수영을 한다는 말을 듣고 놀라움을 나타내는 말로, 여기서 That은 '그렇게, 그 정도'의 의미로 강조를 나타내는 부사로 쓰였다.

❸ 그런데, 그건 그렇고

❹ '우리 ~하자.'라고 함께 할 일을 제안하는 표현이다.
do stretching exercises: 스트레칭을 하다

Q2 Kate는 수영하기 전에 무엇을 하자고 제안했나요?

Listen and Talk A-3

교과서 84쪽

B: Suji, how often do you ❶take bowling lessons?

G: ❷Twice a week. I'm just a beginner. I heard you're very good.

B: Well, I love bowling. Hmm. Your bowling ball ❸looks heavy for you. I suggest you use a lighter ball.

G: OK. I'll look for a lighter ❹one, then.

❶ take lessons: 수업을 받다, 강습을 받다

❷ 횟수는 「숫자+times」로 나타내는데, 보통 '한 번'은 once, '두 번'은 twice로 나타낸다.

❸ look+형용사: ~해 보이다

❹ 앞에서 언급한 명사의 반복을 피하기 위해 사용하며, 여기서는 ball을 가리킨다.

Q3 How often does Suji take bowling lessons? ( )

ⓐ twice a week ⓑ once a week

Q4 소년이 수지에게 제안한 것은 무엇인가요?

Listen and Talk A-4

교과서 84쪽

B: Mina, how often do you come here ❶to run?

G: ❷Every day.

B: ❸Can I run with you today?

G: Sure, but I suggest you wear running shoes. Your shoes ❹aren't good for running.

❶ 목적의 의미를 나타내는 부사적 용법으로 쓰인 to부정사이다.

❷ every day는 '매일'이라는 뜻이며, '이틀에 한 번'이라고 말할 때는 every other day를 사용한다.

❸ Can I ~?는 상대방에게 허락을 요청하는 표현이다.

❹ be good for: ~에 좋다

Q5 미나는 얼마나 자주 달리기를 하나요?

Listen and Talk C

교과서 85쪽

W: Hello. Welcome to Sports World. May I help you?

B: Yes, ❶I came to register for a swimming class.

W: ❷Is this your first time taking swimming lessons?

B: Yes, it is. ❸I don't know how to swim at all.

W: I see. How often do you want to take classes?

B: I want to take classes twice a week. I'd like to take classes ❹on weekdays and not on weekends.

W: Then, I suggest that you take the Beginner 2 class. This class meets ❺on Tuesdays and Thursdays.

B: That sounds good. I'd like to ❻sign up for that class. ❼How big is the class?

W: ❽The class has a limit of 10 people.

B: That's perfect.

❶ to부정사를 사용하여 스포츠 센터에 온 목적을 말하는 문장이다.

❷ 상대방에게 어떤 것을 처음 해 보는지 묻는 말이다. (one's first time -ing: 처음으로 ~해 보는 것)

❸ 「의문사 how+to부정사」는 '~하는 방법'이라는 의미이고, not ~ at all은 '전혀 ~ 않는'이라는 의미로 부정의 의미를 강조하는 표현이다.

❹ on weekdays: 주중에
on weekends: 주말에, 주말마다

❺ 「on+요일-s」 ~요일마다

❻ sign up: (강좌에) 등록하다 (= register)

❼ 강좌의 규모를 묻는 말이다.

❽ limit는 '한도, 제한'이라는 뜻으로, 수업을 들을 수 있는 제한 인원이 10명이라는 의미이다.

Q6 소년은 무슨 요일에 수영 수업을 듣기로 했나요?

Review - 1

교과서 98쪽

B: Mina, how often do you swim?

G: I swim every day.

B: Can I go swimming with you this afternoon?

G: Sure, but I suggest you bring a swimming cap.
❶Without a swimming cap, ❷you aren't allowed in the pool.

❶ Without은 '~이 없으면, ~ 없이는'이라는 의미로 쓰인 전치사이다.

❷ be not allowed는 '허용되지 않다'라는 의미로, 무언가를 금지할 때 사용하는 표현이다.

Q7 They cannot enter the pool if they don't wear swimming caps.　(T / F)

Review - 2

교과서 98쪽

B: Somi, ❶is your piano practice over?

G: Yes, it is.

B: ❷How often do you practice?

G: I practice twice a week.

❶ be over는 '끝나다'라는 의미이고, practice는 '연습'이라는 의미의 명사로 쓰였다.

❷ 빈도를 묻는 질문으로, 이 문장에서 practice는 '연습하다'라는 의미의 동사로 쓰였다.

Q8 소미는 피아노 연습을 얼마나 자주 하나요?

Review - 3

교과서 98쪽

W: Hello. May I help you?

B: Yes, I came to register for a soccer class.

W: I see. How often do you want to take classes?

B: I want to take classes twice a week. ❶I'd like to take classes on weekends.

W: Then, I suggest that you take the Beginner 1 class. ❷This class meets on Saturdays and Sundays.

B: That sounds good.

❶ '일주일에 두 번 수업을 듣고 싶다'고 말한 뒤 주중이 아니라 '주말에 듣고 싶다'고 덧붙이는 말이다.
on weekends: 주말마다

❷ 소년이 '일주일에 두 번, 주말에 수업을 듣고 싶다'고 했으므로 여자가 토요일과 일요일마다 하는 수업을 추천해 주고 있다. 여기서 meet는 '(집회·수업 등이) 열리다'라는 의미로 쓰였다.

Q9 The boy wants to take soccer classes every weekend.　(T / F)

빈칸 채우기

• 주어진 우리말과 일치하도록 교과서 대화문을 완성하시오.

Listen and Talk A-1

B: _____ _____ _____ _____ play basketball?

G: I play _____ _____ _____, but I want to play more _____.

B: I _____ you _____ my basketball club. We play _____ _____ a week.

G: That sounds good! It'll be fun to play with you.

교과서 84쪽

B: 너는 얼마나 자주 농구를 하니?

G: 일주일에 한 번 하는데 더 자주 하고 싶어.

B: 네가 우리 농구 동아리에 가입할 것을 제안해. 우리는 일주일에 세 번 농구를 해.

G: 좋아! 너와 함께 농구 하면 재미있을 거야.

Listen and Talk A-2

B: I don't swim often. How about you, Kate? _____ _____ do you swim?

G: I swim _____ _____ _____ _____.

B: _____ _____? Anyway, it'll be fun swimming together today.

G: Yes, but before we swim, I _____ we _____ stretching exercises.

B: That's a good idea.

교과서 84쪽

B: 나는 수영을 자주 하지 않아. 너는 어때, Kate? 너는 얼마나 자주 수영을 하니?

G: 나는 일주일에 네 번 수영을 해.

B: 그렇게 자주? 어쨌든, 오늘 함께 수영하면 재미있을 거야.

G: 그래, 그런데 수영하기 전에, 우리가 스트레칭하는 것을 제안해.

B: 좋은 생각이야.

Listen and Talk A-3

B: Suji, how often _____ _____ _____ bowling lessons?

G: _____ _____ _____. I'm just a beginner. I heard you're very good.

B: Well, I love bowling. Hmm. Your bowling ball _____ _____ for you. _____ _____ _____ use a lighter ball.

G: OK. I'll look for a lighter one, then.

교과서 84쪽

B: 수지야, 너는 얼마나 자주 볼링 수업을 받니?

G: 일주일에 두 번. 나는 그냥 초보야. 너는 아주 잘한다고 들었어.

B: 음, 나는 볼링을 정말 좋아해. 흠. 네 볼링 공이 너에게 무거워 보여. 더 가벼운 공을 쓰는 걸 권해.

G: 알았어. 그러면 더 가벼운 공을 찾아 볼게.

Listen and Talk A-4

B: Mina, _____ _____ _____ _____ come here to run?

G: _____ _____.

B: Can I run with you today?

G: Sure, but _____ _____ _____ _____ running shoes. Your shoes aren't good for running.

교과서 84쪽

B: 미나야, 너는 이곳에 달리기를 하러 얼마나 자주 오니?

G: 매일 와.

B: 오늘 너랑 같이 달리기를 해도 될까?

G: 물론이야. 그런데 네가 운동화를 신는 것을 권해. 네 신발은 달리기에 적합하지 않아.

Listen and Talk C

W: Hello. Welcome to Sports World. May I help you?

B: Yes, I came _____ _____ _____ a swimming class.

W: Is this your _____ _____ _____ swimming lessons?

B: Yes, it is. I don't know _____ _____ _____ at all.

W: I see. _____ _____ do you want to take classes?

B: I want to take classes twice a week. I'd like to take classes _____ _____ and not _____ _____.

W: Then, I _____ _____ you take the Beginner 2 class. This class meets _____ Tuesdays and Thursdays.

B: That sounds good. I'd like to _____ _____ for that class. _____ _____ is the class?

W: The class has a _____ of 10 people.

B: That's perfect.

Review - 1

B: Mina, how often do you swim?

G: I swim _____ _____.

B: Can I _____ _____ with you this afternoon?

G: Sure, but I _____ _____ _____ a swimming cap. Without a swimming cap, you aren't _____ in the pool.

Review - 2

B: Somi, is your piano practice _____?

G: Yes, it is.

B: How often _____ _____ _____?

G: I practice _____ _____ _____.

Review - 3

W: Hello. May I help you?

B: Yes, I _____ _____ _____ for a soccer class.

W: I see. How _____ do you want to take classes?

B: I want to take classes _____ a week. I'd like to take classes _____ _____.

W: Then, I _____ _____ you take the Beginner 1 class. This class _____ on Saturdays and Sundays.

B: That sounds good.

 해석

교과서 85쪽

W: 안녕하세요. Sports World에 오신 것을 환영합니다. 도와드릴까요?

B: 네, 저는 수영 수업에 등록하려고 왔어요.

W: 수영 강습을 받는 것이 이번이 처음이세요?

B: 네. 저는 수영하는 법을 전혀 몰라요.

W: 그렇군요. 얼마나 자주 수업을 듣고 싶으세요?

B: 일주일에 두 번 수업을 듣고 싶어요. 주말은 아니고 주중에 수업을 듣고 싶습니다.

W: 그러면, 초급 2반을 수강하기를 권해요. 이 수업은 화요일과 목요일에 있습니다.

B: 좋아요. 그 수업으로 등록할게요. 그 수업은 규모가 얼마나 되나요?

W: 그 수업은 제한 인원이 10명이에요.

B: 딱 좋네요.

교과서 98쪽

B: 미나야, 너는 얼마나 자주 수영을 하니?

G: 나는 매일 수영해.

B: 오늘 오후에 너랑 수영하러 가도 될까?

G: 물론이지. 하지만 수영 모자를 가져올 것을 권해. 수영 모자가 없으면 수영장에 들어갈 수가 없거든.

교과서 98쪽

B: 소미야, 피아노 연습은 끝났니?

G: 응, 끝났어.

B: 너는 얼마나 자주 연습하니?

G: 나는 일주일에 두 번 연습해.

교과서 98쪽

W: 안녕하세요. 도와드릴까요?

B: 네, 저는 축구 수업에 등록하러 왔어요.

W: 그렇군요. 얼마나 자주 수업을 듣고 싶으세요?

B: 일주일에 두 번 듣고 싶어요. 주말에 수업을 듣고 싶습니다.

W: 그러면, 초급 1반 수강을 권합니다. 이 수업은 토요일과 일요일에 있어요.

B: 그거 좋네요.

대화 순서 배열하기

1 Listen and Talk A-1

교과서 84쪽

ⓐ I play once a week, but I want to play more often.
ⓑ That sounds good! It'll be fun to play with you.
ⓒ I suggest you join my basketball club. We play three times a week.
ⓓ How often do you play basketball?

(   ) – (   ) – ⓒ – (   )

2 Listen and Talk A-2

교과서 84쪽

ⓐ Yes, but before we swim, I suggest we do stretching exercises.
ⓑ I swim four times a week.
ⓒ I don't swim often. How about you, Kate? How often do you swim?
ⓓ That's a good idea.
ⓔ That often? Anyway, it'll be fun swimming together today.

(   ) – (   ) – ⓔ – (   ) – (   )

3 Listen and Talk A-3

교과서 84쪽

ⓐ Well, I love bowling. Hmm. Your bowling ball looks heavy for you. I suggest you use a lighter ball.
ⓑ Twice a week. I'm just a beginner. I heard you're very good.
ⓒ OK. I'll look for a lighter one, then.
ⓓ Suji, how often do you take bowling lessons?

ⓓ – (   ) – (   ) – (   )

4 Listen and Talk A-4

교과서 84쪽

ⓐ Can I run with you today?
ⓑ Sure, but I suggest you wear running shoes. Your shoes aren't good for running.
ⓒ Every day.
ⓓ Mina, how often do you come here to run?

(   ) – (   ) – (   ) – ⓑ

5 Listen and Talk C

교과서 85쪽

A: Hello. Welcome to Sports World. May I help you?

ⓐ Then, I suggest that you take the Beginner 2 class. This class meets on Tuesdays and Thursdays.

ⓑ The class has a limit of 10 people.

ⓒ Yes, it is. I don't know how to swim at all.

ⓓ I see. How often do you want to take classes?

ⓔ That sounds good. I'd like to sign up for that class. How big is the class?

ⓕ Yes, I came to register for a swimming class.

ⓖ I want to take classes twice a week. I'd like to take classes on weekdays and not on weekends.

ⓗ Is this your first time taking swimming lessons?

B: That's perfect.

A – (   ) – (   ) – ⓒ – ⓓ – (   ) – (   ) – (   ) – (   ) – B

6 Review - 1

교과서 98쪽

ⓐ I swim every day.

ⓑ Mina, how often do you swim?

ⓒ Sure, but I suggest you bring a swimming cap. Without a swimming cap, you aren't allowed in the pool.

ⓓ Can I go swimming with you this afternoon?

(   ) – (   ) – ⓓ – (   )

7 Review - 2

교과서 98쪽

ⓐ How often do you practice?

ⓑ Yes, it is.

ⓒ Somi, is your piano practice over?

ⓓ I practice twice a week.

ⓒ – (   ) – (   ) – (   )

8 Review - 3

교과서 98쪽

ⓐ I want to take classes twice a week. I'd like to take classes on weekends.

ⓑ That sounds good.

ⓒ I see. How often do you want to take classes?

ⓓ Yes, I came to register for a soccer class.

ⓔ Hello. May I help you?

ⓕ Then, I suggest that you take the Beginner 1 class. This class meets on Saturdays and Sundays.

(   ) – (   ) – ⓒ – (   ) – (   ) – ⓑ

01 다음 대화의 빈칸에 들어갈 말로 알맞은 것은?

> A: _____
> B: I read a book twice a month.
> A: I suggest you read more books.
> B: OK. I'll try.

① What's your favorite book?
② How often do you read books?
③ What kind of books do you like?
④ When do you usually read books?
⑤ What are you going to do next month?

02 다음 대화의 빈칸에 들어갈 말로 알맞지 <u>않은</u> 것은?

> A: How often do you take guitar lessons?
> B: _____

① For an hour.
② Twice a week.
③ Four times a month.
④ I take guitar lessons three times a week.
⑤ Once a week, but I practice hard in my free time.

03 다음 대화의 밑줄 친 문장에 담긴 화자의 의도로 알맞은 것은?

> A: Jiseon, how often do you eat fast food?
> B: I eat fast food three times a week.
> A: <u>I suggest you eat it less.</u>

① 빈도 말하기　　　② 정보 제공하기
③ 계획 말하기　　　④ 도움 요청하기
⑤ 제안하기

04 다음 대화의 밑줄 친 부분과 바꿔 쓸 수 있는 것은?

> A: <u>How often</u> do you come here to run?
> B: Every day.

① How long　　　② What time
③ How much　　　④ What kind
⑤ How many times a week

05 자연스러운 대화가 되도록 (A)~(D)를 바르게 배열한 것은?

> A: I don't swim often. How about you, Kate?
> 　 How often do you swim?
> (A) That's a good idea.
> (B) I swim four times a week.
> (C) That often? Anyway, it'll be fun swimming together today.
> (D) Yes, but before we swim, I suggest we do stretching exercises.

① (A) – (D) – (C) – (B)　　② (B) – (A) – (C) – (D)
③ (B) – (C) – (D) – (A)　　④ (C) – (B) – (A) – (D)
⑤ (D) – (B) – (C) – (A)

06 다음 중 짝지어진 대화가 <u>어색한</u> 것은?

① A: I have a terrible headache.
　 B: I suggest you go see a doctor.
② A: I suggest we join the soccer club.
　 B: Sounds great.
③ A: How often do you clean your room?
　 B: I'll clean it soon.
④ A: I play badminton every day. How about you?
　 B: I don't play it that often.
⑤ A: Let's go on a picnic.
　 B: That sounds great. I suggest we bring our cameras.

[07~09] 다음 대화를 읽고, 물음에 답하시오.

Woman: Hello. Welcome to Sports World. May I help you?

Boy: Yes, I came to register for a swimming class.

Woman: Is this your first time taking swimming lessons?

Boy: Yes, it is. (①) I don't know ____ⓐ____ to swim at all.

Woman: I see. (②) How often do you want to take classes?

Boy: (③) I'd like to take classes on weekdays and not on weekends.

Woman: Then, I suggest that you take the Beginner 2 class. This class meets on Tuesdays and Thursdays. (④)

Boy: That sounds good. (⑤) I'd like to sign up for that class. ____ⓑ____ big is the class?

Woman: The class has a limit of 10 people.

Boy: That's perfect.

07 위 대화의 ①~⑤ 중 주어진 문장이 들어갈 위치로 알맞은 것은?

> I want to take classes twice a week.

①   ②   ③   ④   ⑤

08 위 대화의 빈칸 ⓐ와 ⓑ에 공통으로 들어갈 말로 알맞은 것은?

① why(Why)
② how(How)
③ what(What)
④ when(When)
⑤ where(Where)

09 위 대화의 내용과 일치하지 <u>않는</u> 것은?

① 두 사람은 수영 수업 등록에 대해 이야기하고 있다.
② 소년은 이전에 수영 강습을 받아 본 적이 없다.
③ 소년은 주말에 수업을 듣고 싶어 한다.
④ 초급 2반의 수업은 화요일과 목요일에 있다.
⑤ 초급 2반의 수강 제한 인원은 10명이다.

서술형

10 다음 Andy와 Brian의 운동 일정표를 보고, 대화를 완성하시오.

	Mon.	Tue.	Wed.	Thu.	Fri.	Sat.	Sun.
Andy	√		√		√		
Brian				√			

Andy: I exercise _____. How about you? How often do you exercise?

Brian: _____

Andy: I suggest you exercise more often.

Brian: OK. I'll try.

11 다음 대화의 밑줄 친 우리말과 의미가 같도록 괄호 안의 표현을 바르게 배열하여 문장을 쓰시오.

A: How often do you take bowling lessons?

B: Twice a week. I'm just a beginner. I heard you're very good.

A: Well, I love bowling. Hmm. Your bowling ball looks heavy for you. <u>더 가벼운 공을 쓰는 걸 권해.</u>

B: OK. I'll look for a lighter one, then.

→ _____

(I, lighter, you, suggest, use, a, ball)

12 다음 대화의 밑줄 친 ⓐ~ⓓ 중 흐름상 어색한 것을 찾아 기호를 쓰고, 바르게 고쳐 쓰시오. (단, 한 단어만 바꿀 것)

A: ⓐ<u>How often do you play basketball?</u>

B: I play basketball twice a week, but I want to ⓑ<u>play more often.</u>

A: Then, I suggest you ⓒ<u>join my soccer club.</u> We play four times a week.

B: ⓓ<u>That sounds great!</u> It'll be fun to play basketball with you.

(   ) → _____

Grammar
핵심 노트

1 현재분사

읽기 본문 Pacers usually have flags or balloons **showing** their finish time.

<small>앞의 명사 수식</small>

페이서들은 보통 자신들의 완주 시간을 나타내는 깃발이나 풍선들을 가지고 있다.

대표 예문 The girl **waiting** at the bus stop is my sister.

버스 정류장에서 기다리고 있는 소녀는 내 여동생이다.

The bird **singing** in the tree is very big.

나무에서 노래하고 있는 새는 매우 크다.

There are many students **studying** in the library.

도서관에서 공부하고 있는 학생들이 많다.

The woman **wearing** glasses is my teacher.

안경을 쓰고 있는 여자는 우리 선생님이다.

(1) 형태: 동사원형-ing

(2) 의미와 쓰임: 현재분사는 명사의 앞이나 뒤에서 명사를 수식하는 형용사 역할을 한다.

Look at the **sleeping** child. (자고 있는 아이를 봐.)

I know the man **standing** by the gate. (나는 문 옆에 서 있는 남자를 안다.)

현재분사가 단독으로 명사를 수식할 때는 명사 앞에 쓰이고, 뒤따르는 어구가 있을 때는 명사 뒤에 쓰인다. 현재분사가 명사 뒤에 오는 경우, 명사와 현재분사 사이에 「주격 관계대명사＋be동사」가 생략되었다고 볼 수 있다.

Don't go near the **boiling** water. (끓는 물 근처에 가지 마라.)

Do you know the girl (who(that) is) **talking** with Peter?
(너는 Peter와 이야기하고 있는 여자아이를 아니?)

시험 포인트 ❶ point
현재분사 vs. 동명사
「동사원형-ing」로 형태가 같으므로 현재분사와 동명사를 구분하는 문제가 출제될 수 있다. 따라서 형용사 역할을 하는 현재분사와 명사 역할을 하는 동명사를 구분할 수 있도록 한다.
Wearing a baseball cap is not just for baseball players. ▶ 중 1 교과서 5과

시험 포인트 ❷ point
지각동사＋목적어＋현재분사(-ing)/동사원형
현재분사는 5형식 문장에서 지각동사의 목적격보어로도 쓰인다.
Daedalus saw birds **flying**.
▶ 중 2 교과서 6과

한 단계 더!

- 현재분사는 보어의 역할을 할 수 있으며, 능동·진행의 의미를 나타낸다.

He was **running**. (그는 뛰고 있었다.) 〈주격보어〉

I saw Jane **dancing**. (나는 Jane이 춤추고 있는 것을 보았다.) 〈목적격보어〉

- 수식하는 명사와 분사의 관계가 수동일 때는 과거분사를 쓴다.

There is a **broken** vase on the floor. (바닥에 깨진 꽃병이 있다.)

I received a letter **written** in English. (나는 영어로 쓰여진 편지를 받았다.)

QUICK CHECK

1 다음 괄호 안에서 알맞은 것을 고르시오.

(1) Look at the stars (shone / shining) in the sky.

(2) He lives in a house (built / building) ten years ago.

(3) The boys (danced / dancing) in the room are my brothers.

2 다음 빈칸에 괄호 안의 동사를 알맞은 형태로 쓰시오.

(1) Look at the _____ birds. (fly)

(2) The girl _____ glasses is my classmate. (wear)

(3) A man _____ a large bag got off the bus. (carry)

2 as ~ as ...

읽기 본문 They are **as** important **as** the players.
<u>as+형용사의 원급+as</u>

그들은 선수들만큼 중요하다.

대표 예문 Jason can run **as** fast **as** Mike.
<u>as+부사의 원급+as</u>

Jason은 Mike만큼 빠르게 달릴 수 있다.

I am **as** hungry **as** you.

나는 너만큼 배고프다.

Canada is **as** large **as** the USA.

캐나다는 미국만큼 크다.

Today is **as** windy **as** yesterday.

오늘은 어제만큼 바람이 분다.

(1) 형태: as+형용사/부사의 원급+as

(2) 의미와 쓰임

'…만큼 ~한/하게'라는 뜻으로, 비교하는 두 대상의 정도나 상태가 같음을 나타내는 표현이다.

My bag is **as** heavy **as** yours. (내 가방은 네 가방만큼 무겁다.)

This smartphone is **as** expensive **as** yours.
(이 스마트폰은 네 것만큼 비싸다.)

I don't play tennis **as** often **as** you. (나는 너만큼 테니스를 자주 치지 않는다.)

point
시험 포인트 ❶

as ~ as ...는 정도가 같은 두 대상을 비교하는 것이므로 as와 as 사이에 형용사나 부사의 원급 형태가 바르게 들어가 있는지 확인하는 문제가 주로 출제된다. 문맥에 따라 형용사를 써야 하는지 또는 부사를 써야 하는지 구분하는 문제도 출제되므로, 문맥상 적절한 품사를 쓸 수 있도록 한다.

point
시험 포인트 ❷

not as ~ as ... 구문과 의미가 같은 비교급 문장을 고르는 문제도 자주 출제되므로, 문맥에 맞는 비교급 구문으로 바꾸는 연습을 하도록 한다.
「A ~ not as(so)+형용사/부사의 원급+as B」=「B ~ 비교급+than A」

___한 단계 | 더!

「as+형용사/부사의 원급+as」의 부정형은 「not as(so)+형용사/부사의 원급+as」의 형태로 쓰며 '…만큼 ~하지 않은/않게'라는 뜻을 나타낸다. 이는 「비교급+than」의 구문으로 바꿔 쓸 수 있다.

Jim is **not as(so)** tall **as** Bob. (Jim은 Bob만큼 키가 크지 않다.)
= Bob is taller than Jim. (Bob은 Jim보다 키가 더 크다.)
= Jim is shorter than Bob. (Jim은 Bob보다 키가 더 작다.)

QUICK CHECK

1 다음 괄호 안에서 알맞은 것을 고르시오.

(1) I can't run as fast (as / than) you.

(2) My mom is as (old / older) as my dad.

(3) Jenny speaks French as (well / good) as Andrew.

2 다음 밑줄 친 부분을 어법에 맞게 고쳐 쓰시오.

(1) Rita was as <u>busiest</u> as Lucy. → _____

(2) The book is as old <u>than</u> the CD. → _____

(3) This city is <u>as large not</u> as Seoul. → _____

1 현재분사

STEP A

A 다음 밑줄 친 부분을 어법에 맞게 고쳐 쓰시오.

1 The cry boy was looking for his father. → _____

2 There were many students studied in the library. → _____

3 The man work in the garden is my grandfather. → _____

4 The students talking to Mr. Kim is from Canada. → _____

5 The shoes making in this factory are very expensive. → _____

B 다음 빈칸에 알맞은 말을 [보기]에서 골라 어법에 맞게 쓰시오. (단, 중복 사용 불가)

[보기]	play	show	drive	cover

1 The woman _____ the car is Ms. Baker.

2 The girls _____ badminton are my good friends.

3 They climbed up the mountain _____ with snow.

4 I need a map _____ the nearest bus stops and subway stations.

C 다음 문장의 밑줄 친 부분의 쓰임으로 알맞은 것을 고르시오.

1 My job is teaching English. (현재분사 / 동명사)

2 I saw you holding his hand. (현재분사 / 동명사)

3 They waved at the passing train. (현재분사 / 동명사)

4 We met a girl carrying a basket full of vegetables. (현재분사 / 동명사)

D 주어진 우리말과 의미가 같도록 괄호 안의 표현을 어법에 맞게 사용하여 문장을 쓰시오.

1 떨어지고 있는 잎들을 봐. (look at, the, fall, leaves)
→ _____

2 나는 깨진 안경을 버렸다. (throw away, the, break, glasses)
→ _____

3 Jane이 우리에게 충격적인 이야기를 하나 해 주었다. (tell us, shock, story)
→ _____

4 그 지루한 영화는 나를 졸리게 했다. (bore, movie, make me, sleepy)
→ _____

2 as ~ as ...

A 주어진 두 문장의 내용과 같도록 as ~ as ...와 괄호 안의 단어를 어법에 맞게 사용하여 문장을 완성하시오.

1 Sophia is 160 cm tall. Helen is 160 cm tall, too.

→ Sophia is _____ Helen. (tall)

2 The red bag is $50. The blue bag is $70.

→ The red bag is _____ the blue one. (expensive)

3 Jinsu has lived here for 20 years. Sora has lived here for 20 years, too.

→ Jinsu _____ Sora. (long)

4 Nick gets up at 6 o'clock. Amy gets up at 7 o'clock.

→ Amy _____ Nick. (early)

B 다음 문장에서 어법상 틀린 부분을 찾아 바르게 고쳐 쓰시오.

1 Is this exam as more difficult as the last exam? _____ → _____

2 He drove as careful as his sister. _____ → _____

3 Monkeys are as fast not as tigers. _____ → _____

C 다음 두 문장의 의미가 같도록 빈칸에 알맞은 말을 쓰시오.

1 Today is not as cold as yesterday.

= Yesterday was _____ than today.

2 Minji's brother is more diligent than Minji.

= Minji is _____ as her brother.

3 Yuri didn't work as much as Tom.

= Tom _____ than Yuri.

D 주어진 우리말과 의미가 같도록 as ~ as ...와 괄호 안의 표현을 사용하여 문장을 쓰시오.

1 이 책은 내 노트북만큼 무겁다. (heavy, laptop)

→ _____

2 오늘은 어제만큼 바람이 분다. (today, windy, yesterday)

→ _____

3 배드민턴은 스카이다이빙만큼 위험하지 않다. (badminton, dangerous, skydiving)

→ _____

4 치어리더들은 선수들만큼 열심히 일했다. (the cheerleaders, hard, the players)

→ _____

01 다음 빈칸에 들어갈 **wait**의 형태로 알맞은 것은?

The girl _____ at the bus stop is my sister.

① wait ② waits
③ waiting ④ waited
⑤ is waiting

02 다음 빈칸에 들어갈 **heavy**의 형태로 알맞은 것은?

My suitcase is as _____ as yours.

① heavy ② heavier
③ heaviest ④ more heavy
⑤ most heavy

03 다음 문장의 ①~⑤ 중 **reading**이 들어갈 위치로 알맞은 것은?

The (①) boy (②) a book (③) under the tree (④) is (⑤) Dave.

① ② ③ ④ ⑤

한 단계 더!
04 다음 글의 빈칸에 들어갈 말로 알맞은 것은?

Dan and Ryan are my cousins. Dan is _____ Ryan. Dan is 15 years old, and Ryan is 16 years.

① old as ② as old as
③ as old so ④ not as old as
⑤ not old as

05 다음 문장의 밑줄 친 ①~⑤ 중 생략할 수 있는 것은?

The player ①who is ②running in ③the race ④looks ⑤injured.

① ② ③ ④ ⑤

06 다음 두 문장을 한 문장으로 바꿔 쓸 때, 빈칸에 들어갈 말로 알맞은 것은?

The woman is my homeroom teacher. She is wearing glasses.
→ The woman _____ glasses is my homeroom teacher.

① wears ② worn ③ is worn
④ wearing ⑤ is wearing

한 단계 더!
07 다음 빈칸에 들어갈 말이 순서대로 바르게 짝지어진 것은?

This bridge is not as long as that bridge.
= This bridge is _____ than that one.
= That bridge is _____ than this one.

① shorter – longer ② longer – shorter
③ long – shorter ④ shorter – long
⑤ short – longer

08 다음 중 밑줄 친 부분의 쓰임이 나머지와 다른 하나는?

① Collecting old coins is my hobby.
② Who is the girl wearing a blue cap?
③ The chef cooking over there is my father.
④ Look at the old lady carrying a large bag.
⑤ There are many students eating lunch in the cafeteria.

09 고/난도 한 단계 더! 다음 두 문장의 의미가 같도록 할 때, 빈칸에 들어갈 말로 알맞은 것은?

> Suji is not as good at English as Minho.
> = Minho speaks English _____ than Suji.

① well ② good ③ better
④ worse ⑤ best

10 신유형 다음 문장에서 어법상 **틀린** 부분을 찾아 바르게 고쳐 쓴 것은?

> Staying healthy is as more important as making money.

① Staying → Stay
② is → are
③ as → so
④ more important → important
⑤ making → make

11 고/난도 다음 중 빈칸 ⓐ~ⓔ에 들어갈 말로 알맞은 것은?

- The cat ____ⓐ____ on the sofa is so cute.
- The woman ____ⓑ____ cookies is my aunt.
- Do you know the man ____ⓒ____ on the phone over there?
- Turn down the volume not to wake up the ____ⓓ____ baby.
- Do you know the man ____ⓔ____ sunglasses?

① ⓐ: sit ② ⓑ: is baking
③ ⓒ: talks ④ ⓓ: slept
⑤ ⓔ: who is wearing

12 다음 빈칸에 들어갈 말로 알맞은 것을 <u>모두</u> 고르면?

> Look at the birds _____ in the tree.

① sing ② sung
③ singing ④ are singing
⑤ that are singing

[13~14] 다음 그림의 내용에 맞는 문장을 <u>모두</u> 고르시오.

13

① Tom is as tall as Jane.
② Tom is taller than Jane.
③ Tom is as taller as Jane.
④ Tom is not so tall as Jane.
⑤ Tom is the same height as Jane.

14 한 단계 더!

① The green hat is cheaper than the red one.
② The red hat is as expensive as the green one.
③ The red hat is not as expensive as the green one.
④ The green hat is not so expensive as the red one.
⑤ The green hat is more expensive than the red one.

15 다음 중 어법상 <u>틀린</u> 부분을 바르게 고쳐 쓴 것은?

ⓐ The boy takes pictures is my cousin.
ⓑ The train is as fast not as the airplane.
ⓒ Did you see the girl worn a yellow dress?
ⓓ Did you see the tall man carried a big backpack?
ⓔ I think basketball is not as popular than baseball in Korea.

① ⓐ: takes → taken
② ⓑ: as fast not as → not as fast as
③ ⓒ: worn → wore
④ ⓓ: carried → carries
⑤ ⓔ: than → like

16 다음 대화의 빈칸 ⓐ～ⓔ에 들어갈 말로 알맞지 <u>않은</u> 것은?

A: Who is this girl ____ⓐ____ brightly in the picture?
B: That's my cousin, ____ⓑ____ lives in London.
A: What ____ⓒ____ these boys?
B: They're my brothers. The boy ____ⓓ____ a bat is my younger brother.
A: Oh, he's as ____ⓔ____ as you.

① ⓐ: smiling ② ⓑ: who ③ ⓒ: about
④ ⓓ: holds ⑤ ⓔ: tall

17 다음 우리말을 Is로 시작하는 영어 문장으로 옮겨 쓸 때 5번째로 올 단어로 알맞은 것은?

네 방은 내 방만큼 크니?

① room ② as ③ your
④ mine ⑤ big

18 다음 중 어법상 옳은 문장의 개수는?

ⓐ Do you know the boy sitting on the sofa?
ⓑ There was a breaking bottle on the floor.
ⓒ Yesterday I read a book written in English.
ⓓ Be careful when you fill the jar with boiling water.

① 0개 ② 1개 ③ 2개 ④ 3개 ⑤ 4개

19 다음 표의 내용과 일치하지 <u>않는</u> 것은?

Name	Height	Weight	Age
Eric	174 cm	63 kg	17
Jiho	174 cm	65 kg	15

① Eric is as tall as Jiho.
② Eric is older than Jiho.
③ Eric is as heavy as Jiho.
④ Jiho is not as old as Eric.
⑤ Jiho is not as light as Eric.

20 다음 중 어법상 <u>틀린</u> 문장끼리 짝지어진 것은?

ⓐ He is looking for his missing dog.
ⓑ I had to get up as early so my dad.
ⓒ Baseball is not so exciting as soccer.
ⓓ The boy played the musical instrument is Ted.
ⓔ My sister and I had fried eggs and some milk for breakfast.

① ⓐ, ⓑ ② ⓑ, ⓒ
③ ⓑ, ⓓ ④ ⓒ, ⓓ
⑤ ⓒ, ⓓ, ⓔ

서술형

21 다음 그림을 보고, [예시]와 같이 문장을 완성하시오.

[예시] The girl talking with the teacher is Mina.

(1) _____ is Mike. (water)

(2) _____ is Jiho. (music)

(3) _____ is Lucy. (a book)

22 다음 표의 내용과 일치하도록 괄호 안의 단어를 사용하여 두 물건을 비교하는 문장을 완성하시오.

(1) 크기	35×55 cm	35×55 cm	30×45 cm
(2) 가격	$25	$35	$35
(3) 무게	700 g	950 g	700 g

(1) The blue backpack is _____
the red one. (big)

(2) The red backpack is _____
the black one. (expensive)

(3) The black backpack is _____
the blue one. (heavy)

23 주어진 두 문장을 [조건]에 맞게 한 문장으로 바꿔 쓰시오.

(1) Yuna runs 100 m in 16 seconds. Somin also runs 100 m in 16 seconds.

[조건] 1. Somin을 주어로 쓸 것
2. run, fast를 어법에 맞게 사용할 것

→ _____

(2) The man is my new English teacher. He is taking pictures.

[조건] 1. The man을 주어로 쓸 것
2. 9단어로 쓸 것

→ _____

24 다음 중 어법상 틀린 문장 두 개를 찾아 기호를 쓰고, 틀린 부분을 바르게 고쳐 쓰시오.

ⓐ This river is as longer as the Han River.
ⓑ This phone is as not light as my phone.
ⓒ David called me as often as Amy.
ⓓ My watch is as big as my younger brother's.

(1) ( ) _____ → _____
(2) ( ) _____ → _____

25 다음 우리말과 의미가 같도록 괄호 안의 표현을 어법에 맞게 사용하여 주어진 단어 수에 맞게 문장을 쓰시오.

(1) 꽃에 물을 주고 있는 남자는 나의 아빠다. (8단어)

→ _____

(the man, water the flowers, my dad)

(2) 개를 산책시키는 사람들이 많이 있다. (7단어)

→ _____

(there, many people, walk their dogs)

만점 노트

STEP A

스포츠 분야의 숨은 조력자들

01 스포츠에서는 선수들만 트로피나 메달을 받지만, 그들이 혼자 힘으로 우승하는 것은 아니다.

02 그 선수들을 돕는 사람들이 있다.

03 이 사람들은 종종 숨겨져 있고 주목을 받지 못한다.

04 하지만 그들은 선수들만큼 중요하다.

05 여기 몇 가지 예가 있다.

마라톤의 페이서들

06 페이서들은 마라톤에서 다른 선수들과 함께 달리며 그들을 이끈다.

07 페이서들은 경험이 많은 선수들이며, 그들의 역할은 다른 선수들이 경주를 더 잘 운영하도록 돕는 것이다.

08 한 경주에는 여러 명의 페이서들이 있을 수 있다.

09 각각의 페이서는 다른 속도로 달리고 다른 시간대에 경주를 마친다.

10 페이서들은 보통 자신들의 완주 시간을 나타내는 깃발이나 풍선을 가지고 있다.

11 선수들은 자신들의 목표 완주 시간에 따라 페이서를 선택할 수 있다.

12 예를 들어, 한 선수가 4시간 안에 경주를 마치고 싶다면, 그 선수는 4시간 페이서를 따라갈 것이다.

13 페이서가 시간을 계속해서 파악하기 때문에, 선수는 특정 시간 안에 마라톤을 완주하려는 자신의 목표를 더 쉽게 달성할 수 있다.

14 요컨대, 페이서들은 달리기는 하지만 우승을 하기 위해 달리는 것은 아니다.

15 그들은 다른 이들을 위해 달린다.

Hidden People in Sports

01 In sports, only the players <u>get</u> a trophy or medal, but <u>they</u> don't win
= win   = the players
<u>on their own</u>.
on one's own: 혼자서, 혼자 힘으로 (= by oneself)

02 There are people [who help the players].
~가 있다   선행사   주격 관계대명사   관계대명사절

03 These people are often hidden <u>and</u> don't get attention.
= people who   동사 1   동사 2 (등위 접속사 and로 연결된 병렬 구조)
help the players   수동태

04 However, they are as important as the players.
하지만, 그러나   「as+형용사의 원급+as」 …만큼 ~한

05 Here are some examples.

Pacers in a Marathon

06 Pacers run with other runners <u>and</u> lead them in a marathon.
동사 1   형 (그 밖의) 다른   동사 2   = other runners

07 Pacers are experienced runners, and their job is to help other runners
manage their race better.
부 더 잘
to부정사의 명사적 용법 (보어)
「help+목적어+(to+)동사원형」
(목적어)가 ~하는 것을 돕다

08 There can be several pacers in a race.
~가 있을 수 있다   형 몇몇의 (수나 종류가 셋 이상 있는 경우 사용)

09 <u>Each pacer</u> runs at different speeds <u>and</u> finishes the race in different
「each(각각의)+단수명사」 → 주어로 쓰이면 단수 취급   동사 2 (병렬 구조)
동사 1   전 ~ (속도)로
times.

10 Pacers usually have flags or balloons [showing their finish time].
현재분사 (목적어, 보어, 부사구 등 뒤따르는
어구가 있을 때는 명사를 뒤에서 수식)

11 Runners can choose a pacer depending on their target finish time.
= runners'

12 For example, if a runner wants to finish the race in four hours, the
조건을 나타내는 부사절에서는 동사를 현재형으로 사용함
runner will follow the four-hour pacer.
접 (만약) ~라면

13 Since the pacer keeps track of the time, the runner can achieve his or
접 ~ 때문에
동격을 나타내는 전치사 of (전치사+동명사)
her goal of finishing the marathon in a particular time more easily.
keep track of: ~을 파악하다
easily의 비교급

14 In short, pacers run but they don't run to win.
요컨대   = pacers   to부정사의
부사적 용법
(목적)

15 They run for others.
= pacers

Pit Crews in Car Racing

16 You may only see the car and the driver during
　　㉣ ~일지도 모른다 (약한 추측)　　　　　　전 ~ 동안

　　most car races, but there is a team behind the driver.
　　　　　　　　　　┌수동태 「be동사＋과거분사」
17 This team is called a pit crew.
　　= a team behind the driver　「by＋행위자」 생략

18 A pit is a place on the side of the race track, and drivers stop there

　　several times during a race.
　　　　　　　　　　　　┌to부정사의 명사적 용법 (보어)
19 The main job of the pit crew is to check the car and change the tires.
　　　　　　　　　　　　　　└──and로 연결된 to부정사구──┘

20 Changing the tires is especially important because the tires wear out
　　문장의 주어 (동명사구)　단수 취급　　　　　　　　　　닳다, 해지다
　　easily in a high speed race.

21 A pit stop can be as short as 2 seconds, and there are as many as 20

　　members on a crew.
　　　　　　　　　┌'팀, 무리'라는 뜻이지만 단수 취급
22 Therefore, the pit crew has to work in perfect harmony.
　　그러므로 (결과의 의미를 나타내는 연결어)

23 The driver may get all the attention, but as people say,
　　　　　　　　　　　　　　　　　　　　접 ~듯이, ~처럼
　　"Races are won in the pits."
　　　　　수동태 「be동사＋과거분사」
　　　　　(win-won-won)

Sherpas in Mountain Climbing

　　　　　　　　　　　　　　　　　　　관계대명사절
24 The word *Sherpa* comes from the Sherpa tribe, [which lives in the
　　　　└─동격─┘　　　　　　　　선행사　계속적 용법의 주격 관계대명사
　　　　　　　　　　　　　　　　　　　　　(선행사에 대한 추가 정보 제공)
　　eastern part of Nepal].

25 Sherpas have good climbing skills and know their way around the
　　　　　　　동사 1　　　　　　　　　동사 2 (병렬 구조)
　　mountains well.
　　　　　　　　　┌거의 없는
26 They also have little difficulty breathing high up in the mountains.
　　= Sherpas　　have difficulty -ing: ~하는 데 어려움이 있다
　　　　　　　　　　　　　　　　　┌to부정사의 명사적 용법 (목적어)
27 Therefore, mountain climbers started to hire Sherpas
　　　　　　　　　　　　　　　to부정사와 동명사를 모두 목적어로 취하는 동사
　　　　　　　= mountain climbers
　　to help them climb Mount Everest.
　　「help＋목적어＋(to＋)동사원형」 (목적어)가 ~하는 것을 돕다
28 Sherpas lead mountain climbers to the top of the mountain.
　　　　　　　　└lead A to B: A를 B로 이끌다─┘
29 They support climbers in many ways.
　　= Sherpas　　　　　　　way 명 방식, 방법
30 For example, they put up tents and carry climbers' bags.
　　　　　　　　　　　　동사 1　　　　　동사 2 (병렬 구조)
31 Sherpas are often called the invisible people of Mount
　　　　　　　└─수동태─┘　in-＋visible(보이는) → 보이지 않는
　　Everest because people often see a picture of only the
　　　　　　　　　　　　　　종종, 흔히 (빈도부사)
　　climbers at the top of the mountain.

자동차 경주의 피트 크루

16 여러분은 대부분의 자동차 경주에서 자동차와 레이서만 볼지도 모르겠지만, 그 레이서 뒤에는 팀이 있다.

17 이 팀은 피트 크루라고 불린다.

18 피트는 경주 트랙의 옆에 있는 공간으로, 레이서들이 경주 도중에 그곳에 여러 번 정지한다.

19 피트 크루가 하는 주요 역할은 자동차를 점검하고 타이어를 교체하는 것이다.

20 빠른 속도의 경주에서는 타이어가 쉽게 마모되기 때문에 타이어를 교체하는 것이 특히 중요하다.

21 피트에서의 정지는 짧게는 2초 정도가 될 수 있고, 한 크루에 많게는 20명에 이르는 구성원이 있다.

22 그러므로 피트 크루는 완벽한 조화를 이루며 일해야 한다.

23 레이서만 모든 주목을 받을지 모르지만 사람들이 말하는 것처럼, "경주의 우승은 피트에서 이루어진다."

등반에서의 셰르파

24 Sherpa라는 단어는 셰르파족에서 유래되었는데, 셰르파족은 네팔의 동쪽 지역에 산다.

25 셰르파는 훌륭한 등반 기술을 가졌으며 산의 지리에 밝다.

26 그들은 또한 산의 높은 곳에서 호흡하는 데 어려움이 거의 없다.

27 그래서 등산가들은 자신들이 에베레스트산을 등반하는 것을 돕는 셰르파를 고용하기 시작했다.

28 셰르파는 등산가들을 산 정상까지 이끈다.

29 그들은 여러 방식으로 등산가들을 지원한다.

30 예를 들어, 그들은 텐트를 치고 등산가들의 가방을 운반한다.

31 셰르파는 종종 에베레스트산의 보이지 않는 사람들로 불리는데, 왜냐하면 사람들은 흔히 산 정상에서 등산가들만 찍힌 사진을 보기 때문이다.

빈칸 채우기

• 우리말과 의미가 같도록 교과서 본문의 문장을 완성하시오.

01 In sports, only the players get a trophy or medal, but they don't win _____ _____ _____.

01 스포츠에서는 선수들만 트로피나 메달을 받지만, 그들이 혼자 힘으로 우승하는 것은 아니다.

02 There are people _____ help the players.

02 그 선수들을 돕는 사람들이 있다.

03 These people are often _____ and don't _____ _____.

03 이 사람들은 종종 숨겨져 있고 주목을 받지 못한다.

04 However, they are _____ _____ _____ the players.

04 하지만 그들은 선수들만큼 중요하다.

05 Here are some _____.

05 여기 몇 가지 예가 있다.

06 Pacers _____ with other runners _____ _____ them in a marathon.

06 페이서들은 마라톤에서 다른 선수들과 함께 달리며 그들을 이끈다.

07 Pacers are _____ runners, and their job is _____ _____ other runners _____ their race better.

07 페이서들은 경험이 많은 선수들이며, 그들의 역할은 다른 선수들이 경주를 더 잘 운영하도록 돕는 것이다.

08 _____ _____ _____ several pacers in a race.

08 한 경주에는 여러 명의 페이서들이 있을 수 있다.

09 _____ _____ runs at different speeds and _____ the race in different times.

09 각각의 페이서는 다른 속도로 달리고 다른 시간대에 경주를 마친다.

10 Pacers usually have flags or balloons _____ their finish time.

10 페이서들은 보통 자신들의 완주 시간을 나타내는 깃발이나 풍선을 가지고 있다.

11 Runners can choose a pacer _____ _____ their _____ finish time.

11 선수들은 자신들의 목표 완주 시간에 따라 페이서를 선택할 수 있다.

12 For example, _____ a runner _____ to finish the race in four hours, the runner will _____ the four-hour pacer.

12 예를 들어, 한 선수가 4시간 안에 경주를 마치고 싶다면, 그 선수는 4시간 페이서를 따라갈 것이다.

13 Since the pacer _____ _____ _____ the time, the runner can achieve his or her _____ _____ _____ the marathon in a particular time more easily.

13 페이서가 시간을 계속해서 파악하기 때문에, 선수는 특정 시간 안에 마라톤을 완주하려는 자신의 목표를 더 쉽게 달성할 수 있다.

14 _____ _____, pacers run but they don't run _____ _____.

14 요컨대, 페이서들은 달리기는 하지만 우승을 하기 위해 달리는 것은 아니다.

15 They _____ _____ others.

15 그들은 다른 이들을 위해 달린다.

16 You _____ only see the car and the driver _____ most car races, but there is a team _____ the driver.

17 This team _____ _____ a pit crew.

18 A pit is a place _____ _____ _____ _____ the race track, and drivers stop there several times _____ a race.

19 The main job of the pit crew is to _____ the car and _____ the tires.

20 Changing the tires is _____ _____ because the tires _____ _____ easily in a high speed race.

21 A pit stop can be _____ _____ _____ 2 seconds, and there are as many as 20 members on a crew.

22 _____, the pit crew has to work in _____ _____.

23 The driver may _____ all the _____, but _____ people say, "Races are won in the pits."

24 The word *Sherpa* comes from the Sherpa tribe, _____ lives in the _____ part of Nepal.

25 Sherpas have good climbing skills and _____ _____ _____ _____ the mountains well.

26 They also _____ _____ _____ _____ high up in the mountains.

27 Therefore, mountain climbers started to _____ Sherpas to _____ _____ _____ Mount Everest.

28 Sherpas _____ mountain climbers _____ the top of the mountain.

29 They support climbers _____ _____ _____.

30 For example, they _____ _____ tents and carry climbers' bags.

31 Sherpas _____ _____ _____ the _____ people of Mount Everest because people often see a picture of only the climbers at the top of the mountain.

16 여러분은 대부분의 자동차 경주에서 자동차와 레이서만 볼지도 모르겠지만, 그 레이서 뒤에는 팀이 있다.

17 이 팀은 피트 크루라고 불린다.

18 피트는 경주 트랙의 옆에 있는 공간으로, 레이서들이 경주 도중에 그곳에 여러 번 정지한다.

19 피트 크루가 하는 주요 역할은 자동차를 점검하고 타이어를 교체하는 것이다.

20 빠른 속도의 경주에서는 타이어가 쉽게 마모되기 때문에 타이어를 교체하는 것이 특히 중요하다.

21 피트에서의 정지는 짧게는 2초 정도가 될 수 있고, 한 크루에 많게는 20명에 이르는 구성원이 있다.

22 그러므로 피트 크루는 완벽한 조화를 이루며 일해야 한다.

23 레이서만 모든 주목을 받을지 모르지만 사람들이 말하는 것처럼, "경주의 우승은 피트에서 이루어진다."

24 Sherpa라는 단어는 셰르파족에서 유래되었는데, 셰르파족은 네팔의 동쪽 지역에 산다.

25 셰르파는 훌륭한 등반 기술을 가졌으며 산의 지리에 밝다.

26 그들은 또한 산의 높은 곳에서 호흡하는 데 어려움이 거의 없다.

27 그래서 등산가들은 자신들이 에베레스트산을 등반하는 것을 돕는 셰르파를 고용하기 시작했다.

28 셰르파는 등산가들을 산 정상까지 이끈다.

29 그들은 여러 방식으로 등산가들을 지원한다.

30 예를 들어, 그들은 텐트를 치고 등산가들의 가방을 운반한다.

31 셰르파는 종종 에베레스트산의 보이지 않는 사람들로 불리는데, 왜냐하면 사람들은 흔히 산 정상에서 등산가들만 찍힌 사진을 보기 때문이다.

바른 어휘·어법 고르기

STEP A

01 In sports, only the players get a trophy or medal, but they don't win (on / by) their own.

02 There are people (who / whom) help the players.

03 These people are often (hidden / hide) and don't get attention.

04 However, they are as (important / more important) as the players.

05 Here (is / are) some examples.

06 Pacers (running / run) with other runners and lead them in a marathon.

07 Pacers are experienced runners, and their job is to help other runners (manage / managing) their race better.

08 There can be several (pacer / pacers) in a race.

09 Each pacer runs at different speeds and (finish / finishes) the race in different times.

10 Pacers usually have flags or balloons (shown / showing) their finish time.

11 Runners can choose a pacer depending (on / with) their target finish time.

12 For example, if a runner (wants / want) to finish the race in four hours, the runner (will / will not) follow the four-hour pacer.

13 Since the pacer keeps track of the (goal / time), the runner can achieve his or her goal of (finish / finishing) the marathon in a particular time more easily.

14 (Shortly / In short), pacers run but they don't run to win.

15 They run for (others / themselves).

16 You may only see the car and the driver (while / during) most car races, but there is a team behind the driver.

17 This team (calls / is called) a pit crew.

18   A (crew / pit) is a place on the side of the race track, and drivers stop there several times during a race.

19   The main job of the pit crew is (checking / to check) the car and change the tires.

20   Changing the tires is especially important because the tires wear (off / out) easily in a high speed race.

21   A pit stop can be as short (as / than) 2 seconds, and there are as many as 20 members on a crew.

22   Therefore, the pit crew (has to / doesn't have to) work in perfect harmony.

23   The driver may get all the attention, but as people say, "Races (are won / are winning) in the pits."

24   The word *Sherpa* comes from the Sherpa tribe, (which / that) lives in the eastern part of Nepal.

25   Sherpas have good climbing skills and (knowing / know) their way around the mountains well.

26   They also (have difficulty / have little difficulty) breathing high up in the mountains.

27   Therefore, mountain climbers started to hire Sherpas to help them (climb / climbing) Mount Everest.

28   Sherpas lead mountain climbers (to / of) the top of the mountain.

29   They support climbers (in / for) many ways.

30   (However / For example), they put up tents and carry climbers' bags.

31   Sherpas are often called the (visible / invisible) people of Mount Everest because people often see a picture of only the climbers at the top of the mountain.

Reading

틀린 문장 고치기

• 밑줄 친 부분이 내용이나 어법상 올바르면 ○에, 틀리면 ×에 동그라미 하고 틀린 부분을 바르게 고쳐 쓰시오.

01 In sports, only the players get a trophy or medal, but they don't win <u>on their own</u>. ○ ×

02 There are people <u>who helps</u> the players. ○ ×

03 These people are often <u>hide</u> and don't get attention. ○ ×

04 However, they are <u>such important</u> as the players. ○ ×

05 Here are <u>some examples</u>. ○ ×

06 Pacers run with other runners and <u>leading them</u> in a marathon. ○ ×

07 Pacers are experienced runners, and their job is to help <u>other runners managed</u> their race better. ○ ×

08 <u>There can be</u> several pacers in a race. ○ ×

09 Each pacer <u>run at different speeds</u> and finishes the race in different times. ○ ×

10 Pacers usually have flags or balloons <u>show</u> their finish time. ○ ×

11 Runners can choose a pacer <u>depending on</u> their target finish time. ○ ×

12 For example, if a runner <u>wants finishing</u> the race in four hours, the runner will follow the four-hour pacer. ○ ×

13 Since the pacer keeps track of the time, the runner can achieve his or her goal <u>of finishing</u> the marathon in a particular time more easily. ○ ×

14 In short, pacers run but they don't run <u>to win</u>. ○ ×

15 They run <u>for others</u>. ○ ×

16 You <u>may only see</u> the car and the driver during most car races, but there is a team behind the driver. ○ ×

17 This team <u>called</u> a pit crew. ○ ×

18   A pit is a place on the side of the race track, and drivers stop there several times while a race.

◯ ☓

19   The main job of the pit crew is to check the car and changed the tires.

◯ ☓

20   Changing the tires are especially important because the tires wear out easily in a high speed race.

◯ ☓

21   A pit stop can be as shorter as 2 seconds, and there are as many as 20 members on a crew.

◯ ☓

22   Therefore, the pit crew has to work in perfect harmony.

◯ ☓

23   The driver may get all the attention, but as people say, "Races are won in the pits."

◯ ☓

24   The word *Sherpa* comes from the Sherpa tribe, which lives in the eastern part of Nepal.

◯ ☓

25   Sherpas have good climbing skills and know their way around the mountains well.

◯ ☓

26   They also have little difficulty breathe high up in the mountains.

◯ ☓

27   Therefore, mountain climbers started to hire Sherpas to help them climb Mount Everest.

◯ ☓

28   Sherpas leading mountain climbers to the top of the mountain.

◯ ☓

29   They support climbers to many ways.

◯ ☓

30   For example, they put up tents and carry climbers' bags.

◯ ☓

31   Sherpas are often called the invisible people of Mount Everest because people are often seen a picture of only the climbers at the top of the mountain.

◯ ☓

Reading
배열로 문장 완성하기

01 스포츠에서는, 선수들만 트로피나 메달을 받지만, 그들이 혼자 힘으로 우승하는 것은 아니다.
(a trophy or medal / their own / only the players / don't / in sports / but / on / win / they / get)

>

02 그 선수들을 돕는 사람들이 있다. (are / who / there / the players / people / help)

>

03 이 사람들은 종종 숨겨져 있고 주목을 받지 못한다. (and / attention / get / hidden / are / these people / often / don't)

>

04 하지만, 그들은 선수들만큼 중요하다. (as / are / the players / as / they / however / important)

>

05 여기 몇 가지 예가 있다. (some / are / examples / here)

>

06 페이서들은 마라톤에서 다른 선수들과 함께 달리며 그들을 이끈다.
(run / and / other runners / pacers / in a marathon / with / them / lead)

>

07 페이서들은 경험이 많은 선수들이며, 그들의 역할은 다른 선수들이 경주를 더 잘 운영하도록 돕는 것이다.
(their race / is / manage / better / other runners / are / and / their job / experienced runners / to help / pacers)

>

08 한 경주에는 여러 명의 페이서들이 있을 수 있다. (be / several pacers / there / in a race / can)

>

09 각각의 페이서는 다른 속도로 달리고 다른 시간대에 경주를 마친다.
(in different times / at different speeds / and / each pacer / the race / finishes / runs)

>

10 페이서들은 보통 자신들의 완주 시간을 나타내는 깃발이나 풍선을 가지고 있다.
(flags or balloons / their finish time / pacers / showing / usually / have)

>

11 선수들은 자신들의 목표 완주 시간에 따라 페이서를 선택할 수 있다.
(depending on / can choose / a pacer / their target finish time / runners)

>

12 예를 들어, 한 선수가 4시간 안에 경주를 마치고 싶다면, 그 선수는 4시간 페이서를 따라갈 것이다.
(will follow / the race / for example / in four hours / the four-hour pacer / a runner wants / the runner / if / to finish)

>

13 페이서가 시간을 계속해서 파악하기 때문에, 선수는 특정 시간 안에 마라톤을 완주하려는 자신의 목표를 더 쉽게 달성할 수 있다.
(of finishing the marathon / keeps track of / can achieve / in a particular time / the runner / the pacer / his or her goal / more easily / since / the time)

>

14 요컨대, 페이서들은 달리기는 하지만 우승을 하기 위해 달리는 것은 아니다. (don't run / run / to win / in short / but / pacers / they)

>

15 그들은 다른 이들을 위해 달린다. (run / others / they / for)

>

16 여러분은 대부분의 자동차 경주에서 자동차와 레이서만 볼지도 모르겠지만, 그 레이서 뒤에는 팀이 있다.
(during / a team / most car races / there / but / only see / is / behind the driver / you / the car and the driver / may)

>

17 이 팀은 피트 크루라고 불린다. (called / this team / a pit crew / is)

>

18 피트는 경주 트랙의 옆에 있는 공간으로, 레이서들이 경주 도중에 그곳에 여러 번 정지한다.
(on the side of / and / a place / the race track / during a race / drivers / a pit / stop / several times / is / there)

>

19 피트 크루가 하는 주요 역할은 자동차를 점검하고 타이어를 교체하는 것이다.
(to check / the tires / change / the main job / and / of the pit crew / the car / is)

>

20 빠른 속도의 경주에서는 타이어가 쉽게 마모되기 때문에 타이어를 교체하는 것이 특히 중요하다.
(because / is / in a high speed race / changing the tires / especially important / the tires / wear out easily)

>

21 피트에서의 정지는 짧게는 2초 정도가 될 수 있고, 한 크루에 많게는 20명에 이르는 구성원이 있다.
(and / 20 members / there are / as short as / 2 seconds / on a crew / can be / as many as / a pit stop)

>

22 그러므로 피트 크루는 완벽한 조화를 이루며 일해야 한다. (has to / in perfect harmony / the pit crew / work / therefore)

>

23 레이서만 모든 주목을 받을지 모르지만, 사람들이 말하는 것처럼, "경주의 우승은 피트에서 이루어진다."
(say / the driver / people / get / as / but / may / all the attention / "Races are won in the pits.")

>

24 Sherpa라는 단어는 셰르파족에서 유래되었는데, 셰르파족은 네팔의 동쪽 지역에 산다.
(which / in / the Sherpa tribe / the eastern part / of Nepal / the word *Sherpa* / lives / comes from)

>

25 셰르파는 훌륭한 등반 기술을 가졌으며 산의 지리에 밝다.
(know / well / and / Sherpas / good climbing skills / the mountains / their way / have / around)

>

26 그들은 또한 산의 높은 곳에서 호흡하는 데 어려움이 거의 없다.
(in the mountains / little difficulty / they / breathing / high up / also have)

>

27 그래서, 등산가들은 자신들이 에베레스트산을 등반하는 것을 돕는 셰르파를 고용하기 시작했다.
(started / to help / therefore / climb / mountain climbers / to hire / Mount Everest / Sherpas / them)

>

28 셰르파는 등산가들을 산 정상까지 이끈다. (mountain climbers / the top of / lead / the mountain / Sherpas / to)

>

29 그들은 여러 방식으로 등산가들을 지원한다. (many / climbers / they / in / ways / support)

>

30 예를 들어, 그들은 텐트를 치고 등산가들의 가방을 운반한다. (put up / carry / for example / tents / climbers' bags / they / and)

>

31 셰르파는 종종 에베레스트산의 보이지 않는 사람들로 불리는데, 왜냐하면 사람들은 흔히 산 정상에서 등산가들만 찍힌 사진을 보기 때문이다.
(people / of Mount Everest / Sherpas / at the top of / because / often see / the invisible people / a picture of / the mountain / are often called / only the climbers)

>

[01~03] 다음 글을 읽고, 물음에 답하시오.

_____ ⓐ _____ sports, only the players get a trophy or medal, but they don't win _____ ⓑ _____ their own. There are people _____ ⓒ _____ help the players. These people are often _____ ⓓ _____ and don't get attention. However, (A)그들은 선수들만큼 중요하다. Here _____ ⓔ _____ some examples.

01 윗글의 빈칸 ⓐ~ⓔ에 들어갈 말로 알맞지 <u>않은</u> 것은?

① ⓐ: In   ② ⓑ: on   ③ ⓒ: who

④ ⓓ: hide   ⑤ ⓔ: are

02 윗글의 밑줄 친 우리말 (A)를 영어로 바르게 옮긴 것은?

① they are as important as the players

② they are less important than the players

③ they are not as important as the players

④ they are more important than the players

⑤ the players are more important than them

03 윗글 다음에 이어질 내용으로 가장 알맞은 것은?

① 메달을 받은 우승자들의 예시

② 스포츠에서 팀워크의 중요성

③ 비인기 스포츠 종목의 예시

④ 운동 선수들이 갖추어야 할 자질

⑤ 스포츠에서 숨은 조력자들의 예시

[04~09] 다음 글을 읽고, 물음에 답하시오.

Pacers in a Marathon

Pacers run with other runners and lead them in a marathon. Pacers are ⓐexperienced runners, and their job is to help other runners ⓑmanage their race better. There can be several pacers in a race. Each pacer runs at different speeds and finishes the race in different times. Pacers usually have flags or balloons ⓒshow their finish time.

Runners can choose a pacer depending _____ (A) _____ their target finish time. For example, if a runner wants ⓓto finish the race in four hours, the runner will follow the four-hour pacer. Since the pacer keeps track _____ (B) _____ the time, the runner can achieve his or her goal of ⓔfinishing the marathon in a particular time more easily. _____ (C) _____, pacers run but they don't run (D)to win. They run for others.

04 윗글의 밑줄 친 ⓐ~ⓔ 중 어법상 틀린 것을 바르게 고친 사람은?

① 미나: ⓐ → experiencing

② 준호: ⓑ → managed

③ 유준: ⓒ → showing

④ 윤지: ⓓ → finishing

⑤ 세경: ⓔ → to finish

05 윗글의 빈칸 (A)와 (B)에 들어갈 말이 순서대로 바르게 짝 지어진 것은?

① in – of   ② in – for

③ on – of   ④ on – for

⑤ on – with

06 윗글의 빈칸 (C)에 들어갈 말로 알맞은 것은?

① By the way   ② In short
③ For example   ④ In addition
⑤ On the other hand

07 윗글의 밑줄 친 (D)to win과 쓰임이 같은 것은?

① He has a lot of homework to do today.
② I hope to climb Mount Everest someday.
③ It was surprising to meet him in person.
④ My future dream is to be a robot scientist.
⑤ They hurried to the station to catch the last train.

08 윗글을 읽고 pacers에 대해 알 수 있는 것은?

① 나이   ② 성별   ③ 복장
④ 역할   ⑤ 국적

09 윗글의 pacers에 대한 설명으로 틀린 것은?

① They lead other runners in a marathon.
② They help other runners do better in a marathon.
③ Each of them has to run with one runner.
④ They run with flags or balloons.
⑤ They don't run for themselves but for others.

[10~14] 다음 글을 읽고, 물음에 답하시오.

You may only see the car and the driver during most car races, but there is a team behind the driver. This team is (A)calling / called a pit crew. A pit is a place on the side of the race track, and drivers stop there several times during a race. The main job of the pit crew is to check the car and change the tires. (B)Change / Changing the tires is especially important ____ⓐ____ the tires wear out easily in a high speed race.

A pit stop can be as (C)short / shortly as 2 seconds, and there are as many as 20 members on a crew. Therefore, the pit crew has to work in perfect harmony. The driver may get all the attention, but as people say, "Races are won in the pits."

10 윗글의 제목으로 가장 알맞은 것은?

① How to Win a Car Race
② Pit Crews in Car Racing
③ The Main Job of Car Racers
④ Several Tips for Safe Car Racing
⑤ The Importance of Changing Tires

11 윗글 (A)~(C)의 각 네모 안에 주어진 말 중에서 어법상 알맞은 것끼리 짝지어진 것은?

	(A)		(B)		(C)
①	calling	⋯	Change	⋯	shortly
②	calling	⋯	Changing	⋯	short
③	called	⋯	Change	⋯	shortly
④	called	⋯	Changing	⋯	shortly
⑤	called	⋯	Changing	⋯	short

12 윗글의 흐름상 빈칸 ⓐ에 들어갈 말로 알맞은 것은?

① that   ② unless   ③ because
④ until   ⑤ though

13 다음 영영풀이에 해당하는 단어를 윗글에서 찾아 쓰시오.

> a group of people with particular skills who work together

→ _____

14 윗글을 읽고 답할 수 <u>없는</u> 질문은?

① What is a pit in car racing?

② Where does a pit crew work during a race?

③ What is the main job of a pit crew?

④ How many times can car racers change tires in each race?

⑤ Why is it especially important to change tires in a car race?

15 윗글의 밑줄 친 ⓐ~ⓔ 중 어법상 <u>틀린</u> 것은?

① ⓐ   ② ⓑ   ③ ⓒ

④ ⓓ   ⑤ ⓔ

16 윗글의 ①~⑤ 중 주어진 문장이 들어갈 위치로 알맞은 것은?

> For example, they put up tents and carry climbers' bags.

①   ②   ③   ④   ⑤

17 윗글의 흐름상 빈칸 (A)에 들어갈 말로 가장 알맞은 것은?

① climbing   ② formal   ③ eastern

④ difficult   ⑤ invisible

[15~18] 다음 글을 읽고, 물음에 답하시오.

Sherpas in Mountain Climbing

The word *Sherpa* comes from the Sherpa tribe, ⓐ<u>which</u> lives in the eastern part of Nepal. (①) Sherpas have good climbing skills and know their way around the mountains well. (②) They also have little difficulty ⓑ<u>to breathe</u> high up in the mountains. (③) Therefore, mountain climbers started ⓒ<u>to hire</u> Sherpas to help them ⓓ<u>climb</u> Mount Everest.

Sherpas ⓔ<u>lead</u> mountain climbers to the top of the mountain. (④) They support climbers in many ways. (⑤) Sherpas are often called the _____(A)_____ people of Mount Everest because people often see a picture of only the climbers at the top of the mountain.

18 윗글을 읽고 알 수 <u>없는</u> 내용은?

① the origin of the word *Sherpa*

② what Sherpas are good at

③ why mountain climbers hire Sherpas

④ how to hire Sherpas

⑤ the role of Sherpas in mountain climbing

[19~20] 다음 글을 읽고, 물음에 답하시오.

Runners can choose a pacer depending on their target finish time. For example, if a runner wants to finish the race in four hours, the runner will follow the four-hour pacer. Since the pacer keeps track of the time, the runner can achieve ⓐhis or her goal of finishing the marathon in a particular time more easily. In short, pacers run but they don't run to win. They run for others.

19 윗글의 밑줄 친 ⓐ가 가리키는 것을 우리말로 쓰시오.

→ _____

20 윗글의 내용과 일치하도록 다음 질문에 대한 답을 쓰시오.

> **Q.** If a runner wants to finish the race in three hours, which pacer will the runner follow?

→ The runner will _____ .

[21~22] 다음 글을 읽고, 물음에 답하시오.

You may only see the car and the driver during most car races, but there is a team behind the driver.

(A) Therefore, the pit crew has to work in perfect harmony. The driver may get all the attention, but as people say, "Races ⓐare won in the pits."

(B) This team is called a pit crew. A pit is a place on the side of the race track, and drivers stop there several times during a race. The main job of the pit crew is ⓑto check the car and change the tires.

(C) Changing the tires ⓒare especially important because the tires wear out easily in a high speed race. A pit stop can be as ⓓshort as 2 seconds, and there are as ⓔmany as 20 members on a crew.

21 윗글의 흐름에 맞게 (A)~(C)를 바르게 배열하시오.

(   ) – (   ) – (   )

22 윗글의 밑줄 친 ⓐ~ⓔ 중 어법상 틀린 것의 기호를 쓰고, 바르게 고쳐 쓰시오.

(   ) → _____

[23~24] 다음 글을 읽고, 물음에 답하시오.

The word *Sherpa* comes from the Sherpa tribe, which lives in the eastern part of Nepal. Sherpas have good climbing skills and know their way around the mountains well. ⓐ그들은 또한 산의 높은 곳에서 호흡하는 데 어려움이 거의 없다. Therefore, mountain climbers started to hire Sherpas to help them climb Mount Everest.

Sherpas lead mountain climbers to the top of the mountain. They support climbers in many ways. For example, they put up tents and carry climbers' bags. Sherpas are often called the invisible people of Mount Everest because people often see a picture of only the climbers at the top of the mountain.

23 윗글의 밑줄 친 우리말 ⓐ와 의미가 같도록 [보기]의 표현을 바르게 배열하여 쓰시오.

> [보기]   they, difficulty, high up, also, little, have, breathing, in the mountains

→ _____

24 윗글의 내용과 일치하도록 Sherpas에 관한 다음 글의 빈칸에 알맞은 말을 본문에서 찾아 쓰시오.

> They _____ mountain climbers climb Mount Everest. They _____ the climbers to the _____ of the mountain and _____ them in many ways.

만점 노트

Listen and Talk D

교과서 85쪽

Do you ❶like riding a bike? Then, ❷I suggest you join our club, Fun Wheels. We ride bikes ❸once a week, on Saturdays. We ride along the river or in parks. ❹It's fun to ride bikes together.

자전거 타는 것을 좋아하나요? 그렇다면, 우리 동아리 Fun Wheels에 가입하는 것을 제안합니다. 우리는 일주일에 한 번, 토요일마다 자전거를 타요. 강을 따라 자전거를 타거나 공원에서 탑니다. 함께 자전거를 타면 재미있어요.

❶ like는 to부정사와 동명사를 모두 목적어로 취할 수 있다.
❷ 상대방에게 어떤 일을 하도록 제안할 때 「I suggest (that) you (should)+동사원형 ~.」으로 표현한다.
❸ once a week는 '일주일에 한 번'을 의미하고, 「on+요일-s」는 '~요일마다'를 의미한다.
❹ It은 가주어이고 to ride bikes together가 진주어로 쓰인 문장이다.

Around the World

교과서 93쪽

· In swimming, a tapper uses a long pole to ❶help a blind swimmer swim.
· In a race, a guide runner runs with a blind runner and ❷helps him or her stay on the track.
· In blind football, a shooting assistant ❸tells his or her team players which direction to shoot.

· 수영 경기에서 tapper는 시각장애인 수영 선수가 수영하는 것을 돕기 위해 장대를 사용한다.
· 달리기 경주에서 guide runner는 시각장애인 선수와 함께 달리며 그들이 트랙에서 벗어나지 않도록 돕는다.
· 시각장애인 축구에서 shooting assistant는 자신의 팀 선수들에게 어느 방향으로 슛을 해야 하는지 말해 준다.

❶, ❷ 동사 help는 「help+목적어+(to+)동사원형(목적격 보어)」의 형태로 '(목적어)가 ~하는 것을 돕다'라는 의미를 나타낸다.
❸ 「tell+간접목적어(his or her team players)+직접목적어(which direction to shoot)」의 4형식 문장으로, 직접목적어가 「의문사+to부정사」 형태로 쓰였다.

Think and Write

교과서 96쪽

Cheerleaders in Football Games

❶Although people usually don't think that cheerleaders are a part of a football team, they ❷play an important role in a football game. ❸By cheering at a game, they create team spirit. They also encourage their team and fans. ❹To do their job well, cheerleaders ❺need to be fit and strong. They also need to ❻be good at jumping and dancing. ❼Most of all, they need to work as hard as the players.

미식축구 경기의 치어리더들
사람들은 보통 치어리더들이 미식축구 팀의 일원이라고 생각하지 않지만, 그들은 미식축구 경기에서 중요한 역할을 한다. 경기에서 응원을 함으로써 그들은 공동체 정신을 만들어 낸다. 그들은 또한 팀과 팬들을 격려한다. 자신의 역할을 잘 해내기 위해서, 치어리더들은 건강하고 튼튼해야 한다. 그들은 또한 점프와 춤에 능숙해야 한다. 무엇보다도, 그들은 선수들만큼 열심히 일해야 한다.

❶ Although는 '~에도 불구하고'라는 의미의 접속사이며, that은 don't think의 목적어 역할을 하는 명사절을 이끄는 접속사로 쓰였다.
❷ play a role: 역할을 하다
❸ 「by+동명사」는 '~함으로써'라는 뜻을 나타내며, team spirit은 '공동체 정신'이라는 의미이다.
❹ To do는 '~하기 위해'라는 의미의 목적을 나타내는 부사적 용법의 to부정사이다.
❺ 「need to+동사원형」은 '~할 필요가 있다'라는 의미이다.
❻ be good at은 '~에 능숙하다'라는 의미이고 전치사 at 뒤에 동사가 올 경우에는 동명사 형태가 되어야 한다.
❼ most of all: 무엇보다도

실전 TEST

[01~02] 다음 글을 읽고, 물음에 답하시오.

Do you like riding a bike? Then, ⓐI suggest you join our club, Fun Wheels. ⓑWe ride bikes once a week, on Saturdays. We ride along the river or in parks. It's fun to ride bikes together.

01 윗글의 밑줄 친 ⓐ와 바꿔 쓸 수 있는 것을 모두 고르면?

① Did you join our club, Fun Wheels?
② You can't join our club, Fun Wheels.
③ Why don't you join our club, Fun Wheels?
④ What do you think of our club, Fun Wheels?
⑤ I think you should join our club, Fun Wheels.

02 윗글의 밑줄 친 ⓑ가 대답이 될 수 있는 질문으로 알맞은 것은?

① Why don't we ride bikes?
② Who do you ride bikes with?
③ How often do you ride bikes?
④ Where do you usually ride bikes?
⑤ Do you know how to ride a bike?

03 다음 글의 내용을 요약한 아래 문장의 빈칸에 알맞은 말을 쓰시오.

- In swimming, a tapper uses a long pole to help a blind swimmer swim.
- In a race, a guide runner runs with a blind runner and helps him or her stay on the track.
- In blind football, a shooting assistant tells his or her team players which direction to shoot.

↓

In sports games, helpers such as a tapper, a guide runner, and a shooting assistant help _____ players.

[04~06] 다음 글을 읽고, 물음에 답하시오.

Cheerleaders in Football Games

Although people usually don't think that cheerleaders are a part of a football team, they _____ⓐ_____ in a football game. By cheering at a game, they create team spirit. They also encourage their team and fans. To do their job well, cheerleaders need to be fit and strong. They also need to be good at jumping and dancing. Most of all, they need to work ⓑ선수들만큼 열심히.

04 윗글의 빈칸 ⓐ에 들어갈 말로 가장 알맞은 것은?

① play with a ball
② give the players balls
③ play an important role
④ cheer for the other team
⑤ don't need to work hard

05 윗글의 밑줄 친 우리말 ⓑ를 괄호 안에 주어진 단어를 사용하여 영어로 쓰시오. (5단어)

→ _____ (hard)

06 윗글의 cheerleaders가 자신의 역할을 잘 해내기 위해 필요한 것 세 가지를 우리말로 쓰시오.

(1) _____

(2) _____

(3) _____

Words

고득점 맞기

01 Which word has the following definition?

> to take air into your body and let it out again

① hide   ② register   ③ breathe
④ achieve   ⑤ suggest

02 다음 중 짝지어진 단어의 관계가 서로 같지 <u>않은</u> 것은?

① light : heavy = cheer : encourage
② target : goal = particular : specific
③ visible : invisible = direct : indirect
④ achieve : achievement = breathe : breath
⑤ register : registration = suggest : suggestion

03 다음 빈칸에 들어갈 말이 순서대로 바르게 짝지어진 것은?

> • A turtle can _____ itself in its shell when it is in danger.
> • The botanical garden has a _____ on the number of visitors so that it doesn't get crowded.

① hire – spirit   ② cheer – flag
③ hide – limit   ④ join – target
⑤ suggest – tribe

04 다음 빈칸에 공통으로 들어갈 말을 주어진 철자로 시작하여 쓰시오.

> • Her first shot missed the t_____ by an inch.
> • We're raising money for our school, and our t_____ is $3,000.

05 Which can replace the underlined part?

> A: I'm making a house for my dog, Bamtori.
> B: Wow. Are you building it <u>on your own</u>?

① on time   ② by yourself
③ for a living   ④ in your case
⑤ on your way home

신/유형
06 다음 짝지어진 단어의 관계가 반의어일 때, 빈칸에 들어갈 접두어가 나머지와 <u>다른</u> 하나는?

① polite – __polite   ② formal – __formal
③ perfect – __perfect   ④ patient – __patient
⑤ possible – __possible

07 다음 우리말과 의미가 같도록 빈칸에 알맞은 말을 쓰시오.

> 내 남동생은 많은 야외 활동을 즐겨서 바지가 쉽게 닳는다.

→ My brother enjoys many outdoor activities, so his pants _____ _____ easily.

08 다음 빈칸에 공통으로 들어갈 말로 알맞은 것은?

> • All the athletes were running along the _____.
> • The presentation is only 10 minutes. You should keep _____ of the time carefully.

① pit   ② race   ③ target
④ track   ⑤ attention

고_{난도} 신_{유형}

09 다음 단어의 영영풀이를 완성할 때 빈칸에 알맞은 것은?

> achieve: *v.* to _____ in doing or getting
> something you want

① expect   ② lose   ③ create
④ receive   ⑤ succeed

10 다음 중 밑줄 친 부분의 우리말 의미가 알맞지 <u>않은</u> 것은?

① The president will <u>give a speech</u> at one o'clock.
(연설하다)
② The price can be determined <u>depending on</u>
the producer. (~에 따라)
③ Wear a cap if you don't want to <u>get people's
attention</u>. (사람들의 관심을 받다)
④ <u>In short</u>, we won't take a final exam at the end
of this semester. (무엇보다)
⑤ If you <u>sign up</u> before the end of this month,
you can get a 20% discount. (등록하다)

고_{난도}

11 다음 중 밑줄 친 부분의 쓰임이 문맥상 <u>어색한</u> 것은?

① Some <u>flags</u> were blowing in the wind.
② He waved his hand until his son was <u>invisible</u>.
③ Can you <u>allow</u> some interesting places to
visit?
④ She gave us <u>several</u> tips for a good night's
sleep.
⑤ Explore Machu Picchu with an <u>experienced</u>
local guide.

12 다음 중 밑줄 친 단어의 쓰임이 나머지와 <u>다른</u> 하나는?

① I <u>once</u> lived in Hawaii.
② Can I try it on <u>once</u> again?
③ I do aerobics <u>once</u> a week.
④ I'll do it <u>once</u>. Look carefully.
⑤ This chance comes <u>once</u> in a lifetime.

13 다음 밑줄 친 단어의 영영풀이로 알맞은 것은?

> Mr. Harris decided to <u>support</u> children in need.

① to put someone's name on an official list
② to hold something up to stop it from falling down
③ to employ or pay someone to do a particular
job
④ to put something in a place where no one can
see it
⑤ to help someone, often when they are having
problems

고_{난도} 신_{유형}

14 다음 빈칸 ⓐ~ⓓ의 어느 곳에도 들어갈 수 <u>없는</u> 단어는?

> • I'll _____ⓐ_____ the cooking club tomorrow.
> • The club members have a strong team
> _____ⓑ_____ .
> • My cats and dogs are living in perfect
> _____ⓒ_____ .
> • The temple is in the _____ⓓ_____ part of the
> mountain.

① join   ② spirit   ③ tribe
④ eastern   ⑤ harmony

고_{난도}

15 다음 (A)~(C)의 각 네모 안에 주어진 단어 중 문맥상 알맞
은 것끼리 짝지어진 것은?

> • They (A) hired / hid two painters to paint
> their house.
> • Daniel did his best to achieve his (B) limit /
> target score.
> • Did you (C) hold / register for the English
> speech contest?

	(A)		(B)		(C)
①	hired	⋯	limit	⋯	hold
②	hired	⋯	target	⋯	register
③	hired	⋯	limit	⋯	register
④	hid	⋯	target	⋯	hold
⑤	hid	⋯	limit	⋯	register

Listen and Talk

영작하기

• 주어진 우리말과 일치하도록 교과서 대화문을 쓰시오.

Listen and Talk A-1

B: _____

G: _____

B: _____

G: _____

교과서 84쪽

해석

B: 너는 얼마나 자주 농구를 하니?

G: 일주일에 한 번 하는데 더 자주 하고 싶어.

B: 네가 우리 농구 동아리에 가입할 것을 제안해. 우리는 일주일에 세 번 농구를 해.

G: 좋아! 너와 함께 농구 하면 재미있을 거야.

Listen and Talk A-2

B: _____

G: _____

B: _____

G: _____

B: _____

교과서 84쪽

B: 나는 수영을 자주 하지 않아. 너는 어때, Kate? 너는 얼마나 자주 수영을 하니?

G: 나는 일주일에 네 번 수영을 해.

B: 그렇게 자주? 어쨌든, 오늘 함께 수영하면 재미있을 거야.

G: 그래, 그런데 수영하기 전에, 우리가 스트레칭하는 것을 제안해.

B: 좋은 생각이야.

Listen and Talk A-3

B: _____

G: _____

B: _____

G: _____

교과서 84쪽

B: 수지야, 너는 얼마나 자주 볼링 수업을 받니?

G: 일주일에 두 번. 나는 그냥 초보야. 너는 아주 잘한다고 들었어.

B: 음, 나는 볼링을 정말 좋아해. 흠, 네 볼링 공이 너에게 무거워 보여. 더 가벼운 공을 쓰는 걸 권해.

G: 알았어. 그러면 더 가벼운 공을 찾아 볼게.

Listen and Talk A-4

B: _____

G: _____

B: _____

G: _____

교과서 84쪽

B: 미나야, 너는 이곳에 달리기를 하러 얼마나 자주 오니?

G: 매일 와.

B: 오늘 너랑 같이 달리기를 해도 될까?

G: 물론이야. 그런데 네가 운동화를 신는 것을 권해. 네 신발은 달리기에 적합하지 않아.

Listen and Talk C

W: _____

B: _____

W: _____

B: _____

W: _____

B: _____

W: _____

B: _____

W: _____

B: _____

Answers: 본문 pp. 14~15 참고

교과서 85쪽

해석

W: 안녕하세요. Sports World에 오신 것을 환영합니다. 도와드릴까요?

B: 네, 저는 수영 수업에 등록하려고 왔어요.

W: 수영 강습을 받는 것이 이번이 처음이세요?

B: 네. 저는 수영하는 법을 전혀 몰라요.

W: 그렇군요. 얼마나 자주 수업을 듣고 싶으세요?

B: 일주일에 두 번 수업을 듣고 싶어요. 주말은 아니고 주중에 수업을 듣고 싶습니다.

W: 그러면, 초급 2반을 수강하기를 권해요. 이 수업은 화요일과 목요일에 있습니다.

B: 좋아요. 그 수업으로 등록할게요. 그 수업은 규모가 얼마나 되나요?

W: 그 수업은 제한 인원이 10명이에요.

B: 딱 좋네요.

Review - 1

B: _____

G: _____

B: _____

G: _____

교과서 98쪽

B: 미나야, 너는 얼마나 자주 수영을 하니?

G: 나는 매일 수영해.

B: 오늘 오후에 너랑 수영하러 가도 될까?

G: 물론이지, 하지만 수영 모자를 가져올 것을 권해. 수영 모자가 없으면 수영장에 들어갈 수가 없거든.

Review - 2

B: _____

G: _____

B: _____

G: _____

교과서 98쪽

B: 소미야, 피아노 연습은 끝났니?

G: 응, 끝났어.

B: 너는 얼마나 자주 연습하니?

G: 나는 일주일에 두 번 연습해.

Review - 3

W: _____

B: _____

W: _____

B: _____

W: _____

B: _____

교과서 98쪽

W: 안녕하세요. 도와드릴까요?

B: 네, 저는 축구 수업에 등록하러 왔어요.

W: 그렇군요. 얼마나 자주 수업을 듣고 싶으세요?

B: 일주일에 두 번 듣고 싶어요. 주말에 수업을 듣고 싶습니다.

W: 그러면, 초급 1반 수강을 권합니다. 이 수업은 토요일과 일요일에 있어요.

B: 그거 좋네요.

Listen and Talk

고득점 맞기

01 다음 대화의 빈칸에 들어갈 말로 알맞지 <u>않은</u> 것을 <u>모두</u> 고르면?

> A: How often do you go to the movies?
> B: _____

① Almost every week.
② I like action movies.
③ I go to the movies once a week.
④ I go see a movie three times a month.
⑤ I usually go to the movies with my friends.

02 다음 중 짝지어진 대화가 <u>어색한</u> 것은?

① A: How often do you play soccer?
  B: Three times a week.
② A: I exercise with my brother every morning.
  B: Well, I suggest you exercise regularly.
③ A: Let's go for a bike ride today.
  B: Sure. I suggest you bring your helmet and knee pads.
④ A: I clean my room once a week.
  B: I think you should clean your room more often.
⑤ A: Can I run with you today?
  B: Sure, but I suggest you wear running shoes. Your shoes aren't good for running.

03 다음 대화의 밑줄 친 ①~⑤ 중 흐름상 <u>어색한</u> 것은?

> A: ①How often do you take bowling lessons?
> B: Twice a week. I'm just a beginner. ②I heard you're very good.
> A: ③Well, I love bowling. Hmm. ④Your bowling ball looks heavy for you. I suggest you use a lighter ball.
> B: OK. ⑤I'll look for a heavier one, then.

①   ②   ③   ④   ⑤

04 다음과 같은 상황에서 준호가 지수에게 할 말로 가장 알맞은 것은?

> Jisu likes eating fast food such as French fries, hamburgers, and pizza. She eats fast food almost every day. Junho thinks fast food is bad for her health. He wants Jisu to eat less fast food.

① I want to eat less fast food.
② I think you should lose weight.
③ I suggest you eat less fast food.
④ I think I should eat less fast food.
⑤ I'm glad that you eat less fast food.

[05~06] 다음 대화를 읽고, 물음에 답하시오.

> Boy: I don't swim often. How about you, Kate? How often do you swim?
> Girl: I swim four times a week.
> Boy: That often? Anyway, it'll be fun swimming together today.
> Girl: Yes, but before we swim, _____ⓐ_____.
> Boy: That's a good idea.

05 Which are suitable for blank ⓐ in the dialog above? Choose TWO.

① I suggest we do stretching exercises
② we don't have to do stretching exercises
③ I think we should do stretching exercises
④ I agree we should do stretching exercises
⑤ I'm not allowed to do stretching exercises

06 위 대화를 읽고 답할 수 <u>없는</u> 질문을 <u>모두</u> 고르면?

① Does the boy swim often?
② How often does the boy swim?
③ How many times a week does the girl swim?
④ When does the girl usually swim?
⑤ What will the girl and the boy do together today?

[07~08] 다음 대화를 읽고, 물음에 답하시오.

Woman: Hello. Welcome to Sports World. May I help you?

Boy: Yes, I came to register for a swimming class.

Woman: Is this your first time taking swimming lessons?

Boy: Yes, it is. I don't know how to swim at all.

Woman: I see. ⓐ얼마나 자주 수업을 듣고 싶으세요?

Boy: I want to take classes twice a week. I'd like to take classes on weekdays and not on weekends.

Woman: Then, I suggest that you take the Beginner 2 class. This class meets on Tuesdays and Thursdays.

Boy: That sounds good. I'd like to sign up for that class. How big is the class?

Woman: The class has a limit of 10 people.

Boy: That's perfect.

07 위 대화의 밑줄 친 우리말 ⓐ와 의미가 같도록 8단어의 완전한 문장으로 쓰시오.

→ _____

08 위 대화의 내용과 일치하지 <u>않는</u> 것을 찾아 기호를 쓰고, 바르게 고쳐 문장을 다시 쓰시오.

> ⓐ The boy has never learned how to swim.
> ⓑ The boy wants to take classes twice a month.
> ⓒ The boy doesn't want to take classes on weekends.
> ⓓ The boy will take the Beginner 2 class.
> ⓔ The class the boy wants to sign up for has a limit of 10 people.

(   ) → _____

09 다음 대화의 내용과 일치하도록 주어진 글을 완성하시오.

A: Mina, how often do you swim?

B: I swim every day.

A: Can I go swimming with you this afternoon?

B: Sure, Hojun. But I suggest you bring a swimming cap. Without a swimming cap, you aren't allowed in the pool.

↓

> Mina and Hojun will _____ _____ together this afternoon. Mina told Hojun to _____ _____ _____ _____.

10 주어진 [조건]에 맞게 다음 대화를 완성하시오.

A: I think I have a cold.

B: _____

> [조건] 1. A의 상황에 맞는 제안하는 말을 쓸 것
>   2. suggest를 사용할 것

11 다음은 수지의 습관을 정리한 표이다. 표를 보고 [조건]에 맞게 대화를 완성하시오.

	월	화	수	목	금	토	일
운동	○	○	○	○	○	○	○
아침 식사	×	×	×	×	×	○	○

> [조건] (1)에는 빈도를 묻는 표현, (2)에는 빈도를 말하는 표현, (3)에는 제안이나 권유하는 표현을 사용할 것

A: Suji, (1)_____?

B: I exercise every day.

A: That's good. Then, how often do you have breakfast?

B: (2)_____

A: (3)_____ Having breakfast is good for your health.

B: OK. I'll try.

Grammar
고득점 맞기

01 다음 빈칸에 들어갈 말이 순서대로 바르게 짝지어진 것은?

> • The boy _____ the ball is my best friend.
> • There were many people _____ in the park.

① kicked – walked ② kicked – walking
③ kicking – walked ④ kicking – walking
⑤ to kicking – to walk

한 단계 더!

02 다음 중 문장의 의미가 나머지와 다른 하나는?

① Soccer is as popular as baseball in the USA.
② Soccer isn't as popular as baseball in the USA.
③ Soccer isn't so popular as baseball in the USA.
④ Soccer is less popular than baseball in the USA.
⑤ Baseball is more popular than soccer in the USA.

03 다음 중 어법상 올바른 문장을 모두 고르면?

① Korea isn't as large as Australia.
② Nothing is as hardest as a diamond.
③ My mom does yoga as good as my sister.
④ The woman driving the red car is my English teacher.
⑤ The lady sang a song on the stage is a famous movie star.

04 다음 우리말과 의미가 같도록 괄호 안의 단어를 배열할 때 6번째로 올 단어로 알맞은 것은?

> 저쪽에서 자고 있는 고양이는 Tom의 고양이이다.
> (Tom's, there, cat, the, is, over, sleeping)

① is ② over ③ there
④ sleeping ⑤ Tom's

05 다음 우리말을 영어로 옮길 때 반드시 필요한 단어를 모두 고르면?

> 나는 그녀만큼 수영을 잘한다.

① well ② as ③ better
④ so ⑤ than

한 단계 더!

06 다음 중 밑줄 친 부분이 어법상 틀린 것은?

① She threw away the vase <u>broken</u> by me.
② The spaghetti <u>cooked</u> by Bill was too salty.
③ Do you know the boy <u>eating</u> a hamburger?
④ There was a room <u>filled</u> with a lot of old books.
⑤ The girl <u>waited</u> in front of the bakery is my sister.

07 다음 두 문장을 한 문장으로 바르게 바꿔 쓴 것은?

> Jisu gets up at 6. Her mom also gets up at 6.

① Jisu gets up as early as her mom.
② Jisu gets up earlier than her mom.
③ Jisu gets up less early than her mom.
④ Jisu doesn't get up as late as her mom.
⑤ Jisu doesn't get up as early as her mom.

한 단계 더!

08 다음 문장의 빈칸에 들어갈 수 없는 것은?

> ⓐ The girl _____ behind me is Alice.
> ⓑ I know the woman _____ an umbrella.
> ⓒ Tom ate up the cake _____ on the table.
> ⓓ They live in a house _____ in the 1970s.
> ⓔ She read the story about a family _____ around the world.

① standing ② holding ③ placing
④ built ⑤ traveling

09 다음 ⓐ~ⓔ 중 밑줄 친 부분의 쓰임이 같은 것끼리 짝지어진 것은?

> ⓐ I know the boys playing tennis.
> ⓑ I saw Tom crossing the street a few minutes ago.
> ⓒ Kate stopped driving after she had a car accident.
> ⓓ My problem is spending too much money on clothes.
> ⓔ The man waving his hands over there is my uncle.

① ⓐ, ⓒ   ② ⓑ, ⓓ   ③ ⓒ, ⓔ
④ ⓐ, ⓑ, ⓔ   ⑤ ⓑ, ⓒ, ⓔ

한 단계 │ 더!

10 다음 표의 내용과 일치하지 않는 문장은?

	Phone A	Phone B
크기	7×15 cm	7×15 cm
무게	155 g	170 g
가격	$250	$200
출시 연도	2020	2020

① Phone A is as big as Phone B.
② Phone B is as old as Phone A.
③ Phone B is heavier than Phone A.
④ Phone A is not as light as Phone B.
⑤ Phone B is not as expensive as Phone A.

한 단계 │ 더!

11 다음 중 밑줄 친 부분을 어법상 바르게 고치지 않은 것은?

> ⓐ The man worked at the zoo is very kind.
> ⓑ Sharks aren't as dangerous than alligators.
> ⓒ Pick up the trash throwing away by people.
> ⓓ These apples are more expensive as organic apples.
> ⓔ Nick is as patience as his old brother.

① ⓐ → working   ② ⓑ → as
③ ⓒ → thrown   ④ ⓓ → expensive
⑤ ⓔ → patient

한 단계 │ 더!

12 다음 중 짝지어진 두 문장의 의미가 같지 않은 것은?

> ① Tigers are faster than monkeys.
> = Monkeys are not so fast as tigers.
> ② This book isn't as helpful as that book.
> = This book is less helpful than that book.
> ③ The new park isn't as good as the old one.
> = The new park is better than the old one.
> ④ This hat is as expensive as that bag.
> = The price of this hat and that bag is the same.
> ⑤ The result isn't as important as the process.
> = The process is more important than the result.

13 다음 글의 밑줄 친 ⓐ~ⓔ 중 어법상 틀린 것은?

> There are two boys ⓐplay badminton. A girl is ⓑreading a book ⓒwritten in English. A boy is ⓓlooking at the birds ⓔsinging in the tree.

① ⓐ   ② ⓑ   ③ ⓒ   ④ ⓓ   ⑤ ⓔ

14 다음 문장들을 잘못 이해한 사람은?

> ⓐ A man was climbing up the tree.
> ⓑ My free time activity is watching a movie.
> ⓒ The dog running after Katie is not her pet.
> ⓓ Do you know the girl who is dancing on the street?

① 수미: ⓐ의 climbing은 진행 중인 동작을 나타내.
② 지호: ⓑ의 watching은 현재분사야.
③ 태영: ⓒ의 running은 The dog를 수식해.
④ 희진: ⓒ의 running 앞에는 that is가 생략되어 있다고 볼 수도 있어.
⑤ 미성: ⓓ에서 who is는 생략할 수 있어.

한 단계 더!

15 다음 두 문장을 분사를 사용하여 주어진 단어 수에 맞게 한 문장으로 쓰시오.

(1) The woman is my grandma. She is carrying books. (7단어)

→ _____

(2) She cleared up the plate. The plate was broken by Tom. (8단어)

→ _____

한 단계 더!

16 다음 두 문장의 의미가 같도록 빈칸에 알맞은 말을 쓰시오.

His new song is less popular than his first song.
= His new song _____ _____ _____ _____ _____ his first song.

17 다음 우리말과 의미가 같도록 괄호 안의 표현을 바르게 배열하여 문장을 쓰시오. (단, 필요한 단어만 사용할 것)

그 관현악단에서 연주하고 있는 바이올린 연주자들은 오스트리아 출신이다.

(from, in the orchestra, the violinists, are, played, playing, Austria, is)

→ _____

한 단계 더!

18 다음 문장에서 어법상 틀린 부분을 찾아 바르게 고쳐 쓰시오.

Mom was satisfied with the pictures taking by the professional photographer.

_____ → _____

19 다음 그림을 보고, as ~ as ...와 괄호 안의 단어를 사용하여 문장을 쓰시오.

(1)  (2)

(3) 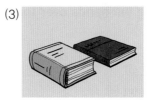 (4)

(1) _____ (fast)
(2) _____ (tall)
(3) _____ (thick)
(4) _____

(expensive)

20 다음 그림을 보고, ⟨A⟩와 ⟨B⟩의 표현을 각각 하나씩 사용하여 아래 글을 완성하시오. (단, 4단어 이하로 쓸 것)

A	run	hold	play
B	basketball	on the track	a soccer ball

I'll introduce my sports club to you. The boys (1)_____ are my classmates, Minsu, Yunho, and Jiho. The girl (2)_____ is my sister. The man (3)_____ is my coach.

영작하기

• 주어진 우리말과 일치하도록 문장을 쓰시오.

01
_____
스포츠에서는 선수들만 트로피나 메달을 받지만, 그들이 혼자 힘으로 우승하는 것은 아니다.

02
_____
그 선수들을 돕는 사람들이 있다.

03
_____
이 사람들은 종종 숨겨져 있고 주목을 받지 못한다.

04
_____
하지만 그들은 선수들만큼 중요하다.☆

05
_____
여기 몇 가지 예가 있다.

06
_____
페이서들은 마라톤에서 다른 선수들과 함께 달리며 그들을 이끈다.

07
_____
페이서들은 경험이 많은 선수들이며, 그들의 역할은 다른 선수들이 경주를 더 잘 운영하도록 돕는 것이다.

08
_____
한 경주에는 여러 명의 페이서들이 있을 수 있다.

09
_____
각각의 페이서는 다른 속도로 달리고 다른 시간대에 경주를 마친다.

10
_____
페이서들은 보통 자신들의 완주 시간을 나타내는 깃발이나 풍선을 가지고 있다.☆

11
_____
선수들은 자신들의 목표 완주 시간에 따라 페이서를 선택할 수 있다.

12
_____
예를 들어, 한 선수가 4시간 안에 경주를 마치고 싶다면, 그 선수는 4시간 페이서를 따라갈 것이다.

13
_____
페이서가 시간을 계속해서 파악하기 때문에, 선수는 특정 시간 안에 마라톤을 완주하려는 자신의 목표를 더 쉽게 달성할 수 있다.

14
_____
요컨대, 페이서들은 달리기는 하지만 우승을 하기 위해 달리는 것은 아니다.

15
_____
그들은 다른 이들을 위해 달린다.

16
_____
여러분은 대부분의 자동차 경주에서 자동차와 레이서만 볼지도 모르겠지만, 그 레이서 뒤에는 팀이 있다.

17
_____
이 팀은 피트 크루라고 불린다.

18
_____

피트는 경주 트랙의 옆에 있는 공간으로, 레이서들이 경주 도중에 그곳에 여러 번 정지한다.

19
_____

피트 크루가 하는 주요 역할은 자동차를 점검하고 타이어를 교체하는 것이다.

20
_____

빠른 속도의 경주에서는 타이어가 쉽게 마모되기 때문에 타이어를 교체하는 것이 특히 중요하다.

21
_____

피트에서의 정지는 짧게는 2초 정도가 될 수 있고, 한 크루에 많게는 20명에 이르는 구성원이 있다.☆

22
_____

그러므로 피트 크루는 완벽한 조화를 이루며 일해야 한다.

23
_____

레이서만 모든 주목을 받을지 모르지만 사람들이 말하는 것처럼, "경주의 우승은 피트에서 이루어진다."

24
_____

Sherpa라는 단어는 셰르파족에서 유래되었는데, 셰르파족은 네팔의 동쪽 지역에 산다.

25
_____

셰르파는 훌륭한 등반 기술을 가졌으며 산의 지리에 밝다.

26
_____

그들은 또한 산의 높은 곳에서 호흡하는 데 어려움이 거의 없다.

27
_____

그래서 등산가들은 자신들이 에베레스트산을 등반하는 것을 돕는 셰르파를 고용하기 시작했다.

28
_____

셰르파는 등산가들을 산 정상까지 이끈다.

29
_____

그들은 여러 방식으로 등산가들을 지원한다.

30
_____

예를 들어, 그들은 텐트를 치고 등산가들의 가방을 운반한다.

31
_____

셰르파는 종종 에베레스트산의 보이지 않는 사람들로 불리는데, 왜냐하면 사람들은 흔히 산 정상에서 등산가들만 찍힌 사진을 보기 때문이다.

고득점 맞기

[01~02] 다음 글을 읽고, 물음에 답하시오.

In sports, only the players get a trophy or medal, but they _____ⓐ_____ on their own. There are people who help the players. These people are often _____ⓑ_____ and don't get attention. However, ⓒthey are as important as the players. Here are some examples.

01 윗글의 빈칸 ⓐ와 ⓑ에 들어갈 말이 순서대로 바르게 짝지어진 것은?

① win – hidden   ② win – famous
③ don't win – hidden   ④ don't win – famous
⑤ don't win – visible

02 What does the underlined ⓒthey indicate in the passage above?

① sports   ② some examples
③ the players   ④ medals or trophies
⑤ people who help the players

[03~06] 다음 글을 읽고, 물음에 답하시오.

Pacers run with other runners and lead them in a marathon. Pacers are experienced runners, and their job is to help other runners manage their race better. There can be several pacers in a race. Each pacer runs at (A)同same / different┃ speeds and finishes the race in different times. Pacers usually have flags or balloons ⓐshowing their finish time.

Runners can choose a pacer depending on their target finish time. _____ⓑ_____, if a runner wants to finish the race in four hours, the runner will follow the four-hour pacer. Since the pacer keeps track of the time, the runner can (B)┃achieve / plan┃ his or her goal of finishing the marathon in a particular time more easily. _____ⓒ_____, pacers run but they don't run to win. They run for (C)┃others / themselves┃.

03 윗글 (A)~(C)의 각 네모 안에서 문맥상 알맞은 말이 순서대로 바르게 짝지어진 것은?

	(A)	(B)	(C)
①	same	⋯ achieve	⋯ others
②	same	⋯ plan	⋯ themselves
③	different	⋯ achieve	⋯ others
④	different	⋯ plan	⋯ themselves
⑤	different	⋯ achieve	⋯ themselves

**고
난도
04** 윗글의 밑줄 친 ⓐshowing과 쓰임이 같은 것을 모두 고르면?

① She imagined winning a gold medal.
② What do you enjoy doing on weekends?
③ Look at the children playing hide-and-seek.
④ The man talking on the phone is my grandpa.
⑤ They looked forward to winning the car race.

05 윗글의 흐름상 빈칸 ⓑ와 ⓒ에 들어갈 말이 순서대로 바르게 짝지어진 것은?

① However – In short
② However – For example
③ For example – In short
④ For example – However
⑤ Therefore – For example

**신
유형
06** 윗글의 pacers에 관한 설명으로 올바른 문장의 개수는?

ⓐ They run with other runners and help them.
ⓑ Only one pacer can run in each marathon.
ⓒ All of them have to finish the race at the same time.
ⓓ They have flags or balloons, which show their start time.

① 0개   ② 1개   ③ 2개   ④ 3개   ⑤ 4개

STEP
B

[07~09] 다음 글을 읽고, 물음에 답하시오.

You may only see the car and the driver @during most car races, but there is a team behind the driver. (①) A pit is a place on the side of the race track, and drivers stop there several times during a race. (②) The main job of the pit crew is to check the car and change the tires. (③) Changing the tires is especially important ⓑbecause of the tires wear out easily in a high speed race. (④) A pit stop can be as ©shortest as 2 seconds, and there are as many as 20 members on a crew. (⑤) Therefore, the pit crew has to work @in perfect harmony. The driver may get all the attention, but ⓔas people say, "Races ⓕare won in the pits."

07 윗글의 ①~⑤ 중 주어진 문장이 들어갈 위치로 알맞은 것은?

This team is called a pit crew.

①   ②   ③   ④   ⑤

08 윗글의 밑줄 친 @~ⓕ 중 어법상 틀린 것끼리 짝지어진 것은?

① @, ©   ② @, @, ⓔ   ③ ⓑ, ©
④ ⓑ, ⓕ   ⑤ ©, ⓔ, ⓕ

09 다음 질문과 응답 중 윗글의 내용과 일치하지 <u>않는</u> 것은?

① A: What is a pit?
   B: It is a place on the side of the race track.
② A: How often can drivers make a pit stop?
   B: They can make it once during a race.
③ A: What is the main job of a pit crew?
   B: It's checking the car and changing the tires.
④ A: Why is changing the tires important in a car race?
   B: The tires wear out easily during a car race.
⑤ A: How long is a pit stop?
   B: It can be as short as 2 seconds.

[10~12] 다음 글을 읽고, 물음에 답하시오.

The word *Sherpa* comes from the Sherpa tribe, @that lives in the eastern part of Nepal. Sherpas have good climbing skills and know their way around the mountains well. They also have ⓑfew difficulty breathing high up in the mountains. Therefore, mountain climbers started to hire Sherpas to help them ©climbed Mount Everest.

Sherpas lead mountain climbers to the top of the mountain. They support climbers in @much ways. For example, they put up tents and carry climbers' bags. Sherpas are often called _____(A)_____ of Mount Everest because people ⓔare often seen a picture of only the climbers at the top of the mountain.

10 윗글의 밑줄 친 @~ⓔ를 바르게 고쳐 쓴 것 중 어법상 <u>틀린</u> 것은?

① @ → which   ② ⓑ → little
③ © → climbing   ④ @ → many
⑤ ⓔ → often see

11 윗글의 빈칸 (A)에 들어갈 말로 가장 알맞은 것은?

① the photographers
② the invisible people
③ the climbing people
④ the famous climbers
⑤ the good mountain climbers

12 Which CANNOT be answered from the passage above?

① Where did the word *Sherpa* come from?
② Where does the Sherpa tribe live?
③ How do Sherpas learn climbing skills?
④ Why did mountain climbers start to hire Sherpas?
⑤ What do Sherpas do for mountain climbers?

[13~15] 다음 글을 읽고, 물음에 답하시오.

Pacers run with other runners and lead them in a marathon. Pacers are experienced runners, and their job is to help other runners manage their race better. There can be several pacers in a race. Each pacer runs at different speeds and finishes the race in different times. Pacers usually have ⓐ그들의 완주 시간을 나타내는 깃발이나 풍선들.

Runners can choose a pacer depending on their target finish time. For example, if a runner wants to finish the race in four hours, the runner will follow the four-hour pacer. Since the pacer keeps track of the time, the runner can achieve his or her goal of finishing the marathon in a particular time more easily. In short, pacers run but they don't run to win. They run for others.

고난도

13 괄호 안의 표현을 어법에 맞게 사용하여 윗글의 밑줄 친 우리말 ⓐ를 영어로 쓰시오. (7단어)

→ _____

(show, finish time, flags, balloons)

고난도

14 다음 문장의 빈칸에 알맞은 말을 윗글에서 찾아 쓰시오.

You can make various types of Gimbap _____ _____ the ingredients.

15 윗글의 내용과 일치하도록 다음 질문에 완전한 영어 문장으로 답하시오.

(1) How do runners choose a pacer in a marathon?

→ _____

(2) Who do pacers run for?

→ _____

[16~18] 다음 글을 읽고, 물음에 답하시오.

You may only see the car and the driver during most car races, but there is a team behind the driver. This team is called a pit crew. A pit is a place on the side of the race track, and drivers stop there several times during a race. The main job of the pit crew is to check the car and change the tires. Changing the tires is especially important because the tires wear out easily in a high speed race.

A pit stop can be as short as 2 seconds, and there are as many as 20 members on a crew. Therefore, the pit crew has to work in perfect harmony. The driver may get all the attention, but as people say, "ⓐRaces are won in the pits."

16 다음 영영풀이에 해당하는 단어를 윗글에서 찾아 쓰시오.

the act of watching or listening to something carefully

→ _____

고난도

17 윗글의 밑줄 친 ⓐ와 같이 말하는 이유를 우리말로 간단히 설명하시오.

→ _____
_____

신유형

18 윗글의 a pit crew에 대해 **잘못** 설명한 것을 찾아 기호를 쓰고, 잘못된 부분을 바르게 고쳐 쓰시오.

ⓐ It is a team behind the driver in car races.
ⓑ It checks the driver and changes the tires during car races.
ⓒ It consists of as many as 20 members.

( ) _____ → _____

서술형 100% TEST

01 다음 영영풀이에 해당하는 단어를 [보기]에서 골라 쓰시오.

> [보기] register   hide   particular   achieve

(1) _____ : relating to a specific person, thing, or place

(2) _____ : to succeed in doing or getting something you want

(3) _____ : to put something in a place where no one can see it

(4) _____ : to put someone's or something's name on an official list

02 다음 우리말과 의미가 같도록 빈칸에 알맞은 말을 쓰시오.

(1) 그는 혼자 힘으로 그 로봇을 만들었다.

→ He made the robot _____ _____ _____.

(2) 연구자들은 나이에 따라 참가자들을 분류했다.

→ The researchers grouped the participants _____ _____ their ages.

(3) 내가 수영할 때 시간을 계속해서 파악해 주겠니?

→ Can you _____ _____ _____ the time when I swim?

고난도

03 다음 [보기]에 제시된 단어의 반의어를 사용하여 각각의 문장을 완성하시오. (단, 중복 사용 불가)

> [보기] patient   visible   formal   polite

(1) I think it is _____ to ask someone's age.

(2) Although air is everywhere, it is _____ to the eye.

(3) You don't have to wear a suit because it's an _____ meeting.

(4) We're getting _____ because we've been waiting for half an hour.

04 다음 민지의 운동 일과표를 보고, 빈도를 묻고 말하는 대화를 완성하시오.

SUN	MON	TUE	WED	THU	FRI	SAT
	🏀		🏀		🏀	
🏃	🏃	🏃	🏃	🏃	🏃	🏃
		🎳				

A: Minji, _____ _____ _____ _____ _____ _____ ?

B: I play basketball _____ _____ a week.

A: Then, _____ _____ _____ _____ run on the track?

B: _____ _____.

A: That often? What about bowling lessons? How often do you take them?

B: _____ a week, on _____.

05 다음 대화를 읽고, 소년이 등록한 수업의 수강증을 완성하시오.

Woman: Hello. May I help you?

Boy: Yes, I came to register for a soccer class.

Woman: I see. How often do you want to take classes?

Boy: I want to take classes twice a week. I'd like to take classes on weekends.

Woman: Then, I think you can take the Beginner 1 class. This class meets on Saturdays and Sundays.

Boy: That sounds good.

Sports Center Registration	
Sport	Soccer
Class	(1)_____
How often	(2)_____
Day	(3)_____

[06~07] 다음 대화를 읽고, 물음에 답하시오.

Woman: Hello. Welcome to Sports World. May I help you?

Boy: Yes, I came to register for a swimming class.

Woman: Is this your first time taking swimming lessons?

Boy: Yes, it is. I don't know how to swim at all.

Woman: I see. How often do you want to take classes?

Boy: I want to take classes twice a week. I'd like to take classes on weekdays and not on weekends.

Woman: Then, @초급 2반을 수강하기를 권해요. This class meets on Tuesdays and Thursdays.

Boy: That sounds good. I'd like to sign up for that class. How big is the class?

Woman: The class has a limit of 10 people.

Boy: That's perfect.

06 위 대화의 밑줄 친 우리말 @와 의미가 같도록 주어진 표현을 바르게 배열하여 문장을 쓰시오.

> you, I, the Beginner 2 class, suggest, take, that

→ _____

07 위 대화의 내용과 일치하도록 소년의 일기를 완성하시오.

> Today I _____ for a swimming class at Sports World. As I don't _____ _____ _____ _____, I signed up for a beginners' class. I'll go swimming _____ a week on _____ _____ _____ from now on.

08 다음 두 문장을 분사를 사용하여 주어진 단어 수에 맞게 한 문장으로 바꿔 쓰시오.

(1) The dog is Jina's. It's following me. (6단어)

→ _____

(2) The boy is Mike. He is shaking his legs. (7단어)

→ _____

(3) The woman is my English teacher. She is wearing glasses. (8단어)

→ _____

09 다음 그림을 보고, as ~ as ...와 괄호 안의 단어를 사용하여 문장을 완성하시오.

(1)  (2)

(1) The express train is _____ the airplane. (fast)

(2) Some dogs are _____ dolphins. (smart)

10 다음 그림과 일치하도록 [보기]의 표현을 어법에 맞게 사용하여 문장을 완성하시오. (단, 필요시 두 개의 표현을 함께 사용할 것)

> [보기]   play   swim   sleep
>   with sand   under the umbrella

(1) The _____ woman is my mom.

(2) The man _____ _____ _____ _____ is my dad.

(3) The boys _____ _____ _____ _____ my brothers.

11 다음 중 어법상 **틀린** 문장을 **두 개** 골라 기호를 쓰고, 바르게 고쳐 문장을 다시 쓰시오.

> ⓐ Jake caught a falling leaf.
> ⓑ I know the girl wait for a bus.
> ⓒ Sujin is as creative as her sisters.
> ⓓ My dad cooks as good as the chef.
> ⓔ Do you know the boy band singing a song on TV?

(1) (　　) → _____

(2) (　　) → _____

12 다음 [조건]에 맞게 문장을 완성하시오.

A		B	
be		fast	
run		well	
sing		good	

> [조건]　1. as ~ as ...를 사용할 것
> 　　　　2. A와 B에서 각각 한 단어씩 중복되지 않게 사용할 것

(1) Jina _____ Minji. They both have beautiful voices.

(2) Your laptop _____ mine. You don't have to buy a new one.

(3) Lions cannot _____ cheetahs. Cheetahs are the fastest land animals.

[13~14] 다음 글을 읽고, 물음에 답하시오.

> Pacers run with other runners and ⓐunderline lead them in a marathon. Pacers are ⓑexperienced runners, and their job is _____(A)_____. There can be several ⓒpacers in a race. Each pacer runs at different speeds and ⓓfinish the race in different times. Pacers usually have flags or balloons ⓔshowing their finish time.

13 윗글의 빈칸 (A)에 들어갈 말을 [보기]에 주어진 표현을 바르게 배열하여 쓰시오.

> [보기]　better, to, manage, help, their race, other runners

→ _____

14 윗글의 밑줄 친 ⓐ~ⓔ 중 어법상 **틀린** 것을 찾아 바르게 고쳐 쓰고, 틀린 이유를 쓰시오.

(1) 틀린 부분: (　　) → _____

(2) 틀린 이유: _____

_____

15 다음 글의 내용과 일치하도록 페이서와의 인터뷰를 완성하시오.

> Runners can choose a pacer depending on their target finish time. For example, if a runner wants to finish the race in four hours, the runner will follow the four-hour pacer. Since the pacer keeps track of the time, the runner can achieve his or her goal of finishing the marathon in a particular time more easily. In short, pacers run but they don't run to win. They run for others.

↓

> Interviewer: How do runners choose a pacer?
> Pacer: They can choose a pacer _____ _____ _____ _____ _____ _____.
> Interviewer: What do you keep track of during a race?
> Pacer: We _____ _____ _____ _____ _____ to help runners achieve their goals _____ _____.
> Interviewer: You don't run to win, do you?
> Pacer: Of course not. We run _____ _____.

[16~18] 다음 글을 읽고, 물음에 답하시오.

You may only see the car and the driver during most car races, but there is a team behind the driver. This team is called a pit crew. A pit is a place on the side of the race track, and drivers stop there several times during a race. The main job of the pit crew is to check the car and change the tires. Changing the tires is especially important because the tires wear out easily in a high speed race.

A pit stop can be as short as 2 seconds, and there are as many as 20 members on a crew. Therefore, the pit crew has to work in perfect harmony. The driver may get all the attention, but as people say, "ⓐ경주의 우승은 피트에서 이루어진다."

16 pit의 정의를 윗글에서 찾아 9단어로 쓰시오.

→ _____

17 윗글의 밑줄 친 우리말 ⓐ를 [조건]에 맞게 영어로 쓰시오.

[조건] 1. Races를 주어로 하여 6단어로 쓸 것
2. win, in, the pits를 어법에 맞게 사용할 것

→ _____

18 윗글의 내용과 일치하도록 다음 질문에 대한 답을 완전한 영어 문장으로 쓰시오.

(1) What is a pit crew's main job?

→ _____

_____

(2) Why is changing the tires especially important in a car race?

→ _____

_____

[19~20] 다음 글을 읽고, 물음에 답하시오.

The word *Sherpa* comes from the Sherpa tribe, ⓐthat lives in the eastern part of Nepal. Sherpas have good climbing skills and ⓑknow their way around the mountains well. They also have ⓒfew difficulty breathing high up in the mountains. Therefore, mountain climbers started to hire Sherpas to help them ⓓto climb Mount Everest.

Sherpas lead mountain climbers to the top of the mountain. They support climbers in many ways. For example, they put up tents and carry climbers' bags. Sherpas are often ⓔcalling the invisible people of Mount Everest because people often see a picture of only the climbers at the top of the mountain.

19 윗글의 밑줄 친 ⓐ~ⓔ 중 어법상 틀린 것을 모두 찾아 기호를 쓰고, 바르게 고쳐 쓰시오.

(1) (　　) → _____

(2) (　　) → _____

(3) (　　) → _____

20 다음 질문에 대한 답 세 가지를 윗글에서 찾아 우리말로 쓰시오.

Why did mountain climbers start to hire Sherpas to help them climb Mount Everest?

(1) _____

(2) _____

(3) _____

01 다음 중 짝지어진 두 단어의 관계가 나머지와 <u>다른</u> 하나는?

2점

① direct – indirect　② target – goal
③ formal – informal　④ polite – impolite
⑤ possible – impossible

02 다음 영영풀이에 해당하는 단어로 알맞은 것은?

3점

> to put someone's or something's name on an official list

① hide　② achieve　③ suggest
④ support　⑤ register

서술형 1

03 다음 빈칸에 공통으로 들어갈 말을 쓰시오.

3점

> • My right shoe seems to _____ out easily.
> • Have you decided what to _____ to the party?

→ _____

신유형

04 다음 중 빈칸에 들어갈 수 있는 단어가 <u>아닌</u> 것은?

4점

> ⓐ The Apache are one of the native American _____(e)s.
> ⓑ He suddenly stood up and sang a song to get _____.
> ⓒ The _____ on the airplane was wearing blue uniforms.
> ⓓ The winner of this game will get a _____ and 500 dollars.

① track　② crew　③ tribe
④ trophy　⑤ attention

서술형 2

05 다음 대화의 빈칸에 들어갈 말을 7단어로 쓰시오.

5점

> A: _____?
> B: I stay up late three or four times a week.

06 자연스러운 대화가 되도록 (A)~(D)를 바르게 배열한 것은?

3점

> (A) I play once a week, but I want to play more often.
> (B) That sounds good! It'll be fun to play with you.
> (C) How often do you play basketball?
> (D) I suggest you join my basketball club. We play three times a week.

① (A) – (C) – (D) – (B)
② (A) – (D) – (C) – (B)
③ (B) – (C) – (A) – (D)
④ (C) – (A) – (D) – (B)
⑤ (C) – (B) – (D) – (A)

07 다음 대화의 흐름상 빈칸에 들어갈 말로 알맞은 것은?

3점

> A: Mina, how often do you come here to run?
> B: Every day.
> A: Can I run with you today?
> B: Sure, but _____. Your shoes aren't good for running.

① I think you should wear shoes
② I suggest you wear running shoes
③ I want you to change your clothes
④ I don't think you should change your shoes
⑤ I can recommend you a good place for running

[08~09] 다음 대화를 읽고, 물음에 답하시오.

> Woman: Hello. Welcome to Sports World. May I help you?
>
> Boy: Yes, I came to register for a swimming class.
>
> Woman: Is this your first time taking swimming lessons?
>
> Boy: Yes, it is. I don't know how to swim at all.
>
> Woman: I see. _____ ⓐ _____
>
> Boy: I want to take classes twice a week. I'd like to take classes on weekdays and not on weekends.
>
> Woman: Then, I suggest that you take the Beginner 2 class. This class meets on Tuesdays and Thursdays.
>
> Boy: That sounds good. I'd like to sign up for that class.

08 위 대화의 흐름상 빈칸 ⓐ에 들어갈 말로 알맞은 것은? 3점

① When did you start swimming?
② How many classes do you have?
③ What kind of sports do you like?
④ How long have you been swimming?
⑤ How often do you want to take classes?

서술형3

09 위 대화의 내용과 일치하도록 다음 문장의 빈칸에 알맞은 말을 쓰시오. 각 3점

(1) The boy has not learned _____ _____ _____ before.

(2) The boy wants to take swimming classes _____ a week, on _____.

(3) The boy will take the Beginner 2 class on _____ _____ _____.

10 다음 빈칸에 들어갈 말이 순서대로 바르게 짝지어진 것은? 3점

> • The girl _____ a book on the bench is my sister.
> • Canada is as _____ as the USA.

① read – larger ② reads – large
③ reads – larger ④ reading – largest
⑤ reading – large

서술형4

11 다음 우리말과 의미가 같도록 괄호 안의 단어를 어법에 맞게 사용하여 문장을 완성하시오. 5점

> 이 의자는 저 의자만큼 편안하다. (comfortable)

→ This chair is _____.

고
난도

12 다음 중 밑줄 친 부분의 쓰임이 [보기]와 같지 않은 것은? 4점

> [보기] There were many students borrowing books in the library.

① Don't wake up the sleeping dog.
② I know the girls waving their hands.
③ The man driving the car is my uncle.
④ My parents enjoy watching SF movies.
⑤ Did you see the boy playing the guitar?

한 단계 더!

13 다음 문장에서 어법상 틀린 부분을 바르게 고친 것은? 4점

> The red sunglasses are as not expensive as the brown ones.

① are → is
② as not → not as
③ not expensive → expensive not
④ expensive → more expensive
⑤ as → than

[14~15] 다음 글을 읽고, 물음에 답하시오.

In sports, only the players get a trophy or medal, but they don't win on their own. There are people who help the players. ⓐThese people are often hidden and don't get attention. However, ⓑthey are as important as the players. Here are some examples.

14 윗글의 밑줄 친 ⓐThese people에 대한 설명으로 알맞은 것을 <u>모두</u> 고르면? 4점

① They help the players.
② They like to get attention.
③ They are not well-known to people.
④ They are more important than the players.
⑤ They win a trophy or medal with other players.

서술형5

15 윗글의 밑줄 친 ⓑthey가 가리키는 것을 본문에서 찾아 다섯 단어로 쓰시오. 5점

→ _____

고난도

16 다음 글의 흐름상 빈칸 ⓐ~ⓔ에 들어갈 말로 알맞지 <u>않은</u> 것은? 4점

Pacers in a Marathon

Pacers ____ⓐ____ with other runners and lead them in a marathon. Pacers are ____ⓑ____ runners, and their job is to help other ____ⓒ____ manage their race ____ⓓ____. There can be several pacers in a ____ⓔ____.

① ⓐ: run
② ⓑ: experienced
③ ⓒ: pacers
④ ⓓ: better
⑤ ⓔ: race

[17~19] 다음 글을 읽고, 물음에 답하시오.

Each ⓐpacer runs at different speeds and finishes the race in different times. Pacers usually have flags or balloons ⓑshown their finish time. Runners can choose a pacer depending (A)⟨on / with⟩ their target finish time. For example, if a runner ⓒwants to finish the race in four hours, the runner will follow the four-hour pacer. Since the pacer keeps track (B)⟨of / on⟩ the time, the runner can achieve his or her goal of ⓓfinishing the marathon in a particular time more easily. (C)⟨At / In⟩ short, pacers run but they don't run ⓔto win. They run for others.

17 윗글의 밑줄 친 ⓐ~ⓔ 중 어법상 틀린 것은? 3점

① ⓐ ② ⓑ ③ ⓒ ④ ⓓ ⑤ ⓔ

18 윗글 (A)~(C)의 각 네모 안에 주어진 말 중에서 어법상 알맞은 것끼리 짝지어진 것은? 3점

	(A)	(B)	(C)
①	on	on	In
②	on	of	In
③	with	of	At
④	with	of	In
⑤	with	on	At

고난도

19 윗글의 내용과 일치하는 것은? 5점

① Runners cannot choose pacers on their own.
② Pacers usually have flags and balloons for other pacers.
③ Pacers and runners keep track of the time together.
④ Runners can meet their target finish time more easily by following a particular pacer.
⑤ Pacers run not for others but for themselves.

[20~22] 다음 글을 읽고, 물음에 답하시오.

You may only see the car and the driver during most car races, but there is a ____ⓐ____ behind the driver. This team is called a pit crew. A pit is a place on the side of the race ____ⓑ____, and drivers stop there several times during a race. The main job of the pit crew is to check the car and change the tires. ____(A)____ is especially important because the tires wear out easily in a high speed race.

A pit stop can be as ____ⓒ____ as 2 seconds, and there are as many as 20 members on a crew. Therefore, the pit crew has to work in ____ⓓ____ harmony. The ____ⓔ____ may get all the attention, but as people say, "Races are won in the pits."

고산도

20 윗글의 빈칸 ⓐ~ⓔ에 들어갈 수 있는 단어가 <u>아닌</u> 것은?

4점

① track   ② team   ③ pit
④ short   ⑤ perfect

21 윗글의 흐름상 빈칸 (A)에 들어갈 말로 알맞은 것은?   3점

① Driving fast
② Winning races
③ Getting attention
④ Changing the tires
⑤ Checking the driver

서술형6

22 다음 영영풀이에 해당하는 단어를 윗글에서 찾아 쓰시오.

3점

a situation in which people are peaceful and agree with each other

→ _____

[23~25] 다음 글을 읽고, 물음에 답하시오.

The word *Sherpa* comes from the Sherpa tribe, which lives in the eastern part of Nepal. Sherpas have good climbing skills and know their way around the mountains well. ⓐ<u>그들은 또한 산의 높은 곳에서 호흡하는 데 어려움이 거의 없다.</u> Therefore, mountain climbers started to hire Sherpas to help ⓑ<u>them</u> climb Mount Everest.

Sherpas lead mountain climbers to the top of the mountain. ⓒ<u>They</u> support climbers in many ways. For example, they put up tents and carry climbers' bags. Sherpas are often called the invisible people of Mount Everest because people often see a picture of only the climbers at the top of the mountain.

서술형7

23 윗글의 밑줄 친 우리말 ⓐ와 의미가 같도록 괄호 안의 단어를 어법에 맞게 사용하여 문장을 완성하시오.   5점

→ They also _____
_____ in the mountains.
(little, difficulty, breathe)

24 윗글의 내용과 일치하도록 할 때, 다음 질문에 대한 답으로 가장 알맞은 것은?   4점

> **Q.** Why are Sherpas often called the invisible people of Mount Everest?

① They only carry climbers' bags.
② The Sherpa tribe lives in hidden places.
③ They don't go to the top of the mountain.
④ They put up tents on top of the mountain.
⑤ They are not in the pictures of the climbers at the mountain top.

서술형8

25 윗글의 밑줄 친 ⓑ<u>them</u>과 ⓒ<u>They</u>가 각각 가리키는 것을 본문에서 찾아 쓰시오.   각 3점

ⓑ _____

ⓒ _____

01 다음 빈칸에 들어갈 말로 알맞은 것은?   2점

> A lot of stars are _____ to the human eye.

① light   ② formal   ③ particular
④ invisible   ⑤ impossible

서술형**1**

02 다음 빈칸에 공통으로 들어갈 말을 쓰시오.   3점

> • The young children couldn't find the way home _____ their own.
> • The price is different depending _____ the size.

→ _____

03 다음 중 밑줄 친 target의 의미가 나머지와 다른 하나는?
3점

① They couldn't achieve their target.
② The arrow hit the center of the target.
③ What's your sales target for next month?
④ The company has set a new target for next year.
⑤ The university will reach its target of 3,000 students soon.

04 다음 중 밑줄 친 부분의 우리말 뜻이 알맞지 않은 것은? 3점

① Sally did not take any drawing lessons.
            └──(수업을 듣다)──┘
② They worked together in perfect harmony.
                 └(조화를 이루며)┘
③ Mom decided to sign up for yoga classes.
                  (~을 위해 서명하다)
④ We'll keep track of our spending from now on.
        (~을 파악하다)
⑤ In short, we are living in the age of technology.
   (요컨대)

서술형**2**

05 다음 대화의 빈칸 ⓐ와 ⓑ에 공통으로 들어갈 말을 쓰시오.
4점

> A: How _____ⓐ_____ do you play basketball?
> B: I play once a week, but I want to play more _____ⓑ_____.

→ _____

06 자연스러운 대화가 되도록 (A)~(D)를 바르게 배열한 것은?   3점

> (A) That often? Anyway, it'll be fun swimming together today.
> (B) I don't swim often. How about you, Kate? How often do you swim?
> (C) Yes, but before we swim, I suggest we do stretching exercises.
> (D) I swim four times a week.
> A: That's a good idea.

① (B) – (C) – (A) – (D)   ② (B) – (D) – (A) – (C)
③ (C) – (A) – (D) – (B)   ④ (D) – (A) – (C) – (B)
⑤ (D) – (B) – (C) – (A)

07 다음 중 짝지어진 대화가 어색한 것은?   4점

① A: I think I have a cold.
   B: I suggest you go see a doctor.
② A: How often do you want to take classes?
   B: I want to take a baking class.
③ A: I suggest you eat less fast food.
   B: OK. I'll try.
④ A: Can I run with you today?
   B: Sure, but I suggest you wear running shoes.
⑤ A: How many times a week do you exercise?
   B: I exercise every day.

[08~10] 다음 대화를 읽고, 물음에 답하시오.

> **Woman:** Hello. Welcome to Sports World. May I help you?
> **Boy:** Yes, I came to register for a swimming class.
> **Woman:** Is this your first time taking swimming lessons? (①)
> **Boy:** Yes, it is. I don't know how to swim at all.
> **Woman:** I see. (②) How often do you want to take classes?
> **Boy:** I want to take classes twice a week. I'd like to take classes on weekdays and not on weekends.
> **Woman:** (③) This class meets on Tuesdays and Thursdays. (④)
> **Boy:** That sounds good. I'd like to sign up for that class. _____ ⓐ _____
> **Woman:** The class has a limit of 10 people. (⑤)
> **Boy:** That's perfect.

08 위 대화의 ①~⑤ 중 주어진 문장이 들어갈 위치로 알맞은 것은? 3점

> Then, I suggest that you take the Beginner 2 class.

①   ②   ③   ④   ⑤

09 위 대화의 흐름상 빈칸 ⓐ에 들어갈 말로 가장 알맞은 것은? 3점

① How big is the class?
② How long is the class?
③ When does the class meet?
④ What time does the class start?
⑤ How often does the class meet?

서술형 3

10 위 대화의 내용과 일치하도록 주어진 질문에 대한 답을 완성하시오. 각 3점

(1) How often will the boy take swimming lessons?
  → He'll take lessons _____.

(2) On what days will the boy take lessons?
  → He'll take lessons _____.

11 다음 빈칸에 들어갈 말이 순서대로 바르게 짝지어진 것은? 3점

> • Look at the cat _____ on the chair.
> • My baseball cap is as _____ as yours.

① sleeps − better   ② sleeps − well
③ sleeping − well   ④ sleeping − good
⑤ sleeping − better

12 다음 중 어법상 틀린 문장은? 3점

① Look at the falling leaves.
② You should be careful of boiling water.
③ The students playing soccer are my classmates.
④ The people live in the building need to move out in a month.
⑤ Do you know the girls taking a picture in front of the gate?

한 단계 더!

13 다음 중 빈칸에 as가 들어갈 수 없는 것은? 3점

① My bike is _____ old as my sister's.
② Today isn't so cold _____ yesterday.
③ Are you able to run _____ fast as Jake?
④ Is this watch _____ expensive than that one?
⑤ This movie is not _____ exciting as the movie I saw last week.

서술형 4   고난도

14 다음 우리말을 영어로 옮긴 문장에서 어법상 틀린 부분을 찾아 바르게 고쳐 쓰시오. 4점

> Jane은 저기 서 있는 자신의 언니만큼 노래를 아름답게 한다.
> → Jane sings as beautifully as her sister stands over there.

_____ → _____

[15~16] 다음 글을 읽고, 물음에 답하시오.

In sports, only the players get a trophy or medal, but they don't win on their own. There are people who help the players. These people are often hidden and don't get attention. However, they are as ___ⓐ___ as the players. Here are some examples.

15 윗글의 흐름상 빈칸 ⓐ에 들어갈 말로 알맞은 것은? 3점

① fast   ② well   ③ hidden

④ invisible   ⑤ important

16 윗글에 이어질 내용으로 가장 알맞은 것은? 4점

① various kinds of sports

② hidden people in sports

③ famous players who won on their own

④ sports players who get a lot of attention

⑤ hidden people who are as famous as players

[17~20] 다음 글을 읽고, 물음에 답하시오.

Pacers in a Marathon

Pacers run with other runners and lead ⓐthem in a marathon. Pacers are experienced runners, and ⓑtheir job is to help other runners manage their race better. There can be several pacers in a race. (A)Each pacers runs at different speeds and finishes the race in different times. Pacers usually have flags or balloons showing ⓒtheir finish time.

Runners can choose a pacer depending on ⓓtheir target finish time. For example, if a runner ___(B)___ to finish the race in four hours, the runner will follow the four-hour pacer. Since the pacer keeps track of the time, the runner can achieve his or her goal of ___(C)___ the marathon in a particular time more easily. In short, pacers run but they don't run to win. ⓔThey run for others.

17 윗글의 밑줄 친 ⓐ~ⓔ 중 가리키는 대상이 같은 것끼리 짝지어진 것은? 4점

① ⓐ, ⓑ, ⓓ – ⓒ, ⓔ

② ⓐ, ⓑ, ⓔ – ⓒ, ⓓ

③ ⓐ, ⓒ – ⓑ, ⓓ, ⓔ

④ ⓐ, ⓒ, ⓔ – ⓑ, ⓓ

⑤ ⓐ, ⓓ – ⓑ, ⓒ, ⓔ

서술형5

18 윗글의 밑줄 친 문장 (A)에서 어법상 틀린 부분을 찾아 바르게 고쳐 쓰시오. (단, 한 단어만 고칠 것) 4점

_____ → _____

19 윗글의 빈칸 (B)와 (C)에 들어갈 동사의 올바른 형태가 순서대로 바르게 짝지어진 것은? 3점

① wants – finish   ② will want – finish

③ wants – finishing   ④ will want – to finish

⑤ wants – finishes

서술형6 고난도

20 윗글의 내용과 일치하도록 다음 요약문을 완성하시오. 6점

Pacers are (1)_____ runners who (2)_____ other runners in a marathon. Runners can follow pacers that have flags or balloons depending on their (3)_____ _____ time. Pacers help runners finish the race in a particular time more easily by keeping track of the (4)_____.

[21~22] 다음 글을 읽고, 물음에 답하시오.

You may only see the car and the driver during most car races, but there is a team behind the driver. This team ⓐ피트 크루라고 불린다. A pit is a place on the side of the race track, and drivers stop there several times during a race. The main job of the pit crew is to check the car and change the tires. Changing the tires is especially important because the tires wear out easily in a high speed race.

A pit stop can be ⓑ2초만큼 짧은, and there are as many as 20 members on a crew. Therefore, the pit crew has to work in perfect harmony. The driver may get all the attention, but as people say, "Races are won in the pits."

서술형**7**

21 윗글의 밑줄 친 우리말 ⓐ와 ⓑ를 [조건]에 맞게 영어로 쓰시오. 각 **4**점

> [조건] 1. 괄호 안의 표현을 어법에 맞게 사용할 것
>   2. 각각 5단어로 쓸 것

ⓐ _____

(call, a pit crew)

ⓑ _____

(short, two seconds)

22 윗글의 피트 크루에 관한 내용으로 알맞지 <u>않은</u> 것은? **3**점

① 자동차 경주 트랙 옆의 공간에서 일한다.
② 차를 정비하고 타이어를 교체하는 것이 주된 일이다.
③ 레이서가 경기 중 단 한 번만 피트에 정지할 수 있기 때문에 완벽한 조화를 이루며 일해야 한다.
④ 자동차 경주에서 타이어가 쉽게 닳기 때문에 타이어를 교체하는 작업이 특히 중요하다.
⑤ 레이서만큼 주목을 받지는 못하지만 중요한 역할을 한다.

[23~25] 다음 글을 읽고, 물음에 답하시오.

Sherpas have good climbing skills and know their way around the mountains well. They also have little difficulty ____ⓐ____ high up in the mountains well. Therefore, mountain climbers started to ____ⓑ____ Sherpas to help them climb Mount Everest.

Sherpas ____ⓒ____ mountain climbers to the top of the mountain. They ____ⓓ____ climbers (A)in many ways. For example, they put up tents and carry climbers' bags. Sherpas are often called the ____ⓔ____ people of Mount Everest because people often see a picture of only the climbers at the top of the mountain.

23 윗글의 빈칸 ⓐ~ⓔ에 들어갈 말로 알맞지 <u>않은</u> 것은? **3**점

① ⓐ: breathing   ② ⓑ: hide   ③ ⓒ: lead
④ ⓓ: support   ⑤ ⓔ: invisible

24 윗글의 밑줄 친 (A)에 해당하는 내용으로 알맞은 것은? **3**점

① to live on Mount Everest
② to teach climbers climbing skills
③ to take pictures with the climbers
④ to put up tents and carry climbers' bags
⑤ to introduce Sherpas to mountain climbers

서술형**8**

25 다음 그림 속 각 사람을 소개하는 문장을 [보기]에 주어진 표현을 사용하여 [예시]와 같이 쓰시오. 각 **4**점

[보기]	write a card	blow up a balloon
	make a cake	play the piano

[예시] The girl writing a card is Sujin.

(1) _____

(2) _____

(3) _____

01 다음 중 짝지어진 단어의 관계가 [보기]와 같지 <u>않은</u> 것은?

2점

[보기] register – registration

① breathe – breath
② weekday – weekend
③ suggest – suggestion
④ achieve – achievement
⑤ recommend – recommendation

02 다음 중 단어와 영영풀이가 바르지 <u>않은</u> 것은? 3점

① **particular**: relating to a specific person, thing, or place
② **target**: the aim or result that you try to achieve
③ **hire**: to help someone, often when they are having problems
④ **crew**: a group of people with particular skills who work together
⑤ **tribe**: a group of people who have their own language and ways of living

서술형 1

03 다음 두 문장의 의미가 같도록 빈칸에 알맞은 말을 한 단어로 쓰시오. 4점

David planned his vacation on his own.
= David planned his vacation by _____.

04 다음 중 밑줄 친 부분의 쓰임이 <u>어색한</u> 것은? 3점

① The team worked <u>in perfect harmony</u>.
② Divers always <u>breathe</u> deeply before diving.
③ Carol didn't <u>sign up</u> for the swimming class.
④ Mr. Jones will <u>give a speech</u> at the conference.
⑤ Ron is an <u>experienced</u> player. He has never played in a game.

05 다음 대화의 빈칸에 들어갈 말로 알맞지 <u>않은</u> 것은? 3점

A: Mina, how often do you come here to run?
B: _____
A: Can I run with you today?
B: Sure, but I suggest you wear running shoes. Your shoes aren't good for running.

① Every day.
② Once a month.
③ Three times a week.
④ I want to run more often.
⑤ I come here four times a week.

서술형 2 고난도

06 다음 대화의 빈칸에 들어갈 말을 [조건]에 맞게 쓰시오. 5점

A: Minsu, how often do you exercise?
B: I exercise once a week.
A: _____
B: OK. I'll try.

[조건] 1. I, suggest, more often을 사용할 것
2. 6단어의 완전한 문장으로 쓸 것

07 다음 대화를 읽고 답할 수 <u>없는</u> 질문은? 3점

Andy: I don't swim often. How about you, Kate? How often do you swim?
Kate: I swim four times a week.
Andy: That often? Anyway, it'll be fun swimming together today.
Kate: Yes, but before we swim, I suggest we do stretching exercises.
Andy: That's a good idea.

① Does Andy swim often?
② How often does Kate swim?
③ Is Andy going to swim today?
④ Who suggests doing stretching exercises?
⑤ How long will they do stretching exercises?

[08~09] 다음 대화를 읽고, 물음에 답하시오.

Woman: Hello. Welcome to Sports World. May I help you?

Boy: Yes, I came to ____ⓐ____ for a swimming class.

Woman: Is this your first time taking swimming lessons?

Boy: Yes, it is. I don't know how to swim at all.

Woman: I see. How ____ⓑ____ do you want to take classes?

Boy: I want to take classes twice ____ⓒ____ week. I'd like to take classes on ____ⓓ____ and not on weekends.

Woman: Then, I suggest that you take the Beginner 2 class. (A)This class meets on Tuesdays and Thursdays.

Boy: That sounds good. I'd like to ____ⓔ____ for that class. How big is the class?

Woman: The class has a limit of 10 people.

Boy: That's perfect.

08 위 대화의 흐름상 빈칸 ⓐ~ⓔ에 들어갈 말로 알맞지 <u>않은</u> 것은? 3점

① ⓐ: register
② ⓑ: often
③ ⓒ: for
④ ⓓ: weekdays
⑤ ⓔ: sign up

09 위 대화를 읽고 밑줄 친 (A)This class에 관해 알 수 <u>없는</u> 것을 <u>모두</u> 고르면? 3점

① 수업명
② 수강료
③ 수강 요일
④ 수업 시간
⑤ 수강 제한 인원 수

10 다음 중 밑줄 친 부분이 어법상 <u>틀린</u> 것은? 3점

① Ted's bike is <u>as old as</u> mine.
② I try to laugh <u>as often as</u> Betty.
③ The lamp is <u>as tall as</u> the bookshelf.
④ Amy dances <u>as beautiful as</u> her sister.
⑤ His latest movie isn't <u>as interesting as</u> his other movies.

11 다음 중 밑줄 친 부분의 쓰임이 [보기]와 같은 것은? 3점

[보기] The girl <u>running</u> for the bus is my sister.

① They stopped <u>talking</u> for a while.
② My hobby is <u>playing</u> computer games.
③ Do you enjoy <u>listening</u> to hip hop music?
④ I have a map <u>showing</u> the way to the zoo.
⑤ By <u>following</u> the rule, you can manage your money better.

서술형3 고난도

12 다음 그림을 보고, 두 대상을 비교하는 문장을 [조건]에 맞게 쓰시오. 각 4점

[조건] 1. as ~ as ...를 사용할 것
2. 괄호 안의 단어를 사용할 것

(1)
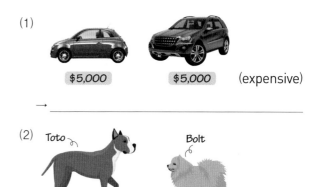
$5,000 $5,000   (expensive)

→ _____

(2) Toto   Bolt

2 years old   8 years old   (old)

→ _____

서술형4

13 다음 두 문장을 분사를 사용하여 주어진 단어 수에 맞게 한 문장으로 쓰시오. 각 3점

(1) The boy is my friend. He is looking at us. (8단어)
→ _____

(2) The man is the mayor. He is shaking hands with people. (9단어)
→ _____

(3) The woman is a famous singer. She is singing on the stage. (10단어)
→ _____

14 다음 중 어법상 올바른 문장의 개수는? 4점

> ⓐ Peter is as taller as his father.
> ⓑ The man wearing a suit is my teacher.
> ⓒ The lady reads a book there is a writer.
> ⓓ This issue is as serious not as the air pollution.
> ⓔ The girl making a speech on the stage is my classmate.

① 1개 ② 2개 ③ 3개 ④ 4개 ⑤ 5개

15 다음 글의 밑줄 친 ①~⑤ 중 흐름상 어색한 것은? 3점

> ### Hidden People in Sports
>
> In sports, only the players get ①a trophy or medal, but they don't win ②on their own. There are people ③who help the players. These people are often hidden and ④get a lot of attention. However, they are as ⑤important as the players.

① ② ③ ④ ⑤

[16~18] 다음 글을 읽고, 물음에 답하시오.

> Pacers run with other runners and lead them in a marathon. Pacers are experienced runners, and their job is to help other runners manage their race better. There can be several pacers in a race. Each pacer runs at different speeds and finishes the race in different times. (①) Pacers usually have flags or balloons showing their finish time. (②)
>
> Runners can choose a pacer depending on their target finish time. (③) For example, if a runner wants to finish the race in four hours, the runner will follow the four-hour pacer. (④) Since the pacer keeps track ___ⓐ___ the time, the runner can achieve his or her goal ___ⓑ___ finishing the marathon in a particular time more easily. (⑤) They run for others.

16 윗글의 ①~⑤ 중 주어진 문장이 들어갈 위치로 알맞은 것은? 3점

> In short, pacers run but they don't run to win.

① ② ③ ④ ⑤

17 윗글의 빈칸 ⓐ와 ⓑ에 공통으로 들어갈 말로 알맞은 것은? 3점

① of ② on ③ for ④ to ⑤ with

서술형5 고난도 신유형

18 다음 중 윗글을 읽고 답할 수 있는 것을 골라 기호를 쓰고, 알맞은 답을 완전한 영어 문장으로 쓰시오. 각 4점

> ⓐ What is a pacer's job in a marathon?
> ⓑ How do pacers choose their runners?
> ⓒ What do the pacers' flags or balloons show?
> ⓓ What does a pacer do to win?

(1) (   ) → _____

(2) (   ) → _____

[19~21] 다음 글을 읽고, 물음에 답하시오.

> You may only see the car and the driver during most car races, but there is a team behind the driver. This team is called a pit crew. A pit is a place on the side of the race track, and drivers stop there several times during a race. The main job of the pit crew is to check the car and change the tires. Changing the tires is especially important because the tires wear out easily in a high speed race.
>
> A pit stop can be as short as 2 seconds, and there are as many as 20 members on a crew. ___ⓐ___, the pit crew has to work in perfect harmony. The driver may get all the attention, but ⓑas people say, "Races are won in the pits."

19 윗글의 빈칸 ⓐ에 들어갈 말로 알맞은 것은?   3점

① However   ② Since   ③ For example

④ Because   ⑤ Therefore

20 윗글의 밑줄 친 ⓑas와 쓰임이 같은 것은?   4점

① As it's cold, you should wear a coat.

② I wanted to listen to music as I had lunch.

③ She was late for school as she got up late.

④ As he was taking a shower, the phone rang.

⑤ As I told you before, I want to play the drums.

서술형**6**

21 윗글의 내용과 일치하도록 피트 크루와의 인터뷰를 완성하시오.   6점

> A: What is your team called?
> B: Our team (1)_____.
> A: What is your main job?
> B: It is to (2)_____.
> A: Is there anything important about your job?
> B: A pit stop can be (3)_____,
>   so we have to work (4)_____.

[22~24] 다음 글을 읽고, 물음에 답하시오.

The word *Sherpa* comes from the Sherpa tribe, which lives in the eastern part of Nepal. Sherpas have good climbing skills and know their way around the mountains well. ⓐThey also have little difficulty breathe high up in the mountains. Therefore, mountain climbers started to hire Sherpas to help them climb Mount Everest.

Sherpas lead mountain climbers to the top of the mountain. They support climbers in many ways. For example, they put up tents and carry climbers' bags. ⓑSherpas are often called the invisible people of Mount Everest because people often see a picture of only the climbers at the top of the mountain.

22 윗글의 밑줄 친 문장 ⓐ에서 어법상 틀린 부분을 바르게 고쳐 쓴 것은?   3점

① little → few   ② difficulty → difficult

③ breathe → breathing   ④ high → highly

⑤ in → to

서술형**7**

23 윗글의 밑줄 친 ⓑ의 이유를 본문에서 찾아 우리말로 쓰시오.   4점

→ _____

_____

24 윗글의 Sherpas에 대해 <u>잘못</u> 이해한 사람은?   3점

① Mina: They are good at climbing mountains.

② Sue: They are hired by mountain climbers.

③ Jake: Mountain climbers lead them to the top of the mountains.

④ Carol: People call them the invisible people of Mount Everest.

⑤ Alex: People often can't see them in the pictures of climbers at the top of the mountain.

25 다음 글의 흐름상 빈칸 ⓐ와 ⓑ에 들어갈 말이 순서대로 바르게 짝지어진 것은?   4점

> ____ⓐ____ people usually don't think that cheerleaders are a part of a football team, they play an important role in a football game. By cheering at a game, they create team spirit. They also encourage their team and fans. To do their job well, cheerleaders need to be fit and strong. They also need to be good at jumping and dancing. ____ⓑ____, they need to work as hard as the players.

① If – However

② As – However

③ Since – Most of all

④ Although – Most of all

⑤ Because – For example

01 다음 영영풀이 중 어느 것에도 해당하지 <u>않는</u> 단어는? 3점

> ⓐ to take air into your body and let it out again
> ⓑ a group of people who have their own language and ways of living
> ⓒ a situation in which people are peaceful and agree with each other
> ⓓ to put something in a place where no one can see it

① hide ② tribe ③ hire
④ harmony ⑤ breathe

02 다음 중 밑줄 친 부분의 쓰임이 <u>어색한</u> 것은? 3점

① This tire <u>doesn't wear out</u> easily.
② Anyone can <u>sign up</u> for the art class.
③ The bank failed to <u>keep track of</u> the money.
④ The prices of the pots are different <u>depending on</u> the size.
⑤ My friends helped me with my project, so I did it <u>on my own</u>.

03 다음 대화의 빈칸에 들어갈 수 <u>없는</u> 것은? 3점

> A: How often do you exercise?
> B: _____

① Twice a week.
② I rarely exercise.
③ As often as I can.
④ I exercise every day.
⑤ I exercised last Sunday.

서술형1 고/난도

04 다음과 같은 상황에서 Lucy에게 할 권유의 말을 suggest 를 사용하여 쓰시오. 5점

> Lucy: I think I have a bad cold. I have a runny nose and a fever.

→ _____

05 다음 대화의 빈칸 (A)~(C)에 들어갈 말로 알맞은 것을 [보기] 에서 골라 순서대로 바르게 짝지은 것은? 3점

> A: How often do you play basketball?
> B: ___(A)___, but I want to play more often.
> A: ___(B)___. We play three times a week.
> B: ___(C)___! It'll be fun to play with you.

> [보기] ⓐ That sounds good
> ⓑ I play once a week
> ⓒ I suggest you join my basketball club

① ⓐ – ⓒ – ⓑ ② ⓑ – ⓐ – ⓒ
③ ⓑ – ⓒ – ⓐ ④ ⓒ – ⓐ – ⓑ
⑤ ⓒ – ⓑ – ⓐ

[06~07] 다음 대화를 읽고, 물음에 답하시오.

> Boy: Suji, how often do you take bowling lessons?
> Girl: Twice a week. I'm just a beginner. I heard you're very good.
> Boy: Well, I love bowling. Hmm. Your bowling ball looks heavy for you. I suggest ___ⓐ___.
> Girl: OK. I'll look for a lighter one, then.

06 위 대화의 흐름상 빈칸 ⓐ에 들어갈 말로 가장 알맞은 것은? 3점

① you practice more
② you use a lighter ball
③ you use a heavier one
④ you take bowling lessons
⑤ you look for a light-colored ball

07 Which is NOT true about the dialog above? 4점

① The girl takes bowling lessons.
② The boy goes bowling twice a week.
③ The girl thinks she is at the beginning stage in bowling.
④ The girl heard that the boy is good at bowling.
⑤ The boy gave advice to the girl.

[08~10] 다음 대화를 읽고, 물음에 답하시오.

> Woman: Hello. Welcome to Sports World. May I help you?
> Boy: ⓐYes, I came to register for a swimming class.
> Woman: Have you ever taken swimming lessons before?
> Boy: ⓑNo, I haven't. I don't know how to swim at all.
> Woman: I see. _____(A)_____?
> Boy: I want to take classes twice a week. ⓒI'd like to take classes on weekends and not on weekdays.
> Woman: Then, I suggest you take the Beginner 2 class. This class meets on Tuesdays and Thursdays.
> Boy: ⓓThat sounds good. I'd like to sign up for that class. ⓔHow big is the class?
> Woman: The class has a limit of 10 people.
> Boy: That's perfect.

08 위 대화의 밑줄 친 ⓐ~ⓔ 중 흐름상 어색한 것은? 3점

① ⓐ   ② ⓑ   ③ ⓒ   ④ ⓓ   ⑤ ⓔ

서술형2
09 위 대화의 흐름상 빈칸 (A)에 알맞은 말을 8단어로 쓰시오. 5점

→ _____

서술형3 고난도
10 위 대화의 내용과 일치하도록 소년의 수강증에서 잘못된 정보를 찾아 기호를 쓰고, 바르게 고쳐 쓰시오. 5점

Sports World Registration	
Sport	ⓐSwimming
Class	ⓑBeginner 2 (ⓒa minimum of 10 people)
Day	ⓓTwice a week ⓔTuesdays and Thursdays

(　　　) → _____

11 다음 우리말을 영어로 쓸 때 반드시 필요한 단어는? 4점

> 그의 방은 내 방만큼 크다.

① as   ② he   ③ bigger
④ largely   ⑤ me

12 다음 중 밑줄 친 부분의 쓰임이 [보기]와 같은 것끼리 짝지어진 것은? 4점

> [보기] I saw a crying boy on my way home.

> ⓐ He is looking forward to going to Italy.
> ⓑ There are two boys dancing on the street.
> ⓒ A lady carrying a big box fell on the floor.
> ⓓ Collecting magnets is my brother's hobby.

① ⓐ, ⓒ   ② ⓑ, ⓒ   ③ ⓒ, ⓓ
④ ⓐ, ⓑ, ⓒ   ⑤ ⓑ, ⓒ, ⓓ

고난도 한 단계 더!

13 다음 중 의미가 같은 문장을 <u>모두</u> 고르면? 4점

① Health is as important as money.
② Money is less important than health.
③ Money is not as important as health.
④ Money is more important than health.
⑤ Health is more important than money.

14 다음 중 밑줄 친 부분을 어법상 바르게 고친 것은? 4점

① Don't wake the baby <u>sleeping</u>.
　　　　　→ baby sleeps
② Tom can jump as <u>higher</u> as John.
　　　　　→ highly
③ He plays the piano as <u>good</u> as I.
　　　　　→ better
④ The man wearing jeans <u>are</u> my uncle.
　　　　　→ is
⑤ Amy is <u>as not outgoing as</u> Lisa.
　　　　　→ not as outgoing than

[15~16] 다음 글을 읽고, 물음에 답하시오.

In sports, only the players get a trophy or medal, but they don't win on ⓐ<u>his</u> own. There are people ⓑ<u>that</u> help the players. These people are often ⓒ<u>hide</u> and don't get attention. However, they are as ⓓ<u>importantly</u> as the players. Here ⓔ<u>is</u> some examples.

15 윗글의 밑줄 친 ⓐ~ⓔ 중 어법상 올바른 것은? 3점

　① ⓐ　　② ⓑ　　③ ⓒ　　④ ⓓ　　⑤ ⓔ

16 윗글의 주제로 가장 알맞은 것은? 3점

① how to get a lot of attention in sports
② sports players who help people secretly
③ hidden people who help players in sports
④ sports players who win trophies and medals
⑤ how to become an important player in sports

[17~19] 다음 글을 읽고, 물음에 답하시오.

Pacers run with other runners and 　ⓐ　 them in a marathon. Pacers are experienced runners, and their job is 　ⓑ　 other runners 　ⓒ　 their race better. There can be several pacers in a race. (A)각각의 페이서는 다른 속도로 달리고 다른 시간대에 경주를 마친다. Pacers usually have flags or balloons (B)<u>showing</u> their finish time.

서술형4

17 윗글의 빈칸 ⓐ~ⓒ에 들어갈 말을 [보기]에서 골라 쓰시오. 각 3점

[보기]	manage	lead	to help

ⓐ _____

ⓑ _____

ⓒ _____

고난도

18 윗글의 밑줄 친 우리말 (A)를 영어로 바르게 옮긴 것은? 4점

① Each pacers run at different speeds and finish the race in different times.
② Each pacer runs at different speeds and finish the race in different times.
③ All the pacers run at different speeds and finishing the race in different time.
④ Each pacer runs at different speeds and finishes the race in different times.
⑤ All pacer runs at different speeds and finishes the race in different times.

신유형

19 윗글의 (B)<u>showing</u>과 밑줄 친 부분의 쓰임이 같은 문장의 개수는? 4점

ⓐ The boy avoided <u>showing</u> his hands.
ⓑ Thank you for <u>showing</u> me your work.
ⓒ There was a picture <u>showing</u> fancy cars.
ⓓ Jane doesn't like <u>showing</u> her pictures to other people.

　① 0개　　② 1개　　③ 2개　　④ 3개　　⑤ 4개

[20~21] 다음 글을 읽고, 물음에 답하시오.

Runners can choose a pacer depending on their target finish time. For example, if a runner wants to finish the race in four hours, the runner will follow the four-hour pacer. Since the pacer keeps track of the time, the runner can achieve his or her goal of finishing the marathon in a particular time more easily.

서술형 **5**

20 다음 빈칸에 해당하는 단어를 윗글에서 찾아 쓰시오. 3점

Jenny _____(e)d her goal of passing the exam.

21 윗글을 다음과 같이 요약할 때, ⓐ~ⓓ 중 윗글의 내용과 일치하지 <u>않는</u> 것끼리 짝지어진 것은? 4점

Runners	ⓐ have their target finish time ⓑ keep track of the time for other runners
Pacers	ⓒ don't run to win a race ⓓ run to support other pacers

① ⓐ, ⓒ   ② ⓐ, ⓓ   ③ ⓑ, ⓒ
④ ⓑ, ⓓ   ⑤ ⓒ, ⓓ

[22~24] 다음 글을 읽고, 물음에 답하시오.

You may only see the car and the driver __(A)__ most car races, but there is a team behind the driver. People call this team a pit crew. A pit is a place on the side of the race track, and drivers stop there several times __(B)__ a race. ⓐThe main job of the pit crew is checking the car and changing the tires. ⓑChanging the tires is especially important because the tires wear out easily in a high speed race. (C)피트에서의 정지는 짧게는 2초 정도가 될 수 있다, and there are as many as 20 members on a crew. Therefore, the pit crew has to work in perfect harmony. The driver may get all the attention, but as people say, "ⓒRaces win in the pits."

22 윗글의 빈칸 (A)와 (B)에 공통으로 들어갈 말로 알맞은 것은? 3점

① of   ② from   ③ during
④ when   ⑤ while

서술형 **6**

23 윗글의 밑줄 친 우리말 (C)와 의미가 같도록 괄호 안의 단어를 바르게 배열하여 문장을 완성하시오. 5점

→ _____

(be, 2 seconds, can, as, as, short, pit stop, a)

서술형 **7**

24 윗글의 밑줄 친 ⓐ~ⓒ 중 어법상 <u>틀린</u> 문장을 찾아 기호를 쓰고, 바르게 고쳐 문장을 다시 쓰시오. 5점

(   ) → _____

25 다음 글의 흐름에 맞게 (A)~(C)를 바르게 배열한 것은? 4점

The word *Sherpa* comes from the Sherpa tribe, which lives in the eastern part of Nepal.

(A) Therefore, mountain climbers started to hire Sherpas to help them climb Mount Everest. Sherpas lead mountain climbers to the top of the mountain. They support climbers in many ways.

(B) Sherpas have good climbing skills and know their way around the mountains well. They also have little difficulty breathing high up in the mountains.

(C) For example, they put up tents and carry climbers' bags. Sherpas are often called the invisible people of Mount Everest because people often see a picture of only the climbers at the top of the mountain.

① (A) – (C) – (B)   ② (B) – (A) – (C)
③ (B) – (C) – (A)   ④ (C) – (A) – (B)
⑤ (C) – (B) – (A)

● 틀린 문항을 표시해 보세요.

〈제1회〉 대표 기출로 내신 **적중** 모의고사   총점 _____ / 100

문항	영역	문항	영역	문항	영역
01	p.10(W)	10	pp.22~23(G)	19	p.30(R)
02	p.10(W)	11	p.23(G)	20	p.31(R)
03	p.8(W)	12	p.22(G)	21	p.31(R)
04	p.8(W)	13	p.23(G)	22	p.31(R)
05	p.13(L&T)	14	p.30(R)	23	p.31(R)
06	p.14(L&T)	15	p.30(R)	24	p.31(R)
07	p.14(L&T)	16	p.30(R)	25	p.31(R)
08	p.15(L&T)	17	p.30(R)		
09	p.15(L&T)	18	p.30(R)		

〈제2회〉 대표 기출로 내신 **적중** 모의고사   총점 _____ / 100

문항	영역	문항	영역	문항	영역
01	p.8(W)	10	p.15(L&T)	19	p.30(R)
02	p.8(W)	11	pp.22~23(G)	20	p.30(R)
03	p.10(W)	12	p.22(G)	21	p.31(R)
04	p.8(W)	13	p.23(G)	22	p.31(R)
05	p.13(L&T)	14	p.22(G)	23	p.31(R)
06	p.14(L&T)	15	p.30(R)	24	p.31(R)
07	p.13(L&T)	16	p.30(R)	25	p.22(G)
08	p.15(L&T)	17	p.30(R)		
09	p.15(L&T)	18	p.30(R)		

〈제3회〉 대표 기출로 내신 **적중** 모의고사   총점 _____ / 100

문항	영역	문항	영역	문항	영역
01	p.10(W)	10	p.23(G)	19	p.31(R)
02	p.10(W)	11	p.22(G)	20	p.31(R)
03	p.8(W)	12	p.23(G)	21	p.31(R)
04	p.8(W)	13	p.22(G)	22	p.31(R)
05	p.14(L&T)	14	pp.22~23(G)	23	p.31(R)
06	p.13(L&T)	15	p.30(R)	24	p.31(R)
07	p.14(L&T)	16	p.30(R)	25	p.44(R)
08	p.15(L&T)	17	p.30(R)		
09	p.15(L&T)	18	p.30(R)		

〈제4회〉 고난도로 내신 **적중** 모의고사   총점 _____ / 100

문항	영역	문항	영역	문항	영역
01	p.10(W)	10	p.15(L&T)	19	p.30(R)
02	p.8(W)	11	p.23(G)	20	p.30(R)
03	p.13(L&T)	12	p.22(G)	21	p.30(R)
04	p.13(L&T)	13	p.23(G)	22	p.31(R)
05	p.14(L&T)	14	pp.22~23(G)	23	p.31(R)
06	p.14(L&T)	15	p.30(R)	24	p.31(R)
07	p.14(L&T)	16	p.30(R)	25	p.31(R)
08	p.15(L&T)	17	p.30(R)		
09	p.15(L&T)	18	p.30(R)		

● 부족한 영역을 점검하고 어떻게 더 학습할지 계획을 적어 보세요.

제1회 오답 공략
부족한 영역
학습 계획

제2회 오답 공략
부족한 영역
학습 계획

제3회 오답 공략
부족한 영역
학습 계획

제4회 오답 공략
부족한 영역
학습 계획

Lesson 6

Stories for All Time

주요 학습 내용	의사소통 기능	축하·유감 표현하기	Congratulations on winning the gold medal. (금메달 딴 것을 축하해.) I'm sorry to hear that. (그 말을 들으니 유감이야.)
		감정 표현하기	A: What's up? (무슨 일이니?) B: My smartphone is broken. I'm very upset. (내 스마트폰이 고장 났어. 나는 너무 속상해.)
	언어 형식	과거완료	People asked him where he **had got** the furniture. (사람들은 그에게 가구를 어디에서 구했는지 물었다.)
		관계대명사 what	The table was **what** every dealer dreamed of. (그 탁자는 모든 판매상이 꿈꾸는 것이었다.)

학습 단계 PREVIEW	STEP A	Words	Listen and Talk	Grammar	Reading	기타 지문
	STEP B	Words	Listen and Talk	Grammar	Reading	서술형 100% Test
	내신 적중 모의고사	제 1 회	제 2 회	제 3 회	제 4 회	

Words

만점 노트

Listen and Talk

* 완벽히 외운 단어는 □ 안에 √표 해 봅시다.

□□ announcement　명 발표, 소식

□□ anyway　부 어쨌든, 그런데

□□ congratulation☆　명 (-s) 축하 (인사)　감 (-s) 축하해

□□ disappointed☆　형 실망한

□□ elect　동 (선거로) 선출하다

□□ flu　명 독감

□□ main　형 주된, 중요한

□□ practice　명 연습　동 연습하다

□□ president　명 회장

□□ role　명 역할

□□ unfortunately　부 불행하게도, 유감스럽게도

□□ upset☆　형 화가 난, 속상한

□□ be proud of　～을 자랑스러워하다

□□ do one's best　최선을 다하다

Talk and Play

□□ method　명 방법

□□ spot　명 곳, 장소

Reading

□□ add　동 첨가하다; (말을) 덧붙이다

□□ antique☆　형 (귀중한) 골동품인　명 (귀중한) 골동품

□□ attach　동 붙이다, 첨부하다

□□ charge　동 (요금·값을) 청구하다

□□ dealer　명 (특정 물건을 사고파는) 판매상, 중개인

□□ favor　명 호의, 친절

□□ final　형 최종의, 마지막의

□□ furniture☆　명 가구

□□ knock　동 두드리다, 노크하다

□□ luck　명 행운, 운 (cf. lucky 형 운이 좋은)

□□ offer　명 제안, 제의

□□ owner　명 주인, 소유자

□□ pay　동 (값·비용·대가 등을) 지불하다

□□ price　명 값, 가격

□□ priceless☆　형 대단히 귀중한

□□ reproduction☆　명 (예술 작품의) 복제품, 복제

□□ saw　명 톱　동 톱질하다

□□ shocked　형 충격을 받은, 깜짝 놀란

□□ valuable☆　형 값비싼, 귀중한

□□ worth☆　형 (어떤 금액의) 가치가 있는, ～의 값어치가 있는

□□ be known for☆　～으로 알려져 있다, 유명하다

□□ can't help -ing☆　～하지 않을 수 없다

□□ cut off　～을 잘라 내다

□□ fall over　넘어지다, 넘어지며 구르다

□□ on one's way (to)☆　(～로) 가는 길에

□□ take a look　한번 보다

□□ take advantage of　～을 이용하다, 기회로 활용하다

□□ What if ~?　～면 어쩌지?

□□ with a straight face　정색하며, 시치미를 떼고

Language in Use

□□ careless　형 부주의한

□□ collection　명 소장품, 수집물

□□ endless　형 무한한

□□ exactly　부 정확하게

□□ receive　동 받다

□□ replay　동 재생하다, 다시 듣다/보다

□□ whole　형 전부의

□□ help yourself　맘껏 드세요

Think and Write

□□ review　명 논평, 비평

□□ recommendation　명 추천

Review

□□ chance　명 기회

□□ backpack　명 배낭

Words

연습 문제

A 다음 단어의 우리말 뜻을 쓰시오.

01 charge _____

02 dealer _____

03 announcement _____

04 favor _____

05 elect _____

06 careless _____

07 add _____

08 reproduction _____

09 congratulation(s) _____

10 attach _____

11 anyway _____

12 offer _____

13 priceless _____

14 unfortunately _____

15 spot _____

16 whole _____

17 collection _____

18 endless _____

19 valuable _____

20 receive _____

B 다음 우리말 뜻에 알맞은 영어 단어를 쓰시오.

01 톱; 톱질하다 _____

02 가구 _____

03 역할 _____

04 화가 난, 속상한 _____

05 주인, 소유자 _____

06 최종의, 마지막의 _____

07 골동품(인) _____

08 실망한 _____

09 값, 가격 _____

10 독감 _____

11 충격을 받은, 깜짝 놀란 _____

12 정확하게 _____

13 행운, 운 _____

14 두드리다, 노크하다 _____

15 주된, 중요한 _____

16 연습; 연습하다 _____

17 회장 _____

18 (값·비용·대가 등을) 지불하다 _____

19 재생하다, 다시 듣다/보다 _____

20 (어떤 금액의) 가치가 있는 _____

C 다음 영어 표현의 우리말 뜻을 쓰시오.

01 fall over _____

02 take advantage of _____

03 take a look _____

04 on one's way (to) _____

05 can't help -ing _____

06 be known for _____

07 cut off _____

08 with a straight face _____

09 be proud of _____

10 help yourself _____

D 다음 우리말 뜻에 알맞은 영어 표현을 쓰시오.

01 한번 보다 _____

02 ~으로 알려져 있다, 유명하다 _____

03 정색하며, 시치미를 떼고 _____

04 ~하지 않을 수 없다 _____

05 ~면 어쩌지? _____

06 ~을 잘라 내다 _____

07 ~을 이용하다 _____

08 최선을 다하다 _____

09 넘어지다, 넘어지며 구르다 _____

10 (~로) 가는 길에 _____

 **Words Plus**
만점 노트

영영풀이

□□	antique	골동품인	old and often valuable or beautiful
□□	attach	붙이다	to fasten or join one thing to another
□□	charge	(요금을) 청구하다	to ask people to pay a particular amount of money for something
□□	congratulation(s)	축하 (인사)	the act of congratulating someone
□□	dealer	판매상	a person whose job is to buy and sell things
□□	favor	호의, 친절	something that you do to help someone
□□	furniture	가구	things such as chairs, beds, tables, and bookshelves, etc.
□□	knock	두드리다	to hit a door with your hand so that someone inside knows you are there
□□	offer	제안, 제의	an act of asking someone if they would like something
□□	priceless	대단히 귀중한	extremely valuable
□□	reproduction	복제품	a copy of something such as a picture
□□	saw	톱	a tool for cutting wood or other materials, typically with a long, thin, steel blade
□□	shocked	충격을 받은	very surprised and upset
□□	valuable	값비싼, 귀중한	worth a lot of money
□□	worth	가치가 있는	having a specific value
□□	be known for	~으로 유명하다	to be famous or well known because of something
□□	cut off	~을 잘라 내다	to separate something by cutting it away from the main part
□□	on one's way to	~로 가는 길(도중)에	in the process of traveling to or leaving someplace
□□	take advantage of	~을 이용하다	to make good or unfair use of

단어의 의미 관계

- 유의어
  priceless (대단히 귀중한) = valuable
  be known for (~으로 유명하다) = be famous for

- 동사 – 명사
  announce (발표하다) – announcement (발표)
  elect (선거로 선출하다) – election (선거, 당선)
  congratulate (축하하다) – congratulation (축하)
  reproduce (복제하다) – reproduction (복제품, 복제)

- 동사 – 동사
  produce (생산하다) – reproduce (복제하다)
  play (틀다) – replay (재생하다, 다시 듣다/보다)

- 명사 – 형용사
  price (값, 가격) – priceless (대단히 귀중한)
  end (끝) – endless (무한한)
  care (주의) – careless (부주의한)
  luck (행운, 운) – lucky (운이 좋은, 행운의)

다의어

- **charge** 1. 동 (요금·값을) 청구하다 2. 명 요금
  1. The restaurant **charged** $40 for dinner.
     (그 식당은 저녁 식사비로 40달러를 청구했다.)
  2. Delivery is free of **charge**. (배달은 무료입니다.)

- **saw** 1. 명 톱 2. 동 톱질하다 3. 동 (see의 과거형) 보았다
  1. Grandpa is cutting wood with a **saw**.
     (할아버지는 톱으로 나무를 자르고 계신다.)
  2. There was a woman **sawing** some wood.
     (나무를 톱질하는 여자가 한 명 있었다.)
  3. We **saw** lions there. (우리는 그곳에서 사자들을 보았다.)

- **worth** 1. 형 ~의 가치가 있는 2. 명 가치, 값어치
  1. This house is **worth** £200,000.
     (이 집은 20만 파운드의 가치가 있다.)
  2. The company didn't appreciate her true **worth**.
     (그 회사는 그녀의 진가를 알아주지 않았다.)

Words **Plus**

연습 문제

A 다음 영영풀이에 해당하는 단어를 [보기]에서 골라 쓴 후, 우리말 뜻을 쓰시오.

[보기]	reproduction	furniture	dealer	antique	offer	worth	charge	attach

1 _____ : having a specific value : _____
2 _____ : old and often valuable or beautiful : _____
3 _____ : to fasten or join one thing to another : _____
4 _____ : a copy of something such as a picture : _____
5 _____ : a person whose job is to buy and sell things : _____
6 _____ : an act of asking someone if they would like something : _____
7 _____ : things such as chairs, beds, tables, and bookshelves, etc. : _____
8 _____ : to ask people to pay a particular amount of money for something : _____

B 다음 빈칸에 알맞은 단어를 [보기]에서 골라 쓰시오. (단, 중복 사용 불가)

[보기]	offer	disappointed	saw	unfortunately	valuable

1 Cut the branch off the tree with a _____.
2 _____, there is nothing I can do about it.
3 He accepted the company's _____ to hire him.
4 Be careful not to lose this ring. It's very _____.
5 Visitors were _____ to find out that the museum was closed.

C 우리말과 의미가 같도록 빈칸에 알맞은 말을 쓰시오.

1 나는 그 소식을 듣고 울지 않을 수 없었다. → I _____ _____ crying when I heard the news.
2 우리는 집에 가는 길에 Jake를 만났다. → We met Jake _____ _____ _____ home.
3 그 도시는 온화한 날씨로 유명하다. → The city _____ _____ _____ its mild weather.
4 그는 정색하며 내게 거짓말을 했다. → He lied to me _____ _____ _____.
5 더 많은 학교들이 인터넷을 최대한으로 이용할 필요가 있다.
  → More schools need to take full _____ _____ the Internet.

D 다음 짝지어진 두 단어의 관계가 같도록 빈칸에 알맞은 단어를 쓰시오.

1 end : endless = care : _____
2 play : replay = produce : _____
3 be known for : be famous for = valuable : _____
4 congratulate : congratulation = reproduce : _____

Words

실전 TEST

01 다음 영영풀이에 해당하는 단어로 알맞은 것은?

> a copy of something such as a picture

① saw   ② dealer   ③ antique
④ exhibition   ⑤ reproduction

02 다음 짝지어진 두 단어의 관계가 같도록 빈칸에 알맞은 단어를 쓰시오.

> elect : election = congratulate : _____

03 다음 문장의 밑줄 친 단어와 바꿔 쓸 수 있는 것은?

> The project was a <u>valuable</u> experience for me.

① useless   ② antique   ③ endless
④ priceless   ⑤ disappointed

04 다음 중 밑줄 친 부분의 우리말 뜻이 알맞지 <u>않은</u> 것은?

① He <u>fell over</u> and hurt his knee.
(뛰어넘었다)
② She said no <u>with a straight face</u>.
(정색하며)
③ They met Jennifer <u>on their way</u> to school.
(~로 가는 길에)
④ The café is <u>known for</u> its excellent desserts.
(~으로 유명하다)
⑤ Please <u>cut off</u> this thread with the scissors.
(~을 잘라 내다)

05 다음 빈칸에 공통으로 들어갈 말로 알맞은 것은?

> • I just want to _____ a look.
> • Don't let other people _____ advantage of you.

① do   ② take   ③ use
④ make   ⑤ charge

06 다음 중 밑줄 친 **saw**의 의미가 [보기]와 같은 것은?

> [보기] You can use a power <u>saw</u> over there.

① Please <u>saw</u> the board in half.
② We <u>saw</u> no footprints in the snow.
③ My parents and I <u>saw</u> a movie last night.
④ I don't think I can cut the tree with a <u>saw</u>.
⑤ Did you see them <u>saw</u> the wood into pieces?

07 다음 우리말과 의미가 같도록 괄호 안의 단어를 알맞은 형태로 바꿔 문장을 완성하시오.

> 유감스럽게도, 우리는 당신의 의견에 동의할 수 없습니다.

→ _____, we cannot agree with you.
   (fortunate)

08 다음 우리말과 의미가 같도록 빈칸에 알맞은 말을 쓰시오.

> 나는 그 문제에 대해 생각하지 않을 수 없었다.

→ I _____ _____ _____ about the problem.

Listen and Talk

핵심 노트

1 축하·유감 표현하기

· **Congratulations** on winning the gold medal.

· **I'm sorry to hear that.**

금메달 딴 것을 축하해.

그 말을 들으니 유감이야.

시험 포인트 point

상대방에게 축하의 말을 건네야 하는지, 또는 위로의 말을 건네야 하는지를 묻는 문제가 자주 출제된다. 또한, 축하나 위로의 말로 보아 상대방에게 어떤 일이 일어났는지를 고르는 문제가 자주 출제되므로, 축하할 일과 유감스러운 일을 잘 구분하도록 한다.

(1) 축하 표현하기

상대방에게 좋은 일이 생겨 축하의 말을 할 때 Congratulations!라고 한다. 축하하는 일을 구체적으로 표현할 때는 congratulations 뒤에 「on+축하하는 일」을 덧붙여 말한다. That's great. / Good for you. / I'm so happy for you. 등으로도 말할 수 있다.

· **A:** I passed the driving test. (나 운전 면허 시험에 합격했어.)
  B: Congratulations! (축하해!)

· **A:** Kevin, congratulations on winning the game! (Kevin, 경기에서 이긴 것을 축하해!)
  B: Thanks. (고마워.)

(2) 유감 표현하기

상대방에게 좋지 않은 일이 생겨 유감을 나타낼 때는 I'm sorry to hear that. 또는 That's too bad.로 말한다.

· **A:** I lost my bag yesterday. (나 어제 가방을 잃어버렸어.)
  B: I'm sorry to hear that. (그 말을 들으니 유감이야.)

· **A:** My brother hurt his arm. He's in hospital now.
  (남동생이 팔을 다쳤어. 그 애는 지금 병원에 있어.)
  B: That's too bad. (안됐구나.)

2 감정 표현하기

A: What's up?

B: My smartphone is broken. **I'm** very **upset.**

무슨 일이니?

내 스마트폰이 고장 났어. 나는 너무 속상해.

자신의 감정을 표현할 때 감정 형용사를 사용하여 「I am(feel)+감정 형용사」로 말한다. 기분이 좋을 때는 happy, excited, glad, 슬플 때는 sad, 화가 났을 때는 angry, upset, 이 밖에도 worried, scared, disappointed 등의 감정 형용사를 사용한다.

시험 포인트 point

각 사건으로 화자의 감정이나 적절한 응답을 유추해 보는 문제가 자주 출제되므로, 감정을 나타내는 다양한 감정 형용사들을 숙지해 두도록 한다.

· **A:** What's the matter? (무슨 일 있니?)
  B: I lost my dog. I feel so sad. (내 개를 잃어버렸어. 너무 슬퍼.)

감정 형용사 뒤에 부사적 용법의 to부정사를 덧붙여 '~해서'라는 의미로 그 감정의 원인을 구체적으로 나타낼 수도 있다.

· **A:** What's up? (무슨 일이니?)
  B: I was chosen as the leader of the club. I'm happy to work for my club.
  (내가 동아리의 리더로 뽑혔어. 동아리를 위해 일할 수 있어서 기뻐.)

만점 노트

Listen and Talk A-1

교과서 102쪽

B: Sue, you look excited. ❶What's up?

G: I was elected as class president. ❷I'm so excited.

B: That's wonderful. ❸Congratulations!

G: Thanks. ❹I'm really happy to have a chance to work for my class.

❶ 신나 보이는 상대방에게 무슨 일이 있는지 묻는 의미로 쓰였다. What's the matter?와 같이 상대방에게 안 좋은 일이 있어 보일 때 무슨 일이 있는지 묻는 표현으로도 쓰일 수 있다.

❷ 자신의 감정은 「I'm+감정 형용사」로 표현할 수 있다.

❸ 상대방에게 좋은 일이 있을 때 축하해 주는 표현으로, 반드시 복수 형태(-s)로 쓰인다.

❹ 감정 형용사 뒤에 부사적 용법의 to부정사가 쓰여 '~해서'라는 의미로 그 감정의 원인을 나타낸다.

Q1 소년은 왜 Sue에게 축하의 말을 하나요?

Listen and Talk A-2

교과서 102쪽

G: Tim, ❶congratulations on winning the gold medal in the school marathon.

B: Thanks, Suji. I'm very happy.

G: ❷You must be very proud of yourself.

B: Yes, I am. I ❸did my best.

❶ 축하하는 일을 구체적으로 말할 때는 congratulations 뒤에 「on+축하하는 일」을 덧붙인다.

❷ 조동사 must가 '~임에 틀림없다'라는 뜻으로 강한 추측을 나타낸다.
be proud of: ~을 자랑스러워하다

❸ do one's best: 최선을 다하다

Q2 Tim is happy to win the gold medal in the school marathon. (T / F)

Listen and Talk A-3

교과서 102쪽

B: Mina, ❶is anything wrong?

G: Well, I lost my smartphone. ❷I'm upset.

B: Oh, ❸I'm so sorry to hear that. Do you remember when you used it last?

G: Well, I ❹remember taking it out of my bag at the snack shop.

B: Then, let's go back to the snack shop to look for it.

❶ 상대방에게 안 좋은 일이 있어 보일 때 무슨 일이 있는지 묻는 표현이다. (= What's the matter? / What's wrong? / What's up?)

❷ 속상한 감정을 표현하는 말이다.

❸ 좋지 않은 일이 있는 상대방에게 유감을 표현하며 위로하는 말이다. (= That's too bad.)

❹ remember+동명사: (이전에) ~한 것을 기억하다

Q3 How does Mina feel now? (　　) 　　ⓐ upset　ⓑ sorry　ⓒ excited

Listen and Talk A-4

교과서 102쪽

G: You don't look so good, Inho. ❶What's the matter?

B: I have the flu.

G: ❷That's too bad. Did you see the doctor?

B: Yes. I'm ❸taking medicine.

G: Well, ❹I hope you feel better soon.

B: Thanks.

❶ 상대방에게 안 좋은 일이 있어 보일 때 무슨 일이 있는지 묻는 말이다.

❷ 좋지 않은 일이 있는 상대방에게 유감을 표현하며 위로하는 말이다.

❸ take medicine: 약을 먹다

❹ 자신이 상대방에게 소망하는 것을 말할 때 「I hope (that) you+동사원형 ~.」으로 표현할 수 있다.

Q4 What's wrong with Inho?

He _____ _____ _____.

Listen and Talk C

교과서 103쪽

B: Excuse me, Ms. Carter. ❶Can I ask you a question? Did I get the ❷main role in the play?

W: Yes, you did. Congratulations, Jiho! You're going to be Romeo in our school play, *Romeo and Juliet*.

B: Really? I'm so excited. Thank you so much, Ms. Carter.

W: ❸I know how much you wanted the role. ❹I'm so happy for you.

B: Thank you. ❺What about Sumi? Did she get the role she wanted, too?

W: ❻Unfortunately, no. ❼She's very disappointed.

B: Oh, ❽I'm sorry to hear that. Anyway, when is the first practice?

W: ❾It's at 2 p.m. on September 20th, in the acting club room. You'll get a text message about it soon.

B: OK. ❿I'll be there.

Q5 Carter 선생님은 지호를 왜 축하해 주고 있나요?

Q6 ❽과 같은 의미로 쓰이는 표현이 <u>아닌</u> 것은? (　　)

❶ Can I ~?는 '(제가) ~해도 될까요?'라는 뜻으로 상대방에게 허락을 구하는 표현이다.

❷ 주인공 역할

❸ I know 뒤에 목적어로 「의문사(how much)+주어(you)+동사(wanted) ~」 형태의 간접의문문이 쓰였다.

❹ 좋은 일이 생긴 상대방을 축하하는 말이다.

❺ '수미는 어떻게 됐어요?'라는 뜻으로, How about Sumi?라고도 말할 수 있다.

❻ 유감스럽게도, 불행하게도

❼ disappointed: 실망한

❽ 수미가 원하는 역할을 맡지 못해 실망했다는 말을 듣고 유감을 표현하는 말이다.

❾ It은 the first practice를 가리키며 시각(2시) 앞에는 전치사 at, 날짜(9월 20일) 앞에는 on을 쓴다.

❿ 약속 시간과 장소에 맞춰 가겠다는 의미의 표현이다.

ⓐ That's too bad. ⓑ Good for her.

Talk and Play

교과서 104쪽

A: What's up?

B: My bike ❶is broken. ❷I'm very upset.

A: That's too bad. I'm sorry to hear that.

Q7 B가 속상한 이유는 무엇인가요? (　　)

❶ be broken: 고장 나다, 깨지다, 부러지다

❷ 자신의 감정을 표현하는 말로, 속상하거나 화가 났을 때 하는 말이다.

ⓐ 자전거를 잃어버려서　ⓑ 자전거가 고장 나서

Review - 1

교과서 116쪽

B: You ❶look excited, Sally. What's up?

G: I'm going to go to the Dream Concert.

B: ❷Congratulations! I know how much you wanted to go.

G: Thanks. ❸I'm so happy to get a chance to see my favorite singer.

Q8 Sally is excited to go to the Dream Concert.

❶ look+형용사: ~해 보이다

❷ 상대방에게 좋은 일이 있을 때 축하해 주는 표현이다.

❸ 감정 형용사(happy) 뒤에 부사적 용법의 to부정사(to get)가 쓰여 '~해서'라는 의미로 그 감정의 원인을 나타낸다.

(T / F)

Review - 2

교과서 116쪽

B: ❶You don't look good, Sumi. What's the matter?

G: Well, I didn't get a role in the school play. ❷I'm very disappointed.

B: Oh, I'm so sorry to hear that. But ❸I'm sure you can get a role next time.

G: Thanks. ❹I'll try harder next time.

Q9 Sumi is very _____ because she didn't get a role in the play.

❶ 상대방에게 안 좋은 일이 있어 보일 때 하는 말이다.

❷ 자신의 감정을 표현할 때 「I'm+감정 형용사」로 말한다.

❸ '나는 ~을 확신해'라는 뜻으로 어떤 일에 대한 확신을 표현할 때 「I'm sure (that)+주어+동사 ~」로 말한다.

❹ try harder는 '더 열심히 노력하다'라는 의미이고 next time은 '다음번에는'이라는 뜻이다.

Listen and Talk
빈칸 채우기

• 주어진 우리말과 일치하도록 교과서 대화문을 완성하시오.

Listen and Talk A-1

B: Sue, you look excited. _____ _____?

G: I was _____ as class president. I'm so _____.

B: That's wonderful. _____!

G: Thanks. I'm really _____ _____ have a chance to work for my class.

 해석

교과서 102쪽

B: Sue, 너 신나 보인다. 무슨 일 있어?

G: 내가 학급 회장으로 당선되었어. 정말 신나.

B: 멋지다. 축하해!

G: 고마워. 우리 반을 위해 일할 기회가 생겨서 나는 정말 기뻐.

Listen and Talk A-2

G: Tim, _____ _____ _____ the gold medal in the school marathon.

B: Thanks, Suji. I'm very happy.

G: You _____ _____ very proud of yourself.

B: Yes, I am. I _____ _____ _____.

교과서 102쪽

G: Tim, 학교 마라톤에서 금메달 딴 것을 축하해.

B: 고마워, 수지야. 나는 정말 기뻐.

G: 네 스스로가 매우 자랑스럽겠구나.

B: 응, 맞아. 나는 최선을 다했어.

Listen and Talk A-3

B: Mina, is _____ _____?

G: Well, I lost my smartphone. I'm _____.

B: Oh, I'm so _____ _____ _____ _____. Do you remember when you used it last?

G: Well, I _____ _____ it out of my bag at the snack shop.

B: Then, let's go back to the snack shop to look for it.

교과서 102쪽

B: 미나야, 안 좋은 일 있니?

G: 음, 내 스마트폰을 잃어버렸어. 속상해.

B: 아, 그 말을 들으니 정말 유감이야. 마지막으로 언제 사용했는지 기억나니?

G: 음, 매점에서 그것을 가방에서 꺼낸 것은 기억나.

B: 그럼 그것을 찾으러 매점에 다시 가 보자.

Listen and Talk A-4

G: You don't look so good, Inho. What's _____ _____?

B: I have the flu.

G: _____ _____ _____. Did you see the doctor?

B: Yes. I'm taking medicine.

G: Well, I hope you feel _____ _____.

B: Thanks.

교과서 102쪽

G: 너 몸이 안 좋아 보인다. 인호야. 무슨 일 있어?

B: 나는 독감에 걸렸어.

G: 안됐구나. 병원은 가 봤어?

B: 응. 약을 먹고 있어.

G: 음, 네가 곧 낫기를 바라.

B: 고마워.

Listen and Talk C

B: Excuse me, Ms. Carter. _____ _____ _____ _____ a question? Did I get the _____ _____ in the play?

W: Yes, you did. _____, Jiho! You're going to be Romeo in our school play, *Romeo and Juliet*.

B: Really? I'm so excited. Thank you so much, Ms. Carter.

W: I know _____ _____ _____ _____ the role. I'm so _____ _____ you.

B: Thank you. _____ _____ Sumi? Did she get the role she wanted, too?

W: Unfortunately, no. She's very _____.

B: Oh, I'm _____ _____ _____ that. Anyway, when is the first practice?

W: It's _____ 2 p.m. _____ September 20th, in the acting club room. You'll get a _____ _____ about it soon.

B: OK. I'll be there.

Talk and Play

A: What's up?

B: My bike is _____. I'm very _____.

A: That's ___ ___ _____. I'm sorry to hear that.

Review - 1

B: You _____ _____, Sally. What's up?

G: I'm going to go to the Dream Concert.

B: Congratulations! I know _____ _____ you wanted to go.

G: Thanks. I'm so _____ _____ _____ a chance to see my favorite singer.

Review - 2

B: You don't _____ _____, Sumi. What's the matter?

G: Well, I didn't _____ _____ _____ in the school play. I'm very disappointed.

B: Oh, _____ _____ to hear that. But I'm _____ you can get a role next time.

G: Thanks. I'll try harder next time.

Answers p. 22

 해석

교과서 103쪽

B: 실례합니다. Carter 선생님. 질문 하나 해도 될까요? 연극에서 제가 주인공 역할을 맡게 됐나요?

W: 그렇단다. 축하해, 지호야! 너는 우리 학교 연극 '로미오와 줄리엣'에서 로미오가 될 거야.

B: 정말이요? 너무 신나요. 정말 고맙습니다. Carter 선생님.

W: 네가 얼마나 그 역할을 원했는지 알고 있단다. 나도 정말 기쁘구나.

B: 고맙습니다. 수미는 어떻게 됐어요? 수미도 원했던 역할을 맡게 됐나요?

W: 안타깝게도, 아니란다. 그녀는 매우 실망했어.

B: 아, 그 말을 들으니 유감이네요. 그런데, 첫 연습은 언제예요?

W: 9월 20일 오후 2시에 연극 동아리방에서 할 거야. 그것에 관한 문자 메시지를 곧 받을 거야.

B: 알겠습니다. 거기에서 뵐게요.

교과서 104쪽

A: 무슨 일 있니?

B: 내 자전거가 고장 났어. 정말 속상해.

A: 안됐구나. 그 말을 들으니 유감이야.

교과서 116쪽

B: 너 신나 보인다, Sally. 무슨 일 있어?

G: 나는 Dream 콘서트에 갈 거야.

B: 축하해! 네가 얼마나 가고 싶어 했는지 내가 알지.

G: 고마워. 내가 가장 좋아하는 가수를 볼 기회가 생겨서 정말 기뻐.

교과서 116쪽

B: 수미야, 너 기분 안 좋아 보인다. 무슨 일 있니?

G: 음, 나는 학교 연극에서 역할을 맡지 못했어. 나는 정말 실망했어.

B: 아, 그 말을 들으니 정말 유감이야. 그렇지만 너는 분명히 다음번에는 역할을 맡을 수 있을 거야.

G: 고마워. 다음번에는 더 열심히 노력할 거야.

대화 순서 배열하기

1 Listen and Talk A-1

교과서 102쪽

ⓐ I was elected as class president. I'm so excited.

ⓑ Thanks. I'm really happy to have a chance to work for my class.

ⓒ That's wonderful. Congratulations!

ⓓ Sue, you look excited. What's up?

(   ) – (   ) – ⓒ – (   )

2 Listen and Talk A-2

교과서 102쪽

ⓐ Thanks, Suji. I'm very happy.

ⓑ Tim, congratulations on winning the gold medal in the school marathon.

ⓒ You must be very proud of yourself.

ⓓ Yes, I am. I did my best.

(   ) – (   ) – ⓒ – (   )

3 Listen and Talk A-3

교과서 102쪽

A: Mina, is anything wrong?

ⓐ Oh, I'm so sorry to hear that. Do you remember when you used it last?

ⓑ Well, I remember taking it out of my bag at the snack shop.

ⓒ Well, I lost my smartphone. I'm upset.

ⓓ Then, let's go back to the snack shop to look for it.

A – (   ) – (   ) – (   ) – (   )

4 Listen and Talk A-4

교과서 102쪽

ⓐ Yes. I'm taking medicine.

ⓑ Thanks.

ⓒ You don't look so good, Inho. What's the matter?

ⓓ Well, I hope you feel better soon.

ⓔ That's too bad. Did you see the doctor?

ⓕ I have the flu.

(   ) – (   ) – ⓔ – (   ) – (   ) – ⓑ

5 Listen and Talk C

교과서 103쪽

A: Excuse me, Ms. Carter. Can I ask you a question? Did I get the main role in the play?

ⓐ Unfortunately, no. She's very disappointed.

ⓑ I know how much you wanted the role. I'm so happy for you.

ⓒ It's at 2 p.m. on September 20th, in the acting club room. You'll get a text message about it soon.

ⓓ Thank you. What about Sumi? Did she get the role she wanted, too?

ⓔ Oh, I'm sorry to hear that. Anyway, when is the first practice?

ⓕ Really? I'm so excited. Thank you so much, Ms. Carter.

ⓖ Yes, you did. Congratulations, Jiho! You're going to be Romeo in our school play, *Romeo and Juliet*.

ⓗ OK. I'll be there.

A – (　　) – (　　) – (　　) – ⓓ – (　　) – ⓔ – (　　) – (　　)

6 Talk and Play

교과서 104쪽

ⓐ That's too bad. I'm sorry to hear that.

ⓑ My bike is broken. I'm very upset.

ⓒ What's up?

(　　) – (　　) – (　　)

7 Review - 1

교과서 116쪽

ⓐ Congratulations! I know how much you wanted to go.

ⓑ I'm going to go to the Dream Concert.

ⓒ Thanks. I'm so happy to get a chance to see my favorite singer.

ⓓ You look excited, Sally. What's up?

ⓓ – (　　) – (　　) – (　　)

8 Review - 2

교과서 116쪽

ⓐ Well, I didn't get a role in the school play. I'm very disappointed.

ⓑ You don't look good, Sumi. What's the matter?

ⓒ Thanks. I'll try harder next time.

ⓓ Oh, I'm so sorry to hear that. But I'm sure you can get a role next time.

(　　) – (　　) – (　　) – (　　)

[01~02] 대화의 빈칸에 들어갈 말로 알맞은 것을 고르시오.

01

A: Tim, congratulations on winning the gold medal in the school marathon.
B: Thanks, Suji. I'm very _____.
A: You must be very proud of yourself.
B: Yes, I am. I did my best.

① sad   ② upset   ③ worried
④ happy   ⑤ disappointed

02

A: You don't look so good, Inho. What's the matter?
B: I have the flu.
A: _____ Did you see the doctor?
B: Yes. I'm taking medicine.
A: Well, I hope you feel better soon.
B: Thanks.

① Congratulations!   ② Good for you.
③ I'm happy for you.   ④ That's too bad.
⑤ I'm glad to hear that.

03 다음 중 짝지어진 대화가 어색한 것은?

① A: Is anything wrong?
  B: My computer broke down. I'm upset.
② A: My best friend forgot my birthday.
  B: Congratulations!
③ A: I got a ticket for the baseball game.
  B: Good for you!
④ A: You look excited. What's up?
  B: I won first prize in the cooking contest.
⑤ A: I failed the math test. I'm very disappointed.
  B: Oh, I'm sorry to hear that.

04 다음 대화의 빈칸에 들어갈 말로 알맞지 <u>않은</u> 것은?

A: You don't look good. What's the matter?
B: _____
A: That's too bad.

① My dog is sick. I'm sad.
② I passed the driving test.
③ I have a terrible headache.
④ My bike was stolen last night.
⑤ My laptop is broken. I'm upset.

05 다음 대화의 빈칸에 들어갈 말로 알맞은 것을 <u>모두</u> 고르면?

A: What's up?
B: _____
A: Congratulations!

① I broke my leg.
② I have a toothache.
③ I left my wallet on the bus.
④ My team won the soccer game.
⑤ I got the main role in the school play.

06 자연스러운 대화가 되도록 (A)~(D)를 바르게 배열한 것은?

(A) That's wonderful. Congratulations!
(B) I was elected as class president. I'm so excited.
(C) Sue, you look excited. What's up?
(D) Thanks. I'm really happy to have a chance to work for my class.

① (A) – (D) – (B) – (C)   ② (B) – (A) – (C) – (D)
③ (B) – (C) – (A) – (D)   ④ (C) – (A) – (B) – (D)
⑤ (C) – (B) – (A) – (D)

07 다음 대화의 밑줄 친 ①~⑤ 중 흐름상 어색한 것은?

A: ①You don't look good. What's up?

B: I lost my smartphone. ②I'm upset.

A: ③I'm so happy for you. ④Do you remember when you used it last?

B: Well, I remember taking it out of my bag at the snack shop.

A: ⑤Let's go back to the shop to look for it.

①   ②   ③   ④   ⑤

[08~09] 다음 대화를 읽고, 물음에 답하시오.

A: Excuse me, Ms. Carter. Can I ask you a question? Did I get the main role in the play?

B: Yes, you did. Congratulations, Jiho! You're going to be Romeo in our school play, *Romeo and Juliet*.

A: Really? I'm so excited. Thank you so much, Ms. Carter.

B: I know how much you wanted the role. I'm so happy for you.

A: Thank you. What about Sumi? Did she get the role she wanted, too?

B: Unfortunately, no. She's very ___ ⓐ ___.

A: Oh, I'm sorry to hear that. Anyway, when is the first practice?

B: It's at 2 p.m. on September 20th, in the acting club room. You'll get a text message about it soon.

A: OK. I'll be there.

08 위 대화의 빈칸 ⓐ에 들어갈 말로 알맞은 것은?

① sorry   ② excited   ③ pleased

④ happy   ⑤ disappointed

09 위 대화의 내용과 일치하지 <u>않는</u> 것은?

① 지호는 연극에서 로미오 역할을 맡게 되었다.

② Carter 선생님은 지호에게 축하의 말을 건넸다.

③ 수미는 연극에서 원했던 역할을 맡지 못했다.

④ 첫 연극 공연은 9월 20일 오후 2시에 있다.

⑤ 첫 연극 연습에 관한 안내는 문자 메시지로 전달될 것이다.

서술형

10 다음 대화의 밑줄 친 우리말과 의미가 같도록 괄호 안의 단어를 사용하여 문장을 완성하시오.

A: What's up?

B: I lost my cat. I'm so sad.

A: <u>그 말을 들으니 유감이구나.</u> (hear, that)

→ _____ .

11 자연스러운 대화가 되도록 빈칸에 알맞은 말을 [보기]에서 골라 쓰시오.

[보기]	
What's up?	What's wrong?
I'm very happy.	I'm so worried.
That's too bad.	Congratulations!

A: You look excited. (1)_____

B: I got a ticket to the Dream Concert. (2)_____

A: (3)_____ I know how much you wanted to go to the concert.

B: Thanks. I'm really excited to have a chance to see my favorite singer.

12 다음 대화를 읽고, 아래 요약문을 완성하시오.

A: Congratulations, Jane! I heard you were chosen as the leader of the school band.

B: Thanks, Minho. I'm so excited. I'll do my best for the band.

↓

Minho is congratulating Jane because she was (1)_____. Jane says she is very (2)_____ and she will (3)_____.

STEP A

1 과거완료

읽기 본문 People <u>asked</u> him where he **had got** the furniture.
　　　└─ 물어본 시점 (과거)　　　└─ 물어본 시점 이전의 일 (과거완료)

사람들은 그에게 가구를 어디에서 구했는지 물었다.

대표 예문 When Mr. Boggis <u>came</u> back, the legs **had been cut** off.

Boggis 씨가 돌아왔을 때, 탁자 다리는 잘려 있었다.

When I <u>came</u> home, everybody **had gone** to bed.

내가 집에 왔을 때, 모두가 잠자리에 들어 있었다.

I <u>was shocked</u> that somebody **had stolen** my bike during the night.

누군가 밤중에 내 자전거를 훔쳐가 버려서 나는 충격을 받았다.

He <u>told</u> me that he **had** already **seen** the movie.

그는 그 영화를 이미 봤다고 내게 말했다.

(1) 형태: had+과거분사

(2) 쓰임: 과거의 특정 시점보다 앞서 일어난 일이나 과거에 일어난 두 가지 일 중 먼저 일어난 일을 명확하게 나타낼 때 쓴다.

I <u>lost</u> the new bag that I **had bought** the day before.
(나는 전날 산 새 가방을 잃어버렸다.)

When Mr. Smith <u>came</u>, his students **had** already **taken** their seats.
(Smith 선생님이 왔을 때, 학생들은 이미 자리에 앉아 있었다.)

I **had** never **ridden** a bike until I <u>was</u> ten.
(나는 10살이 될 때까지 자전거를 타 본 적이 없었다.)

She **had been** ill for a week when I <u>visited</u> her.
(내가 그녀를 방문했을 때 그녀는 일주일째 아팠다.)

Tom <u>found</u> that he **had left** his smartphone at home.
(Tom은 스마트폰을 집에 놓고 왔다는 것을 알았다.)

> **시험 포인트 ❶** point
> 과거완료는 과거의 특정 시점보다 더 이전에 일어난 일을 나타낼 때 사용되므로 어떤 일이 먼저 일어났는지 전후 관계를 파악하도록 한다.

> **시험 포인트 ❷** point
> **현재완료 vs. 과거완료**
> 현재완료는 과거의 일과 현재의 일의 연관성을 나타내고, 과거완료는 과거의 특정 시점을 기준으로 그때까지 계속된 동작이나 상태, 완료된 일, 경험 등을 나타낸다.
> I've never **seen** a blue sky. 〈현재완료〉
> ▶ 중 2 교과서 7과

한 단계 더!

before, after 등과 같이 일어난 일의 전후 관계를 명확히 나타내는 말이 쓰일 때는 과거완료를 쓰지 않고 과거시제를 쓸 수 있다.

He **called** me <u>before</u> he left for Busan. (그는 부산으로 떠나기 전에 나에게 전화했다.)

QUICK CHECK

1 다음 괄호 안에서 알맞은 것을 고르시오.

(1) I had no money because I had (lose / lost) my wallet.

(2) He found out that the thief (has broken / had broken) the window.

(3) I (have known / had known) him for 10 years before he became a singer.

2 다음 괄호 안의 동사를 어법에 맞게 사용하여 문장을 완성하시오.

(1) He asked me where I _____ _____ the bag. (buy)

(2) They _____ already _____ when we arrived. (leave)

(3) I _____ _____ this bag for five years until I bought a new bag. (use)

2 관계대명사 what

읽기 본문
The table was [**what** every dealer dreamed of].

was의 보어 역할을 하는 명사절

그 탁자는 모든 판매상이 꿈꾸던 것이었다.

대표 예문
We ate **what** Mom had cooked for us.

우리는 엄마가 우리에게 요리해 주신 것을 먹었다.

This is exactly **what** I want.

이것은 정확히 내가 원하는 것이다.

I haven't received **what** I ordered yet.

나는 주문한 것을 아직 받지 못했다.

She loved **what** Joe gave her as a birthday present.

그녀는 Joe가 생일 선물로 그녀에게 준 것을 아주 좋아했다.

(1) 쓰임: what은 선행사를 포함하는 관계대명사로, '~하는 것'을 의미하며 the thing(s) that(which)로 바꿔 쓸 수 있다.

(2) 역할: 관계대명사 what이 이끄는 절은 명사절이며, 문장 내에서 주어, 보어, 목적어 역할을 한다.

What she said is not true.   〈주어〉 (그녀가 말한 것은 사실이 아니다.)

= The thing that(which) she said is not true.

This is not **what** I want.   〈보어〉 (이것은 내가 원하는 것이 아니다.)

Do you believe **what** she said? 〈목적어〉 (너는 그녀가 말한 것을 믿니?)

point
시험 포인트

선행사를 수식하는 which, who, that과 같은 관계대명사와 선행사를 포함하는 관계대명사 what을 구분하는 문제가 자주 출제된다. 관계대명사 what은 선행사를 포함하므로, 앞에 선행사가 없는 것에 유의한다.

This book is **what** I read recently.
(이 책이 내가 최근에 읽은 것이다.)

This is the book **that** I read recently.

선행사
(이것이 내가 최근에 읽은 책이다.)

한 단계 더!

- 관계대명사 what은 계속적 용법으로 사용하지 않는다.

You can order **what** you want to eat. (네가 먹고 싶은 것을 주문해도 된다.)

You can order, what you want to eat. (×)

- 관계대명사 what은 '~하는 것'이라고 해석하고, 의문사 what은 '무엇'이라고 해석하는데, 해석 방법에 따라 어느 것으로도 볼 수 있는 경우도 많다.

Mom asked Bill **what** he had eaten for lunch. 〈의문사〉
(엄마는 Bill에게 점심으로 무엇을 먹었는지 물으셨다.)

QUICK CHECK

1 다음 괄호 안에서 알맞은 것을 고르시오.

(1) That's not (what / which) we need.

(2) (When / What) I wanted to say is that I'm honest.

(3) This is the book (that / what) everyone is talking about.

2 다음 두 문장의 의미가 같도록 빈칸에 알맞은 말을 쓰시오.

(1) I like the thing that Dad gave me.

= I like _____ _____ _____ _____.

(2) This is exactly what we were looking for.

= This is exactly _____ _____ _____ we were looking for.

(3) The thing that I want to do on my birthday is to have a party.

= _____ _____ _____ _____ _____ on my birthday is to have a party.

G Grammar
연습 문제

1 과거완료

A 다음 [보기]에서 알맞은 동사를 골라 자연스러운 문장이 되도록 어법에 맞게 문장을 완성하시오. (단, 한 번씩만 쓸 것)

[보기]	steal	leave	eat	begin

1 I wasn't hungry because I _____ just _____ pizza.

2 He _____ already _____ the restaurant when I got there.

3 When he arrived at the theater, the movie _____ already _____.

4 Jimin was shocked that somebody _____ _____ his bag during the night.

B 다음 괄호 안의 단어를 어법에 맞게 사용하여 문장을 완성하시오.

1 He didn't know that the meeting _____ _____ already. (end)

2 I _____ _____ _____ the story until you told me. (never, hear)

3 She _____ _____ _____ to big cities before she visited Seoul. (not, be)

4 When I came home, Dad _____ _____ _____ my room. (already, clean)

C 다음 문장의 밑줄 친 부분을 어법상 바르게 고쳐 쓰시오.

1 He asked me if I <u>had saw</u> the movie before.   → _____

2 When Mike went to the bus stop, the bus <u>has already left</u>.   → _____

3 I thought that my sister <u>already gone</u> to bed, but she hadn't.   → _____

4 I was very tired because I <u>didn't have slept</u> well for several days.   → _____

D 다음 우리말과 의미가 같도록 괄호 안의 표현을 바르게 배열하여 문장을 완성하시오.

1 Tom은 다리를 다쳐서 축구를 할 수 없었다.

→ Tom _____.

(because, play, hurt, couldn't, had, soccer, his leg, he)

2 그는 누군가가 자신의 집에 침입했다는 것을 알았다.

→ He _____.

(his house, broken, someone, that, found, had, into)

3 내가 그곳에 도착했을 때, 모두가 저녁 식사를 마친 상태였다.

→ When _____.

(dinner, everyone, there, finished, arrived, I, had)

2 관계대명사 what

A 다음 빈칸에 알맞은 관계대명사를 쓰시오.

1 _____ she said made me cry.

2 I haven't received _____ I ordered yet.

3 The bike _____ I wanted to buy was pink.

4 That is the woman _____ let me use her phone.

B 다음 문장에서 어법상 틀린 부분을 찾아 바르게 고쳐 쓰시오. (단, 한 단어만 고쳐 쓸 것)

1 This is exactly which he wants.   _____ → _____

2 We couldn't believe that we saw there.   _____ → _____

3 I need a knife with what I can cut meat.   _____ → _____

4 My sister, what is 15 years old, is going to study in New York.   _____ → _____

C 다음 우리말과 의미가 같도록 괄호 안의 표현을 바르게 배열하여 문장을 쓰시오.

1 그 소년에 관해 내가 마음에 드는 것은 그의 정직성이다.

→ _____

(his honesty, the boy, like, what, is, about, I)

2 김 선생님은 그녀가 전시회에서 본 것을 묘사했다.

→ _____

(at the exhibition, what, described, she, had seen, Ms. Kim)

3 그가 하는 말은 그가 행동하는 것과 다르다.

→ _____

(different from, says, what, does, what, he, is, he)

D 다음 우리말과 의미가 같도록 괄호 안의 표현을 사용하여 문장을 완성하시오.

1 엄마가 우리를 위해 요리하신 것을 먹자. (what, cooked, for)

→ Let's eat _____.

2 이것이 바로 내가 쓰고 싶은 것이다. (what, write about)

→ This is exactly _____.

3 그 가게에는 그가 찾고 있는 것이 없었다. (what, looking for)

→ The store didn't have _____.

01 다음 빈칸에 들어갈 말로 알맞은 것은?

> Jennifer loved _____ Mike gave her as a birthday present.

① that   ② who   ③ what
④ which   ⑤ when

02 다음 빈칸에 들어갈 see의 형태로 알맞은 것은?

> Tony told me that he _____ the movie already.

① seen   ② seeing   ③ was seen
④ has seen   ⑤ had seen

[03~04] 다음 중 어법상 틀린 문장을 고르시오.

03 ① Tom had gone out when I visited him.
   ② I wondered who had broken the window.
   ③ I had no money because I had used it up.
   ④ Katie has been ill for a week when I called her.
   ⑤ When I arrived at the theater, the movie had already begun.

04 ① This is exactly what I wanted.
   ② He read what I had written to him.
   ③ We ate what Joe had cooked for us.
   ④ You can choose what you want to have.
   ⑤ Show me the thing what you have in your hand.

05 다음 대화의 빈칸에 들어갈 말로 알맞은 것은?

> A: I'm so hungry. Let's have lunch.
> B: OK. What do you want to eat?
> A: _____ is pizza.

① I want to eat the most
② I want to eat what the most
③ What I want to eat the most
④ What do I want to eat the most
⑤ The thing what I want to eat the most

06 다음 두 문장을 한 문장으로 나타낼 때, 빈칸에 알맞은 말이 순서대로 바르게 짝지어진 것은?

> Mom bought me a backpack a week ago.
> I lost it today.
> → I _____ the backpack that Mom _____ for me.

① lost – have bought
② lost – had bought
③ have lost – have bought
④ had lost – bought
⑤ had lost – had bought

07 다음 빈칸에 들어갈 말이 나머지와 다른 하나는?

① _____ she told you is not true.
② Sally loved _____ I made for her.
③ I didn't understand _____ he said.
④ I couldn't believe _____ I saw in the forest.
⑤ I've found the keys _____ you were looking for.

08 다음 우리말을 영어로 바르게 옮긴 것은?

점심시간은 내가 우리 학교에서 좋아하는 것이다.

① That I like about my school is lunchtime.
② Lunchtime is what I like about my school.
③ When I like about my school is lunchtime.
④ Lunchtime is which I like about my school.
⑤ Lunchtime is the thing what I like about my school.

09 다음 빈칸에 들어갈 말로 알맞지 <u>않은</u> 것을 <u>모두</u> 고르면?

I hadn't seen Laura before _____.

① I came here last year
② she moved here in 2015
③ we are in the same class
④ you introduced her to me
⑤ I will join the drawing club

한 단계 │ 더!
10 다음 중 빈칸에 what(What)이 들어갈 수 없는 문장은?

① We couldn't believe _____ we heard.
② _____ I need now is a new smartphone.
③ Do you know _____ the picnic is canceled?
④ _____ I want to know is her phone number.
⑤ It's a bad habit to buy _____ you don't need.

[11~12] 다음 빈칸에 들어갈 말로 알맞은 것을 <u>모두</u> 고르시오.
고난도 한 단계 │ 더!
11
He felt better after he _____ a long nap.

① takes ② took ③ has taken
④ had taken ⑤ will take

12
I haven't received _____ I ordered last week.

① when ② what
③ which ④ the thing what
⑤ the thing that

한 단계 │ 더!
13 다음 빈칸에 공통으로 들어갈 말로 알맞은 것은?

• The lake is _____ I like about the park.
• They didn't know _____ to do next.

① this ② what ③ who
④ which ⑤ that

14 다음 중 밑줄 친 부분을 어법상 바르게 고치지 <u>않은</u> 것은?

ⓐ Tony <u>have</u> already left when we arrived.
ⓑ This dress is <u>that</u> I want to wear at the party.
ⓒ <u>The thing what</u> I want to do now is to ride a bike.
ⓓ I had never heard the rumor until you <u>had told</u> me.
ⓔ When I came home, everybody <u>goes</u> to bed already.

① ⓐ → had
② ⓑ → what
③ ⓒ → The thing that
④ ⓓ → told
⑤ ⓔ → has gone

15 다음 빈칸에 알맞은 말이 순서대로 바르게 짝지어진 것은?

> I _____ shocked that somebody _____ my bike during the night.

① was – steals
② was – has stolen
③ was – had stolen
④ had been – stole
⑤ had been – had stolen

16 다음 우리말과 의미가 같도록 괄호 안의 단어를 배열할 때 6번째로 올 단어로 알맞은 것은?

> 나는 그에게 그 가구를 어디에서 샀는지 물었다.
> (where, I, him, had, furniture, the, asked, bought, he)

① him   ② where   ③ bought
④ had   ⑤ furniture

^고/_{난도} 한 단계 더!
17 다음 중 어법상 올바른 문장의 개수는?

> ⓐ What I want to buy is that T-shirt.
> ⓑ You can choose, what you want to eat.
> ⓒ What I want to say is that I'm really sorry.
> ⓓ Swimming is the thing that they do in their free time.
> ⓔ This is the TV show what everyone is talking about recently.

① 1개   ② 2개   ③ 3개   ④ 4개   ⑤ 5개

18 다음 중 빈칸에 had가 들어갈 수 <u>없는</u> 것은?

① I _____ been at the beach until the sun set.
② Kevin asked me if I _____ been to Italy before.
③ I heard that they _____ already finished the project.
④ The pianist _____ played the piano since he was five.
⑤ I _____ lived with my grandparents before I moved to Seoul.

^신/_{유형}
19 다음 문장에 대해 <u>잘못</u> 설명한 사람은?

> Playing soccer is what I want to do after school.

① 정민: 이 문장의 주어는 Playing soccer야.
② 희진: 이 문장의 동사는 is야.
③ 준상: what은 선행사를 포함하는 관계대명사야.
④ 성희: what은 '무엇'으로 해석해.
⑤ 경아: what이 이끄는 절이 보어 역할을 해.

^고/_{난도}
20 다음 중 어법상 <u>틀린</u> 문장끼리 짝지어진 것은?

> ⓐ I asked him if he had visited Europe before.
> ⓑ I found out that my brother had broken the vase.
> ⓒ I lost my umbrella that I have bought the day before.
> ⓓ He showed me the pictures what he had taken during the vacation.
> ⓔ When they arrived at the airport, the plane had already landed.

① ⓐ, ⓑ   ② ⓐ, ⓓ   ③ ⓑ, ⓒ, ⓔ
④ ⓑ, ⓔ   ⑤ ⓒ, ⓓ

21 [보기]와 같이 주어진 문장을 과거완료와 already를 사용한 문장으로 바꿔 쓰시오.

> [보기] My family finished eating dinner before I came home.
> → When I came home, my family had already finished eating dinner.

(1) The train left before we arrived at the station.
→ When _____,
_____.

(2) I woke up before my alarm clock rang.
→ When _____,
_____.

(3) I finished my homework before Mom came home.
→ When _____,
_____.

22 다음 우리말과 의미가 같도록 괄호 안의 말을 어법에 맞게 사용하여 문장을 완성하시오.

(1) 전화벨이 울렸을 때 나는 막 목욕을 한 참이었다.
→ I _____ _____ _____ a bath when the phone rang. (just, take)

(2) 그는 집에 오는 길에 잃어버렸던 그의 열쇠를 찾았다.
→ He found his key that _____ _____ _____ on his way home. (lose)

(3) 나는 그녀가 이미 제주도로 떠났다고 생각했지만 아니었다.
→ I thought that _____ _____ _____ for Jeju-do, but she hadn't. (already, leave)

(4) 우리가 야구장에 도착했을 때 표는 매진되고 없었다.
→ When we arrived at the baseball stadium, _____ _____ _____ _____ _____. (the tickets, be sold out)

23 다음 문장에서 어법상 틀린 부분을 바르게 고쳐 문장을 다시 쓰시오.

(1) That I really want is your support.
→ _____

(2) When the police arrived, the man has already run away.
→ _____

(3) That is not the thing what I wanted to say.
→ _____

(4) He told me that he doesn't meet the movie star before.
→ _____

[24~25] 다음 표를 보고, 물음에 답하시오.

	☺	☹
Jason	draw cartoons	play basketball
Luna	ride a bike	swim
Dan	play soccer	do yoga

24 세 사람이 좋아하는 것을 말하는 다음 글을 완성하시오.

What Jason likes is to draw cartoons. _____ _____ _____ is to ride a bike. What Dan likes is _____ _____ _____.

25 세 사람이 좋아하지 않는 것을 말하는 다음 글을 완성하시오.

Playing basketball is what Jason doesn't like. _____ is what Luna doesn't like. _____ _____ _____ _____ is doing yoga.

Reading
만점 노트

STEP A

어느 운수 좋은 일요일

One Lucky Sunday

01 Cyril Boggis는 런던의 골동품 가구 판매상이었다.

01 Cyril Boggis was an antique furniture dealer in London.
　　　　　　　　　　　　　　　　　　　　　　　명 (특정 물건을 사고파는)
　　　　　　　　　　　　　　　　　　　　　　　판매상, 중개인

02 그는 좋은 물건을 낮은 가격에 사서 높은 가격에 파는 것으로 유명했다.

02 He was known for buying good things at a low price and then selling
　　　　　　　　　　　└── 전치사 for의 목적어인 동명사 buying과 selling이 ──┘
them at a high price.　　　　　and then으로 연결된 병렬 구조
= good things

03 사람들은 그에게 가구를 어디에서 구했는지 물었지만, 그는 "그건 비밀이에요."라고만 말했다.

　　　　　　　　　간접목적어┐　　┌ 간접의문문: 「의문사+주어+동사 ~」 (asked의 직접목적어)
03 People asked him [where he had got the furniture], but he just said,
　　　　　　　 ~에게 …을 질문했다　　　　　과거완료(had+과거분사):
"It's a secret."　　　　　　　　　　'사람들이 질문한(asked)' 과거 시점보다 더 이전에 일어난 일
　└─where he had got the furniture를 가리킴

04 Boggis 씨의 비밀은 단순했다.

04 Mr. Boggis' secret was simple.
　　　　-s로 끝나는 단어의 소유격: 아포스트로피(')만 붙이고 s는 생략 가능

05 그는 매주 일요일에 작은 마을들을 방문해서 문을 두드렸다.

05 He went to small towns every Sunday and knocked on doors.
　　　　　　　　　　　　　　　　매주 일요일마다 (= on Sundays)

06 그는 사람들에게 자신이 가구 판매상이라고 말했다.

　　　┌~에게 …을 말했다
06 He told people [that he was a furniture dealer].
　　　간접목적어 접속사 that이 이끄는 명사절 (told의 직접목적어)

07 사람들은 자신들의 물건이 얼마나 값진 것인지 몰랐으므로 Boggis 씨는 그들을 이용했다.

　　　　　　　　　　┌간접의문문 (didn't know의 목적어)
07 People didn't know [how valuable their things were], so Mr. Boggis
　　　　　　　= people┘ 의문사+형용사　　주어　　　동사　접 그래서
took advantage of them.
take advantage of: ~을 이용하다

08 그는 물건들을 매우 싸게 살 수 있었다.

　　　　　┌= could
08 He was able to buy things very cheaply.
　　　be able to: ~할 수 있다

09 일요일이 또 찾아왔고, Boggis 씨는 다시 어느 작은 마을에 있었다.

09 Now it was another Sunday, and Mr. Boggis was in a small town again.
　　　비인칭주어　　또 하나의
　　　(요일)

10 그는 방문한 집에서 두 남자를 만났다.

10 At a house he visited, he met two men.
　　　　　목적격 관계대명사 which(that) 생략

11 한 명은 주인인 Rummins였고, 다른 한 명은 그의 아들인 Bert였다.

11 One was Rummins, the owner, and the other was his son Bert.
　　둘 중 하나　　└──=──┘　　　　　나머지 하나　　　└─=─┘

12 "저는 고가구를 삽니다.

12 "I buy old furniture.
　　　　　셀 수 없는 명사
　　　　　(수량을 나타낼 때: a piece of, two pieces of ~)

13 고가구가 있으신가요?" Boggis 씨가 물었다.

13 Do you have any?" asked Mr. Boggis.
　　　　　　　　furniture 생략

14 "아니요." Rummins가 말했다.

14 "No, I don't," said Rummins.

15 "한번 둘러봐도 될까요?" Boggis 씨가 물었다.

　　　┌~해도 될까요? (허락 구하기)
15 "Can I just take a look?" asked Mr. Boggis.
　　　　　　　부 그저, 단지

16 "그럼요. 들어오세요." Rummins가 말했다.

16 "Sure. Please come in," said Rummins.

17 Mr. Boggis first went to the kitchen, and there was nothing.
       (부) 우선, 맨 먼저

17 Boggis 씨는 먼저 부엌에 갔는데 아무것도 없었다.

18 He then moved to the living room.
       move to: ~로 이동하다

18 그런 다음 그는 거실로 옮겨 갔다.

19 And there it was!

19 그리고 그곳에 그것이 있었다!

20 A table [which was a priceless piece of eighteenth-century English
      선행사   주격 관계대명사   = valuable
     ┌─── 관계대명사절
furniture].

20 매우 귀중한 18세기 영국 가구인 탁자가.

21 He was so excited that he almost fell over.
         ┌fall over: 넘어지다
     「so+형용사/부사+that+주어+동사」 매우(너무) ~해서 …하다

21 그는 몹시 흥분해서 거의 넘어질 뻔했다.

22 "What's wrong?" Bert asked.

22 "무슨 일이세요?" Bert가 물었다.

23 "Oh, nothing. Nothing at all," Mr. Boggis lied.
          lie (동) 거짓말하다 (-lied-lied)

23 "아, 아무것도 아니에요. 전혀 아무 일도 아닙니다." Boggis 씨는 거짓말을 했다.

24 He then said with a straight face, "This table is a reproduction.
                   (명) 복제품

24 그리고 나서 그는 정색하며 말했다. "이 탁자는 복제품입니다.

25 It's worth only a few pounds."
    ┌a few+복수 명사: 약간의 ~
  be worth+명사(구): ~의 가치가 있다

25 몇 파운드의 가치밖에 안 돼요."

26 He then added, "Hmm, I think I may buy it.
     add (동) 덧붙이다   접속사 that 생략   = this table
                    ┌~일 수도 있다, ~일지도 모른다

26 그리고 그는 덧붙였다. "흠, 제가 살 수도 있을 것 같아요.

27 The legs of my table at home are broken.
             수 일치 (복수)   수동태(be동사+과거분사)

27 우리 집에 있는 탁자 다리가 부러졌거든요.

28 I can cut off the legs of your table and attach them to mine."
                        = the legs of your table = my table

28 당신의 탁자 다리를 잘라서 제 탁자에 붙일 수 있겠어요."

29 "How much?" Rummins asked.
    가격을 묻는 표현 (= How much will(can) you pay?)

29 "얼마를 줄 건가요?" Rummins가 물었다.

30 "Not much, I'm afraid. This is just a reproduction," said Mr. Boggis.
    ~인 것 같다. (유감이지만) ~이다
    (유감스러운 내용을 말할 때 예의상 덧붙이는 표현)

30 "유감이지만 많이 줄 수는 없어요. 이것은 복제품일 뿐이니까요." Boggis 씨가 말했다.

31 "So how much?"

31 "그래서 얼마를 줄 수 있는데요?"

32 "Ten pounds."

32 "10파운드요."

33 "Ten? It's worth more than that."
    └Rummins의 탁자   = ten
      를 가리킴   pounds

33 "10이요? 그것보다는 가치가 더 나가요."

34 "How about fifteen?"
    = What about ~? (제안하는 표현)

34 "15는 어때요?"

STEP
A

35 "50으로 하지요."

35 "Make it fifty."
(가격) ~에 합시다

36 "음, 30이요. 이게 제 마지막 제안입니다."

36 "Well, thirty. This is my final offer."
= Thirty (pounds)

37 "그렇죠, 이건 당신 겁니다. 그런데 이걸 어떻게 가져갈 건가요?

37 "OK, it's yours, but how are you going to take it?
= your table   be going to+동사원형: ~할 예정이다

38 이게 차에 들어가지 않을 텐데요!"

38 This thing will not go in a car!"
= This table   (어떤 장소에) 넣어지다, 들어가다

39 "한번 보죠." Boggis 씨가 말하고는 자신의 차를 가지러 밖으로 나갔다.

39 "We'll see," Mr. Boggis said and went out to bring his car.
한번 보죠. / 곧 알게 되겠죠.   └병렬 구조┘   to부정사의 부사적 용법 (목적)

40 차로 가는 길에 Boggis 씨는 웃지 않을 수 없었다.

40 On his way to the car, Mr. Boggis couldn't help smiling.
┌= couldn't help but smile
on one's way to: ~로 가는 길에   can't help -ing: ~하지 않을 수 없다

41 그 탁자는 모든 판매상이 꿈꾸는 것이었다.

41 The table was [what every dealer dreamed of].
명사절 (보어)   ┌dream of: ~을 꿈꾸다
선행사를 포함하는 관계대명사 (= the thing that(which))

42 그는 자신의 행운을 믿을 수가 없었다.

42 He couldn't believe his luck.
매우 귀중한 탁자를 싼 가격에 사게 된 행운

43 "아버지, 만약 이게 그의 차에 안 들어가면 어쩌죠?

43 "Dad, what if this thing doesn't go in his car?
┌= this table
What if+절(주어+동사): ~면 어쩌지?

44 그가 값을 지불하지 않을 수도 있어요." Bert가 말했다.

44 He might not pay you," said Bert.
┌= Mr. Boggis
~하지 않을지도 모른다

45 Rummins는 그때 생각이 떠올랐다.

45 Rummins then had an idea.
have an idea: 생각이 떠오르다

46 "그가 원하는 건 오직 탁자의 다리뿐이야.

46 "What he wants is only the legs.
관계대명사 what이 이끄는 명사절 주어 (단수 취급)

47 그를 위해서 다리를 자르자." Rummins가 말했다.

47 Let's cut the legs off for him," said Rummins.
= cut off the legs / cut them off
(「동사+부사」의 목적어가 대명사일 경우, 대명사는 동사와 부사 사이에 위치해야 함)

48 "좋은 생각이에요!" Bert가 말했다.

48 "Great idea!" said Bert.
= That's a great idea! / Sounds great! 등

49 그런 다음 Bert는 톱을 꺼내서 탁자 다리를 자르기 시작했다.

49 Bert then took out a saw and began to cut off the legs.
┌to부정사와 동명사 모두 목적어로 취하는 동사
take out: (명) 톱   명사적 용법의 to부정사
꺼내다

50 Boggis 씨가 돌아왔을 때, 탁자 다리는 잘려 있었다.

50 When Mr. Boggis came back, the legs had been cut off.
과거완료 수동태 (had been+과거분사):
탁자 다리가 잘린 것이 Boggis 씨가
돌아온(came back) 것보다 앞서 일어난 일

51 "걱정하지 마세요. 이건 호의로 한 거예요.

51 "Don't worry, this was a favor.
탁자 다리를 자른 일

52 이것에 대해 비용을 청구하지는 않을게요." Rummins가 말했다.

52 I won't charge you for this," said Rummins.
┌탁자 다리를 자른 일
charge A for B: B에 대해 A에게(를) 청구하다

53 Boggis 씨는 너무 충격을 받아서 아무 말도 할 수 없었다.

53 Mr. Boggis was so shocked that he couldn't say anything.
「so+형용사/부사+that+주어+can't+동사원형」
매우(너무) ~해서 …할 수 없다

빈칸 채우기

• 우리말과 의미가 같도록 교과서 본문의 문장을 완성하시오.

01 Cyril Boggis was an _____ _____ dealer in London.

02 He _____ _____ _____ buying good things at a low price and then selling them at a _____ _____.

03 People asked him where _____ _____ _____ the furniture, but he just said, "It's a secret."

04 Mr. Boggis' secret was _____.

05 He went to small towns every Sunday and _____ _____ doors.

06 He _____ _____ that he was a furniture dealer.

07 People didn't know _____ _____ their things were, so Mr. Boggis _____ _____ _____ them.

08 He _____ _____ _____ buy things very cheaply.

09 Now it was _____ _____, and Mr. Boggis was in a small town again.

10 At a house _____ _____, he met two men.

11 _____ was Rummins, the owner, and _____ _____ was his son Bert.

12 "I buy old _____.

13 Do you have _____?" asked Mr. Boggis.

14 "No, _____ _____," said Rummins.

15 "Can I just _____ _____ _____?" asked Mr. Boggis.

16 "Sure. Please _____ _____," said Rummins.

17 Mr. Boggis _____ went to the kitchen, and there was _____.

18 He then _____ _____ the living room.

19 And there it _____!

20 A table which was a _____ piece of _____-_____ English furniture.

21 He was so _____ that he almost _____ _____.

22 "What's _____?" Bert asked.

23 "Oh, nothing. Nothing _____ _____," Mr. Boggis _____.

24 He then said with a _____ _____, "This table is a _____.

25 It's _____ only _____ _____ pounds."

01 Cyril Boggis는 런던의 골동품 가구 판매상이었다.

02 그는 좋은 물건을 낮은 가격에 사서 높은 가격에 파는 것으로 유명했다.

03 사람들은 그에게 가구를 어디에서 구했는지 물었지만, 그는 "그건 비밀이에요."라고만 말했다.

04 Boggis 씨의 비밀은 단순했다.

05 그는 매주 일요일에 작은 마을들을 방문해서 문을 두드렸다.

06 그는 사람들에게 자신이 가구 판매상이라고 말했다.

07 사람들은 자신들의 물건이 얼마나 값진 것인지 몰랐으므로 Boggis 씨는 그들을 이용했다.

08 그는 물건들을 매우 싸게 살 수 있었다.

09 일요일이 또 찾아왔고, Boggis 씨는 다시 어느 작은 마을에 있었다.

10 그는 방문한 집에서 두 남자를 만났다.

11 한 명은 주인인 Rummins였고, 다른 한 명은 그의 아들인 Bert였다.

12 "저는 고가구를 삽니다.

13 고가구가 있으신가요?" Boggis 씨가 물었다.

14 "아니요." Rummins가 말했다.

15 "한번 둘러봐도 될까요?" Boggis 씨가 물었다.

16 "그럼요. 들어오세요." Rummins가 말했다.

17 Boggis 씨는 먼저 부엌에 갔는데 아무것도 없었다.

18 그런 다음 그는 거실로 옮겨 갔다.

19 그리고 그곳에 그것이 있었다!

20 매우 귀중한 18세기 영국 가구인 탁자가.

21 그는 몹시 흥분해서 거의 넘어질 뻔했다.

22 "무슨 일이세요?" Bert가 물었다.

23 "아, 아무것도 아니에요. 전혀 아무 일도 아닙니다." Boggis 씨는 거짓말을 했다.

24 그리고 나서 그는 정색하며 말했다. "이 탁자는 복제품입니다.

25 몇 파운드의 가치밖에 안 돼요."

26 그리고 그는 덧붙였다. "흠, 제가 살 수도 있을 것 같아요.

27 우리 집에 있는 탁자 다리가 부러졌거든요.

28 당신의 탁자 다리를 잘라서 제 탁자에 붙일 수 있겠어요."

29 "얼마를 줄 건가요?" Rummins가 물었다.

30 "유감이지만 많이 줄 수는 없어요. 이것은 복제품일 뿐이니까요." Boggis 씨가 말했다.

31 "그래서 얼마를 줄 수 있는데요?"

32 "10파운드요."

33 "10이요? 그것보다는 가치가 더 나가요."

34 "15는 어때요?"

35 "50으로 하지요."

36 "음, 30이요. 이게 제 마지막 제안입니다."

37 "그러죠, 이건 당신 겁니다. 그런데 이걸 어떻게 가져갈 건가요?

38 이게 차에 들어가지 않을 텐데요!"

39 "한번 보죠." Boggis 씨가 말하고는 자신의 차를 가지러 밖으로 나갔다.

40 차로 가는 길에 Boggis 씨는 웃지 않을 수 없었다.

41 그 탁자는 모든 판매상이 꿈꾸는 것이었다.

42 그는 자신의 행운을 믿을 수가 없었다.

43 "아버지, 만약 이게 그의 차에 안 들어가면 어쩌죠?

44 그가 값을 지불하지 않을 수도 있어요." Bert가 말했다.

45 Rummins는 그때 생각이 떠올랐다.

46 "그가 원하는 건 오직 탁자의 다리뿐이야.

47 그를 위해서 다리를 자르자." Rummins가 말했다.

48 "좋은 생각이에요!" Bert가 말했다.

49 그런 다음 Bert는 톱을 꺼내서 탁자 다리를 자르기 시작했다.

50 Boggis 씨가 돌아왔을 때, 탁자 다리는 잘려 있었다.

51 "걱정하지 마세요. 이건 호의로 한 거예요.

52 이것에 대해 비용을 청구하지는 않을게요." Rummins가 말했다.

53 Boggis 씨는 너무 충격을 받아서 아무 말도 할 수 없었다.

26 He then _____, "Hmm, I think I _____ _____ it.

27 The legs of my table at home _____ _____.

28 I can _____ _____ the legs of your table and _____ them to mine."

29 "_____ _____?" Rummins asked.

30 "Not much, _____ _____. This is just a reproduction," said Mr. Boggis.

31 "So _____ _____?"

32 "Ten _____."

33 "Ten? It's worth _____ _____ that."

34 "_____ _____ fifteen?"

35 "_____ it fifty."

36 "Well, thirty. This is my _____ _____."

37 "OK, it's _____, but how are you going to _____ it?

38 This thing will not _____ _____ a car!"

39 "We'll _____," Mr. Boggis said and went out _____ _____ his car.

40 On his way to the car, Mr. Boggis couldn't _____ _____.

41 The table was _____ every dealer _____ _____.

42 He couldn't believe _____ _____.

43 "Dad, _____ _____ this thing doesn't go in his car?

44 He might _____ _____ you," said Bert.

45 Rummins then _____ an _____.

46 "_____ _____ _____ is only the legs.

47 Let's _____ the legs _____ for him," said Rummins.

48 "Great _____!" said Bert.

49 Bert then _____ _____ a saw and began to cut off the legs.

50 When Mr. Boggis came back, the legs _____ _____ _____ off.

51 "Don't worry, this was a _____.

52 I won't _____ you _____ this," said Rummins.

53 Mr. Boggis was _____ _____ _____ he couldn't say anything.

바른 어휘 · 어법 고르기

01 Cyril Boggis was an antique furniture dealer (on / in) London.

02 He was known (for / to) buying good things at a low price and then selling them at a high price.

03 People asked him where (he had / had he) got the furniture, but he just said, "It's a secret."

04 Mr. Boggis' secret was (simply / simple).

05 He went to small towns every Sunday and (knocked / knocking) on doors.

06 He told people (that / which) he was a furniture dealer.

07 People didn't know how valuable their things were, so Mr. Boggis took advantage (for / of) them.

08 He was able to (buy / buying) things very cheaply.

09 Now (it / this) was another Sunday, and Mr. Boggis was in a small town again.

10 At a house he visited, he met two (men / mans).

11 One was Rummins, the owner, and (another / the other) was his son Bert.

12 "I buy old (furniture / furnitures).

13 Do you have (any / another)?" asked Mr. Boggis.

14 "No, I (am not / don't)," said Rummins.

15 "Can I just (take / make) a look?" asked Mr. Boggis.

16 "Sure. Please come (in / out)," said Rummins.

17 Mr. Boggis first went to the kitchen, and there (were / was) nothing.

18 He then moved (on / to) the living room.

19 And there (was it / it was)!

20 A table which was a (priceless / useless) piece of eighteenth-century English furniture.

21 He was (so excited that / so that excited) he almost fell over.

22 "What's wrong?" Bert (asked / was asked).

23 "Oh, nothing. Nothing at all," Mr. Boggis (lied / lay).

24 He then said (from / with) a straight face, "This table is a reproduction.

25 It's (worth / worthy) only a few pounds."

26　He then added, "Hmm, I think I (may / may not) buy it.

27　The legs of my table at home (broken / are broken).

28　I can cut off the legs of your table and (attach / attached) them to mine."

29　"How (much / many)?" Rummins asked.

30　"(A lot / Not much), I'm afraid. This is just a reproduction," said Mr. Boggis.

31　"So (what / how) much?"

32　"Ten (pound / pounds)."

33　"Ten? It's worth (more / less) than that."

34　"(Which / How) about fifteen?"

35　"(Let / Make) it fifty."

36　"Well, thirty. This is my (first / final) offer."

37　"OK, it's yours, but (what / how) are you going to take it?

38　This thing (will / will not) go in a car!"

39　"We'll see," Mr. Boggis said and went out (to bring / brought) his car.

40　On his way to the car, Mr. Boggis couldn't help (smile / smiling).

41　The table was (what / which) every dealer dreamed of.

42　He couldn't believe his (luck / lucky).

43　"Dad, (what if / if what) this thing doesn't go in his car?

44　He might not (to pay / pay) you," said Bert.

45　Rummins then (has / had) an idea.

46　"What (he wants / does he want) is only the legs.

47　Let's cut the legs off (for / from) him," said Rummins.

48　"(Great / Terrible) idea!" said Bert.

49　Bert then took (off / out) a saw and began to cut off the legs.

50　When Mr. Boggis came back, the legs (had / had been) cut off.

51　"Don't (worry / worried), this was a favor.

52　I won't charge you (at / for) this," said Rummins.

53　Mr. Boggis was so (shocked / shocking) that he couldn't say anything.

• 밑줄 친 부분이 내용이나 어법상 올바르면 ○에, 틀리면 ×에 동그라미 하고 틀린 부분을 바르게 고쳐 쓰시오.

01	Cyril Boggis was an antique furniture dealer <u>in London</u>.	○ ×
02	He was known for buying good things at a low price and then <u>sell them</u> at a high price.	○ ×
03	People asked him where <u>he has got</u> the furniture, but he just said, "It's a secret."	○ ×
04	Mr. Boggis' secret <u>was simple</u>.	○ ×
05	He went to small towns every Sunday and <u>knocked on doors</u>.	○ ×
06	He told people <u>what</u> he was a furniture dealer.	○ ×
07	People didn't know how <u>valuable were their things</u>, so Mr. Boggis took advantage of them.	○ ×
08	He <u>could able to</u> buy things very cheaply.	○ ×
09	Now it was <u>another Sunday</u>, and Mr. Boggis was in a small town again.	○ ×
10	<u>At a house he visited</u>, he met two men.	○ ×
11	One was Rummins, the owner, and <u>others</u> was his son Bert.	○ ×
12	"I buy <u>old furniture</u>.	○ ×
13	Do you <u>have any</u>?" asked Mr. Boggis.	○ ×
14	"<u>No, I don't</u>," said Rummins.	○ ×
15	"Can I just <u>taking a look</u>?" asked Mr. Boggis.	○ ×
16	"Sure. <u>Please come in</u>," said Rummins.	○ ×
17	Mr. Boggis first went to the kitchen, and <u>there is nothing</u>.	○ ×
18	He then <u>moved from</u> the living room.	○ ×
19	And there <u>it was</u>!	○ ×
20	A table which was a priceless <u>eighteenth-century English furniture</u>.	○ ×
21	He was so <u>exciting</u> that he almost fell over.	○ ×
22	"<u>What's wrong</u>?" Bert asked.	○ ×
23	"Oh, nothing. <u>Nothing at all</u>," Mr. Boggis lied.	○ ×
24	He then said <u>on a straight face</u>, "This table is a reproduction.	○ ×
25	It's worth only <u>a little</u> pounds."	○ ×
26	He then added, "Hmm, I think <u>I may buy</u> it.	○ ×

27 The legs of my table at home <u>are broke</u>. ☐ ○ ☐ ×

28 I can cut off the legs of your table and attach <u>it</u> to mine." ☐ ○ ☐ ×

29 "<u>How much</u>?" Rummins asked. ☐ ○ ☐ ×

30 "Not much, <u>I'm afraid</u>. This is just a reproduction," said Mr. Boggis. ☐ ○ ☐ ×

31 "<u>So how much?</u>" ☐ ○ ☐ ×

32 "<u>Ten pounds</u>." ☐ ○ ☐ ×

33 "Ten? It's <u>worth of</u> more than that." ☐ ○ ☐ ×

34 "<u>How about</u> fifteen?" ☐ ○ ☐ ×

35 "<u>Make it fifty</u>." ☐ ○ ☐ ×

36 "Well, thirty. This is my <u>finally offer</u>." ☐ ○ ☐ ×

37 "OK, it's <u>your</u>, but how are you going to take it? ☐ ○ ☐ ×

38 This thing <u>will not go</u> in a car!" ☐ ○ ☐ ×

39 "We'll see," Mr. Boggis said and went out <u>to bring</u> his car. ☐ ○ ☐ ×

40 <u>For his way</u> to the car, Mr. Boggis couldn't help smiling. ☐ ○ ☐ ×

41 The table was <u>that</u> every dealer dreamed of. ☐ ○ ☐ ×

42 He couldn't believe <u>his luck</u>. ☐ ○ ☐ ×

43 "Dad, <u>if what</u> this thing doesn't go in his car? ☐ ○ ☐ ×

44 He <u>might not pay you</u>," said Bert. ☐ ○ ☐ ×

45 Rummins then <u>had an idea</u>. ☐ ○ ☐ ×

46 "<u>Which he wants</u> is only the legs. ☐ ○ ☐ ×

47 Let's <u>cut the legs off</u> for him," said Rummins. ☐ ○ ☐ ×

48 "<u>Great idea!</u>" said Bert. ☐ ○ ☐ ×

49 Bert then took out a saw and began to <u>cutting off</u> the legs. ☐ ○ ☐ ×

50 When Mr. Boggis came back, the legs <u>have been cut off</u>. ☐ ○ ☐ ×

51 "Don't worry, <u>this was a favor</u>. ☐ ○ ☐ ×

52 I won't <u>charge you for this</u>," said Rummins. ☐ ○ ☐ ×

53 Mr. Boggis was so shocked that he couldn't say <u>nothing</u>. ☐ ○ ☐ ×

배열로 문장 완성하기

01 Cyril Boggis는 런던의 골동품 가구 판매상이었다. (an antique furniture dealer / Cyril Boggis / in London / was)
>

02 그는 좋은 물건을 낮은 가격에 사서 높은 가격에 파는 것으로 유명했다.
(them / buying / selling / good things / he / at a low price / was known for / at a high price / and then)
>

03 사람들은 그에게 가구를 어디에서 구했는지 물었지만, 그는 "그건 비밀이에요."라고만 말했다.
(he had got / him / the furniture / people / but / asked / he just said, / where / "It's a secret.")
>

04 Boggis 씨의 비밀은 단순했다. (was / Mr. Boggis' / simple / secret)
>

05 그는 매주 일요일에 작은 마을들을 방문해서 문을 두드렸다. (every Sunday / doors / and / went to / he / knocked on / small towns)
>

06 그는 사람들에게 자신이 가구 판매상이라고 말했다. (that / he / told / a furniture dealer / people / he was)
>

07 사람들은 자신들의 물건이 얼마나 값진 것인지 몰랐으므로 Boggis 씨는 그들을 이용했다.
(their things / people / valuable / were / Mr. Boggis / didn't know / took advantage of / how / them / so)
>

08 그는 물건들을 매우 싸게 살 수 있었다. (buy / he / things / was / to / very cheaply / able)
>

09 일요일이 또 찾아왔고, Boggis 씨는 다시 어느 작은 마을에 있었다.
(and / another Sunday / in / now it / again / Mr. Boggis was / was / a small town)
>

10 그는 방문한 집에서 두 남자를 만났다. (visited / at a house / he / two men / he met)
>

11 한 명은 주인인 Rummins였고, 다른 한 명은 그의 아들인 Bert였다.
(Rummins / his son Bert / one was / the other was / the owner / and)
>

12 "저는 고가구를 삽니다. (old / I / furniture / buy)
>

13 고가구가 있으신가요?" Boggis 씨가 물었다. (Mr. Boggis / have / you / do / any / asked)
>

14 "아니요." Rummins가 말했다. (said / no / Rummins / I don't)
>

15 "한번 둘러봐도 될까요?" Boggis 씨가 물었다. (Mr. Boggis / I / can / asked / take a look / just)
>

16 "그럼요. 들어오세요." Rummins가 말했다. (please come in / Rummins / sure / said)
>

17 Boggis 씨는 먼저 부엌에 갔는데 아무것도 없었다. (first went to / there / the kitchen / nothing / and / Mr. Boggis / was)
>

STEP
A

18 그런 다음 그는 거실로 옮겨 갔다. (moved / he then / the living room / to)
>

19 그리고 그곳에 그것이 있었다! (it / and / was / there)
>

20 매우 귀중한 18세기 영국 가구인 탁자가. (a priceless piece of / was / eighteenth-century / a table / English furniture / which)
>

21 그는 몹시 흥분해서 거의 넘어질 뻔했다. (that / fell over / he / he was / almost / excited / so)
>

22 "무슨 일이세요?" Bert가 물었다. (what's / Bert / wrong / asked)
>

23 "아, 아무것도 아니에요. 전혀 아무 일도 아닙니다." Boggis 씨는 거짓말을 했다. (lied / nothing / Mr. Boggis / Oh, nothing. / at all)
>

24 그러고 나서 그는 정색하며 말했다. "이 탁자는 복제품입니다. (with / is / this table / then said / a reproduction / a straight face / he)
>

25 몇 파운드의 가치밖에 안 돼요." (it's / pounds / a few / worth / only)
>

26 그리고 그는 덧붙였다. "흠, 제가 살 수도 있을 것 같아요. (hmm / then added / I may / he / buy it / I think)
>

27 우리 집에 있는 탁자 다리가 부러졌거든요. (at home / the legs / are broken / of my table)
>

28 당신의 탁자 다리를 잘라서 제 탁자에 붙일 수 있겠어요."
(the legs / them / I / cut off / of your table / and / to mine / attach / can)
>

29 "얼마를 줄 건가요?" Rummins가 물었다. (how / Rummins / much / asked)
>

30 "유감이지만 많이 줄 수는 없어요. 이것은 복제품일 뿐이니까요." Boggis 씨가 말했다.
(afraid / I'm / not much / Mr. Boggis / this is / said / a reproduction / just)
>

31 "그래서 얼마를 줄 수 있는데요?" (much / how / so)
>

32 "10파운드요." (pounds / ten)
>

33 "10이요? 그것보다는 가치가 더 나가요." (more / worth / ten / than / that / it's)
>

34 "15는 어때요?" (about / how / fifteen)
>

35 "50으로 하지요." (it / fifty / make)
>

36 음, 30이요. 이게 제 마지막 제안입니다." (is / thirty / final offer / my / well / this)
>

37 "그러죠, 이건 당신 겁니다. 그런데 이걸 어떻게 가져갈 건가요? (how / OK, it's yours / are / it / to / you / take / but / going)
>

38 이게 차에 들어가지 않을 텐데요!" (go / this thing / in a car / will not)
>

39 "한번 보죠." Boggis 씨가 말하고는 자신의 차를 가지러 밖으로 나갔다.
(said / his car / Mr. Boggis / and / went out / we'll see / to bring)
>

40 차로 가는 길에 Boggis 씨는 웃지 않을 수 없었다. (Mr. Boggis / on his way / couldn't help smiling / to the car)
>

41 그 탁자는 모든 판매상이 꿈꾸는 것이었다. (what / the table / dreamed of / was / every dealer)
>

42 그는 자신의 행운을 믿을 수가 없었다. (believe / he / his luck / couldn't)
>

43 "아버지, 만약 이게 그의 차에 안 들어가면 어쩌죠? (doesn't / Dad / in his car / this thing / go / what if)
>

44 그가 값을 지불하지 않을 수도 있어요." Bert가 말했다. (you / Bert / he / said / pay / might not)
>

45 Rummins는 그때 생각이 떠올랐다. (then had / Rummins / an idea)
>

46 "그가 원하는 건 오직 탁자의 다리뿐이야. (what / the legs / is only / he / wants)
>

47 그를 위해서 다리를 자르자." Rummins가 말했다. (for him / said / let's / the legs off / Rummins / cut)
>

48 "좋은 생각이에요!" Bert가 말했다. (said / idea / great / Bert)
>

49 그런 다음 Bert는 톱을 꺼내서 탁자 다리를 자르기 시작했다. (took out / the legs / and / Bert then / began to / cut off / a saw)
>

50 Boggis 씨가 돌아왔을 때, 탁자 다리는 잘려 있었다. (the legs / cut off / had / came back / when / been / Mr. Boggis)
>

51 "걱정하지 마세요. 이건 호의로 한 거예요. (this / a favor / don't worry / was)
>

52 이것에 대해 비용을 청구하지는 않을게요." Rummins가 말했다. (you / I / for this / said / won't / Rummins / charge)
>

53 Boggis 씨는 너무 충격을 받아서 아무 말도 할 수 없었다. (shocked / couldn't / so / anything / that / he / say / Mr. Boggis / was)
>

[01~05] 다음 글을 읽고, 물음에 답하시오.

Cyril Boggis was an antique furniture dealer in London. (①) He was known ___(A)___ buying good things at a low price and then selling them at a ⓐhigh price. (②) People asked him where he ___(B)___ the furniture, but he just said, "It's a secret."

(③) He went to small towns every Sunday and ⓑknocked on doors. (④) He told people that he was a ⓒfurniture dealer. People didn't know how ⓓvaluable their things were, so Mr. Boggis took advantage ___(C)___ them. (⑤) He was able to buy things very ⓔexpensively.

01 윗글의 빈칸 (A)와 (C)에 들어갈 말이 순서대로 바르게 짝 지어진 것은?

① to – of   ② to – for   ③ for – of
④ for – from   ⑤ as – from

02 윗글의 빈칸 (B)에 들어갈 동사 get의 형태로 알맞은 것은?

① gets   ② getting   ③ has got
④ had got   ⑤ was got

03 윗글의 ①~⑤ 중 주어진 문장이 들어갈 위치로 가장 알맞은 것은?

Mr. Boggis' secret was simple.

①   ②   ③   ④   ⑤

04 윗글의 밑줄 친 ⓐ~ⓔ 중 문맥상 어색한 것은?

① ⓐ   ② ⓑ   ③ ⓒ   ④ ⓓ   ⑤ ⓔ

05 윗글을 읽고 답할 수 없는 질문은?

① What was Mr. Boggis' job?
② What was Mr. Boggis famous for?
③ Where did Mr. Boggis go on Sundays?
④ When did Mr. Boggis sell furniture?
⑤ How could Mr. Boggis buy good furniture at a low price?

[06~10] 다음 글을 읽고, 물음에 답하시오.

Now it was another Sunday, and Mr. Boggis was in a small town again. At a house he visited, he met two men. One was Rummins, the owner, and ___ⓐ___ was his son Bert.

"I buy old (A)furniture / furnitures. Do you have any?" asked Mr. Boggis.

"No, I don't," said Rummins.

"Can I just take a look?" asked Mr. Boggis.

"Sure. Please come in," said Rummins.

Mr. Boggis first went to the kitchen, and there was nothing. He then moved to the living room. And there it was! A table (B)what / which was a priceless piece of eighteenth-century English furniture. ⓑ그는 몹시 흥분해서 거의 넘어질 뻔했다.

"What's wrong?" Bert asked.

"Oh, nothing. Nothing at all," Mr. Boggis lied. He then said with a straight face, "This table is a reproduction. It's worth only (C)a little / a few pounds."

06 윗글의 빈칸 ⓐ에 들어갈 말로 알맞은 것은?

① other   ② others   ③ another
④ the other   ⑤ the others

07 윗글 (A)~(C)의 각 네모 안에 주어진 말 중에서 어법상 알맞은 것끼리 짝지어진 것은?

	(A)		(B)		(C)
①	furniture	…	what	…	a little
②	furniture	…	which	…	a few
③	furnitures	…	what	…	a few
④	furnitures	…	which	…	a little
⑤	furnitures	…	which	…	a few

08 윗글의 밑줄 친 우리말 ⓑ와 의미가 같도록 할 때, 다음 문장의 빈칸에 알맞은 말이 순서대로 바르게 짝지어진 것은?

> He was _____ excited _____ he almost fell over.

① so – but   ② so – that
③ so – then   ④ such – then
⑤ such – as

09 다음 영영풀이에 해당하는 단어를 윗글에서 찾아 쓰시오.

> a copy of something such as a picture

→ _____

10 윗글의 내용과 일치하도록 할 때, 빈칸에 들어갈 말로 알맞은 것은?

> Q: What did Mr. Boggis find in the living room of Rummins' house?
> A: He found _____.

① nothing   ② a reproduction
③ a few pounds   ④ new furniture
⑤ a very valuable table

[11~13] 다음 글을 읽고, 물음에 답하시오.

He then added, "Hmm, I think I may buy ①it. The legs of my table at home ⓐis broken. I can cut off the legs of your table and ⓑattach them to mine."

"How much?" Rummins asked.

"Not ⓒmuch, I'm afraid. ②This is just a reproduction," said Mr. Boggis.

"So how much?"

"Ten pounds."

"Ten? It's ⓓworth more than ③that."

"How about fifteen?"

"Make it fifty."

"Well, thirty. This is my final offer."

"OK, ④it's yours, but how are you going to take it? ⑤This thing will not go in a car!"

"We'll see," Mr. Boggis said and went out ⓔto bring his car.

11 윗글의 밑줄 친 ①~⑤ 중 가리키는 대상이 나머지와 다른 하나는?

①   ②   ③   ④   ⑤

12 윗글의 밑줄 친 ⓐ~ⓔ 중 어법상 틀린 것을 바르게 고친 것은?

① ⓐ → are   ② ⓑ → attaching
③ ⓒ → many   ④ ⓓ → worthy
⑤ ⓔ → brought

13 윗글의 내용과 일치하지 않는 것은?

① Rummins의 탁자는 다리가 부러졌기 때문에 Boggis 씨가 싸게 사려고 했다.
② Rummins는 자신의 탁자가 10파운드보다 값어치가 있다고 생각했다.
③ Boggis 씨가 마지막으로 제안한 금액은 30파운드였다.
④ Rummins는 Boggis 씨에게 탁자를 팔기로 했다.
⑤ Boggis 씨는 차를 가져오려고 밖으로 나갔다.

[14~16] 다음 글을 읽고, 물음에 답하시오.

On his way to the car, Mr. Boggis couldn't help ____ⓐ____. The table was ____(A)____ every dealer dreamed of. He couldn't believe his ____ⓑ____.

"Dad, what if this thing doesn't go in his car? He might not pay you," said Bert.

Rummins then had an idea. "____(B)____ he wants is only the legs. Let's cut the legs off for him," said Rummins. "Great idea!" said Bert. Bert then took out a ____ⓒ____ and began to cut off the legs.

When Mr. Boggis came back, the legs (C)cut off. "Don't worry, this was a favor. I won't ____ⓓ____ you for this," said Rummins. Mr. Boggis was so ____ⓔ____ that he couldn't say anything.

14 윗글의 흐름상 빈칸 ⓐ~ⓔ에 들어갈 말로 알맞지 <u>않은</u> 것은?

① ⓐ: smiling
② ⓑ: luck
③ ⓒ: saw
④ ⓓ: charge
⑤ ⓔ: happy

15 윗글의 빈칸 (A)와 (B)에 공통으로 들어갈 말로 알맞은 것은?

① that(That)
② what(What)
③ who(Who)
④ which(Which)
⑤ whom(Whom)

16 윗글의 밑줄 친 (C)cut off의 형태로 어법상 알맞은 것은?

① cut off
② were cutting off
③ had cut off
④ have been cut off
⑤ had been cut off

서술형

[17~19] 다음 글을 읽고, 물음에 답하시오.

Cyril Boggis was an antique furniture dealer in London. He was known for buying good things at a low price and then selling them at a high price. People asked him where he had got the furniture, but he just said, "ⓐIt's a secret."

Mr. Boggis' secret was simple. He went to small towns every Sunday and knocked on doors. He told people that he was a furniture dealer. People didn't know _____ⓑ_____, so Mr. Boggis took advantage of them. He was able to buy things very cheaply.

17 윗글의 밑줄 친 ⓐIt이 가리키는 것을 본문에서 찾아 쓰시오. (6단어)

→ _____

18 윗글의 빈칸 ⓑ에 알맞은 말을 괄호 안의 단어를 배열하여 쓰시오.

→ _____

(were, valuable, how, things, their)

19 윗글의 내용과 일치하도록 다음 질문에 대한 답을 완성하시오.

(1) What did Cyril Boggis do for a living?

→ He was _____ _____

_____.

(2) When and where did Cyril Boggis go to buy things at a low price?

→ He went to _____ _____ _____

_____.

[20~22] 다음 글을 읽고, 물음에 답하시오.

Mr. Boggis first went to the kitchen, and there was ⓐ<u>nothing</u>. He then moved to the living room. And there it was! A table ⓑ<u>which</u> was a priceless piece of eighteenth-century English furniture. He was so ⓒ<u>exciting</u> that he almost fell over.

"What's wrong?" Bert asked.

"Oh, nothing. Nothing at all," Mr. Boggis lied. He then said ⓓ<u>with</u> a straight face, "This table is a reproduction. It's worth only a few pounds."

He then added, "Hmm, I think I may buy it. The legs of my table at home ⓔ<u>are broken</u>. I can cut off the legs of your table and attach (A)<u>them</u> to (B)<u>mine</u>."

20 윗글의 밑줄 친 ⓐ~ⓔ 중 어법상 어색한 것의 기호를 쓰고 바르게 고쳐 쓰시오.

(   ) → _____

21 윗글의 밑줄 친 (A)와 (B)가 각각 가리키는 것을 본문에서 찾아 쓰시오.

(A) _____

(B) _____

22 윗글을 다음과 같이 요약할 때, 빈칸에 알맞은 말을 본문에서 찾아 쓰시오.

Mr. Boggis found a piece of _____ _____ in Rummins' living room. He lied that it was a(n) _____ and said he would _____ it.

[23~25] 다음 글을 읽고, 물음에 답하시오.

"OK, it's yours, but how are you going to take it? This thing will not go in a car!"

"We'll see," Mr. Boggis said and went out to bring his car.

On his way to the car, ⓐ<u>Boggis 씨는 웃지 않을 수 없었다</u>. The table was what every dealer dreamed of. He couldn't believe his luck.

"Dad, what if this thing doesn't go in his car? He might not pay you," said Bert.

Rummins then had an idea. "What he wants is only the legs. Let's cut the legs off for him," said Rummins. "Great idea!" said Bert. Bert then took out a saw and began to cut off the legs.

When Mr. Boggis came back, the legs had been cut off. "Don't worry, this was a favor. I won't charge you for ⓑ<u>this</u>," said Rummins. Mr. Boggis was so shocked that he couldn't say anything.

23 괄호 안의 단어를 어법에 맞게 사용하여 윗글의 밑줄 친 우리말 ⓐ를 영어로 쓰시오.

→ _____

(help, smile)

24 윗글의 내용과 일치하도록 다음 세 사람의 말을 완성하시오.

Mr. Boggis	I got a _____ that every dealer wants to buy. I can't believe my _____!
Bert	I think this table is too big to go in Mr. Boggis' _____. Then, he might not _____ my father.
Rummins	Mr. Boggis said he only needed the _____. Let's _____ them _____.

25 윗글의 밑줄 친 ⓑthis가 가리키는 것을 10자 내외의 우리말로 쓰시오.

→ _____

만점 노트

Listen and Talk D

교과서 103쪽

Last summer, I lost my dog, Bomi. She disappeared ❶while I was drinking water in the park. ❷Luckily, I ❸was able to find her two days later. ❹I was so happy that I hugged her tightly.

작년 여름에 나는 내 강아지 보미를 잃어버렸어. 내가 공원에서 물을 마시는 사이에 그녀가 사라졌어. 다행히, 이틀 뒤에 그녀를 찾을 수 있었어. 나는 너무 기뻐서 그녀를 품에 꼭 안았어.

❶ 접속사 while이 '~하는 동안에'라는 의미로 쓰였다.
❷ luckily는 '다행히, 운 좋게'라는 의미로, fortunately로 바꿔 쓸 수 있다. (↔ unfortunately)
❸ be able to는 '~할 수 있다'라는 의미의 표현으로, was able to는 조동사 could로 바꿔 쓸 수 있다.
❹ 「so+형용사/부사+that+주어+동사」는 '매우(너무) ~해서 (그 결과) …하다'라는 의미를 나타낸다.

Around the World

교과서 111쪽

· *Fantastic Mr. Fox*: A fox ❶protects his family from three mean farmers.
· *Matilda*: A girl uses her special powers ❷to help her friends.
· *Charlie and the Chocolate Factory*: A boy visits ❸the best chocolate factory in the world.

· '멋진 여우 씨': 한 여우가 3명의 못된 농부들로부터 자신의 가족을 지켜 낸다.
· '마틸다': 한 소녀가 친구들을 돕기 위해 자신의 특별한 힘을 사용한다.
· '찰리와 초콜릿 공장': 한 소년이 세계 최고의 초콜릿 공장을 방문한다.

❶ protect A from B는 'B로부터 A를 보호하다'의 뜻이고, mean은 '비열한, 심술궂은, 못된'이라는 의미의 형용사로 쓰였다.
❷ '~하기 위해'라는 뜻의 목적을 나타내는 부사적 용법의 to부정사이다.
❸ 「the+형용사의 최상급+명사(구)+in+장소나 집단」(…에서 가장 ~한) 형태의 최상급 표현이다.

Think and Write

교과서 114쪽

Review of the Story, *One Lucky Sunday*

This story ❶was written by Roald Dahl. It is about Mr. Boggis, ❷who was an antique furniture dealer. In the story, ❸he lied to Rummins that his table was a reproduction and ❹offered 30 pounds to buy it. Mr. Boggis said he only wanted the legs of the table, so Bert ❺cut them off for him. This surprised Mr. Boggis ❻who really wanted the whole table. I think Mr. Boggis was not a good man because he lied to people. ❼What I like the most about this story is the surprising ending. I think this story is very interesting.

독후감, '어느 운수 좋은 일요일'

이 이야기는 Roald Dahl이 썼다. 이것은 Boggis 씨에 관한 것인데, 그는 골동품 가구 판매상이었다. 이 이야기에서, 그는 Rummins에게 그의 탁자가 복제품이라고 거짓말을 했고, 그것을 사는 데 30파운드를 주겠다고 제안했다. Boggis 씨는 탁자의 다리만을 원한다고 말했고, 그래서 Bert는 그를 위해 탁자 다리를 잘랐다. 이것은 실제로는 탁자 전부를 원했던 Boggis 씨를 놀라게 했다. 나는 Boggis 씨가 사람들에게 거짓말을 했기 때문에 좋은 사람이 아니라고 생각한다. 이 이야기에서 내가 가장 마음에 드는 것은 놀라운 결말이다. 나는 이 이야기가 매우 흥미롭다고 생각한다.

❶ 「be동사+과거분사+by+행위자」 형태의 수동태 문장이다.
❷ 계속적 용법의 관계대명사 who가 이끄는 관계대명사절로, 선행사인 Mr. Boggis에 대해 부연 설명해 준다.
❸ lie to는 '~에게 거짓말하다'라는 의미이며, 접속사 that이 이끄는 명사절이 거짓말의 내용을 가리킨다.
❹ lied와 offered가 등위접속사 and로 병렬 연결되어 있다.
❺ 「동사+부사」로 이루어진 cut off는 이어동사이고, 이어동사의 목적어가 대명사인 경우에는 동사와 부사 사이에 목적어가 온다.
❻ 주격 관계대명사 who가 이끄는 관계대명사절이 선행사인 Mr. Boggis를 수식한다.
❼ What I ~ story는 선행사를 포함하는 관계대명사 what이 이끄는 명사절로, 문장에서 주어 역할을 한다.

실전 TEST

[01~02] 다음 글을 읽고, 물음에 답하시오.

ⓐLast summer, I lost my dog, Bomi. She disappeared while I was drinking water in the park. Luckily, I was able to find her two days later. I was so happy that I hugged her tightly.

01 윗글의 밑줄 친 ⓐ에 대해 해 줄 수 있는 말로 알맞은 것을 <u>모두</u> 고르면?

① Good for you.
② That's too bad.
③ Congratulations!
④ I'm so happy for you.
⑤ I'm sorry to hear that.

02 윗글을 읽고 답할 수 <u>없는</u> 질문은?

① Where did the writer lose Bomi?
② What was the writer doing when Bomi disappeared?
③ Where did the writer find Bomi?
④ How long did it take to find Bomi?
⑤ How did the writer feel when he or she found Bomi?

03 다음 글의 빈칸 ⓐ와 ⓑ에 들어갈 말이 순서대로 바르게 짝지어진 것은?

· *Fantastic Mr. Fox*: A fox protects his family ____ⓐ___ three mean farmers.
· *Matilda*: A girl uses her special powers ____ⓑ___ her friends.
· *Charlie and the Chocolate Factory*: A boy visits the best chocolate factory in the world.

① to – helps
② to – to help
③ from – helps
④ from – to help
⑤ for – helping

[04~06] 다음 글을 읽고, 물음에 답하시오.

Review of the Story, *One Lucky Sunday*

This story ①was written by Roald Dahl. It is about Mr. Boggis, ②who was an antique furniture dealer. In the story, he lied to Rummins that his table was a reproduction and offered 30 pounds ③to buy it. Mr. Boggis said he only wanted the legs of the table, so Bert ④cut off them for him. This surprised Mr. Boggis who really wanted the whole table. I think Mr. Boggis was not a good man ⑤because he lied to people. (A)<u>이 이야기에서 내가 가장 마음에 드는 것</u> is the surprising ending. I think this story is very interesting.

04 윗글의 밑줄 친 ①~⑤ 중 어법상 <u>틀린</u> 것은?

①　　②　　③　　④　　⑤

05 윗글의 밑줄 친 우리말 (A)와 의미가 같도록 빈칸에 알맞은 말을 쓰시오.

→ _____ _____ _____ _____
_____ about this story

06 윗글의 내용과 일치하지 <u>않는</u> 것은?

① Roald Dahl wrote *One Lucky Sunday*.
② Mr. Boggis was an antique furniture dealer.
③ Mr. Boggis told Rummins that his table was a reproduction.
④ Bert cut off the legs of the table because Mr. Boggis told him to do so.
⑤ The writer likes the surprising ending of the story the most.

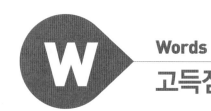

Words
고득점 맞기

01 다음 영영풀이에 해당하는 단어로 알맞은 것은?

> to ask people to pay a particular amount of money for something

① add   ② charge   ③ offer
④ attach   ⑤ reproduce

02 Which pair is correct for the blanks?

> • He accepted our _____ to help him on his project.
> • She _____ a red leather patch on her bag.

① saw – paid   ② dealer – charged
③ offer – attached   ④ method – knocked
⑤ announcement – elected

03 다음 대화의 빈칸에 들어갈 말로 가장 알맞은 것은?

> A: Did you do well on your math exam?
> B: _____, no. I don't feel good about it.

① Luckily   ② Thankfully   ③ Anyway
④ Suddenly   ⑤ Unfortunately

고난도 신유형
04 [보기]에서 알맞은 단어를 골라 단어의 앞이나 뒤에 re- 또는 -less를 붙여 문장을 완성하시오.

> [보기]   price   care   play   cycle

(1) We need to _____ more to save the Earth.

(2) I was disappointed with his _____ behavior.

(3) People will get bored if you _____ the music so many times.

05 다음 빈칸에 공통으로 들어갈 말을 쓰시오.

> • She _____ a mouse sitting under the chair yesterday.
> • He is cutting wood with a(n) _____ to make a swing for his son.

→ _____

06 다음 두 문장의 뜻이 같도록 할 때, 빈칸에 들어갈 말로 알맞은 것은?

> How much do these sneakers cost?
> = What is the _____ of these sneakers?

① pay   ② price   ③ offer
④ method   ⑤ collection

07 다음 밑줄 친 단어의 영영풀이로 알맞은 것은?

> The painting is <u>worth</u> more than $50,000.

① all of something
② having a specific value
③ very surprised and upset
④ without any care or thought
⑤ not having any value, or not useful

08 다음 중 밑줄 친 부분과 바꿔 쓸 수 없는 것은?

① James was <u>known</u> for solving mysteries.
(= famous)
② The <u>whole</u> city was filled with yellow dust.
(= entire)
③ She raised her hand to ask her <u>final</u> question.
(= first)
④ The museum has a lot of <u>priceless</u> works of art. (= valuable)
⑤ You can <u>take advantage of</u> this vacation to improve your English. (= make good use of)

09 다음 ⓐ～ⓓ의 빈칸 중 어느 곳에도 들어갈 수 <u>없는</u> 것은?

> ⓐ My uncle is the _____ of the restaurant.
> ⓑ His job is to make _____s of famous artworks.
> ⓒ They wanted some new _____ for their new house.
> ⓓ My sister got the main _____ in the school play.

① role　　　② owner　　　③ furniture
④ favor　　　⑤ reproduction

10 다음 우리말과 의미가 같도록 빈칸에 알맞은 말을 쓰시오.

> 정색하며, 그녀는 그 소문이 사실이 아니라고 말했다.

→ With _____ _____ _____, she said that the rumor wasn't true.

[11~12] 다음 중 밑줄 친 부분의 쓰임이 의미상 <u>어색한</u> 것을 고르시오.

11
① Parents' love for their children is <u>endless</u>.
② I asked him for a <u>favor</u>, but he didn't help me.
③ I don't keep <u>priceless</u> things in the basement.
④ Dad found an <u>antique</u> oak table in the garage.
⑤ Every time I got <u>disappointed</u>, he congratulated me.

12
① Henry <u>fell over</u> and broke his leg.
② Kate began to <u>cut off</u> her long hair.
③ He heard a strange sound <u>on his way home</u>.
④ <u>Take a look</u> at this picture and guess its title.
⑤ The story was so sad that she <u>couldn't help</u> <u>laughing</u>.

13 다음 영영풀이의 빈칸 ⓐ～ⓔ에 들어갈 말로 알맞지 <u>않은</u> 것은?

> · **attach**: to fasten or ____ⓐ____ one thing to another
> · **dealer**: a person whose job is to ____ⓑ____ things
> · **reproduction**: a(n)____ⓒ____ of something such as a picture
> · **favor**: something that you do to ____ⓓ____ someone
> · **knock**: to ____ⓔ____ a door with your hand so that someone inside knows you are there

① ⓐ: join　　　② ⓑ: buy and sell
③ ⓒ: copy　　　④ ⓓ: hurt
⑤ ⓔ: hit

14 Which underlined word has the same meaning as in the example?

> [보기] The restaurant <u>charges</u> high prices for its food.

① Is there a <u>charge</u> for children?
② How much is the shipping <u>charge</u>?
③ They fixed my smartphone free of <u>charge</u>.
④ A service <u>charge</u> is not included on your bill.
⑤ The Art Museum doesn't <u>charge</u> for admission.

15 다음 중 단어와 영영풀이가 바르게 연결되지 <u>않은</u> 것끼리 짝지어진 것은?

> ⓐ **valuable**: worth little money
> ⓑ **shocked**: very surprised and upset
> ⓒ **luck**: an act of asking someone if they would like something
> ⓓ **furniture**: things such as chairs, beds, tables, and bookshelves, etc.
> ⓔ **saw**: a tool for cutting wood or other materials, typically with a long, thin, steel blade

① ⓐ, ⓒ　　　② ⓐ, ⓓ　　　③ ⓑ, ⓔ
④ ⓒ, ⓓ　　　⑤ ⓑ, ⓓ, ⓔ

Listen and Talk

영작하기

• 주어진 우리말과 일치하도록 교과서 대화문을 쓰시오.

Listen and Talk A-1

B: _____

G: _____

B: _____

G: _____

 해석

교과서 102쪽

B: Sue, 너 신나 보인다. 무슨 일 있어?

G: 내가 학급 회장으로 당선되었어. 정말 신나.

B: 멋지다. 축하해!

G: 고마워. 우리 반을 위해 일할 기회가 생겨서 나는 정말 기뻐.

Listen and Talk A-2

G: _____

B: _____

G: _____

B: _____

교과서 102쪽

G: Tim, 학교 마라톤에서 금메달 딴 것을 축하해.

B: 고마워, 수지야. 나는 정말 기뻐.

G: 네 스스로가 매우 자랑스럽겠구나.

B: 응. 맞아. 나는 최선을 다했어.

Listen and Talk A-3

B: _____

G: _____

B: _____

G: _____

B: _____

교과서 102쪽

B: 미나야, 안 좋은 일 있니?

G: 음, 내 스마트폰을 잃어버렸어. 속상해.

B: 아, 그 말을 들으니 정말 유감이야. 마지막으로 언제 사용했는지 기억나니?

G: 음, 매점에서 그것을 가방에서 꺼낸 것은 기억나.

B: 그럼 그것을 찾으러 매점에 다시 가 보자.

Listen and Talk A-4

G: _____

B: _____

G: _____

B: _____

G: _____

B: _____

교과서 102쪽

G: 너 몸이 안 좋아 보인다, 인호야. 무슨 일 있어?

B: 나는 독감에 걸렸어.

G: 안됐구나. 병원은 가 봤어?

B: 응. 약을 먹고 있어.

G: 음, 네가 곧 낫기를 바라.

B: 고마워.

Listen and Talk C

B: _____

_____

W: _____

_____

B: _____

W: _____

B: _____

_____

W: _____

B: _____

W: _____

_____

B: _____

 해석

교과서 103쪽

B: 실례합니다, Carter 선생님. 질문 하나 해도 될까요? 연극에서 제가 주인공 역할을 맡게 됐나요?

W: 그렇단다. 축하해, 지호야! 너는 우리 학교 연극 '로미오와 줄리엣'에서 로미오가 될 거야.

B: 정말이요? 너무 신나요. 정말 고맙습니다, Carter 선생님.

W: 네가 얼마나 그 역할을 원했는지 알고 있단다. 나도 정말 기쁘구나.

B: 고맙습니다. 수미는 어떻게 됐어요? 수미도 원했던 역할을 맡게 됐나요?

W: 안타깝게도, 아니란다. 그녀는 매우 실망했어.

B: 아, 그 말을 들으니 유감이네요. 그런데, 첫 연습은 언제예요?

W: 9월 20일 오후 2시에 연극 동아리방에서 할 거야. 그것에 관한 문자 메시지를 곧 받을 거야.

B: 알겠습니다. 거기에서 뵐게요.

Talk and Play

A: _____

B: _____

A: _____

교과서 104쪽

A: 무슨 일 있니?

B: 내 자전거가 고장 났어. 정말 속상해.

A: 안됐구나. 그 말을 들으니 유감이야.

Review - 1

B: _____

G: _____

B: _____

G: _____

교과서 116쪽

B: 너 신나 보인다. Sally. 무슨 일 있어?

G: 나는 Dream 콘서트에 갈 거야.

B: 축하해! 네가 얼마나 가고 싶어 했는지 내가 알지.

G: 고마워. 내가 가장 좋아하는 가수를 볼 기회가 생겨서 정말 기뻐.

Review - 2

B: _____

G: _____

B: _____

_____

G: _____

교과서 116쪽

B: 수미야, 너 기분 안 좋아 보인다. 무슨 일 있니?

G: 음, 나는 학교 연극에서 역할을 맡지 못했어. 나는 정말 실망했어.

B: 아, 그 말을 들으니 정말 유감이야. 그렇지만 너는 분명히 다음번에는 역할을 맡을 수 있을 거야.

G: 고마워. 다음번에는 더 열심히 노력할 거야.

01 다음 대화의 빈칸에 들어갈 말로 알맞지 <u>않은</u> 것은?

> A: _____
>
> B: That's wonderful. Congratulations!

① I passed the entrance exam.
② I finally got a ticket to the musical.
③ I won first prize in the singing contest.
④ I finished a full marathon. I'm so happy.
⑤ I dropped my new smartphone, and it broke.

02 다음 대화의 밑줄 친 ①~⑤ 중 흐름상 <u>어색한</u> 것은?

> A: ①<u>You don't look good.</u> What's the matter?
> B: Well, I didn't get a role in the school play.
> ②<u>I'm very excited.</u>
> A: ③<u>Oh, I'm so sorry to hear that.</u> ④<u>But I'm sure you can get a role next time.</u>
> B: Thanks. ⑤<u>I'll try harder next time.</u>

①   ②   ③   ④   ⑤

03 다음 중 짝지어진 대화가 <u>어색한</u> 것을 <u>모두</u> 고르면?

① A: I was elected as class president. I'm so happy.
  B: That's wonderful. Congratulations!
② A: I lost my dog in the park this morning.
  B: I'm sorry to hear that. I hope you find him soon.
③ A: I'm going to go to the BTS concert.
  B: That's too bad. I know how much you wanted to go.
④ A: My best friend will move to another country. I'm so sad.
  B: That's too bad. I'm sorry to hear that.
⑤ A: Congratulations on winning the tennis match. You must be very proud of yourself.
  B: Thanks. I'm very disappointed.

04 다음과 같은 상황에서 글쓴이에게 해 줄 말로 가장 적절한 것은?

> Last weekend, my sister lost my bag. She left it on the bus and couldn't find it. I was so upset. It was a present from my mother on my birthday.

① You did a good job!
② I'm afraid I can't do it.
③ I'm really happy for you!
④ That's wonderful. Congratulations!
⑤ That's too bad. I'm sorry to hear that.

[05~06] 다음 대화를 읽고, 물음에 답하시오.

> A: You don't look so good, Inho. What's the matter?
> B: I have the flu.
> A: _____ⓐ_____ Did you see the doctor?
> B: Yes. I'm taking medicine.
> A: Well, I hope you feel better soon.
> B: Thanks, Sumi.

05 위 대화의 빈칸 ⓐ에 들어갈 말로 알맞지 <u>않은</u> 것을 <u>모두</u> 고르면?

① That's terrible.
② That's too bad.
③ I'm happy for you.
④ That's wonderful.
⑤ I'm sorry to hear that.

06 위 대화를 읽고 답할 수 있는 질문은?

① What's the problem with Sumi?
② Why did Inho go to the doctor?
③ What does Inho advise Sumi to do?
④ How often does Inho take medicine?
⑤ What will Inho do after the conversation?

서술형

[07~09] 다음 대화를 읽고, 물음에 답하시오.

A: Excuse me, Ms. Carter. Can I ask you a question? Did I get the main role in the play?
B: Yes, you did. ⓐCongratulations, Jiho! You're going to be Romeo in our school play, *Romeo and Juliet*.
A: Really? ⓑI'm so upset. Thank you so much, Ms. Carter.
B: I know how much you wanted the role. ⓒI'm so happy for you.
A: Thank you. What about Sumi? Did she get the role she wanted, too?
B: Unfortunately, no. ⓓShe's very disappointed.
A: Oh, (A)I'm sorry to hear that. Anyway, when is the first practice?
B: It's at 2 p.m. on September 20th, in the acting club room. You'll get a text message about it soon.
A: OK. ⓔI'll be there.

07 위 대화의 밑줄 친 ⓐ~ⓔ 중 흐름상 어색한 것을 찾아 기호를 쓰고 바르게 고쳐 쓰시오.

( ) → _____

08 위 대화의 밑줄 친 (A)와 바꿔 쓸 수 있는 말을 완성하시오.

→ That's _____ _____.

09 위 대화의 내용과 일치하도록 다음 질문에 대한 답을 완전한 영어 문장으로 쓰시오.

(1) Which role did Jiho get in the school play?
→ _____

(2) When and where is the first practice?
→ _____

10 다음 대화의 빈칸에 알맞은 말을 [조건]에 맞게 쓰시오.

A: (1)_____
_____ (win first prize)
B: Thanks. (2)_____ (so)
A: You must be very proud of yourself.
B: Yes, I am. I did my best.

[조건] 1. (1)은 축하하는 말, (2)는 감정을 나타내는 말을 쓸 것
2. 괄호 안의 말을 어법에 맞게 사용할 것

[11~12] 다음 대화를 읽고, 물음에 답하시오.

Tim: Mina, is anything wrong?
Mina: Well, I lost my smartphone. I'm upset.
Tim: Oh, _____ⓐ_____. Do you remember when you used it last?
Mina: Well, I remember taking it out of my bag at the snack shop.
Tim: Then, let's go back to the snack shop to look for it.
Mina: OK, thanks.

11 위 대화의 흐름상 빈칸 ⓐ에 들어갈 알맞은 말을 sorry를 사용하여 쓰시오.

→ _____ _____ _____
_____

12 위 대화의 내용과 일치하도록 빈칸에 알맞은 말을 쓰시오.

Mina lost her _____, so she's _____. She remembers using it last at _____ _____ _____. After the conversation, she will go there to _____ _____ it with Tim.

Grammar
고득점 맞기

01 다음 빈칸에 들어갈 말이 순서대로 바르게 짝지어진 것은?

> • He said he _____ the song before.
> • Mina plays the cello very well. She _____ the cello since she was very young.

① heard – had played
② has heard – played
③ has heard – had played
④ had heard – played
⑤ had heard – has played

02 다음 빈칸에 공통으로 들어갈 말로 알맞은 것은?

> • I haven't decided _____ to wear.
> • Alice read _____ I had written to her.
> • _____ he wants to be is a robot scientist.

① if(If)
② that(That)
③ what(What)
④ which(Which)
⑤ whether(Whether)

03 다음 우리말을 영어로 바르게 옮긴 것은?

> 그는 나에게 그 신발을 어디에서 샀는지 물었다.

① He asks me where I bought the shoes.
② He asked me where I had bought the shoes.
③ He had asked me where I bought the shoes.
④ He asked me where I have bought the shoes.
⑤ He has asked me where I've bought the shoes.

04 다음 대화의 밑줄 친 ①～⑤ 중 어법상 틀린 것은?

> A: ①Why did you ②miss the concert yesterday?
> B: The traffic ③was so heavy ④that I was late for it. When I arrived at the hall, it ⑤has already started.

①   ②   ③   ④   ⑤

05 다음 두 문장을 한 문장으로 바르게 쓴 것을 모두 고르면?

> The thief stole the thing. It was in the safe.

① The thief stole that was in the safe.
② The thief stole what was in the safe.
③ The thief stole which was in the safe.
④ The thief stole the thing that was in the safe.
⑤ The thief stole the thing what was in the safe.

06 다음 글의 빈칸에 들어갈 말이 순서대로 바르게 짝지어진 것은?

> I'm sorry I'm late. I _____ the train this morning. The train _____ when I got to the station.

① miss – had left
② had missed – left
③ missed – has left
④ missed – had left
⑤ had missed – has left

고/난도
07 다음 글에서 어법상 틀린 부분을 바르게 고친 것은?

> I ordered the T-shirt online last month. But the color was different from that I had seen on the website.

① ordered → have ordered
② last month → next month
③ was → has been
④ that → what
⑤ had seen → have seen

08 다음 중 빈칸에 들어갈 관계대명사가 나머지와 다른 하나는?

① The cake is _____ Mom was baking.
② I haven't received _____ he sent yet.
③ This camera is _____ I've wanted to have.
④ We ate _____ my parents had cooked for us.
⑤ I can't find the book _____ I want to borrow.

09 다음 중 밑줄 친 부분이 어법상 **틀린** 것은?

① Where <u>had</u> you <u>lived</u> before you came here?
② I <u>had</u> never <u>used</u> an oven before I took the baking class.
③ Amy liked my desk. She <u>had asked</u> me where I <u>had got</u> it.
④ I was late for the test. The test <u>had</u> already <u>begun</u> when I arrived at the classroom.
⑤ Mom and I couldn't go in. Mom told me that she <u>had lost</u> the key on her way home.

10 다음 중 어법상 올바른 문장끼리 짝지어진 것은?

ⓐ This is different from what I expected.
ⓑ *Spiderman* is who I want to watch with you.
ⓒ Sam hasn't received it what he bought last week.
ⓓ What I know about him is that he likes to wear jeans.

① ⓐ, ⓑ   ② ⓐ, ⓒ
③ ⓐ, ⓓ   ④ ⓑ, ⓓ
⑤ ⓒ, ⓓ

11 다음 중 어법상 **틀린** 문장의 개수는?

ⓐ I'll cook what you want to eat for dinner.
ⓑ Which they need now is a house to live in.
ⓒ They have never seen snow before they came to Seoul.
ⓓ Grandpa's garden is what I like the most about his house.
ⓔ The house had been empty for ten years until Tom's family moved into it.

① 1개   ② 2개   ③ 3개   ④ 4개   ⑤ 5개

서술형

[12~13] 주어진 두 문장을 괄호 안의 단어를 사용하여 한 문장으로 쓰시오.

12
His parents went to bed. After that, he got home. (when)

→ _____

13
Jake didn't understand the thing. The teacher was talking about it. (what)

→ _____

14 다음 중 어법상 **틀린** 문장을 **두 개** 찾아 기호를 쓰고, 틀린 부분을 바르게 고쳐 쓰시오.

ⓐ I can't believe that she said.
ⓑ Jim told me what he had seen on his way home.
ⓒ The movie was quite different from what I had imagined.
ⓓ Michael shouted out that he has finally solved the problem.

(1) ( ) _____ → _____
(2) ( ) _____ → _____

15 다음 우리말과 의미가 같도록 주어진 표현을 배열하여 문장을 쓰시오. (단, 필요한 표현만 사용할 것)

그들이 말하는 것은 내가 예상했던 것과 비슷하다.
(similar to, what, expected, say, that, which, I, what, is, they)

→ _____

⬤ 서술형 ⬤

16 다음 두 문장을 [조건]에 맞게 한 문장으로 쓰시오.

> [조건] 1. 괄호 안의 접속사와 과거완료를 사용할 것
> 2. 첫 문장을 주절로 앞에 쓸 것

(1) She ran out of allowance. She bought the sneakers. (after)

→ _____

(2) I couldn't use my laptop. My brother broke it. (because)

→ _____

17 다음 두 가지 일이 일어난 시간을 보고, [조건]에 맞게 두 문장을 한 문장으로 완성해 쓰시오.

> **7:00** A.M.   Dad went to work.
> **7:10** A.M.   I woke up.

> [조건] 1. When으로 시작하여 쓸 것
> 2. already를 포함하여 10단어로 쓸 것

→ _____

18 다음 표를 보고, 미나에 대해 [예시]와 같이 쓰시오.

Questions for Mina	Answers
[예시] What are you good at?	taking pictures
(1) What are you interested in?	singing and dancing
(2) What do you like to do in your free time?	playing badminton
(3) What do you want to be in the future?	a movie director

[예시] What Mina is good at is taking pictures.

(1) _____

(2) _____

(3) _____

19 민수가 집에 왔을 때 있었던 일들을 나타낸 다음 그림을 보고, [보기]에 주어진 표현을 어법에 맞게 사용하여 [예시]와 같이 문장을 완성하시오.

> [보기] go to bed   write him a card
> be cleaned   prepare a surprise party

[예시]    (1)

(2)    (3)

[예시] When Minsu came home, his sister <u>had gone to bed</u>.

(1) When Minsu came home, his room _____

_____ .

(2) When Minsu came home, his parents _____

_____ .

(3) When Minsu came home, his grandparents

_____ .

20 다음 우리말과 의미가 같도록 [조건]에 맞게 영어로 쓰시오.

> 이 책은 그녀가 찾고 있는 것이다.

> [조건] 1. look for를 어법에 맞게 사용할 것
> 2. (1)에는 관계대명사 what, (2)에는 관계대명사 that을 사용할 것

(1) _____

(2) _____

• 주어진 우리말과 일치하도록 문장을 쓰시오.

01 _____

Cyril Boggis는 런던의 골동품 가구 판매상이었다.

02 _____

그는 좋은 물건을 낮은 가격에 사서 높은 가격에 파는 것으로 유명했다.

03 _____

사람들은 그에게 가구를 어디에서 구했는지 물었지만, 그는 "그 건 비밀이에요."라고만 말했다.☆

04 _____

Boggis 씨의 비밀은 단순했다.

05 _____

그는 매주 일요일에 작은 마을들을 방문해서 문을 두드렸다.

06 _____

그는 사람들에게 자신이 가구 판매상이라고 말했다.

07 _____

사람들은 자신들의 물건이 얼마나 값진 것인지 몰랐으므로 Boggis 씨는 그들을 이용했다.

08 _____

그는 물건들을 매우 싸게 살 수 있었다.

09 _____

일요일이 또 찾아왔고, Boggis 씨는 다시 어느 작은 마을에 있 었다.

10 _____

그는 방문한 집에서 두 남자를 만났다.

11 _____

한 명은 주인인 Rummins였고, 다른 한 명은 그의 아들인 Bert였다.

12 _____

"저는 고가구를 삽니다.

13 _____

고가구가 있으신가요?" Boggis 씨가 물었다.

14 _____

"아니요." Rummins가 말했다.

15 _____

"한번 둘러봐도 될까요?" Boggis 씨가 물었다.

16 _____

"그럼요. 들어오세요." Rummins가 말했다.

17 _____

Boggis 씨는 먼저 부엌에 갔는데 아무것도 없었다.

18 _____

그런 다음 그는 거실로 옮겨 갔다.

19 _____

그리고 그곳에 그것이 있었다!

20 _____

매우 귀중한 18세기 영국 가구인 탁자가.

21 _____

그는 몹시 흥분해서 거의 넘어질 뻔했다.

22 _____

"무슨 일이세요?" Bert가 물었다.

23 _____

"아, 아무것도 아니에요. 전혀 아무 일도 아닙니다." Boggis 씨는 거짓말을 했다.

24 _____

그러고 나서 그는 정색하며 말했다. "이 탁자는 복제품입니다.

25 _____

몇 파운드의 가치밖에 안 돼요."

26 _____

그리고 그는 덧붙였다. "흠, 제가 살 수도 있을 것 같아요.

27 _____

우리 집에 있는 탁자 다리가 부러졌거든요.

28 _____

당신의 탁자 다리를 잘라서 제 탁자에 붙일 수 있겠어요."

29 _____

"얼마를 줄 건가요?" Rummins가 물었다.

30 _____

"유감이지만 많이 줄 수는 없어요. 이것은 복제품일 뿐이니까
요." Boggis 씨가 말했다.

31 _____

"그래서 얼마를 줄 수 있는데요?"

32 _____

"10파운드요."

33 _____

"10이요? 그것보다는 가치가 더 나가요."

34 _____

"15는 어때요?"

35 _____

"50으로 하지요."

36 _____

"음, 30이요. 이게 제 마지막 제안입니다."

37 _____

"그러죠, 이건 당신 겁니다. 그런데 이걸 어떻게 가져갈 건가요?

38 _____

이게 차에 들어가지 않을 텐데요!"

39 _____

"한번 보죠." Boggis 씨가 말하고는 자신의 차를 가지러 밖으
로 나갔다.

40 _____

차로 가는 길에 Boggis 씨는 웃지 않을 수 없었다.

41 _____

그 탁자는 모든 판매상이 꿈꾸는 것이었다.☆

42 _____

그는 자신의 행운을 믿을 수가 없었다.

43 _____

"아버지, 만약 이게 그의 차에 안 들어가면 어쩌죠?

44 _____

그가 값을 지불하지 않을 수도 있어요." Bert가 말했다.

45 _____

Rummins는 그때 생각이 떠올랐다.

46 _____

"그가 원하는 건 오직 탁자의 다리뿐이야.☆

47 _____

그를 위해서 다리를 자르자." Rummins가 말했다.

48 _____

"좋은 생각이에요!" Bert가 말했다.

49 _____

그런 다음 Bert는 톱을 꺼내서 탁자 다리를 자르기 시작했다.

50 _____

Boggis 씨가 돌아왔을 때, 탁자 다리는 잘려 있었다.☆

51 _____

"걱정하지 마세요. 이건 호의로 한 거예요.

52 _____

이것에 대해 비용을 청구하지는 않을게요." Rummins가 말
했다.

53 _____

Boggis 씨는 너무 충격을 받아서 아무 말도 할 수 없었다.

Reading
고득점 맞기

[01~03] 다음 글을 읽고, 물음에 답하시오.

Cyril Boggis was an antique furniture dealer in London. He was known ___ⓐ___ buying good things ___ⓑ___ a low price and then selling them ___ⓒ___ a high price. People asked him where he (A) has / had got the furniture, but he just said, "It's a secret."

Mr. Boggis' secret was simple. He went to small towns every Sunday and knocked ___ⓓ___ doors. He told people (B) what / that he was a furniture dealer. People didn't know (C) how / why valuable their things were, so Mr. Boggis took advantage ___ⓔ___ them. He (D) was / could able to buy things very cheaply.

01 윗글의 빈칸 ⓐ~ⓔ 중 어느 곳에도 들어갈 수 없는 것은?

① at   ② to   ③ of
④ on   ⑤ for

02 윗글 (A)~(D)의 각 네모 안에 주어진 말 중 어법상 올바른 것끼리 짝지어진 것은?

	(A)	(B)	(C)	(D)
①	has	what	how	was
②	has	that	why	was
③	had	what	how	could
④	had	that	how	was
⑤	had	that	why	could

03 윗글의 Cyril Boggis에 대해 잘못 이해한 사람은?

① 유미: 골동품 가구 판매상이었어.
② 수지: 좋은 가구를 싸게 사서 비싸게 팔았어.
③ 지우: 사람들에게 자신만의 요령을 공유했어.
④ 영호: 일요일마다 작은 마을들을 방문했어.
⑤ 인하: 자신이 갖고 있는 가구의 가치를 잘 모르는 사람들에 게서 가구를 샀어.

[04~05] 다음 글을 읽고, 물음에 답하시오.

Now it was another Sunday, and Mr. Boggis was in a small town again. At a house he visited, he met two men. One was Rummins, the owner, and ⓐother was his son Bert.

"I buy old ⓑfurnitures. Do you have any?" asked Mr. Boggis.

"No, I don't," said Rummins.

"Can I just take a look?" asked Mr. Boggis.

"Sure. Please come in," said Rummins.

Mr. Boggis first went to the kitchen, and there was nothing. He then moved to the living room. And there it was! A table ⓒwhat was a priceless piece of eighteenth-century English furniture. He was ⓓvery excited that he almost fell over.

"What's wrong?" Bert asked.

"Oh, nothing. Nothing at all," Mr. Boggis lied. He then said with a straight face, "This table is a reproduction. It's worth only ⓔa little pounds."

04 윗글의 밑줄 친 ⓐ~ⓔ를 어법상 바르게 고쳐 쓰지 않은 것은?

① ⓐ → the other   ② ⓑ → furniture
③ ⓒ → which   ④ ⓓ → such
⑤ ⓔ → a few

05 Which are correct according to the passage above? Choose TWO.

① Mr. Boggis visited Rummins' house on Sunday.
② Rummins allowed Mr. Boggis to enter his house.
③ There were many pieces of antique furniture in Rummins' house.
④ Mr. Boggis found a piece of valuable furniture in Rummins' kitchen.
⑤ Rummins had a nice old table, which was a reproduction.

[06~09] 다음 글을 읽고, 물음에 답하시오.

He then added, "Hmm, I think I may buy it. (①) The legs of my table at home are broken. I can cut off the legs of your table and attach them to ⓐmine. (②)"

"How much?" Rummins asked.

"Not much, I'm afraid. (③) This is just a reproduction," said Mr. Boggis.

"So how much?"

"Ten pounds."

"Ten? It's worth more than ⓑthat."

"How about fifteen?"

"Make it fifty."

"Well, thirty. This is my final offer. (④)"

"OK, it's yours, but how are you going to take it? (⑤)"

"We'll see," Mr. Boggis said and went out to bring his car.

On his way to the car, Mr. Boggis couldn't help smiling. The table was (A)what every dealer dreamed of. He couldn't believe his luck.

06 윗글의 ①~⑤ 중 주어진 문장이 들어갈 위치로 알맞은 것은?

> This thing will not go in a car!

①   ②   ③   ④   ⑤

07 윗글의 밑줄 친 ⓐ와 ⓑ가 각각 가리키는 것이 순서대로 바르게 짝지어진 것은?

① Rummins' table – the reproduction
② Rummins' table – Mr. Boggis' table
③ Mr. Boggis' table – ten pounds
④ Mr. Boggis' table – fifty pounds
⑤ the legs of Rummins' table – Rummins' table

08 윗글의 밑줄 친 (A)what과 쓰임이 같은 것끼리 짝지어진 것은?

> ⓐ We ate what Dad had cooked for us.
> ⓑ I asked Grandma what to buy for her.
> ⓒ What do you think about my new shoes?
> ⓓ I gave what I bought to my sister yesterday.
> ⓔ He wanted to know what kind of music she likes.

① ⓐ, ⓑ, ⓔ   ② ⓐ, ⓓ   ③ ⓑ, ⓒ
④ ⓑ, ⓔ   ⑤ ⓒ, ⓓ, ⓔ.

09 Which CANNOT be answered from the passage above?

① What did Mr. Boggis decide to buy?
② What was Mr. Boggis' first offer for the table?
③ How much did Rummins want to get for the table at first?
④ Where did Rummins get the table?
⑤ Why did Mr. Boggis smile on his way to his car?

10 다음 글의 흐름상 빈칸 ⓐ~ⓔ에 들어갈 말로 알맞지 않은 것은?

"Dad, _____ⓐ_____ this thing doesn't go in his car? He might not pay you," said Bert.

Rummins then had an idea. "_____ⓑ_____ he wants is only the legs. Let's _____ⓒ_____," said Rummins. "Great idea!" said Bert. Bert then took out a saw and began to cut off the legs.

When Mr. Boggis came back, the legs had been cut off. "Don't worry, this was a favor. I won't _____ⓓ_____," said Rummins. Mr. Boggis was so shocked that he _____ⓔ_____.

① ⓐ: what if
② ⓑ: What
③ ⓒ: sell the table cheaply
④ ⓓ: charge you for this
⑤ ⓔ: couldn't say anything

[11~13] 다음 글을 읽고, 물음에 답하시오.

Cyril Boggis was an antique furniture dealer in London. He was known for buying good things at a low price and then selling them at a high price. ⓐ사람들은 그에게 그 가구를 어디에서 구했는지 물었다, but he just said, "It's a secret."

Mr. Boggis' secret was simple. He went to small towns every Sunday and knocked on doors. He told people that he was a furniture dealer. People didn't know how valuable their things were, so Mr. Boggis took advantage of them. He was able to buy things very cheaply.

11 윗글의 밑줄 친 우리말 ⓐ와 의미가 같도록 괄호 안에 주어진 단어를 어법에 맞게 사용하여 문장을 완성하시오.

→ People asked _____ _____ _____

_____ _____ _____ (get)

12 윗글의 내용을 다음과 같이 요약할 때, 빈칸에 알맞은 말을 쓰시오.

> Mr. Boggis was a dealer who bought and sold _____ _____. He could buy good things very _____ because people in small towns didn't know _____ _____ their things were.

13 윗글을 읽고 답할 수 있는 질문을 골라 기호를 쓰고, 완전한 영어 문장으로 답하시오.

> ⓐ What was Mr. Boggis famous for?
> ⓑ When did Mr. Boggis start to visit small towns?
> ⓒ How many pieces of furniture did Mr. Boggis buy in small towns?

( ) → _____

_____

[14~16] 다음 글을 읽고, 물음에 답하시오.

On his way to the car, Mr. Boggis couldn't help smiling. The table was what every dealer dreamed of. He couldn't believe his luck.

"Dad, what if this thing doesn't go in his car? He might not pay you," said Bert.

Rummins then had ⓐan idea. "What he wants is only the legs. Let's cut the legs off for him," said Rummins. "Great idea!" said Bert. Bert then took out a saw and began to cut off the legs.

When Mr. Boggis came back, the legs had been cut off. "Don't worry, this was a favor. I won't charge you for this," said Rummins. _____ⓑ_____

14 윗글의 밑줄 친 ⓐan idea가 가리키는 말을 본문에서 찾아 완전한 문장으로 쓰시오.

→ _____

15 다음 문장과 같은 의미가 되도록 윗글의 빈칸 ⓑ에 알맞은 문장을 so ~ that ...을 사용하여 쓰시오.

> Mr. Boggis couldn't say anything because he was very shocked.

→ _____

16 윗글의 내용과 일치하도록 빈칸에 알맞은 말을 쓰시오.

(1) _____ was worried that Mr. Boggis wouldn't pay for _____ _____.

(2) Rummins didn't want to charge Mr. Boggis for cutting off _____ _____ of the table.

서술형 100% TEST

01 다음 영영풀이에 해당하는 단어를 [보기]에서 골라 쓰시오.

> [보기] favor   offer   charge   worth

(1) _____ : having a specific value

(2) _____ : something that you do to help someone

(3) _____ : an act of asking someone if they would like something

(4) _____ : to ask people to pay a particular amount of money for something

02 다음 우리말과 의미가 같도록 빈칸에 알맞은 말을 쓰시오.

(1) 너는 모든 기회를 이용해야 한다.
   → You should take _____ _____ all the chances.

(2) 엄마는 출근하시는 길에 내게 전화하셨다.
   → Mom called me _____ _____ _____ to work.

(3) 그녀는 그 소식을 듣고 넘어질 뻔했다.
   → She almost _____ _____ when she heard the news.

03 다음 글을 읽고, (A)~(C)의 각 네모 안에서 어법상 알맞은 것을 골라 쓰시오.

> Charlie is known (A) for / to being funny. Whenever he jokes (B) on / with a straight face, we can't help (C) laugh / laughing .

(A) _____

(B) _____

(C) _____

[04~05] 다음 대화를 읽고, 물음에 답하시오.

> A: Sue, you look excited. What's up?
> B: I was elected as class president. (A)난 정말 신나.
> A: That's wonderful. (B)축하해!
> B: Thanks. _____ ⓐ _____

04 위 대화의 밑줄 친 (A), (B)의 우리말과 의미가 같도록 영어로 쓰시오.

(A) _____

(B) _____

05 위 대화의 빈칸 ⓐ에 들어갈 말을 주어진 표현을 바르게 배열하여 쓰시오.

> work for, to, a chance, really happy, have, I'm, to, my class

→ _____

06 다음 글의 내용과 일치하도록 대화를 완성하시오.

> Inho doesn't feel good because he has the flu. He went to the doctor, and he's taking medicine now. Sumi hopes that he feels better soon.

> A: You don't look so good, Inho. What's (1)_____ _____?
> B: I have the flu.
> A: That's (2) _____ _____. Did you see the doctor?
> B: Yes. I'm taking medicine.
> A: Well, I hope you (3)_____ _____ _____.
> B: Thanks, Sumi.

[07~09] 다음 대화를 읽고, 물음에 답하시오.

> A: Excuse me, Ms. Carter. ⓐCan I ask you a question? Did I get the main role in the play?
> B: Yes, you did. ⓑCongratulations, Jiho! You're going to be Romeo in our school play, *Romeo and Juliet*.
> A: Really? I'm so excited. Thank you so much, Ms. Carter.
> B: I know how much you wanted the role. ⓒI'm upset.
> A: Thank you. ⓓWhat about Sumi? Did she get the role she wanted, too?
> B: Unfortunately, no. She's very disappointed.
> A: ⓔOh, I'm sorry to hear that. Anyway, when is the first practice?
> B: It's at 2 p.m. on September 20th, in the acting club room. You'll get a text message about it soon.
> A: OK. I'll be there.

07 위 대화의 밑줄 친 ⓐ~ⓔ 중 흐름상 어색한 것을 찾아 기호를 쓰고, 바르게 고쳐 문장 전체를 쓰시오.

( ) → _____

08 다음 중 위 대화의 내용과 일치하지 <u>않는</u> 것을 찾아 기호를 쓰고 바르게 고쳐 쓰시오.

> ⓐ Jiho got the role he wanted in the school play.
> ⓑ Sumi didn't get the role she wanted in *Romeo and Juliet*.
> ⓒ Jiho will get a call about the first practice for the play soon.

( ) _____ → _____

09 위 대화의 내용과 일치하도록 지호와 엄마가 주고받은 문자 메시지를 완성하시오.

Mom, I'm going to be _____ in *Romeo and Juliet*. I'm so _____.

Mom: That's wonderful. _____!

Thanks, Mom.

Mom: How about Sumi?

She didn't _____ _____.

Mom: That's _____.

Yeah, Ms. Carter said Sumi was very _____.

10 그림을 보고, 주어진 표현과 과거완료를 사용하여 문장을 완성하시오.

(1)

→ When I _____ Suji last night, she _____ to bed. (call, go)

(2) 5/10~16   5/17 yesterday

→ Jackson _____ tired yesterday because he _____ for a week. (feel, busy)

STEP B

11 다음 문장을 관계대명사를 사용한 문장으로 바꿔 쓸 때, 빈칸에 알맞은 말을 쓰시오.

(1) He gave me his new novel.

→ _____ _____ _____ _____
was his new novel.

(2) She wanted to relax at home.

→ _____ _____ _____ _____
_____ was to relax at home.

(3) Mr. Wilson was known for his entertaining speeches.

→ _____ Mr. Wilson _____ _____
_____ was his entertaining speeches.

12 다음 우리말과 의미가 같도록 [조건]에 맞게 문장을 완성하시오.

> Mark는 그 전날에 차를 도난당했다고 경찰에 신고했다.

> [조건] 1. that절의 주어를 his car로 하고, steal을 사용할 것
> 2. 필요시 단어의 형태를 바꿀 것
> 3. 5단어로 쓸 것

→ Mark reported to the police that _____
_____ the previous day.

13 다음 중 어법상 틀린 문장을 두 개 골라 기호를 쓰고, 틀린 부분을 바르게 고쳐 문장을 다시 쓰시오.

> ⓐ She said that she had been ill for a week.
> ⓑ The thing what he bought for her was a scarf.
> ⓒ Junsu has never ridden a bike before he was 15.
> ⓓ We should be thankful for what parents do for us.

(1) ( ) → _____

(2) ( ) → _____

[14~16] 다음 글을 읽고, 물음에 답하시오.

Mr. Boggis' secret was simple. He went to small towns every Sunday and knocked on doors. He told people that he was a furniture dealer. ⓐPeople didn't know how valuable were their things, so Mr. Boggis took advantage of them. He was able to buy things very cheaply.

Now it was another Sunday, and Mr. Boggis was in a small town again. At a house he visited, he met two men. One was Rummins, the owner, and the other was his son Bert.

"I buy old furniture. Do you have any?" asked Mr. Boggis.

"No, I don't," said Rummins.

"Can I just take a look?" asked Mr. Boggis.

"Sure. Please come in," said Rummins.

Mr. Boggis first went to the kitchen, and there was nothing. He then moved to the living room. And there it was! A table which was a priceless piece of eighteenth-century English furniture. ⓑ그는 몹시 흥분해서 거의 넘어질 뻔했다.

"What's wrong?" Bert asked.

"Oh, nothing. Nothing at all," Mr. Boggis lied. He then said with a straight face, "This table is a reproduction. It's worth only a few pounds."

14 윗글의 밑줄 친 ⓐ에서 어법상 틀린 부분을 바르게 고쳐 다시 쓰시오.

→ _____

15 윗글의 밑줄 친 우리말 ⓑ와 의미가 같도록 [조건]에 맞게 영어로 쓰시오.

> [조건] 1. so ~ that ... 구문으로 나타낼 것
> 2. excited, almost, fall over를 어법에 맞게 사용할 것
> 3. 9단어의 완전한 문장으로 쓸 것

→ _____

16 윗글의 내용과 일치하도록 주어진 질문에 대한 답을 완성하시오.

(1) What did Mr. Boggis find in the living room of Rummins' house?

→ He found _____

_____ there.

(2) What did Mr. Boggis lie to Rummins and Bert about?

→ He lied to them that _____

_____.

[17~21] 다음 글을 읽고, 물음에 답하시오.

"So how much?"

"Ten pounds."

"Ten? It's worth more than that."

"Make it fifty."

"Well, thirty. This is my final offer."

"OK, it's yours, but how are you going to take it? This thing will not go in a car!"

"We'll see," Mr. Boggis said and went out (A)bring his car.

On his way to the car, Mr. Boggis couldn't help (B)smile. The table was ___ⓐ___ every dealer dreamed of. He couldn't believe his luck.

"Dad, what if this thing doesn't go in his car? He might not pay you," said Bert.

Rummins then had an idea. "___ⓑ___ he wants is only the legs. Let's cut the legs off for him," said Rummins. "Great idea!" said Bert. Bert then took out a saw and (C)begin to cut off the legs.

ⓒBoggis 씨가 돌아왔을 때, (탁자의) 다리는 잘려 있었다. "Don't worry, this was a ⓓfavor. I won't charge you for this," said Rummins. ⓔMr. Boggis was so excited that he couldn't say anything.

17 윗글의 밑줄 친 (A)~(C)를 어법상 올바른 형태로 쓰시오.

(A) _____

(B) _____

(C) _____

18 윗글의 빈칸 ⓐ와 ⓑ에 공통으로 들어갈 말을 한 단어로 쓰시오.

→ _____

19 윗글의 밑줄 친 우리말 ⓒ와 의미가 같도록 [조건]에 맞게 영어 문장을 쓰시오.

[조건] 1. 과거완료를 사용할 것
2. come back, the legs, cut off를 어법에 맞게 사용할 것

→ _____

20 윗글의 밑줄 친 ⓓfavor에 해당하는 내용을 [조건]에 맞게 영어로 쓰시오. 고난도

[조건] 1. 윗글에 쓰인 표현을 이용할 것
2. 동명사를 사용하여 4단어로 쓸 것

→ _____

21 윗글의 밑줄 친 문장 ⓔ에서 문맥상 <u>어색한</u> 부분을 바르게 고쳐 쓰시오.

_____ → _____

01 다음 영영풀이에 해당하는 단어로 알맞은 것은? 3점

> to fasten or join one thing to another

① elect ② move ③ knock
④ attach ⑤ charge

02 다음 중 밑줄 친 단어의 우리말 뜻이 알맞지 <u>않은</u> 것은? 3점

① This scarf is <u>worth</u> fifty dollars.
　　(~의 값어치가 있는)
② These ancient vases are <u>priceless</u>.
　　　　　　(가격표가 없는)
③ Dad <u>cut off</u> some branches from the tree.
　　(~을 잘라 냈다)
④ I <u>was shocked</u> to find a snake in the grass.
　　(깜짝 놀랐다)
⑤ This picture is a <u>reproduction</u> of *The Kiss* by Klimt. (복제품)

03 다음 빈칸에 알맞은 말이 순서대로 바르게 짝지어진 것은? 4점

> • I met Jim _____ my way to the airport.
> • You need to take advantage _____ this chance.
> • That small restaurant is known _____ its excellent food.

① to – with – as　　② to – of – for
③ on – for – for　　④ on – with – as
⑤ on – of – for

서술형1

04 다음 우리말과 의미가 같도록 괄호 안의 표현을 어법에 맞게 사용하여 문장을 완성하시오. 4점

> 우리는 그 시험을 앞두고 긴장하지 않을 수가 없었다.

→ We _____ _____ _____ _____
　before the test. (help, feel nervous)

05 다음 대화의 빈칸에 들어갈 말로 알맞지 <u>않은</u> 것은? 3점

> A: Sue, you look excited. What's up?
> B: I was elected as class president. I'm so excited.
> A: _____

① Good for you.
② Congratulations!
③ That's wonderful.
④ I'm so happy for you.
⑤ I'm sorry to hear that.

서술형2

06 자연스러운 대화가 되도록 (A)~(D)를 바르게 배열하시오. 4점

> (A) I have the flu.
> (B) Yes. I'm taking medicine.
> (C) That's too bad. Did you see the doctor?
> (D) You don't look so good, Inho. What's the matter?
> A: Well, I hope you feel better soon.

(　　) – (　　) – (　　) – (　　)

07 다음 대화의 밑줄 친 ①~⑤ 중 흐름상 어색한 것은? 4점

> A: Mina, ①is anything wrong?
> B: Well, I lost my smartphone. ②<u>I'm so excited.</u>
> A: Oh, ③I'm so sorry to hear that. Do you remember ④when you used it last?
> B: Well, I remember taking it out of my bag at the snack shop.
> A: Then, let's go back to the snack shop ⑤to look for it.

①　　②　　③　　④　　⑤

[08~10] 다음 대화를 읽고, 물음에 답하시오.

A: Excuse me, Ms. Carter. Can I ask you a question? Did I get the main role in the play?

B: Yes, you did. Congratulations, Jiho! You're going to be Romeo in our school play, *Romeo and Juliet*.

A: Really? I'm so excited. Thank you so much, Ms. Carter.

B: I know how much you wanted the role.
_____ⓐ_____

A: Thank you. What about Sumi? Did she get the role she wanted, too?

B: Unfortunately, no. She's very disappointed.

A: Oh, ⓑI'm sorry to hear that. Anyway, when is the first practice?

B: It's at 2 p.m. on September 20th, in the acting club room. You'll get a text message about it soon.

A: OK. I'll be there.

08 위 대화의 빈칸 ⓐ에 들어갈 말로 알맞은 것은? **3점**

① Try harder next time.
② I'm so happy for you.
③ I'm so sorry to hear that.
④ I'm really proud of myself.
⑤ I hope you'll get the role next time.

서술형3 고난도

09 위 대화에서 지호가 밑줄 친 ⓑ와 같이 말한 이유를 본문에서 찾아 문장을 완성하시오. **6점**

→ Sumi _____ _____ _____
_____ _____.

10 위 대화의 내용과 일치하지 <u>않는</u> 것은? **4점**

① Jiho is very excited to get the role he wanted.
② Jiho really wanted to be Romeo in the school play.
③ Ms. Carter says that Sumi is disappointed.
④ Jiho will take part in the first practice of *Romeo and Juliet*.
⑤ Jiho will get an email about the first practice soon.

11 다음 빈칸에 들어갈 말로 알맞은 것은? **3점**

The small playground is _____ I don't like about my school.

① who   ② when   ③ that
④ what   ⑤ which

서술형4

12 다음 우리말과 의미가 같도록 괄호 안의 단어를 배열할 때, 앞에서 **6번째**로 올 단어를 쓰시오. **5점**

그는 그 영화를 본 적이 있다고 내게 말했다.
(seen, told, he, me, movie, he, had, that, the)

→ _____

13 다음 중 빈칸에 **what**이 들어갈 수 <u>없는</u> 것은? **4점**

① Susan found _____ I had hidden.
② She loved _____ I gave her for Christmas.
③ I forgot to bring _____ I had made for you.
④ I haven't received _____ I ordered last week.
⑤ The restaurant _____ you recommended was closed today.

고난도

14 다음 ⓐ~ⓔ의 어법상 <u>틀린</u> 부분을 바르게 고친 것을 <u>모두</u> 고르면? **5점**

ⓐ He said that he had ate insects before.
ⓑ Santa didn't give me which I wanted to get.
ⓒ The T-shirt is that every student wants to wear.
ⓓ When Mike returned to the classroom, everybody has already gone home.
ⓔ I was shocked that somebody had steal my bike during the night.

① ⓐ: had → has   ② ⓑ: which → who
③ ⓒ: that → what   ④ ⓓ: has → had
⑤ ⓔ: had steal → has stolen

[15~17] 다음 글을 읽고, 물음에 답하시오.

Cyril Boggis was an antique furniture dealer in London. He ⓐwas known for buying good things at a low price and then ⓑsold them at a high price. People asked him where he had got the furniture, but he just said, "(A)It's a secret."

Mr. Boggis' secret was simple. He went to small towns every ⓒSunday and knocked on doors. He told people that he was a furniture dealer. People didn't know how valuable ⓓtheir things were, so Mr. Boggis took advantage of them. He ⓔwas able to buy things very cheaply.

서술형5

15 윗글의 밑줄 친 ⓐ~ⓔ 중 어법상 **틀린** 것의 기호를 쓰고 바르게 고쳐 쓰시오.   5점

(   ) → _____

16 윗글의 밑줄 친 (A)It이 의미하는 것으로 알맞은 것은? 3점

① who the furniture dealer was
② how much Mr. Boggis' furniture was
③ where Mr. Boggis had sold the furniture
④ why Mr. Boggis' furniture was expensive
⑤ where Mr. Boggis had bought the furniture

17 Which is NOT true about Mr. Boggis?   4점

① He bought and sold old furniture.
② He was good at buying good things cheaply.
③ He went to small towns on Sundays to buy old furniture.
④ He bought things from people who knew the value of their furniture.
⑤ He took advantage of people in small towns.

[18~20] 다음 글을 읽고, 물음에 답하시오.

Now it was another Sunday, and Mr. Boggis was in a small town again. At a house he visited, he met two men. (①) One was Rummins, the owner, and _____ⓐ_____ was his son Bert. (②)

"I buy old furniture. Do you have _____ⓑ_____?" asked Mr. Boggis.

"No, I don't," said Rummins.

"Can I just take a look?" asked Mr. Boggis.

"Sure. Please come in," said Rummins. (③)

Mr. Boggis first went to the kitchen, and there _____ⓒ_____ nothing. (④) He then moved to the living room. (⑤) A table _____ⓓ_____ was a priceless piece of eighteenth-century English furniture. He was _____ⓔ_____ excited that he almost fell over.

18 윗글의 ①~⑤ 중 주어진 문장이 들어갈 위치로 알맞은 것은?   3점

And there it was!

①   ②   ③   ④   ⑤

19 윗글의 빈칸 ⓐ~ⓔ에 들어갈 말로 어법상 알맞지 <u>않은</u> 것은?   4점

① ⓐ: the other   ② ⓑ: any
③ ⓒ: was   ④ ⓓ: which
⑤ ⓔ: very

서술형6

20 다음 영영풀이에 해당하는 단어를 윗글에서 찾아 쓰시오.   4점

extremely valuable

→ _____

[21~23] 다음 글을 읽고, 물음에 답하시오.

> "What's wrong?" Bert asked.
>
> "Oh, nothing. Nothing at all," Mr. Boggis lied. He then said with a straight face, "ⓐThis table is a reproduction. It's worth only a few pounds."
>
> He then added, "Hmm, I think I may buy ⓑit. The legs of my table at home are broken. I can cut off the legs of your table and attach them to ⓒmine."
>
> "How much?" Rummins asked.
>
> "Not much, I'm afraid. This is just a reproduction," said Mr. Boggis.
>
> "So how much?"
>
> "Ten pounds."
>
> "Ten? ⓓIt's worth more than that."
>
> "How about fifteen?"
>
> "Make it fifty."
>
> "Well, thirty. (A)This is my final offer."
>
> "OK, it's yours, but how are you going to take it? ⓔThis thing will not go in a car!"
>
> "We'll see," Mr. Boggis said and went out to bring his car.
>
> On his way to the car, Mr. Boggis couldn't help smiling. The table was what every dealer dreamed of. He couldn't believe his luck.

21 윗글의 밑줄 친 ⓐ~ⓔ 중 가리키는 대상이 나머지와 다른 하나는? **3점**

① ⓐ　　② ⓑ　　③ ⓒ　　④ ⓓ　　⑤ ⓔ

22 윗글의 밑줄 친 (A)This가 의미하는 것을 두 단어의 영어로 쓰시오. **4점**

→ _____

23 윗글을 읽고 답할 수 없는 질문은? **5점**

① Why did Mr. Boggis tell Rummins and Bert that the table was a reproduction?
② How much did Mr. Boggis want to pay for the table at first?
③ How much did Rummins pay for his table?
④ Why did Mr. Boggis go out of Rummins' house?
⑤ Why did Mr. Boggis think that he was lucky?

[24~25] 다음 글을 읽고, 물음에 답하시오.

> "Dad, what ____ⓐ____ this thing doesn't go in his car? He might not ____ⓑ____ you," said Bert.
>
> Rummins then had an idea. "(A)그가 원하는 것은 오직 다리뿐이야. Let's cut the legs off for him," said Rummins. "Great idea!" said Bert. Bert then took out a(n) ____ⓒ____ and began to cut off the legs.
>
> When Mr. Boggis came back, the legs had been cut off. "Don't worry, this was a(n) ____ⓓ____. I won't charge you for this," said Rummins. Mr. Boggis was so ____ⓔ____ that he couldn't say anything.

24 윗글의 흐름상 빈칸 ⓐ~ⓔ 중 어디에도 들어갈 수 없는 것은? **5점**

① saw　　② pay　　③ favor
④ about　　⑤ shocked

25 윗글의 밑줄 친 우리말 (A)와 의미가 같도록 [보기]에서 필요한 단어만 골라 바르게 배열하시오. (7단어) **5점**

[보기] wants, what, the, he, is, legs, only, that

→ _____

01 다음 중 짝지어진 단어의 관계가 [보기]와 같은 것은? 3점

> [보기]   cheap – expensive

① play – replay   ② low – high
③ exciting – excited   ④ upset – angry
⑤ priceless – valuable

02 다음 빈칸에 공통으로 들어갈 말로 알맞은 것은? 3점

> • I met my classmate Jeff _____ my way to the library.
> • She went to her neighbor's house and knocked _____ the door.

① to   ② in   ③ on
④ for   ⑤ at

서술형1

03 다음 영영풀이에 해당하는 단어를 사용하여 문장을 완성하시오. 4점

> old and often valuable or beautiful

→ The museum has a collection of a_____ pianos.

04 다음 빈칸에 들어갈 표현으로 가장 알맞은 것은? 3점

> Don't let anyone _____ your weak points.

① cut off   ② fall over
③ take a look   ④ be known for
⑤ take advantage of

05 다음 대화의 빈칸에 들어갈 말로 알맞지 <u>않은</u> 것은? 3점

> A: _____
> B: Oh, I'm sorry to hear that.

① My new camera was broken.
② I lost my puppy last Saturday.
③ I failed the final exam. I'm upset.
④ I won first place in the school marathon.
⑤ My best friend is moving to another city. I'm sad.

06 다음 대화의 빈칸 (A)와 (B)에 들어갈 말이 순서대로 바르게 짝지어진 것은? 4점

> A: You look excited, Sally. _____(A)_____
> B: I'm going to go to the Dream Concert. I finally got a ticket.
> A: _____(B)_____ I know how much you wanted to go.

    (A)   (B)
① What's up?   ⋯   Congratulations!
② Are you sure?   ⋯   I did my best.
③ That's too bad.   ⋯   Good for you.
④ Congratulations!   ⋯   Don't mention it.
⑤ Is anything wrong?   ⋯   Thanks a lot.

07 다음 글의 흐름상 빈칸에 들어갈 알맞은 말을 <u>모두</u> 고르면? 4점

> Last summer, I lost my dog, Bomi. She disappeared while I was drinking water in the park. Luckily, I was able to find her two days later. I was so _____ that I hugged her tightly.

① nervous   ② bored   ③ happy
④ pleased   ⑤ disappointed

[08~09] 다음 대화를 읽고, 물음에 답하시오.

> **A:** Excuse me, Ms. Carter. Can I ask you a question? _____ (A) _____
>
> **B:** Yes, you did. ⓐCongratulations, Jiho! You're going to be Romeo in our school play, *Romeo and Juliet*.
>
> **A:** Really? ⓑI'm so excited. Thank you so much, Ms. Carter.
>
> **B:** I know how much you wanted the role. ⓒI'm so happy for you.
>
> **A:** Thank you. What about Sumi? Did she get the role she wanted, too?
>
> **B:** ⓓUnfortunately, no. She's very disappointed.
>
> **A:** Oh, ⓔI'm glad to hear that.

08 위 대화의 흐름상 빈칸 (A)에 들어갈 말로 가장 알맞은 것은? **3점**

① What's up?
② Is anything wrong?
③ Did you see the school play?
④ Did I get the main role in the play?
⑤ What are we going to do for the school play?

09 위 대화의 밑줄 친 ⓐ~ⓔ 중 흐름상 어색한 것은? **4점**

① ⓐ　② ⓑ　③ ⓒ　④ ⓓ　⑤ ⓔ

서술형2

10 다음 문장과 의미가 같도록 할 때, 빈칸에 알맞은 말을 3단어로 쓰시오. **4점**

> We will consider the thing that you suggest.
> = We will consider _____.

11 다음 중 빈칸에 **had**가 들어갈 수 없는 것은? **3점**

① Ted said that he _____ read the book.
② I _____ done the dishes before you called me.
③ Sue said that she _____ been there several times.
④ I couldn't ride my bike because it _____ been broken.
⑤ When Dad _____ got home, I had already eaten dinner.

서술형3 고 산도

12 다음 우리말과 의미가 같도록 괄호 안의 단어를 어법에 맞게 사용하여 문장을 완성하시오. **5점**

> 할머니가 집에 오셨을 때 우리는 요리를 끝낸 상태였다.
> (finish, cook)

→ When Grandma came home, _____
_____.

13 다음 빈칸에 들어갈 말이 순서대로 바르게 짝지어진 것은? **4점**

> Sue really liked _____ her sister _____ for her.

① that – makes
② that – has made
③ what – has made
④ what – had made
⑤ which – had made

14 다음 중 밑줄 친 부분이 어법상 틀린 것은? **4점**

① He shared <u>what</u> he had with others.
② Eric said that he <u>had been</u> to Alaska before.
③ Jogging is <u>which</u> Susan likes to do in the morning.
④ My sister <u>had</u> just <u>eaten</u> a whole pizza when I went to the kitchen.
⑤ The students <u>had</u> already <u>cleaned</u> the classroom when Mr. Kim came back.

[15~17] 다음 글을 읽고, 물음에 답하시오.

Cyril Boggis was an antique furniture dealer in London. He was known for ⓐbuy good things at a low price and then selling them at a high price. People asked him where he ⓑget the furniture, but he just said, "It's a secret."

Mr. Boggis' secret was simple. He went to small towns every Sunday and knocked on doors. He told people that he was a furniture dealer. People didn't know how valuable their things were, so _____ⓒ_____. He was able to buy things very cheaply.

15 윗글의 밑줄 친 ⓐbuy와 ⓑget의 어법상 올바른 형태가 바르게 짝지어진 것은? 3점

① buys – got
② buys – had got
③ buying – has got
④ buying – had got
⑤ to buy – has got

16 윗글의 흐름상 빈칸 ⓒ에 들어갈 말로 가장 알맞은 것은? 4점

① people didn't want to sell them
② people sold them at a high price
③ Mr. Boggis took advantage of them
④ Mr. Boggis gave enough money to them
⑤ they didn't want Mr. Boggis to buy their things

서술형4 고난도
17 윗글의 내용과 일치하도록 다음 질문에 대한 답을 완성하시오. 5점

Q: What was Mr. Boggis' secret of buying things cheaply?
A: He bought things from people who _____
_____.

[18~19] 다음 글을 읽고, 물음에 답하시오.

Now it was another Sunday, and Mr. Boggis was in a small town again. At a house he visited, he met two men. One was Rummins, the owner, and ⓐanother was his son Bert.

"I buy old furniture. Do you have any?" asked Mr. Boggis.

"No, I don't," said Rummins.

"Can I just take a look?" asked Mr. Boggis.

"Sure. Please come in," said Rummins.

Mr. Boggis first went to the kitchen, and there was nothing. He then moved to the living room. And ⓑthere was it! A table ⓒwhat was a priceless piece of eighteenth-century English furniture. He was ⓓso exciting that he almost fell over.

"What's wrong?" Bert asked.

"Oh, nothing. Nothing at all," Mr. Boggis lied. He then said with a straight face, "This table is a reproduction. It's worth only ⓔa little pounds."

18 윗글의 밑줄 친 ⓐ~ⓔ를 어법상 바르게 고쳐 쓰지 않은 것은? 4점

① ⓐ → the other
② ⓑ → there it was
③ ⓒ → which
④ ⓓ → excited so that
⑤ ⓔ → a few pounds

고난도
19 윗글의 내용과 일치하지 않는 것은? 5점

① Rummins and Bert live in a small town.
② Rummins told Mr. Boggis that he didn't have any old furniture.
③ Rummins let Mr. Boggis take a look around his house.
④ Rummins was surprised to know that his table was priceless.
⑤ Mr. Boggis didn't tell the truth to Rummins and Bert.

[20~22] 다음 글을 읽고, 물음에 답하시오.

He then added, "Hmm, I think I may buy it. The legs of my table at home are broken. I can cut off the legs of your table and attach them to mine."

"How much?" Rummins asked.

"Not much, I'm afraid. This is just a(n) ___ⓐ___," said Mr. Boggis.

"So how much?"

"Ten pounds."

"Ten? It's worth more than that."

"How about fifteen?"

"Make it fifty."

"Well, thirty. This is my final offer."

"OK, it's yours, but how are you going to take it? This thing will not go in a car!"

"We'll see," Mr. Boggis said and went out to bring his car.

On his way to the car, Mr. Boggis couldn't help smiling. ⓑThe table was the thing what every dealer dreamed of. He couldn't believe his luck.

서술형5

20 윗글의 빈칸 ⓐ에 들어갈 단어를 다음 영영풀이에 맞게 쓰시오. **4점**

a copy of something such as a picture

→ _____

21 윗글의 내용을 잘못 이해한 사람은? **4점**

① 혜인: Boggis 씨는 Rummins의 탁자 다리를 잘라 자신의 탁자에 붙일 수 있겠다고 말했어.

② 민호: Rummins는 자신의 탁자가 10파운드보다 가치가 있다고 생각했어.

③ 연주: Boggis 씨는 Rummins의 탁자를 30파운드에 사기로 했어.

④ 예서: Boggis 씨는 돈을 가지러 차에 갔어.

⑤ 진영: Boggis 씨는 자신이 운이 좋다고 생각했어.

서술형6

22 윗글의 밑줄 친 문장 ⓑ에서 어법상 틀린 부분을 찾아 바르게 고쳐 쓰시오. **4점**

_____ → _____

[23~25] 다음 글을 읽고, 물음에 답하시오.

"OK, it's yours, but how are you going to take it? This thing will not go in a car!"

"We'll see," Mr. Boggis said and went out to bring his car.

"Dad, ___ⓐ___? He might not pay you," said Bert.

Rummins then had an ①idea. "(A) Which / What he wants is only the legs. Let's cut the legs off for him," said Rummins. "Great idea!" said Bert. Bert then took out a ②saw and began to ③cut off the legs.

When Mr. Boggis came back, the legs (B) had / have been cut off. "Don't worry, this was a ④favor. I won't ⑤pay you for this," said Rummins. Mr. Boggis was so shocked (C) what / that he couldn't say anything.

서술형7

23 윗글의 흐름에 맞게 빈칸 ⓐ에 들어갈 말을 괄호 안의 표현을 배열하여 완성하시오. **5점**

→ Dad, _____?

(go in, if, his car, this thing, what, doesn't)

서술형8

24 윗글 (A)~(C)의 각 네모 안에 주어진 말 중 어법상 올바른 말을 골라 쓰시오. **각 2점**

(A) _____ (B) _____ (C) _____

고난도

25 윗글의 밑줄 친 ①~⑤ 중 문맥상 어색한 것은? **5점**

① ② ③ ④ ⑤

모의고사

01 다음 빈칸에 공통으로 들어갈 말로 알맞은 것은? 3점

> • Delivery is free of _____.
> • They won't _____ you for delivery.

① luck ② offer ③ buy
④ price ⑤ charge

02 다음 빈칸에 알맞은 말이 순서대로 바르게 짝지어진 것은? 3점

> • The man lied _____ a straight face.
> • I cut _____ the bottom of my old jeans.
> • I fell _____ because the bus started suddenly.

① on – off – for ② on – over – for
③ with – off – over ④ with – over – over
⑤ for – off – from

03 다음 중 밑줄 친 단어의 쓰임이 의미상 어색한 것은? 4점

① Careless drivers can cause accidents.
② Mr. Davis bought a truck from a car dealer.
③ Unfortunately, I won first prize in the dance contest.
④ People got bored because he replayed the music so many times.
⑤ This picture is cheap. It's a reproduction of *Sunflowers* by van Gogh.

04 다음 빈칸 ⓐ~ⓓ 중 어디에도 들어갈 수 없는 것은? 4점

> • Please _____ⓐ a note on the box.
> • The antique chair is _____ⓑ more than $500.
> • I need to move some _____ⓒ in my room.
> • We saw many _____ⓓ paintings in the museum.

① favor ② worth ③ attach
④ priceless ⑤ furniture

서술형1

05 다음 대화의 빈칸에 들어갈 말을 괄호 안의 단어를 사용하여 5단어로 쓰시오. 4점

> A: Mina, is anything wrong?
> B: Well, I lost my smartphone. I'm upset.
> A: Oh, I'm _____.
>   (so, sorry, hear)

06 다음 중 짝지어진 대화가 어색한 것은? 3점

① A: Min, what's wrong?
   B: Well, I lost the game. I'm upset.
② A: Sue, you look excited. What's up?
   B: I was elected as class president.
③ A: My smartphone is broken.
   B: That's too bad.
④ A: Congratulations on winning the gold medal in the school marathon.
   B: That's wonderful! You did a good job.
⑤ A: I won first prize in the speech contest. I'm so happy.
   B: That's wonderful. Congratulations!

07 다음 대화의 ①~⑤ 중 주어진 문장이 들어갈 위치로 알맞은 것은? 3점

> That's too bad.

> A: You don't look so good, Inho. What's the matter?
> B: (①) I have the flu.
> A: (②) Did you see the doctor?
> B: Yes. (③) I'm taking medicine. (④)
> A: Well, I hope you feel better soon.
> B: Thanks. (⑤)

① ② ③ ④ ⑤

[08~09] 다음 대화를 읽고, 물음에 답하시오.

> A: Excuse me, Ms. Carter. ___ⓐ___ Did I get the main role in the play?
> B: Yes, you did. Congratulations, Jiho! You're going to be Romeo in our school play, *Romeo and Juliet*.
> A: Really? ___ⓑ___ Thank you so much, Ms. Carter.
> B: I know how much you wanted the role. ___ⓒ___
> A: Thank you. What about Sumi? Did she get the role she wanted, too?
> B: Unfortunately, no. ___ⓓ___
> A: Oh, I'm sorry to hear that. Anyway, when is the first practice?
> B: It's at 2 p.m. on September 20th, in the acting club room. ___ⓔ___
> A: OK. I'll be there.

08 위 대화의 빈칸 ⓐ~ⓔ에 들어갈 말로 알맞지 <u>않은</u> 것은?

4점

① ⓐ: Can I ask you a question?
② ⓑ: I'm so excited.
③ ⓒ: I'm so happy for you.
④ ⓓ: She must be proud of herself.
⑤ ⓔ: You'll get a text message about it soon.

09 위 대화를 읽고 답할 수 <u>없는</u> 질문은?

4점

① Why is Ms. Carter congratulating Jiho?
② Who will play Romeo in the school play?
③ Which role did Jiho want to get?
④ Which role did Sumi want to get?
⑤ When and where is the first practice?

서술형 2

10 다음 대화의 빈칸에 들어갈 알맞은 말을 한 단어로 쓰시오.

4점

> A: What did you buy at the store?
> B: Nothing. The store didn't have _____ I wanted to buy.

고난도

11 다음 중 어법상 틀린 부분을 바르게 고친 것은?

4점

> The living room had already cleaned by my brother when I came back.

① had → has
② had already → already had
③ cleaned → been cleaned
④ by → with
⑤ came back → had come back

한 단계 더!

12 다음 대화의 빈칸에 공통으로 들어갈 말로 알맞은 것은? 4점

> A: I don't know _____ to buy for my sister.
> B: Why don't you buy _____ she needs the most?

① who   ② that   ③ where
④ what   ⑤ which

서술형 3

13 다음 두 문장과 의미가 같도록 빈칸에 알맞은 말을 써서 문장을 완성하시오.

4점

> We arrived at the theater. Before that, the movie started.

→ When we _____ at the theater, the movie _____ _____ already.

14 다음 중 어법상 틀린 문장은?

4점

① This is what I was looking for.
② They had left when we got there.
③ I thought you had already gone to bed.
④ What my dad cooked for us was delicious.
⑤ Mom liked the sunglasses what we bought for her birthday.

[15~17] 다음 글을 읽고, 물음에 답하시오.

Cyril Boggis was an antique furniture dealer in London. He was known ___(A)___ buying good things ⓐat a low price and then selling them at a high price. People asked him where he had got the furniture, but he just said, "It's a secret."

Mr. Boggis' secret was simple. He went to small towns every Sunday and knocked ___(B)___ doors. He told people that he was a furniture dealer. People didn't know how valuable their things were, so Mr. Boggis took advantage ___(C)___ them. He was able to buy things very cheaply.

서술형 **4**

15 윗글의 빈칸 (A)~(C)에 들어갈 알맞은 말을 쓰시오. 각 2점

(A) _____

(B) _____

(C) _____

서술형 **5**

16 윗글의 밑줄 친 ⓐ와 바꿔 쓸 수 있는 말을 본문에서 찾아 한 단어로 쓰시오. 4점

→ _____

17 윗글을 읽고 Cyril Boggis에 대해 알 수 없는 것을 두 개 고르면? 3점

① how old he was

② what his job was

③ where he sold things

④ what he was famous for

⑤ how he bought good things at a low price

[18~20] 다음 글을 읽고, 물음에 답하시오.

Now it was another Sunday, and Mr. Boggis was in a small town again. At a house he visited, he met two men. (A)한 명은 주인인 Rummins였고, 나머지 한 명은 그의 아들인 Bert였다.

"I buy old furniture. ___ⓐ___" asked Mr. Boggis.

"No, I don't," said Rummins.

"___ⓑ___" asked Mr. Boggis.

"Sure. Please come in," said Rummins.

Mr. Boggis first went to the kitchen, and there was nothing. He then moved to the living room. And there it was! A table which was a priceless piece of eighteenth-century English furniture. He was so excited that he almost fell over.

"___ⓒ___" Bert asked.

"___ⓓ___," Mr. Boggis lied. He then said with a straight face, "This table is a reproduction. ___ⓔ___"

서술형 **6**

18 윗글의 밑줄 친 우리말 (A)와 의미가 같도록 다음 빈칸에 알맞은 말을 각각 쓰시오. 4점

→ _____ was Rummins, the owner, and _____ _____ was his son Bert.

19 윗글의 흐름상 빈칸 ⓐ~ⓔ에 들어갈 말로 알맞지 않은 것은? 4점

① ⓐ: Do you have any?

② ⓑ: Can I just take a look?

③ ⓒ: What's wrong?

④ ⓓ: I think your table is really valuable

⑤ ⓔ: It's worth only a few pounds.

[08~09] 다음 대화를 읽고, 물음에 답하시오.

> A: Excuse me, Ms. Carter. Can I ask you a question? Did I get the main role in the play?
> B: Yes, you did. Congratulations, Jiho! You're going to be Romeo in our school play, *Romeo and Juliet*.
> A: Really? I'm so excited. Thank you so much, Ms. Carter.
> B: (A)<u>나는 네가 얼마나 그 역할을 원했는지 알고 있어.</u> I'm so happy for you.
> A: Thank you. What about Sumi? Did she get the role she wanted, too?
> B: Unfortunately, no. She's very disappointed.
> A: _____(B)_____ Anyway, when is the first practice?
> B: It's at 2 p.m. on September 20th, in the acting club room. You'll get a text message about it soon.
> A: OK. I'll be there.

08 주어진 단어를 배열하여 위 대화의 밑줄 친 우리말 (A)를 영어로 옮길 때, 5번째로 올 단어로 알맞은 것은? **4점**

> how, I, wanted, know, much, you, role, the

① how ② role ③ know
④ you ⑤ wanted

서술형4

09 위 대화의 빈칸 (B)에 들어갈 말을 **hear**를 사용하여 완성하시오. **4점**

→ Oh, I'm _____ _____ _____ _____.

10 다음 빈칸에 들어갈 수 있는 것을 <u>모두</u> 고르면? **4점**

> When Tom came home, his sister _____.

① had fallen asleep
② was reading a book
③ listens to loud music
④ has been using his laptop
⑤ has finished her homework

서술형5

11 다음 우리말과 의미가 같도록 관계대명사와 괄호 안의 단어를 사용하여 문장을 완성하시오. **4점**

> 나는 우리가 그 호수에서 본 것을 잊지 못할 것이다.

→ I won't forget _____ _____ _____ at the lake. (see)

12 [보기]에 주어진 표현 중 다음 문장의 빈칸에 들어갈 수 있는 것의 개수는? **4점**

> _____ she gave to me was a small box.

> [보기] Which   The things   What
>   The thing which   The things that

① 1개 ② 2개 ③ 3개 ④ 4개 ⑤ 5개

한 단계 더!

13 다음 ⓐ~ⓓ 중 어법상 <u>틀린</u> 것끼리 짝지어진 것은? **3점**

> ⓐ What we heard there was amazing.
> ⓑ Emma understood, what the teacher said.
> ⓒ They had finished dinner when I got there.
> ⓓ The house has been built before I was born.

① ⓐ, ⓑ   ② ⓐ, ⓒ   ③ ⓐ, ⓓ
④ ⓑ, ⓓ   ⑤ ⓒ, ⓓ

서술형6 고난도

14 괄호 안의 표현을 어법에 맞게 써서 다음 그림의 내용에 맞게 문장을 완성하시오. **6점**

→ Ted thinks he did well on the science test yesterday. He _____ the problems when _____.
(already finish, solve, the bell, ring)

[15~17] 다음 글을 읽고, 물음에 답하시오.

Cyril Boggis was an antique furniture dealer in London. He was ⓐfamous for buying good things ⓑat a low price and then selling them at a high price. People asked him where he had got the furniture, but he just said, "It's a secret."

Mr. Boggis' secret was simple. He went to small towns ⓒevery Sunday and knocked on doors. He told people __(A)__ he was a furniture dealer. People didn't know how ⓓpriceless their things were, so Mr. Boggis took advantage of them. He ⓔcould buy things very cheaply.

Now it was another Sunday, and Mr. Boggis was in a small town again. At a house __(B)__ he visited, he met two men. One was Rummins, the owner, and the other was his son Bert.

15 윗글의 밑줄 친 ⓐ~ⓔ와 바꿔 쓸 수 없는 것은? 3점

① ⓐ → known
② ⓑ → cheaply
③ ⓒ → on Sundays
④ ⓓ → cheap
⑤ ⓔ → was able to

서술형7

16 윗글의 빈칸 (A)와 (B)에 공통으로 들어갈 알맞은 말을 한 단어로 쓰시오. 4점

→ _____

17 윗글의 Cyril Boggis에 관한 내용으로 알맞지 않은 것끼리 짝지어진 것은? 4점

ⓐ He bought and sold old furniture for a living.
ⓑ Where he had bought furniture was a secret.
ⓒ He took advantage of people who asked him where he had got the furniture.
ⓓ He went to Rummins and Bert's house to sell antique furniture.

① ⓐ, ⓒ
② ⓐ, ⓓ
③ ⓑ, ⓒ
④ ⓑ, ⓓ
⑤ ⓒ, ⓓ

[18~23] 다음 글을 읽고, 물음에 답하시오.

"I buy old furniture. Do you have any?" asked Mr. Boggis.

"No, I don't," said Rummins. (①)

"Can I just take a look?" asked Mr. Boggis.

"Sure. Please come in," said Rummins. (②)

Mr. Boggis first went to the kitchen, and there was nothing. He then moved to the living room. And there it was! A table which was a priceless piece of eighteenth-century English furniture. (③)

"What's wrong?" Bert asked. (④)

"Oh, nothing. Nothing at all," Mr. Boggis lied. He then said with a straight face, "This table is a reproduction. It's __ⓐ__ only a few pounds." (⑤)

He then added, "Hmm, I think I may buy it. The legs of my table at home are broken. I can cut off the legs of your table and __ⓑ__ them to mine."

"How much?" Rummins asked.

"Not much, I'm afraid. This is just a reproduction," said Mr. Boggis.

"So how much?"

"Ten pounds."

"Ten? It's worth more than that."

"How about fifteen?"

"Make it fifty."

"Well, thirty. This is my final offer."

"OK, it's yours, but how are you going to take it? This thing will not go in a car!"

"We'll see," Mr. Boggis said and went out to bring his car.

On his way to the car, Mr. Boggis couldn't help ⓒsmiling. The table was the thing that every dealer dreamed of. He couldn't believe his luck.

서술형8

18 윗글의 빈칸 ⓐ와 ⓑ에 들어갈 단어를 다음 영영풀이를 참고하여 쓰시오. 각 2점

ⓐ having a specific value
ⓑ to fasten or join one thing to another

ⓐ _____

ⓑ _____

19 윗글의 ①~⑤ 중 주어진 문장이 들어갈 위치로 알맞은 것은? 3점

> He was so excited that he almost fell over.

① ② ③ ④ ⑤

20 윗글의 밑줄 친 ⓒ와 쓰임이 다른 것을 모두 고르면? 4점

① Andy is good at taking pictures.
② He cut the wood by using a saw.
③ They are playing computer games.
④ She is looking forward to going fishing.
⑤ I could hear my uncle snoring in his room.

21 According to the passage above, what are the characteristics of Mr. Boggis? 4점

① honest and kind
② clever but dishonest
③ kind and generous
④ humorous and honest
⑤ smart but lazy

22 윗글의 내용과 일치하는 문장의 개수는? 4점

> ⓐ Rummins and Bert invited Mr. Boggis.
> ⓑ Rummins knew that he had something expensive in his house.
> ⓒ Mr. Boggis found a valuable table in Rummins' living room.
> ⓓ Rummins' table was a piece of eighteenth-century English furniture.
> ⓔ Mr. Boggis lied to Rummins that Rummins' table was priceless.

① 1개 ② 2개 ③ 3개 ④ 4개 ⑤ 5개

서술형 **9**

23 윗글의 내용과 일치하도록 Boggis 씨의 생각을 유추한 다음 글을 완성하시오. 6점

> Wow! This table is a _____ piece of furniture. I have to tell Rummins and Bert that it's just _____ _____ so that I can buy it _____.

[24~25] 다음 글을 읽고, 물음에 답하시오.

> "Dad, what if this thing doesn't go in his car? He might not pay you," said Bert.
> Rummins then had an idea. "ⓐThe thing what he wants is only the legs. Let's cut the legs off for him," said Rummins. "Great idea!" said Bert. Bert then took out a saw and began to cut off the legs.
> ⓑWhen Mr. Boggis had come back, the legs had been cut off. "Don't worry, (A)this was a favor. I won't charge you for this," said Rummins. ⓒMr. Boggis was such shocked that he couldn't say anything.

서술형 **10**

24 윗글의 밑줄 친 문장 ⓐ~ⓒ에서 어법상 틀린 부분을 각각 바르게 고쳐 쓰시오. 각 2점

ⓐ _____ → _____

ⓑ _____ → _____

ⓒ _____ → _____

25 윗글의 밑줄 친 (A)this가 가리키는 내용으로 알맞은 것은? 3점

① not selling the table
② putting the table in Mr. Boggis' car
③ attaching the legs to Mr. Boggis' broken table
④ cutting off the legs of the table for Mr. Boggis
⑤ not telling anyone that Mr. Boggis bought the table

● 틀린 문항을 표시해 보세요.

● 부족한 영역을 점검하고 어떻게 더 학습할지 계획을 적어 보세요.

〈제1회〉 대표 기출로 내신 **적중** 모의고사 　　총점 _____ / 100

문항	영역	문항	영역	문항	영역
01	p.84(W)	10	p.89(L&T)	19	pp.104~105(R)
02	p.82(W)	11	p.97(G)	20	pp.104~105(R)
03	p.82(W)	12	p.96(G)	21	pp.105~106(R)
04	p.82(W)	13	p.97(G)	22	pp.105~106(R)
05	p.87(L&T)	14	pp.96~97(G)	23	pp.105~106(R)
06	p.88(L&T)	15	p.104(R)	24	p.106(R)
07	p.87(L&T)	16	p.104(R)	25	p.106(R)
08	p.89(L&T)	17	p.104(R)		
09	p.89(L&T)	18	pp.104~105(R)		

제1회 오답 공략
부족한 영역
학습 계획

〈제2회〉 대표 기출로 내신 **적중** 모의고사 　　총점 _____ / 100

문항	영역	문항	영역	문항	영역
01	p.84(W)	10	p.97(G)	19	pp.104~105(R)
02	p.82(W)	11	p.96(G)	20	pp.105~106(R)
03	p.84(W)	12	p.96(G)	21	pp.105~106(R)
04	p.82(W)	13	pp.96~97(G)	22	pp.105~106(R)
05	p.87(L&T)	14	pp.96~97(G)	23	p.106(R)
06	p.87(L&T)	15	p.104(R)	24	p.106(R)
07	p.87(L&T)	16	p.104(R)	25	p.106(R)
08	p.89(L&T)	17	p.104(R)		
09	p.89(L&T)	18	pp.104~105(R)		

제2회 오답 공략
부족한 영역
학습 계획

〈제3회〉 대표 기출로 내신 **적중** 모의고사 　　총점 _____ / 100

문항	영역	문항	영역	문항	영역
01	p.84(W)	10	p.97(G)	19	pp.104~105(R)
02	p.82(W)	11	p.96(G)	20	pp.104~105(R)
03	p.82(W)	12	p.97(G)	21	pp.105~106(R)
04	p.82(W)	13	p.96(G)	22	pp.105~106(R)
05	p.87(L&T)	14	pp.96~97(G)	23	pp.105~106(R)
06	p.87(L&T)	15	p.104(R)	24	p.106(R)
07	p.88(L&T)	16	p.104(R)	25	p.106(R)
08	p.89(L&T)	17	p.104(R)		
09	p.89(L&T)	18	pp.104~105(R)		

제3회 오답 공략
부족한 영역
학습 계획

〈제4회〉 고난도로 내신 **적중** 모의고사 　　총점 _____ / 100

문항	영역	문항	영역	문항	영역
01	p.84(W)	10	p.96(G)	19	pp.104~106(R)
02	p.84(W)	11	p.97(G)	20	pp.104~106(R)
03	p.82(W)	12	p.97(G)	21	pp.104~106(R)
04	p.89(L&T)	13	pp.96~97(G)	22	pp.104~106(R)
05	p.89(L&T)	14	p.96(G)	23	pp.104~106(R)
06	p.88(L&T)	15	p.104(R)	24	p.106(R)
07	p.89(L&T)	16	p.104(R)	25	p.106(R)
08	p.89(L&T)	17	p.104(R)		
09	p.89(L&T)	18	pp.104~106(R)		

제4회 오답 공략
부족한 영역
학습 계획

Lesson 7

Technology in Our Lives

주요 학습 내용			
의사소통 기능	방법·절차 묻고 답하기	A: Do you know how to return these books? (이 책들을 어떻게 반납하는지 아세요?) B: Sure. First, insert the card. Then put the books in this box. (그럼요. 먼저 카드를 넣으세요. 그런 다음 이 상자에 책들을 넣으세요.)	
	감사 표현하기	I really appreciate your help. (도와주셔서 정말 고맙습니다.)	
언어 형식	분사구문	**Using** various methods, experts analyze big data. (전문가들은 다양한 방법들을 사용하여 빅데이터를 분석한다.)	
	접속사 as	**As** information and communication technology develops, the amount of data we have is getting much greater than before. (정보 통신 기술이 발달함에 따라 우리가 갖고 있는 데이터의 양이 이전보다 훨씬 더 많아지고 있다.)	

학습 단계 PREVIEW

STEP **A**	Words	Listen and Talk	Grammar	Reading	기타 지문
STEP **B**	Words	Listen and Talk	Grammar	Reading	서술형 100% Test

내신 적중 모의고사	제 1 회	제 2 회	제 3 회	제 4 회

Words
만점 노트

Listen & Talk

□□ amount	명 양, 액수	□□ press	동 (버튼 등을) 누르다
□□ appreciate☆	동 고마워하다	□□ rent	동 (사용료를 내고) 빌리다
□□ front desk	안내 데스크, 접수처	□□ transportation	명 교통수단, 탈것; 운송, 수송
□□ insert	동 넣다, 삽입하다	□□ type	동 (자판기로) 타자를 치다, 입력하다
□□ place	동 놓다, 두다	□□ unlock	동 (잠긴 것을) 열다

Reading

□□ analysis	명 분석	□□ leave	동 남기다; 떠나다
□□ analyze☆	동 분석하다	□□ mainly	부 주로, 대개
□□ avoid	동 피하다, 방지하다	□□ meaningful☆	형 의미 있는
□□ collect	동 모으다, 수집하다	□□ method	명 방법, 방식
□□ communication	명 의사소통, 연락	□□ national	형 국가의, 국가를 대표하는
□□ complex	형 복잡한	□□ performance	명 경기력, 수행, 성과; 공연
□□ crime	명 범죄	□□ predict☆	동 예측하다
□□ database	명 데이터베이스	□□ prevention☆	명 예방, 방지
□□ develop	동 성장하다, 발달하다	□□ purchase	명 구입, 구매 동 구입하다, 구매하다
□□ disease	명 질병, 병	□□ spread	명 확산, 전파 동 퍼지다, 퍼뜨리다
□□ draw	동 (결과를) 이끌어 내다	□□ symptom	명 증상
□□ flu	명 독감	□□ technology	명 기술
□□ forecast☆	명 예측, 예보 동 예측하다, 예보하다	□□ trace	명 흔적, 자취, 발자국
□□ further	형 추가의, 더 이상의	□□ upload	동 ~을 전송하다, 업로드하다
□□ identify☆	동 알아보다, 확인하다, 식별하다	□□ be likely to☆	~할 것 같다
□□ improve	동 개선하다, 향상하다	□□ focus on☆	~에 집중하다
□□ include	동 포함하다	□□ play a role☆	역할을 하다
□□ industry	명 산업	□□ recommend A for B	A를 B에게 추천하다
□□ influence	동 영향을 미치다 명 영향	□□ thanks to	~ 덕분에

Language in Use

□□ generally	부 일반적으로 (cf. general 형 일반적인)	□□ society	명 사회
□□ possibly	부 아마 (cf. possible 형 가능한)	□□ from now on	이제부터
□□ regularly	부 규칙적으로 (cf. regular 형 규칙적인)	□□ take off	~을 벗다 (↔ put on)

Think and Write & Team Project

| □□ actually | 부 실제로, 사실은 | □□ gap | 명 차이, 격차 |
| □□ distance | 명 거리 | □□ based on | ~에 근거하여 |

Review

| □□ dig | 동 (땅을) 파다 (-dug-dug) | □□ dirt | 명 흙, 먼지 |

Words
연습 문제

A 다음 단어의 우리말 뜻을 쓰시오.

01	disease
02	regularly
03	meaningful
04	forecast
05	identify
06	transportation
07	industry
08	symptom
09	trace
10	method
11	amount
12	improve
13	unlock
14	predict
15	analyze
16	complex
17	further
18	purchase
19	include
20	spread

B 다음 우리말 뜻에 알맞은 영어 단어를 쓰시오.

01	국가의, 국가를 대표하는
02	(결과를) 이끌어 내다
03	피하다, 방지하다
04	의사소통, 연락
05	범죄
06	놓다, 두다
07	모으다, 수집하다
08	기술
09	영향(을 미치다)
10	경기력, 수행, 성과; 공연
11	예방, 방지
12	남기다; 떠나다
13	고마워하다
14	넣다, 삽입하다
15	데이터베이스
16	(사용료를 내고) 빌리다
17	성장하다, 발달하다
18	독감
19	(버튼 등을) 누르다
20	분석

C 다음 영어 표현의 우리말 뜻을 쓰시오.

01	play a role
02	from now on
03	based on
04	be likely to
05	focus on
06	recommend A for B
07	thanks to
08	take off

D 다음 우리말 뜻에 알맞은 영어 표현을 쓰시오.

01	~에 집중하다
02	~을 벗다
03	역할을 하다
04	~에 근거하여
05	~ 덕분에
06	이제부터
07	~할 것 같다
08	A를 B에게 추천하다

Words Plus
만점 노트

영영풀이

☐☐ **analyze**   분석하다   to examine something carefully

☐☐ **avoid**   피하다   to stay away from someone or something

☐☐ **communication**   의사소통   the sharing or exchange of messages, information, or ideas

☐☐ **crime**   범죄   an action that the law does not allow

☐☐ **database**   데이터베이스   a large amount of information stored in a computer system

☐☐ **develop**   성장하다, 발달하다   to grow and change into something bigger, better, or more important

☐☐ **flu**   독감   an illness that is like a bad cold but can be very serious

☐☐ **identify**   알아보다, 확인하다, 식별하다   to realize who someone is or what something is

☐☐ **improve**   개선하다, 향상하다   to become better or to make something better

☐☐ **include**   포함하다   to contain something as a part of a whole

☐☐ **industry**   산업   the work or business of manufacturing products or providing services

☐☐ **influence**   영향을 미치다   to change or affect something

☐☐ **method**   방법, 방식   a way of doing something

☐☐ **performance**   경기력, 수행   the action or process of accomplishing a task or function

☐☐ **predict**   예측하다   to say that something is going to happen

☐☐ **purchase**   구입(품), 구매(품)   the action of buying something; a thing that has been bought

☐☐ **spread**   확산, 전파   the growth or development of something, so that it affects a larger area or a larger number of people

☐☐ **symptom**   증상   something that shows you may have a particular illness

☐☐ **trace**   흔적, 자취, 발자국   a mark or sign of a past event or thing

단어의 의미 관계

● **유의어**
disease (병) = illness   forecast (예측하다) = predict
method (방법) = way   complex (복잡한) = complicated

● **반의어**
lock (잠그다) ↔ unlock (열다)
simple (간단한) ↔ complex (복잡한)

● **형용사 – 부사**
general (일반적인) – generally (일반적으로)
possible (가능한) – possibly (아마)
regular (규칙적인) – regularly (규칙적으로)
wise (현명한) – wisely (현명하게)

● **명사 – 형용사**
help (도움) – helpful (도움이 되는)
meaning (의미) – meaningful (의미 있는)
nation (국가) – national (국가의)

다의어

● **draw** 1. ⑧ (결과를) 이끌어 내다, 도출하다   2. ⑧ 그리다
1. What results did you **draw** from the survey?
(그 설문 조사에서 어떤 결과를 도출했나요?)
2. Tom likes to **draw** trees.
(Tom은 나무 그리는 것을 좋아한다.)

● **leave** 1. ⑧ 남기다   2. ⑧ 떠나다
1. The thief **left** no trace behind.
(그 도둑은 아무 흔적도 남기지 않았다.)
2. The train will **leave** soon. (기차는 곧 떠날 것이다.)

● **performance** 1. ⑲ 경기력, 수행   2. ⑲ 공연
1. I was impressed by the team's **performance**.
(나는 그 팀의 경기력에 깊은 인상을 받았다.)
2. This evening's **performance** will begin at 8:00 p.m.
(오늘 저녁 공연은 8시에 시작할 것이다.)

Words Plus
연습 문제

Answers p. 42

A 다음 영영풀이에 해당하는 단어를 [보기]에서 골라 쓴 후, 우리말 뜻을 쓰시오.

[보기]	purchase	include	method	symptom	flu	avoid	database	improve

1 _____ : a way of doing something : _____
2 _____ : to contain something as a part of a whole : _____
3 _____ : to stay away from someone or something : _____
4 _____ : to become better or to make something better : _____
5 _____ : something that shows you may have a particular illness : _____
6 _____ : an illness that is like a bad cold but can be very serious : _____
7 _____ : a large amount of information stored in a computer system : _____
8 _____ : the action of buying something; a thing that has been bought : _____

B 다음 빈칸에 알맞은 단어를 [보기]에서 골라 쓰시오. (단, 중복 사용 불가)

[보기]	crime	analyze	trace	spread	identify

1 Babies can easily _____ their mothers.
2 The woman disappeared without a _____.
3 The police worked hard to prevent _____.
4 This software is used to _____ marketing data.
5 You can stop the _____ of this disease by washing your hands.

C 우리말과 의미가 같도록 빈칸에 알맞은 말을 쓰시오.

1 그 영화는 실화에 기반을 두고 있다. → The film is _____ _____ a real-life story.
2 들어오기 전에 신발을 벗렴. → _____ _____ your shoes before you come in.
3 많은 사람들이 환경 문제에 집중한다. → Many people _____ _____ environmental issues.
4 학교는 우리 사회에서 중요한 역할을 한다.
   → Schools _____ _____ important _____ in our society.
5 그 지역들에서는 지진이 일어날 가능성이 더 크다.
   → Earthquakes _____ more _____ _____ happen in those areas.

D 다음 짝지어진 두 단어의 관계가 같도록 빈칸에 알맞은 단어를 쓰시오.

1 lock : unlock = simple : _____
2 help : helpful = meaning : _____
3 regular : regularly = wise : _____
4 forecast : predict = illness : _____
5 possible : possibly = general : _____

Words
실전 TEST

01 다음 영영풀이에 해당하는 단어로 알맞은 것은?

> to change or affect something

① rent　　　② predict　　　③ avoid
④ identify　　⑤ influence

02 다음 중 짝지어진 단어의 관계가 [보기]와 같은 것은?

> [보기]　　　forecast – predict

① lock – unlock　　　② nation – national
③ simple – complex　　④ disease – illness
⑤ general – generally

[03~04] 다음 빈칸에 공통으로 들어갈 말로 알맞은 것을 고르시오.

03
> • Jim tried to focus _____ his project.
> • I'll stop playing mobile games from now _____.

① in　　　② of　　　③ with
④ to　　　⑤ on

04
> • The thief didn't _____ any trace at the scene of the crime.
> • They will _____ for Yeosu this weekend.

① avoid　　　② draw　　　③ leave
④ collect　　　⑤ develop

05 다음 짝지어진 두 단어의 관계가 같도록 빈칸에 알맞은 단어를 쓰시오.

> regular : regularly = possible : _____

06 다음 빈칸 ⓐ~ⓔ에 들어갈 말로 알맞지 <u>않은</u> 것은?

> • I _____ⓐ_____ a lot of pictures on my blog every day.
> • The weather _____ⓑ_____ says it will rain tomorrow.
> • Can you _____ⓒ_____ a good place to visit in London?
> • They are _____ⓓ_____ to arrive at the station at around 12.
> • The first _____ⓔ_____ of the disease is coughing.

① ⓐ: upload　　　② ⓑ: method
③ ⓒ: recommend　　④ ⓓ: likely
⑤ ⓔ: symptom

[07~08] 주어진 우리말과 의미가 같도록 빈칸에 알맞은 말을 쓰시오.

07
> 그는 과학 프로젝트에서 중요한 역할을 했다.

→ He _____ _____ important _____ in the science project.

08
> 방에 들어가기 전에 모자를 벗어라.

→ _____ your hat _____ before you enter the room.

Listen and Talk
핵심 노트

1 방법 · 절차 묻고 답하기

A: Do you know how to return these books?

B: Sure. **First**, insert the card. **Then** put the books in this box.

이 책들을 어떻게 반납하는지 아세요?

그럼요. 먼저 카드를 넣으세요. 그런 다음 이 상자에 책들을 넣으세요.

상대방에게 어떤 일을 하는 방법이나 절차를 물을 때 「Can you tell me how to +동사원형 ~?」 또는 「Do you know how to+동사원형 ~?」으로 말한다. 이에 대한 답으로 방법이나 절차를 설명할 때는 동사원형으로 시작하는 명령문으로 말하는데, 보통 first(첫 번째로), second(두 번째로), then(그다음에), last(마지막으로)와 같이 순서를 나타내는 말을 문장 앞에 넣어 방법이나 절차의 순서를 명확하게 알려 준다.

시험 포인트 **point**
어떤 일의 순서나 절차를 바르게 배열하는 문제가 글 또는 그림으로 출제되므로, 순서를 나타내는 주요 어휘를 충분히 숙지하고, 내용의 순서를 파악하는 연습을 하도록 한다.

A: Can you tell me how to boil eggs? (달걀 삶는 방법을 알려 주시겠어요?)

B: Of course. First, put water and the eggs in a pot. Then, boil the water and the eggs for 10 to 12 minutes.
(그럼요. 먼저, 냄비에 물과 달걀을 넣으세요. 그런 다음, 10~12분간 물과 달걀을 끓이세요.)

A: OK. And then? (알겠어요. 그다음에는요?)

B: Last, take the eggs out and cool them.
(마지막으로, 달걀을 꺼내서 식히세요.)

2 감사 표현하기

A: I really **appreciate your help.**

B: You're welcome.

도와주셔서 정말 고맙습니다.

천만에요.

상대방에게 고마움을 표현할 때 Thank you (very much). / Thanks (a lot). 또는 Thank you for ~. / I (really) appreciate ~. / I can't thank you enough. 등으로 말한다. 이에 답할 때는 You're welcome.이나 Don't mention it. 또는 It's my pleasure. 등으로 말한다.

시험 포인트 **point**
앞에서 언급된 내용에 대한 응답으로 감사 표현을 고르는 문제, 또는 감사 표현에 대한 알맞은 응답을 고르는 문제가 출제되므로, 감사하는 표현과 이에 답하는 여러 표현을 잘 익혀 두도록 한다.

• A: Thank you for sharing it with me. (그것을 나와 공유해 줘서 고마워.)
  B: Don't mention it. (별일 아닌 걸.)

• A: I really appreciate everything you've done for us.
  (저희를 위해 해 주신 모든 것에 정말 감사해요.)
  B: You're welcome. (천만에요.)

• A: I can't thank you enough. (뭐라고 감사해야 할지 모르겠네요.)
  B: It's my pleasure. (제가 좋아서 한 일이에요.)

STEP
A

B: Excuse me. ❶Can you tell me how to add money to my transportation card?

G: Of course. ❷First, put your card in the machine. Second, choose ❸the amount of money you want to add.

B: OK.

G: ❹Last, insert your money into the machine.

B: That ❺sounds simple. Thanks.

❶ 상대방에게 어떤 일을 하는 방법이나 절차를 물을 때 「Can you tell me how to+동사원형 ~?」으로 말할 수 있다.
add A to B: A를 B에 넣다
transportation card: 교통 카드

❷ 방법이나 절차를 설명할 때, first, second, then 등의 순서를 나타내는 연결어를 사용하여 순서를 명확하게 알려 줄 수 있다.

❸ the amount of money는 '돈의 액수, 금액'이라는 의미이고, you want to add는 선행사 the amount of money를 수식하는 관계대명사절이다.

❹ Last(마지막으로)는 방법이나 절차를 설명하면서 마지막 순서를 말할 때 사용한다.

❺ sound+형용사: ~하게 들리다

Q1 소녀는 소년에게 무엇을 알려 주고 있나요? _____

Q2 **The boy needs to put his transportation card in the machine first.** (T / F)

B: I want to buy a snack. ❶Do you know how to use this snack machine?

G: Yeah. First, choose ❷the snack you want.

B: I already did. ❸What's next?

G: Just put in the money. ❹Then take the snack out.

B: ❺Got it. Thanks.

❶ 상대방에게 방법이나 절차를 물을 때 「Do you know how to+동사원형 ~?」으로도 말할 수 있다.
snack machine: 과자 자판기

❷ 관계대명사절인 you want가 선행사 the snack을 수식하는 형태이다.

❸ 절차를 설명하는 상대방에게 그다음 절차는 무엇인지 묻는 표현이다. (= Then what?)

❹ Then은 '그다음에, 그리고 나서'라는 뜻으로, 다음 순서를 말할 때 주로 사용한다.

❺ 상대방의 말을 듣고 '알았다.' 또는 '이해했다.'라고 말할 때 (I) Got it.이라고 한다.

Q3 **The girl doesn't know how to use the snack machine.** (T / F)

Q4 **What does the boy have to do first to use the snack machine?** He has to _____.

G: Excuse me. I want to ❶rent a bike. Can you tell me how to use this application?

M: Sure. First, ❷log in to the application. Then find the RENT button and touch it.

G: ❸Then what?

M: Then the application will give you ❹a number to unlock a bike with.

G: Thank you. ❺I really appreciate your help.

❶ (사용료를 내고) 자전거를 빌리다

❷ ~에 로그인하다

❸ 절차를 설명하는 상대방에게 그다음 절차는 무엇인지 묻는 표현이다. (= What's next? / And then?)

❹ '자전거 잠금을 해제할 수 있는 번호'라는 의미로, to unlock a bike with가 a number를 뒤에서 수식하는 형태이다.

❺ 도와줘서 고맙다는 의미의 표현으로, Thank you for your help. 또는 간단히 Thanks (a lot). 등으로 바꿔 말할 수 있다.

Q5 두 사람은 무엇에 관해 대화하고 있나요? (   )

ⓐ 자전거 타는 법   ⓑ 앱 사용법

Listen and Talk C

G: Excuse me, but ❶what's this robot for?

B: Oh, it's a robot that finds books for you.

G: Really? ❷Can you tell me how to use it?

B: Sure. First, ❸place your library card on the robot's screen.

G: OK.

B: Second, ❹type the title of the book you're looking for and then press ENTER.

G: ❺Is that all?

B: Yes. Then, the robot will find the book and take it to the front desk.

G: ❻So I can just go to the front desk and get the book?

B: Right. It's so easy, ❼isn't it?

G: ❽Yes, it's really amazing. Thank you.

Q6 What is the robot used for? (　　)

Q7 A library card is needed when the girl uses the robot.

❶ What's ~ for?는 물건의 용도를 묻는 표현이다.

❷ 물건의 사용법을 묻는 말이며, it은 this robot을 가리킨다.

❸ place A on B: A를 B 위에 놓다

❹ type이 '타자를 치다, 입력하다'라는 의미의 동사로 쓰였고, 목적격 관계대명사가 생략된 관계대명사절인 you're looking for가 선행사 the book을 수식하고 있다.

❺ 상대방이 말한 것이 전부인지 묻는 표현이다.

❻ 「주어+동사 ~」 형태의 평서문 어순인데 끝에 물음표가 붙었다. 이는 자신의 말이 맞는지 확인하는 표현이다.

❼ 확인이나 동의를 구할 때 문장 뒤에 덧붙여 '그렇지 않니?'라는 뜻으로 묻는 부가의문문이다. 긍정문 뒤에는 부정형 부가의문문을 덧붙인다.

❽ 부가의문문으로 묻는 질문에 답할 때는 묻는 말의 내용이 맞으면 Yes로, 맞지 않으면 No로 말한다.

ⓐ finding books　ⓑ reading books

(T / F)

Talk and Play

A: ❶Do you know how to make tea?

B: Sure. First, put a tea bag in a cup.

A: OK.

B: Then, ❷pour hot water in the cup.

A: ❸And then?

B: Last, ❹take the tea bag out after 3 minutes.

A: ❺I got it. I really appreciate your help.

Q8 차를 만들 때 두 번째로 할 일은 무엇인가요?

❶ 상대방에게 절차나 방법을 묻는 표현이다.
make tea: 차를 끓이다(만들다)

❷ pour A in B: A를 B에 붓다

❸ 이어지는 절차가 무엇인지 묻는 표현으로, What's next? / Then what? 등으로 바꿔 말할 수 있다.

❹ take out: ~을 꺼내다

❺ 상대방의 말을 듣고 '알았다.' 또는 '이해했다.'라고 말하는 표현이다.

Review - 1

G: Can you tell me how to ❶plant a potato?

B: Sure. First, ❷cut a potato into small pieces. Second, dig holes in the ground.

G: ❸Then?

B: Then put the potato pieces in the holes and ❹cover the holes with dirt.

G: ❺That sounds simple. Thanks.

Q9 감자를 구멍에 넣은 후에 무엇을 해야 하나요? (　　)

❶ 감자를 심다

❷ cut ~ into pieces: ~을 여러 조각으로 자르다

❸ = What's next? / And then? / Then what?

❹ cover A with B: A를 B로 덮다

❺ '~하게 들리다'는 「sound+형용사」로 나타낸다.

ⓐ 감자를 작은 조각으로 자르기　ⓑ 흙으로 덮기

L&T Listen and Talk
빈칸 채우기

• 주어진 우리말과 일치하도록 교과서 대화문을 완성하시오.

Listen and Talk A-1

B: Excuse me. ＿＿＿＿ ＿＿＿＿ ＿＿＿＿ ＿＿＿＿ how to add money to my transportation card?

G: Of course. ＿＿＿＿, put your card in the machine. ＿＿＿＿, choose ＿＿＿＿ ＿＿＿＿ ＿＿＿＿ ＿＿＿＿ you want to add.

B: OK.

G: ＿＿＿＿, ＿＿＿＿ your money ＿＿＿＿ the machine.

B: That sounds ＿＿＿＿. Thanks.

 해석

교과서 120쪽

B: 실례합니다. 교통 카드에 돈을 충전하는 방법을 알려 주시겠어요?

G: 그럼요. 먼저, 기계에 카드를 넣으세요. 두 번째로, 충전하고 싶은 금액을 선택하세요.

B: 알겠어요.

G: 마지막으로, 기계에 돈을 넣으세요.

B: 간단한 것 같네요. 고맙습니다.

Listen and Talk A-2

B: I want to buy a snack. Do you know ＿＿＿＿ ＿＿＿＿ ＿＿＿＿ this snack machine?

G: Yeah. ＿＿＿＿, choose the snack you want.

B: I already did. What's ＿＿＿＿?

G: Just put in the money. Then ＿＿＿＿ the snack ＿＿＿＿.

B: ＿＿＿＿ it. Thanks.

교과서 120쪽

B: 저는 과자를 사고 싶어요. 이 과자 자판기를 어떻게 사용하는지 아세요?

G: 네. 먼저, 원하는 과자를 고르세요.

B: 이미 했어요. 그다음은 뭔가요?

G: 돈을 넣으세요. 그런 다음 과자를 꺼내세요.

B: 알겠어요. 고마워요.

Listen and Talk A-3

G: Excuse me. I want to ＿＿＿＿ ＿＿＿＿ ＿＿＿＿. Can you ＿＿＿＿ ＿＿＿＿ ＿＿＿＿ ＿＿＿＿ ＿＿＿＿ this application?

M: Sure. First, ＿＿＿＿ ＿＿＿＿ ＿＿＿＿ the application. ＿＿＿＿ find the RENT button and touch it.

G: Then ＿＿＿＿?

M: Then the application will give you a number ＿＿＿＿ ＿＿＿＿ a bike with.

G: Thank you. I really ＿＿＿＿ ＿＿＿＿ ＿＿＿＿.

교과서 120쪽

G: 실례합니다. 자전거를 빌리고 싶은데요. 이 앱을 어떻게 사용하는지 알려 주시겠어요?

M: 그럼요. 먼저, 앱에 로그인하세요. 그런 다음 RENT 버튼을 찾아서 터치하세요.

G: 그다음에는 뭘 하죠?

M: 그러면 앱이 자전거 잠금을 해제할 수 있는 번호를 알려 줄 거예요.

G: 고맙습니다. 도와주셔서 정말 감사해요.

Listen and Talk C

교과서 121쪽

G: Excuse me, but what's this _____ _____?

B: Oh, it's a robot that finds books for you.

G: Really? Can _____ _____ _____ _____ to use it?

B: Sure. First, _____ your library card on the robot's _____.

G: OK.

B: _____, _____ the title of the book you're _____ _____ and then press ENTER.

G: Is _____ _____?

B: Yes. Then, the robot will find the book and _____ it _____ the front desk.

G: So I can just go to the front desk and get the book?

B: Right. It's so easy, _____ _____?

G: _____, it's really _____. Thank you.

G: 실례합니다만, 이 로봇은 용도가 뭔가요?

B: 아, 그것은 책을 찾아 주는 로봇이에요.

G: 정말요? 어떻게 사용하는지 알려 주시겠어요?

B: 그럼요. 먼저, 도서 대출 카드를 로봇 화면 위에 대세요.

G: 알겠어요.

B: 두 번째로, 당신이 찾고 있는 책의 제목을 입력한 다음 ENTER를 누르세요.

G: 그게 다인가요?

B: 네. 그러면, 로봇이 그 책을 찾아서 안내 데스크로 가져다줄 거예요.

G: 그러면 저는 그냥 안내 데스크로 가서 책을 받을 수 있네요?

B: 그렇습니다. 아주 쉬워요, 그렇지 않아요?

G: 네, 정말 놀랍네요. 고마워요.

Talk and Play

교과서 122쪽

A: _____ _____ _____ how to make tea?

B: Sure. First, _____ _____ _____ _____ in a cup.

A: OK.

B: Then, _____ _____ _____ in the cup.

A: And _____?

B: _____, take the tea bag out after 3 minutes.

A: _____ _____ _____. I really _____ your help.

A: 너는 차 만드는 방법을 아니?

B: 그럼. 먼저, 컵에 티백을 넣어.

A: 알겠어.

B: 그런 다음, 그 컵에 뜨거운 물을 부어.

A: 그다음에는?

B: 마지막으로, 3분 뒤에 티백을 꺼내.

A: 알겠어. 도와줘서 정말 고마워.

Review - 1

교과서 134쪽

G: Can you tell me _____ _____ _____ _____ _____?

B: Sure. _____, _____ a potato _____ _____ _____.
_____, dig holes in the ground.

G: Then?

B: _____ put the potato pieces in the holes and _____ _____ _____ with dirt.

G: That _____ _____. Thanks.

G: 감자 심는 방법을 알려 주겠니?

B: 그럼. 먼저, 감자를 작은 조각으로 잘라. 둘째로, 땅에 구멍을 파.

G: 그다음에는?

B: 그런 다음 구멍에 감자 조각들을 넣고 흙으로 구멍을 덮어.

G: 간단한 것 같네. 고마워.

Listen and Talk

대화 순서 배열하기

1 Listen and Talk A-1

교과서 120쪽

ⓐ Last, insert your money into the machine.

ⓑ Of course. First, put your card in the machine. Second, choose the amount of money you want to add.

ⓒ OK.

ⓓ That sounds simple. Thanks.

ⓔ Excuse me. Can you tell me how to add money to my transportation card?

(　　) – (　　) – ⓒ – (　　) – (　　)

2 Listen and Talk A-2

교과서 120쪽

ⓐ Yeah. First, choose the snack you want.

ⓑ I want to buy a snack. Do you know how to use this snack machine?

ⓒ Just put in the money. Then take the snack out.

ⓓ I already did. What's next?

ⓔ Got it. Thanks.

(　　) – (　　) – (　　) – (　　) – (　　)

3 Listen and Talk A-3

교과서 120쪽

ⓐ Then what?

ⓑ Sure. First, log in to the application. Then find the RENT button and touch it.

ⓒ Excuse me. I want to rent a bike. Can you tell me how to use this application?

ⓓ Then the application will give you a number to unlock a bike with.

ⓔ Thank you. I really appreciate your help.

(　　) – (　　) – (　　) – (　　) – (　　)

4 Listen and Talk C

교과서 121쪽

A: Excuse me, but what's this robot for?

ⓐ So I can just go to the front desk and get the book?

ⓑ Really? Can you tell me how to use it?

ⓒ Yes. Then, the robot will find the book and take it to the front desk.

ⓓ OK.

ⓔ Sure. First, place your library card on the robot's screen.

ⓕ Is that all?

ⓖ Right. It's so easy, isn't it?

ⓗ Oh, it's a robot that finds books for you.

ⓘ Second, type the title of the book you're looking for and then press ENTER.

ⓙ Yes, it's really amazing. Thank you.

A – (   ) – (   ) – (   ) – ⓓ – (   ) – ⓕ – (   ) – (   ) – ⓖ – ⓙ

5 Talk and Play

교과서 122쪽

ⓐ Sure. First, put a tea bag in a cup.

ⓑ And then?

ⓒ OK.

ⓓ Do you know how to make tea?

ⓔ I got it. I really appreciate your help.

ⓕ Last, take the tea bag out after 3 minutes.

ⓖ Then, pour hot water in the cup.

(   ) – (   ) – ⓒ – (   ) – ⓑ – (   ) – (   )

6 Review - 1

교과서 134쪽

ⓐ Sure. First, cut a potato into small pieces. Second, dig holes in the ground.

ⓑ That sounds simple. Thanks.

ⓒ Then?

ⓓ Then put the potato pieces in the holes and cover the holes with dirt.

ⓔ Can you tell me how to plant a potato?

(   ) – (   ) – (   ) – (   ) – ⓑ

STEP
A

[01~02] 다음 대화의 빈칸에 들어갈 말로 알맞은 것을 고르시오.

01

A: I want to buy a snack. _____
B: Yes. Choose the snack you want and put in the money. Then take the snack out.

① Can you buy me some snacks?
② How do I get to the snack shop?
③ Where can I find a snack machine?
④ Is there any place I can buy a snack?
⑤ Do you know how to use this snack machine?

02

A: Can you tell me how to use a copy machine?
B: Sure. First, put the paper on the copy machine. Then choose the paper size and the number of copies. Last, press the START button.
A: I got it. _____

① That's all right.
② Don't mention it.
③ Do you need some help?
④ I really appreciate your help.
⑤ Thank you for copying it for me.

03 다음 대화의 밑줄 친 ①~⑤ 중 흐름상 어색한 것은?

A: ①Excuse me. Can you tell me how to add money to my transportation card?
B: ②No, I'm afraid not. First, put your card in the machine. ③Second, choose the amount of money you want to add.
A: OK.
B: ④Last, insert your money into the machine.
A: That sounds simple. ⑤Thanks.

①   ②   ③   ④   ⑤

04 다음 대화의 밑줄 친 문장과 바꿔 쓸 수 있는 것은?

A: Do you know how to get to the park?
B: Sure. Walk straight two blocks and turn left.
A: I appreciate it.

① Excuse me.   ② That's too bad.
③ You can't miss it.   ④ It's my pleasure.
⑤ Thank you for your help.

05 자연스러운 대화가 되도록 (A)~(D)를 바르게 배열한 것은?

A: Excuse me. I want to rent a bike. Can you tell me how to use this application?
(A) Then what?
(B) Sure. First, log in to the application. Then find the RENT button and touch it.
(C) Thank you. I really appreciate your help.
(D) Then the application will give you a number to unlock a bike with.

① (A) – (C) – (B) – (D)   ② (A) – (D) – (C) – (B)
③ (B) – (A) – (D) – (C)   ④ (B) – (D) – (C) – (A)
⑤ (C) – (D) – (B) – (A)

06 다음 대화의 빈칸 ⓐ~ⓔ에 들어갈 말로 알맞지 <u>않은</u> 것은?

A: Do you know _____ⓐ_____ to plant a potato?
B: Sure. _____ⓑ_____, cut a potato into small pieces.
A: OK.
B: _____ⓒ_____, dig holes in the ground.
A: And then?
B: _____ⓓ_____, put the potato pieces in the holes.
A: Is that all?
B: No. _____ⓔ_____, cover the holes with dirt.
A: That sounds simple. Thanks.

① ⓐ: how   ② ⓑ: First   ③ ⓒ: Then
④ ⓓ: Second   ⑤ ⓔ: Last

[07~09] 다음 대화를 읽고, 물음에 답하시오.

A: Excuse me, but what's ⓐ<u>this robot</u> for?
B: Oh, it's a robot that finds books for you.
A: Really? (①)
B: Sure. First, place your library card on the robot's screen.
A: OK. (②)
B: Second, type the title of the book you're looking for and then press ENTER.
A: Is that all? (③)
B: Yes. Then, the robot will find the book and take it to the front desk.
A: So I can just go to the front desk and get the book? (④)
B: Right. It's so easy, isn't it? (⑤)
A: Yes, it's really amazing. _____ ⓑ

07 위 대화의 ①~⑤ 중 주어진 문장이 들어갈 위치로 알맞은 것은?

> Can you tell me how to use it?

①   ②   ③   ④   ⑤

08 위 대화의 밑줄 친 ⓐ<u>this robot</u>에 대해 알 수 있는 것을 <u>모두</u> 고르면?

① 용도   ② 개발자   ③ 사용료
④ 사용법   ⑤ 사용 후기

09 위 대화의 빈칸 ⓑ에 들어갈 말로 알맞은 것을 <u>모두</u> 고르면?

① That's OK.
② Thank you.
③ You're welcome.
④ I appreciate your help.
⑤ I'm sorry to hear that.

---

10 괄호 안의 단어를 배열하여 다음 대화를 완성하시오.

A: (1)_____?
    (you, how, do, to, make, know, tea)
B: Sure. First, put a tea bag in a cup. Then, pour hot water in the cup.
A: And then?
B: Last, take the tea bag out after 3 minutes.
A: I got it. (2)_____.
    (I, your, appreciate, really, help)

11 다음 메모의 내용과 일치하도록 대화를 완성하시오.

How to Boil Eggs
1. Put water and the eggs in a pot.
2. Boil the water and the eggs for 10 to 12 minutes.
3. Take the eggs out and cool them.

A: Do you know how to boil eggs?
B: Sure. First, (1)_____.
   Then, (2)_____.
A: And then?
B: (3)_____, take the eggs out and cool them.

12 다음 글에서 설명하는 절차에 따라 그림에 번호를 쓰시오.

Let me tell you how to use the drink machine. First, insert money into the machine. Second, choose the drink you want. Then just take the drink out of the machine.

(   ) － (   ) － (   )

Grammar
핵심 노트

1 분사구문

읽기 본문 **Using** various methods, experts analyze big data.
분사구문 (~하면서)

전문가들은 다양한 방법들을 사용하여 빅데이터를 분석한다.

대표 예문 Big data is improving the performance of players,
making sports more exciting.
Walking along the street, I saw a man with five dogs.
Waving his hand, he walked out of the house.
Eating a sandwich, she waited for the train.

빅데이터는 스포츠를 더욱 흥미진진하게 만들면서 선수들의 경기력을 향상하고 있다.

나는 길을 따라 걷다가 개 다섯 마리와 함께 있는 남자를 보았다.

그는 손을 흔들면서 집 밖으로 걸어 나갔다.

그녀는 샌드위치를 먹으면서 기차를 기다렸다.

분사가 동사와 접속사의 역할을 동시에 하며, 그 분사가 이끄는 구가 문장 내에서 부사구로 쓰이는 것을 분사구문이라고 한다. 분사구문은 문맥에 따라 다양한 의미를 나타내며, 「접속사+주어 +동사 ~」 형태의 부사절로 바꿔 쓸 수 있다.

(1) 동시동작(~하면서): as, while
Eating breakfast, we watched TV. (우리는 아침 식사를 하면서 TV를 봤다.)
= While we were eating breakfast, we watched TV.
(2) 시간(~할 때, ~하자마자): when, as soon as 등
Seeing me, the baby stopped crying. (그 아기는 나를 보자 울음을 그쳤다.)
(3) 이유(~해서, ~하기 때문에): because, as, since
Having no money, he couldn't buy the bag. (그는 돈이 없어서 그 가방을 살 수 없었다.)
(4) 조건(~하면): if
Turning left, you will see the museum. (왼쪽으로 돌면 박물관이 보일 것이다.)

한 단계 더!

- 분사구문의 뜻을 명확하게 하기 위해 분사구문 앞에 접속사를 쓰기도 한다.
<u>While</u> **working** in Paris, he met Sue. (그는 파리에서 일하는 동안 Sue를 만났다.)
- 분사구문의 부정은 분사 앞에 부정어 not이나 never를 써서 나타낸다.
<u>Not</u> **knowing** French, I couldn't read the book. (프랑스어를 몰라서 나는 그 책을 읽을 수 없었다.)
- 분사구문에서 Being은 생략할 수 있다.
(**Being**) Too tired, I fell asleep right away. (나는 너무 피곤해서 바로 잠들어 버렸다.)

point
시험 포인트 ❶
부사절을 분사구문으로 바꾸는 문제가 자주 출제되므로 부사절을 분사구문으로 만드는 법을 충분히 익혀 두도록 한다.
① 부사절의 접속사를 생략한다.
② 부사절의 주어를 생략한다.
(단, 주절의 주어와 같을 때)
③ 부사절의 동사를 「동사원형+-ing」 형태로 바꾼다. (단, 주절과 시제가 같을 때)

point
시험 포인트 ❷
분사구문의 의미를 구별하여 알맞은 부사절로 바꾸는 문제가 자주 출제되므로 주절과의 맥락을 잘 파악하도록 한다. 다만, 분사구문은 경우에 따라서는 한 가지 이상의 의미로 해석될 수도 있다.

QUICK CHECK

1 다음 빈칸에 괄호 안의 동사를 알맞은 형태로 쓰시오.
(1) _____ his homework, he felt sleepy. (do)
(2) _____ the news, she started to cry. (hear)
(3) _____ with her dad, she smiled brightly. (dance)

2 다음 밑줄 친 부분을 어법에 맞게 고쳐 쓰시오. (단, 한 단어만 바꿔 쓸 것)
(1) <u>Waited</u> for the bus, I met Tom. → _____
(2) <u>Don't feeling</u> well, I stayed home. → _____
(3) <u>Call</u> my name, Anne walked towards us. → _____

2 접속사 as

읽기 본문 **As** information and communication technology develops,
~함에 따라
the amount of data we have is getting much greater than
before.

정보 통신 기술이 발달함에 따라, 우리가 갖고 있는 데이터의 양이 이전보다 훨씬 더 많아지고 있다.

대표 예문 Health professionals can now forecast a disease just **as**
weather experts forecast the weather.
~하듯이

날씨 전문가들이 날씨를 예측하는 것과 같이, 현재 건강 전문가들이 질병을 예측할 수 있다.

As I told you, we will meet at 6:00 in front of the bus stop.
~하듯이

내가 너에게 말했듯이, 우리는 버스 정류장 앞에서 6시에 만날 것이다.

She got wiser **as** she got older.
~함에 따라

그녀는 나이가 더 들어감에 따라 더 현명해졌다.

As it was late at night, we went back home.
~ 때문에

밤이 늦었기 때문에 우리는 집으로 돌아갔다.

접속사로 쓰이는 as는 부사절을 이끌면서 다음과 같이 다양한 의미를 나타낸다.

(1) ~하면서, ~할 때

As I left the building, I saw Amy. (나는 그 건물을 떠날 때 Amy를 봤다.)

(2) ~ 때문에

As it is getting dark, we should go home. (어두워지고 있으니 우리는 집에 가야 한다.)

(3) ~하듯이

As you know, he will come back soon. (너도 알다시피, 그는 곧 돌아올 거야.)

(4) ~함에 따라, 할수록

As she grew older, she became much weaker. (그녀는 나이가 들면서 훨씬 더 약해졌다.)

(5) ~하는 대로

Don't change the story **as** you want. (원하는 대로 이야기를 바꾸지 마.)

시험 포인트 ❶ **point**

접속사 as의 의미를 구별하는 문제가 주로 출제되므로 부사절과 주절의 논리 관계를 파악할 수 있어야 한다. 다양한 예시 문장을 통해 의미를 구분하여 익혀 두도록 한다.

시험 포인트 ❷ **point**

접속사 as와 전치사 as를 구분하는 문제도 출제되므로 as의 쓰임을 잘 구분하도록 한다.
• 접속사 as+주어+동사 ~
• 전치사 as+명사(구)

한 단계 더!

전치사 as+명사(구)

(1) ~처럼: They were all dressed **as** clowns. (그들은 모두 광대처럼 입었다.)

(2) ~로서: She is leading the team **as** a captain. (그녀는 주장으로서 팀을 이끌고 있다.)

QUICK CHECK

1 다음 괄호 안에서 알맞은 것을 고르시오.

(1) The meeting started (if / as) I arrived there.

(2) (As / Unless) I mentioned earlier, we will meet at six.

(3) (As / Though) it is raining outside, we won't go out today.

2 자연스러운 문장이 되도록 연결하시오. (단, 중복 연결 불가)

(1) He felt great • • ⓐ we get wiser.

(2) As we get older, • • ⓑ as he stood on the mountaintop.

(3) I didn't go to the gym today • • ⓒ as I had a lot of homework to do.

G

Grammar

연습 문제

STEP A

1 분사구문

A 자연스러운 문장이 되도록 연결하시오. (단, 중복 연결 불가)

1 Being too sick, •   • ⓐ I read a book all night long.

2 Taking this bus, •   • ⓑ she had to be in the hospital for a week.

3 Going into the theater, •   • ⓒ you can get to the City Hall in ten minutes.

4 Not feeling sleepy at all, •   • ⓓ we turned off our cell phones.

B 다음 두 문장의 의미가 같도록 주어진 접속사를 사용하여 문장을 완성하시오.

1 Waiting for the train, she ate a sandwich.

= _____, she ate a sandwich. (while)

2 Being too busy, they couldn't go camping with us.

= _____, they couldn't go camping with us. (because)

3 Solving this problem, you will get a prize.

= _____, you will get a prize. (if)

C 다음 밑줄 친 분사구문에서 어법상 **틀린** 부분을 찾아 바르게 고쳐 쓰시오.

1 <u>Seen me on the street</u>, he ran away.   _____ → _____

2 <u>When use this knife</u>, you should be very careful.   _____ → _____

3 <u>Knowing not what to do</u>, he asked for my help.   _____ → _____

4 <u>Not heard the phone call</u>, I couldn't answer.   _____ → _____

D 주어진 우리말과 의미가 같도록 괄호 안의 표현을 어법에 맞게 사용하여 문장을 완성하시오.

1 나는 음악을 들으면서 화초에 물을 주었다. (listen to, water the plants)

→ _____ _____ music, I _____ _____ _____.

2 집에 도착하자마자 그녀는 창문을 모두 열었다. (arrive home, all the windows)

→ _____ _____, she _____ _____ _____ _____.

3 그는 친구가 없기 때문에 항상 외로웠다. (have friends, always lonely)

→ _____ _____ _____, he _____ _____ _____.

2 접속사 as

A [보기]에서 알맞은 말을 골라 문장을 완성하시오. (단, 중복 사용 불가)

| [보기] | • we made a fire | • as it snowed a lot |
| | • as I walked out of the café | • the leaves will turn yellow and red |

1 As time goes by, _____.

2 I spilled my coffee _____.

3 As it was getting cold, _____.

4 The picnic was canceled _____.

B 주어진 문장과 의미가 같도록 because나 when을 사용하여 문장을 완성하시오.

1 As I entered the room, I dropped my smartphone.

= _____, I dropped my smartphone.

2 I'm really hungry as I haven't eaten anything since this morning.

= I'm really hungry _____.

3 Some people listen to music as they study.

= Some people listen to music _____.

C 주어진 우리말과 의미가 같도록 접속사 as와 괄호 안의 단어를 사용하여 문장을 완성하시오. (단, 필요시 단어의 형태를 바꿀 것)

1 너도 알듯이, 김 선생님은 운동을 좋아하지 않으셔. (know)

→ _____, Mr. Kim doesn't like exercising.

2 그녀가 그곳에 없어서 나는 메모를 남겼다. (not, there)

→ I left a note _____.

3 봄이 옴에 따라 날씨가 점점 더 따뜻해진다. (spring, come)

→ _____, it gets warmer and warmer.

D 주어진 우리말과 의미가 같도록 괄호 안의 단어를 바르게 배열하여 문장을 쓰시오.

1 그들은 우리가 요청한 대로 그 일을 했다. (as, they, had asked, did, we, the work)

→ _____

2 그녀는 나이가 들어감에 따라 더 현명해졌다. (older, wiser, as, got, she, became, she)

→ _____

3 매우 늦었기 때문에 우리는 집으로 갔다. (went, late, it, as, home, we, was, very)

→ _____

01 다음 빈칸에 들어갈 **wave**의 형태로 알맞은 것은?

> _____ her hand, she got on the train.

① Wave ② Waving ③ Waved
④ Waves ⑤ Being waved

02 다음 문장의 밑줄 친 부분과 바꿔 쓸 수 있는 것은?

> I joined the cooking club <u>as</u> I was interested in cooking.

① if ② but ③ whether
④ though ⑤ because

03 다음 두 문장의 의미가 같도록 할 때, 빈칸에 들어갈 말로 알맞은 것은?

> Since I drink too much coffee, I can't fall asleep easily.
> = _____, I can't fall asleep easily.

① Drink too much coffee
② Drunk too much coffee
③ Drinking too much coffee
④ I drinking too much coffee
⑤ When drank too much coffee

04 다음 중 밑줄 친 **As**의 우리말 의미가 알맞지 <u>않은</u> 것은?

① <u>As</u> he had the flu, he didn't go out.
　(～ 때문에)
② <u>As</u> it grew darker, it became colder.
　(～하듯이)
③ They didn't do <u>as</u> I had asked them to do.
　(～하는 대로)
④ <u>As</u> I grow older, I enjoy reading books more.
　(～함에 따라)
⑤ <u>As</u> everyone knows, Sujin is the best player.
　(～하듯이)

05 다음 밑줄 친 부분을 바르게 바꿔 쓴 것은?

> <u>Taking a shower</u>, I heard someone knocking.

① If I took a shower
② Unless I take a shower
③ While I was taking a shower
④ Though I didn't take a shower
⑤ Because I wasn't taking a shower

06 다음 빈칸에 들어갈 말로 알맞지 <u>않은</u> 것은?

> As it rained heavily, _____.

① Jina couldn't drive
② I put on a raincoat
③ the land became drier
④ the picnic was canceled
⑤ they couldn't play tennis

한 단계 더!
07 다음 우리말을 영어로 바르게 옮긴 것을 <u>모두</u> 고르면?

> 나는 무엇을 해야 할지 몰라서 가만히 서 있었다.

① Not known what to do, I just stood still.
② Didn't know what to do, I just stood still.
③ Not knowing what to do, I just stood still.
④ Knowing not what to do, I just stood still.
⑤ As I didn't know what to do, I just stood still.

08 다음 문장에서 어법상 <u>틀린</u> 부분을 바르게 고친 것은?

> Walked along the river, I saw a man with five dogs.

① Walked → Walking ② along → on
③ saw → see ④ with → from
⑤ dogs → dog

09 다음 중 밑줄 친 **As(as)**의 의미가 [보기]와 같은 것은?

> [보기] As she was tired, she went to bed early.

① I'll do it as you wish.
② As I was cooking dinner, the phone rang.
③ As you know, this is not a good question.
④ As she grew up, she became more beautiful.
⑤ As it snowed a lot, the camping was canceled.

10 다음 중 어법상 틀린 문장은?

① He rode his bike, listening to music.
② Having dinner, I watched a TV show.
③ Was too hungry, I ate a whole pizza.
④ Turning to the left, you'll see the bank.
⑤ Reading a book, Tim ate some cookies.

11 다음 중 빈칸에 **As**가 들어가기에 어색한 것은?

① _____ he didn't answer my phone, I texted him.
② _____ they are twins, they look totally different.
③ _____ it gets colder, people wear thicker clothes.
④ _____ I was cleaning my room, Mom came home.
⑤ _____ Dad told you, you should not eat too much fast food.

12 다음 중 밑줄 친 부분의 쓰임이 나머지와 다른 하나는?

① She watched TV, eating an apple.
② Talking to himself, he drove a car.
③ Playing online games is very exciting.
④ Sending text messages, he ate breakfast.
⑤ Looking out the window, I drank some tea.

고/난도
13 다음 중 어법상 틀린 문장끼리 짝지어진 것은?

ⓐ Played soccer, he hurt his leg.
ⓑ As you can see, I'm not a good singer.
ⓒ He prepared dinner, listening to the radio.
ⓓ Being too tired, I couldn't focus on the exam.
ⓔ As she had a lot of money, she couldn't buy the shoes.

① ⓐ, ⓓ   ② ⓐ, ⓔ   ③ ⓑ, ⓓ
④ ⓒ, ⓔ   ⑤ ⓓ, ⓔ

고/난도 한 단계 더!
14 다음 두 문장을 한 문장으로 연결하여 쓴 것 중 어법상 틀린 것은?

① Go straight two blocks. Then you'll see the park.
→ Going straight two blocks, you'll see the park.
② Kevin played a mobile game. He ate a sandwich at the same time.
→ Kevin ate a sandwich, playing a mobile game.
③ Mina waited for her friends. She was talking on the phone, too.
→ Mina waited for her friends, talked on the phone.
④ I didn't know about the accident. So I had nothing to say.
→ Not knowing about the accident, I had nothing to say.
⑤ Jessica had a terrible headache. So she stayed in bed all day.
→ Having a terrible headache, Jessica stayed in bed all day.

신유형
15 다음 우리말을 분사구문이 쓰인 영어 문장으로 옮길 때, 빈칸에 필요 <u>없는</u> 단어는?

> 그 소녀는 풀밭에 앉아 새들에게 먹이를 주었다.
> → _____, the girl fed birds.

① grass　　② on　　③ the
④ sat　　⑤ sitting

고난도
16 다음 중 밑줄 친 분사구문을 부사절로 바꾼 것 중 어법상 <u>틀린</u> 것은?

① <u>Seeing the accident</u>, I almost fell over.
　→ When I saw the accident
② <u>Leaving now</u>, you can catch the last train.
　→ If you leave now
③ <u>Getting up late</u>, he is always late for school.
　→ As he gets up late
④ <u>Seeing a burning house</u>, I called 119 for help.
　→ When I see a burning house
⑤ <u>Being injured</u>, he couldn't finish the marathon.
　→ Because he was injured

고난도 신유형
17 다음 문장 (A)~(C)에 대한 설명 중 <u>틀린</u> 것은?

> (A) As we were a little late, we took a taxi.
> (B) Arriving in Jeju-do, I called my friend Tim.
> (C) As winter comes, it gets colder and colder.

① (A)의 As는 Because나 Since로 바꿔 쓸 수 있다.
② (A)의 부사절을 분사구문으로 바꿔 문장을 다시 쓰면 Being a little late, we took a taxi.이다.
③ (B)의 Arriving in Jeju-do는 When I arrived in Jeju-do로 바꿔 쓸 수 있다.
④ (B)의 Arriving은 주절의 시제와 맞춰 Arrived로 고쳐 써야 한다.
⑤ (C)의 As는 '～함에 따라'라는 의미로 쓰였다.

18 다음 빈칸에 공통으로 들어갈 알맞은 접속사를 쓰시오.

> • _____ time went by, things got better.
> • She went home without a word _____ she was very angry.
> • _____ the doctor told you, you should take this medicine.

→ _____

19 다음 그림을 보고, [보기]에서 알맞은 표현을 골라 분사구문을 사용하여 문장을 완성하시오.

[보기]　• drink water
　　　• play the guitar
　　　• eat ice cream
　　　• talk on the phone

(1) _____, Eric read a book.

(2) _____, Yumi sang songs.

(3) _____, Amy walked her dog.

(4) _____, Jiho waited for the bus.

20 다음 글의 밑줄 친 문장을 분사구문을 사용하여 다시 쓰시오.

> My sister and I walked around the shopping mall to buy a birthday present for Mom. <u>As we felt hungry after shopping, we went to the food court to eat something.</u>

→ _____

_____

21 다음 우리말과 의미가 같도록 괄호 안의 단어를 어법에 맞게 사용하여 문장을 완성하시오. (단, 모두 같은 접속사를 사용할 것)

(1) 그는 나이가 들어감에 따라 더욱 명랑해졌다.

→ _____ _____ _____ _____, he became more cheerful. (grow, old)

(2) 내가 전에 말했듯이, 함께 일하는 것은 절대 쉽지 않다.

→ _____ _____ _____ _____, working together is never easy. (say, before)

(3) 우리가 예측한 대로, 영화관은 매우 붐볐다.

→ _____ _____ _____, the movie theater was very crowded. (predict)

한 단계 더!
22 다음 밑줄 친 부분을 분사구문으로 바꿔 쓰시오.

(1) <u>After she finished her homework</u>, she went to bed.

→ _____, she went to bed.

(2) <u>Because he doesn't have enough money</u>, he can't buy the car now.

→ _____, he can't buy the car now.

(3) <u>When I walked on the beach</u>, I saw some people swimming in the sea.

→ _____, I saw some people swimming in the sea.

[23~24] 주어진 우리말과 의미가 같도록 [조건]에 맞게 영어 문장을 쓰시오.

> [조건] 1. 괄호 안의 말을 어법에 맞게 사용할 것
> 2. (1)은 접속사 as로 시작하여 쓰고, (2)는 분사구문으로 시작하여 쓸 것

고난도
23 그는 버스에서 내리면서 내게 인사했다.
(get off, say hello to)

(1) _____

(2) _____

고난도 한 단계 더!
24 나는 배가 별로 고프지 않아서 아무것도 먹지 않았다.
(that hungry, anything)

(1) _____

(2) _____

25 다음 〈A〉와 〈B〉에서 각각 알맞은 말을 하나씩 골라 접속사 as로 시작하는 한 문장으로 연결하여 쓰시오. (단, 중복 사용 불가)

A (1) I arrived late.
(2) I entered the kitchen.
(3) The doctor told me.

B • I will take this medicine every day.
• I missed the beginning of the movie.
• I could smell Mom's cookies.

(1) _____

(2) _____

(3) _____

STEP A

빅데이터와 함께 살아가기

01 당신은 온라인 서점을 방문해서 그 서점이 당신에게 추천한 책들을 보고 놀란 적이 있는가?

02 그 책들 중 다수가 당신에게 흥미로워 보였다.

03 그러면 그 서점은 당신이 무엇을 좋아하는지 어떻게 알았을까?

04 이것은 모두 빅데이터 때문에 가능하다.

빅데이터는 무엇인가?

05 빅데이터는 매우 크고 복잡한 데이터의 집합이다.

06 정보 통신 기술이 발달함에 따라 우리가 갖고 있는 데이터의 양이 이전보다 훨씬 더 많아지고 있다.

07 이것의 주된 이유는 우리가 온라인상에서 하는 거의 모든 것들이 흔적을 남기기 때문이다.

08 예를 들어, 당신이 블로그에 올린 사진들과 온라인 상점에서의 구매 기록들이 모두 빅데이터의 일부이다.

09 하지만 단순히 데이터를 수집하는 것만으로는 충분하지 않다.

10 빅데이터는 분석되어야 하는데, 이것은 빅데이터 전문가들에 의해서 이루어진다.

11 전문가들은 다양한 방법들을 사용하여 빅데이터를 분석하고, 그것으로부터 의미 있는 결과들을 도출한다.

12 그런 다음, 이런 결과들은 의사결정을 하거나 미래를 예측하는 데 사용될 수 있다.

빅데이터는 우리 삶에 어떻게 영향을 미치고 있는가?

13 빅데이터는 우리 삶의 거의 모든 부분에 영향을 미치고 있다.

14 그것은 회사들이 소비자들이 필요로 하는 것을 더 잘 이해하고 더 많은 상품을 팔도록 도와준다.

15 그것은 사람들이 교통 체증을 피하도록 도와준다.

16 그것의 쓰임은 끝이 없는데, 여기 몇 가지 흥미로운 예들이 있다.

Living with Big Data

01 「Have you (ever)+과거분사(visited, been) ~?」 현재완료(경험)
Have you ever visited an online bookstore and been surprised by
수동태 (be동사+과거분사+by+행위자)
the books [that the store recommended for you]?
선행사 목적격 관계대명사 recommend A for B: A를 B에게 추천하다

02 Many of them looked interesting to you.
= the books 「감각동사 look+형용사」 ~해 보이다

03 So how did the bookstore know what you liked?
know의 목적어

04 This is all possible because of big data.
「because of+명사(구)」 ~ 때문에

What is big data?

05 Big data is data sets [that are very big and complex].
관계대명사절
「접」 ~함에 따라 선행사 주격 관계대명사

06 As information and communication technology develops, the amount of
동사 훨씬 (비교급 강조) 선행사 (주어)
data [we have] is getting much greater than before.
목적격 관계대명사 생략 「get+비교급」 더 ~해지다

07 This is mainly because almost everything [that we do online] leaves a
이것은 ~ 때문이다 선행사 (because절의 주어) 목적격 관계대명사 동사 (everything은 단수 취급)
trace.

08 For example, [the photos [you upload on your blog] and the records of
선행사 목적격 관계대명사 생략 동사
your purchases at online stores] are all part of big data.
주어 (the photos ~ and the records ~ stores) 동사 (동명사(구) 주어는 단수 취급)

09 Simply collecting data, however, is not enough.
주어 역할을 하는 동명사구 빅데이터를 분석하는 일

10 Big data has to be analyzed, and this is done by big data experts.
~해야 한다 수동태 (be동사+과거분사) 수동태 (be동사+과거분사+by+행위자)

11 Using various methods, experts analyze big data and draw meaningful
분사구문 「동」 (결과를) 이끌어 내다
results from it.
= big data

12 These results then can be used to make decisions or to predict the
「be used to+동사원형」 ~하는 데 사용되다
future.

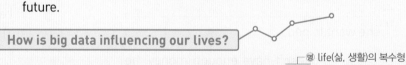

How is big data influencing our lives?

13 Big data is influencing almost all parts of our lives.
「명」 life(삶, 생활)의 복수형
= Big data

14 It helps companies understand their customers' needs better and helps
「help+목적어+(to+)동사원형」 (목적어)가 ~하도록 돕다 = companies' 「명」 (pl.) 요구, 수요
them sell more products.
= companies

15 It helps people avoid heavy traffic.
= Big data 「help+목적어+(to+)동사원형」 (목적어)가 ~하도록 돕다

16 Its uses are endless, and here are some interesting examples.
use 「명」 쓰임 end(「명」 끝)+접미사 -less: 「형」 끝없는, 무한한

Disease Forecast

17 Did you know [that health professionals can now forecast a
　　명사절을 이끄는 접속사
　　　　　　　명사절 (know의 목적어)
disease just as weather experts forecast the weather]?
　　　　　　접 ~하듯이

18 This is possible thanks to big data.
　　앞 문장의 내용을 가리킴　　「thanks to+명사(구)」 ~ 덕분에

19 For example, when the flu season comes,
　　　　　　접 ~할 때　　　　　　when절에서는 미래의
people will buy more flu medicine.　일도 현재시제 사용

20 They will also search online about flu symptoms more.
　= People　　　　　　　　　　　　　　　부사 much의 비교급

21 If this kind of data is analyzed wisely, the spread
　접 (만약) ~하면　　　수동태 (be동사+과거분사)　　명 확산, 전파
of the flu can be predicted.
　　　　수동태 (be동사+과거분사)

Improving Performance in Sports

22 Are you a sports fan?

23 Well, big data is improving the performance of
　　　　　　　분사구문: ~하면서 (동시동작)
players, making sports more exciting.
　　「make+목적어+목적격보어(형용사)」 (목적어)가 ~하게 하다

24 A famous example is Germany's national soccer team.
　　　　　　　　　　by+동명사: ~함으로써
25 The team built a database by collecting and analyzing a huge amount of
　　　　　　　　　　　　　전치사(by)의 목적어
data on players.
　접 ~에 대하여, ~에 관하여　　　　　명사절 (전치사 about의 목적어)

26 For example, the data included information about [how much each

player ran and how long he had the ball].
　　　간접의문문 (의문사+주어+동사 ~)

27 With the help of this database, Germany's national soccer team

was able to improve its performance and win the 2014 World Cup.
　= could　　　　　　　and로 연결된 병렬 구조

Crime Prevention

28 Thanks to big data, police can now predict crime before it happens.
　　　　　　　　　　　　　　　　　　= crime
29 Through the analysis of big data about the type, time and place of crime,
　= By analyzing
police can make a map of crime hot spots.
　　　　　　간접의문문 「의문사+주어+동사」 (identifies의 목적어 역할)
30 This map identifies when and where crime is most likely to happen.
　　　　　　　형 추가의, 더 이상의　　「be likely to+동사원형」 ~할 것 같다
31 Police can prevent further crime by focusing on the areas and the times
　목적격 관계대명사 생략　　　by+동명사: ~함으로써　　선행사
[this map predicts].
관계대명사절 (선행사 수식)
32 Big data has already changed the world greatly.
　　　　　　「have+과거분사」 현재완료(완료)
33 So where will the big data industry go from here?
　　　　　　　　　　　　　　명사절 (agree의 목적어)
34 Nobody knows for sure, but experts agree [that big data
　대 아무도 ~ (않다)　　　　　　명사절을 이끄는 접속사
will play a more and more important role in our lives].
　　「비교급+and+비교급」 점점 더 ~한

질병 예측

17 당신은 날씨 전문가들이 날씨를 예측하는 것과 같이 현재 건강 전문가들이 질병을 예측할 수 있다는 것을 알고 있었는가?

18 이것은 빅데이터 덕분에 가능하다.

19 예를 들어, 독감의 계절이 오면 사람들은 독감 약을 더 많이 구입할 것이다.

20 그들은 또한 온라인상에서 독감 증상에 대해 더 많이 검색해 볼 것이다.

21 이런 종류의 데이터가 현명하게 분석된다면, 독감의 확산은 예측될 수 있다.

스포츠에서의 경기력 향상

22 당신은 스포츠 팬인가?

23 빅데이터는 스포츠를 더 흥미진진하게 만들면서 선수들의 경기력을 향상하고 있다.

24 한 유명한 사례가 독일 국가 대표 축구팀이다.

25 그 팀은 선수들에 관한 엄청난 양의 데이터를 모으고 분석함으로써 데이터베이스를 구축했다.

26 예를 들어, 그 데이터는 각각의 선수들이 얼마나 많이 달렸고, 얼마나 오랫동안 공을 갖고 있었는지에 관한 정보를 포함했다.

27 이 데이터베이스의 도움으로, 독일 국가 대표 축구팀은 경기력을 향상할 수 있었고, 2014년 월드컵에서 우승할 수 있었다.

범죄 예방

28 빅데이터 덕분에 경찰은 이제 범죄가 발생하기 전에 그 범죄를 예측할 수 있다.

29 범죄의 유형, 시간 및 장소에 관한 빅데이터 분석을 통해, 경찰은 범죄 다발 지역의 지도를 만들 수 있다.

30 이 지도는 범죄가 언제, 어디에서 가장 발생할 것 같은지 알려 준다.

31 경찰은 이 지도가 예측하는 지역과 시간대에 집중함으로써 추가 범죄를 예방할 수 있다.

32 빅데이터는 이미 세계를 크게 변화시켰다.

33 그러면 빅데이터 산업은 여기에서부터 어디로 가게 될까?

34 누구도 확실히 알지는 못하지만, 전문가들은 빅데이터가 우리 삶에서 더욱 더 중요한 역할을 할 것이라는 데에는 동의한다.

• 우리말과 의미가 같도록 교과서 본문의 문장을 완성하시오.

STEP A

01 Have you ever visited an online bookstore and _____ _____ _____ the books that the store _____ _____ you?

01 당신은 온라인 서점을 방문해서 그 서점이 당신에게 추천한 책들을 보고 놀란 적이 있는가?

02 Many of them _____ _____ to you.

02 그 책들 중 다수가 당신에게 흥미로워 보였다.

03 So how did the bookstore know _____ _____ _____?

03 그러면 그 서점은 당신이 무엇을 좋아하는지 어떻게 알았을까?

04 This is all possible _____ _____ big data.

04 이것은 모두 빅데이터 때문에 가능하다.

05 Big data is _____ _____ that are very big and _____.

05 빅데이터는 매우 크고 복잡한 데이터의 집합이다.

06 _____ information and communication technology develops, the amount of data we have is getting _____ greater than before.

06 정보 통신 기술이 발달함에 따라 우리가 갖고 있는 데이터의 양이 이전보다 훨씬 더 많아지고 있다.

07 This is mainly _____ almost everything that we do online _____ _____ _____.

07 이것의 주된 이유는 우리가 온라인상에서 하는 거의 모든 것들이 흔적을 남기기 때문이다.

08 _____ _____, the photos you upload on your blog and the _____ of your _____ at online stores are all part of big data.

08 예를 들어, 당신이 블로그에 올린 사진들과 온라인 상점에서의 구매 기록들이 모두 빅데이터의 일부이다.

09 Simply _____ data, however, is _____ _____.

09 하지만 단순히 데이터를 수집하는 것만으로는 충분하지 않다.

10 Big data has to _____ _____, and this _____ _____ by big data experts.

10 빅데이터는 분석되어야 하는데, 이것은 빅데이터 전문가들에 의해서 이루어진다.

11 _____ various methods, experts _____ big data and _____ meaningful results from it.

11 전문가들은 다양한 방법들을 사용하여 빅데이터를 분석하고, 그것으로부터 의미 있는 결과들을 도출한다.

12 These results then can _____ _____ _____ make decisions or to predict the future.

12 그런 다음, 이런 결과들은 의사결정을 하거나 미래를 예측하는 데 사용될 수 있다.

13 Big data _____ _____ almost all parts of our lives.

13 빅데이터는 우리 삶의 거의 모든 부분에 영향을 미치고 있다.

14 It helps companies _____ their customers' _____ better and helps them sell more products.

14 그것은 회사들이 소비자들이 필요로 하는 것을 더 잘 이해하고 더 많은 상품을 팔도록 도와준다.

15 It _____ _____ _____ heavy traffic.

15 그것은 사람들이 교통 체증을 피하도록 도와준다.

16 Its _____ are _____, and here are some interesting examples.

16 그것의 쓰임은 끝이 없는데, 여기 몇 가지 흥미로운 예들이 있다.

17 Did you know that health professionals can now forecast a _____ just _____ weather experts _____ _____ _____?

18 This is possible _____ _____ big data.

19 For example, when the flu season _____, people _____ _____ more _____ medicine.

20 They will also search online about flu _____ more.

21 If this kind of data _____ _____ wisely, the spread of the flu can _____ _____.

22 _____ _____ a sports fan?

23 Well, big data is improving the _____ of players, _____ sports more _____.

24 A famous _____ is Germany's _____ soccer team.

25 The team built a database _____ _____ and _____ a huge amount of data on players.

26 For example, the data included information about _____ _____ each player ran and _____ _____ he had the ball.

27 _____ _____ _____ _____ this database, Germany's national soccer team _____ _____ _____ improve its performance and win the 2014 World Cup.

28 Thanks to big data, police can now _____ _____ before it happens.

29 _____ _____ _____ _____ big data about the type, time and place of crime, police can make a map of crime _____ _____.

30 This map identifies when and where crime _____ _____ _____ _____ happen.

31 Police can _____ further crime _____ _____ _____ the areas and the times this map predicts.

32 Big data _____ already _____ the world greatly.

33 So where will the big data industry go _____ _____?

34 Nobody knows _____ _____, but experts agree that big data will play a more and more _____ _____ in our lives.

17 당신은 날씨 전문가들이 날씨를 예측하는 것과 같이 현재 건강 전문가들이 질병을 예측할 수 있다는 것을 알고 있었는가?

18 이것은 빅데이터 덕분에 가능하다.

19 예를 들어, 독감의 계절이 오면 사람들은 독감 약을 더 많이 구입할 것이다.

20 그들은 또한 온라인상에서 독감 증상에 대해 더 많이 검색해 볼 것이다.

21 이런 종류의 데이터가 현명하게 분석된다면, 독감의 확산은 예측될 수 있다.

22 당신은 스포츠 팬인가?

23 빅데이터는 스포츠를 더 흥미진진하게 만들면서 선수들의 경기력을 향상하고 있다.

24 한 유명한 사례가 독일 국가 대표 축구팀이다.

25 그 팀은 선수들에 관한 엄청난 양의 데이터를 모으고 분석함으로써 데이터베이스를 구축했다.

26 예를 들어, 그 데이터는 각각의 선수들이 얼마나 많이 달렸고, 얼마나 오랫동안 공을 갖고 있었는지에 관한 정보를 포함했다.

27 이 데이터베이스의 도움으로, 독일 국가 대표 축구팀은 경기력을 향상할 수 있었고, 2014년 월드컵에서 우승할 수 있었다.

28 빅데이터 덕분에 경찰은 이제 범죄가 발생하기 전에 그 범죄를 예측할 수 있다.

29 범죄의 유형, 시간 및 장소에 관한 빅데이터 분석을 통해, 경찰은 범죄 다발 지역의 지도를 만들 수 있다.

30 이 지도는 범죄가 언제, 어디에서 가장 발생할 것 같은지 알려 준다.

31 경찰은 이 지도가 예측하는 지역과 시간대에 집중함으로써 추가 범죄를 예방할 수 있다.

32 빅데이터는 이미 세계를 크게 변화시켰다.

33 그러면 빅데이터 산업은 여기에서부터 어디로 가게 될까?

34 누구도 확실히 알지는 못하지만, 전문가들은 빅데이터가 우리 삶에서 더욱 더 중요한 역할을 할 것이라는 데에는 동의한다.

STEP A

01 Have you ever visited an online bookstore and (surprised / been surprised) by the books that the store recommended for you?

02 Many of them looked (interesting / interestingly) to you.

03 So how did the bookstore know (that / what) you liked?

04 This is all possible (because / because of) big data.

05 Big data is data sets (that / what) are very big and complex.

06 As information and communication technology develops, the amount of data we have is getting (very / much) greater than before.

07 This is mainly because almost everything that we do online (leave / leaves) a trace.

08 (However / For example), the photos you upload on your blog and the records of your purchases at online stores are all part of big data.

09 Simply collecting data, however, (is / are) not enough.

10 Big data has to be analyzed, and this is done (by / of) big data experts.

11 (Used / Using) various methods, experts analyze big data and draw meaningful results from it.

12 These results then can be (used / using) to make decisions or to predict the future.

13 Big data is (influencing / influenced) almost all parts of our lives.

14 It helps companies understand their customers' needs better and helps them (sell / selling) more products.

15 It helps people (avoid / protect) heavy traffic.

16 Its uses (is / are) endless, and here are some interesting examples.

17 Did you know that health professionals can now forecast a disease just (as / because) weather experts forecast the weather?

18   This is possible thanks (to / for) big data.

19   For example, when the flu season (comes / will come), people will buy more flu medicine.

20   They will also search online about flu symptoms (less / more).

21   (If / Although) this kind of data is analyzed wisely, the spread of the flu can be predicted.

22   Are you a sports (fan / fans)?

23   Well, big data is improving the performance of players, (makes / making) sports more exciting.

24   A famous example is Germany's (nation / national) soccer team.

25   The team built a database (by / as) collecting and analyzing a huge amount of data on players.

26   For example, the data included information about how much each player ran and how long (he had / did he have) the ball.

27   With the help of this database, Germany's national soccer team was able to improve its performance and (win / winning) the 2014 World Cup.

28   Thanks to big data, police can now predict crime (before / after) it happens.

29   (On / Through) the analysis of big data about the type, time and place of crime, police can make a map of crime hot spots.

30   This map identifies when and where crime is most (like / likely) to happen.

31   Police can prevent further crime by (focus / focusing) on the areas and the times this map predicts.

32   Big data has already (changed / changing) the world greatly.

33   So where will the big data industry go (to / from) here?

34   Nobody (know / knows) for sure, but experts agree that big data will play a more and more important role in our lives.

R Reading

틀린 문장 고치기

• 밑줄 친 부분이 내용이나 어법상 올바르면 ○에, 틀리면 ×에 동그라미 하고 틀린 부분을 바르게 고쳐 쓰시오.

STEP A

01 Have you ever visited an online bookstore and <u>be surprised by</u> the books that the store recommended for you? ○ ×

02 Many of them looked <u>boring</u> to you. ○ ×

03 So how did the bookstore know <u>what you liked</u>? ○ ×

04 This is all possible <u>because of</u> big data. ○ ×

05 Big data is data sets that <u>is</u> very big and complex. ○ ×

06 As information and communication technology develops, the amount of data we have is getting much <u>great</u> than before. ○ ×

07 This is mainly because almost everything <u>that</u> we do online leaves a trace. ○ ×

08 For example, the photos you upload on your blog and the records of your purchases at online stores <u>is</u> all part of big data. ○ ×

09 Simply <u>collecting</u> data, however, is not enough. ○ ×

10 Big data has to be analyzed, and this <u>is done</u> by big data experts. ○ ×

11 <u>Using various methods</u>, experts analyze big data and draw meaningful results from it. ○ ×

12 These results then can be <u>used making</u> decisions or to predict the future. ○ ×

13 Big data <u>is influencing</u> almost all parts of our lives. ○ ×

14 It <u>helps companies understand</u> their customers' needs better and helps them sell more products. ○ ×

15 It helps people <u>avoiding</u> heavy traffic. ○ ×

16 Its uses are <u>endless</u>, and here are some interesting examples. ○ ×

17 Did you know that health professionals can now forecast a disease <u>just as</u> weather experts forecast the weather? ○ ×

18   This is possible <u>thanks to</u> big data.   ○ ✕

19   For example, <u>although</u> the flu season comes, people will buy more flu medicine.   ○ ✕

20   They will also search online about <u>flu symptoms</u> more.   ○ ✕

21   If this kind of data is analyzed wisely, the spread of the flu can <u>predict</u>.   ○ ✕

22   <u>Are you</u> a sports fan?   ○ ✕

23   Well, big data is improving the performance of players, making sports <u>more excited</u>. ○ ✕

24   A famous example <u>is</u> Germany's national soccer team.   ○ ✕

25   The team built a database by <u>collect</u> and analyzing a huge amount of data on players. ○ ✕

26   For example, the data included information about <u>how much each player ran</u> and
      how long he had the ball.   ○ ✕

27   With the help of this database, Germany's national soccer team was able <u>improving</u>
      its performance and win the 2014 World Cup.   ○ ✕

28   Thanks to big data, police can now predict crime before it <u>happens</u>.   ○ ✕

29   Through the <u>analyze</u> of big data about the type, time and place of crime, police can
      make a map of crime hot spot.   ○ ✕

30   This map identifies when and where crime <u>is most likely to happen</u>.   ○ ✕

31   Police can prevent further crime by focusing <u>to</u> the areas and the times this map
      predicts.   ○ ✕

32   Big data <u>has been</u> already changed the world greatly.   ○ ✕

33   So where will the big data industry <u>go from</u> here?   ○ ✕

34   Nobody knows for sure, but experts agree that big data will play a
      <u>more and more important</u> role in our lives.   ○ ✕

배열로 문장 완성하기

01 당신은 온라인 서점을 방문해서 그 서점이 당신에게 추천한 책들을 보고 놀란 적이 있는가? (been surprised / recommended / and / an online bookstore / have you / that / for you / the store / ever visited / by the books)

>

02 그 책들 중 다수가 당신에게 흥미로워 보였다. (interesting / many of them / to you / looked)

>

03 그러면 그 서점은 당신이 무엇을 좋아하는지 어떻게 알았을까? (did / what / the bookstore / so / liked / how / you / know)

>

04 이것은 모두 빅데이터 때문에 가능하다. (all possible / this / big data / is / because of)

>

05 빅데이터는 매우 크고 복잡한 데이터의 집합이다. (that / very big and complex / is / are / big data / data sets)

>

06 정보 통신 기술이 발달함에 따라 우리가 갖고 있는 데이터의 양이 이전보다 훨씬 더 많아지고 있다. (the amount of data / than before / as / we / develops / information and communication technology / have / much greater / is getting)

>

07 이것의 주된 이유는 우리가 온라인상에서 하는 거의 모든 것들이 흔적을 남기기 때문이다.
(almost everything / a trace / is / do online / mainly because / this / that / leaves / we)

>

08 예를 들어, 당신이 블로그에 올린 사진들과 온라인 상점에서의 구매 기록들이 모두 빅데이터의 일부이다. (on your blog / all part of big data / and / at online stores / the records of / the photos / for example / you upload / your purchases / are)

>

09 하지만 단순히 데이터를 수집하는 것만으로는 충분하지 않다. (collecting data / not enough / simply / is / however)

>

10 빅데이터는 분석되어야 하는데, 이것은 빅데이터 전문가들에 의해서 이루어진다.
(be analyzed / and / big data / by big data experts / has to / is done / this)

>

11 전문가들은 다양한 방법들을 사용하여 빅데이터를 분석하고, 그것으로부터 의미 있는 결과들을 도출한다.
(big data / analyze / various methods / and / meaningful results / using / from it / draw / experts)

>

12 그런 다음, 이런 결과들은 의사결정을 하거나 미래를 예측하는 데 사용될 수 있다.
(then can be used / the future / or / to make / these results / decisions / to predict)

>

13 빅데이터는 우리 삶의 거의 모든 부분에 영향을 미치고 있다. (almost / our lives / influencing / big data / all parts of / is)

>

14 그것은 회사들이 소비자들이 필요로 하는 것을 더 잘 이해하고 더 많은 상품을 팔도록 도와준다.
(their customers' needs / more products / helps them / it / sell / helps / understand / better / companies / and)

>

15 그것은 사람들이 교통 체증을 피하도록 도와준다. (people / it / heavy traffic / helps / avoid)

>

16 그것의 쓰임은 끝이 없는데, 여기 몇 가지 흥미로운 예들이 있다.
(and / some / its / are endless / interesting examples / here are / uses)

>

17 당신은 날씨 전문가들이 날씨를 예측하는 것과 같이 현재 건강 전문가들이 질병을 예측할 수 있다는 것을 알고 있었는가?
(forecast / just as / can now / did you know / forecast the weather / weather experts / health professionals / that / a disease)

>

18 이것은 빅데이터 덕분에 가능하다. (thanks to / this / possible / big data / is)

>

19 예를 들어, 독감의 계절이 오면 사람들은 독감 약을 더 많이 구입할 것이다.
(will / people / comes / more flu medicine / for example / when / buy / the flu season)

>

20 그들은 또한 온라인상에서 독감 증상에 대해 더 많이 검색해 볼 것이다.
(online / they / also search / flu symptoms more / will / about)

>

21 이런 종류의 데이터가 현명하게 분석된다면, 독감의 확산은 예측될 수 있다.
(wisely / can / analyzed / if / the spread of the flu / this kind of data / be predicted / is)

>

22 당신은 스포츠 팬인가? (a sports fan / you / are)

>

23 빅데이터는 스포츠를 더 흥미진진하게 만들면서 선수들의 경기력을 향상하고 있다.
(improving / is / making / the performance of players / sports / well, big data / more exciting)

>

24 한 유명한 사례가 독일 국가 대표 축구팀이다. (Germany's / a famous example / national soccer team / is)

>

25 그 팀은 선수들에 관한 엄청난 양의 데이터를 모으고 분석함으로써 데이터베이스를 구축했다.
(by collecting / on players / a huge amount of / analyzing / built / and / the team / data / a database)

>

26 예를 들어, 그 데이터는 각각의 선수들이 얼마나 많이 달렸고, 얼마나 오랫동안 공을 갖고 있었는지에 관한 정보를 포함했다. (information about / he had / ran / the data / for example / how much / how long / the ball / each player / included / and)

>

27 이 데이터베이스의 도움으로, 독일 국가 대표 축구팀은 경기력을 향상할 수 있었고, 2014년 월드컵에서 우승할 수 있었다. (was able to / and / Germany's national soccer team / win / improve / with the help of this database / its performance / the 2014 World Cup)

>

28 빅데이터 덕분에 경찰은 이제 범죄가 발생하기 전에 그 범죄를 예측할 수 있다.
(predict / thanks to / crime / it happens / big data / before / can now / police)

>

29 범죄의 유형, 시간 및 장소에 관한 빅데이터 분석을 통해, 경찰은 범죄 다발 지역의 지도를 만들 수 있다. (the type, time and place of crime / through / police / make / the analysis of big data / a map of / about / can / crime hot spots)

>

30 이 지도는 범죄가 언제, 어디서 가장 발생할 것 같은지 알려 준다.
(crime / this map / most likely / when and where / is / to happen / identifies)

>

31 경찰은 이 지도가 예측하는 지역과 시간대에 집중함으로써 추가 범죄를 예방할 수 있다.
(this map / police / further crime / can / by focusing on / predicts / prevent / the areas and the times)

>

32 빅데이터는 이미 세계를 크게 변화시켰다. (already changed / big data / the world / has / greatly)

>

33 그러면 빅데이터 산업은 여기에서부터 어디로 가게 될까? (the big data industry / so / from here / will / where / go)

>

34 누구도 확실히 알지는 못하지만, 전문가들은 빅데이터가 우리 삶에서 더욱 더 중요한 역할을 할 것이라는 데에는 동의한다. (a more and more / agree that / nobody / important role / for sure / in our lives / knows / but / will / experts / big data / play)

>

01 다음 글의 빈칸에 들어갈 말로 알맞은 것은?

> Have you ever visited an online bookstore and been surprised by the books that the store recommended for you? Many of them looked interesting to you. So how did the bookstore know what you liked? This is all possible _____ big data.

① such as
② thanks for
③ instead of
④ because of
⑤ in addition to

[02~06] 다음 글을 읽고, 물음에 답하시오.

> Big data is data sets that are very big and complex. ⓐAs information and communication technology develops, the amount of data we have is getting (A) much / very greater than before. This is mainly because almost everything that we do online leaves a trace. ___ⓑ___, the photos you upload on your blog and the records of your purchases at online stores are all part of big data.
>
> Simply collecting data, however, is not enough. Big data has to be analyzed, and this is (B) doing / done by big data experts. (C) Using / Used various methods, experts analyze big data and draw meaningful results from it. These results then can be used to make decisions or to predict the future.

02 윗글의 밑줄 친 ⓐAs와 쓰임이 같은 것은?

① She works there as a doctor.
② Please do the work as I asked yesterday.
③ I couldn't take the class as I arrived late.
④ As he grew older, he became even quieter.
⑤ As I was playing a game, Mom came home.

03 윗글의 흐름상 빈칸 ⓑ에 들어갈 말로 알맞은 것은?

① However
② In addition
③ In the end
④ In contrast
⑤ For example

04 윗글 (A)~(C)의 각 네모 안에 주어진 말 중 어법상 올바른 것끼리 짝지어진 것은?

	(A)		(B)		(C)
①	much	···	doing	···	Used
②	much	···	done	···	Using
③	much	···	done	···	Used
④	very	···	done	···	Used
⑤	very	···	doing	···	Using

05 윗글의 내용과 일치하지 <u>않는</u> 것은?

① We had more data in the past than now.
② What we do online can be part of big data.
③ The job of big data experts is to analyze big data.
④ Big data experts draw results from big data.
⑤ Meaningful results from big data can help people make decisions.

06 다음 영영풀이에 해당하는 단어를 윗글에서 찾아 쓰시오.

> to say that something is going to happen

→ _____

[07~10] 다음 글을 읽고, 물음에 답하시오.

Big data is ①influencing almost all parts of our lives. It helps companies understand their customers' needs better and helps ⓐthem sell more products. ⓑIt helps people ②avoid heavy traffic. Its uses are endless, and here are some interesting examples.

(A) This is possible thanks to big data. For example, when the flu season comes, people ③will buy more flu medicine. They will also search online about flu symptoms more.

(B) Did you know that health professionals can now forecast a disease just ④as weather experts forecast the weather?

(C) If this kind of data is analyzed wisely, the spread of the flu can ⑤predict.

07 자연스러운 글이 되도록 (A)~(C)를 바르게 배열한 것은?

① (A) – (B) – (C)　　　② (B) – (A) – (C)
③ (B) – (C) – (A)　　　④ (C) – (A) – (B)
⑤ (C) – (B) – (A)

08 윗글의 밑줄 친 ①~⑤ 중 어법상 틀린 것을 바르게 고친 것은?

① → influenced　　　② → avoiding
③ → bought　　　④ → so
⑤ → be predicted

09 윗글의 밑줄 친 ⓐthem과 ⓑIt이 가리키는 것이 순서대로 바르게 짝지어진 것은?

① our lives – big data
② our lives – company
③ companies – big data
④ companies – company
⑤ customers – big data

고/난도
10 윗글을 읽고 답할 수 없는 질문은?

① How does big data help companies?
② Is there a limit to the uses of big data?
③ What can health professionals now forecast?
④ How do weather experts analyze big data?
⑤ What will people do when the flu season comes?

[11~13] 다음 글을 읽고, 물음에 답하시오.

Are you a sports fan? (①) Well, big data is improving the performance of players, ___ⓐ___ sports more exciting. (②) A famous example is Germany's national soccer team. (③) The team built a database ___ⓑ___ collecting and analyzing a huge amount of data on players. (④) ___ⓒ___ the help of this database, Germany's national soccer team was able to improve its performance and win the 2014 World Cup. (⑤)

11 윗글의 ①~⑤ 중 주어진 문장이 들어갈 위치로 알맞은 것은?

For example, the data included information about how much each player ran and how long he had the ball.

①　　　②　　　③　　　④　　　⑤

12 윗글의 빈칸 ⓐ에 들어갈 make의 형태로 알맞은 것은?

① make　　　② made　　　③ makes
④ making　　　⑤ to make

13 윗글의 빈칸 ⓑ와 ⓒ에 들어갈 말이 순서대로 바르게 짝지어진 것은?

① by – For　　② by – With　　③ for – For
④ for – With　　⑤ on – For

[14~16] 다음 글을 읽고, 물음에 답하시오.

ⓐThanks to big data, police can now ＿＿(A)＿＿ crime before it happens. Through the analysis of big data about the type, time and place of crime, police can make a map of crime hot spots. This map identifies when and where crime ⓑis most likely to happen. Police can ＿＿(B)＿＿ further crime ⓒby focusing on the areas and the times this map predicts.

Big data has already changed the world greatly. So where will the big data industry go from here? Nobody knows ⓓfor sure, but experts agree that big data will ⓔplay a more and more important role in our lives.

14 윗글의 밑줄 친 ⓐ~ⓔ의 우리말 의미가 알맞지 않은 것은?

① ⓐ: ~ 덕분에　　② ⓑ: ~을 가장 좋아하다
③ ⓒ: ~에 집중함으로써　④ ⓓ: 확실히
⑤ ⓔ: 더욱 더 중요한 역할을 하다

15 윗글의 빈칸 (A)와 (B)에 들어갈 말이 순서대로 바르게 짝지어진 것은?

① change – prevent　② analyze – cause
③ predict – cause　④ predict – prevent
⑤ improve – predict

16 윗글의 내용을 잘못 이해한 사람끼리 짝지어진 것은?

- 유나: 경찰은 빅데이터를 분석해서 범죄 다발 지역 지도를 만들 수 있어.
- 지민: 범죄 다발 지역 지도로는 이미 발생한 범죄에 대한 정보만 알 수 있어.
- 소미: 빅데이터는 범죄 발생 후 범죄를 처리하는 과정에서 주로 사용돼.
- 호진: 빅데이터는 세상을 크게 변화시켰어.

① 유나, 지민　② 유나, 호진　③ 지민, 소미
④ 지민, 호진　⑤ 소미, 호진

서술형

[17~19] 다음 글을 읽고, 물음에 답하시오.

Have you ever visited an online bookstore and been ⓐsurprised by the books that the store recommended for you? Many of them looked ⓑinteresting to you. So how did the bookstore know what you liked? This is all possible ⓒbecause big data.

(A)빅데이터는 매우 크고 복잡한 데이터의 집합이다. ⓓAs information and communication technology develops, the amount of data we have is getting much ⓔgreater than before. (B)This is mainly because almost everything that we do online leaves a trace. For example, the photos you upload on your blog and the records of your purchases at online stores are all part of big data.

17 윗글의 밑줄 친 우리말 (A)와 의미가 같도록 괄호 안의 표현을 바르게 배열하여 쓰시오.

→ ＿＿＿＿＿＿＿＿＿＿＿＿＿＿＿＿

(data sets, that, and, very, big data, are, complex, is, big)

18 윗글의 밑줄 친 ⓐ~ⓔ 중 어법상 틀린 것을 골라 기호를 쓰고 바르게 고쳐 쓴 후, 틀린 이유를 우리말로 쓰시오.

(1) 틀린 부분: (　　) → ＿＿＿＿＿＿＿＿＿

(2) 틀린 이유: ＿＿＿＿＿＿＿＿＿＿＿

＿＿＿＿＿＿＿＿＿＿＿＿＿＿＿＿＿

19 윗글의 밑줄 친 (B)This가 의미하는 것을 우리말로 쓰시오.

＿＿＿＿＿＿＿＿＿＿＿＿＿＿＿＿＿

[20~21] 다음 글을 읽고, 물음에 답하시오.

Simply collecting data, however, is not enough. Big data has to ⓐ analyze, and this is done by big data experts. Using various methods, experts analyze big data and draw meaningful results from it. These results then can be used ⓑ make decisions or to predict the future.

20 윗글의 밑줄 친 ⓐanalyze와 ⓑmake의 어법상 올바른 형태를 각각 쓰시오.

ⓐ _____ ⓑ _____

21 윗글의 내용과 일치하도록 다음 질문에 대한 답을 완전한 영어 문장으로 쓰시오.

Q: What do big data experts do?
A: _____

[22~23] 다음 글을 읽고, 물음에 답하시오.

Did you know ____ⓐ____ health professionals can now forecast a disease just ____ⓑ____ weather experts forecast the weather? This is possible thanks to big data. For example, when the flu season comes, people will buy more flu medicine. They will also search online about flu symptoms more. ____ⓒ____ this kind of data is analyzed wisely, the spread of the flu can be predicted.

22 윗글의 빈칸 ⓐ~ⓒ에 알맞은 접속사를 [보기]에서 골라 쓰시오. (단, 중복 사용 불가)

> [보기] as   if   until   that   though

ⓐ _____ ⓑ _____ ⓒ _____

23 윗글의 내용과 일치하도록 할 때, 다음 문장에서 틀린 부분을 찾아 바르게 고쳐 쓰시오.

Big data can help health professionals treat a disease.

_____ → _____

[24~25] 다음 글을 읽고, 물음에 답하시오.

Are you a sports fan? Well, ⓐ빅데이터는 스포츠를 더 흥미진진하게 만들면서 선수들의 경기력을 향상하고 있다. A famous example is Germany's national soccer team. The team built a database by collecting and analyzing a huge amount of data on players. For example, the data included information about how much each player ran and how long he had the ball. With the help of this database, Germany's national soccer team was able to improve its performance and win the 2014 World Cup.

24 윗글의 밑줄 친 우리말 ⓐ와 의미가 같도록 빈칸에 알맞은 말을 [조건]에 맞게 쓰시오.

> [조건] 1. 분사구문과 비교급을 사용할 것
>   2. make와 exciting을 어법에 맞게 사용할 것
>   3. 4단어로 쓸 것

→ big data is improving the performance of players, _____

25 윗글을 다음과 같이 요약할 때, 빈칸에 알맞은 말을 쓰시오.

Thanks to big data on _____, Germany's national soccer team could _____ its performance and _____ the 2014 World Cup.

Listen and Talk D

교과서 121쪽

❶Let me tell you how to use a drink machine. First, insert money into the machine. Then, choose ❷the drink you want. Last, ❸take the drink out of the machine. It's easy.

음료 자판기 사용하는 법을 알려 드리겠습니다. 먼저, 기계에 돈을 넣으세요. 그런 다음, 원하는 음료를 고르세요. 마지막으로, 기계에서 음료를 꺼내세요. 간단하죠.

❶ Let me tell you ~.는 '너에게 ~을 말해(알려) 줄게.'라는 의미로, 「사역동사(let)+목적어(me)+동사원형(tell) ~」 형태의 5형식 문장이다. you는 수여동사 tell의 간접목적어, how to use a drink machine은 직접목적어로 쓰였다.

❷ 목적격 관계대명사 which 또는 that이 생략된 관계대명사절인 you want가 선행사 the drink를 수식하는 형태이다.

❸ take A out of B: A를 B에서 꺼내다

Think and Write

교과서 132쪽

Teens' Free Time Activities

We asked 100 teenagers about their free time activities. ❶The results show that the free time activity the teenagers want to do the most is traveling. 34% said that they want to travel in their free time. ❷However, the free time activity they actually do the most is watching TV. 39% said that they watch TV in their free time. ❸Looking at the results, we see that there is a big gap between what the teenagers want to do and what they actually do in their free time.

청소년들의 여가 시간 활동들

우리는 100명의 청소년들에게 그들의 여가 시간 활동에 대해 질문했습니다. 그 결과 청소년들이 가장 하고 싶어 하는 여가 시간 활동은 여행인 것으로 보입니다. 34%가 여가 시간에 여행을 하고 싶다고 말했습니다. 하지만, 그들이 실제로 가장 많이 하는 여가 시간 활동은 TV 시청입니다. 39%가 여가 시간에 TV를 시청한다고 말했습니다. 이 결과를 보면, 우리는 청소년들이 여가 시간에 하고 싶어 하는 것과 여가 시간에 실제로 하는 것 사이에 큰 차이가 있다는 것을 알 수 있습니다.

❶ that절이 동사 show의 목적어 역할을 하며, 목적격 관계대명사가 생략된 관계대명사절인 the teenagers want to do the most가 선행사 the free time activity를 수식하고 있다.

❷ 설문 조사에서 가장 하고 싶어 하는 여가 활동으로 답한 것과 실제로 가장 많이 하는 여가 활동이 다르다는 상반된 내용이 이어지므로, '그러나, 하지만'이라는 뜻의 연결어 However가 쓰였다.

❸ '~하면'이라는 뜻으로 조건의 의미를 나타내는 분사구문으로, 부사절 If we look at the results로 바꿔 쓸 수 있다.

Team Project

교과서 133쪽

❶Based on our survey, we chose Gyeongju. Ten students think that activities are the most important when choosing a field trip place. After we ❷searched for some data online, we found out that ❸there are many things to see and do in Gyeongju.

설문 조사를 바탕으로, 우리는 경주를 골랐습니다. 10명의 학급 친구들이 졸업 여행지를 고를 때 활동이 가장 중요하다고 생각합니다. 온라인으로 자료를 찾아본 후, 우리는 경주에 볼 것과 할 것이 많이 있다는 것을 알게 되었습니다.

❶ based on: ~에 근거하여

❷ search for: ~을 찾다

❸ to see and do는 many things를 수식하는 형용사적 용법의 to부정사로, see와 do가 등위접속사 and로 연결되어 있다.

[01~02] 다음 글을 읽고, 물음에 답하시오.

(A)음료 자판기 사용하는 법을 알려 드리겠습니다. First, insert money into the machine. ____ⓐ____, choose the drink you want. ____ⓑ____, take the drink out of the machine. It's easy.

01 윗글의 밑줄 친 우리말 (A)와 의미가 같도록 주어진 표현을 바르게 배열하여 문장을 쓰시오.

→ _____

(use, me, how, a drink machine, tell, you, to, let)

02 윗글의 빈칸 ⓐ와 ⓑ에 들어갈 말이 순서대로 바르게 짝지어진 것은?

① Two – Three
② Then – Second
③ Then – Last
④ Second – Three
⑤ Second – First

[03~05] 다음 글을 읽고, 물음에 답하시오.

We asked 100 teenagers about their free time activities. The results show that the free time activity the teenagers want to do the most is traveling. 34% said that they want to travel in their free time. ____ⓐ____, the free time activity they actually do the most is watching TV. 39% said that they watch TV in their free time. ⓑIf we look at the results, we see that there is a big gap between what the teenagers want to do and what they actually do in their free time.

03 윗글의 흐름상 빈칸 ⓐ에 들어갈 말로 알맞은 것은?

① Therefore
② However
③ As a result
④ Most of all
⑤ For example

04 윗글의 밑줄 친 ⓑ를 분사구문으로 바꿔 쓰시오.

→ _____ _____ _____ _____

05 윗글의 내용과 일치하도록 빈칸에 알맞은 말을 쓰시오.

According to the teenagers' answers about their _____ _____ _____, what they want to do the most is _____, but what they actually do the most is _____ _____.

[06~07] 다음 글을 읽고, 물음에 답하시오.

____ⓐ____ on our survey, we ____ⓑ____ Gyeongju. Ten students ____ⓒ____ that activities are the most important when choosing a field trip place. After we ____ⓓ____ for some data online, we found out that there are many things (A)see and ____ⓔ____ in Gyeongju.

06 윗글의 흐름상 빈칸 ⓐ~ⓔ에 들어갈 말로 알맞지 <u>않은</u> 것은?

① ⓐ: Based
② ⓑ: chose
③ ⓒ: think
④ ⓓ: cared
⑤ ⓔ: do

07 윗글의 밑줄 친 (A)see의 형태로 알맞은 것은?

① seen
② saw
③ to see
④ seeing
⑤ have seen

 **Words**

고득점 맞기

01 다음 영영풀이에 해당하는 단어가 순서대로 바르게 짝지어진 것은?

> • an action that the law does not allow
> • to realize who someone is or what something is

① trace – draw   ② purchase – insert
③ crime – identify   ④ distance – predict
⑤ industry – upload

02 다음 빈칸에 들어갈 말로 알맞은 것은?

> Wearing medical masks can help prevent the _____ of the flu.

① method   ② spread   ③ society
④ forecast   ⑤ amount

[03~04] 다음 빈칸에 공통으로 들어갈 말로 알맞은 것을 고르시오.

03

> • They are looking for ways to improve their _____ at work.
> • You're not allowed to use your cell phone during the _____.

① gap   ② analysis   ③ symptom
④ influence   ⑤ performance

04

> • Something is likely _____ happen.
> • Thanks _____ John and his team, we could finish the project on time.

① in   ② to   ③ at
④ on   ⑤ for

05 다음 중 짝지어진 단어들의 관계가 같지 <u>않은</u> 것은? 고/산도

① lock : unlock = simple : complex
② help : helpful = nation : national
③ wise : wisely = possible : possibly
④ regular : regularly = meaning : meaningful
⑤ disease : illness = complex : complicated

06 다음 중 밑줄 친 부분의 우리말 의미가 알맞지 <u>않은</u> 것은?

① <u>Prevention</u> is always better than a cure. (예방)
② May is a very <u>meaningful</u> month in Korea.
     (의미 있는)
③ Mike makes decisions <u>based on</u> his emotions.
     (~에 근거하여)
④ I improved my English pronunciation <u>thanks to</u> Jane. (~에 감사하여)
⑤ The subway is a safe and convenient <u>method</u> of transportation. (교통수단)

07 다음 영영풀이에 해당하는 단어를 빈칸에 쓰시오.

> *n.* something that shows you may have a particular illness

> I think you have some early _____(e)s of a cold.

08 Which can replace the underlined part of the sentence?

> Do you think that it is possible to <u>predict</u> an upcoming earthquake?

① draw   ② leave   ③ develop
④ analyze   ⑤ forecast

09 다음 중 밑줄 친 부분의 쓰임이 어색한 것은?

① Press the button and <u>insert</u> your card here.
② There are several <u>national</u> museums in Seoul.
③ If you need <u>further</u> information, you can call this center.
④ The issue is so <u>complex</u> that everyone can understand it.
⑤ The more science <u>develops</u>, the more convenient the world becomes.

10 다음 우리말과 의미가 같도록 빈칸에 알맞은 말을 쓰시오.

이제부터, 나는 어떤 정크 푸드도 먹지 않겠다.

→ _____ _____ _____, I won't eat any junk food.

11 다음 중 밑줄 친 부분과 바꿔 쓸 수 있는 말로 알맞지 <u>않은</u> 것은?

① They tried their best to <u>avoid</u> mistakes.
  → prevent
② It is the <u>disease</u> that harms your bones.
  → illness
③ He <u>purchased</u> some furniture very cheaply.
  → bought
④ <u>Possibly</u>, he can finish the project by tomorrow.
  → Mainly
⑤ It takes some time to <u>collect</u> all the information.
  → gather

12 다음 빈칸에 들어갈 단어의 영영풀이로 알맞은 것은?

If you practice every day, your cooking skills will _____ quickly.

① to do an action
② to change or affect something
③ to examine something carefully
④ to say that something is going to happen
⑤ to become better or to make something better

13 다음 중 단어와 영영풀이가 바르게 연결되지 <u>않은</u> 것은?

① **analysis**: a way of doing something
② **avoid**: to stay away from someone or something
③ **include**: to contain something as a part of a whole
④ **flu**: an illness that is like a bad cold but can be very serious
⑤ **database**: a large amount of information stored in a computer system

14 다음 중 밑줄 친 leave의 의미가 같은 것끼리 짝지어진 것은?

ⓐ She will <u>leave</u> home at 8 o'clock.
ⓑ The thief didn't <u>leave</u> a single footprint.
ⓒ Why don't you <u>leave</u> some more messages?
ⓓ I'll <u>leave</u> early in the morning to take the first bus.
ⓔ If you <u>leave</u> your name and phone number, you can borrow a bike.

① ⓐ, ⓒ – ⓑ, ⓓ, ⓔ
② ⓐ, ⓓ – ⓑ, ⓒ, ⓔ
③ ⓐ, ⓔ – ⓑ, ⓒ, ⓓ
④ ⓐ, ⓑ, ⓔ – ⓒ, ⓓ
⑤ ⓐ, ⓓ, ⓔ – ⓑ, ⓒ

15 다음 빈칸 ⓐ~ⓓ 중 어느 곳에도 들어갈 수 <u>없는</u> 단어는?

· Music can __ⓐ__ people's feelings.
· What is __ⓑ__ to happen after the story?
· You can __ⓒ__ results from the given data.
· The outdoor activities __ⓓ__ mountain biking and canoeing.

① draw   ② likely   ③ avoid
④ influence   ⑤ include

Listen and Talk

영작하기

• 주어진 우리말과 일치하도록 교과서 대화문을 쓰시오.

STEP
B

Listen and Talk A-1

B: _____

G: _____

_____

B: _____

G: _____

B: _____

해석 교과서 120쪽

B: 실례합니다. 교통 카드에 돈을 충전하는 방법을 알려 주시겠어요?

G: 그럼요. 먼저, 기계에 카드를 넣으세요. 두 번째로, 충전하고 싶은 금액을 선택하세요.

B: 알겠어요.

G: 마지막으로, 기계에 돈을 넣으세요.

B: 간단한 것 같네요. 고맙습니다.

Listen and Talk A-2

B: _____

_____

G: _____

B: _____

G: _____

B: _____

교과서 120쪽

B: 저는 과자를 사고 싶어요. 이 과자 자판기를 어떻게 사용하는지 아세요?

G: 네. 먼저, 원하는 과자를 고르세요.

B: 이미 했어요. 그다음은 뭔가요?

G: 돈을 넣으세요. 그런 다음 과자를 꺼내세요.

B: 알겠어요. 고마워요.

Listen and Talk A-3

G: _____

_____

M: _____

_____

G: _____

M: _____

G: _____

교과서 120쪽

G: 실례합니다. 자전거를 빌리고 싶은데요. 이 앱을 어떻게 사용하는지 알려 주시겠어요?

M: 그럼요. 먼저, 앱에 로그인하세요. 그런 다음 RENT 버튼을 찾아서 터치하세요.

G: 그다음에는 뭘 하죠?

M: 그러면 앱이 자전거 잠금을 해제할 수 있는 번호를 알려 줄 거예요.

G: 고맙습니다. 도와주셔서 정말 감사해요.

Listen and Talk C

G: _____

B: _____

G: _____

B: _____

G: _____

B: _____

G: _____

B: _____

G: _____

B: _____

G: _____

해석   교과서 121쪽

G: 실례합니다만, 이 로봇은 용도가 뭔가요?

B: 아, 그것은 책을 찾아 주는 로봇이에요.

G: 정말요? 어떻게 사용하는지 알려 주시겠어요?

B: 그럼요. 먼저, 도서 대출 카드를 로봇 화면 위에 대세요.

G: 알겠어요.

B: 두 번째로, 당신이 찾고 있는 책의 제목을 입력한 다음 ENTER를 누르세요.

G: 그게 다인가요?

B: 네. 그러면, 로봇이 그 책을 찾아서 안내 데스크로 가져다줄 거예요.

G: 그러면 저는 그냥 안내 데스크로 가서 책을 받을 수 있네요?

B: 그렇습니다. 아주 쉬워요, 그렇지 않아요?

G: 네, 정말 놀랍네요. 고마워요.

Talk and Play

A: _____

B: _____

A: _____

B: _____

A: _____

B: _____

A: _____

교과서 122쪽

A: 너는 차 만드는 방법을 아니?

B: 그럼. 먼저, 컵에 티백을 넣어.

A: 알겠어.

B: 그런 다음, 그 컵에 뜨거운 물을 부어.

A: 그다음엔?

B: 마지막으로, 3분 뒤에 티백을 꺼내.

A: 알겠어. 도와줘서 정말 고마워.

Review - 1

G: _____

B: _____

G: _____

B: _____

G: _____

교과서 134쪽

G: 감자 심는 방법을 알려 주겠니?

B: 그럼. 우선 감자를 작은 조각으로 잘라. 둘째로, 땅에 구멍을 파.

G: 그다음에는?

B: 그런 다음 구멍에 감자 조각들을 넣고 흙으로 구멍을 덮어.

G: 간단한 것 같네. 고마워.

STEP B

01 다음 대화의 빈칸에 들어갈 말로 알맞은 것은?

> A: _____
> B: Sure. First, put a tea bag in a cup. Then, pour hot water in the cup. And after 3 minutes, take the tea bag out.

① Would you like some tea?
② Why don't you have some tea?
③ Do you know how to make tea?
④ Do you want to learn how to make tea?
⑤ Please tell me where I can drink some tea.

02 다음 대화의 빈칸에 들어갈 말로 알맞지 <u>않은</u> 것을 <u>모두</u> 고르면?

> A: Can you tell me how to use this snack machine?
> B: Yeah. First, choose the snack you want. Then, put in the money. Last, take the snack out.
> A: Got it. _____

① Thanks a lot.　　　② It's my pleasure.
③ Don't mention it.　　④ I appreciate your help.
⑤ I can't thank you enough.

03 다음 대화의 밑줄 친 ⓐ~ⓔ 중 흐름상 어색한 것은?

> A: Excuse me. ⓐCan you tell me how to use this machine?
> B: Sure. ⓑFirst, put the paper on the copy machine.
> A: OK.
> B: ⓒLast, choose the paper size and number of the copies.
> A: ⓓAnd then?
> B: Finally, press the START button.
> A: Thank you. ⓔI really appreciate your help.

① ⓐ　　② ⓑ　　③ ⓒ　　④ ⓓ　　⑤ ⓔ

04 Which is the correct order of (A)~(E) to make a natural dialog?

> (A) Then just take your card out.
> (B) Excuse me. I want to return these books. Do you know how to do it?
> (C) What's next?
> (D) I really appreciate your help.
> (E) Sure. It's simple. First, insert the library card into the machine. Second, put the books in this box.

① (A) – (B) – (D) – (C) – (E)
② (B) – (A) – (E) – (C) – (D)
③ (B) – (E) – (C) – (A) – (D)
④ (C) – (B) – (D) – (E) – (A)
⑤ (C) – (D) – (A) – (E) – (B)

[05~06] 다음 대화를 읽고, 물음에 답하시오.

> Girl: Excuse me. I want to rent a bike. Can you tell me _____ⓐ_____?
> Man: Sure. First, log in to the application. Then find the RENT button and touch it.
> Girl: Then what?
> Man: Then the application will give you a number to unlock a bike with.
> Girl: Thank you. I really appreciate your help.

05 위 대화의 빈칸 ⓐ에 들어갈 말로 알맞은 것은?

① how to buy a bike
② where to ride a bike
③ how to use this application
④ how to make an application
⑤ how to get to the bike rental shop

06 위 대화의 내용과 일치하지 <u>않는</u> 것을 <u>모두</u> 고르면?

① The girl wants to rent a bike.
② The man tells the girl how to ride a bike well.
③ The application is used to rent a bike.
④ The man unlocks a bike for the girl.
⑤ The girl thanks the man for his help.

서술형

[07~09] 다음 대화를 읽고, 물음에 답하시오.

Lucy: Excuse me, but what's this robot for?

Seho: Oh, it's a robot that finds books for you.

Lucy: Really? Can you tell me how to use it?

Seho: Sure. First, place your library card on the robot's screen.

Lucy: OK.

Seho: Second, type the title of the book you're looking for and then press ENTER.

Lucy: Is that all?

Seho: Yes. Then, the robot will find the book and take it to the front desk.

Lucy: So I can just go to the front desk and get the book?

Seho: Right. It's so easy, isn't it?

Lucy: Yes, it's really amazing. _____ⓐ_____

07 위 대화의 빈칸 ⓐ에 들어갈 말을 [조건]에 맞게 쓰시오.

> [조건] 1. 감사를 나타낼 것
>   2. I, help를 사용하여 4단어의 문장으로 쓸 것

→ _____

08 위 대화의 내용과 일치하도록 로봇 사용법을 완성하시오.

> 1. Put _____ _____ _____ on the robot's screen.
> 2. _____ _____ _____ of the book you want and then _____ _____.
> 3. Go to _____ _____ _____ and get the book.

09 위 대화의 내용과 일치하도록 다음 질문에 대한 답을 완성하시오.

(1) Where are Lucy and Seho now?

→ They are in the _____.

(2) Where does the robot take the book it finds?

→ It takes it _____ _____ _____
_____.

[10~13] 다음 대화를 읽고, 물음에 답하시오.

Girl: _____ⓐ_____

Boy: Sure. _____ⓑ_____, cut a potato into small pieces.

Girl: OK.

Boy: Then, dig holes in the ground.

Girl: And then?

Boy: _____ⓒ_____, put the potato pieces in the holes.

Girl: Then what?

Boy: Last, cover the holes with dirt.

Girl: I got it. Thank you for your help.

10 위 대화의 빈칸 ⓐ에 들어갈 질문을 괄호 안의 단어를 사용하여 8단어로 쓰시오.

→ _____

(know, plant)

11 위 대화의 빈칸 ⓑ와 ⓒ에 들어갈 알맞은 말을 각각 한 단어로 쓰시오.

ⓑ _____ ⓒ _____

12 According to the dialog above, what does the girl have to do after the first step?

→ She has to _____.

13 위 대화의 내용과 일치하지 <u>않는</u> 문장을 골라 기호를 쓰고, 바르게 고쳐 문장을 다시 쓰시오.

> ⓐ The girl needs to cut a potato into small pieces to plant a potato.
> ⓑ The fourth step of planting a potato is to water the holes.
> ⓒ The girl thanks the boy for helping her.

(   ) → _____

_____

01 다음 빈칸에 들어갈 말이 바르게 짝지어진 것은?

> • _____ to music, he is doing the dishes.
> • _____ in the forest, she saw a squirrel.

① Listen – Walked
② Listening – Walked
③ Listened – To walk
④ Listening – Walking
⑤ Listened – Walking

한 단계 더!

02 다음 빈칸에 공통으로 들어갈 말로 알맞은 것은?

> • He works _____ an assistant cook.
> • Tim didn't come _____ he was too busy.
> • It became more silent _____ it grew darker.

① if
② as
③ when
④ since
⑤ because

한 단계 더!

03 다음 밑줄 친 부분을 분사구문으로 바르게 바꾼 것은?

> <u>Because she wasn't hungry at all</u>, she didn't have lunch.

① Didn't be hungry at all
② Been not hungry at all
③ Not been hungry at all
④ Being not hungry at all
⑤ Not being hungry at all

04 다음 밑줄 친 <u>As</u>와 바꿔 쓸 수 있는 것을 <u>모두</u> 고르면?

> <u>As</u> she had a lot of work to do, she couldn't go out.

① Until
② If
③ Since
④ Because
⑤ That

05 다음 우리말을 영어로 바르게 옮긴 것을 <u>모두</u> 고르면?

> 나는 옛 친구를 봤을 때 기뻐서 소리쳤다.

① Seen my old friend, I shouted with joy.
② Seeing my old friend, I shouted with joy.
③ I seeing my old friend, I shouted with joy.
④ When I saw my old friend, I shouted with joy.
⑤ When I seeing my old friend, I shouted with joy.

06 다음 빈칸에 들어갈 말로 알맞지 <u>않은</u> 것은?

> As she was too tired, _____.

① she went to bed early
② she didn't go swimming
③ she couldn't finish the work
④ she could easily stay up all night
⑤ she canceled an appointment with her friend

07 다음 중 밑줄 친 부분의 쓰임이 나머지와 <u>다른</u> 하나는?

① <u>Eating</u> popcorn, they watched a movie.
② Not <u>feeling</u> well, I came back home early.
③ Peter walked slowly, <u>watching</u> the sunset.
④ <u>Being</u> too sleepy, I went to bed right away.
⑤ She left the classroom without <u>saying</u> goodbye to her friends.

고난도

08 다음 중 어법상 올바른 문장을 <u>두 개</u> 고르면?

① As he told a lie, she trusted him.
② Waited for his sons, he cooked dinner.
③ Not wearing your coat, you'll catch a cold.
④ As the musical started, all the lights went off.
⑤ Been taking a shower, he didn't answer the phone.

09 다음 중 밑줄 친 As(as)의 의미가 [보기]와 같은 것은?

> [보기] <u>As</u> time passed, her English improved.

① <u>As</u> I was going to the library, I met Jane.
② <u>As</u> he grows older, he is getting healthier.
③ <u>As</u> he walked out, everybody looked at him.
④ He was late for school <u>as</u> he missed the bus.
⑤ The man entered the university <u>as</u> he had wished.

10 다음 중 밑줄 친 부분과 바꿔 쓸 수 없는 것은?

① <u>As</u> I got out of the car, I saw Kate.
　(→ When)
② You can't change the story <u>as</u> you want.
　　　　　　　　　　　　　　(→ because)
③ I want to return the shoes <u>as</u> they are too big.
　　　　　　　　　　　　　　(→ since)
④ Turn off the water <u>as</u> you are brushing your teeth.　　　　　　(→ while)
⑤ <u>As</u> I didn't like the movie, I came out of the theater right away. (→ Because)

11 다음 중 어법상 올바른 문장의 개수는?

> ⓐ I watched a movie, eating a hot dog.
> ⓑ Was too surprised, I couldn't say a word.
> ⓒ As it was late at night, we went back home.
> ⓓ As the temperature goes up, the ice melts.
> ⓔ Waiting while at the train station, I met Tommy.

① 1개　② 2개　③ 3개　④ 4개　⑤ 5개

 서술형

12 다음 밑줄 친 부분을 분사구문으로 바꿔 쓰시오.

(1) <u>When she heard a dog bark,</u> she looked outside.
　→ _____

(2) <u>Because I didn't feel well,</u> I couldn't go to school.
　→ _____

13 다음 두 문장을 접속사 as를 사용하여 한 문장으로 연결하시오. (단, 부사절로 시작할 것)

(1) Time passed. Jack felt weaker and weaker.
　→ _____

(2) The bread is very delicious. Jenny buys it every morning.
　→ _____

14 다음 우리말을 영어로 옮길 때, 어법상 틀린 부분을 찾아 바르게 고쳐 쓰시오.

> 그는 자신의 아기를 팔에 안고서 사진을 찍었다.
> → He holding his baby in his arms, he took a picture.

_____ → _____

15 다음 문장과 의미가 같도록 분사구문을 사용하여 한 문장으로 쓰시오. (단, 분사구문으로 시작할 것)

(1) While she was drinking a cup of coffee, she surfed the Internet.
　→ _____

(2) When he doesn't wear glasses, he can't read books.
　→ _____

한 단계 더!

16 다음 중 어법상 틀린 문장 두 개를 찾아 기호를 쓰고, 틀린 부분을 바르게 고쳐 쓰시오.

> ⓐ Staying in New York, I visited my aunt.
> ⓑ Knowing not what to say, she kept silent.
> ⓒ I walked down the street, thinking of her.
> ⓓ Feeling sick, you should take this medicine.
> ⓔ Ran down the stairs, I fell down and hurt my knee.

(1) (　　) ＿＿＿＿＿＿＿ → ＿＿＿＿＿＿＿

(2) (　　) ＿＿＿＿＿＿＿ → ＿＿＿＿＿＿＿

[17~18] 다음 우리말과 의미가 같도록 [조건]에 맞게 영어 문장을 쓰시오.

17

내가 너에게 말했듯이, 너는 스마트폰을 덜 사용해야 한다.
(tell, have to, your smartphone, less)

> [조건] 1. 부사절로 시작할 것
> 　　　 2. 괄호 안의 표현을 어법에 맞게 사용할 것

→ ＿＿＿＿＿＿＿＿＿＿＿＿＿＿＿＿＿

고난도

18

그는 노래를 부르면서 세차를 했다.
(sing a song, clean his car)

> [조건] 1. (1)은 부사절, (2)는 분사구문으로 시작하는 문장을 쓸 것
> 　　　 2. 괄호 안의 표현을 어법에 맞게 사용할 것

(1) ＿＿＿＿＿＿＿＿＿＿＿＿＿＿＿＿＿

(2) ＿＿＿＿＿＿＿＿＿＿＿＿＿＿＿＿＿

19 다음 그림에 알맞는 문장이 되도록 〈A〉, 〈B〉에서 문장을 하나씩 골라 분사구문을 포함한 문장으로 쓰시오.

(1) 　(2)

(3) 　(4)

A　· She played the piano.
　　　· She waited for the bus.
　　　· She rode a bike in the park.
　　　· She saw a mouse in the kitchen.

B　· She fell down.
　　　· She screamed.
　　　· She sang a song.
　　　· She talked on the phone.

(1) ＿＿＿＿＿＿＿＿＿＿＿＿＿＿＿＿＿

(2) ＿＿＿＿＿＿＿＿＿＿＿＿＿＿＿＿＿

(3) ＿＿＿＿＿＿＿＿＿＿＿＿＿＿＿＿＿

(4) ＿＿＿＿＿＿＿＿＿＿＿＿＿＿＿＿＿

신유형

20 다음 괄호 안의 단어를 바르게 배열하여 문장을 완성하고, 문장을 우리말로 해석하시오.

(1) ＿＿＿＿＿＿＿＿＿＿＿＿, the sun rises in the east. (knows, everyone, as)

　→ ＿＿＿＿＿＿＿＿＿＿＿＿＿＿＿＿

(2) ＿＿＿＿＿＿＿＿＿＿＿＿, you'll become healthier. (exercise, as, more, you)

　→ ＿＿＿＿＿＿＿＿＿＿＿＿＿＿＿＿

• 주어진 우리말과 일치하도록 문장을 쓰시오.

01
_____

당신은 온라인 서점을 방문해서 그 서점이 당신에게 추천한 책들을 보고 놀란 적이 있는가?

02
_____

그 책들 중 다수가 당신에게 흥미로워 보였다.

03
_____

그러면 그 서점은 당신이 무엇을 좋아하는지 어떻게 알았을까?

04
_____

이것은 모두 빅데이터 때문에 가능하다.

05
_____

빅데이터는 매우 크고 복잡한 데이터의 집합이다.

06
_____

정보 통신 기술이 발달함에 따라 우리가 갖고 있는 데이터의 양이 이전보다 훨씬 더 많아지고 있다.☆

07
_____

이것의 주된 이유는 우리가 온라인상에서 하는 거의 모든 것들이 흔적을 남기기 때문이다.

08
_____

예를 들어, 당신이 블로그에 올린 사진들과 온라인 상점에서의 구매 기록들이 모두 빅데이터의 일부이다.

09
_____

하지만 단순히 데이터를 수집하는 것만으로는 충분하지 않다.

10
_____

빅데이터는 분석되어야 하는데, 이것은 빅데이터 전문가들에 의해서 이루어진다.

11
_____

전문가들은 다양한 방법들을 사용하여 빅데이터를 분석하고, 그것으로부터 의미 있는 결과들을 도출한다.☆

12
_____

그런 다음, 이런 결과들은 의사결정을 하거나 미래를 예측하는 데 사용될 수 있다.

13
_____

빅데이터는 우리 삶의 거의 모든 부분에 영향을 미치고 있다.

14
_____

그것은 회사들이 소비자들이 필요로 하는 것을 더 잘 이해하고 더 많은 상품을 팔도록 도와준다.

15
_____

그것은 사람들이 교통 체증을 피하도록 도와준다.

16
_____

그것의 쓰임은 끝이 없는데, 여기 몇 가지 흥미로운 예들이 있다.

17
_____

당신은 날씨 전문가들이 날씨를 예측하는 것과 같이 현재 건강 전문가들이 질병을 예측할 수 있다는 것을 알고 있었는가?☆

18

이것은 빅데이터 덕분에 가능하다.

19

예를 들어, 독감의 계절이 오면 사람들은 독감 약을 더 많이 구입할 것이다.

20

그들은 또한 온라인상에서 독감 증상에 대해 더 많이 검색해 볼 것이다.

21

이런 종류의 데이터가 현명하게 분석된다면, 독감의 확산은 예측될 수 있다.

22

당신은 스포츠 팬인가?

23

빅데이터는 스포츠를 더 흥미진진하게 만들면서 선수들의 경기력을 향상하고 있다.☆

24

한 유명한 사례가 독일 국가 대표 축구팀이다.

25

그 팀은 선수들에 관한 엄청난 양의 데이터를 모으고 분석함으로써 데이터베이스를 구축했다.

26

예를 들어, 그 데이터는 각각의 선수들이 얼마나 많이 달렸고, 얼마나 오랫동안 공을 갖고 있었는지에 관한 정보를 포함했다.

27

이 데이터베이스의 도움으로, 독일 국가 대표 축구팀은 경기력을 향상할 수 있었고, 2014년 월드컵에서 우승할 수 있었다.

28

빅데이터 덕분에 경찰은 이제 범죄가 발생하기 전에 그 범죄를 예측할 수 있다.

29

범죄의 유형, 시간 및 장소에 관한 빅데이터 분석을 통해, 경찰은 범죄 다발 지역의 지도를 만들 수 있다.

30

이 지도는 범죄가 언제, 어디에서 가장 발생할 것 같은지 알려 준다.

31

경찰은 이 지도가 예측하는 지역과 시간대에 집중함으로써 추가 범죄를 예방할 수 있다.

32

빅데이터는 이미 세계를 크게 변화시켰다.

33

그러면 빅데이터 산업은 여기에서부터 어디로 가게 될까?

34

누구도 확실히 알지는 못하지만, 전문가들은 빅데이터가 우리 삶에서 더욱 더 중요한 역할을 할 것이라는 데에는 동의한다.

고득점 맞기

[01~02] 다음 글을 읽고, 물음에 답하시오.

Have you ever visited an online bookstore and ___ⓐ___ by the books that the store recommended for you? Many of them looked interesting to you. So how did the bookstore know what you liked? ⓑThis is all possible because of big data.

01 윗글의 빈칸 ⓐ에 들어갈 말로 알맞은 것은?

① surprised
② surprising
③ being surprised
④ been surprised
⑤ been surprising

02 윗글의 밑줄 친 ⓑThis가 가리키는 것은?

① 당신이 온라인 서점을 선호하게 된 것
② 사람들이 온라인 서점을 방문하는 이유
③ 당신이 온라인 서점에서 구입하는 책의 종류
④ 온라인 서점이 당신이 무엇을 좋아하는지 아는 것
⑤ 당신이 온라인 서점에서 다른 사람들에게 책을 추천하는 것

[03~05] 다음 글을 읽고, 물음에 답하시오.

Big data is data sets that are very big and complex. As information and communication technology develops, the amount of data we have is getting ⓐmuch greater than before. This is mainly because almost everything that we do online ⓑleave a trace. For example, the photos you upload on your blog and the records of your purchases at online stores ⓒare all part of big data.

Simply collecting data, however, is not enough. Big data has to ⓓbe analyzed, and this is done by big data experts. ⓔUsed various methods, experts analyze big data and draw meaningful results from it. These results then ⓕcan use to make decisions or to predict the future.

03 윗글의 주제로 가장 알맞은 것은?

① What is big data?
② How big is big data?
③ Where can we find big data?
④ How can we predict the future?
⑤ How fast is information and communication technology developing?

고난도 04 다음 중 윗글에 사용된 단어의 영영풀이가 <u>아닌</u> 것은?

① a way of doing something
② the action of buying something
③ to examine something carefully
④ to stay away from someone or something
⑤ to say that something is going to happen

고난도 05 윗글의 밑줄 친 ⓐ~ⓕ 중 어법상 올바른 것끼리 짝지어진 것은?

① ⓐ, ⓑ
② ⓐ, ⓒ, ⓓ
③ ⓑ, ⓓ, ⓕ
④ ⓑ, ⓔ, ⓕ
⑤ ⓒ, ⓓ, ⓔ, ⓕ

[06~07] 다음 글을 읽고, 물음에 답하시오.

Big data is influencing almost all parts of our lives. It ___ⓐ___ companies understand their customers' needs better and ___ⓑ___ them sell more products. It ___ⓒ___ people avoid heavy traffic. Its uses are endless, and here are some interesting examples.

(①) Did you know that health professionals can now forecast a disease just as weather experts forecast the weather? (②) This is possible thanks to big data. (③) For example, when the flu season comes, people will buy more flu medicine. (④) If this kind of data is analyzed wisely, the spread of the flu can be predicted. (⑤)

06 윗글의 빈칸 ⓐ~ⓒ에 공통으로 들어갈 말로 알맞은 것은?

① helps　　② needs　　③ wants
④ expects　　⑤ influences

07 윗글의 ①~⑤ 중 주어진 문장이 들어갈 위치로 알맞은 것은?

> They will also search online about flu symptoms more.

①　　　②　　　③　　　④　　　⑤

[08~09] 다음 글을 읽고, 물음에 답하시오.

Are you a sports fan? Well, big data is improving the performance of players, making sports more (A) exciting / excitingly. A famous example is Germany's national soccer team. The team built a database by (B) collect / collecting and analyzing a huge amount of data on players. For example, the data included information about how much each player ran and how long he had the ball. With the help of this database, Germany's national soccer team was able to improve its performance and (C) win / winning the 2014 World Cup.

08 윗글 (A)~(C)의 각 네모 안에 주어진 말 중에서 어법상 올바른 것끼리 짝지어진 것은?

	(A)	(B)	(C)
①	exciting	…　collecting	…　winning
②	exciting	…　collecting	…　win
③	exciting	…　collect	…　win
④	excitingly	…　collect	…　winning
⑤	excitingly	…　collecting	…　winning

09 윗글의 **big data**에 대한 설명으로 알맞은 문장의 개수는?

> ⓐ It can affect the performance of sports players.
> ⓑ Germany's national soccer team made its players analyze it.
> ⓒ Germany held the 2014 World Cup thanks to it.
> ⓓ It helped Germany's national soccer team win the 2014 World Cup.

① 0개　　② 1개　　③ 2개　　④ 3개　　⑤ 4개

[10~11] 다음 글을 읽고, 물음에 답하시오.

Thanks to big data, police can now predict crime ＿＿＿＿(A)＿＿＿＿. Through the analysis of big data about the type, time and place of crime, police can make a map of crime hot spots. This map identifies when and where crime is most likely ⓐhappen. Police can prevent further crime by focusing on the areas and the times ⓑwhat this map predicts.

Big data has already changed the world ⓒgreat. So where will the big data industry go from here? Nobody ⓓknow for sure, but experts agree that big data will play a ⓔmuch and much important role in our lives.

10 Which is correct for blank (A) in the passage above?

① after it happens
② before it happens
③ after they prevent it
④ though they analyze big data
⑤ before they analyze big data

11 윗글의 밑줄 친 ⓐ~ⓔ를 바르게 고쳐 쓴 것 중 어법상 틀린 것은?

① ⓐ → happening　　② ⓑ → that
③ ⓒ → greatly　　④ ⓓ → knows
⑤ ⓔ → more and more important

[12~14] 다음 글을 읽고, 물음에 답하시오.

Big data is data sets ⓐthat are very big and complex. As information and communication technology develops, the amount of data ⓑwhat we have is getting much greater than before. This is mainly because almost everything that we do online leaves (A)a trace. For example, the photos you upload on your blog and the records of your purchases at online stores are all part of big data.

Simply ⓒcollecting data, however, is not enough. Big data has to be analyzed, and this is done by big data experts. ⓓUsing various methods, experts analyze big data and draw meaningful results from it. These results then can be used to ⓔmaking decisions or to predict the future.

12 윗글의 밑줄 친 ⓐ~ⓔ 중 어법상 틀린 것을 2개 찾아 기호를 쓰고, 바르게 고쳐 쓰시오.

(1) ( ) → _____

(2) ( ) → _____

13 윗글의 밑줄 친 (A)a trace에 해당하는 예시로 본문에 언급된 것 2개를 우리말로 쓰시오.

→ _____

14 윗글의 내용과 일치하도록 빈칸에 알맞은 말을 쓰시오.

Big data is very _____ and _____ data sets, and its amount is getting greater than before. It is analyzed by _____ _____ _____, and people can use its results to _____ _____ or _____ _____ _____.

15 다음 글을 읽고 답할 수 있는 질문을 ⓐ~ⓒ에서 골라 기호를 쓰고, 완전한 영어 문장으로 답하시오.

Are you a sports fan? Well, big data is improving the performance of players, making sports more exciting. A famous example is Germany's national soccer team. The team built a database by collecting and analyzing a huge amount of data on players. For example, the data included information about how much each player ran and how long he had the ball. With the help of this database, Germany's national soccer team was able to improve its performance and win the 2014 World Cup.

ⓐ How much data did Germany's soccer team collect to build a database?
ⓑ What did the data that Germany's national soccer team collected include?
ⓒ Which team did Germany play against in the 2014 World Cup finals?

( ) → _____

16 다음 글을 읽고, 주어진 질문에 대한 답을 완성하시오.

Thanks to big data, police can now predict crime before it happens. Through the analysis of big data about the type, time and place of crime, police can make a map of crime hot spots. This map identifies when and where crime is most likely to happen. Police can prevent further crime by focusing on the areas and the times this map predicts.

(1) What can police make by analyzing big data?
→ Police can make _____.

(2) How can police prevent further crime?
→ Police can prevent it _____
_____.

서술형 100% TEST

01 다음 영영풀이에 해당하는 단어를 [보기]에서 골라 쓰시오.

> [보기] spread   analyze   develop   symptom

(1) _____ : to examine something carefully

(2) _____ : something that shows you may have a particular illness

(3) _____ : to grow and change into something bigger, better, or more important

(4) _____ : the growth or development of something, so that it affects a larger area or a larger number of people

02 다음 우리말과 의미가 같도록 빈칸에 알맞은 말을 쓰시오.

(1) 곧 비가 올 것 같다.

→ It _____ _____ _____ rain soon.

(2) 스포츠는 사회에서 큰 역할을 한다.

→ Sports _____ _____ huge _____ in society.

(3) 그는 숙제에 집중하기 위해 TV를 껐다.

→ He turned off the TV to _____ _____ his homework.

03 다음 대화의 밑줄 친 우리말과 의미가 같도록 괄호 안의 지시대로 문장을 쓰시오.

> A: Excuse me. I want to rent a bike. (1)이 앱을 어떻게 사용하는지 알려 주시겠어요?
> B: Sure. First, log in to the application. Then find the RENT button and touch it.
> A: Then what?
> B: Then the application will give you a number to unlock a bike with.
> A: Thank you. (2)도와주셔서 정말 감사해요.

(1) (how to를 사용하여 9단어로 쓸 것)

→ _____

(2) (really, appreciate를 사용하여 5단어로 쓸 것)

→ _____

04 다음 대화의 밑줄 친 ⓐ와 ⓑ에서 흐름상 어색한 부분을 찾아 각각 바르게 고쳐 쓰시오.

> A: Excuse me. Can you tell me how to add money to my transportation card?
> B: ⓐOf course. Finally, put your card in the machine. Second, choose the amount of money you want to add.
> A: OK.
> B: Last, insert your money into the machine.
> A: ⓑThat sounds simple. Don't mention it.

ⓐ _____ → _____

ⓑ _____ → _____

[05~07] 다음 대화를 읽고, 물음에 답하시오.

> A: Excuse me, but what's this robot for?
> B: Oh, it's a robot that finds books for you.
> A: Really? _____ ⓐ _____
> B: Sure. First, place your library card on the robot's screen.
> A: OK.
> B: Second, type the title of the book you're looking for and then press ENTER.
> A: ⓑ그게 다인가요?
> B: Yes. Then, the robot will find the book and take it to the front desk.
> A: So I can just go to the front desk and get the book?
> B: Right. ⓒ그건 아주 쉬워요, 그렇지 않아요?
> A: Yes, it's really amazing. Thank you.

05 위 대화의 빈칸 ⓐ에 들어갈 말을 [조건]에 맞게 쓰시오.

> [조건] 1. 사용 방법을 물어볼 것
> 2. know, it을 사용할 것
> 3. 7단어의 완전한 의문문으로 쓸 것

→ _____

06 윗글의 밑줄 친 우리말 ⓑ와 ⓒ를 영어로 옮기시오.

ⓑ _____

ⓒ _____

07 다음 로봇 사용 설명문의 밑줄 친 ⓐ~ⓔ 중 위 대화의 내용과 일치하지 <u>않는</u> 것을 찾아 기호를 쓰고, 내용과 일치하도록 고쳐서 다시 쓰시오.

A ROBOT THAT FINDS BOOKS FOR YOU

ⓐ How to Use This Robot

1. ⓑ Pick your library card on the screen.
2. ⓒ Type the title of the book you're looking for.
3. ⓓ Press FINISH.
4. ⓔ Go to the robot and get the book.

(1) (   ) → _____

(2) (   ) → _____

(3) (   ) → _____

08 다음 두 문장의 의미가 같도록 괄호 안의 접속사를 사용하여 문장을 완성하시오.

(1) The girl watched the sunset, sitting on the grass.

= The girl watched the sunset _____

_____. (while)

(2) Turning left, you can see the bookstore.

= _____, you

can see the bookstore. (if)

(3) Being too busy, she couldn't go to the party.

= _____, she

couldn't go to the party. (because)

09 다음 〈A〉와 〈B〉에서 각각 알맞은 말을 하나씩 골라 접속사 **as**를 사용하여 자연스러운 문장으로 연결하시오. (단, 〈A〉의 내용으로 문장을 시작할 것)

A   (1) The boy soon fell asleep.

       (2) We went up the mountain.

       (3) The teacher announced yesterday.

B   • It became colder.

       • He was very tired.

       • The sports day will be canceled.

(1) _____

(2) _____

(3) _____

한 단계 더!

10 그림의 내용에 맞게 주어진 두 문장을 분사구문을 사용하여 한 문장으로 바꿔 쓰시오. (단, 첫 번째 문장을 분사구문으로 나타낼 것)

(1)

He was talking with me. He kept looking at his cell phone.

→ _____

(2)

She didn't feel comfortable. She left the party early.

→ _____

한 단계 더!

11 다음 대화의 내용과 일치하도록 분사구문을 사용하여 문장을 완성하시오.

(1)
A: Peter, what are you doing?
B: I'm posting some pictures on my blog. I'm also listening to music now.

→ Peter is posting some pictures on his blog, _____ _____ _____.

(2)
A: Minji, why didn't you buy a coat?
B: I didn't have enough money.

→ _____ _____ _____ _____, Minji couldn't buy a coat.

곡 고난도 한 단계 더!

12 다음 우리말과 의미가 같도록 [조건]에 맞게 문장을 쓰시오.

그는 무엇을 해야 할지 몰라서 나에게 도움을 청했다.

[조건] 1. know what to do, ask for my help를 어법에 맞게 사용할 것
2. (1)은 분사구문으로, (2)는 as를 사용하여 쓸 것

(1) _____

(2) _____

[13~15] 다음 글을 읽고, 물음에 답하시오.

Big data is data sets that are very big and complex. ⓐAs information and communication technology develops, the amount of data we have is getting ⓑvery greater than before. This is mainly because almost everything ⓒthat we do online leaves a trace. For example, the photos you upload on your blog and the records of your purchases at online stores are all part of big data.

Simply collecting data, however, is not enough. Big data has to be analyzed, and this ⓓis doing by big data experts. (A)다양한 방법들을 사용하여, experts analyze big data and draw meaningful results from it. These results then can ⓔbe used to make decisions or to predict the future.

13 윗글의 밑줄 친 ⓐ~ⓔ 중에서 어법상 틀린 것 두 개를 골라 기호를 쓰고, 바르게 고쳐 쓰시오.

(1) ( ) → _____

(2) ( ) → _____

14 윗글의 밑줄 친 우리말 (A)와 의미가 같도록 [조건]에 맞게 영어로 쓰시오.

[조건] 1. 분사구문을 사용할 것
2. various methods를 사용할 것

→ _____

15 윗글의 빅데이터에 해당하는 예시 두 가지를 본문에서 찾아 쓰시오.

(1) _____

(2) _____

[16~17] 다음 글을 읽고, 물음에 답하시오.

Big data is influencing almost all parts of our lives. It helps companies understand their customers' needs better and helps them sell more products. (A)(heavy, avoid, people, traffic, helps, it). Its uses are endless, and here are some interesting examples.

Did you know that health professionals can now forecast a disease just as weather experts forecast the weather? This is possible thanks to big data. For example, when the flu season comes, people will buy more flu medicine. They will also search online about flu symptoms more. If this kind of data is analyzed wisely, the spread of the flu can be predicted.

16 윗글의 괄호 (A) 안의 단어를 바르게 배열하여 문장을 완성하시오.

→ _____

17 다음 ⓐ～ⓒ 중 윗글의 내용과 일치하지 <u>않는</u> 문장의 기호를 쓰고, 바르게 고쳐 문장을 다시 쓰시오.

> ⓐ The uses of big data are not limited to certain industries.
> ⓑ Big data can help health professionals forecast a disease.
> ⓒ The symptoms of the flu can be predicted thanks to big data.

(   ) → _____

18 다음 글의 내용과 일치하도록 독일 국가 대표 축구팀 감독과의 가상 인터뷰를 완성하시오.

> Are you a sports fan? Well, big data is improving the performance of players, making sports more exciting. A famous example is Germany's national soccer team. The team built a database by collecting and analyzing a huge amount of data on players. For example, the data included information about how much each player ran and how long he had the ball. With the help of this database, Germany's national soccer team was able to improve its performance and win the 2014 World Cup.

> REPORTER: Your team won the 2014 World Cup. What was the secret?
> COACH: By _____
> _____ on players, my team could improve its performance.
> REPORTER: What kind of data was it?
> COACH: The data included information about
> _____
> _____.
> REPORTER: Wow, big data really makes sports more exciting.

[19~20] 다음 글을 읽고, 물음에 답하시오.

> Thanks to big data, police can now predict crime before it happens. Through the analysis of big data about the type, time and place of crime, police can make a map of crime hot spots. This map identifies when and where crime is most likely to happen. Police can prevent further crime by focusing on the areas and the times this map predicts.
> Big data has already changed the world greatly. So where will the big data industry go from here? Nobody knows for sure, but experts agree that ⓐ빅데이터는 우리 삶에서 점점 더 중요한 역할을 할 것이다.

19 윗글의 밑줄 친 우리말 ⓐ와 의미가 같도록 [조건]에 맞게 영어로 쓰시오.

> [조건] 1. play, role, important, our lives를 사용할 것
>   2. 비교급과 and를 사용할 것

→ _____

_____

20 윗글의 내용과 일치하도록 다음 질문에 대한 답을 완성하시오.

(1) How can police make a map of crime hot spots?
   → They can make it through _____
   _____.

(2) What does a map of crime hot spots do?
   → It _____
   _____.

(3) What can police do by using a map of crime hot spots?
   → Police can _____
   _____.

01 다음 중 짝지어진 단어의 관계가 [보기]와 같은 것은? 3점

> [보기] lock – unlock

① wise – wisely ② simple – complex
③ nation – national ④ possible – possibly
⑤ forecast – predict

02 다음 영영풀이에 해당하는 단어로 알맞은 것은? 3점

> to stay away from someone or something

① collect ② analyze ③ avoid
④ identify ⑤ predict

03 다음 빈칸에 들어갈 말이 순서대로 바르게 짝지어진 것은? 3점

> • Teachers _____ an important role in our society.
> • It's so noisy outside. I can't _____ on my studies.

① take – focus ② play – focus
③ take – forecast ④ play – improve
⑤ make – improve

04 다음 중 밑줄 친 단어의 우리말 의미가 알맞지 **않은** 것은? 3점

① The dog disappeared without a trace. (흔적)
② My parents influence my life the most.
　　　　　　　　　　　　　(격려한다)
③ The movie industry in Korea is growing fast.
　　　　　　　　　　(산업)
④ You can get a discount on the next purchase.
　　　　　　　　　　　　　　　(구매)
⑤ Our goal is to prevent the spread of the disease.
　　　　　　　　　　　　(확산)

05 다음 대화의 빈칸에 들어갈 말로 알맞은 것은? 3점

> A: _____
> B: Sure. First, cut a potato into small pieces.

① Do you want to plant a potato?
② Where did you plant potatoes?
③ Do you know when to plant a potato?
④ Can you tell me how to plant a potato?
⑤ How many potatoes are you going to plant?

서술형 1

06 다음 대화의 빈칸 (A)~(C)에 들어갈 말로 알맞은 것을 [보기]에서 골라 기호를 쓰시오. 4점

> A: I want to buy a snack. _____(A)_____
> B: Yeah. First, choose the snack you want.
> A: I already did. _____(B)_____
> B: Put in the money. Then take the snack out.
> A: _____(C)_____

> [보기] ⓐ What's next?
> 　　　 ⓑ Got it. Thanks.
> 　　　 ⓒ Do you know how to use this snack machine?

(A) _____ (B) _____ (C) _____

서술형 2

07 자연스러운 대화가 되도록 (A)~(D)를 바르게 배열하시오. 4점

> (A) Sure. First, put a tea bag in a cup. Then pour hot water in a cup.
> (B) Last, take the tea bag out after 3 minutes.
> (C) OK.
> (D) Do you know how to make tea?
> A: I got it. I really appreciate your help.

(　　) – (　　) – (　　) – (　　)

[08~10] 다음 대화를 읽고, 물음에 답하시오.

A: Excuse me, but what's this robot for?
B: Oh, it's a robot that finds books for you.
A: Really? _____ ⓐ _____
B: Sure. First, place your library card on the robot's screen.
A: OK.
B: Second, type the title of the book you're looking for and then press ENTER.
A: Is that all?
B: Yes. Then, _____ ⓑ _____ and take it to the front desk.
A: So I can just go to the front desk and get the book?
B: Right. It's so easy, isn't it?
A: Yes, it's really amazing. Thank you.

서술형3

08 위 대화의 빈칸 ⓐ에 들어갈 말을 주어진 [조건]에 맞게 영어로 쓰시오. 5점

[조건] 1. tell, how, it을 사용할 것
2. 8단어의 의문문으로 쓸 것

→ _____

09 위 대화의 빈칸 ⓑ에 들어갈 말로 가장 알맞은 것은? 4점

① you have to help the robot
② the robot will find the book
③ you should pay for the book
④ the robot will read the book
⑤ the robot will give you a library card

서술형4 고/난도

10 위 대화의 내용과 일치하도록 대화 속 단어를 사용하여 다음 문장을 완성하시오. 4점

People can use the robot when they want to _____ books in the library.

11 다음 빈칸에 들어갈 walk의 형태로 알맞은 것은? 3점

_____ along the street, I met my old friend.

① Walk ② Walked ③ Walking
④ To walk ⑤ To walking

12 다음 중 밑줄 친 **As**의 의미가 나머지와 **다른** 하나는? 4점

① <u>As</u> I said before, I keep my promises.
② <u>As</u> Jina was nervous, she made a mistake.
③ <u>As</u> the movie was boring, Jason fell asleep.
④ <u>As</u> we were late for the meeting, we hurried.
⑤ <u>As</u> Jenny didn't come to school, I called her.

서술형5

13 다음 두 문장의 의미가 같도록 빈칸에 알맞은 말을 3단어로 쓰시오. 4점

As Cathy entered the room, she smiled at us.

= Cathy smiled at us, _____.

고/난도

14 다음 중 어법상 올바른 문장끼리 짝지어진 것은? 5점

ⓐ He did as I had asked him to do.
ⓑ We watched TV, eaten sandwiches.
ⓒ As she got older, she became wiser.
ⓓ I feeling cold, I turned on the heater.
ⓔ Working hard, you will definitely pass the test.

① ⓐ, ⓓ ② ⓑ, ⓓ ③ ⓒ, ⓓ
④ ⓐ, ⓒ, ⓔ ⑤ ⓑ, ⓓ, ⓔ

[15~17] 다음 글을 읽고, 물음에 답하시오.

Big data is data sets that are very big and complex. (①) As information and communication technology develops, the amount of data we have is getting much greater than before. (②) For example, the photos you upload on your blog and the records of your purchases at online stores are all part of _____ⓐ_____. Simply collecting data, however, is not enough. (③) Big data has to be analyzed, and ⓑthis is done by big data experts. (④) Using various methods, experts analyze big data and draw meaningful results from it. (⑤) These results then can be used to make decisions or to predict the future.

15 윗글의 ①~⑤ 중 주어진 문장이 들어갈 위치로 알맞은 것은?　　4점

This is mainly because almost everything that we do online leaves a trace.

①　　　②　　　③　　　④　　　⑤

서술형6

16 윗글의 흐름상 빈칸 ⓐ에 들어갈 말을 본문에서 찾아 쓰시오.　　4점

→ _____ _____

17 윗글의 밑줄 친 ⓑthis가 가리키는 것은?　　3점

① collecting big data
② analyzing big data
③ purchasing big data
④ using various methods
⑤ making decisions or predicting the future

[18~19] 다음 글을 읽고, 물음에 답하시오.

Big data is ____ⓐ____ almost all parts of our lives. It helps companies understand their customers' needs better and helps them sell more products. It helps people avoid heavy traffic. Its uses are endless, and here are some interesting examples.

18 윗글의 빈칸 ⓐ에 들어갈 말로 가장 알맞은 것은?　　3점

① leaving　　② avoiding　　③ collecting
④ influencing　　⑤ purchasing

19 윗글 뒤에 이어질 내용으로 가장 알맞은 것은?　　4점

① 빅데이터의 정의
② 빅데이터의 폐해
③ 빅데이터 분석 방법
④ 빅데이터를 발명한 사람
⑤ 빅데이터의 다양한 쓰임새

고
난도

20 다음 글의 빈칸에 들어갈 말로 알맞은 것은?　　4점

_____ Using Big Data
Did you know that health professionals can now forecast a disease just as weather experts forecast the weather? This is possible thanks to big data. For example, when the flu season comes, people will buy more flu medicine. They will also search online about flu symptoms more. If this kind of data is analyzed wisely, the spread of the flu can be predicted.

① Market Research　　② Online Search
③ Disease Forecast　　④ Weather Prediction
⑤ Accident Prevention

[21~22] 다음 글을 읽고, 물음에 답하시오.

Are you a sports fan? Well, big data is ⓐ<u>improving</u> the performance of players, ⓑ<u>made</u> sports more exciting. A famous example is Germany's national soccer team. The team built a database by collecting and ⓒ<u>analyzing</u> a huge amount of data on players. For example, the data ⓓ<u>included</u> information about how much each player ran and how long he had the ball. With the help of (A)<u>this database</u>, Germany's national soccer team was able to improve its performance and ⓔ<u>win</u> the 2014 World Cup.

서술형7 고/난도

21 윗글의 밑줄 친 ⓐ~ⓔ 중 어법상 틀린 것을 찾아 기호를 쓰고 바르게 고쳐 쓴 후, 틀린 이유를 쓰시오. 각 4점

(1) 틀린 부분: ( ) → _____

(2) 틀린 이유: _____

_____

[23~25] 다음 글을 읽고, 물음에 답하시오.

Thanks ____ⓐ____ big data, police can now predict crime before it happens. ____ⓑ____ the analysis of big data about the type, time and place of crime, police can make a map of crime hot spots. This map identifies when and where crime is most likely ____ⓒ____ happen. Police can prevent further crime by focusing ____ⓓ____ the areas and the times this map predicts.

Big data has already changed the world greatly. So where will the big data industry go from here? Nobody knows ____ⓔ____ sure, but experts agree that big data will play a more and more important role in our lives.

23 윗글의 주제로 가장 알맞은 것은? 4점

① what big data is
② the role of police
③ the definition of big data
④ the influence of big data in our lives
⑤ how to collect big data in everyday life

24 윗글의 빈칸 ⓐ~ⓔ에 들어갈 말로 알맞지 <u>않은</u> 것은? 4점

① ⓐ: for ② ⓑ: Through ③ ⓒ: to
④ ⓓ: on ⑤ ⓔ: for

22 윗글의 밑줄 친 (A)<u>this database</u>에 대한 내용으로 알맞지 <u>않은</u> 것은? 4점

① 독일 국가 대표 축구팀이 구축했다.
② 독일 국가 대표 축구 선수들을 분석한 것이다.
③ 독일 국가 대표 축구 선수들의 공 점유 시간에 대한 정보는 제외했다.
④ 독일 국가 대표 축구팀의 경기력을 향상시켰다.
⑤ 독일 국가 대표 축구팀이 2014년 월드컵에서 우승하는 데 도움이 되었다.

서술형8 고/난도

25 윗글의 내용과 일치하도록 빈칸에 알맞은 말을 쓰시오. 각 2점

By (1)_____ big data, police can make a map of (2)_____ _____ _____ and use it to (3)_____ further crime.

01 다음 중 단어의 성격이 나머지와 <u>다른</u> 하나는? 3점

① wisely ② mainly ③ friendly

④ regularly ⑤ generally

02 다음 중 단어와 영영풀이가 바르게 연결되지 <u>않은</u> 것은? 3점

① **influence**: to change or affect something

② **crime**: an action that the law does not allow

③ **avoid**: to stay away from someone or something

④ **include**: to contain something as a part of a whole

⑤ **symptom**: a large amount of information stored in a computer system

서술형**1**

03 다음 빈칸에 공통으로 들어갈 단어를 쓰시오. 4점

• He isn't likely _____ arrive here on time.

• Thanks _____ the Internet, our lives have become more convenient.

→ _____

04 다음 중 밑줄 친 단어의 쓰임이 <u>어색한</u> 것은? 4점

① A fever is a cold <u>symptom</u>.

② As we know, Canada is a <u>huge</u> country.

③ There are many <u>national</u> parks in the USA.

④ I earned a lot of money for the <u>purchase</u> of the car.

⑤ Did you hear about today's weather <u>forecast</u>?

05 다음 대화의 ①~⑤ 중 주어진 문장이 들어갈 위치로 알맞은 것은? 3점

What's next?

A: I want to buy a snack. Do you know how to use this snack machine? (①)

B: Yeah. First, choose the snack you want. (②)

A: I already did. (③)

B: Just put in the money. (④) Then take the snack out.

A: (⑤) Got it. Thanks.

서술형**2**

06 다음 대화의 밑줄 친 우리말과 의미가 같도록 괄호 안의 표현을 바르게 배열하여 문장을 쓰시오. 4점

A: Excuse me. <u>교통 카드에 돈을 충전하는 방법을 알려 주시겠어요?</u>

B: Of course. First, put your card in the machine.

→ _____

(how, you, can, add money, to, me, to, tell, my transportation card)

07 다음 대화의 밑줄 친 ①~⑤ 중 흐름상 <u>어색한</u> 것은? 4점

A: Excuse me. I want to rent a bike. ①<u>Can you tell me how to use this application?</u>

B: Sure. ②<u>First, log in to the application.</u> Then find the RENT button and touch it.

A: ③<u>Then what?</u>

B: ④<u>Then the application will give you a number to unlock a bike with.</u>

A: Thank you. ⑤<u>Don't mention it.</u>

[08~10] 다음 대화를 읽고, 물음에 답하시오.

> A: _____ⓐ_____, but what's this robot for?
> B: Oh, it's a robot that finds books for you.
> A: Really? _____ⓑ_____
> B: Sure. First, place your library card on the robot's screen.
> A: OK.
> B: Second, type the title of the book you're looking for and then press ENTER.
> A: _____ⓒ_____
> B: Yes. _____ⓓ_____, the robot will find the book and take it to the front desk.
> A: So I can just go to the front desk and get the book?
> B: Right. _____ⓔ_____
> A: Yes, it's really amazing. (A)도와주셔서 정말 감사해요.

08 위 대화의 흐름상 빈칸 ⓐ~ⓔ에 들어갈 말로 알맞지 <u>않은</u> 것은? 4점

① ⓐ: Excuse me
② ⓑ: Can you find some books for me?
③ ⓒ: Is that all?
④ ⓓ: Then
⑤ ⓔ: It's so easy, isn't it?

서술형 3

09 위 대화의 밑줄 친 우리말 (A)와 의미가 같도록 괄호 안의 단어를 사용하여 5단어의 영어 문장을 쓰시오. 4점

→ _____

(appreciate, your)

서술형 4

10 위 대화의 내용과 일치하도록 로봇 사용 방법을 나타내는 그림을 순서대로 배열하시오. 4점

(A)  (B)  (C)

( ) – ( ) – ( )

11 다음 문장의 밑줄 친 <u>As</u>와 바꿔 쓸 수 있는 것은? 3점

> <u>As</u> he is kind, everybody likes him.

① If ② Whether ③ Although
④ Because ⑤ Even though

한 단계 더!

12 다음 빈칸에 들어갈 말로 알맞은 것을 <u>모두</u> 고르면? 4점

> _____, she cooked spaghetti.

① Watch TV
② Drank tea
③ Playing loud music
④ While singing a song
⑤ Being talked on the phone

서술형 5

13 다음 두 문장을 as로 시작하는 한 문장으로 쓰시오. 4점

> Tony grew older. He became braver.

→ _____

고난도 한 단계 더!

14 다음 중 짝지어진 두 문장의 의미가 같지 <u>않은</u> 것은? 4점

① As I sang a song, I heard the doorbell.
  = Singing a song, I heard the doorbell.
② When I got home, nobody was at home.
  = As I got home, nobody was at home.
③ Smiling brightly, the baby walked to her mom.
  = The baby smiled brightly, walking to her mom.
④ Going down the stairs, I found a coin.
  = While I was going down the stairs, I found a coin.
⑤ As she didn't know Korean, she couldn't read the book.
  = Although she knew Korean, she couldn't read the book.

15 다음 글의 밑줄 친 ⓐ~ⓓ 중 어법상 올바른 것은? 4점

Have you ever ⓐvisit an online bookstore and been surprised by the books ⓑthat the store recommended for you? Many of them looked ⓒinterested to you. So how did the bookstore know what you liked? This is all possible ⓓbecause big data.

① 없음　　② ⓐ　　③ ⓑ　　④ ⓒ　　⑤ ⓓ

[16~17] 다음 글을 읽고, 물음에 답하시오.

Big data is data sets that are very big and complex. (A)As information and communication technology develops, the amount of data we have is getting much greater than before. This is mainly because almost everything that we do online leaves a trace. For example, the photos you upload on your blog and the records of your purchases at online stores are all part of big data.

Simply collecting data, however, is not enough. Big data has to be analyzed, and this is done by big data experts. Using various methods, experts analyze big data and draw meaningful results from it. These results then can be used to make decisions or to predict the future.

16 윗글의 밑줄 친 (A)As와 의미상 쓰임이 같은 것은? 4점

① Please do as I say.
② As I was sleepy, I hurried to go to bed.
③ Can you turn off the light as you leave?
④ As my car broke down, I was late for work.
⑤ As the population increases, people need more houses.

17 윗글의 내용과 일치하도록 할 때, 빈칸 ⓐ~ⓒ에 알맞은 말이 순서대로 바르게 짝지어진 것은? 5점

_____ ⓐ _____ results from big data that is _____ ⓑ _____ by experts can be used to _____ ⓒ _____ the future.

① Various – analyzed – prevent
② Complex – collected – predict
③ Complex – analyzed – develop
④ Meaningful – analyzed – predict
⑤ Meaningful – collected – develop

[18~20] 다음 글을 읽고, 물음에 답하시오.

Big data is influencing almost all parts of our lives. It helps companies understand their _____ ⓐ _____ needs better and helps them sell more products. It helps people avoid heavy traffic. Its uses are _____ ⓑ _____, and here are some interesting examples.

Did you know that health professionals can now forecast a disease just as weather experts forecast the weather? This is _____ ⓒ _____ thanks to big data. For example, _____ (A) _____ the flu season comes, people will buy more flu medicine. They will also search online about flu _____ ⓓ _____ more. If this kind of data is analyzed wisely, the spread of the flu can be _____ ⓔ _____.

18 윗글의 빈칸 ⓐ~ⓔ에 들어갈 말 중 문맥상 어색한 것은? 4점

① ⓐ: customers'　　② ⓑ: endless
③ ⓒ: impossible　　④ ⓓ: symptoms
⑤ ⓔ: predicted

19 윗글의 흐름상 빈칸 (A)에 들어갈 말로 알맞은 것을 모두 고르면? 4점

① as　　② that　　③ when
④ though　　⑤ unless

서술형 6 고난도

20 윗글의 내용을 다음과 같이 정리할 때, 빈칸에 들어갈 말을 본문에서 찾아 각각 한 단어로 쓰시오. (단, 필요시 형태를 바꿀 것) 각 3점

> the (1)_____ of big data in our lives and how it can be used for (2)_____ forecast

[21~23] 다음 글을 읽고, 물음에 답하시오.

> Are you a sports fan? Well, big data is improving the performance of players, ⓐ(more, sports, exciting, make). A famous example is Germany's national soccer team. The team built a database by collecting and analyzing a huge amount of data on players. For example, the data included information about how much each player ran and how long he had the ball. __ⓑ__ this database, Germany's national soccer team was able to improve its performance and win the 2014 World Cup.

서술형 7

21 윗글의 괄호 ⓐ의 단어를 [조건]에 맞게 배열하여 문장을 완성하시오. 4점

> [조건] 1. '스포츠를 더 흥미진진하게 만들면서'의 의미가 되도록 쓸 것
> 2. 한 단어만 형태를 바꿀 것

→ _____

22 윗글의 흐름상 빈칸 ⓑ에 들어갈 말로 알맞은 것은? 3점

① Instead of
② Thanks for
③ In addition to
④ In contrast with
⑤ With the help of

고난도

23 윗글을 읽고 알 수 없는 것은? 5점

① Big data can be used in sports.
② Germany's national soccer team is a good example of using big data.
③ Germany's national soccer team collected a lot of data on players to build a database.
④ The data collected by Germany's national soccer team showed who ran fastest in the team.
⑤ The database on players helped Germany's national soccer team win the 2014 World Cup.

[24~25] 다음 글을 읽고, 물음에 답하시오.

> Thanks to big data, police can now predict crime before it happens. Through the analysis of big data about the type, time and place of crime, police can make a map of crime hot spots. This map identifies when and where crime is most likely (A)|to happen / happening|. Police can prevent further crime by (B)|focusing / to focus| on the areas and the times this map predicts.
> ⓐBig data has already changed the world greatly. So where will the big data industry go from here? Nobody knows for sure, but experts agree (C)|that / what| big data will play a more and more important role in our lives.

24 윗글 (A)~(C)의 각 네모 안에 주어진 말 중 어법상 올바른 것끼리 짝지어진 것은? 3점

	(A)	(B)	(C)
①	to happen	focusing	that
②	to happen	to focus	what
③	to happen	focusing	what
④	happening	to focus	that
⑤	happening	focusing	what

서술형 8 고난도

25 윗글의 밑줄 친 문장 ⓐ에 해당하는 예시를 본문에서 찾아 문장을 완성하시오. 6점

> By using big data, _____
> _____ now.

01 다음 빈칸에 들어갈 말이 순서대로 바르게 짝지어진 것은?

3점

> • I was able to answer the question _____.
> • To be healthy, we need to eat _____ meals.

① ease – regular
② easily – regular
③ easy – regular
④ easily – regularly
⑤ easy – regularly

02 다음 중 밑줄 친 draw(Draw)의 뜻이 나머지와 다른 하나는?

3점

① I'm drawing an outline of the ship.
② Draw a line at the bottom of the page.
③ Why don't you draw a picture of your family?
④ Did you draw any conclusions at the meeting?
⑤ My brother likes to draw pictures in his free time.

03 다음 빈칸 ⓐ~ⓔ에 들어갈 말로 알맞지 않은 것은?

4점

> • _____ⓐ_____ to Jessica, I could find my watch.
> • He tried to focus _____ⓑ_____ the conversation.
> • This team is most _____ⓒ_____ to win the game.
> • We can save a huge _____ⓓ_____ of energy by recycling.
> • Smartphones are playing an important _____ⓔ_____ in our lives.

① ⓐ: Thanks
② ⓑ: at
③ ⓒ: likely
④ ⓓ: amount
⑤ ⓔ: role

04 다음 대화의 밑줄 친 문장과 바꿔 쓸 수 있는 것을 모두 고르면?

4점

> A: Thank you for inviting me.
> B: Don't mention it.

① I'm afraid I can't invite you.
② I'd like to invite you to dinner.
③ I really appreciate your invitation.
④ I'm truly grateful to you for inviting me.
⑤ I'm sorry to hear that you're not invited.

서술형 **1**

05 다음 대화의 내용과 일치하도록 빈칸에 알맞은 말을 6단어로 쓰시오.

4점

> A: Do you know how to use a drink machine?
> B: Sure. First, insert your money into the machine. Then, choose the drink you want and take the drink out of the machine.
> A: Wow, that's easy.

→ The speakers are talking about _____
_____.

06 다음 중 짝지어진 대화가 어색한 것은?

4점

① A: What's next?
　B: Then, put in the money.
② A: Is that all?
　B: No. Last, take your card out.
③ A: Thanks for your help.
　B: It's my pleasure.
④ A: Do you know how to make tea?
　B: Sure. I got it.
⑤ A: Can you tell me how to use this application?
　B: Sure. First, log in to the application.

[07~09] 다음 대화를 읽고, 물음에 답하시오.

> Lucy: Excuse me, but what's this robot for?
> Seho: Oh, it's a robot that ___ⓐ___ books for you.
> Lucy: Really? Can you tell me how to use it?
> Seho: Sure. First, place your library card on the robot's screen.
> Lucy: OK.
> (A) Second, type the title of the book you're looking for and then press ENTER.
> (B) Yes. Then, the robot will find the book and take it to the front desk.
> (C) Is that all?
> Lucy: So I can just go to the front desk and get the book?
> Seho: Right. It's so easy, isn't it?
> Lucy: Yes, it's really amazing. Thank you.

07 위 대화의 흐름상 빈칸 ⓐ에 들어갈 말로 알맞은 것은? 3점

① finds   ② pays   ③ buys
④ returns   ⑤ makes

서술형2

08 자연스러운 대화가 되도록 (A)~(C)를 바르게 배열하시오.

4점

(   ) – (   ) – (   )

09 위 대화를 읽고 답할 수 <u>없는</u> 질문은? 4점

① Who knows how to use the robot?
② Where can people use the robot?
③ What is needed to use the robot?
④ What is the final step for using the robot?
⑤ How much does it cost to use the robot?

서술형3 한 단계 더!

10 다음 빈칸에 공통으로 알맞은 말을 한 단어로 쓰시오. 4점

> • We decided to go home _____ it was getting dark.
> • Sam is working _____ a librarian at the library.

→ _____

서술형4

11 다음 대화에서 어법상 틀린 부분을 찾아 바르게 고쳐 쓰시오. (단, 한 단어만 고칠 것) 5점

> A: How was your weekend trip to the lake?
> B: As you know, the weather was good. Arrived there, we set up a tent and went fishing at the lake.

_____ → _____

12 다음 중 밑줄 친 **as(As)**의 의미가 [보기]와 같은 것은? 4점

> [보기] Do <u>as</u> you like.

① <u>As</u> the day goes on, it gets colder.
② Why didn't you do <u>as</u> he told you?
③ <u>As</u> it is Sunday, I don't have to get up early.
④ I saw Tom running <u>as</u> I opened the window.
⑤ <u>As</u> he lives near my house, he often sees me.

고난도 한 단계 더!

13 다음 중 어법상 올바른 문장의 개수는? 5점

> ⓐ I didn't call her as I was busy.
> ⓑ Shaking hands, we greeted each other.
> ⓒ Turned to the left, you'll find the building.
> ⓓ Before getting off the bus, she met Jake.
> ⓔ Someone knocked on the door as I was about to go out.

① 1개   ② 2개   ③ 3개   ④ 4개   ⑤ 5개

14 다음 밑줄 친 부분과 바꿔 쓸 수 있는 것은? 3점

> Playing soccer, Tom broke his arm.

① If he played soccer
② When played soccer
③ Since he plays soccer
④ While we played soccer
⑤ While he was playing soccer

17 윗글을 잘못 이해한 사람은? 4점

① 준호: 정보 통신 기술이 발달하면서 많은 양의 데이터가 생겨나고 있어.
② 재민: 온라인 서점에서 구매한 책의 내역은 빅데이터의 일부가 될 수 없어.
③ 수지: 데이터는 수집뿐만 아니라 분석도 필요해.
④ 민하: 전문가들은 데이터를 분석하기 위해 다양한 방법들을 사용해.
⑤ 석진: 빅데이터를 분석하여 의미 있는 결과들을 얻을 수 있어.

[15~17] 다음 글을 읽고, 물음에 답하시오.

> Big data is data sets that are very big and complex. As information and communication technology develops, ⓐthe amount of data we have is getting much greater than before. This is mainly because almost everything that we do online leaves a trace. For example, the photos you upload on your blog and the records of your purchases at online stores are all part of big data.
>
> Simply collecting data, however, is not enough. Big data has to be analyzed, and this is done by big data experts. ___ⓑ___ various methods, experts analyze big data and draw meaningful results from it. These results then can ___ⓒ___ to make decisions or to predict the future.

서술형5

15 윗글의 밑줄 친 ⓐ의 주된 이유를 30자 내외의 우리말로 쓰시오. 4점

→ _____

[18~19] 다음 글을 읽고, 물음에 답하시오.

> Big data is ⓐinfluencing almost all parts of our lives. It helps companies ⓑunderstand their customers' needs better and helps them sell more products. It ⓒhelps people avoid heavy traffic. Its uses are endless, and here are some interesting examples.
>
> Did you know that health professionals can now forecast a disease just ⓓas weather experts forecast the weather? This is possible thanks to big data. For example, when the flu season ⓔwill come, people will buy more flu medicine. They will also search online about flu symptoms more. If this kind of data is analyzed wisely, ___(A)___.

서술형6

18 윗글의 밑줄 친 ⓐ~ⓔ 중 어법상 틀린 것을 찾아 기호를 쓰고 바르게 고쳐 쓰시오. 5점

( ) → _____

19 윗글의 흐름상 빈칸 (A)에 들어갈 말로 가장 알맞은 것은? 4점

① the flu can spread quickly
② the flu medicine has an effect
③ the flu will appear more often
④ the spread of the flu can be predicted
⑤ various flu symptoms won't disappear

16 윗글의 빈칸 ⓑ와 ⓒ에 들어갈 동사 use의 알맞은 형태가 순서대로 바르게 짝지어진 것은? 4점

① Use – use
② Use – be used
③ Using – use
④ Using – be used
⑤ Used – be used

[20~22] 다음 글을 읽고, 물음에 답하시오.

Are you a sports fan? (①) Well, big data is improving the performance of players, making sports more exciting. (②) A famous example is Germany's national soccer team. (③) For example, the data included ⓐ각각의 선수가 얼마나 많이 달렸는지에 관한 정보 and how long he had the ball. (④) With the help of this database, Germany's national soccer team was able to improve its performance and win the 2014 World Cup. (⑤)

20 윗글의 ①~⑤ 중 주어진 문장이 들어갈 위치로 알맞은 것은?   3점

The team built a database by collecting and analyzing a huge amount of data on players.

①   ②   ③   ④   ⑤

서술형7

21 윗글의 밑줄 친 우리말 ⓐ와 의미가 같도록 주어진 단어들을 바르게 배열하시오.   4점

player, how, ran, information, about, much, each

→ _____

서술형8 고난도

22 윗글의 내용과 일치하도록 본문 속 단어를 사용하여 다음 문장을 완성하시오. (단, 필요시 형태를 바꿀 것)   각 2점

The database built by Germany's national soccer team (1)_____ the team improve its (2)_____ and (3)_____ the 2014 World Cup.

[23~24] 다음 글을 읽고, 물음에 답하시오.

Thanks ___ⓐ___ big data, police can now predict crime before it happens. Through the analysis of big data about the type, time and place of crime, police can make a map of crime hot spots. ⓑThis map identifies when and where crime is most likely to happen. Police can prevent further crime ___ⓒ___ focusing on the areas and the times this map predicts.

23 윗글의 빈칸 ⓐ와 ⓒ에 들어갈 말이 순서대로 바르게 짝지어진 것은?   3점

① to − by   ② for − by   ③ to − on
④ for − in   ⑤ in − with

고난도 신유형

24 다음 중 윗글의 밑줄 친 ⓑThis map에 대한 내용으로 알맞지 않은 것의 개수는?   5점

ⓐ It shows crime hot spots.
ⓑ It can be helpful to prevent further crime.
ⓒ It is made through the analysis of big data about crime.
ⓓ It predicts the reasons why crime is likely to happen.

① 0개   ② 1개   ③ 2개   ④ 3개   ⑤ 4개

25 다음 글을 읽고 알 수 있는 것은?   4점

Big data has already changed the world greatly. So where will the big data industry go from here? Nobody knows for sure, but experts agree that big data will play a more and more important role in our lives.

① 빅데이터의 장단점
② 빅데이터 산업의 명암
③ 빅데이터가 가져온 변화들
④ 빅데이터의 다양한 활용 방법
⑤ 빅데이터에 대한 전문가들의 의견

모의고사

01 다음 짝지어진 두 단어의 관계가 같도록 할 때, 빈칸에 들어갈 단어로 알맞은 것은? 3점

> method : way = illness : _____

① flu　　　　② trace　　　　③ disease
④ spread　　　⑤ prevention

서술형1

02 다음 영영풀이에 공통으로 해당하는 단어를 쓰시오. 4점

> *v.* to change or affect something
> *n.* the power to have an effect on people or things

→ _____

고난도

03 다음 중 짝지어진 문장의 밑줄 친 단어가 같은 의미로 쓰인 것은? 4점

① I'm a big fan of soccer.
　The cause of the fire was a fan.
② She has been very kind to me.
　What kind of music do you like?
③ What did he leave on the bus?
　How often do trains leave for Busan?
④ Draw a straight line on a piece of paper.
　What result did you draw from the report?
⑤ Jackson trained every day to improve his performance.
　He praised the members of the soccer team for their great performance.

04 다음 중 의미하는 바가 나머지와 다른 하나는? 3점

① I appreciate your help.
② I can't thank you enough.
③ I would like to thank you.
④ Thank you for helping me.
⑤ I'll appreciate it if you can help me.

05 다음 대화의 빈칸에 들어갈 말로 알맞지 <u>않은</u> 것은? 3점

> A: Do you know how to plant a potato?
> B: Sure. First, cut a potato into small pieces. Second, dig holes in the ground.
> A: _____
> B: Then put the potato pieces in the holes and cover the holes with dirt.
> A: That sounds simple. Thanks.

① OK.　　　　　　　② What's up?
③ And then?　　　　④ What's next?
⑤ Then what?

서술형2 고난도

06 다음과 같은 상황에서 Ryan이 Jane에게 요청할 말을 괄호 안의 단어를 사용하여 쓰시오. 4점

> Ryan went to the library to print out his science report, but he didn't know how to use the printer. Then, he saw Jane, his classmate. She was printing something out on the other computer.

Ryan: Hi, Jane. _____

_____? (tell, how)

서술형3

07 다음 대화의 밑줄 친 ⓐ~ⓔ 중 흐름상 어색한 문장의 기호를 쓰고, 문맥에 맞게 고쳐 다시 쓰시오. 4점

> A: Excuse me. I want to rent a bike. ⓐDo you know how to use this application?
> B: Yes. ⓑFirst, log in to the application. ⓒThen find the RENT button and touch it.
> A: Then what?
> B: ⓓThen the application will give you a number to unlock a bike with.
> A: Got it. ⓔI'm really sorry to hear that.

(　　) → _____

[08~10] 다음 대화를 읽고, 물음에 답하시오.

> **Lucy:** Excuse me, but (A)<u>이 로봇은 용도가 뭔가요?</u>
>
> **Seho:** Oh, it's a robot that finds books for you.
>
> **Lucy:** Really? Can you tell me how to use it?
>
> **Seho:** Sure. First, place your library card on the robot's screen.
>
> **Lucy:** OK.
>
> **Seho:** Second, type the title of the book you're looking for and then press ENTER.
>
> **Lucy:** Is that all?
>
> **Seho:** Yes. Then, the robot will find the book and take it to the front desk.
>
> **Lucy:** So I can just go to the front desk and get the book?
>
> **Seho:** Right. It's so easy, isn't it?
>
> **Lucy:** Yes, it's really amazing. Thank you.

서술형 **4** 고난도

08 위 대화의 밑줄 친 우리말 (A)와 의미가 같도록 [조건]에 맞게 영어로 쓰시오. **5점**

> [조건] 1. what을 포함할 것
> 2. 축약하지 않고 5단어로 쓸 것

→ _____

09 위 대화의 내용과 일치하지 <u>않는</u> 것은? **4점**

① There is a robot that can help people in the library.

② Seho tells Lucy how to use the robot.

③ To use the robot, you need your student ID card.

④ If you type the title of the book you're looking for on the robot, the robot will find it for you.

⑤ Lucy thinks the robot is easy to use.

서술형 **5**

10 위 대화의 내용과 일치하도록 다음을 완성하시오. 각 **2점**

(1) _____ **Use This Robot**
STEP 1. (2) _____ on the screen.
STEP 2. (3) _____.
STEP 3. (4) _____.
STEP 4. (5) _____ and get the book.

11 다음 문장의 밑줄 친 부분을 부사절로 바꿔 쓸 때 사용할 수 있는 단어를 <u>모두</u> 고르면? **4점**

> <u>Talking with her</u>, you can understand her well.

① if   ② they   ③ before
④ talk   ⑤ talked

한 단계 더!

12 다음 중 분사구문을 사용하여 바르게 바꿔 쓴 것은? **3점**

① As soon as the thief saw the police officer, he ran away.
  → Saw the police officer, the thief ran away.

② Because I didn't know his number, I couldn't call him.
  → Didn't know his number, I couldn't call him.

③ If you turn to the right, you can easily find the store.
  → Turn to the right, you can easily find the store.

④ While he was listening to music, he ran in the park.
  → Being listened to music, he ran in the park.

⑤ As Melanie was too surprised, she almost cried.
  → Too surprised, Melanie almost cried.

한 단계 더!

13 다음 밑줄 친 As(as)의 역할이 나머지와 <u>다른</u> 하나는? **3점**

① <u>As</u> Tom got older, he became shyer.

② Lisa felt great <u>as</u> she finished the race.

③ Mom works there <u>as</u> an English teacher.

④ <u>As</u> I mentioned earlier, practice makes perfect.

⑤ <u>As</u> we all know, Andrew is really good at basketball.

고난도 한 단계 더!

14 다음 중 밑줄 친 부분의 쓰임이 같은 것끼리 짝지어진 것은? 4점

> ⓐ He wrote a letter, <u>thinking</u> of his son.
> ⓑ They thanked me for <u>finding</u> their dog.
> ⓒ <u>Having</u> the flu, I couldn't go to the party.
> ⓓ Not <u>being</u> tired, he continued to work out.
> ⓔ <u>Doing</u> the job wasn't easy, but I enjoyed it.

① ⓐ, ⓑ, ⓓ   ② ⓐ, ⓒ, ⓓ   ③ ⓑ, ⓒ, ⓔ
④ ⓑ, ⓓ, ⓔ   ⑤ ⓒ, ⓓ, ⓔ

15 다음 글의 빈칸에 들어갈 말로 알맞은 것을 <u>모두</u> 고르면? 4점

> Have you ever visited an online bookstore and been surprised by the books that the store recommended for you? Many of them looked interesting to you. So how did the bookstore know what you liked? This is all possible _____ big data.

① thanks to   ② instead of
③ because of   ④ with the help of
⑤ in addition to

[16~18] 다음 글을 읽고, 물음에 답하시오.

> Big data is data sets that are very big and _____ⓐ_____. As information and communication technology develops, the _____ⓑ_____ of data we have is getting much greater than before. (①) This is mainly because almost everything that we do online leaves a trace. (②) For example, the photos you upload on your blog and the records of your purchases at online stores are all part of big data.
>   (③) Big data has to be analyzed, and this is done by big data experts. (④) Using various _____ⓒ_____, experts analyze big data and draw _____ⓓ_____ results from it. (⑤) (A) These results then can be used to making decisions or to predict the future.

16 윗글의 빈칸 ⓐ~ⓓ 중 어느 곳에도 들어갈 수 <u>없는</u> 것은? 4점

① amount   ② methods   ③ complex
④ symptoms   ⑤ meaningful

17 윗글의 ①~⑤ 중 주어진 문장이 들어갈 위치로 알맞은 것은? 3점

> Simply collecting data, however, is not enough.

①   ②   ③   ④   ⑤

서술형 6

18 윗글의 밑줄 친 문장 (A)에서 어법상 틀린 부분을 찾아 바르게 고쳐 쓰시오. 4점

_____ → _____

[19~20] 다음 글을 읽고, 물음에 답하시오.

> Big data is influencing almost all parts of our lives. It helps companies understand their customers' needs better and helps them sell more products. It helps people (A) avoid / avoiding heavy traffic. Its uses are endless, and here are some interesting examples.
>   Did you know that health professionals can now forecast a disease just (B) as / because weather experts forecast the weather? This is possible thanks to big data. For example, when the flu season comes, people will buy more flu medicine. They will also search online about flu symptoms more. If this kind of data is analyzed wisely, the spread of the flu can (C) predict / be predicted.

19 윗글 (A)~(C)의 각 네모 안에 주어진 말 중 어법상 올바른 것끼리 짝지어진 것은? 3점

	(A)	(B)	(C)
①	avoid	as	predict
②	avoid	as	be predicted
③	avoid	because	predict
④	avoiding	as	be predicted
⑤	avoiding	because	predict

[서술형7] 고난도

20 다음 중 윗글을 읽고 답할 수 있는 질문을 골라 기호를 쓰고, 완전한 영어 문장으로 답하시오. 4점

> ⓐ How does big data help customers?
> ⓑ When did weather experts begin to use big data?
> ⓒ What can health professionals now forecast using big data?

( ) → _____

[21~22] 다음 글을 읽고, 물음에 답하시오.

> Are you a sports fan? Well, big data is ____ⓐ____ the performance of players, making sports more ____ⓑ____. A famous ____ⓒ____ is Germany's national soccer team. The team built a database by ____ⓓ____ and analyzing a huge amount of data on players. For example, the data included information about (A)각 선수가 얼마나 많이 달렸는지 and (B)그가 얼마나 오랫동안 공을 갖고 있었는지. With the help of this database, Germany's national soccer team ____ⓔ____ improve its performance and win the 2014 World Cup.

21 윗글의 흐름상 빈칸 ⓐ~ⓔ에 들어갈 말로 알맞지 <u>않은</u> 것은? 3점

① ⓐ: improving ② ⓑ: exciting
③ ⓒ: method ④ ⓓ: collecting
⑤ ⓔ: was able to

[서술형8]

22 윗글의 밑줄 친 우리말 (A)와 (B)를 괄호 안의 지시대로 영어로 쓰시오. 각 3점

(A) (how, each player를 사용하여 5단어로 쓸 것)
→ _____

(B) (how, had the ball을 사용하여 6단어로 쓸 것)
→ _____

[23~25] 다음 글을 읽고, 물음에 답하시오.

> Thanks to big data, police can now predict crime before it ⓐis happened. Through the analysis of big data about the type, time and place of crime, police can make a map of crime hot spots. This map identifies when and where crime is most likely ⓑto happen. Police can prevent further crime by ⓒfocusing on the areas and the times this map predicts.
>
> Big data has already changed the world ⓓgreat. So where will the big data industry go from here? (A)누구도 확실히 알지는 못하지만, but experts agree that big data will play a more and ⓔmost important role in our lives.

고난도

23 윗글의 밑줄 친 ⓐ~ⓔ 중 어법상 올바른 것의 개수는? 4점

① 1개 ② 2개 ③ 3개 ④ 4개 ⑤ 5개

신유형

24 윗글의 밑줄 친 우리말 (A)를 영어로 옮길 때 필요하지 <u>않은</u> 단어는? 3점

① for ② nobody ③ knows
④ sure ⑤ didn't

신유형

25 다음 ⓐ~ⓒ에 윗글의 내용과 일치하면 T, 일치하지 않으면 F를 쓸 때, 순서대로 바르게 짝지어진 것은? 4점

> · Thanks to big data, police can make a map of crime hot spots. (ⓐ)
> · The map of crime hot spots identifies why crime is likely to happen. (ⓑ)
> · With the information the map of crime hot spots provides, police can prevent crime. (ⓒ)

① T – T – T ② T – F – T ③ T – F – F
④ F – T – F ⑤ F – F – T

● 틀린 문항을 표시해 보세요.

● 부족한 영역을 점검하고 어떻게 더 학습할지 계획을 적어 보세요.

〈제1회〉 대표 기출로 내신 **적중** 모의고사   총점 _____ / 100

문항	영역	문항	영역	문항	영역
01	p.160(W)	10	p.165(L&T)	19	p.180(R)
02	p.160(W)	11	p.172(G)	20	p.181(R)
03	p.158(W)	12	p.173(G)	21	p.181(R)
04	p.158(W)	13	p.172(G)	22	p.181(R)
05	p.163(L&T)	14	pp.172~173(G)	23	p.181(R)
06	p.164(L&T)	15	p.180(R)	24	p.181(R)
07	p.165(L&T)	16	p.180(R)	25	p.181(R)
08	p.165(L&T)	17	p.180(R)		
09	p.165(L&T)	18	p.180(R)		

제1회 오답 공략
부족한 영역
학습 계획

〈제2회〉 대표 기출로 내신 **적중** 모의고사   총점 _____ / 100

문항	영역	문항	영역	문항	영역
01	p.160(W)	10	p.165(L&T)	19	pp.180~181(R)
02	p.160(W)	11	p.173(G)	20	pp.180~181(R)
03	p.158(W)	12	p.172(G)	21	p.181(R)
04	p.158(W)	13	p.173(G)	22	p.181(R)
05	p.164(L&T)	14	pp.172~173(G)	23	p.181(R)
06	p.163(L&T)	15	p.180(R)	24	p.181(R)
07	p.164(L&T)	16	p.180(R)	25	p.181(R)
08	p.165(L&T)	17	p.180(R)		
09	p.165(L&T)	18	pp.180~181(R)		

제2회 오답 공략
부족한 영역
학습 계획

〈제3회〉 대표 기출로 내신 **적중** 모의고사   총점 _____ / 100

문항	영역	문항	영역	문항	영역
01	p.160(W)	10	p.173(G)	19	pp.180~181(R)
02	p.160(W)	11	p.172(G)	20	p.181(R)
03	p.158(W)	12	p.173(G)	21	p.181(R)
04	p.163(L&T)	13	pp.172~173(G)	22	p.181(R)
05	p.163(L&T)	14	p.172(G)	23	p.181(R)
06	p.163(L&T)	15	p.180(R)	24	p.181(R)
07	p.165(L&T)	16	p.180(R)	25	p.181(R)
08	p.165(L&T)	17	p.180(R)		
09	p.165(L&T)	18	pp.180~181(R)		

제3회 오답 공략
부족한 영역
학습 계획

〈제4회〉 고난도로 내신 **적중** 모의고사   총점 _____ / 100

문항	영역	문항	영역	문항	영역
01	p.160(W)	10	p.165(L&T)	19	pp.180~181(R)
02	p.160(W)	11	p.172(G)	20	pp.180~181(R)
03	p.160(W)	12	p.172(G)	21	p.181(R)
04	p.163(L&T)	13	p.173(G)	22	p.181(R)
05	p.165(L&T)	14	p.172(G)	23	p.181(R)
06	p.163(L&T)	15	p.180(R)	24	p.181(R)
07	p.164(L&T)	16	p.180(R)	25	p.181(R)
08	p.165(L&T)	17	p.180(R)		
09	p.165(L&T)	18	p.180(R)		

제4회 오답 공략
부족한 영역
학습 계획

동아출판 영어 교재 가이드

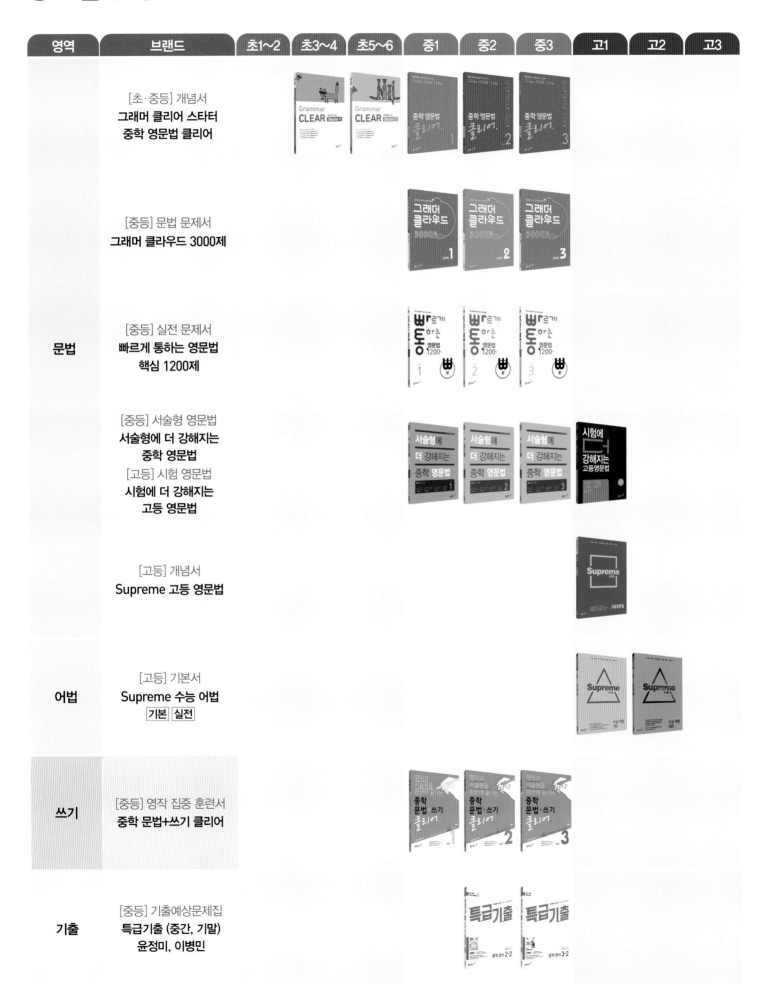

영역	브랜드	초1~2	초3~4	초5~6	중1	중2	중3	고1	고2	고3
문법	[초·중등] 개념서 그래머 클리어 스타터 중학 영문법 클리어									
	[중등] 문법 문제서 그래머 클라우드 3000제									
	[중등] 실전 문제서 빠르게 통하는 영문법 핵심 1200제									
	[중등] 서술형 영문법 서술형에 더 강해지는 중학 영문법 [고등] 시험 영문법 시험에 더 강해지는 고등 영문법									
	[고등] 개념서 Supreme 고등 영문법									
어법	[고등] 기본서 Supreme 수능 어법 기본 실전									
쓰기	[중등] 영작 집중 훈련서 중학 문법+쓰기 클리어									
기출	[중등] 기출예상문제집 특급기출 (중간, 기말) 윤정미, 이병민									

특급기출

중학 영어 3-2

윤정미

정답 및 해설

동아출판

Lesson 5
The Team Behind the Team

STEP A

Words 연습 문제
p. 9

A 01 제안하다, 추천하다
02 보이지 않는, 볼 수 없는
03 동쪽의
04 고용하다
05 달성하다, 성취하다
06 주목, 관심
07 격식을 차린
08 숨 쉬다
09 몇몇의
10 (함께 일하는) 팀, 조
11 지원하다; 지지하다
12 정중한
13 페이서, 보조를 맞춰 걷는 사람
14 허락하다
15 특정한
16 그러므로
17 종족, 부족
18 경험이 풍부한, 능숙한
19 특히
20 숨기다, 감추다

B 01 twice
02 weekday
03 direct
04 flag
05 possible
06 harmony
07 once
08 perfect
09 patient
10 cheer
11 register
12 race
13 target
14 pit
15 spirit
16 limit
17 trophy
18 join
19 recommend
20 hidden

C 01 요컨대, 요약하면
02 (강좌에) 등록하다
03 (낡아서) 닳다, 해지다
04 혼자서, 혼자 힘으로
05 (계속해서) ~을 파악하다
06 연설하다
07 수업을 받다, 강습을 받다
08 무엇보다도
09 역할을 맡다, 한몫을 하다
10 ~에 따라

D 01 wear out
02 most of all
03 lead A to B
04 depending on
05 do stretching exercises
06 in short
07 on one's own
08 sign up
09 give a speech
10 keep track of

Words Plus 연습 문제
p. 11

A 1 invisible, 보이지 않는, 볼 수 없는 2 several, 몇몇의
3 target, 목표 4 particular, 특정한 5 breathe, 숨 쉬다
6 hire, 고용하다 7 support, 돕다, 지원하다
8 tribe, 종족, 부족

B 1 register 2 attention 3 hide 4 harmony
5 suggest

C 1 wear out 2 on his own 3 sign up 4 depending
on 5 In short

D 1 particular 2 impolite 3 invisible 4 register
5 breathe

A |해석| 1 보이지 않는
2 몇몇, 그러나 많지 않은
3 성취하고자 노력하는 목표나 결과
4 특정한 사람, 사물 또는 장소와 관련된
5 체내로 공기를 들여보내고 그것을 다시 내보내다
6 특정 일을 하도록 누군가를 고용하거나 돈을 지불하다
7 종종 문제에 맞닥뜨린 누군가를 돕다
8 자신들만의 언어와 생활방식을 가진 사람들의 집단

B |해석| 1 요리 수업에 등록하고 싶어요.
2 그는 관심을 받기 위해 아픈 척했다.
3 그 개는 뼈를 숨기기 위해 구멍을 파고 있었다.
4 그 학생들은 완벽한 조화를 이루며 함께 일했다.
5 김 선생님은 우리에게 매일 책을 읽으라고 제안했다.

D |해석| 1 목표 : 목표 = 특정한 : 특정한
2 직접적인 : 간접적인 = 정중한 : 무례한
3 참을성 있는 : 못 견디는 = (눈에) 보이는 : 보이지 않는
4 제안하다 : 제안 = 등록하다 : 등록
5 추천하다 : 추천 = 숨 쉬다 : 숨

Words 실전 TEST
p. 12

01 ④ 02 breath 03 twice 04 ④ 05 ② 06 ①
07 ③ 08 track of

01 |해석| ① 사실인 – 사실이 아닌 ② 보이는 – 보이지 않는
③ 정중한 – 무례한 ④ 특정한 – 특정한 ⑤ 참을성 있는 – 못 견디는
|해설| ④는 유의어 관계이고, 나머지는 모두 반의어 관계이다.

02 |해석| 제안하다 : 제안 = 숨 쉬다 : 숨
|해설| '동사(제안하다) : 명사(제안)'의 관계이므로 breathe(숨 쉬다)의
명사형 breath(숨, 호흡)가 알맞다.

03 |해석| 하나 : 한 번 = 둘 : 두 번
|해설| '하나 : 한 번'과 같은 관계가 되도록 빈도를 나타내는 twice(두
번)가 들어가는 것이 알맞다.

04 |해석| ① 고용하다: 특정 일을 하도록 누군가를 고용하거나 돈을 지불
하다

② 목표: 성취하고자 노력하는 목표나 결과
③ 주목: 무언가를 주의 깊게 보거나 듣는 행위
④ 등록하다: 종종 문제에 맞닥뜨린 누군가를 돕다 (×)
⑤ 팀, 조: 함께 일하는 특정한 기술을 가진 사람들
|해설| ④ register(등록하다)의 영영풀이는 to put someone's or something's name on an official list이다. 주어진 영영풀이는 support(돕다, 지원하다)에 해당한다.

05 |해설| Angela는 혼자 힘으로 그 문제를 해결했다.
① 쉽게 ② 그녀 혼자서 ③ 함께 ④ 하나씩 ⑤ 즉석에서
|해설| on one's own은 '혼자서, 혼자 힘으로'라는 뜻으로 by oneself로 바꿔 쓸 수 있다.

06 |해석| • 날씨에 따라 우리는 캠핑을 갈 수도 있고 안 갈 수도 있다.
• 요컨대, 우리는 정보로 가득 찬 세상에서 살고 있다.
|해설| 첫 번째 문장은 '~에 따라'라는 의미의 depending on, 두 번째 문장은 '요컨대, 요약하면'이라는 의미의 In short가 되어야 알맞다.

07 |해석| • 그들은 일 년에 두 번 뉴욕에 간다.
• 우리를 도와줄 경험이 풍부한 안내원이 있나요?
• 나는 항상 비밀 장소에 내 일기장을 고용한다(→ 숨긴다).
• 경기의 승자는 트로피나 메달을 받을 것이다.
• 그녀는 가수가 되는 꿈을 성취하기 위해 열심히 노력했다.
|해설| ⓒ에는 '고용하다'라는 뜻의 hire가 아니라 '숨기다'라는 뜻의 hide가 알맞다.

08 |해설| '~을 파악하다'는 keep track of로 나타낸다.

Listen and Talk 만점 노트   pp. 14~15

Q1 ⓑ   Q2 스트레칭을 할 것을 제안했다   Q3 ⓐ   Q4 더 가벼운 공을 사용할 것   Q5 매일   Q6 화요일과 목요일   Q7 T   Q8 일주일에 두 번   Q9 T

Listen and Talk 빈칸 채우기   pp. 16~17

Listen and Talk A-1 How often do you, once a week, often, suggest, join, three times
Listen and Talk A-2 How often, four times a week, That often, suggest, do
Listen and Talk A-3 do you take, Twice a week, looks heavy, I suggest you
Listen and Talk A-4 how often do you, Every day, I suggest you wear
Listen and Talk C to register for, first time taking, how to swim, How often, on weekdays, on weekends, suggest that, on, sign up, How big, limit
Review - 1 every day, go swimming, suggest you bring, allowed

Review - 2 over, do you practice, twice a week
Review - 3 came to register, often, twice, on weekends, suggest that, meets

Listen and Talk 대화 순서 배열하기   pp. 18~19

1 ⓓ – ⓐ, ⓑ   2 ⓒ – ⓑ, ⓐ – ⓓ
3 ⓑ – ⓐ – ⓒ   4 ⓓ – ⓒ – ⓐ
5 ⓕ – ⓗ, ⓖ – ⓐ – ⓔ – ⓑ   6 ⓑ – ⓐ, ⓒ
7 ⓑ – ⓐ – ⓓ   8 ⓔ – ⓓ, ⓐ – ⓕ

Listen and Talk 실전 TEST   pp. 20~21

01 ②   02 ①   03 ⑤   04 ⑤   05 ③   06 ③   07 ③
08 ②   09 ③

[서술형]
10 three times a week, (I exercise) Once a week.
11 I suggest you use a lighter ball.   12 ⓒ → join my basketball club

01 |해석| A: 너는 얼마나 자주 책을 읽니?
B: 나는 한 달에 두 번 책을 읽어.
A: 네가 책을 더 많이 읽는 것을 제안해.
B: 알았어. 해 볼게.
① 네가 가장 좋아하는 책은 뭐니?
③ 너는 어떤 종류의 책을 좋아하니?
④ 너는 보통 언제 책을 읽니?
⑤ 너는 다음 달에 무엇을 할 거니?
|해설| 대답으로 책을 읽는 빈도를 말하고 있으므로 책을 얼마나 자주 읽는지 묻는 말이 빈칸에 알맞다.

02 |해석| A: 너는 얼마나 자주 기타 수업을 듣니?
B: _____
① 한 시간 동안 들어.
② 일주일에 두 번 들어.
③ 한 달에 네 번 들어.
④ 나는 일주일에 세 번 기타 수업을 들어.
⑤ 일주일에 한 번 듣지만, 여가 시간에 열심히 연습해.
|해설| 빈도를 묻는 말에 대한 답이므로 빈도나 횟수를 나타내는 「횟수＋a week/month」로 답하는 것이 알맞다. 횟수는 「숫자＋times」로 표현하는데, 보통 '한 번'은 once로, '두 번'은 twice로 쓴다. ①은 걸리는 시간을 나타내는 표현이다.

03 |해석| A: 지선아, 너는 패스트푸드를 얼마나 자주 먹니?
B: 나는 일주일에 세 번 패스트푸드를 먹어.
A: 네가 그것을 덜 먹는 것을 제안해.
|해설| 「I suggest (that) you (should)＋동사원형 ~.」은 상대방에게 어떤 일을 할 것을 제안하거나 권유할 때 사용하는 표현이다.

04 │해석│ A: 너는 이곳에 달리기를 하러 얼마나 자주 오니?
　　 B: 매일 와.
　　 ① 얼마나 오랫동안 ② 몇 시에 ③ 얼마나 많이 ④ 어떤 종류
　　 ⑤ 일주일에 몇 번
　　│해설│ How often do you ~?는 어떤 일을 얼마나 자주 하는지 묻는
　　 표현으로, How many times a day/week/month do you ~?로
　　 바꿔 쓸 수 있다.

05 │해석│ A: 나는 수영을 자주 하지 않아. 너는 어때, Kate? 너는 얼마나
　　　　 자주 수영을 하니?
　　 (B) 나는 일주일에 네 번 수영을 해.
　　 (C) 그렇게 자주? 어쨌든, 오늘 함께 수영하면 재미있을 거야.
　　 (D) 그래. 그런데 수영하기 전에, 우리가 스트레칭 하는 것을 제안해.
　　 (A) 좋은 생각이야.
　　│해설│ 얼마나 자주 수영을 하는지 묻는 말에 일주일에 네 번 한다고(B)
　　 대답하자 그렇게 자주 하냐고 놀란 후 오늘 함께 수영을 해서 재미있
　　 겠다고 말하고(C), 그 말을 듣고 수영하기 전에 스트레칭부터 먼저 하
　　 자고 제안하는 말(D)을 하는 흐름이 자연스럽다.

06 │해석│ ① A: 나 두통이 심해.
　　　　 B: 병원에 가는 것을 제안해.
　　 ② A: 우리가 축구 동아리에 가입하는 것을 제안해.
　　　　 B: 좋아.
　　 ③ A: 너는 방 청소를 얼마나 자주 하니?
　　　　 B: 곧 청소할 거야.
　　 ④ A: 나는 매일 배드민턴을 쳐. 너는 어때?
　　　　 B: 나는 그렇게 자주 치지 않아.
　　 ⑤ A: 소풍 가자.
　　　　 B: 좋아. 우리가 카메라를 가져가는 것을 제안해.
　　│해설│ ③ 방 청소를 얼마나 자주 하는지 묻는 말에 곧 방 청소를 할 거
　　 라고 답하는 것은 어색하다.

[07~09] │해석│
여자: 안녕하세요. Sports World에 오신 것을 환영합니다. 도와드릴까요?
소년: 네, 저는 수영 수업에 등록하려고 왔어요.
여자: 수영 강습을 받는 것이 이번이 처음이세요?
소년: 네. 저는 수영하는 법을 전혀 몰라요.
여자: 그렇군요. 얼마나 자주 수업을 듣고 싶으세요?
소년: 일주일에 두 번 수업을 듣고 싶어요. 주말은 아니고 주중에 수업을 듣
　　　고 싶습니다.
여자: 그러면, 초급 2반을 수강하기를 권해요. 이 수업은 화요일과 목요일
　　　에 있습니다.
소년: 좋아요. 그 수업으로 등록할게요. 그 수업은 규모가 얼마나 되나요?
여자: 그 수업은 제한 인원이 10명이에요.
소년: 딱 좋네요.

07 │해설│ 주어진 문장은 일주일에 두 번 수강하고 싶다는 말로 횟수를 나
　　 타내므로, 빈도를 묻는 말 바로 뒤인 ③에 들어가는 것이 알맞다.

08 │해설│ 첫 번째 빈칸에는 '수영하는 방법'을 나타내는 how to swim의
　　 how가 알맞고, 두 번째 빈칸에는 어떤 것의 규모를 물을 때 사용하는
　　 How big ~?의 How가 알맞다.

09 │해설│ ③ 소년은 주말이 아니라 주중에 두 번 수업을 듣고 싶어 한다.

10 │해석│ Andy: 나는 일주일에 세 번 운동해. 너는 어때? 너는 얼마나 자
　　　　　주 운동을 하니?

Brian: 나는 일주일에 한 번 운동해.
Andy: 네가 더 자주 운동하는 것을 제안해.
Brian: 알았어. 해 볼게.
│해설│ Andy는 일주일에 운동을 세 번 하므로 three times a week라
고 말하고, 얼마나 자주 운동을 하는지 묻는 말에 Brian은 일주일에 한
번 운동하므로 once a week를 사용하여 대답하는 것이 자연스럽다.

11 │해석│ A: 너는 얼마나 자주 볼링 수업을 받니?
　　 B: 일주일에 두 번. 나는 그냥 초보야. 너는 아주 잘한다고 들었어.
　　 A: 음, 나는 볼링을 정말 좋아해. 흠. 네 볼링 공이 너에게 무거워 보여.
　　　　 더 가벼운 공을 쓰는 걸 권해.
　　 B: 알았어. 그러면 더 가벼운 공을 찾아 볼게.
　　│해설│ 상대방에게 어떤 일을 할 것을 제안하거나 권유할 때 「I suggest
　　 (that) you (should)+동사원형 ~.」으로 말한다.

12 │해석│ A: 너는 얼마나 자주 농구를 하니?
　　 B: 일주일에 두 번 농구를 하는데, 더 자주 하고 싶어.
　　 A: 우리 축구(→ 농구) 동아리에 가입하는 것을 제안해. 우리는 일주일
　　　　 에 네 번 농구를 해.
　　 B: 좋아! 너와 함께 농구 하면 재미있을 거야.
　　│해설│ ⓒ 농구를 더 자주 하고 싶다는 상대방의 말에 대한 제안으로 일
　　 주일에 네 번 농구를 하는 자신의 농구(basketball) 동아리에 가입하
　　 라는 내용이 알맞다.

Ⓖ Grammar 핵심 노트 1 QUICK CHECK　　p. 22

1 (1) shining　(2) built　(3) dancing
2 (1) flying　(2) wearing　(3) carrying

1 │해석│ (1) 하늘에서 빛나고 있는 별을 봐라.
　　 (2) 그는 10년 전에 지어진 집에서 산다.
　　 (3) 방에서 춤추고 있는 소년들은 내 남동생들이다.
2 │해석│ (1) 날아다니고 있는 새들을 봐라.
　　 (2) 안경을 쓰고 있는 소녀는 내 반 친구이다.
　　 (3) 큰 가방을 들고 있는 한 남자가 버스에서 내렸다.

Ⓖ Grammar 핵심 노트 2 QUICK CHECK　　p. 23

1 (1) as　(2) old　(3) well
2 (1) busy　(2) as　(3) not as(so) large

1 │해석│ (1) 나는 너만큼 빨리 달리지 못한다.
　　 (2) 엄마는 아빠와 연세가 같으시다.
　　 (3) Jenny는 Andrew 만큼 프랑스어를 잘한다.
2 │해석│ (1) Rita는 Lucy만큼 바빴다.
　　 (2) 그 책은 그 CD만큼 오래되었다.
　　 (3) 이 도시는 서울만큼 크지 않다.

A 1 crying   2 studying   3 working   4 are   5 made
B 1 driving   2 playing   3 covered   4 showing
C 1 동명사   2 현재분사   3 현재분사   4 현재분사
D 1 Look at the falling leaves.
  2 I threw away the broken glasses.
  3 Jane told us a shocking story.
  4 The boring movie made me sleepy.

A |해석| 1 울고 있는 소년은 자신의 아버지를 찾고 있었다.
  2 도서관에서 공부하고 있는 학생들이 많이 있었다.
  3 정원에서 일하고 있는 남자는 나의 할아버지이다.
  4 김 선생님과 대화하고 있는 학생들은 캐나다에서 왔다.
  5 이 공장에서 만들어진 신발들은 매우 비싸다.
|해설| 1~3 명사를 앞이나 뒤에서 수식하는 현재분사 형태가 되어야 알맞다. 현재분사 뒤에 이어지는 어구가 있을 때는 명사를 뒤에서 수식한다.
  4 현재분사가 수식하는 명사인 The students가 주어이므로 be동사 are를 써야 한다.
  5 수식하는 명사와 분사의 관계가 수동일 때는 과거분사를 사용한다.

B |해석| 1 차를 운전하고 있는 여자는 Baker 선생님이다.
  2 배드민턴을 치고 있는 소녀들은 내 좋은 친구들이다.
  3 그들은 눈으로 덮인 산을 올라갔다.
  4 나는 가장 가까운 버스 정류장과 지하철역을 보여 주는 지도가 필요하다.
|해설| 뒤따르는 어구와 함께 명사를 수식하는 현재분사의 형태로 쓰는 것이 알맞다. 단, 3과 같이 수식하는 명사와 분사의 관계가 수동일 때는 과거분사를 쓴다.

C |해석| 1 내 직업은 영어를 가르치는 것이다.
  2 나는 네가 그의 손을 잡고 있는 것을 봤다.
  3 그들은 지나가는 기차에 손을 흔들었다.
  4 우리는 채소가 가득 담긴 바구니를 들고 있는 한 소녀를 만났다.
|해설| 1 보어 역할을 하는 동명사
  2 지각동사 saw의 목적격보어로 쓰인 현재분사
  3 명사 train을 수식하는 현재분사
  4 명사 a girl을 뒤에서 수식하는 현재분사

D |해설| 수식하는 명사와의 관계가 능동일 때는 현재분사를, 수동일 때는 과거분사를 사용하여 문장을 쓴다.

A 1 as tall as   2 not as expensive as   3 has lived here as long as   4 doesn't(does not) get up as early as
B 1 more difficult → difficult
  2 careful → carefully
  3 as fast not as → not as(so) fast as
C 1 colder   2 not as(so) diligent   3 worked more

D 1 This book is as heavy as my laptop.
  2 Today is as windy as yesterday.
  3 Badminton is not as(so) dangerous as skydiving.
  4 The cheerleaders worked as hard as the players.

A |해석| 1 Sophia는 키가 160cm이다. Helen도 키가 160cm이다.
  → Sophia는 Helen만큼 키가 크다.
  2 빨간색 가방은 50달러이다. 파란색 가방은 70달러이다.
  → 빨간색 가방은 파란색 가방만큼 비싸지 않다.
  3 진수는 20년 동안 여기서 살았다. Sora도 여기서 20년 동안 살았다.
  → 진수는 Sora만큼 여기서 오래 살았다.
  4 Nick은 6시에 일어난다. Amy는 7시에 일어난다.
  → Amy는 Nick만큼 일찍 일어나지 않는다.
|해설| 비교 대상의 정도가 같으면 「as+형용사/부사의 원급+as」의 형태로 나타내고, 같지 않으면 「not as(so)+형용사/부사의 원급+as」의 형태로 쓴다.

B |해석| 1 이 시험은 지난번 시험만큼 어렵니?
  2 그는 자신의 여동생만큼 조심스럽게 운전했다.
  3 원숭이는 호랑이만큼 빠르지 않다.
|해설| 1 「as+형용사의 원급+as」로 써야 한다.
  2 동사를 수식하는 부사의 원급이 쓰여야 한다.
  3 '…만큼 ~하지 않은'은 「not as(so)+형용사의 원급+as」의 형태로 쓴다.

C |해석| 1 오늘은 어제만큼 춥지 않다.
  = 어제는 오늘보다 더 추웠다.
  2 민지의 오빠는 민지보다 더 부지런하다.
  = 민지는 자신의 오빠만큼 부지런하지 않다.
  3 유리는 Tom만큼 일을 많이 하지 않았다.
  = Tom은 유리보다 일을 더 많이 했다.
|해설| '…만큼 ~하지 않은/않게'를 뜻하는 「A ~ not as(so)+형용사/부사의 원급+as B」는 「B ~ 비교급+than A」 형태로 바꿔 쓸 수 있다.

D |해설| '…만큼 ~한/하게'는 「as+형용사/부사의 원급+as」의 형태로 나타내고, '…만큼 ~하지 않는/않게'는 「not as(so)+형용사/부사의 원급+as」의 형태로 쓴다.

01 ③   02 ①   03 ②   04 ④   05 ①   06 ④   07 ①
08 ①   09 ③   10 ④   11 ⑤   12 ③, ⑤   13 ①, ⑤
14 ③, ⑤   15 ②   16 ④   17 ⑤   18 ④   19 ③
20 ③

[서술형]
21 (1) The boy drinking water (2) The boy listening to music (3) The girl reading a book   22 (1) as big as (2) as expensive as (3) as heavy as   23 (1) Somin runs as fast as Yuna. (2) The man taking pictures is my new English teacher.   24 (1) ⓐ longer → long (2) ⓑ as not

→ not as(so) **25** (1) The man watering the flowers is my dad. (2) There are many people walking their dogs.

01 |해석| 버스정류장에서 <u>기다리고 있는</u> 소녀는 내 여동생이다.
|해설| 주어가 The girl이고 동사가 is인 문장이므로 빈칸에는 주어인 The girl을 뒤에서 수식하는 현재분사 형태가 알맞다.

02 |해석| 내 여행 가방은 네 것만큼 <u>무겁다</u>.
|해설| '…만큼 ~한'을 나타내는 「as+형용사의 원급+as」의 형태가 되어야 한다.

03 |해석| 나무 아래에서 책을 <u>읽고 있는</u> 소년은 Dave다.
|해설| 현재분사가 단독으로 명사를 수식할 때는 명사 앞에 오지만, 현재분사에 뒤따르는 어구가 있을 경우에는 명사를 뒤에서 수식한다. 따라서 reading의 목적어에 해당하는 a book이 이어지고 앞에 수식할 명사가 있는 ②에 들어가는 것이 알맞다.

04 |해석| Dan과 Ryan은 나의 사촌들이다. Dan은 Ryan만큼 나이가 많지 <u>않다</u>. Dan은 15살이고, Ryan은 16살이다.
|해설| ④ 15살인 Dan은 16살인 Ryan과 나이가 같지 않으므로 「A ~ not as(so)+형용사의 원급+as B」로 나타내는 것이 알맞다.

05 |해석| 경주에서 달리고 있는 선수는 다친 것 같아 보인다.
|해설| 명사와 현재분사 사이의 「주격 관계대명사+be동사」는 생략할 수 있다.

06 |해석| 그 여자는 나의 담임 선생님이다. 그녀는 안경을 쓰고 있다.
→ 안경을 <u>쓰고 있는</u> 여자는 나의 담임 선생님이다.
|해설| 문장의 동사가 is이므로 빈칸에는 앞에 있는 주어 The woman을 수식하는 형용사 역할을 하는 현재분사 형태가 알맞다.

07 |해석| 이 다리는 저 다리만큼 길지 않다.
= 이 다리는 저 다리보다 더 <u>짧다</u>.
= 저 다리는 이 다리보다 더 <u>길다</u>.
|해설| 「A ~ not as(so)+형용사/부사의 원급+as B」의 형태는 'A는 B만큼 ~하지 않다'라는 뜻을 나타내며 「B ~ 비교급+than A」 형태로 바꿔 쓸 수 있다.

08 |해석| ① 오래된 동전을 <u>모으는</u> 것은 나의 취미다.
② 파란 모자를 <u>쓰고 있는</u> 소녀는 누구니?
③ 저기에서 <u>요리하고 있는</u> 요리사는 나의 아버지다.
④ 큰 가방을 <u>들고 있는</u> 노부인을 봐.
⑤ 구내 식당에는 점심을 <u>먹고 있는</u> 학생들이 많이 있다.
|해설| ①은 주어 역할을 하는 동명사이고, 나머지는 모두 앞에 있는 명사를 수식하는 현재분사이다.

09 |해석| 수지는 민호만큼 영어를 잘하지 못한다.
= 민호는 수지보다 영어를 더 <u>잘한다</u>.
|해설| 「A ~ not as+원급+as B」는 「B ~ 비교급+than A」로 바꿔 쓸 수 있다. 민호가 수지보다 영어를 더 잘한다는 내용이 되도록 부사 well의 비교급 better를 사용하는 것이 알맞다.

10 |해석| 건강을 유지하는 것은 돈을 버는 것만큼 중요하다.
|해설| '…만큼 ~한'을 나타내는 「as+형용사의 원급+as」 형태가 되도록 형용사의 원급인 important가 쓰여야 한다.

11 |해석| • 소파에 <u>앉아 있는</u> 고양이는 정말 귀엽다.
• 쿠키를 <u>굽고 있는</u> 여자는 나의 이모이다.
• 저기서 전화 <u>통화하고 있는</u> 남자를 아니?

• 잠자고 있는 아기를 깨우지 않도록 볼륨을 낮춰라.
• 선글라스를 <u>쓰고 있는</u> 남자를 아니?
|해설| 모두 명사를 수식하는 형용사 역할을 하는 현재분사 형태가 들어가는 것이 알맞다. ⓐ, ⓑ, ⓒ, ⓔ와 같이 현재분사가 뒤따르는 어구와 함께 명사를 수식할 때는 명사와 현재분사 사이에 「주격 관계대명사+be동사」가 생략되었다고 볼 수 있다.

12 |해석| 나무에서 <u>노래하는(노래하고 있는)</u> 새들을 봐.
|해설| 빈칸에는 명사 the birds를 뒤에서 수식하는 현재분사나 주격 관계대명사가 이끄는 관계대명사절 형태가 알맞다. 이때 관계대명사절의 주격 관계대명사(which/that)와 be동사(are)는 생략할 수 있다.

13 |해석| ① Tom은 Jane만큼 키가 크다.
② Tom은 Jane보다 키가 더 크다.
④ Tom은 Jane만큼 키가 크지 않다.
⑤ Tom은 Jane과 키가 같다.
|해설| 'Tom은 Jane과 키가 같다.'라는 의미의 ①과 ⑤가 알맞다.

14 |해석| ① 초록색 모자가 빨간색 모자보다 더 싸다.
② 빨간색 모자는 초록색 모자만큼 비싸다.
③ 빨간색 모자는 초록색 모자만큼 비싸지 않다.
④ 초록색 모자는 빨간색 모자만큼 비싸지 않다.
⑤ 초록색 모자는 빨간색 모자보다 더 비싸다.
|해설| '빨간색 모자는 초록색 모자만큼 비싸지 않다.', '초록색 모자가 빨간색 모자보다 더 비싸다.'가 그림의 내용에 맞는 문장이다. 「A ~ not as+형용사/부사의 원급+as B」는 'A는 B만큼 ~하지 않다'라는 뜻을 나타내며, 「B ~ 비교급+than A」로 바꿔 쓸 수 있다.

15 |해석| ⓐ 사진을 찍고 있는 소년은 내 사촌이다.
ⓑ 기차는 비행기만큼 빠르지 않다.
ⓒ 너는 노란색 드레스를 입고 있는 여자아이를 보았니?
ⓓ 너는 큰 배낭을 가지고 다니는 키 큰 남자를 보았니?
ⓔ 한국에서는 농구가 야구만큼 인기 있는 것 같지 않아.
|해설| ⓑ, ⓔ '…만큼 ~하지 않은'은 「not as(so)+형용사의 원급+as」 형태로 나타낸다. ⓐ, ⓒ, ⓓ는 모두 명사를 뒤에서 수식하는 현재분사 형태가 알맞다.

16 |해석| A: 사진에서 밝게 <u>웃고 있는</u> 이 여자아이는 누구니?
B: 런던에 사는 내 사촌이야.
A: 이 남자아이들은?
B: 내 남자 형제들이야. 야구 배트를 <u>들고 있는</u> 남자아이가 내 남동생이야.
A: 아, 그는 너만큼 <u>키가 크구나</u>.
|해설| ⓓ '야구 방망이를 들고 있는 남자아이'라는 의미가 되어야 하므로 The boy를 뒤에서 수식하는 현재분사 형태가 되어야 알맞다.
(→ holding)

17 |해설| Is your room as big as mine?이 되어야 하므로 5번째로 올 단어는 big이다.

18 |해석| ⓐ 너는 소파에 앉아 있는 소년을 아니?
ⓑ 바닥에 깨진 병이 있었다.
ⓒ 어제 나는 영어로 쓰여진 책을 읽었다.
ⓓ 병에 끓는 물을 채울 때는 조심해라.
|해설| ⓑ 명사와 명사를 수식하는 분사의 관계가 수동일 때는 과거분사를 쓴다. (breaking → broken)

19 |해석| ① Eric은 지호만큼 키가 크다.

② Eric은 지호보다 나이가 더 많다.

③ Eric은 지호만큼 몸무게가 나간다.

④ 지호는 Eric만큼 나이가 많지 않다.

⑤ 지호는 Eric만큼 가볍지 않다.

|해설| ③ Eric은 지호만큼 몸무게가 나가지 않으므로 Eric is not as (so) heavy as Jiho.가 되어야 알맞다.

20 |해석| ⓐ 그는 잃어버린 개를 찾고 있다.

ⓑ 나는 아빠만큼 일찍 일어나야 했다.

ⓒ 야구는 축구만큼 흥미진진하지 않다.

ⓓ 악기를 연주하고 있는 소년은 Ted이다.

ⓔ 내 여동생과 나는 아침으로 계란프라이와 우유를 좀 먹었다.

|해설| ⓑ '아빠만큼 일찍'은 as early as my dad로 나타낸다. (so → as)

ⓓ 명사를 수식하는 분사와 명사의 관계가 능동이므로 현재분사를 써야 한다. (played → playing)

21 |해석| [예시] 선생님과 대화하고 있는 소녀는 미나이다.

(1) 물을 마시고 있는 소년은 Mike이다.

(2) 음악을 듣고 있는 소년은 지호다.

(3) 책을 읽고 있는 소녀는 Lucy다.

|해설| 뒤따르는 어구와 함께 명사를 뒤에서 수식하는 현재분사 형태로 문장을 완성한다. (1) 물을 마시고 있으므로 drinking water, (2) 음악을 듣고 있으므로 listening to music, (3) 책을 읽고 있으므로 reading a book을 사용한다.

22 |해석| (1) 파란색 배낭은 빨간색 배낭만큼 크다.

(2) 빨간색 배낭은 검은색 배낭만큼 비싸다.

(3) 검은색 배낭은 파란색 배낭만큼 무겁다.

|해설| 가격, 크기, 무게가 같은 두 배낭을 「as+형용사의 원급+as」의 형태로 써서 비교한다. 크기는 big, 가격은 expensive, 무게는 heavy를 사용하여 나타낸다.

23 |해석| (1) 유나는 100m를 16초에 달린다. 소민도 100m를 16초에 달린다.

→ 소민이는 유나만큼 빠르게 달린다.

(2) 그 남자는 나의 새로운 영어 선생님이다. 그는 사진을 찍고 있다.

→ 사진을 찍고 있는 남자는 나의 새로운 영어 선생님이다.

|해설| (1) 「as+부사의 원급+as」의 형태로 써서 두 사람의 100미터 달리기 속력이 같음을 나타낸다.

(2) '사진을 찍고 있는 남자'라는 의미가 되도록 두 번째 문장을 현재분사구가 되도록 수정하여 문장을 연결한다.

24 |해석| ⓐ 이 강은 한강만큼 길다.

ⓑ 이 전화기는 내 전화기만큼 가볍지 않다.

ⓒ David는 Amy만큼 자주 나에게 전화를 했다.

ⓓ 내 손목시계는 내 남동생의 손목시계만큼 크다.

|해설| ⓐ '…만큼 ~한'은 「as+형용사의 원급+as」로 나타낸다.

ⓑ '…만큼 ~하지 않은'은 「not as(so)+형용사의 원급+as」 형태로 나타낸다.

25 |해설| 현재분사에 뒤따르는 어구가 있을 경우에는 명사를 뒤에서 수식한다. (1)은 주어 The man 뒤에 현재분사구 watering the flowers를 쓰고 is my dad를 덧붙인다. (2)는 There are many people 뒤에 현재분사구 walking their dogs를 쓴다.

Ⓡ Reading 빈칸 채우기
pp. 32~33

01 on their own **02** who **03** hidden, get attention **04** as important as **05** examples **06** run, and lead **07** experienced, to help, manage **08** There can be **09** Each pacer, finishes **10** showing **11** depending on, target **12** if, wants, follow **13** keeps track of, goal of finishing **14** In short, to win **15** run for **16** may, during, behind **17** is called **18** on the side of, during **19** check, change **20** especially important, wear out **21** as short as **22** Therefore, perfect harmony **23** get, attention, as **24** which, eastern **25** know their way around **26** have little difficulty breathing **27** hire, help them climb **28** lead, to **29** in many ways **30** put up **31** are often called, invisible

---

Ⓡ Reading 바른 어휘·어법 고르기
pp. 34~35

01 on **02** who **03** hidden **04** important **05** are **06** run **07** manage **08** pacers **09** finishes **10** showing **11** on **12** wants, will **13** time, finishing **14** In short **15** others **16** during **17** is called **18** pit **19** to check **20** out **21** as **22** has to **23** are won **24** which **25** know **26** have little difficulty **27** climb **28** to **29** in **30** For example **31** invisible

---

Ⓡ Reading 틀린 문장 고치기
pp. 36~37

01 ○ **02** ×, who help **03** ×, hidden **04** ×, as important **05** ○ **06** ×, lead them **07** ×, other runners manage **08** ○ **09** ×, runs at different speeds **10** ×, showing **11** ○ **12** ×, wants to finish **13** ○ **14** ○ **15** ○ **16** ○ **17** ×, is called **18** ×, during **19** ×, change the tires **20** ×, is **21** ×, as short as **22** ○ **23** ○ **24** ○ **25** ○ **26** ×, have little difficulty breathing **27** ○ **28** ×, lead **29** ×, in many ways **30** ○ **31** ×, often see

---

Ⓡ Reading 실전 TEST
pp. 40~43

01 ④ **02** ① **03** ⑤ **04** ③ **05** ③ **06** ② **07** ⑤
08 ④ **09** ③ **10** ② **11** ⑤ **12** ③ **13** crew
14 ④ **15** ② **16** ⑤ **17** ⑤ **18** ④

[01~03] |해석|

스포츠에서는 선수들만 트로피나 메달을 받지만, 그들이 혼자 힘으로 우승하는 것은 아니다. 그 선수들을 돕는 사람들이 있다. 이 사람들은 종종 숨겨져 있고 주목을 받지 못한다. 하지만 그들은 선수들만큼 중요하다. 여기 몇 가지 예가 있다.

01 |해설| ⓓ '숨겨져 있다'라는 의미의 수동태(be동사＋과거분사) 형태가 되어야 하므로 과거분사 hidden이 알맞다.

02 |해석| ② 그들은 선수들보다 덜 중요하다
③ 그들은 선수들만큼 중요하지 않다
④ 그들은 선수들보다 더 중요하다
⑤ 선수들은 그들보다 더 중요하다
|해설| '…만큼 ~한'은 「as＋형용사의 원급＋as」 형태로 나타낸다.

03 |해설| 스포츠 분야에서 우승자들을 돕는 조력자들이 있고 그 조력자들의 예시가 여기 있다고 말하고 있으므로 이 글 다음에는 스포츠에서 숨은 조력자들의 예시가 이어질 것이다.

[04~09] |해석|

마라톤의 페이서들

페이서들은 마라톤에서 다른 선수들과 함께 달리며 그들을 이끈다. 페이서들은 경험이 많은 선수들이며, 그들의 역할은 다른 선수들이 경주를 더 잘 운영하도록 돕는 것이다. 한 경주에는 여러 명의 페이서들이 있을 수 있다. 각각의 페이서는 다른 속도로 달리고 다른 시간대에 경주를 마친다. 페이서들은 보통 자신들의 완주 시간을 나타내는 깃발이나 풍선을 가지고 있다.
선수들은 자신들의 목표 완주 시간에 따라 페이서를 선택할 수 있다. 예를 들어, 한 선수가 4시간 안에 경주를 미치고 싶다면, 그 선수는 4시간 페이서를 따라갈 것이다. 페이서가 시간을 계속해서 파악하기 때문에, 선수는 특정 시간 안에 마라톤을 완주하려는 자신의 목표를 더 쉽게 달성할 수 있다. 요컨대, 페이서들은 달리기는 하지만 우승을 하기 위해 달리는 것은 아니다. 그들은 다른 이들을 위해 달린다.

04 |해설| ⓒ 앞에 있는 flags or balloons를 수식하는 현재분사 형태인 showing이 되어야 한다. 나머지는 모두 어법상 올바르다.

05 |해설| (A) depending on: ~에 따라
(B) keep track of: (계속해서) ~을 파악하다, ~에 주의를 기울이다

06 |해석| ① 그런데 ③ 예를 들어 ④ 게다가 ⑤ 반면에
|해설| 앞서 언급한 내용을 요약하는 문장이 이어지므로 '요컨대'라는 의미의 연결어 In short가 알맞다.

07 |해석| ① 그는 오늘 해야 할 숙제가 많다.
② 나는 언젠가 에베레스트산을 오르고 싶다.
③ 그를 직접 만나는 것은 놀라운 일이었다.
④ 내 장래희망은 로봇 과학자가 되는 것이다.
⑤ 그들은 마지막 기차를 타기 위해 역으로 서둘러 갔다.
|해설| (D)와 ⑤는 목적을 나타내는 부사적 용법의 to부정사로 쓰였다.
(① 형용사적 용법의 to부정사 ② 목적어 역할을 하는 명사적 용법의 to부정사 ③ 진주어로 쓰인 명사적 용법의 to부정사 ④ 보어 역할을

하는 명사적 용법의 to부정사)

08 |해설| 마라톤 경주에서 페이서가 하는 역할을 설명하는 글이다.

09 |해석| ① 그들은 마라톤에서 다른 선수들을 이끈다.
② 그들은 다른 선수들이 마라톤에서 더 잘하도록 돕는다.
③ 그들은 각자 한 명의 선수와 달려야 한다.
④ 그들은 깃발이나 풍선을 가지고 달린다.
⑤ 그들은 자신들을 위해서가 아니라 다른 사람들을 위해서 뛴다.
|해설| ③ 한 경주에는 여러 명의 페이서가 있고 선수들은 자신들이 원하는 목표 시간에 맞는 페이서를 따라간다고 했다.

[10~14] |해석|

여러분은 대부분의 자동차 경주에서 자동차와 레이서만 볼지도 모르겠지만, 그 레이서 뒤에는 팀이 있다. 이 팀은 피트 크루라고 불린다. 피트는 경주 트랙의 옆에 있는 공간으로, 레이서들이 경주 도중에 그곳에 여러 번 정지한다. 피트 크루가 하는 주요 역할은 자동차를 점검하고 타이어를 교체하는 것이다. 빠른 속도의 경주에서는 타이어가 쉽게 마모되기 <u>때문에</u> 타이어를 교체하는 것이 특히 중요하다.
피트에서의 정지는 짧게는 2초 정도가 될 수 있고, 한 크루에 많게는 20명에 이르는 구성원이 있다. 그러므로 피트 크루는 완벽한 조화를 이루며 일해야 한다. 레이서만 모든 주목을 받을지 모르지만 사람들이 말하는 것처럼, "경주의 우승은 피트에서 이루어진다."

10 |해석| ① 자동차 경주에서 우승하는 방법
② 자동차 경주에서의 피트 크루
③ 자동차 레이서의 주요 업무
④ 안전한 자동차 경주를 위한 몇 가지 조언
⑤ 타이어 교체의 중요성
|해설| 자동차 경주에서 중요한 역할을 하는 피트 크루에 관한 내용이다.

11 |해설| (A) '~으로 불린다'라는 의미의 수동태(be동사＋과거분사) 형태가 알맞다.
(B) 문장의 주어 역할을 하는 동명사 형태가 알맞다.
(C) 「as＋형용사의 원급＋as」의 형태가 되어야 하므로 short가 알맞다.

12 |해설| 타이어 교체가 특히 중요한 이유가 빈칸 뒤에 이어지므로 이유를 나타내는 접속사 because가 알맞다.

13 |해석| 함께 일하는 특정한 기술을 가진 사람들
|해설| crew(팀, 조)의 영영풀이이다.

14 |해석| ① 자동차 경주에서 피트는 무엇인가?
② 피트 크루는 경주를 하는 동안 어디에서 일하는가?
③ 피트 크루의 주요 업무는 무엇인가?
④ 레이서들은 각 경주에서 타이어를 몇 번 교체할 수 있는가?
⑤ 자동차 경주에서 타이어를 교체하는 것이 왜 특히 중요한가?
|해설| ④ 각 경주에서 타이어를 몇 번 교체할 수 있는지는 언급되지 않았다.

[15~18] |해석|

등반에서의 셰르파

Sherpa라는 단어는 셰르파족에서 유래되었는데, 셰르파족은 네팔의 동쪽 지역에 산다. 셰르파는 훌륭한 등반 기술을 가졌으며 산의 지리에 밝다. 그들은 또한 산의 높은 곳에서 호흡하는 데 어려움이 거의 없다. 그래서 등산가들은 자신들이 에베레스트산을 등반하는 것을 돕는 셰르파를 고용하기 시작했다.
셰르파는 등산가들을 산 정상까지 이끈다. 그들은 여러 방식으로 등산가들

을 지원한다. 예를 들어, 그들은 텐트를 치고 등산가들의 가방을 운반한다. 셰르파는 종종 에베레스트산의 보이지 않는 사람들로 불리는데, 왜냐하면 사람들은 흔히 산 정상에서 등산가들만 찍힌 사진을 보기 때문이다.

15 |해설| ⓑ '~하는 데 어려움이 있다'는 have difficulty -ing로 표현하므로 breathing이 되어야 한다.

16 |해설| 주어진 문장은 셰르파가 등산가들을 지원하는 방법의 예시이므로 '셰르파는 여러 방식으로 등산가들을 지원한다.'라는 문장 바로 뒤인 ⑤에 들어가는 것이 자연스럽다.

17 |해석| ① 등산 ② 격식을 차린 ③ 동쪽의 ④ 어려운
|해설| 사람들이 흔히 사진에서 그들을 볼 수 없고 등산가들만 볼 수 있다는 이유가 이어지는 것으로 보아 셰르파들은 '보이지 않는 사람들'로 불린다는 내용이 되는 것이 자연스럽다.

18 |해석| ① Sherpa라는 단어의 기원
② 셰르파가 잘하는 것
③ 등반가들이 셰르파를 고용하는 이유
④ 셰르파를 고용하는 방법
⑤ 등산에서 셰르파의 역할
|해설| ④ 셰르파를 고용하는 방법에 대해서는 언급되지 않았다.

[19~20] |해석|
선수들은 자신들의 목표 완주 시간에 따라 페이서를 선택할 수 있다. 예를 들어, 한 선수가 4시간 안에 경주를 마치고 싶다면, 그 선수는 4시간 페이서를 따라갈 것이다. 페이서가 시간을 계속해서 파악하기 때문에, 선수는 특정 시간 안에 마라톤을 완주하려는 자신의 목표를 더 쉽게 달성할 수 있다. 요컨대, 페이서들은 달리기는 하지만 우승을 하기 위해 달리는 것은 아니다. 그들은 다른 이들을 위해 달린다.

19 |해설| his or her goal은 of 뒤에 이어지는 finishing the marathon in a particular time과 동격이다.

20 |해설| Q. 만약 한 선수가 3시간 안에 경주를 완주하고 싶으면, 어떤 페이서를 따라갈 것인가?
→ 선수는 3시간 페이서를 따라갈 것이다.
|해설| 선수들은 자신의 목표 완주 시간에 맞는 페이서를 따라간다고 했으므로 '3시간 페이서'를 따라갈 것이다.

[21~22] |해석|
여러분은 대부분의 자동차 경주에서 자동차와 레이서만 볼지도 모르겠지만, 그 레이서 뒤에는 팀이 있다.
(B) 이 팀은 피트 크루라고 불린다. 피트는 경주 트랙의 옆에 있는 공간으로, 레이서들이 경주 도중에 그곳에 여러 번 정지한다. 피트 크루가 하는 주요 역할은 자동차를 점검하고 타이어를 교체하는 것이다.
(C) 빠른 속도의 경주에서는 타이어가 쉽게 마모되기 때문에 타이어를 교체하는 것이 특히 중요하다. 피트에서의 정지는 짧게는 2초 정도가 될 수 있고, 한 크루에 많게는 20명에 이르는 구성원이 있다.
(A) 그러므로 피트 크루는 완벽한 조화를 이루며 일해야 한다. 레이서만 모든 주목을 받을지 모르지만 사람들이 말하는 것처럼, "경주의 우승은 피트에서 이루어진다."

21 |해설| 레이서 뒤에 팀이 있다는 문장 뒤에 그 팀을 소개하는 내용(B)이 나오고 그에 대한 자세한 설명(C)과 함께 피트 크루가 하는 일의 중요성을 강조하는 내용(A)이 이어지는 것이 자연스럽다.

22 |해설| ⓒ 동명사가 주어 역할을 할 때는 단수 취급하므로 are가 아니라 is가 되어야 한다.

[23~24] |해석|
Sherpa라는 단어는 셰르파족에서 유래되었는데, 셰르파족은 네팔의 동쪽 지역에 산다. 셰르파는 훌륭한 등반 기술을 가졌으며 산의 지리에 밝다. 그들은 또한 산의 높은 곳에서 호흡하는 데 어려움이 거의 없다. 그래서 등산가들은 자신들이 에베레스트산을 등반하는 것을 돕는 셰르파를 고용하기 시작했다.
셰르파는 등산가들을 산 정상까지 이끈다. 그들은 여러 방식으로 등산가들을 지원한다. 예를 들어, 그들은 텐트를 치고 등산가들의 가방을 운반한다. 셰르파는 종종 에베레스트산의 보이지 않는 사람들로 불리는데, 왜냐하면 사람들은 흔히 산 정상에서 등산가들만 찍힌 사진을 보기 때문이다.

23 |해설| '거의 ~않는'을 의미하는 little을 사용하여 have little difficulty -ing로 '~하는 데 어려움이 거의 없다'라는 의미를 나타낸다.

24 |해석| 그들은 등산가들이 에베레스트산을 오르는 것을 돕는다. 그들은 등산가들을 산 정상으로 이끌고 여러 방식으로 그들을 지원한다.
|해설| 셰르파들은 등산가들이 산을 오르는 것을 돕고(help) 산의 정상(top)까지 이끌며(lead), 그들을 여러 방식으로 지원한다(돕는다)(support(help)).

Ⓜ 기타 지문 실전 TEST   p. 45

01 ③, ⑤   **02** ③   **03** blind   **04** ③   **05** as hard as the players   **06** (1) 건강하고 튼튼해야 한다. (2) 점프와 춤에 능숙해야 한다. (3) 선수들만큼 열심히 일해야 한다.

[01~02] |해석|
자전거 타는 것을 좋아하나요? 그렇다면, 우리 동아리 Fun Wheels에 가입하는 것을 제안합니다. 우리는 일주일에 한 번, 토요일마다 자전거를 타요. 강을 따라 자전거를 타거나 공원에서 탑니다. 함께 자전거를 타면 재미있어요.

01 |해석| ① 당신은 우리 동아리 Fun Wheels에 가입했나요?
② 당신은 우리 동아리 Fun Wheels에 가입할 수 없어요.
③ 우리 동아리 Fun Wheels에 가입하는 게 어떠세요?
④ 우리 동아리 Fun Wheels에 대해 어떻게 생각하나요?
⑤ 당신이 우리 동아리 Fun Wheels에 가입해야 한다고 생각해요.
|해설| 「I suggest you+동사원형 ~.」은 상대방에게 어떤 일을 할 것을 제안하거나 권유하는 표현이다.

02 |해석| ① 우리 자전거 타는 게 어때요?
② 자전거를 누구와 타나요?
③ 자전거를 얼마나 자주 타나요?
④ 자전거를 보통 어디서 타나요?
⑤ 자전거 타는 법을 아세요?
|해설| 일주일에 한 번 자전거를 탄다는 대답에 대한 질문은 자전거를 얼마나 자주 타는지 빈도를 묻는 ③이 알맞다.

03 |해석| • 수영 경기에서 tapper는 시각장애인 수영 선수가 수영하는 것을 돕기 위해 장대를 사용한다.
• 달리기 경주에서 guide runner는 시각장애인 선수와 함께 달리며 그들이 트랙에서 벗어나지 않도록 돕는다.

- 시각장애인 축구에서 shooting assistant는 자신의 팀 선수들에게 어느 방향으로 슛을 해야 하는지 말해 준다.
→ 스포츠 경기에서는 tapper, guide runner, 그리고 shooting assistant 같은 조력자들이 <u>시각장애인</u> 선수들을 돕는다.

|해설| 스포츠 경기에서 시각장애인 선수들을 돕는 다양한 조력자들에 관한 내용이다.

[04~06] |해석|

미식축구 경기의 치어리더들

사람들은 보통 치어리더들이 미식축구 팀의 일원이라고 생각하지 않지만, 그들은 미식축구 경기에서 중요한 역할을 한다. 경기에서 응원을 함으로써 그들은 공동체 정신을 만들어 낸다. 그들은 또한 팀과 팬들을 격려한다. 자신의 역할을 잘 해내기 위해서, 치어리더들은 건강하고 튼튼해야 한다. 그들은 또한 점프와 춤에 능숙해야 한다. 무엇보다도, 그들은 선수들만큼 열심히 일해야 한다.

04 |해석| ① 공을 가지고 논다　② 선수들에게 공을 준다
④ 상대 팀을 응원한다　⑤ 열심히 일할 필요가 없다
|해설| 응원을 함으로써 공동체 정신을 만들어 내고 팀과 팬들을 격려한다는 내용이 이어지는 것으로 보아, 빈칸에는 치어리더가 미식축구 경기에서 중요한 역할을 한다는 내용이 들어가는 것이 가장 알맞다.

05 |해설| '…만큼 ~하게'는 「as+부사의 원급+as」의 형태로 나타낸다.

06 |해설| 치어리더들이 역할을 잘 해내기 위해 필요한 것들은 「need to+동사원형」(~할 필요가 있다)의 형태로 제시되었다.

STEP B

W Words 고득점 맞기　　pp. 46~47

01 ③	02 ①	03 ③	04 (t)arget	05 ②	06 ②
07 wear out	08 ④	09 ⑤	10 ④	11 ③	12 ①
13 ⑤	14 ③	15 ②			

01 |해석| 다음 정의를 가진 단어는 무엇인가?
체내로 공기를 들여보내고 그것을 다시 내보내다
① 숨기다　② 등록하다　③ 숨 쉬다　④ 성취하다　⑤ 제안하다
|해설| breathe(숨 쉬다)에 대한 영영풀이이다.

02 |해석| ① 가벼운 : 무거운 ≠ 응원하다 : 격려하다
② 목표 : 목표 = 특정한 : 특정한
③ 보이는 : 보이지 않는 = 직접적인 : 간접적인
④ 성취하다 : 성취 = 숨 쉬다 : 숨, 호흡
⑤ 등록하다 : 등록 = 제안하다 : 제안
|해설| ① light와 heavy는 반의어 관계이고, cheer와 encourage는 유의어 관계이다. (② 유의어　③ 반의어　④, ⑤ 동사 – 명사)

03 |해석| • 거북은 위험에 처했을 때 껍데기에 자신을 숨길 수 있다.
• 그 식물원은 붐비지 않도록 방문객 수에 제한을 둔다.
① 고용하다 – 정신　② 응원하다 – 깃발　④ 가입하다 – 목표
⑤ 제안하다 – 부족

04 |해석| • 그녀의 첫 발은 1인치 차이로 <u>과녁</u>을 빗나갔다.
• 우리는 학교를 위해 모금을 하고 있는데, 우리의 <u>목표</u>는 3,000달러이다.
|해설| 첫 번째 빈칸에는 '과녁'이라는 뜻으로, 두 번째 빈칸에는 '목표'라는 뜻으로 사용되는 target이 알맞다.

05 |해설| 밑줄 친 부분을 대체할 수 있는 것은?
A: 나는 우리 강아지 밤토리를 위해 집을 짓고 있어.
B: 와. 너는 그것을 <u>혼자 힘</u>으로 만들고 있는 거야?
① 정각에　② 혼자 힘으로　③ 생계 수단으로　④ 너의 경우에는
⑤ 네가 집에 가는 길에
|해설| on one's own: 혼자서, 혼자 힘으로 (= by oneself)

06 |해설| ① 정중한 – 무례한　② 격식을 차린 – 격식에 얽매이지 않는
③ 완전한 – 불완전한　④ 참을성 있는 – 못 견디는
⑤ 가능한 – 불가능한
|해설| ② formal의 반의어는 앞에 in-을 써서 informal로 나타내고, 나머지는 모두 앞에 im-을 써서 반의어를 나타낸다.

07 |해설| wear out: (물건이) 닳다, 해지다

08 |해설| • 모든 선수들이 <u>트랙</u>을 따라 달리고 있었다.
• 발표는 10분 정도 밖에 안 된다. 너는 시간을 주의 깊게 <u>파악</u>해야 한다.
① 피트　② 경주　③ 목표　⑤ 주의
|해설| track: (경주) 트랙, keep track of: ~을 파악하다

09 |해설| 달성하다, 성취하다: ⑧ 원하는 것을 하거나 얻는 데 <u>성공하다</u>
① 기대하다　② 잃다　③ 창조하다　④ 받다

10 |해석| ① 대통령은 1시에 연설을 할 것이다.
② 가격은 생산자에 따라 결정될 수 있다.
③ 사람들의 관심을 받기 싫으면 모자를 써.
④ 요컨대, 우리는 이번 학기 말에 기말고사를 보지 않을 것이다.
⑤ 이달 말 이전에 등록하면 20% 할인을 받을 수 있다.
|해설| ④ in short: 요컨대, 요약하자면

11 |해석| ① 깃발 몇 개가 바람에 펄럭이고 있었다.
② 그는 아들이 보이지 않을 때까지 손을 흔들었다.
③ 방문할 만한 흥미로운 곳을 허락(→ 제안)해 주겠니?
④ 그녀는 우리에게 숙면을 위한 몇 가지 조언을 해 주었다.
⑤ 숙련된 현지 가이드와 함께 마추픽추를 탐험해 보아라.
|해설| ③ 방문할 만한 흥미로운 곳을 '허락해' 달라는 것은 어색하다. allow(허락하다) 대신 suggest(제안하다), recommend(추천하다) 등의 단어가 적절하다.

12 |해석| ① 나는 <u>한때</u> 하와이에 살았다.
② 그것을 다시 <u>한 번</u> 입어 봐도 될까요?
③ 나는 일주일에 <u>한 번</u> 에어로빅을 한다.
④ <u>한 번</u>만 할 거야. 잘 봐.
⑤ 이 기회는 일생에 <u>한 번</u> 온다.
|해설| ①은 '(과거의) 언젠가, 한때'를, 나머지는 모두 '한 번'을 나타낸다.

13 |해석| Harris 씨는 도움이 필요한 아이들을 <u>지원하기</u>로 결정했다.
① 누군가의 이름을 공식 목록에 올리다
② 무언가가 넘어지지 않도록 잡고 있다
③ 특정 일을 하도록 누군가를 고용하거나 금액을 지불하다
④ 아무도 볼 수 없는 곳에 무언가를 두다

⑤ 종종 문제에 맞닥뜨린 누군가를 돕다

|해설| 밑줄 친 support는 '지원하다'라는 의미로 쓰였으므로 ⑤가 알맞다.

14 |해석| • 나는 내일 요리 동아리에 가입할 것이다.
   • 그 동아리 회원들은 강한 팀 정신을 가지고 있다.
   • 나의 고양이들과 개들은 완벽한 조화를 이루며 살고 있다.
   • 그 사원은 산의 동쪽에 있다.

|해설| tribe는 '종족, 부족'이라는 뜻으로 빈칸 중 어느 곳에도 들어갈 수 없다. (ⓐ join: 가입하다 ⓑ spirit: 정신 ⓒ harmony: 조화 ⓓ eastern: 동쪽의)

15 |해석| • 그들은 집을 페인트칠 하도록 두 명의 페인트공을 고용했다.
   • Daniel은 자신의 목표 점수를 달성하기 위해 최선을 다했다.
   • 너는 영어 말하기 대회에 등록했니?

|해설| (A) 페인트칠 하도록 페인트공을 고용했다(hired)는 의미가 알맞다.
(B) 목표(target) 점수를 달성하기 위해 최선을 다했다는 의미가 자연스럽다.
(C) 영어 말하기 대회에 '등록하다(register)'라는 의미가 자연스럽다.

L·T Listen and Talk 고득점 맞기 · pp. 50~51

01 ②, ⑤   02 ②   03 ⑤   04 ③   05 ①, ③   06 ②, ④

[서술형]

07 How often do you want to take classes?   08 ⓑ → The boy wants to take classes twice a week.   09 go swimming, bring a swimming cap   10 |모범 답| I suggest (that) you (should) go see a doctor.   11 (1) how often do you exercise (2) (I have breakfast) Twice a week. (3) |모범 답| I suggest (that) you (should) have breakfast more often.

01 |해석| A: 너는 얼마나 자주 영화를 보러 가니?
   B: _____
   ① 거의 매주 보러 가.
   ② 나는 액션 영화를 좋아해.
   ③ 나는 일주일에 한 번 영화를 보러 가.
   ④ 나는 한 달에 세 번 영화를 보러 가.
   ⑤ 나는 보통 친구들과 영화를 보러 가.

|해설| How often do you ~?는 상대방이 무언가를 얼마나 자주 하는지 빈도를 묻는 말이므로 빈도를 나타내는 말로 답해야 한다.

02 |해석| ① A: 너는 얼마나 자주 축구를 하니?
        B: 일주일에 세 번 해.
      ② A: 나는 매일 아침 형과 함께 운동해.
        B: 음, 네가 규칙적으로 운동하는 것을 제안해.
      ③ A: 오늘 자전거 타러 가자.
        B: 그래. 네 헬멧과 무릎 패드를 가지고 오는 것을 제안해.
      ④ A: 나는 일주일에 한 번 내 방을 청소해.
        B: 내 생각에 너는 네 방 청소를 좀 더 자주 해야 할 것 같아.

⑤ A: 내가 오늘 너와 같이 뛰어도 될까?
   B: 물론이지, 하지만 네가 운동화를 신는 것을 제안해. 네 신발은 달리기에 좋지 않아.

|해설| ② 매일 아침 운동을 한다는 상대방에게 운동을 규칙적으로 할 것을 제안하는 것은 어색하다.

03 |해석| A: 너는 얼마나 자주 볼링 수업을 받니?
   B: 일주일에 두 번. 나는 그냥 초보야. 너는 아주 잘한다고 들었어.
   A: 음, 나는 볼링을 정말 좋아해. 흠. 네 볼링공이 너에게 무거워 보여. 더 가벼운 공을 쓰는 걸 권해.
   B: 알았어. 그러면 더 무거운(→ 더 가벼운) 공을 찾아 볼게.

|해설| ⑤ A는 B에게 볼링공이 무거워 보인다고 말하면서 더 가벼운 공을 사용할 것을 제안했고, B가 그러겠다고 답했으므로 이어서 더 무거운 공을 찾아 보겠다고 말하는 것은 흐름상 어색하다.

04 |해석| 지수는 감자튀김, 햄버거, 피자 같은 패스트푸드를 먹는 것을 좋아한다. 그녀는 거의 매일 패스트푸드를 먹는다. 준호는 패스트푸드가 그녀의 건강에 해롭다고 생각한다. 그는 지수가 패스트푸드를 덜 먹기를 원한다.
   ① 나는 패스트푸드를 덜 먹고 싶어.
   ② 나는 네가 살을 빼야 한다고 생각해.
   ③ 네가 패스트푸드를 덜 먹는 것을 제안해.
   ④ 나는 패스트푸드를 덜 먹어야겠어.
   ⑤ 나는 네가 패스트푸드를 덜 먹어서 기뻐.

|해설| 준호는 지수가 건강에 해로운 패스트푸드를 덜 먹기를 바라는 상황이므로, 지수에게 패스트푸드를 덜 먹을 것을 제안하는 말을 하는 것이 자연스럽다.

05 |해설| 위 대화의 빈칸 ⓐ에 적합한 것은? 두 개 고르시오.
   ① 나는 우리가 스트레칭을 할 것을 제안해
   ② 우리는 스트레칭을 할 필요가 없어
   ③ 우리는 스트레칭을 해야겠어
   ④ 나는 우리가 스트레칭을 해야 한다는 것에 동의해
   ⑤ 나는 스트레칭을 해서는 안 돼

|해설| 빈칸 다음에 '좋은 생각이야.'라고 동의하는 말이 이어지므로, 문맥상 수영하기 전에 스트레칭을 하자고 제안하는 내용이 알맞다. 어떤 일을 하자고 제안할 때 「I suggest (that) we (should)+동사원형 ~.」 또는 「(I think) We should+동사원형 ~.」 등을 사용할 수 있다.

06 |해설| ① 소년은 수영을 자주 하는가?
   ② 소년은 얼마나 자주 수영을 하는가?
   ③ 소녀는 일주일에 몇 번 수영을 하는가?
   ④ 소녀는 보통 언제 수영을 하는가?
   ⑤ 소녀와 소년은 오늘 무엇을 함께 할 것인가?

|해설| ② 소년이 얼마나 자주 수영하는지는 알 수 없다.
④ 소녀는 일주일에 4번 수영을 한다고 했지만 언제 수영하는지는 언급하지 않았다.

07 |해설| 빈도를 물을 때는 How often do you ~?라고 말한다.

08 |해석| ⓐ 소년은 수영하는 법을 배운 적이 없다.
   ⓑ 소년은 한 달에(→ 일주일에) 두 번 수업을 듣기를 원한다.
   ⓒ 소년은 주말에 수업을 듣고 싶어 하지 않는다.
   ⓓ 소년은 초급 2반 수업을 수강할 것이다.
   ⓔ 소년이 등록하고자 하는 수업은 제한 인원이 10명이다.

|해설| 소년은 일주일에 두 번(twice a week) 수업을 받고 싶다고 했다.

09 |해석| A: 미나야, 너는 얼마나 자주 수영을 하니?

B: 나는 매일 수영해.

A: 오늘 오후에 너랑 수영하러 가도 될까?

B: 물론이지, 호준아. 하지만 네가 수영 모자를 가져오는 것을 제안해. 수영 모자가 없으면 수영장에 들어갈 수가 없거든.

→ 미나와 호준이는 오늘 오후에 함께 <u>수영하러</u> 갈 것이다. 미나는 호준이에게 수영 모자를 가져오라고 말했다.

|해설| 미나와 호준이는 오늘 오후에 함께 수영하러 갈 것이고, 미나는 호준이에게 수영 모자를 가져올 것을 제안했다.

10 |해석| A: 나 감기에 걸린 것 같아.

|해설| 상대방에게 제안할 때는 I suggest (that) you (should) ~.로 말할 수 있다.

11 |해석| A: <u>수지야, 너는 얼마나 자주 운동하니?</u>

B: 나는 매일 운동해.

A: 좋다. 그러면 얼마나 자주 아침을 먹니?

B: <u>(나는)</u> 일주일에 두 번 (아침을 먹어).

A: <u>네가 더 자주 아침을 먹는 것을 제안해.</u> 아침을 먹는 것이 건강에 좋아.

B: 알았어. 해 볼게.

|해설| 빈도를 물을 때는 How often do you ~?를 사용해서 말할 수 있고, 제안이나 권유를 할 때는 I suggest (that) you (should) ~.를 사용하여 말할 수 있다.

Ⓖ Grammar 고득점 맞기   pp. 52~54

01 ④   02 ①   03 ①, ④   04 ①   05 ①, ②   06 ⑤
07 ①   08 ③   09 ④   10 ④   11 ④   12 ③   13 ①
14 ②

[서술형]

15 (1) The woman carrying books is my grandma. (2) She cleared up the plate broken by Tom.   16 is not as(so) popular as   17 The violinists playing in the orchestra are from Austria.   18 taking → taken   19 (1) Tom runs as fast as Jerry. 또는 Jerry runs as fast as Tom. (2) Ted is as tall as the tree. 또는 The tree is as tall as Ted. (3) The red book is not as thick as the yellow book. (4) The smartphone(cell phone) is not as expensive as the laptop.   20 (1) running on the track (2) playing basketball (3) holding a soccer ball

01 |해석| • 공을 <u>차고 있는</u> 소년은 나의 가장 친한 친구다.

• 공원에는 <u>걷고 있는</u> 사람들이 많이 있었다.

|해설| 첫 번째 빈칸에는 '공을 차고 있는 소년'이라는 의미가 되도록 현재분사 kicking이 알맞고, 두 번째 빈칸에는 '걷고 있는 사람들'이라는 의미가 되도록 현재분사 walking이 알맞다.

02 |해석| ① 미국에서는 축구가 야구만큼 인기 있다.

②, ③ 미국에서는 축구가 야구만큼 인기 있지 않다.

④ 미국에서는 축구가 야구보다 덜 인기 있다.

⑤ 미국에서는 야구가 축구보다 더 인기 있다.

|해설| ①은 미국에서 축구가 야구만큼 인기 있다는 의미이고, 나머지는 모두 미국에서 야구가 축구보다 더 인기 있다는 의미이다.

03 |해석| ① 한국은 호주만큼 크지 않다.

② 다이아몬드만큼 단단한 것은 없다.

③ 우리 엄마는 내 여동생만큼 요가를 잘하신다.

④ 빨간색 차를 운전하고 있는 여자는 나의 영어 선생님이다.

⑤ 무대에서 노래를 부르고 있는 여자는 유명한 영화배우다.

|해설| ② 「as+형용사의 원급+as」의 형태가 되어야 알맞다. (hardest → hard)

③ 요가를 '잘' 한다는 의미이므로 부사 well의 원급이 쓰여야 한다. (good → well)

⑤ '노래하고 있는 여자'라는 의미가 되어야 하므로 현재분사 singing을 사용해야 한다. (sang → singing)

04 |해설| The cat sleeping over there is Tom's.가 알맞은 문장이므로 6번째로 올 단어는 is이다.

05 |해설| I swim as well as her.가 되어야 하므로 as와 well이 반드시 필요하다.

06 |해석| ① 그녀는 내가 깨뜨린 꽃병을 버렸다.

② Bill이 만든 스파게티는 너무 짰다.

③ 너는 햄버거를 먹고 있는 소년을 아니?

④ 많은 오래된 책들로 가득 찬 방이 있었다.

⑤ 제과점 앞에서 기다리고 있는 소녀는 내 여동생이다.

|해설| ⑤ 소녀가 '기다리고 있는' 것이므로 진행·능동의 의미를 나타내는 현재분사 waiting으로 써야 한다.

07 |해석| 지수는 6시에 일어난다. 그녀의 엄마도 6시에 일어난다.

① 지수는 자신의 엄마만큼 일찍 일어난다.

② 지수는 자신의 엄마보다 일찍 일어난다.

③ 지수는 자신의 엄마보다 덜 일찍 일어난다.

④ 지수는 자신의 엄마만큼 늦게 일어나지 않는다.

⑤ 지수는 자신의 엄마만큼 일찍 일어나지 않는다.

|해설| 지수와 엄마는 둘 다 6시에 일어난다고 했으므로 as ~ as ... 구문을 사용한 ①이 알맞다.

08 |해석| ⓐ 내 뒤에 <u>서 있는</u> 소녀는 Alice이다.

ⓑ 나는 우산을 들고 있는 여자를 안다.

ⓒ Tom은 식탁에 놓인 케이크를 다 먹어 치웠다.

ⓓ 그들은 1970년대에 <u>지어진</u> 집에서 산다.

ⓔ 그녀는 전 세계를 <u>여행하는</u> 한 가족에 관한 소설을 읽었다.

|해설| ⓒ 명사를 뒤에서 수식하는 분사가 들어가야 하는데, 케이크가 탁자 위에 '놓여 있는' 것이므로 과거분사 placed를 써야 한다. (ⓐ standing ⓑ holding ⓓ built ⓔ traveling)

09 |해석| ⓐ 나는 테니스를 치고 있는 소년들을 안다.

ⓑ 나는 몇 분 전에 Tom이 길을 건너는 것을 보았다.

ⓒ Kate는 교통사고를 당한 후 운전하는 것을 멈췄다.

ⓓ 내 문제는 옷에 너무 많은 돈을 쓰는 것이다.

ⓔ 저기서 손을 흔들고 있는 남자는 나의 삼촌이야.

| 해설| ⓐ, ⓑ, ⓔ는 현재분사로 쓰였고, ⓒ와 ⓓ는 동명사로 쓰였다.

10 | 해석| ① A폰은 B폰만큼 크다.

② B폰은 A폰만큼 오래되었다.

③ B폰은 A폰보다 더 무겁다.

④ A폰은 B폰만큼 가볍지 않다.

⑤ B폰은 A폰만큼 비싸지 않다.

| 해설| ④ Phone A가 Phone B보다 무겁지 않다(not as heavy as)는 내용이 되어야 알맞다.

11 | 해석| ⓐ 동물원에서 일하는 남자는 매우 친절하다.

ⓑ 상어는 악어만큼 위험하지 않다.

ⓒ 사람들이 버린 쓰레기를 주워라.

ⓓ 이 사과들은 유기농 사과만큼 비싸다.

ⓔ Nick은 그의 형만큼 참을성이 있다.

| 해설| ⓓ 「as+형용사의 원급+as」의 형태로 써야 한다.

(→ as expensive)

12 | 해석| ① 호랑이는 원숭이보다 더 빠르다.

= 원숭이는 호랑이만큼 빠르지 않다.

② 이 책은 저 책만큼 유용하지 않다.

= 이 책은 저 책보다 덜 유용하다.

③ 새 공원은 예전 공원만큼 좋지 않다.

≠ 새 공원은 예전 공원보다 더 좋다.

④ 이 모자는 저 가방만큼 비싸다.

= 이 모자와 저 가방의 가격은 같다.

⑤ 결과는 과정만큼 중요하지 않다.

= 과정이 결과보다 더 중요하다.

13 | 해설| 배드민턴을 치고 있는 두 소년이 있다. 한 소녀는 영어로 쓰여진 책을 읽고 있다. 한 소년은 나무에서 노래하고 있는 새들을 보고 있다.

| 해설| ⓐ '배드민턴을 치고 있는 두 소년'이라는 의미가 되도록 현재분사 playing을 사용하는 것이 알맞다.

14 | 해석| ⓐ 한 남자가 나무에 오르고 있었다.

ⓑ 나의 여가 활동은 영화 감상이다.

ⓒ Katie를 따라 뛰고 있는 개는 그녀의 애완동물이 아니다.

ⓓ 너는 길거리에서 춤추고 있는 소녀를 아니?

| 해설| ⓑ의 watching은 주격보어로 쓰인 동명사이다.

15 | 해석| (1) 그 여자는 나의 할머니이다. 그녀는 책을 나르고 있다.

→ 책을 나르고 있는 여자는 나의 할머니이다.

(2) 그녀는 접시를 치웠다. 그 접시는 Tom에 의해 깨졌다.

→ 그녀는 Tom에 의해 깨진 접시를 치웠다.

| 해설| (1) 현재분사를 사용하여 carrying books가 주어 The woman을 뒤에서 수식하는 형태로 문장을 연결한다.

(2) 과거분사를 사용하여 broken by Tom이 목적어 the plate를 뒤에서 수식하는 형태로 문장을 연결한다.

16 | 해석| 그의 새 노래는 그의 첫 번째 노래보다 덜 인기 있다.

= 그의 새 노래는 그의 첫 번째 노래만큼 인기 있지 않다.

| 해설| '그의 새 노래는 그의 첫 번째 노래보다 덜 인기 있다.'는 「not as(so)+형용사/부사의 원급+as」를 사용하여 '그의 새 노래는 그의 첫 번째 노래만큼 인기 있지 않다.'로 바꿔 쓸 수 있다.

17 | 해설| 바이올린 연주자들이 '연주하고 있는' 것이므로 현재분사 playing을 사용하여 주어인 The violinists를 playing in the

orchestra가 뒤에서 수식하는 형태로 쓰고, 주어가 복수이므로 동사는 are를 쓴다.

18 | 해석| 엄마는 전문 사진작가가 찍은 사진에 만족했다.

| 해설| 사진은 '찍히는' 것이므로 명사 the pictures를 뒤에서 수식하는 분사의 형태는 수동의 의미를 나타내는 과거분사 taken이 되어야 한다.

19 | 해석| (1) Tom은 Jerry만큼 빠르게 달린다. / Jerry는 Tom만큼 빠르게 달린다.

(2) Ted는 나무만큼 키가 크다. / 나무는 Ted만큼 키가 크다.

(3) 빨간색 책은 노란색 책만큼 두껍지 않다.

(4) 스마트폰은 노트북만큼 비싸지 않다.

| 해설| 비교하는 두 대상의 정도나 상태가 같을 때 「as+형용사/부사의 원급+as」로 표현하고, 부정형은 「not as(so)+형용사/부사의 원급+as」로 표현한다.

20 | 해석| 내 운동 동아리를 너에게 소개할게. 트랙을 달리고 있는 소년들은 내 반 친구인 민수, 윤호, 지호야. 농구를 하고 있는 소녀는 내 여동생이야. 축구공을 들고 있는 남자는 코치님이야.

| 해설| 각 사람의 행동을 묘사하는 표현을 현재분사를 사용하여 목적어나 부사구와 함께 주어를 뒤에서 수식하는 형태로 쓴다.

R Reading 고득점 맞기   pp. 57~59

01 ③   **02** ⑤   **03** ③   **04** ③, ④   **05** ③   **06** ②

07 ①   **08** ③   **09** ②   **10** ③   **11** ②   **12** ③

[서술형]

13 flags or balloons showing their finish time

14 depending on   **15** | 모범 답| (1) They choose a pacer depending on their target finish time. (2) They run for others(other runners).   **16** attention   **17** | 모범 답| 경주 도중 피트 크루가 레이서의 자동차를 점검하고 타이어를 교체해 주는 중요한 일을 하는 공간이기 때문이다.   **18** ⓑ driver → car

01 | 해설| ⓐ 스포츠에서 선수들만 트로피나 메달을 받지만 혼자 힘으로 이기는 것이 아니라(don't win on their own)는 내용이 되는 것이 문맥상 알맞다.

ⓑ '그리고 주목을 받지 못한다'라는 말이 이어지는 것으로 보아 종종 숨겨져 있다(hidden)는 내용이 되는 것이 알맞다.

02 | 해설| 윗글에서 밑줄 친 ⓒthey는 무엇을 나타내는가?

① 스포츠 ② 몇 가지 예시 ③ 선수들 ④ 메달 또는 트로피들

⑤ 선수들을 도와주는 사람들

| 해설| they는 앞부분의 people who help the players, 즉 '선수들을 도와주는 사람들'을 가리킨다.

03 | 해설| (A) 각각의 페이서는 '다른(different)' 속도로 달리고 다른 시간대에 경주를 마친다는 내용이 알맞다.

(B) 목표를 쉽게 '달성할(achieve)' 수 있다는 내용이 알맞다.

(C) 페이서들은 자신들이 아니라 '다른 사람들(others)'을 위해 달린다는 내용이 알맞다.

04 |해석| ① 그녀는 금메달을 따는 것을 상상했다.

② 너는 주말에 무엇을 하는 것을 즐기니?

③ 숨바꼭질을 하고 있는 아이들을 봐.

④ 전화 통화하는 남자는 나의 할아버지다.

⑤ 그들은 자동차 경주에서 우승하기를 고대했다.

|해설| ⓐ와 ③, ④의 밑줄 친 부분은 뒤따르는 어구와 함께 명사를 뒤에서 수식하는 현재분사이고, ①, ②, ⑤는 동명사이다. look forward to -ing는 '~하기를 고대하다'라는 뜻으로 여기서 to는 전치사이므로 뒤에 동명사를 쓴다.

05 |해설| ⓑ 선수들이 목표 완주 시간에 따라 페이서를 선택하는 예시가 이어지므로 For example(예를 들어)이 알맞다.

ⓒ 앞의 내용을 요약하는 내용이 이어지므로 In short(요컨대)가 알맞다.

06 |해석| ⓐ 그들은 다른 선수들과 함께 달리고 그들을 돕는다.

ⓑ 각 마라톤에서 오직 한 명의 페이서만이 달릴 수 있다.

ⓒ 그들은 모두 동시에 경주를 마쳐야 한다.

ⓓ 그들은 깃발이나 풍선을 가지고 있는데, 그것은 그들의 시작 시간을 보여 준다.

|해설| ⓑ 한 경주에 여러 명의 페이서(several pacers)가 있을 수 있다고 했다.

ⓒ 페이서들은 모두 다른 시간대(in different times)에 경주를 마친다고 했다.

ⓓ 페이서들은 완주 시간(finish time)을 나타내는 깃발이나 풍선을 가지고 있다고 했다.

07 |해석| 이 팀은 피트 크루라고 불린다.

|해설| 주어진 문장의 This team은 첫 번째 문장의 a team behind the driver를 가리키므로 ①에 들어가는 것이 자연스럽다.

08 |해설| ⓑ 뒤에 「주어+동사」 형태의 절이 이어지므로 접속사 because가 쓰여야 한다. (→ because)

ⓒ '2초만큼 짧은'이라는 의미를 나타내는 「as+형용사의 원급+as」 형태가 알맞다. (→ short)

09 |해석| ① A: 피트란 무엇인가?

B: 경주 트랙의 옆에 있는 장소이다.

② A: 레이서들은 얼마나 자주 피트에 정지할 수 있는가?

B: 그들은 경주 중에 한 번 정지할 수 있다.

③ A: 피트 크루의 주요 업무는 무엇인가?

B: 차를 점검하고 타이어를 교체하는 것이다.

④ A: 자동차 경주에서 타이어를 교체하는 것은 왜 중요한가?

B: 타이어는 자동차 경주 중에 쉽게 마모된다.

⑤ A: 피트 정지는 시간이 얼마나 걸리는가?

B: 그것은 2초만큼 짧을 수 있다.

|해설| ② 레이서들은 경주 중에 피트에 여러 번(several times) 정지한다.

10 |해설| ⓒ 준사역동사 help는 목적격보어로 동사원형이나 to부정사를 쓰므로 climb이나 to climb으로 고쳐야 한다.

11 |해석| ① 사진작가들

② 보이지 않는 사람들

③ 등산하는 사람들

④ 유명한 등산가들

⑤ 훌륭한 등산가들

|해설| 셰르파들은 등산가들을 돕기 위해 함께 등반하지만 사람들은 정상에서 등산가들만 찍힌 사진을 보기 때문에 셰르파를 빈칸과 같이 부른다는 내용이므로, 빈칸에는 ② '보이지 않는 사람들'이 적절하다.

12 |해석| 윗글에서 답할 수 없는 것은?

① Sherpa라는 단어는 어디에서 유래되었는가?

② 셰르파 부족은 어디에 사는가?

③ 셰르파는 어떻게 등반 기술을 배우는가?

④ 등산가들은 왜 셰르파를 고용하기 시작했는가?

⑤ 셰르파는 등산가들을 위해 무엇을 하는가?

|해설| ③ 셰르파가 등반 기술을 어떻게 배우는지는 언급되지 않았다.

13 |해설| 현재분사를 사용하여 showing their finish time이 목적어로 쓰인 명사구 flags or balloons를 뒤에서 수식하는 형태로 쓴다.

14 |해석| 재료에 따라 다양한 종류의 김밥을 만들 수 있다.

|해설| '재료에 따라'라는 의미가 적절하므로 빈칸에는 본문에 사용된 depending on(~에 따라)이 알맞다.

15 |해석| (1) 마라톤에서 선수들은 어떻게 페이서를 선택하는가?

(2) 페이서는 누구를 위해 달리는가?

|해설| (1) 선수들은 자신의 목표 완주 시간에 따라 페이서를 선택한다.

(2) 페이서들은 우승하기 위해서가 아니라 다른 사람들(선수들)을 위해 달린다고 했다.

16 |해석| 어떤 것을 주의 깊게 보거나 듣는 행동

|해설| attention(관심, 주목)의 영영풀이이다.

17 |해설| 완벽한 조화를 이룬 피트 크루의 역할이 레이서의 우승을 좌우할 수 있을 정도로 중요하다는 내용이다.

18 |해석| ⓐ 자동차 경주에서 레이서 뒤에 있는 팀이다.

ⓑ 자동차 경주 도중에 운전자(→ 자동차)를 점검하고 타이어를 교체한다.

ⓒ 많게는 20명에 이르는 구성원이 있다.

|해설| ⓑ 피트 크루의 주요 역할은 자동차를 점검하고 타이어를 교체하는 일이라고 했다.

서술형 **100% TEST**	pp. 60~63

01 (1) particular (2) achieve (3) hide (4) register

02 (1) on his own (2) depending on (3) keep track of

03 (1) impolite (2) invisible (3) informal (4) impatient

04 how often do you play basketball, three times, how often do you, Every day, Once, Tuesdays

05 (1) Beginner 1 (2) twice a week (3) (on) Saturdays and Sundays   **06** I suggest that you take the Beginner 2 class.   **07** registered, know how to swim, twice, Tuesdays and Thursdays   **08** (1) The dog following me is Jina's. (2) The boy shaking his legs is Mike. (3) The woman wearing glasses is my English teacher.

09 (1) as fast as (2) not as smart as   **10** (1) swimming

(2) sleeping under the umbrella (3) playing with sand are
11 (1) ⓑ → I know the girl waiting for a bus. (2) ⓓ → My
dad cooks as well as the chef. **12** (1) sings as well as
(2) is as good as (3) run as fast as **13** to help other
runners manage their race better **14** (1) ⓓ → finishes
(2) |모범답| 주어가 Each pacer로 단수이므로 동사 finishes를 써
야 한다. **15** depending on their target finish time, keep
track of the time, more easily, for others **16** a place on
the side of the race track **17** Races are won in the pits.
18 (1) It(A pit crew's main job) is to check the car and
change the tires. (2) (It is because) The tires wear out
easily in a high speed race. **19** (1) ⓐ → which (2) ⓒ →
little (3) ⓔ → called **20** (1) 셰르파는 훌륭한 등반 기술을 가졌다.
(2) 셰르파는 산의 지리에 밝다. (3) 셰르파는 높은 산에서 호흡하는
데 어려움이 거의 없다.

01 |해석| (1) 특정한: 특정한 사람, 사물 또는 장소와 관련된
(2) 성취하다: 원하는 것을 하거나 얻는 데 성공하다
(3) 숨기다: 무언가를 아무도 볼 수 없는 곳에 두다
(4) 등록하다: 누군가 또는 무언가의 이름을 공식적인 목록에 올리다

02 |해설| (1) on one's own: 혼자서, 혼자 힘으로
(2) depending on: ~에 따라
(3) keep track of: (계속해서) ~을 파악하다

03 |해석| (1) 나는 누군가의 나이를 물어보는 것은 무례하다고 생각한다.
(2) 공기는 어디에나 있지만 눈에 보이지 않는다.
(3) 그것은 격식에 얽매이지 않는 회의이므로 너는 정장을 입을 필요가
없다.
(4) 우리는 30분째 계속 기다리고 있어서 참을성이 없어지고 있다.
|해설| 접두어 in- 또는 im-을 앞에 붙여 반의어를 만들어 맥락에 맞게
문장을 완성한다. ((1) impolite: 무례한 (2) invisible: 보이지 않는
(3) informal: 격식에 얽매이지 않는 (4) impatient: 참을성 없는)

04 |해석| A: 민지야, 너는 얼마나 자주 농구를 하니?
B: 나는 일주일에 세 번 농구를 해.
A: 그럼 너는 얼마나 자주 트랙에서 달리기를 하니?
B: 매일 해.
A: 그렇게 자주? 볼링 수업은 어때? 얼마나 자주 볼링 수업을 받니?
B: 일주일에 한 번, 화요일에 받아.
|해설| 상대방이 하는 일의 빈도를 물을 때는 How often do you ~?로
말한다. 횟수를 말할 때 '세 번'은 three times, '한 번'은 once로 나타
내고 '매일'은 every day, '~요일마다'는 「on+요일-s」로 나타낸다.

05 |해석| 여자: 안녕하세요. 도와드릴까요?
소년: 네, 저는 축구 수업에 등록하러 왔어요.
여자: 그렇군요. 얼마나 자주 수업을 듣고 싶으세요?
소년: 일주일에 두 번 듣고 싶어요. 주말에 수업을 듣고 싶습니다.
여자: 그러면, 초급 1반을 수강하실 수 있어요. 이 수업은 토요일과 일
요일마다 있어요.
소년: 그거 좋네요.
|해설| 소년이 축구 수업을 일주일에 두 번, 주말에 수강하고 싶다고 하
자 여자가 토요일과 일요일마다 하는 Beginner 1 수업을 제안하였
고, 소년이 좋다고 대답하였다.

06 |해설| 상대방에게 어떤 일을 할 것을 제안하거나 권유할 때 「I suggest
(that) you (should)+동사원형 ~.」으로 표현한다.

07 |해석| 오늘 나는 Sports World에서 수영 수업에 등록했다. 나는 수영
하는 법을 알지 못하기 때문에 초급 반에 등록했다. 나는 지금부터 일
주일에 두 번 화요일과 목요일마다 수영하러 갈 것이다.
|해설| 소년은 수영할 줄을 전혀 모르며, 일주일에 두 번 화요일과 목요
일에 하는 초보 수영 수업에 등록했다.

08 |해석| (1) 그 개는 지나의 개이다. 그것은 나를 따라오고 있다.
→ 나를 따라오고 있는 개는 지나의 개이다.
(2) 그 소년은 Mike이다. 그는 다리를 흔들고 있다.
→ 다리를 흔들고 있는 소년은 Mike이다.
(3) 그 여자는 나의 영어 선생님이다. 그녀는 안경을 쓰고 있다.
→ 안경을 쓰고 있는 여자는 나의 영어 선생님이다.
|해설| 현재분사가 이끄는 구가 주어를 뒤에서 수식하는 형태로 바꿔 쓴다.

09 |해석| (1) 고속철도는 비행기만큼 빠르다.
(2) 어떤 개들은 돌고래만큼 영리하지 않다.
|해설| (1) as fast as를 사용하여 고속철도가 비행기만큼 빠르다는 것
을 표현한다.
(2) 어떤 개들은 돌고래만큼 영리하지 않다는 내용이므로 not as
smart as를 사용한다.

10 |해석| (1) 수영하고 있는 여자는 우리 엄마야.
(2) 우산 아래에서 자고 있는 남자는 우리 아빠야.
(3) 모래를 가지고 노는 남자아이들은 내 남동생들이야.
|해설| (1)과 같이 현재분사가 단독으로 명사를 수식할 때는 명사 앞에
위치하지만, (2), (3)과 같이 뒤따르는 어구가 있을 경우에는 명사를 뒤
에서 수식한다. (3)에서는 주어와 동사의 수 일치에 유의한다.

11 |해석| ⓐ Jake는 떨어지는 낙엽을 잡았다.
ⓑ 나는 버스를 기다리고 있는 소녀를 안다.
ⓒ 수진이는 자신의 언니들만큼 창의적이다.
ⓓ 우리 아빠는 그 요리사만큼 요리를 잘하신다.
ⓔ 너는 TV에서 노래하고 있는 남자 그룹을 아니?
|해설| ⓑ '버스를 기다리고 있는'의 의미가 되어야 하므로 현재분사
waiting이 알맞다.
ⓓ as와 as 사이에 '잘'이라는 의미의 부사 well의 원급을 써야 한다.

12 |해석| (1) 지나는 민지만큼 노래를 잘한다. 그들은 둘 다 목소리가 아름
답다.
(2) 네 노트북은 내 것만큼 좋아. 너는 새것을 살 필요가 없어.
(3) 사자는 치타만큼 빨리 달리지 못한다. 치타는 가장 빠른 육지 동물
이다.
|해설| 비교하는 대상의 정도나 상태가 동등함을 나타낼 때는 「as+형
용사/부사의 원급+as」의 형태로 나타내고, '…만큼 ~하지 않은/않게'
는 「not as(so)+형용사/부사의 원급+as」 형태로 나타낸다.

13 |해설| '다른 선수들이 자신의 경주를 더 잘 관리하도록 돕는 것'의 의미
가 되도록 명사적 용법의 to부정사(to help)가 이끄는 to부정사구를
완성한다. '(목적어)가 ~하는 것을 돕다'는 「help+목적어+(to+)동사
원형」으로 나타낸다.

14 |해설| 주어가 Each pacer로 단수이고 등위접속사 and에 의해 동사
runs와 이어지므로 finishes가 알맞다.

15 |해설| |해석| 인터뷰 진행자: 선수들은 페이서를 어떻게 선택하나요?

페이서: 그들은 <u>그들의 목표 완주 시간에 따라</u> 페이서를 선택할 수 있습니다.

인터뷰 진행자: 경주 도중에 당신은 무엇을 계속해서 파악하나요?

페이서: 우리는 선수들이 자신의 목표를 <u>더 쉽게</u> 달성하도록 돕기 위해 시간을 계속해서 파악합니다.

인터뷰 진행자: 당신은 이기려고 달리는 건 아니시죠, 그렇죠?

페이서: 물론 아니죠. 우리는 <u>다른 이들을 위해</u> 달립니다.

16 |해설| 피트는 '경주 트랙의 옆에 있는 공간'이라고 했다.

17 |해설| Races와 동사 win은 수동의 관계이므로 수동태(are won)를 사용해서 나타낸다.

18 |해석| (1) 피트 크루의 주요 업무는 무엇인가?
(2) 자동차 경주에서 타이어를 교체하는 것은 왜 특히 중요한가?
|해설| (1) 피트 크루가 하는 주요 업무는 자동차를 점검하고 타이어를 교체하는 것이라고 했다.
(2) 빠른 속도의 경주에서는 타이어가 쉽게 마모되기 때문에 타이어를 교체하는 것이 특히 중요하다고 했다.

19 |해설| ⓐ 선행사 the Sherpa tribe를 부연 설명하는 관계대명사절을 이끄는 계속적 용법의 관계대명사이므로 which가 알맞다.
ⓒ 셀 수 없는 명사 앞에서 '거의 없는'이라는 의미를 나타낼 때는 little을 써야 한다.
ⓔ '~로 불린다'라는 의미가 되어야 하므로 수동태(be동사+과거분사)가 되도록 과거분사를 써야 한다.

20 |해석| 왜 등산가들은 자신들이 에베레스트산을 오르는 것을 돕도록 셰르파를 고용하기 시작했는가?
|해설| 등산가들이 셰르파를 고용하기 시작한 이유는 앞부분에 언급된 셰르파들이 가지고 있는 장점 때문이다.

모의고사

제 1 회 대표 기출로 내신 **적중** 모의고사　　pp. 64~67

01 ②　02 ⑤　03 wear　04 ①　05 How often do you stay up late　06 ④　07 ②　08 ⑤　09 (1) how to swim　(2) twice, weekdays　(3) Tuesdays and Thursdays
10 ⑤　11 as comfortable as that chair(one)　12 ④
13 ②　14 ①, ③　15 people who help the players
16 ③　17 ②　18 ②　19 ④　20 ③　21 ④
22 harmony　23 have little difficulty breathing high up
24 ⑤　25 ⓑ mountain climbers ⓒ Sherpas

01 |해석| ① 직접적인 – 간접적인　② 목표 – 목표
③ 격식을 차린 – 격식에 얽매이지 않은　④ 정중한 – 무례한
⑤ 가능한 – 불가능한
|해설| ②는 유의어 관계이고, 나머지는 모두 반의어 관계이다.

02 |해석| 누군가 혹은 무언가의 이름을 공식 목록에 올리다
① 숨기다　② 성취하다　③ 제안하다　④ 지원하다

|해설| register(등록하다)의 영영풀이이다.

03 |해석| • 내 오른쪽 신발은 쉽게 닳는 것 같다.
• 너는 파티에 무엇을 입을지 결정했니?
|해설| 첫 번째 빈칸에는 '(낡아서) 닳다, 해지다'라는 의미인 wear out의 wear가 알맞고, 두 번째 빈칸에는 '무엇을 입을지'라는 의미인 what to wear의 wear가 알맞다.

04 |해석| ⓐ Apache는 미국의 원주민 부족 중 하나이다.
ⓑ 그는 주목을 받기 위해 갑자기 일어나서 노래를 불렀다.
ⓒ 비행기에 탄 승무원들은 파란색 유니폼을 입고 있었다.
ⓓ 이 경기의 승자는 트로피와 500달러를 받을 것이다.

05 |해석| A: 너는 얼마나 자주 늦게까지 잠을 안 자니?
B: 나는 일주일에 서너 번 늦게까지 잠을 안 자.
|해설| 일주일에 서너 번 늦게까지 잠을 안 잔다고 답했으므로 상대방이 무언가를 얼마나 자주 하는지 빈도나 횟수를 묻는 표현인 How often do you ~?를 사용해 묻는 것이 알맞다.

06 |해석| (C) 너는 얼마나 자주 농구를 하니?
(A) 일주일에 한 번 하는데 더 자주 하고 싶어.
(D) 네가 우리 농구 동아리에 가입할 것을 제안해. 우리는 일주일에 세 번 농구를 해.
(B) 좋아! 너와 함께 농구 하면 재미있을 거야.
|해설| 얼마나 자주 농구를 하는지 묻고(C) 답한(A) 후 농구를 더 자주 하고 싶다는 상대방의 말에 자신의 농구 동아리에 가입할 것을 제안하자(D) 이를 승낙하는(B) 흐름이 되는 것이 자연스럽다.

07 |해석| A: 미나야, 너는 이곳에 달리기를 하러 얼마나 자주 오니?
B: 매일 와.
A: 오늘 너랑 같이 달리기를 해도 될까?
B: 물론이야. 그런데 네가 운동화를 신는 것을 권해. 네 신발은 달리기에 적합하지 않아.
① 나는 네가 신발을 신어야 한다고 생각해
③ 네가 옷을 갈아입으면 좋겠어
④ 나는 네가 신발을 바꿔 신어야 한다고 생각하지 않아
⑤ 너에게 달리기 하기 좋은 장소를 추천해 줄 수 있어
|해설| 이어지는 말로 보아 빈칸에는 운동화를 신을 것을 제안하는 말이 들어가는 것이 알맞다.

08 |해설| ⑤ 빈칸 뒤에 일주일에 두 번 수강하고 싶다는 말이 이어지므로, 수업을 얼마나 자주 듣고 싶은지 빈도를 묻는 말이 들어가야 알맞다.

09 |해석| (1) 소년은 전에 수영하는 방법을 배운 적이 없다.
(2) 소년은 일주일에 두 번, 주중에 수영 강습을 받고 싶어 한다.
(3) 소년은 화요일과 목요일마다 초급 2반을 수강할 것이다.

10 |해석| • 벤치에서 책을 읽고 있는 소녀는 내 여동생이다.
• 캐나다는 미국만큼 크다.
|해설| 첫 번째 빈칸에는 뒤따르는 어구와 함께 명사 The girl을 뒤에서 수식하는 현재분사 형태가 오는 것이 알맞다. 비교하는 두 대상의 정도나 상태가 같을 때 as와 as 사이에는 형용사나 부사의 원급을 쓰므로 두 번째 빈칸에는 large가 알맞다.

11 |해설| 비교하는 두 대상의 정도나 상태가 같을 때 「as+형용사/부사의 원급+as」의 형태로 써서 '…만큼 ~한/하게'의 뜻을 나타낸다.

12 |해석| [보기] 도서관에는 책을 빌리는 학생들이 많이 있었다.
① 잠자고 있는 개를 깨우지 마라.

② 나는 손을 흔들고 있는 소녀들을 안다.

③ 그 차를 운전하고 있는 남자는 나의 삼촌이다.

④ 나의 부모님은 공상 과학 영화를 보는 것을 즐기신다.

⑤ 너는 기타 치고 있는 소년을 보았니?

|해설| ④는 enjoy의 목적어로 쓰인 동명사이고, [보기]와 나머지의 밑줄 친 부분은 명사를 앞이나 뒤에서 수식하는 현재분사이다.

13 |해석| 빨간색 선글라스는 갈색 선글라스만큼 비싸지 않다.

|해설| '…만큼 ~하지 않은'은 「not as(so)+형용사의 원급+as」의 형태로 나타낸다.

14 |해석| ① 그들은 선수들을 돕는다.

② 그들은 주목 받는 것을 좋아한다.

③ 그들은 사람들에게 잘 알려져 있지 않다.

④ 그들은 선수들보다 더 중요하다.

⑤ 그들은 다른 선수들과 함께 트로피나 메달을 받는다.

|해설| 스포츠에서 선수들을 돕지만 숨겨져 있고, 주목을 받지 못하지만 선수들만큼 중요한 역할을 하는 사람들에 대한 글이다.

15 |해설| 앞부분에 언급된 '선수들을 돕는 사람들'을 가리킨다.

16 |해석| **마라톤의 페이서들**

페이서들은 마라톤에서 다른 선수들과 함께 달리며 그들을 이끈다. 페이서들은 경험이 많은 선수들이며, 그들의 역할은 다른 페이서들(→ 선수들)이 경주를 더 잘 운영하도록 돕는 것이다. 한 경주에는 여러 명의 페이서들이 있을 수 있다.

|해설| ⓒ 첫 번째 문장에서 페이서는 마라톤에서 다른 선수들을 이끈다고 하였으므로 그들의 역할은 다른 선수들(runners)이 경주를 더 잘 운영할 수 있도록 돕는 것이라고 해야 알맞다.

17 |해설| ⓑ '자신들의 완주 시간을 나타내는'이라는 의미로 flags or balloons를 뒤에서 수식하는 현재분사 형태(showing)로 써야 한다.

18 |해설| (A) depending on: ~에 따라

(B) keep track of: (계속해서) ~을 파악하다

(C) in short: 요컨대, 요약하면

19 |해석| ① 선수들은 혼자 힘으로 페이서를 선택할 수 없다.

② 페이서들은 보통 다른 페이서들을 위한 깃발과 풍선을 가지고 있다.

③ 페이서들과 선수들은 함께 계속해서 시간을 파악한다.

④ 선수들은 특정 페이서를 따라감으로써 목표 완주 시간을 더 쉽게 달성할 수 있다.

⑤ 페이서들은 다른 사람들을 위해서가 아니라 자기 자신들을 위해서 뛴다.

|해설| ① 선수들이 자신의 목표 완주 시간에 맞게 페이서를 따라간다.

② 페이서들은 선수들을 위해서 완주 시간을 나타내는 깃발이나 풍선을 가지고 있다.

③ 시간을 계속해서 파악하는 사람은 페이서들이다.

⑤ 페이서들은 자신들을 위해서 달리는 것이 아니라 다른 선수들을 위해서 달린다.

20 |해설| ⓐ team ⓑ track ⓒ short ⓓ perfect ⓔ driver

21 |해석| ① 빠르게 주행하는 것

② 경주에서 우승하는 것

③ 주목을 받는 것

④ 타이어를 교체하는 것

⑤ 운전자를 점검하는 것

|해설| 타이어가 쉽게 닳기 때문이라는 말이 이어지는 것으로 보아 피트 크루가 하는 차를 점검하는 일과 타이어를 교체하는 일 중에서 '타이어를 교체하는 것'이 특히 중요하다는 내용이 되는 것이 자연스럽다.

22 |해석| 사람들이 평화롭고 서로의 의견이 일치하는 상황

|해설| harmony(조화, 화합)의 영영풀이이다.

23 |해설| have difficulty -ing: ~하는 데 어려움이 있다. little: 거의 없는

24 |해설| **Q.** 왜 셰르파는 종종 에베레스트산의 보이지 않는 사람들이라고 불리는가?

① 그들은 등산가들의 가방을 운반하기만 한다.

② 셰르파 부족은 숨겨진 장소에 산다.

③ 그들은 산 정상에 가지 않는다.

④ 그들은 산 정상에 텐트를 친다.

⑤ 그들은 산 정상에 있는 등산가들의 사진에 없다.

|해설| 셰르파들이 종종 에베레스트산의 보이지 않는 사람들이라고 불리는 이유는 사람들이 흔히 산 정상에서 등산가들만 찍힌 사진을 보기 때문이라고 했다.

25 |해설| ⓑ는 셰르파들이 돕는 등산가들, ⓒ는 셰르파들을 가리킨다.

제 2 회 대표 기출로 내신 **적중** 모의고사   pp. 68~71

01 ④   02 on   03 ②   04 ③   05 often   06 ②
07 ②   08 ③   09 ①   10 (1) twice a week (2) on
Tuesdays and Thursdays   11 ④   12 ④   13 ④
14 stands → standing   15 ⑤   16 ②   17 ⑤
18 pacers → pacer   19 ③   20 (1) experienced (2) help
(lead) (3) target finish (4) time   21 ⓐ is called a pit
crew ⓑ as short as two seconds   22 ③   23 ②
24 ④   25 (1) The boy making a cake is Tim. (2) The girl
playing the piano is Yeji. (3) The boy blowing up a balloon
is Jiho.

01 |해석| 많은 별들은 인간의 눈에 보이지 않는다.

|해설| 많은 별들은 눈에 '보이지 않는다'는 내용이 되어야 알맞다.

(① 가벼운 ② 격식을 차린 ③ 특정한 ⑤ 불가능한)

02 |해석| • 어린 아이들은 혼자 힘으로 집에 가는 길을 찾지 못했다.

• 가격은 크기에 따라 다르다.

|해설| on one's own: 혼자서, 혼자 힘으로 / depending on: ~에 따라

03 |해석| ① 그들은 자신들의 목표를 달성하지 못했다.

② 화살이 과녁 한가운데에 명중했다.

③ 당신의 다음 달 판매 목표는 어떻게 되나요?

④ 그 회사는 내년을 위한 새로운 목표를 세웠다.

⑤ 그 대학은 곧 학생 수 3,000명이라는 목표를 달성할 것이다.

|해설| ②의 target은 '과녁'이라는 의미로 쓰였고, 나머지는 모두 '목표, 목표로 하는 대상'의 의미로 쓰였다.

04 |해석| ① Sally는 그림 수업을 듣지 않았다.

② 그들은 완벽한 조화를 이루며 함께 일했다.

③ 엄마는 요가 수업에 등록하기로 결정했다.

④ 우리는 지금부터 우리의 지출을 계속 파악할 것이다.

⑤ 요컨대, 우리는 기술의 시대에 살고 있다.

|해설| ③ sign up for: ~에 등록하다

05 |해석| A: 너는 얼마나 <u>자주</u> 농구를 하니?

B: 일주일에 한 번 하는데, 더 <u>자주</u> 하고 싶어.

|해설| ⓐ 답변으로 빈도를 말하고 있으므로 무언가를 얼마나 자주 하는지 묻는 How often do you ~?가 되는 것이 알맞다.

ⓑ 문맥상 더 자주(often) 농구를 하고 싶다고 말하는 것이 자연스럽다.

06 |해석| (B) 나는 수영을 자주 하지 않아. 너는 어때, Kate? 너는 얼마나 자주 수영을 하니?

(D) 나는 일주일에 네 번 수영을 해.

(A) 그렇게 자주? 어쨌든, 오늘 함께 수영하면 재미있을 거야.

(C) 그래, 그런데 수영하기 전에, 우리가 스트레칭하는 것을 제안해.

A: 좋은 생각이야.

|해설| 수영을 얼마나 자주 하는지 묻는 말(B)에 일주일에 네 번 한다고 대답하자(D) 그렇게 자주 하냐고 놀란 뒤, 오늘 함께 수영하면 재미있을 거라고 말하고(A) 수영하기 전에 스트레칭을 하자고 제안하는(C) 흐름이 자연스럽다.

07 |해석| ① A: 나 감기에 걸린 것 같아.

B: 병원에 가는 것을 제안해.

② A: 얼마나 자주 수업을 듣고 싶으세요?

B: 저는 제빵 수업을 듣고 싶어요.

③ A: 네가 패스트 푸드를 덜 먹을 것을 제안해.

B: 알았어. 해 볼게.

④ A: 내가 오늘 너와 같이 달리기를 해도 될까?

B: 물론이야, 하지만 네가 운동화를 신는 것을 제안해.

⑤ A: 너는 일주일에 몇 번 운동하니?

B: 나는 매일 운동해.

|해설| ② 얼마나 자주 수업을 듣고 싶은지 묻는 말에 어떤 수업을 듣고 싶은지 답하는 것은 어색하다. 빈도를 말하는 표현으로 답하는 것이 자연스럽다.

08 |해석| 그러면, 초급 2반을 수강하기를 권해요.

|해설| 주어진 문장은 수강할 수업을 제안하는 말로, 수강하고 싶어 하는 횟수와 요일을 말한 소년의 말에 대한 대답이므로 이어지는 문장에서 This class ~.로 부연 설명을 하고 있는 ③에 들어가는 것이 알맞다.

09 |해석| ① 그 수업은 규모가 얼마나 되나요?

② 그 수업은 시간이 얼마나 걸리나요?

③ 그 수업은 언제 하나요?

④ 그 수업은 몇 시에 시작하나요?

⑤ 그 수업은 얼마나 자주 하나요?

|해설| 이어지는 대답에서 제한 인원이 10명이라고 수업의 규모를 말하고 있으므로 ①이 알맞다.

10 |해석| (1) 소년은 얼마나 자주 수영 강습을 받을 것인가?

→ 그는 <u>일주일에 두 번</u> 강습을 받을 것이다.

(2) 소년은 무슨 요일에 강습을 받을 것인가?

→ 그는 <u>화요일과 목요일</u>에 강습을 받을 것이다.

11 |해설| • 의자 위에서 자고 있는 고양이를 봐.

• 내 야구모자는 네 것만큼 좋다.

|해설| 첫 번째 빈칸에는 the cat을 뒤에서 수식하는 현재분사 sleeping이 알맞다. 두 번째 빈칸에는 '네 것만큼 좋은'이라는 의미가 되도록 형용사 원급 good이 알맞다.

12 |해석| ① 떨어지는 나뭇잎들을 봐.

② 너는 끓고 있는 물을 조심해야 해.

③ 축구를 하고 있는 학생들은 나의 반 친구들이다.

④ 그 건물에 살고 있는 사람들은 한 달 안에 이사를 가야 한다.

⑤ 너는 정문 앞에서 사진 찍고 있는 소녀들을 아니?

|해설| 「동사원형-ing」 형태의 현재분사는 명사를 앞이나 뒤에서 수식한다. ④는 문장의 동사가 need이므로 live는 주어 The people을 수식하는 현재분사 형태인 living으로 써야 한다.

13 |해석| ① 내 자전거는 내 여동생 것만큼 오래되었다.

② 오늘은 어제만큼 춥지 않다.

③ 너는 Jake만큼 빠르게 달릴 수 있니?

④ 이 손목시계는 저 손목시계보다 더 비싸니?

⑤ 이 영화는 내가 지난주에 본 영화만큼 흥미진진하지 않다.

|해설| ①과 ③은 '…만큼 ~한/하게'를 의미하는 「as+형용사/부사의 원급+as」, ②와 ⑤는 '…만큼 ~하지 않은'을 의미하는 「not as〔so〕+형용사/부사의 원급+as」 형태로 쓰였다. ④의 빈칸에는 뒤에 than이 있으므로 비교급 more가 들어가야 한다.

14 |해설| '서 있는'의 의미로 앞에 있는 명사(her sister)를 수식하는 현재분사 standing으로 써야 한다.

15 |해석| ① 빠른 ② 잘 ③ 숨겨진 ④ 보이지 않는 ⑤ 중요한

|해설| 선수들을 돕는 사람들은 숨겨져 있고 주목받지 못한다는 내용 뒤에 하지만(However) 그들은 선수들만큼 '중요하다'는 내용이 이어지는 것이 자연스럽다.

16 |해석| ① 다양한 종류의 스포츠들

② 스포츠에서 숨겨진 사람들

③ 혼자 힘으로 우승한 유명한 선수들

④ 주목을 많이 받는 스포츠 선수들

⑤ 선수들만큼 유명한 숨겨진 사람들

|해설| 스포츠 선수들을 돕는 사람들은 숨겨져 있고 주목을 받지 못하지만 그들은 선수들만큼 중요하다고 하며 그 예시가 다음과 같다고 하였으므로, 스포츠에서 숨은 조력자들의 예시가 이어질 것임을 알 수 있다.

17 |해설| ⓐ, ⓓ는 선수들(runners), ⓑ, ⓒ, ⓔ는 페이서들(pacers)을 가리킨다.

18 |해설| each(각각의) 뒤에는 단수명사가 쓰이므로 pacers를 pacer로 고쳐야 한다.

19 |해설| (B) 조건을 나타내는 부사절에서는 미래의 의미를 현재시제로 나타내므로 wants가 알맞다.

(C) 전치사(of)의 목적어로 동사가 쓰일 때는 동명사 형태로 쓴다.

20 |해석| 페이서들은 마라톤에서 다른 선수들을 돕는(이끄는) 경험이 많은 달리기 선수들이다. 선수들은 자신들의 <u>목표</u> 완주 시간에 따라 깃발이나 풍선을 가진 페이서를 따라갈 수 있다. 페이서들은 <u>시간</u>을 계속 파악함으로써 선수들이 더 쉽게 특정 시간 안에 경주를 완주하도록 돕는다.

21 |해설| ⓐ '~라고 불리는' 것이므로 수동태(be동사+과거분사) 형태로 쓴다.

ⓑ 「as+형용사의 원급+as」의 형태로 '…만큼 ~한'의 의미를 나타낸다.

22 |해설| ③ 레이서는 경기 중에 여러 번 피트에 정지할 수 있으며, 피트 크루가 완벽한 조화를 이루며 일해야 하는 이유는 매우 짧은 시간에 많은 구성원이 함께 일해야 하기 때문이다.

23 |해설| ⓑ 셰르파들이 등반 기술이 좋고 지리를 잘 알기 때문에 등반가들이 셰르파를 '고용하기(hire)' 시작했다는 내용이 자연스럽다.

24 |해석| ① 에베레스트산에서 사는 것
② 등산가들에게 등반 기술을 가르치는 것
③ 등산가들과 사진을 찍는 것
④ 텐트를 치고 등산가들의 가방을 운반하는 것
⑤ 등산가들에게 셰르파를 소개하는 것
|해설| For example로 시작하여 이어지는 내용이 등산가들을 지원하는 예시이므로 ④가 알맞다.

25 |해석| 카드를 쓰고 있는 소녀는 수진이다.
(1) 케이크를 만들고 있는 소년은 Tim이다.
(2) 피아노를 치고 있는 소녀는 예지이다.
(3) 풍선을 불고 있는 소년은 지호이다.
|해설| 그림 속 인물의 행동을 묘사하는 표현을 현재분사구로 나타내어 주어를 뒤에서 수식하는 형태로 쓴다.

제 3 회 대표 기출로 내신 **적중** 모의고사   pp. 72~75

01 ② **02** ③ **03** himself **04** ⑤ **05** ④ **06** I suggest you exercise more often. **07** ⑤ **08** ③
09 ②, ④ **10** ④ **11** ④ **12** (1) The red car is as expensive as the black car(one). / The black car is as expensive as the red car(one). (2) Toto is not as old as Bolt. **13** (1) The boy looking at us is my friend. (2) The man shaking hands with people is the mayor. (3) The woman singing on the stage is a famous singer. **14** ②
15 ④ **16** ⑤ **17** ① **18** (1) ⓐ → It is to help (other) runners manage their race better. (2) ⓒ → They show the pacers' finish time. **19** ⑤ **20** ⑤ **21** (1) is called a pit crew (2) check the car and change the tires (3) as short as two seconds (4) in perfect harmony **22** ③
23 셰르파들은 등산가들과 함께 등반하지만 사람들은 정상에서 등산가들만 찍힌 사진을 보기 때문이다. **24** ③ **25** ④

01 |해석| [보기] 등록하다 – 등록
① 숨 쉬다 – 숨 ② 평일 – 주말 ③ 제안하다 – 제안
④ 성취하다 – 성취 ⑤ 추천하다 – 추천
|해설| ②는 '명사(평일) – 명사(주말)'의 관계이고, [보기]와 나머지는 모두 '동사 – 명사'의 관계이다.

02 |해석| ① 특정한: 특정한 사람, 사물 또는 장소와 관련된
② 목표: 성취하고자 노력하는 목적이나 결과
③ 고용하다: 종종 문제에 맞닥뜨린 누군가를 돕다 (×)
④ 팀, 조: 함께 일하는 특별한 기술을 가진 사람들
⑤ 종족, 부족: 자신들만의 언어와 생활방식을 가진 사람들의 집단

|해설| ③ hire는 '고용하다'라는 의미이고, '종종 문제에 맞닥뜨린 누군가를 돕다'는 support(지원하다)의 영영풀이이다.

03 |해석| David는 혼자서 방학을 계획했다.
|해설| on one's own: 혼자서, 혼자 힘으로 (= by oneself)

04 |해석| ① 그 팀은 완벽한 조화를 이루며 일했다.
② 잠수부들은 다이빙하기 전에 항상 숨을 깊게 쉰다.
③ Carol은 수영 수업에 등록하지 않았다.
④ Jones 씨는 학회에서 연설을 할 것이다.
⑤ Ron은 경험이 풍부한 선수이다. 그는 아직 경기를 해 본 적이 없다.
|해설| ⑤ 경기를 해 본 적이 없다는 이어지는 내용과 경험이 풍부한 (experienced) 선수라는 첫 번째 문장의 내용은 자연스럽게 연결되지 않는다.

05 |해석| A: 미나야, 너는 이곳에 달리기를 하러 얼마나 자주 오니?
B: _____
A: 오늘 너랑 같이 달리기를 해도 될까?
B: 물론이야, 그런데 네가 운동화를 신는 것을 권해. 네 신발은 달리기에 적합하지 않아.
① 매일 와.
② 한 달에 한 번 와.
③ 일주일에 세 번 와.
④ 나는 더 자주 달리고 싶어.
⑤ 나는 일주일에 네 번 이곳에 와.
|해설| 달리기를 하러 얼마나 자주 이곳에 오는지를 물었으므로 빈도를 나타내는 말로 답하는 것이 자연스럽다. ④ '나는 더 자주 달리고 싶어.'는 적절한 응답이 아니다.

06 |해석| A: 민수야, 너는 운동을 얼마나 자주 하니?
B: 나는 일주일에 한 번 운동해.
A: 네가 더 자주 운동하는 것을 제안해.
B: 알았어. 해 볼게.
|해설| 일주일에 한 번 운동한다는 민수에게 suggest를 사용하여 더 자주 운동할 것을 제안하는 대화의 흐름이 알맞으므로, 「I suggest (that) you (should)+동사원형 ~.」의 형태로 쓴다.

07 |해석| Andy: 나는 수영을 자주 하지 않아. 너는 어때, Kate? 너는 얼마나 자주 수영을 하니?
Kate: 나는 일주일에 네 번 수영을 해.
Andy: 그렇게 자주? 어쨌든, 오늘 함께 수영하면 재미있을 거야.
Kate: 그래, 그런데 수영하기 전에, 우리가 스트레칭 하는 것을 제안해.
Andy: 좋은 생각이야.
① Andy는 수영을 자주 하는가?
② Kate는 얼마나 자주 수영을 하는가?
③ Andy는 오늘 수영을 할 것인가?
④ 누가 스트레칭 할 것을 제안하는가?
⑤ 그들은 스트레칭을 얼마나 오랫동안 할 것인가?
|해설| ⑤ Kate가 수영하기 전에 스트레칭 할 것을 제안했지만 얼마나 오랫동안 할 것인지는 언급하지 않았다.

08 |해설| 빈도를 말할 때는 「횟수+a day/week/month/year」로 나타내므로 ⓒ에는 a가 알맞다.

09 |해설| This class는 소년이 등록할 Beginner 2 수업으로, 화요일과 목요일마다 수업이 있으며 총 10명이 수강할 수 있다. 수강료와 수업 시간은 언급되지 않았다.

10 |해석| ① Ted의 자전거는 내 것만큼 오래되었다.

② 나는 Betty만큼 자주 웃으려고 노력한다.

③ 그 램프는 책장만큼 키가 크다.

④ Amy는 자신의 여동생만큼 춤을 아름답게 춘다.

⑤ 그의 가장 최근 영화는 그의 다른 영화들만큼 재미가 있지 않다.

|해설| ④ as와 as 사이에 일반동사(dances)를 수식하는 부사의 원급이 들어가서 '~만큼 아름답게'의 의미로 쓰이는 것이 알맞다. (→ as beautifully as)

11 |해석| [보기] 버스를 잡으려고 달리고 있는 소녀는 내 여동생이다.

① 그들은 잠시 말하는 것을 멈췄다.

② 내 취미는 컴퓨터 게임을 하는 것이다.

③ 너는 힙합 음악 듣는 것을 즐기니?

④ 나는 동물원으로 가는 길을 보여 주는 지도가 있다.

⑤ 그 규칙을 따름으로써 당신은 돈을 더 잘 관리할 수 있다.

|해설| [보기]와 ④의 밑줄 친 부분은 명사를 뒤에서 수식하는 현재분사이고, 나머지는 모두 동명사이다. (①, ③ 목적어 ② 보어 ⑤ 전치사의 목적어)

12 |해석| (1) 빨간색 자동차는 검정색 자동차만큼 비싸다. / 검정색 자동차는 빨간색 자동차만큼 비싸다.

(2) Toto는 Bolt만큼 나이가 많지 않다.

|해설| 비교하는 대상의 정도나 상태가 동등함을 나타낼 때는 「as+형용사/부사의 원급+as」 형태로 나타내고, '…만큼 ~하지 않은'은 「not as(so)+형용사의 원급+as」 형태로 나타낸다.

13 |해석| (1) 그 소년은 내 친구이다. 그는 우리를 보고 있다.

→ 우리를 보고 있는 소년은 내 친구이다.

(2) 그 남자는 시장이다. 그는 사람들과 악수하고 있다.

→ 사람들과 악수하고 있는 남자는 시장이다.

(3) 그 여자는 유명한 가수이다. 그녀는 무대에서 노래를 부르고 있다.

→ 무대에서 노래를 부르고 있는 여자는 유명한 가수이다.

|해설| 현재진행형 문장에 쓰인 분사와 이어지는 어구를 명사 뒤에 써서 명사를 수식하는 형태로 쓴다.

14 |해석| ⓐ Peter는 자신의 아버지만큼 키가 크다.

ⓑ 정장을 입고 있는 남자는 나의 선생님이다.

ⓒ 저기서 책을 읽고 있는 여자는 작가이다.

ⓓ 이 문제는 대기 오염만큼 심각하지 않다.

ⓔ 무대에서 연설을 하고 있는 소녀는 나의 반 친구이다.

|해설| ⓐ 비교 대상의 정도가 같으면 「as+형용사/부사의 원급+as」의 형태로 나타낸다. (taller → tall)

ⓒ 명사를 뒤에서 수식하며 진행·능동의 의미를 나타내므로 현재분사로 쓴다. (reads → reading)

ⓓ 비교 대상의 정도가 같지 않으면 「not as(so)+형용사/부사의 원급+as」의 형태로 나타낸다. (as serious not as → not as(so) serious as)

15 |해설| ④ 스포츠 선수들을 돕는 사람들은 종종 숨겨져 있다(are often hidden)고 했으므로, don't get attention(주목을 받지 못한다)으로 바꾸는 것이 흐름상 알맞다.

16 |해석| 요컨대, 페이서들은 달리기는 하지만 우승을 하기 위해 달리는 것은 아니다.

|해설| 주어진 문장은 '요컨대, 페이서들은 우승을 하기 위해 달리는 것이 아니다.'라는 의미로 글의 내용을 요약해 주는 문장이므로 '그들은

다른 이들을 위해 달린다.'라는 말 앞인 ⑤에 들어가는 것이 알맞다.

17 |해설| ⓐ keep track of: (계속해서) ~을 파악하다

ⓑ 동격 관계인 his or her goal과 finishing ~ easily를 연결하는 전치사 of가 알맞다.

18 |해석| ⓐ 마라톤에서 페이서의 역할은 무엇인가?

ⓑ 페이서들은 자신의 선수들을 어떻게 선택하는가?

ⓒ 페이서들의 깃발이나 풍선은 무엇을 보여 주는가?

ⓓ 페이서는 우승하기 위해 무엇을 하는가?

|해설| ⓑ 페이서들이 선수들을 선택하는 것이 아니라 선수들이 자신들의 목표 완주 시간에 따라 페이서를 선택하는 것이므로 답할 수 없다.

ⓓ 페이서들은 우승하기 위해 달리는 것이 아니므로 답할 수 없다.

19 |해석| ① 그러나 ② ~한 이후로/~ 때문에 ③ 예를 들어

④ ~ 때문에 ⑤ 그러므로, 따라서

|해설| 빈칸 앞의 내용이 빈칸 뒤의 내용의 원인이므로, 빈칸에는 Therefore(그러므로)가 알맞다.

20 |해석| ① 추우니까 너는 코트를 입어야 한다.

② 나는 점심을 먹으면서 음악을 듣고 싶었다.

③ 그녀는 늦게 일어나서 학교에 늦었다.

④ 그가 샤워를 하고 있을 때, 전화벨이 울렸다.

⑤ 전에 말했듯이 나는 드럼을 치고 싶다.

|해설| ⓑ와 ⑤의 밑줄 친 as는 '~하듯이'라는 뜻의 접속사로 쓰였다. (①, ③ ~ 때문에 ②, ④ ~할 때)

21 |해석| A: 당신의 팀은 뭐라고 불리나요?

B: 우리 팀은 피트 크루라고 불립니다.

A: 당신의 주요 업무는 무엇인가요?

B: 자동차를 점검하고 타이어를 교체하는 것입니다.

A: 당신의 업무에 중요한 사항이 있나요?

B: 피트에서의 정지는 2초만큼 짧을 수 있으므로, 우리는 완벽한 조화를 이루어서 일해야 합니다.

|해설| 피트 크루의 주요 업무는 자동차를 점검하고 타이어를 교체하는 것이다. 레이서는 피트에 짧게는 2초 머무를 수 있기 때문에 피트 크루는 완벽한 조화를 이루며 일해야 한다.

22 |해설| have difficulty -ing가 '~하는 데 어려움이 있다'라는 의미이므로 breathe를 동명사 형태인 breathing으로 고쳐야 한다.

23 |해설| 셰르파들은 등산가들을 돕기 위해 함께 등반하지만 사람들은 정상에서 등산가들만 찍힌 사진을 보기 때문에 셰르파를 에베레스트 산의 보이지 않는 사람이라고 부른다고 했다.

24 |해석| ① 미나: 그들은 등반을 잘한다.

② Sue: 그들은 등산가들에 의해 고용된다.

③ Jake: 등산가들은 그들을 산 정상까지 이끈다.

④ Carol: 사람들은 그들을 에베레스트산의 보이지 않는 사람들이라고 부른다.

⑤ Alex: 사람들은 흔히 산 정상에 있는 등산가들의 사진에서 그들을 볼 수 없다.

|해설| ③ 등산가들이 셰르파들을 산 정상까지 이끄는 것이 아니라 셰르파들이 여러 방식으로 지원하면서 등산가들을 이끈다.

25 |해설| ⓐ 주절과 부사절의 내용이 상반되므로 '~에도 불구하고'를 의미하는 Although가 알맞다.

ⓑ '무엇보다도'를 의미하는 Most of all이 문맥상 알맞다.

01 ③   02 ⑤   03 ⑤   04 |모범 답| I suggest you go see a doctor. / I suggest you take some medicine.   05 ③   06 ②   07 ②   08 ③   09 How often do you want to take classes   10 ⓒ → a limit(maximum) of 10 people   11 ①   12 ②   13 ②, ③, ⑤   14 ④   15 ②   16 ③   17 ⓐ lead ⓑ to help ⓒ manage   18 ④   19 ②   20 achieve   21 ④   22 ③   23 A pit stop can be as short as 2 seconds   24 ⓒ → Races are won in the pits.   25 ②

01 |해석| ⓐ 체내로 공기를 들여보내고 그것을 다시 내보내다
ⓑ 자신들만의 언어와 생활방식을 가진 사람들의 집단
ⓒ 사람들이 평화롭고 서로 동의하는 상황
ⓓ 무언가를 아무도 볼 수 없는 곳에 두다
① 숨기다 ② 종족, 부족 ③ 고용하다 ④ 조화 ⑤ 숨 쉬다
|해설| hire(고용하다)의 영영풀이는 없다. (ⓐ breathe ⓑ tribe ⓒ harmony ⓓ hide)

02 |해석| ① 이 타이어는 쉽게 닳지 않는다.
② 누구나 미술 수업을 신청할 수 있다.
③ 은행은 그 돈을 파악하는 데 실패했다.
④ 냄비의 가격은 크기에 따라 다르다.
⑤ 내 친구들이 내 프로젝트를 도와줘서 나는 그것을 혼자 힘으로 했다.
|해설| ⑤ 친구들이 프로젝트를 도와줘서 혼자 힘으로(on my own) 해 냈다는 내용은 자연스럽게 연결되지 않는다.

03 |해석| A: 너는 얼마나 자주 운동을 하니?
B: _____
① 일주일에 두 번 해.
② 나는 운동을 거의 하지 않아.
③ 가능한 한 자주 해.
④ 나는 매일 운동을 해.
⑤ 나는 지난주 일요일에 운동을 했어.
|해설| 운동을 하는 빈도를 묻고 있으므로 '지난주 일요일에 운동을 했다'는 대답은 알맞지 않다.

04 |해석| 나 심한 감기에 걸린 것 같아. 콧물이 나고 열이 있어.
|해설| 「I suggest (that) you (should)+동사원형 ~.」을 사용하여 아픈 상대방에게 제안이나 권유의 말을 한다.

05 |해석| A: 너는 얼마나 자주 농구를 하니?
B: 나는 일주일에 한 번 해, 하지만 나는 더 자주 하고 싶어.
A: 네가 우리 농구 동아리에 가입하는 것을 제안해. 우리는 일주일에 세 번 농구를 해.
B: 좋아! 너와 함께 농구 하면 재미있을 거야.
|해설| (A)에는 농구를 얼마나 자주 하는지 답하는 말, (B)에는 농구 동아리에 가입할 것을 제안하는 말, (C)에는 제안을 수락하는 말이 각각 알맞다.

06 |해석| ① 네가 더 연습하는 것을
② 네가 더 가벼운 공을 쓰는 것을
③ 네가 더 무거운 것을 쓰는 것을
④ 네가 볼링 강습을 받는 것을
⑤ 네가 밝은색 공을 찾는 것을
|해설| 소녀의 볼링 공이 너무 무거워 보인다고 말한 후에 I suggest ~. 로 제안하는 말이므로 더 가벼운 공을 사용하라고 제안하는 것이 자연스럽다.

07 |해석| 위의 대화의 내용으로 사실이 아닌 것은?
① 소녀는 볼링 강습을 받는다.
② 소년은 일주일에 두 번 볼링을 치러 간다.
③ 소녀는 자신이 볼링의 시작 단계에 있다고 생각한다.
④ 소녀는 소년이 볼링을 잘 친다고 들었다.
⑤ 소년은 소녀에게 조언을 했다.
|해설| ② 소년이 볼링을 치는 횟수는 언급되지 않았다.

08 |해설| ⓒ 화요일과 목요일에 진행되는 수업을 선택하였으므로 주말이 아닌 주중에 수업을 듣기를 원한다는 내용의 I'd like to take classes on weekdays and not on weekends.가 되어야 자연스럽다.

09 |해석| 얼마나 자주 수업을 듣고 싶으세요?
|해설| 대답으로 빈도를 말하는 것으로 보아 빈도를 묻는 How often do you ~?를 사용한다.

10 |해석| Sports World 등록증
운동: 수영
수업: 초급 2반
(최소 10명(→ 최대(제한 인원) 10명))
요일: 일주일에 두 번
화요일과 목요일마다
|해설| ⓒ 수업 제한 인원이 10명이므로 a limit(maximum) of 10 people이 알맞다.

11 |해설| His room is as large(big) as mine.이므로 반드시 필요한 말은 as이다.

12 |해석| [보기] 나는 집에 오는 길에 울고 있는 소년을 보았다.
ⓐ 그는 이탈리아에 가는 것을 고대하고 있다.
ⓑ 거리에서 춤을 추고 있는 두 소년이 있다.
ⓒ 큰 상자를 들고 있던 한 여성이 바닥에 쓰러졌다.
ⓓ 자석을 수집하는 것은 우리 형의 취미이다.
|해설| [보기]와 ⓑ, ⓒ는 현재분사이다. ⓐ와 ⓓ는 동명사이다.

13 |해석| ① 건강은 돈만큼 중요하다.
② 돈은 건강보다 덜 중요하다.
③ 돈은 건강만큼 중요하지 않다.
④ 돈이 건강보다 더 중요하다.
⑤ 건강은 돈보다 더 중요하다.
|해설| ②, ③, ⑤는 모두 '건강이 돈보다 더 중요하다'라는 의미이다.

14 |해석| ① 잠자고 있는 아기를 깨우지 마라.
② Tom은 John만큼 높이 뛸 수 있다.
③ 그는 나만큼 피아노를 잘 친다.
④ 청바지를 입고 있는 남자는 나의 삼촌이다.
⑤ Amy는 Lisa만큼 외향적이지 않다.
|해설| ④ wearing jeans가 수식하는 주어가 The man이므로 동사로 is가 알맞다. (① sleeping baby ② high ③ well ⑤ not as

outgoing as)

15 |해설| ⓑ 선행사가 사람(people)이므로 주격 관계대명사 who 또는 that이 알맞다. (ⓐ → their ⓒ → hidden ⓓ → important ⓔ → are)

16 |해석| ① 스포츠에서 많은 주목을 받는 방법
② 비밀리에 사람들을 돕는 스포츠 선수들
③ 스포츠에서 선수들을 돕는 숨겨진 사람들
④ 트로피와 메달을 따는 스포츠 선수들
⑤ 스포츠에서 중요한 선수가 되는 방법
|해설| 스포츠 선수들을 돕는 숨겨진 사람들은 숨겨져 있고 주목을 받지 못하지만 선수들만큼 중요하다는 내용이다.

17 |해설| ⓐ 등위접속사 and에 의해 run과 연결되어 있으므로 lead가 알맞다.
ⓑ 문장의 보어로 쓰인 to help가 알맞다.
ⓒ help의 목적격보어로 manage가 알맞다.

18 |해설| ④ 「each(각각의)+단수명사」가 주어로 쓰일 때는 단수 취급하므로 동사 runs와 finishes를 써야 한다. '다른 속도로'는 at different speeds, '다른 시간대에'는 in different times로 나타낸다.

19 |해석| ⓐ 소년은 자신의 손을 <u>보여 주는</u> 것을 피했다.
ⓑ 네 작품을 내게 <u>보여 줘서</u> 고마워.
ⓒ 멋진 차들을 <u>보여 주는</u> 사진이 있었다.
ⓓ Jane은 자신의 사진을 다른 사람들에게 <u>보여 주는</u> 것을 좋아하지 않는다.
|해설| 밑줄 친 (B)와 ⓒ의 showing은 '보여 주는'이라는 의미의 현재분사이고, 나머지는 모두 동명사이다.

20 |해석| Jenny는 그 시험에 합격하는 목표를 <u>성취했다</u>.
|해설| '달성하다, 성취하다'라는 뜻의 achieve가 알맞다.

21 |해석| **선수들:** ⓐ 자신들의 목표 완주 시간이 있다
ⓑ 다른 선수들을 위해 시간을 계속해서 파악한다
페이서들: ⓒ 경주에서 우승하기 위해 달리지 않는다
ⓓ 다른 페이서들을 지원하기 위해 달린다
|해설| ⓑ 달리는 동안 다른 선수들을 위해 시간을 계속해서 파악하는 것은 선수들이 아니라 페이서들이다.
ⓓ 페이서들은 다른 페이서들이 아니라 선수들을 위해 달린다.

22 |해설| '~ 동안'의 의미를 갖는 전치사 during이 알맞다.

23 |해설| '…만큼 ~한'을 나타내는 「as+형용사의 원급+as」를 사용한다.

24 |해설| ⓒ Races와 win의 관계는 수동이므로 수동태(be동사+과거분사) 형태로 쓰는 것이 알맞다.

25 |해설| 등반에 적합한 셰르파의 특징을 소개하고(B) 그래서 등산가들이 셰르파를 고용하며 셰르파는 등산가를 지원한다는 내용(A)이 이어진 후, 그 예와 함께 셰르파가 보이지 않는 사람들이라고 불린다는 내용(C)이 이어지는 것이 자연스럽다.

Lesson 6
Stories for All Time

STEP A

W Words 연습 문제　　　　　　p. 83

A 01 (요금·값을) 청구하다
02 판매상, 중개인
03 발표, 소식
04 호의, 친절
05 (선거로) 선출하다
06 부주의한
07 첨가하다; (말을) 덧붙이다
08 (예술 작품의) 복제품, 복제
09 축하 (인사); 축하해
10 붙이다, 첨부하다
11 어쨌든, 그런데
12 제안, 제의
13 대단히 귀중한
14 불행하게도, 유감스럽게도
15 곳, 장소
16 전부의
17 소장품, 수집물
18 무한한
19 값비싼, 귀중한
20 받다

B 01 saw
02 furniture
03 role
04 upset
05 owner
06 final
07 antique
08 disappointed
09 price
10 flu
11 shocked
12 exactly
13 luck
14 knock
15 main
16 practice
17 president
18 pay
19 replay
20 worth

C 01 넘어지다, 넘어지며 구르다
02 ~을 이용하다, 기회로 활용하다
03 한번 보다
04 (~로) 가는 길에
05 ~하지 않을 수 없다
06 ~으로 알려져 있다, 유명하다
07 ~을 잘라 내다
08 정색하며, 시치미를 떼고
09 ~을 자랑스러워하다
10 맘껏 드세요

D 01 take a look
02 be known for
03 with a straight face
04 can't help -ing
05 What if ~?
06 cut off
07 take advantage of
08 do one's best
09 fall over
10 on one's way (to)

A 1 worth, 가치가 있는   2 antique, 골동품인   3 attach, 붙이다   4 reproduction, 복제품   5 dealer, 판매상
    6 offer, 제안, 제의   7 furniture, 가구   8 charge, (요금을) 청구하다

B 1 saw   2 Unfortunately   3 offer   4 valuable
    5 disappointed

C 1 couldn't help   2 on our way   3 is known(famous) for   4 with a straight face   5 advantage of

D 1 careless   2 reproduce   3 priceless
    4 reproduction

A |해석| 1 특정한 가치를 가지고 있는
   2 오래되고 종종 귀중하거나 아름다운
   3 어떤 것을 다른 것에 고정시키거나 결합하다
   4 그림과 같은 물건의 복제본
   5 물건을 사고파는 직업을 가진 사람
   6 누군가에게 무언가를 원하는지 묻는 행동
   7 의자, 침대, 탁자, 책장과 같은 물건들
   8 사람들에게 어떤 것에 대해 특정 금액의 돈을 지불하라고 요구하다

B |해석| 1 톱으로 나뭇가지를 나무에서 잘라 내라.
   2 불행하게도 내가 할 수 있는 것은 아무것도 없다.
   3 그는 그를 고용하겠다는 회사의 제안을 받아들였다.
   4 이 반지를 잃어버리지 않도록 조심해라. 이것은 매우 귀중하다.
   5 박물관이 문을 닫은 것을 알고 방문객들은 실망했다.

D |해석| 1 끝 : 무한한 = 주의 : 부주의한
   2 틀다 : 재생하다, 다시 듣다/보다 = 생산하다 : 복제하다
   3 ~으로 유명하다 : ~으로 유명하다 = 귀중한 : 대단히 귀중한
   4 축하하다 : 축하 = 복제하다 : 복제

---

② 그녀는 정색하며 싫다고 말했다.
③ 그들은 학교로 가는 길에 Jennifer를 만났다.
④ 그 카페는 훌륭한 디저트로 유명하다.
⑤ 가위로 이 실을 잘라 주세요.
|해설| ① fall over는 '넘어지다'라는 뜻이다.

05 |해석| • 나는 그저 한번 보고 싶다.
   • 다른 사람이 너를 이용하게 두지 말아라.
|해설| 첫 번째 문장은 '한번 보다'라는 뜻의 take a look이 알맞고, 두 번째 문장은 '~을 이용하다'라는 뜻의 take advantage of가 알맞다. 따라서 공통으로 들어갈 말은 take이다.

06 |해석| [보기] 저쪽에 있는 전기톱을 사용하면 된다.
   ① 판자를 반으로 톱질해 주세요.
   ② 우리는 눈에서 아무 발자국도 못 봤다.
   ③ 부모님과 나는 어젯밤에 영화를 보았다.
   ④ 나는 내가 톱으로 나무를 자를 수 있을 것 같지 않다.
   ⑤ 너는 그들이 나무를 조각으로 톱질하는 것을 봤니?
|해설| [보기]와 ④의 saw는 '톱'이라는 의미로 쓰였고, ①과 ⑤는 '톱질하다', ②와 ③은 '보았다'라는 의미로 쓰였다.

07 |해설| unfortunately: 유감스럽게도

08 |해설| '~하지 않을 수 없다'는 can't help -ing로 나타낸다. 과거시제이므로 couldn't를 쓰는 것에 유의한다.

Q1 Sue가 학급 회장으로 당선되어서   **Q2** T   **Q3** ⓐ
Q4 has the flu   **Q5** 지호가 로미오(주인공) 역할을 맡게 되어서
Q6 ⓑ   **Q7** ⓑ   **Q8** T   **Q9** disappointed

---

01 ⑤   **02** congratulation   **03** ④   **04** ①   **05** ②
06 ④   **07** Unfortunately   **08** couldn't help thinking

01 |해석| ① 톱 ② 판매상, 중개인 ③ 골동품 ④ 전시회 ⑤ 복제품
   |해설| '그림과 같은 물건의 복제본'은 reproduction(복제품)의 영영풀이이다.

02 |해석| (선거로) 선출하다 : 선거 = 축하하다 : 축하
   |해설| '(선거로) 선출하다 : 선거'는 '동사 : 명사'의 관계이므로 congratulate (축하하다)의 명사형인 congratulation(축하)이 빈칸에 알맞다.

03 |해석| 그 프로젝트는 나에게 귀중한 경험이었다.
   ① 쓸모없는 ② 골동품의 ③ 무한한 ④ 대단히 귀중한 ⑤ 실망한
   |해설| valuable은 '귀중한'이라는 의미로 priceless(대단히 귀중한)와 바꿔 쓸 수 있다.

04 |해석| ① 그는 넘어져서 무릎을 다쳤다.

Listen and Talk A-1 What's up, elected, excited, Congratulations, happy to
Listen and Talk A-2 congratulations on winning, must be, did my best
Listen and Talk A-3 anything wrong, upset, sorry to hear that, remember taking
Listen and Talk A-4 the matter, That's too bad, better soon
Listen and Talk C Can I ask you, main role, Congratulations, how much you wanted, happy for, What about, disappointed, sorry to hear, at, on, text message
Talk and Play broken, upset, too bad
Review - 1 look excited, how much, happy to get
Review - 2 look good, get a role, I'm so sorry, sure

1 ⓓ – ⓐ, ⓑ	**2** ⓑ – ⓐ, ⓓ
3 ⓒ – ⓐ – ⓑ – ⓓ	**4** ⓒ – ⓕ, ⓐ – ⓓ
5 ⓖ – ⓕ – ⓑ, ⓐ, ⓒ – ⓗ	**6** ⓒ – ⓑ – ⓐ
7 ⓑ – ⓐ – ⓒ	**8** ⓑ – ⓐ – ⓓ – ⓒ

01 ④	02 ④	03 ②	04 ②	05 ④, ⑤	06 ⑤
07 ③	08 ⑤	09 ④			

[서술형]

10 I'm sorry to hear that　11 (1) What's up? (2) I'm very happy. (3) Congratulations!　12 (1) chosen as the leader of the school band (2) excited (3) do her best for the band

01 |해석| A: Tim, 학교 마라톤에서 금메달 딴 것을 축하해.
　B: 고마워, 수지야. 나는 정말 기뻐.
　A: 네 스스로가 매우 자랑스럽겠구나.
　B: 응, 맞아. 나는 최선을 다했어.
　① 슬픈 ② 속상한 ③ 걱정하는 ⑤ 실망한
　|해설| 학교 마라톤에서 금메달을 딴 상황이므로 기쁘다고 말하는 것이 자연스럽다.

02 |해석| A: 너 몸이 안 좋아 보인다. 인호야. 무슨 일 있어?
　B: 나는 독감에 걸렸어.
　A: 안됐구나. 병원은 가 봤어?
　B: 응. 약을 먹고 있어.
　A: 음, 네가 곧 낫기를 바라.
　B: 고마워.
　① 축하해! ②, ③ 잘됐다. ⑤ 그 말을 들으니 기쁘다.
　|해설| 독감에 걸렸다고 말하는 사람에게 유감을 표현하는 말을 하는 것이 자연스럽다.

03 |해석| ① A: 안 좋은 일 있니?
　　B: 내 컴퓨터가 고장 났어. 속상해.
　② A: 내 가장 친한 친구가 내 생일을 잊어버렸어.
　　B: 축하해!
　③ A: 나는 야구 경기 티켓을 구했어.
　　B: 잘됐다!
　④ A: 너 신나 보인다. 무슨 일이야?
　　B: 내가 요리 대회에서 1등을 했어.
　⑤ A: 나는 수학 시험에 불합격했어. 매우 실망했어.
　　B: 아, 그 말을 들으니 유감이야.
　|해설| ② 가장 친한 친구가 자신의 생일을 잊어버렸다고 말하는 상대방에게 축하한다고 말하는 것은 어색하다.

04 |해석| A: 너 안 좋아 보인다. 무슨 일 있니?

B: ＿＿＿＿＿＿＿＿＿＿＿＿
A: 안됐구나.
① 우리 개가 아파. 나는 슬퍼.
② 나 운전 면허 시험에 합격했어.
③ 나는 두통이 심해.
④ 어젯밤에 내 자전거를 도둑맞았어.
⑤ 내 노트북이 고장 났어. 나는 속상해.
|해설| 유감을 표현하는 말이 이어지는 것으로 보아 빈칸에는 좋지 않은 일이 들어가는 것이 알맞다. 축하의 말을 해야 할 좋은 일인 ②는 알맞지 않다.

05 |해석| A: 무슨 일 있니?
B: ＿＿＿＿＿＿＿＿＿＿＿＿
A: 축하해!
① 나는 다리가 부러졌어.
② 나는 치통이 있어.
③ 내가 버스에 지갑을 두고 내렸어.
④ 우리 팀이 축구 경기에서 이겼어.
⑤ 내가 학교 연극에서 주인공 역할을 맡게 되었어.
|해설| 축하하는 말이 이어지는 것으로 보아 빈칸에는 기쁘거나 즐거운 일이 들어가는 것이 알맞다.

06 |해석| (C) Sue, 너 신나 보인다. 무슨 일 있어?
(B) 내가 학급 회장으로 당선되었어. 정말 신나.
(A) 멋지다. 축하해!
(D) 고마워. 우리 반을 위해 일할 기회가 생겨서 나는 정말 기뻐.
|해설| 신나 보인다고 하며 무슨 일이 있는지 묻는 말(C)에 신난 이유를 말하자(B) 그것에 대해 축하하는 말을 하고(A), 그 말에 감사의 표현을 하는(D) 흐름이 자연스럽다.

07 |해석| A: 너 안 좋아 보인다. 무슨 일 있니?
B: 내 스마트폰을 잃어버렸어. 속상해.
A: 정말 잘됐다(→ 그 말을 들으니 (정말) 유감이야.) 마지막으로 언제 사용했는지 기억나니?
B: 음, 매점에서 그것을 가방에서 꺼낸 것은 기억나.
A: 그것을 찾으러 매점에 다시 가 보자.
|해설| ③ 스마트폰을 잃어버려서 속상해하는 상대방에게 축하하는 말을 하는 것은 어색하다. That's too bad.나 I'm (so) sorry to hear that.과 같은 유감을 표현하는 말을 하는 것이 적절하다.

[08~09] |해석|
A: 실례합니다. Carter 선생님. 질문 하나 해도 될까요? 연극에서 제가 주인공 역할을 맡게 됐나요?
B: 그렇단다. 축하해, 지호야! 너는 우리 학교 연극 '로미오와 줄리엣'에서 로미오가 될 거야.
A: 정말이요? 너무 신나요. 정말 고맙습니다. Carter 선생님.
B: 네가 얼마나 그 역할을 원했는지 알고 있단다. 나도 정말 기쁘구나.
A: 고맙습니다. 수미는 어떻게 됐어요? 수미도 원했던 역할을 맡게 됐나요?
B: 안타깝게도, 아니란다. 그녀는 매우 실망했어.
A: 아, 그 말을 들으니 유감이네요. 그런데, 첫 연습은 언제예요?
B: 9월 20일 오후 2시에 연극 동아리방에서 할 거야. 그것에 관한 문자 메시지를 곧 받을 거야.
A: 알겠습니다. 거기에서 뵐게요.

08 |해석| ① 미안한 ② 신난 ③, ④ 기쁜
|해설| 수미가 연극에서 원했던 역할을 맡지 못한 상황이므로 실망했다고 말하는 것이 알맞다.

09 |해설| ④ 9월 20일 오후 2시에는 첫 연극 공연이 아니라 첫 연극 연습이 있다.

10 |해석| A: 무슨 일 있어?
B: 내 고양이를 잃어버렸어. 너무 슬퍼.
A: 그 말을 들으니 유감이구나.
|해설| 좋지 않은 일이 있는 상대방에게 유감을 표현하며 위로할 때 I'm sorry to hear that.으로 말할 수 있다.

11 |해석| 무슨 일 있니?　　　　　무슨 문제 있니?
나는 정말 기뻐.　　　　　나 너무 걱정돼.
그거 안됐다.　　　　　　축하해!
A: 너 신나 보인다. 무슨 일 있어?
B: Dream 콘서트 표를 구했어. 나는 정말 기뻐.
A: 축하해! 나는 네가 그 콘서트에 얼마나 가고 싶어 했는지 알아.
B: 고마워. 내가 가장 좋아하는 가수를 볼 기회가 생겨서 정말 신나.
|해설| (1) 신나 보이는 상대방에게 무슨 일이 있는지 묻는 표현이 알맞다.
(2) 자신에게 일어난 좋은 일을 말한 후에 정말 기쁘다고 감정을 표현하는 말이 이어지는 것이 자연스럽다.
(3) 그 콘서트에 매우 가고 싶어 했던 상대방에게 축하의 말을 건네는 것이 자연스럽다.

12 |해석| A: 축하해, Jane! 네가 학교 밴드의 리더로 뽑혔다고 들었어.
B: 민호야, 고마워. 정말 신나. 나는 밴드를 위해 최선을 다할 거야.
|해설| 민호는 Jane이 학교 밴드의 리더로 뽑혀서 그녀를 축하하고 있다. Jane은 매우 신난다고 말하고 밴드를 위해서 최선을 다하겠다고 말한다.

G Grammar 핵심 노트 1 QUICK CHECK　　p. 96

1 (1) lost (2) had broken (3) had known
2 (1) had bought (2) had, left (3) had used

1 |해석| (1) 나는 지갑을 잃어버려서 돈이 없었다.
(2) 그는 도둑이 창문을 깼다는 것을 알게 되었다.
(3) 그가 가수가 되기 전에 나는 그를 10년 동안 알고 지냈었다.
2 |해석| (1) 그는 나에게 그 가방을 어디서 샀는지 물었다.
(2) 우리가 도착했을 때 그들은 이미 떠나고 없었다.
(3) 나는 새 가방을 살 때까지 5년간 이 가방을 사용했었다.

G Grammar 핵심 노트 2 QUICK CHECK　　p. 97

1 (1) what (2) What (3) that
2 (1) what Dad gave me (2) the thing that(which)
(3) What I want to do

1 |해석| (1) 그것은 우리에게 필요한 것이 아니다.
(2) 내가 말하고 싶었던 것은 나는 정직하다는 것이다.
(3) 이것이 모두가 이야기하고 있는 그 책이다.
2 |해석| (1) 나는 아빠가 내게 주신 것이 마음에 든다.
(2) 이것이 바로 우리가 찾고 있던 것이다.
(3) 내 생일에 내가 하고 싶은 것은 파티를 하는 것이다.

G Grammar 연습 문제 1　　p. 98

A 1 had, eaten　2 had, left　3 had, begun
4 had stolen
B 1 had ended　2 had never heard
3 had not been　4 had already cleaned
C 1 had seen　2 had already left
3 had already gone　4 hadn't(had not) slept
D 1 couldn't play soccer because he had hurt his leg
2 found that someone had broken into his house
3 I arrived there, everyone had finished dinner

A |해석| 1 나는 막 피자를 먹었었기 때문에 배가 고프지 않았다.
2 내가 거기에 도착했을 때 그는 이미 식당을 떠나고 없었다.
3 그가 영화관에 도착했을 때 영화는 이미 시작했었다.
4 지민이는 밤사이에 누군가가 자신의 가방을 훔쳐가서 충격을 받았다.
|해설| 과거의 특정 시점에 일어난 일보다 더 이전에 일어난 일이나 상태를 나타낼 때 「had+과거분사」 형태의 과거완료를 쓴다.
B |해석| 1 그는 회의가 이미 끝났다는 것을 몰랐다.
2 네가 내게 말하기 전까지 나는 그 이야기를 들은 적이 없었다.
3 그녀는 서울에 가기 전에 대도시에 가 본 적이 없었다.
4 내가 집에 돌아왔을 때, 아빠는 내 방을 이미 청소해 놓으셨다.
|해설| 1, 4 과거의 특정 시점 이전에 이미 완료된 일을 나타내므로 과거완료로 쓴다. already는 had와 과거분사 사이, 또는 문장의 끝에 쓴다.
2, 3 과거의 특정 시점 이전에 경험해 보지 못한 일을 나타내므로 과거완료로 쓴다. 과거완료 부정문은 had 뒤에 not이나 never를 써서 나타낸다.
C |해석| 1 그는 나에게 전에 그 영화를 본 적이 있는지 물었다.
2 Mike가 버스 정류장에 갔을 때, 버스는 이미 떠나고 없었다.
3 나는 내 여동생이 이미 잠자리에 든 줄 알았는데, 아니었다.
4 나는 며칠 동안 잠을 잘 못 잤기 때문에 매우 피곤했다.
|해설| 과거의 특정 시점 이전에 이미 일어난 일이나 상태를 나타낼 때는 「had+과거분사」 형태의 과거완료를 쓴다. 과거완료 부정문은 had 뒤에 not이나 never를 써서 나타낸다.
D |해석| 과거의 특정 시점보다 앞서 일어난 일이나 과거에 일어난 두 가지 일 중 먼저 일어난 일을 명확하게 나타낼 때 과거완료(had+과거분사)를 쓴다.

G Grammar 연습 문제 2

A 1 What   2 what   3 which(that)   4 who(that)

B 1 which → what   2 that → what
3 what → which   4 what → who

C 1 What I like about the boy is his honesty.
2 Ms. Kim described what she had seen at the exhibition.
3 What he says is different from what he does.

D 1 what Mom cooked for us
2 what I want to write about
3 what he was looking for

A |해석| 1 그녀가 말한 것은 나를 울게 만들었다.
2 나는 주문한 것을 아직 받지 못했다.
3 내가 사고 싶었던 자전거는 분홍색이었다.
4 저분이 나에게 자신의 핸드폰을 쓰게 해 준 여자이다.
|해설| 1, 2 선행사가 없으므로 선행사를 포함하는 관계대명사 what이 알맞다.
3 선행사가 사물(The bike)이므로 주격 관계대명사 which나 that이 알맞다.
4 선행사(the woman)가 사람이므로 주격 관계대명사 who 또는 that이 알맞다.

B |해석| 1 이것이 바로 그가 원하는 것이다.
2 우리는 거기서 본 것을 믿을 수 없었다.
3 나는 고기를 자를 수 있는 칼이 필요하다.
4 내 여동생은 15살인데, 뉴욕에서 공부할 것이다.
|해설| 1 is의 보어 역할을 하는 명사절을 이끄는 관계대명사 what이 쓰이는 것이 알맞다.
2 couldn't believe의 목적어 역할을 하는 명사절을 이끄는 관계대명사 what이 쓰이는 것이 알맞다.
3 선행사(a knife)를 수식하는 관계대명사절이 쓰였으며, 전치사(with) 뒤이므로 목적격 관계대명사 which가 쓰이는 것이 알맞다.
4 선행사(My sister)를 보충 설명하는 계속적 용법의 관계대명사절이 이어지므로 관계대명사 who를 써야 한다. 관계대명사 what은 계속적 용법으로 쓰이지 않는다.

C |해설| '~하는 것'을 의미하는 관계대명사 what이 각각 문장의 주어 역할과 목적어 역할, 전치사(from)의 목적어 역할을 하는 명사절을 이끄는 형태로 문장을 배열한다.

D |해설| 각각 목적어 또는 보어 역할을 하는 명사절을 이끄는 관계대명사 what을 사용하여 문장을 완성한다.

G Grammar 실전 TEST

01 ③	02 ⑤	03 ④	04 ⑤	05 ③	06 ②	07 ⑤
08 ②	09 ③, ⑤	10 ③	11 ②, ④	12 ②, ⑤	13 ②	
14 ⑤	15 ③	16 ④	17 ③	18 ④	19 ④	20 ⑤

[서술형]

21 (1) we arrived at the station, the train had already left (2) my alarm clock rang, I had already woken up (3) Mom came home, I had already finished my homework
22 (1) had just taken (2) he had lost (3) she had already left (4) the tickets had been sold out   **23** (1) What I really want is your support. (2) When the police arrived, the man had already run away. (3) That is not what I wanted to say. / That is not the thing that(which) I wanted to say. (4) He told me that he had not(never) met the movie star before.   **24** What Luna likes, to play soccer
25 Swimming, What Dan doesn't like

---

01 |해석| Jennifer는 Mike가 그녀에게 생일 선물로 준 것을 아주 좋아했다.
|해설| loved의 목적어로 선행사를 포함하는 관계대명사 what이 이끄는 명사절이 오는 형태가 알맞다.

02 |해석| Tony는 나에게 그 영화를 이미 봤다고 말했다.
|해설| 말한(told) 과거 시점보다 영화를 본 것이 더 먼저 일어난 일이므로 과거완료(had+과거분사)로 쓰는 것이 알맞다.

03 |해석| ① Tom은 내가 그를 방문했을 때 외출하고 없었다.
② 나는 누가 창문을 깼는지 궁금했다.
③ 나는 다 써 버려서 돈이 없었다.
④ 내가 Katie에게 전화했을 때 그녀는 일주일 동안 아팠다.
⑤ 내가 극장에 도착했을 때, 영화는 이미 시작해 있었다.
|해설| ④ 전화한(called) 과거 시점 이전부터 아팠던 것이므로 과거완료(had+과거분사)로 써야 한다. (has been → had been)

04 |해석| ① 이것이 바로 내가 원했던 것이다.
② 그는 내가 그에게 쓴 것을 읽었다.
③ 우리는 Joe가 우리에게 요리해 준 것을 먹었다.
④ 네가 갖고 싶은 것을 선택하면 돼.
⑤ 네 손에 있는 것을 보여줘.
|해설| ⑤ what은 선행사를 포함하는 관계대명사이다. 앞에 선행사 the thing이 있으므로 what을 that 또는 which로 바꾸거나 the thing을 삭제하고 what으로만 써야 한다. (the thing what → the thing 삭제 또는 the thing that(which))

05 |해석| A: 나 너무 배고파. 점심 먹자.
B: 알았어. 너는 무엇을 먹고 싶니?
A: 내가 가장 먹고 싶은 것은 피자야.
|해설| 문장의 주어 역할을 해야 하므로 선행사를 포함하는 관계대명사 What이 이끄는 명사절이 오는 것이 적절하다. ⑤는 선행사 The thing이 있으므로 The thing that(which) I want to eat the most가 되어야 가능하다.

06 |해석| 엄마가 일주일 전에 내게 배낭을 사 주셨다.
나는 그것을 오늘 잃어버렸다.
→ 나는 엄마가 사 주셨던 배낭을 잃어버렸다.
|해설| 엄마가 배낭을 사 주신 것이 잃어버린(lost) 시점 이전의 일이므로 과거완료(had+과거분사)로 나타낸다.

07 |해석| ① 그녀가 네게 말한 것은 사실이 아니다.
② Sally는 내가 그녀에게 만들어 준 것을 정말 좋아했다.

③ 나는 그가 말한 것을 이해하지 못했다.

④ 나는 내가 숲에서 본 것을 믿을 수가 없었다.

⑤ 나는 네가 찾고 있던 열쇠를 찾았다.

|해설| ①~④에는 선행사를 포함하는 관계대명사 what(What)이 알맞고, ⑤에는 앞에 선행사(the keys)가 있으므로 목적격 관계대명사 which나 that이 들어가는 것이 알맞다.

08 |해설| ② 문장의 보어로 선행사를 포함하는 관계대명사 what이 이끄는 명사절이 오는 것이 알맞으며, 관계대명사 what은 the thing that(which)로 바꿔 쓸 수 있다. (① That → What, ③ When → What, ④ which → what, ⑤ what → that(which))

09 |해석| 나는 Laura를 _____ 전에 본 적이 없었다.

① 내가 작년에 이곳에 오기

② 그녀가 2015년에 이곳으로 이사 오기

③ 우리는 같은 반이다

④ 네가 내게 그녀를 소개해 주기

⑤ 나는 그림 동아리에 가입할 것이다

|해설| 주절에 과거의 특정 시점 이전에 일어난 일이나 상태를 나타내는 과거완료(had+과거분사)가 쓰였으므로, before 다음에는 과거 시점을 나타내는 말이 들어가야 한다.

10 |해석| ① 우리는 우리가 들은 것을 믿을 수 없었다.

② 내게 지금 필요한 것은 새 스마트폰이다.

③ 너 소풍이 취소된 것을 알고 있니?

④ 내가 알고 싶은 것은 그녀의 전화번호이다.

⑤ 필요하지 않은 것을 사는 것은 나쁜 습관이다.

|해설| ③에는 know의 목적어 역할을 하는 명사절을 이끄는 접속사 that이 들어가는 것이 알맞고, 나머지는 모두 선행사를 포함하는 관계대명사 what(What)이 알맞다.

11 |해석| 그는 낮잠을 오래 잔 후에 몸이 나아졌다.

|해설| 몸이 나아진(felt better) 과거 시점보다 낮잠을 잔 시점이 더 이전이므로 과거완료를 쓴다. 다만, 시간의 전후가 나타나는 접속사 after가 쓰였으므로 과거완료 대신 과거시제를 쓸 수도 있다.

12 |해석| 나는 지난주에 주문한 것을 아직 받지 못했다.

|해설| 빈칸 앞에 선행사가 없으므로 빈칸에는 선행사를 포함하는 관계대명사 what이나 the thing that(which)가 알맞다.

13 |해석| • 호수는 내가 그 공원에서 좋아하는 것이다.

• 그들은 다음에 무엇을 해야 할지 몰랐다.

|해설| 첫 번째 빈칸에는 선행사를 포함하는 관계대명사 what이 알맞고, 두 번째 빈칸에는 의문사 what이 알맞다.

14 |해석| ⓐ 우리가 도착했을 때 Tony는 이미 떠나고 없었다.

ⓑ 이 드레스는 내가 파티에서 입고 싶은 것이다.

ⓒ 지금 내가 하고 싶은 것은 자전거를 타는 것이다.

ⓓ 네가 나에게 말하기 전까지 나는 그 소문을 들은 적이 없었다.

ⓔ 내가 집에 왔을 때, 모두가 이미 잠자리에 들어 있었다.

|해설| ⓔ 모두가 이미 잠자리에 든 것이 집에 온(came home) 시점 이전의 일이므로 과거완료(had+과거분사)로 나타낸다. (→ had gone)

15 |해석| 나는 누군가가 밤중에 내 자전거를 훔쳐 갔다는 사실에 충격을 받았다.

|해설| 과거의 특정 시점에 일어난 일보다 더 이전에 일어난 일이나 상태는 과거완료(had+과거분사)로 나타낸다. 충격을 받은 것은 과거 시

점이므로 was shocked, 누군가가 자전거를 훔친 것은 그보다 이전에 일어난 일이므로 had stolen으로 쓰는 것이 알맞다.

16 |해설| 주어진 단어를 배열하여 문장을 완성하면 I asked him where he had bought the furniture.이므로 6번째로 올 단어는 had이다.

17 |해석| ⓐ 내가 사고 싶은 것은 저 티셔츠이다.

ⓑ 네가 먹고 싶은 것을 선택하면 된다.

ⓒ 내가 말하고 싶은 것은 정말 미안하다는 것이다.

ⓓ 수영은 그들이 여가 시간에 하는 것이다.

ⓔ 이것이 최근에 모두가 이야기하고 있는 TV 프로그램이다.

|해설| ⓑ 관계대명사 what은 계속적 용법으로 쓰이지 않는다. (→ 콤마(,) 삭제)

ⓔ 앞에 선행사(the TV show)가 있으므로 선행사를 포함하는 관계대명사 what을 쓸 수 없고, 목적격 관계대명사 which나 that으로 써야 한다. (what → which(that))

18 |해석| ① 나는 해가 질 때까지 바닷가에 있었다.

② Kevin은 나에게 전에 이탈리아에 가 본 적이 있느냐고 물었다.

③ 나는 그들이 이미 그 프로젝트를 끝냈다고 들었다.

④ 그 피아니스트는 다섯 살 때부터 피아노를 쳐 왔다.

⑤ 나는 서울로 이사 오기 전에 조부모님과 함께 살았었다.

|해설| ④는 과거의 일이 현재까지 계속됨을 나타내므로 현재완료의 has가 쓰이는 것이 알맞다. 나머지는 모두 과거의 특정 시점에 일어난 일보다 더 이전에 일어난 일이나 상태를 나타내므로 과거완료의 had가 들어가는 것이 알맞다.

19 |해석| 축구는 내가 방과 후에 하고 싶은 것이다.

|해설| ④ 선행사를 포함하는 관계대명사 what은 '~하는 것'으로 해석한다.

20 |해석| ⓐ 나는 그에게 전에 유럽을 방문한 적이 있었는지 물었다.

ⓑ 나는 내 남동생이 꽃병을 깨뜨렸다는 것을 알게 되었다.

ⓒ 나는 그 전날 샀던 우산을 잃어버렸다.

ⓓ 그는 나에게 방학 동안 찍은 사진을 보여주었다.

ⓔ 그들이 공항에 도착했을 때 비행기는 이미 착륙한 상태였다.

|해설| ⓒ 우산을 산 시점이 우산을 잃어버린(lost) 과거 시점보다 더 이전의 일이므로 현재완료가 아니라 과거완료(had+과거분사)를 써야 한다. (have bought → had bought)

ⓓ 선행사(the pictures)가 있으므로 선행사를 포함하는 관계대명사 what은 쓸 수 없다. (what → which(that))

21 |해석| [보기] 내가 집에 오기 전에 우리 가족은 저녁 식사를 다 마쳤다.

→ 내가 집에 왔을 때, 우리 가족은 이미 저녁 식사를 마친 상태였다.

(1) 우리가 역에 도착하기 전에 기차는 떠났다.

→ 우리가 역에 도착했을 때, 기차는 이미 떠나고 없었다.

(2) 나는 알람 시계가 울리기 전에 일어났다.

→ 알람 시계가 울렸을 때, 나는 이미 일어나 있었다.

(3) 나는 엄마가 집에 오시기 전에 숙제를 끝냈다.

→ 엄마가 집에 오셨을 때, 나는 이미 숙제를 끝마친 상태였다.

|해설| 과거에 일어난 두 가지 일 중 이미 먼저 일어난 일은 과거완료(had+과거분사)를 사용하여 문장을 완성한다.

22 |해설| 과거의 특정 시점에 일어난 일들보다 더 이전에 일어난 일들이므로 모두 과거완료(had+과거분사)로 나타낸다. just와 already는 주로 had와 과거분사 사이에 쓴다.

23 |해석| (1) 내가 진정으로 원하는 것은 너의 지지이다.

(2) 경찰이 도착했을 때, 그 남자는 이미 달아난 상태였다.

(3) 그것은 내가 말하고 싶었던 것이 아니다.

(4) 그는 그 영화배우를 전에 만난 적이 없다고 나에게 말했다.

|해설| (1), (3) 선행사를 포함하는 관계대명사가 각각 주어와 목적어 역할을 하는 명사절을 이끄는 것이 알맞다.

(2) 경찰이 도착한(arrived) 과거 시점 이전에 남자가 도망간 것이므로 과거완료(had+과거분사) 형태로 쓰는 것이 알맞다.

(4) 말한(told) 과거 시점 이전에 경험해 본 적이 없다는 내용이므로 과거완료(had+과거분사) 형태로 쓰는 것이 알맞다.

24 |해석| Jason이 좋아하는 것은 만화를 그리는 것이다. Luna가 좋아하는 것은 자전거를 타는 것이다. Dan이 좋아하는 것은 축구 하는 것이다.

|해설| '~가 좋아하는 것'은 선행사를 포함하는 관계대명사 what을 사용하여 what ~ like(s)로 표현할 수 있다.

25 |해석| 농구하는 것은 Jason이 좋아하지 않는 것이다. 수영하는 것은 Luna가 좋아하지 않는 것이다. Dan이 좋아하지 않는 것은 요가 하는 것이다.

|해설| '~가 좋아하지 않는 것'은 what ~ don't(doesn't) like로 나타낼 수 있다.

ⓡ Reading 빈칸 채우기 pp. 107~108

01 antique furniture   02 was known for, high price
03 he had got   04 simple   05 knocked on   06 told people   07 how valuable, took advantage of   08 was able to   09 another Sunday   10 he visited   11 One, the other   12 furniture   13 any   14 I don't   15 take a look   16 come in   17 first, nothing   18 moved to   19 was   20 priceless, eighteenth-century   21 excited, fell over   22 wrong   23 at all, lied   24 straight face, reproduction   25 worth, a few   26 added, may buy   27 are broken   28 cut off, attach   29 How much   30 I'm afraid   31 how much   32 pounds   33 more than   34 How about   35 Make   36 final offer   37 yours, take   38 go in   39 see, to bring   40 help smiling   41 what, dreamed of   42 his luck   43 what if   44 not pay   45 had, idea   46 What he wants   47 cut, off   48 idea   49 took out   50 had been cut   51 favor   52 charge, for   53 so shocked that

---

ⓡ Reading 바른 어휘 · 어법 고르기 pp. 109~110

01 in   02 for   03 he had   04 simple   05 knocked   06 that   07 of   08 buy   09 it   10 men   11 the other   12 furniture   13 any   14 don't   15 take

---

16 in   17 was   18 to   19 it was   20 priceless   21 so excited that   22 asked   23 lied   24 with   25 worth   26 may   27 are broken   28 attach   29 much   30 Not much   31 how   32 pounds   33 more   34 How   35 Make   36 final   37 how   38 will not   39 to bring   40 smiling   41 what   42 luck   43 what if   44 pay   45 had   46 he wants   47 for   48 Great   49 out   50 had been   51 worry   52 for   53 shocked

---

ⓡ Reading 틀린 문장 고치기 pp. 111~112

01 ○   02 ×, selling them   03 ×, he had got   04 ○
05 ○   06 ×, that   07 ×, valuable their things were
08 ×, was able to 또는 could   09 ○   10 ○   11 ×, the other   12 ○   13 ○   14 ○   15 ×, take a look
16 ○   17 ×, there was nothing   18 ×, moved to
19 ○   20 ×, piece of eighteenth-century English furniture   21 ×, excited   22 ○   23 ○   24 ×, with a straight face   25 ×, a few   26 ○   27 ×, are broken
28 ×, them   29 ○   30 ○   31 ○   32 ○   33 ×, worth   34 ○   35 ○   36 ×, final offer   37 ×, yours
38 ○   39 ○   40 ×, On his way   41 ×, what   42 ○
43 ×, what if   44 ○   45 ○   46 ×, What he wants
47 ○   48 ○   49 ×, cut off   50 ×, had been cut off
51 ○   52 ○   53 ×, anything

ⓡ Reading 실전 TEST pp. 116~119

01 ③   02 ④   03 ③   04 ⑤   05 ④   06 ④   07 ②
08 ②   09 reproduction   10 ⑤   11 ③   12 ①
13 ①   14 ⑤   15 ②   16 ⑤

[서술형]
17 where he had got the furniture   18 how valuable their things were   19 (1) an antique furniture dealer (2) small towns every Sunday(on Sundays)   20 ⓒ → excited   21 (A) the legs of your table   (B) my table (at home)   22 priceless furniture, reproduction, buy
23 Mr. Boggis couldn't(could not) help smiling
24 table, luck, car, pay, legs, cut, off   25 탁자의 다리를 자른 것

[01~05] |해석|
Cyril Boggis는 런던의 골동품 가구 판매상이었다. 그는 좋은 물건을 낮은 가격에 사서 높은 가격에 파는 것으로 유명했다. 사람들은 그에게 가구

를 어디에서 <u>구했는지</u> 물었지만, 그는 "그건 비밀이에요."라고만 말했다. <u>Boggis 씨의 비밀</u>은 단순했다. 그는 매주 일요일에 작은 마을들을 방문해서 문을 두드렸다. 그는 사람들에게 자신이 가구 판매상이라고 말했다. 사람들은 자신들의 물건이 얼마나 값진 것인지 몰랐으므로 Boggis 씨는 그들을 이용했다. 그는 물건들을 매우 <u>비싸게(→ 싸게)</u> 살 수 있었다.

01 |해설| (A) be known for: ~으로 유명하다
　　　(C) take advantage of: ~을 이용하다

02 |해설| 사람들이 물어본(asked) 과거 시점보다 가구를 구한 것이 더 이전에 일어난 일이므로 과거완료(had+과거분사)를 쓴다.

03 |해설| secret(비밀)은 '어디에서 가구를 구했는지'에 대한 내용이므로, 주어진 문장은 Boggis 씨가 가구를 구하는 방법을 구체적으로 알려 주는 내용 앞인 ③에 들어가는 것이 자연스럽다.

04 |해설| ⓔ Cyril Boggis는 좋은 물건을 낮은 가격에 사서 높은 가격에 파는 가구 판매상이었으므로 물건들을 싸게(cheaply) 살 수 있었다는 내용이 되어야 자연스럽다.

05 |해석| ① Boggis 씨의 직업은 무엇이었는가?
　　　② Boggis 씨는 무엇으로 유명했는가?
　　　③ Boggis 씨는 일요일마다 어디에 가는가?
　　　④ Boggis 씨는 가구를 언제 팔았는가?
　　　⑤ Boggis 씨는 어떻게 낮은 가격에 좋은 가구를 살 수 있었는가?
　　|해설| ④ Boggis 씨가 언제 가구를 팔았는지는 언급되지 않았다.

[06~10] |해석|
일요일이 또 찾아왔고, Boggis 씨는 다시 어느 작은 마을에 있었다. 그는 방문한 집에서 두 남자를 만났다. 한 명은 주인인 Rummins였고, <u>다른 한 명</u>은 그의 아들인 Bert였다.
"저는 고가구를 삽니다. 고가구가 있으신가요?" Boggis 씨가 물었다.
"아니요." Rummins가 말했다.
"한번 둘러봐도 될까요?" Boggis 씨가 물었다.
"그럼요. 들어오세요." Rummins가 말했다.
Boggis 씨는 먼저 부엌에 갔는데 아무것도 없었다. 그런 다음 그는 거실로 옮겨 갔다. 그리고 그곳에 그것이 있었다! 매우 귀중한 18세기 영국 가구인 탁자가. 그는 몹시 흥분해서 거의 넘어질 뻔했다.
"무슨 일이세요?" Bert가 물었다.
"아, 아무것도 아니에요. 전혀 아무 일도 아닙니다." Boggis 씨는 거짓말을 했다. 그러고 나서 그는 정색하며 말했다. "이 탁자는 복제품입니다. 몇 파운드의 가치밖에 안 돼요."

06 |해설| 둘 중 하나는 one, 나머지 하나는 the other로 나타낸다.

07 |해설| (A) furniture(가구)는 셀 수 없는 명사이다.
　　　(B) 선행사(A table)를 수식하는 관계대명사절을 이끄는 주격 관계대명사 which가 알맞다.
　　　(C) 뒤에 복수 명사(pounds)가 있으므로 a few(약간의)가 알맞다.

08 |해석| 그는 몹시 흥분해서 거의 넘어질 뻔했다.
　　|해설| '너무[매우] ~해서 …하다'는 「so+형용사/부사+that+주어+동사」로 나타낸다.

09 |해설| '그림과 같은 무언가의 복제본'은 reproduction(복제품)의 영영 풀이이다.

10 |해석| Q: Boggis 씨는 Rummins의 집 거실에서 무엇을 발견했는가?
　　　A: 그는 <u>매우 값진 탁자</u>를 발견했다.
　　|해설| Boggis 씨는 Rummins의 집 거실에서 매우 귀중한 18세기 영국 가구인 탁자를 발견했다.

[11~13] |해석|
그리고 그는 덧붙였다. "흠, 제가 살 수도 있을 것 같아요. 우리 집에 있는 탁자 다리가 부러졌거든요. 당신의 탁자 다리를 잘라서 제 탁자에 붙일 수 있겠어요."
"얼마를 줄 건가요?" Rummins가 물었다.
"유감이지만 많이 줄 수는 없어요. 이것은 복제품일 뿐이니까요." Boggis 씨가 말했다.
"그래서 얼마를 줄 수 있는데요?"
"10파운드요."
"10이요? 그것보다는 가치가 더 나가요."
"15는 어때요?"
"50으로 하지요."
"음, 30이요. 이게 제 마지막 제안입니다."
"그러죠, 이건 당신 겁니다. 그런데 이걸 어떻게 가져갈 건가요? 이게 차에 들어가지 않을 텐데요!"
"한번 보죠." Boggis 씨가 말하고는 자신의 차를 가지러 밖으로 나갔다.

11 |해설| ③을 제외한 나머지는 모두 'Rummins의 탁자'를 가리킨다. ③은 앞에서 언급된 ten pounds를 가리킨다.

12 |해설| ⓐ 문장의 주어(The legs ~ home)가 복수이므로 동사는 is가 아니라 are를 써야 한다.

13 |해설| ① Boggis 씨는 자신의 탁자의 다리가 부러져서, Rummins의 탁자를 사서 그 다리를 잘라 자신의 탁자에 붙일 것이라고 말했고, 탁자가 복제품이라고 말하며 싸게 사려고 했다.

[14~16] |해석|
차로 가는 길에 Boggis 씨는 웃지 않을 수 없었다. 그 탁자는 모든 판매상이 꿈꾸는 <u>것</u>이었다. 그는 자신의 <u>행운</u>을 믿을 수가 없었다.
"아버지, 만약 이게 그의 차에 안 들어가면 어쩌죠? 그가 값을 지불하지 않을 수도 있어요." Bert가 말했다.
Rummins는 그때 생각이 떠올랐다. "그가 원하는 <u>것</u>은 오직 탁자의 다리뿐이야. 그를 위해서 다리를 자르자." Rummins가 말했다. "좋은 생각이에요!" Bert가 말했다. 그런 다음 Bert는 톱을 꺼내서 탁자 다리를 자르기 시작했다.
Boggis 씨가 돌아왔을 때, 탁자 다리는 <u>잘려</u> 있었다. "걱정하지 마세요. 이건 호의로 한 거예요. 이것에 대해 비용을 청구하지는 않을게요." Rummins가 말했다. Boggis 씨는 너무 충격을 받아서 아무 말도 할 수 없었다.

14 |해설| ⓔ 모든 판매상이 꿈꾸는 귀중한 가구의 다리가 잘린 것을 본 Boggis 씨는 충격을 받아서 아무 말도 하지 못했을 것이므로 happy(기쁜)가 아니라 shocked(충격을 받은) 또는 surprised(놀란) 등이 알맞다.

15 |해설| 각각 보어와 주어로 쓰인 명사절을 이끄는 관계대명사 what(What)이 알맞다. what은 '~하는 것'이라는 의미로 선행사를 포함하는 관계대명사이다.

16 |해설| Boggis 씨가 돌아온(came back) 과거 시점보다 탁자 다리가 잘린 것이 더 이전에 일어난 일이고 다리가 '잘려진' 것이므로 과거완료 수동태(had been+과거분사)로 쓰는 것이 알맞다.

[17~19] |해석|
Cyril Boggis는 런던의 골동품 가구 판매상이었다. 그는 좋은 물건을 낮은 가격에 사서 높은 가격에 파는 것으로 유명했다. 사람들은 그에게 가구

를 어디에서 구했는지 물었지만, 그는 "그건 비밀이에요."라고만 말했다. Boggis 씨의 비밀은 단순했다. 그는 매주 일요일에 작은 마을들을 방문해서 문을 두드렸다. 그는 사람들에게 자신이 가구 판매상이라고 말했다. 사람들은 자신들의 물건이 얼마나 값진 것인지 몰랐으므로 Boggis 씨는 그들을 이용했다. 그는 물건들을 매우 싸게 살 수 있었다.

17 |해설| 그가 어디에서 가구를 구했는지(where he had got the furniture)를 가리킨다.

18 |해설| didn't know의 목적어 역할을 하는 간접의문문이므로 「의문사＋주어＋동사」의 어순으로 쓴다.

19 |해석| (1) Cyril Boggis의 직업은 무엇이었는가?
→ 그는 골동품 가구 판매상이었다.
(2) Cyril Boggis는 낮은 가격에 물건을 사기 위해 언제 어디로 갔는가?
→ 그는 매주 일요일에 작은 마을에 갔다.

[20~22] |해석|
Boggis 씨는 먼저 부엌에 갔는데 아무것도 없었다. 그런 다음 그는 거실로 옮겨 갔다. 그리고 그곳에 그것이 있었다! 매우 귀중한 18세기 영국 가구인 탁자가. 그는 몹시 흥분해서 거의 넘어질 뻔했다.
"무슨 일이세요?" Bert가 물었다.
"아, 아무것도 아니에요. 전혀 아무 일도 아닙니다." Boggis 씨는 거짓말을 했다. 그러고 나서 그는 정색하며 말했다. "이 탁자는 복제품입니다. 몇 파운드의 가치밖에 안 돼요."
그리고 그는 덧붙였다. "흠, 제가 살 수도 있을 것 같아요. 우리 집에 있는 탁자 다리가 부러졌거든요. 당신의 탁자 다리를 잘라서 제 탁자에 붙일 수 있겠어요."

20 |해설| ⓒ 감정을 느끼게 되는 수동의 의미가 되어야 하므로 '흥분한'을 뜻하는 과거분사형 형용사 excited가 알맞다.

21 |해설| (A) 앞부분에 있는 'Rummins의 탁자 다리'를 가리킨다.
(B) (집에 있는) 자신의 탁자를 가리킨다.

22 |해설| Boggis 씨는 Rummins의 거실에서 매우 귀중한 가구 한 점을 발견했다. 그는 그것이 복제품이라고 거짓말을 했고 그것을 사겠다고 말했다.

[23~25] |해석|
"그렇죠, 이건 당신 겁니다. 그런데 이걸 어떻게 가져갈 건가요? 이게 차에 들어가지 않을 텐데요!"
"한번 보죠." Boggis 씨가 말하고는 자신의 차를 가지러 밖으로 나갔다.
차로 가는 길에 Boggis 씨는 웃지 않을 수 없었다. 그 탁자는 모든 판매상이 꿈꾸던 것이었다. 그는 자신의 행운을 믿을 수가 없었다.
"아버지, 만약 이게 그의 차에 안 들어가면 어쩌죠? 그가 값을 지불하지 않을 수도 있어요." Bert가 말했다.
Rummins는 그때 생각이 떠올랐다. "그가 원하는 건 오직 탁자의 다리뿐이야. 그를 위해서 다리를 자르자." Rummins가 말했다. "좋은 생각이에요!" Bert가 말했다. 그런 다음 Bert는 톱을 꺼내서 탁자 다리를 자르기 시작했다.
Boggis 씨가 돌아왔을 때, 탁자 다리는 잘려 있었다. "걱정하지 마세요. 이건 호의로 한 거예요. 이것에 대해 비용을 청구하지는 않을게요." Rummins가 말했다. Boggis 씨는 너무 충격을 받아서 아무 말도 할 수 없었다.

23 |해설| '~하지 않을 수 없다'는 can't help -ing로 나타낸다. 시제가 과거이므로 couldn't help smiling으로 쓴다.

24 |해석| Boggis 씨: 내가 모든 판매상이 사고 싶어 하는 탁자를 구했어. 내 행운을 믿을 수가 없어!
Bert: 이 탁자는 너무 커서 Boggis 씨의 차에 들어갈 수 없을 것 같아. 그러면 그는 아버지께 값을 지불하지 않을지도 몰라.
Rummins: Boggis 씨는 탁자 다리만 필요하다고 말했어. 그것을 자르자.

25 |해설| 밑줄 친 this는 Rummins와 그의 아들이 앞에서 한 행동을 말하므로 '탁자의 다리를 자른 것'을 가리킨다.

기타 지문 **실전 TEST** p. 121

01 ②, ⑤ **02** ③ **03** ④ **04** ④ **05** What I like the most **06** ④

[01~02] |해석|
작년 여름에 나는 내 강아지 보미를 잃어버렸어. 내가 공원에서 물을 마시는 사이에 그녀가 사라졌어. 다행히, 이틀 뒤에 그녀를 찾을 수 있었어. 나는 너무 기뻐서 그녀를 품에 꼭 안았어.

01 |해석| ① 잘됐다. ② 안됐구나. ③ 축하해! ④ 정말 기쁘다.
⑤ 그 말을 들으니 유감이야.
|해설| 상대방에게 안 좋은 일이 생겨 유감을 표현할 때 That's too bad. 또는 I'm sorry to hear that.으로 말할 수 있다.

02 |해석| ① 글쓴이는 어디에서 보미를 잃어버렸는가?
② 보미가 사라졌을 때 글쓴이는 무엇을 하고 있었는가?
③ 글쓴이는 보미를 어디에서 찾았는가?
④ 보미를 찾는 데 얼마나 오래 걸렸는가?
⑤ 글쓴이가 보미를 찾았을 때 심정이 어땠는가?
|해설| ③ 글쓴이가 자신의 강아지 보미를 어디에서 찾았는지는 언급되지 않았다.

03 |해석| • '멋진 여우 씨': 한 여우가 3명의 못된 농부들로부터 자신의 가족을 지켜 낸다.
• '마틸다': 한 소녀가 친구들을 돕기 위해 자신의 특별한 힘을 사용한다.
• '찰리와 초콜릿 공장': 한 소년이 세계 최고의 초콜릿 공장을 방문한다.
|해설| ⓐ protect A from B: A를 B로부터 보호하다
ⓑ 친구들을 돕기 위해 자신의 특별한 힘을 사용한다는 내용이므로 목적을 나타내는 부사적 용법의 to부정사 형태가 알맞다.

[04~06] |해석|
독후감, '어느 운수 좋은 일요일'
이 이야기는 Roald Dahl이 썼다. 이것은 Boggis 씨에 관한 것인데, 그는 골동품 가구 판매상이었다. 이 이야기에서, 그는 Rummins에게 그의 탁자가 복제품이라고 거짓말을 했고, 그것을 사는 데 30파운드를 주겠다고 제안했다. Boggis 씨는 탁자의 다리만 원한다고 말했고, 그래서 Bert는 그를 위해 탁자 다리를 잘랐다. 이것은 실제로는 탁자 전부를 원했던 Boggis 씨를 놀라게 했다. 나는 Boggis 씨가 사람들에게 거짓말을 했기 때문에 좋은 사람이 아니라고 생각한다. 이 이야기에서 내가 가장 마음에 드는 것은 놀라운 결말이다. 나는 이 이야기가 매우 흥미롭다고 생각한다.

04 |해설| ④ 「동사＋부사」로 이루어진 이어동사는 목적어가 대명사인 경우에 동사와 부사 사이에 목적어가 와야 한다. (→ cut them off)

05 |해설| 문장의 주어 역할을 하는 명사절을 이끌고 '~하는 것'이라는 의미를 나타내는 관계대명사 what을 사용하여, 「What+주어+동사 ~」의 어순으로 쓴다.

06 |해석| ① Roald Dahl은 '어느 운수 좋은 일요일'을 썼다.
② Boggis 씨는 골동품 가구 판매상이었다.
③ Boggis 씨는 Rummins에게 그의 탁자가 복제품이라고 말했다.
④ Bert는 Boggis 씨가 그에게 그렇게 하라고 말했기 때문에 탁자의 다리를 잘랐다.
⑤ 글쓴이는 그 이야기의 놀라운 결말을 가장 좋아한다.
|해설| ④ Boggis 씨가 탁자 다리를 잘라 달라고 말한 것이 아니라, Boggis 씨가 탁자 다리만 원한다고 생각해서 Bert가 탁자의 다리를 잘랐다는 내용이다.

STEP B

W Words 고득점 맞기　　　　　　pp. 122~123

01 ②　02 ③　03 ⑤　04 (1) recycle (2) careless
(3) replay　05 saw　06 ②　07 ②　08 ③　09 ④
10 a straight face　11 ⑤　12 ⑤　13 ④　14 ⑤
15 ①

01 |해석| 사람들에게 어떤 것에 대해 특정 금액의 돈을 지불하라고 요구하다
① 첨가하다, 덧붙이다　③ 제안하다, 제의하다　④ 붙이다　⑤ 복제하다
|해설| charge((요금·값을) 청구하다)의 영영풀이이다.

02 |해석| 빈칸에 알맞은 말끼리 짝지어진 것은?
• 그는 프로젝트를 도와주겠다는 우리의 제안을 받아들였다.
• 그녀는 자신의 가방에 빨간색 가죽 조각을 붙였다.
① 톱 – 지불했다　② 판매상 – 청구했다　④ 방법 – 두드렸다
⑤ 발표 – 선출했다

03 |해석| A: 너는 수학 시험을 잘 봤니?
B: 유감스럽게도, 아니. 나는 그것에 기분이 좋지 않아.
① 운 좋게　② 고맙게도　③ 그런데　④ 갑자기
|해설| 수학 시험을 잘 봤는지 묻는 말에 그렇지 않다고 답하고 그 때문에 기분이 좋지 않다고 했으므로 빈칸에는 Unfortunately(불행하게도, 유감스럽게도)가 알맞다.

04 |해석| (1) 우리는 지구를 구하기 위해 더 많이 재활용해야 한다.
(2) 나는 그의 부주의한 행동에 실망했다.
(3) 네가 그 음악을 너무 많이 재생하면 사람들이 지루해할 거야.
|해설| (1) '재활용하다'라는 의미가 되도록 동사 cycle에 '다시'라는 의미를 나타내는 접두사 re-를 붙인다.
(2) '부주의한'의 의미가 되도록 명사 care에 '~이 없는'을 의미하는 접미사 -less를 붙인다.
(3) '재생하다, 다시 듣다'의 의미가 되도록 동사 play에 접두사 re-를 붙인다.

05 |해석| • 그녀는 어제 쥐가 의자 밑에 앉아 있는 것을 보았다.
• 그는 아들을 위한 그네를 만들기 위해 톱으로 나무를 자르고 있다.
|해설| 첫 번째 문장에는 동사 see의 과거형 saw가 알맞고, 두 번째 문장에는 '톱'이라는 뜻의 명사 saw가 알맞다.

06 |해석| 이 운동화는 얼마인가요?
= 이 운동화의 가격은 얼마인가요?
① 지불하다　③ 제안　④ 방법　⑤ 소장품
|해설| How much ~ cost?는 '~가 얼마인가요?'라는 뜻으로 가격을 물어보는 표현이며 '가격'을 의미하는 price를 사용하여 What is the price of ~?로 바꿔 쓸 수 있다.

07 |해석| 그 그림은 5만 달러 이상의 가치가 있다.
① 무언가의 모든 것
② 특정한 가치를 가지고 있는
③ 매우 놀라고 속상한
④ 아무 걱정이나 생각 없이
⑤ 아무런 가치가 없거나 쓸모가 없는
|해설| '(어떤 금액의) 가치가 있는'이라는 뜻으로 쓰였으므로 영영풀이로 ②가 알맞다.

08 |해석| ① James는 수수께끼들을 푸는 것으로 유명했다.
② 도시 전체가 황사로 가득 차 있었다.
③ 그녀는 마지막 질문을 하기 위해 손을 들었다.
④ 그 박물관에는 대단히 귀중한 미술 작품들이 많이 있다.
⑤ 너는 영어 실력을 향상시키기 위해 이번 방학을 이용할 수 있다.
|해설| ③ final은 '마지막의'라는 의미이므로 last와 바꿔 쓸 수 있다.

09 |해석| ⓐ 나의 삼촌은 그 식당의 주인이다.
ⓑ 그의 직업은 유명한 예술 작품의 복제품을 만드는 것이다.
ⓒ 그들은 새 집을 위한 새 가구를 원했다.
ⓓ 내 여동생이 학교 연극에서 주인공 역할을 맡았다.
① 역할　② 주인　③ 가구　④ 호의　⑤ 복제품
|해설| ⓐ에는 owner(주인), ⓑ에는 reproduction(복제품), ⓒ에는 furniture(가구), ⓓ에는 role(역할)이 알맞다.

10 |해설| with a straight face: 정색하며, 시치미를 떼고

11 |해석| ① 자녀에 대한 부모의 사랑은 끝이 없다.
② 내가 그에게 부탁을 했지만, 그는 나를 도와주지 않았다.
③ 나는 지하실에 값진 물건을 보관하지 않는다.
④ 아빠는 차고에서 골동품 오크 탁자를 발견했다.
⑤ 내가 실망할 때마다 그는 나를 축하해 주었다. (×)
|해설| ⑤ 실망할 때마다 축하한다는 내용은 어색하다.

12 |해석| ① Henry는 넘어져서 다리가 부러졌다.
② Kate는 자신의 긴 머리를 자르기 시작했다.
③ 그는 집에 가는 길에 이상한 소리를 들었다.
④ 이 그림을 한번 보고 제목을 맞춰 보아라.
⑤ 그 이야기가 너무 슬퍼서 그녀는 웃지(→ 울지) 않을 수 없었다.
|해설| ⑤ 문맥상 이야기가 너무 슬퍼서 울지 않을 수 없었다는 의미가 되어야 자연스럽다. (→ couldn't help crying)

13 |해석| • 붙이다: 어떤 것을 다른 것에 고정시키거나 결합하다
• 판매상: 물건을 사고파는 직업을 가진 사람
• 복제품: 그림과 같은 물건의 복제본
• 호의, 친절: 누군가를 돕기 위해 하는 일

• 두드리다: 손으로 문을 쳐서 안에 있는 누군가에게 당신이 거기 있다는 것을 알리다

|해설| ⓓ favor는 '호의, 친절'이라는 뜻이며 영영풀이로 something that you do to help someone이 알맞다.

14 **|해석|** 다음 밑줄 친 단어 중 [보기]와 의미가 같은 것은?

[보기] 그 식당은 음식값을 비싸게 청구한다.

① 어린이 요금이 있나요?

② 배송 요금은 얼마인가요?

③ 그들은 내 스마트폰을 요금 없이 무료로 고쳐 주었다.

④ 서비스 요금은 청구서에 포함되지 않습니다.

⑤ 그 미술관은 입장료를 청구하지 않는다.

|해설| [보기]와 ⑤는 '요금을 청구하다'라는 뜻의 동사로 쓰였고, 나머지는 모두 '요금'이라는 뜻의 명사로 쓰였다.

15 **|해석|** ⓐ 귀중한: 거의 가치가 없는(→ 많은 돈의 가치가 있는)

ⓑ 충격을 받은: 매우 놀라고 속상한

ⓒ 운, 행운(→ 제안): 누군가에게 무언가를 원하는지 묻는 행동

ⓓ 가구: 의자, 침대, 탁자, 책장과 같은 물건들

ⓔ 톱: 주로 길고 가는 철로 된 날이 있으며 나무나 다른 물질을 자르는 용도의 도구

|해설| ⓐ valuable은 '값비싼, 귀중한'이라는 뜻이므로 영영풀이로 worth a lot of money가 알맞다.

ⓒ '누군가에게 무언가를 원하는지 묻는 행동'은 offer(제안)의 영영풀이이다.

L&T Listen and Talk 고득점 맞기   pp. 126~127

01 ⑤   **02** ②   **03** ③, ⑤   **04** ⑤   **05** ③, ④   **06** ②

[서술형]

07 ⓑ → **|모범 답|** I'm so excited/happy.   **08** too bad

09 (1) He got the main role, Romeo.   (2) It's at 2 p.m. on September 20th, in the acting club room.

10 (1) Congratulations on winning first prize.

(2) **|모범 답|** I'm so happy/pleased/excited.   **11** I'm sorry to hear that   **12** smartphone, upset, the snack shop, look for

01 **|해석|** A: _____

B: 잘됐다. 축하해!

① 나 입학 시험에 합격했어.

② 내가 드디어 뮤지컬 티켓을 구했어.

③ 내가 노래자랑 대회에서 1등을 했어.

④ 내가 마라톤을 완주했어. 정말 기뻐.

⑤ 내가 새 스마트폰을 떨어뜨렸는데, 고장 났어.

|해설| 상대방에게 잘됐다고 말하며 축하해 주고 있으므로 유감의 말을 해야 할 좋지 않은 일인 ⑤는 알맞지 않다.

02 **|해석|** A: 너 기분 안 좋아 보인다. 무슨 일 있니?

B: 음, 나는 학교 연극에서 역할을 맡지 못했어. 정말 신나.(→ 정말 실망했어.)

A: 아, 그 말을 들으니 정말 유감이야. 그렇지만 너는 분명히 다음번에는 역할을 맡을 수 있을 거야.

B: 고마워. 다음번에는 더 열심히 노력할 거야.

|해설| ② 연극에서 역할을 맡지 못했다는 말을 하며 자신의 감정을 표현하는 말이므로 disappointed(실망한)나 upset(속상한)과 같은 감정 형용사를 사용하는 것이 적절하다.

03 **|해석|** ① A: 내가 학급 회장으로 당선되었어. 정말 기뻐.

B: 멋지다. 축하해!

② A: 나는 오늘 아침에 공원에서 내 개를 잃어버렸어.

B: 그 말을 들으니 유감이야. 네가 그를 빨리 찾기를 바라.

③ A: 나는 BTS 콘서트에 갈 거야.

B: 안됐구나. 나는 네가 얼마나 가고 싶어 했는지 알아.

④ A: 내 가장 친한 친구가 다른 나라로 이사 갈 거야. 너무 슬퍼.

B: 안됐구나. 그 말을 들으니 유감이야.

⑤ A: 테니스 경기에서 이긴 것을 축하해. 네 스스로가 매우 자랑스럽겠구나.

B: 고마워. 나는 매우 실망했어.

|해설| ③ 콘서트에 가게 되었다는 말을 듣고 상대방이 얼마나 그 콘서트에 가고 싶어 했는지 안다고 말하면서 유감을 표현하는 것은 어색하다.

⑤ 우승을 축하하는 말을 듣고 고맙다고 답한 후 실망했다고 이어서 말하는 것은 어색하다.

04 **|해석|** 지난 주말에 내 여동생이 내 가방을 잃어버렸어. 그녀는 그것을 버스에 두고 내렸고 찾지 못했어. 나는 정말 속상했어. 그것은 내 생일에 엄마가 주신 선물이었거든.

① 너는 잘했어!

② 나는 그것을 할 수 없을 것 같아.

③ 정말 잘됐다!

④ 멋지다. 축하해!

⑤ 안됐구나. 그 말을 들으니 유감이야.

|해설| 여동생이 글쓴이의 가방을 버스에 두고 내려 찾지 못하고 있는 상황이므로 유감의 말을 하는 것이 적절하다.

05 **|해석|** ① 끔찍하다. ② 안됐구나. ③ 잘됐구나. ④ 멋지다.

⑤ 그 말을 들으니 유감이야.

|해설| 독감에 걸린 친구에게 유감의 말을 하는 것이 적절하다.

06 **|해석|** ① 수미에게 무슨 문제가 있는가?

② 인호는 왜 병원에 갔는가?

③ 인호는 수미에게 무엇을 하라고 조언하는가?

④ 인호는 얼마나 자주 약을 먹는가?

⑤ 인호는 대화 후에 무엇을 할 것인가?

|해설| ② 인호는 독감에 걸려서 병원에 갔다고 했다.

07 **|해설|** ⓑ 지호가 학교 연극에서 자신이 원했던 주인공 역할을 맡게 되었다고 했으므로 지호의 감정은 속상한 것이 아니라 신나거나 기쁜 감정이 되어야 알맞다.

08 **|해설|** I'm sorry to hear that.은 유감을 표현하는 말로, That's too bad.로 바꿔 쓸 수 있다.

09 **|해석|** (1) 학교 연극에서 지호는 어떤 역할을 맡았는가?

→ 그는 주인공인 로미오 역할을 맡았다.

(2) 첫 번째 연습은 언제 어디서 하는가?

→ 그것은 9월 20일 오후 2시에 연극 동아리방에서 한다.

|해설| (1) 지호는 학교 연극에서 주인공인 로미오 역할을 맡게 되었다고 했다.

(2) 첫 번째 연습은 9월 20일 오후 2시에 연극 동아리방에서 할 것이라고 했다.

10 |해석| A: 1등 한 것을 축하해.

B: 고마워. 나는 정말 기뻐/신나.

A: 네 스스로가 매우 자랑스럽겠구나.

B: 응, 맞아. 나는 최선을 다했어.

|해설| (1) '~에 대해 축하해.'와 같이 축하하는 일을 구체적으로 표현할 때는 Congratulations on ~.을 사용하며, on 뒤에는 명사나 동명사가 온다.

(2) 좋은 일에 대해 축하의 말을 들었으므로 기쁜 감정을 표현하는 것이 알맞다.

11 |해설| 상대방이 스마트폰을 잃어버려 속상해하고 있으므로 유감을 표현하는 말을 하는 것이 자연스럽다.

12 |해석| 미나는 스마트폰을 잃어버렸고, 그래서 속상하다. 그녀는 그것을 매점에서 마지막으로 사용한 것을 기억한다. 대화가 끝난 후에 그녀는 Tim과 함께 그것을 찾으러 그곳에 갈 것이다.

|해설| 미나는 스마트폰을 잃어버려 속상해하고 있으며, 마지막으로 매점에서 그것을 가방에서 꺼낸 것을 기억했고, Tim의 제안대로 그것을 찾으러 매점에 다시 가기로 했다.

G Grammar 고득점 맞기 pp. 128~130

01 ⑤ **02** ③ **03** ② **04** ⑤ **05** ②, ④ **06** ④
07 ④ **08** ⑤ **09** ③ **10** ③ **11** ②

[서술형]

12 His parents had (already) gone to bed when he got home. 또는 When he got home, his parents had (already) gone to bed. **13** Jake didn't understand what the teacher was talking about. **14** (1) ⓐ that → what (2) ⓓ has → had **15** What they say is similar to what I expected. **16** (1) She ran out of allowance after she had bought the sneakers. (2) I couldn't use my laptop because my brother had broken it. **17** When I woke up, Dad had already gone to work(had gone to work already). **18** (1) What Mina is interested in is singing and dancing. (2) What Mina likes to do in her free time is playing badminton. (3) What Mina wants to be in the future is a movie director. **19** (1) had been cleaned (2) had written him a card (3) had prepared a surprise party **20** (1) This(The) book is what she is looking for. (2) This(The) book is the thing that she is looking for.

01 |해석| • 그는 전에 그 노래를 들어 본 적이 있다고 말했다.

• 미나는 첼로를 매우 잘 연주한다. 그녀는 아주 어렸을 때부터 첼로를 연주해 왔다.

|해설| 첫 번째 빈칸에는 과거에 말한(said) 시점보다 더 이전에 경험한

일이므로 과거완료(had+과거분사)가 알맞다. 두 번째 빈칸에는 매우 어릴 때부터 현재까지 첼로를 연주해 오고 있는 상황이므로 현재완료(have(has)+과거분사)가 알맞다.

02 |해석| • 나는 무엇을 입어야 할지 정하지 않았다.

• Alice는 내가 그녀에게 쓴 것을 읽었다.

• 그가 되고 싶은 것은 로봇 과학자이다.

|해설| 첫 번째 빈칸에는 의문사 what이 알맞고, 두 번째와 세 번째 빈칸에는 선행사를 포함하는 관계대명사 what이 알맞다.

03 |해설| 그가 물은 것은 과거시제(asked)로 쓰고, 내가 신발을 산 것은 그것보다 더 이전의 일이므로 과거완료(had bought)로 쓴다.

04 |해석| A: 너 어제 콘서트를 왜 놓쳤니?

B: 교통 체증이 심해서 나는 콘서트에 늦었어. 내가 홀에 도착했을 때, 콘서트는 이미 시작한 상태였어.

|해설| ⑤ 도착한(arrived) 과거 시점보다 콘서트가 시작한 것이 더 먼저 일어난 일이므로 현재완료가 아닌 과거완료로 써야 한다.

05 |해석| 도둑은 그 물건을 훔쳤다. 그것은 금고 안에 있었다.

②, ④ 도둑은 금고 안에 있던 것을 훔쳤다.

|해설| 두 번째 문장의 It은 첫 번째 문장의 the thing을 가리키므로 주격 관계대명사 that이나 which를 사용하여 The thief stole the thing that(which) was in the safe.로 쓸 수 있고, the thing that(which)는 선행사를 포함하는 관계대명사 what으로 바꿔 쓸 수 있다.

06 |해석| 늦어서 미안해. 나는 오늘 아침 기차를 놓쳤어. 내가 역에 도착했을 때 기차는 떠나고 없었어.

|해설| 첫 번째 빈칸은 과거의 상황을 나타내므로 과거시제로, 두 번째 빈칸은 역에 도착한(got) 과거 시점보다 더 이전에 기차가 떠났음을 나타내는 과거완료로 써야 한다.

07 |해석| 나는 지난달에 온라인으로 그 티셔츠를 주문했다. 그런데 색깔이 내가 사이트에서 봤던 것과는 달랐다.

|해설| ④ 전치사 from의 목적어인 명사절을 이끌며 '~하는 것'이라는 뜻으로 선행사를 포함하는 관계대명사 what을 써야 한다.

08 |해석| ① 그 케이크는 엄마가 굽고 있던 것이다.

② 나는 그가 보낸 것을 아직 받지 못했다.

③ 이 카메라는 내가 갖고 싶었던 것이다.

④ 우리는 부모님이 우리에게 요리해 주신 것을 먹었다.

⑤ 나는 내가 빌리고 싶은 책을 못 찾겠다.

|해설| ⑤에는 목적격 관계대명사 that 또는 which가 들어가고, 나머지에는 선행사를 포함하는 관계대명사 what이 들어간다.

09 |해석| ① 여기에 오기 전에 너는 어디서 살았니?

② 제빵 수업을 듣기 전에 나는 오븐을 사용해 본 적이 한 번도 없었다.

③ Amy는 내 책상을 마음에 들어 했다. 그녀는 나에게 그것을 어디서 구했는지 물었다.

④ 나는 시험에 늦었다. 내가 교실에 도착했을 때, 시험은 이미 시작해 있었다.

⑤ 엄마와 나는 들어갈 수 없었다. 엄마는 내게 집에 오는 길에 열쇠를 잃어버렸다고 말했다.

|해설| ③ 책상을 구한 시점이 물어본 시점보다 더 이전에 일어난 일이므로 She asked me where I had got it.이 되어야 알맞다.

10 |해석| ⓐ 이것은 내가 예상했던 것과 다르다.

ⓑ 'Spiderman'이 내가 너와 함께 보고 싶은 것이다.

ⓒ Sam은 지난주에 산 것을 못 받았다.

ⓓ 내가 그에 대해 아는 것은 그가 청바지 입기를 좋아한다는 것이다.

|해설| ⓑ is의 보어가 '내가 너와 함께 보고 싶은 것'이 되어야 하므로 선행사를 포함하는 관계대명사 what이 명사절을 이끄는 것이 알맞다. (who → what)

ⓒ hasn't received의 목적어 역할을 하는 it과 선행사를 포함하는 관계대명사 what으로 시작하는 명사절은 동시에 쓰일 수 없다. (it what → what)

11 |해석| ⓐ 나는 네가 저녁으로 먹고 싶어 하는 것을 요리할 것이다.

ⓑ 지금 그들에게 필요한 것은 살 집이다.

ⓒ 그들은 서울에 오기 전에는 눈을 본 적이 없었다.

ⓓ 할아버지의 정원은 그의 집에서 내가 가장 좋아하는 것이다.

ⓔ Tom의 가족이 이사 올 때까지 그 집은 10년 동안 비어 있던 상태였다.

|해설| ⓑ 주어가 '지금 그들이 필요한 것'이 되어야 하므로 선행사를 포함하는 관계대명사 What을 사용해야 한다. (Which → What)

ⓒ 서울에 온(came) 과거 시점 이전에는 눈을 본 적이 없었다는 내용이므로 과거완료(had+과거분사)로 써야 한다. (have → had)

12 |해석| 그의 부모님은 잠자리에 들었다. 그 후에 그는 집에 왔다.

→ 그가 왔을 때 그의 부모님은 (이미) 잠자리에 들어 있었다.

|해설| 집에 온(got home) 과거 시점 이전에 부모님이 잠자리에 든 것이므로 주절은 과거완료(had+과거분사)로 나타낸다.

13 |해석| Jake는 그것을 이해하지 못했다. 선생님은 그것에 관해 이야기하고 있었다.

→ Jake는 선생님이 이야기하고 있는 것을 이해하지 못했다.

|해설| 두 번째 문장에서 about의 목적어 it이 첫 번째 문장의 the thing을 가리키므로 목적격 관계대명사 that 또는 which를 사용해 한 문장으로 연결할 수 있으며, 이때 the thing that(which)는 선행사를 포함하는 관계대명사 what으로 바꿔 쓸 수 있다.

14 |해석| ⓐ 나는 그녀가 말한 것을 못 믿겠다.

ⓑ Jim은 내게 그가 집에 오는 길에 본 것을 말했다.

ⓒ 그 영화는 내가 상상했던 것과는 상당히 달랐다.

ⓓ Michael은 마침내 그 문제를 풀었다고 소리쳤다.

|해설| ⓐ believe의 목적어로 선행사를 포함하는 관계대명사 what이 이끄는 명사절이 오는 것이 알맞다.

ⓓ 문제를 푼 시점이 소리친(shouted out) 과거 시점보다 더 이전의 일이므로 현재완료가 아닌 과거완료로 나타낸다.

15 |해설| 선행사를 포함하는 관계대명사 what을 사용하여 '그들이 말하는 것'은 what they say로, '내가 예상했던 것'은 what I expected로 표현할 수 있다. 관계대명사 that이나 which를 쓰려면 선행사 the thing이 있어야 한다.

16 |해석| (1) 그녀는 용돈을 다 썼다. 그녀는 운동화를 샀다.

→ 그녀는 운동화를 산 후에 용돈을 다 썼다.

(2) 나는 내 노트북을 사용할 수 없었다. 내 형이 그것을 고장 냈다.

→ 나는 형이 내 노트북을 고장 내서 그것을 쓸 수가 없었다.

|해설| 특정 과거 시점보다 앞서 일어난 일을 과거완료(had+과거분사)로 나타낸다.

(1) 운동화를 산 것이 용돈을 다 쓴 것보다 이전의 일이므로 두 번째 문장을 과거완료로 나타낸다.

(2) 노트북을 고장 낸 것이 노트북을 사용할 수 없었던 것보다 이전의 일이므로 두 번째 문장을 과거완료로 나타낸다.

17 |해석| 오전 7시 – 아빠는 출근하셨다.

오전 7시 10분 – 나는 일어났다.

|해설| '내가 일어났을 때 아빠는 이미 출근하고 안 계셨다.'라는 의미가 되도록 문장을 완성한다. 아빠가 출근한 것이 내가 일어난(woke up) 과거 시점보다 이전의 일이므로 과거완료로 나타낸다.

18 |해석| [예시] 미나가 잘하는 것은 사진 찍는 것이다.

(1) 미나가 흥미 있는 것은 노래하고 춤추는 것이다.

(2) 미나가 여가 시간에 하기 좋아하는 것은 배드민턴 치는 것이다.

(3) 미나가 장래에 되고 싶은 것은 영화 감독이다.

|해설| 선행사를 포함하는 관계대명사 what이 이끄는 명사절이 주어 역할을 하도록 문장을 쓴다.

19 |해석| [예시] 민수가 집에 왔을 때, 그의 여동생은 잠자리에 들어 있었다.

(1) 민수가 집에 왔을 때, 그의 방은 청소되어 있었다.

(2) 민수가 집에 왔을 때, 그의 부모님은 그에게 카드를 써 두셨다.

(3) 민수가 집에 왔을 때, 그의 조부모님은 깜짝 파티를 준비해 두셨다.

|해설| 과거의 특정 시점에 일어난 일보다 더 이전에 일어난 일은 과거완료(had+과거분사)로 나타낸다.

20 |해설| '~하는 것'은 선행사를 포함하는 관계대명사 what으로 쓸 수 있고 what은 the thing that(which)로 바꿔 쓸 수 있다.

R Reading 고득점 맞기   pp. 133~135

01 ②   **02** ④   **03** ③   **04** ④   **05** ①, ②   **06** ⑤

07 ③   **08** ②   **09** ④   **10** ③

[서술형]

11 him where he had got(gotten) the furniture

12 antique furniture, cheaply, how valuable   **13** ⓐ → He was famous for buying good things at a low price and then selling them at a high price.   **14** Let's cut the legs off for him.   **15** Mr. Boggis was so shocked that he couldn't say anything.   **16** (1) Bert, the table (2) the legs

01 |해설| ⓐ be known for: ~으로 유명하다

ⓑ, ⓒ at a low/high price: 낮은/높은 가격으로

ⓓ knock on: ~을 두드리다

ⓔ take advantage of: ~을 이용하다

02 |해설| (A) 가구를 구한 것이 사람들이 물어본(asked) 시점보다 더 이전의 일이므로 과거완료의 had가 쓰이는 것이 알맞다.

(B) 뒤에 완전한 절이 이어지고 있으므로 명사절을 이끄는 접속사 that이 알맞다.

(C) '얼마나 귀중한지'는 how valuable로 나타낸다.

(D) '~할 수 있다'는 can이나 be able to로 나타낸다.

03 |해설| ③ Cyril Boggis는 사람들이 가구를 어디에서 구했는지 묻자 비밀이라고 하며 알려주지 않았다.

04 |해설| ⓓ '너무〔매우〕 ~해서 …하다'는 「so+형용사/부사+that+주어+동사」로 나타내므로 such가 아니라 so를 써야 한다.

05 |해석| 윗글의 내용과 일치하는 것은? 두 개 고르시오.
① Boggis 씨는 일요일에 Rummins의 집을 방문했다.
② Rummins는 Boggis 씨가 자신의 집에 들어오는 것을 허락했다.
③ Rummins의 집에는 골동품 가구들이 많이 있었다.
④ Boggis 씨는 Rummins의 부엌에서 귀중한 가구를 발견했다.
⑤ Rummins는 멋지고 오래된 탁자를 가지고 있었는데, 그것은 복제품이었다.
|해설| ① 글의 시작 부분에 일요일에 작은 마을에 가서 Rummins의 집을 방문했다고 언급되어 있다.
② Rummins는 Boggis 씨를 집에 들어오게 해서 안을 둘러보게 해 주었다.

06 |해설| 주어진 문장은 '이것이 차에 들어가지 않을 텐데요!'라는 의미이므로 탁자를 어떻게 가져갈 것인지 묻는 말 다음인 ⑤에 들어가는 것이 자연스럽다.

07 |해석| ① Rummins의 탁자 – 복제품
② Rummins의 탁자 – Boggis 씨의 탁자
③ Boggis 씨의 탁자 – 10파운드
④ Boggis 씨의 탁자 – 50파운드
⑤ Rummins의 탁자 다리 – Rummins의 탁자
|해설| ⓐ mine은 Boggis 씨가 자신의 탁자를 가리켜 하는 말이므로 Mr. Boggis' table이 알맞다.
ⓑ that은 앞에서 Boggis 씨가 말한 ten pounds를 가리킨다.

08 |해석| ⓐ 우리는 아빠가 우리에게 요리해 주신 것을 먹었다.
ⓑ 나는 할머니께 무엇을 사 드려야 할지 물었다.
ⓒ 너는 내 새 신발에 대해 어떻게 생각하니?
ⓓ 나는 어제 내가 산 것을 여동생에게 주었다.
ⓔ 그는 그녀가 어떤 종류의 음악을 좋아하는지 알고 싶었다.
|해설| (A)와 ⓐ, ⓓ는 관계대명사로 쓰였고, ⓑ, ⓒ, ⓔ는 모두 의문사로 쓰였다.

09 |해석| 윗글을 읽고 답할 수 없는 질문은?
① Boggis 씨는 무엇을 사기로 결정했는가?
② 탁자에 대한 Boggis 씨의 첫 번째 제안은 무엇이었는가?
③ Rummins는 처음에 탁자 가격으로 얼마를 받고 싶어 했는가?
④ Rummins는 탁자를 어디에서 구했는가?
⑤ Boggis 씨는 왜 자신의 차로 가는 길에 웃었는가?
|해설| ④ Rummins가 탁자를 어디에서 구했는지는 언급되지 않았다.

10 |해석| "아버지, 만약 이게 그의 차에 안 들어가면 어쩌죠? 그가 값을 지불하지 않을 수도 있어요." Bert가 말했다.
Rummins는 그때 생각이 떠올랐다. "그가 원하는 것은 오직 탁자의 다리뿐이야. 그를 위해서 다리를 자르자." Rummins가 말했다. "좋은 생각이에요!" Bert가 말했다. 그런 다음 Bert는 톱을 꺼내서 탁자 다리를 자르기 시작했다.
Boggis 씨가 돌아왔을 때, 탁자 다리는 잘려 있었다. "걱정하지 마세요. 이건 호의로 한 거예요. 이것에 대해 비용을 청구하지는 않을게요." Rummins가 말했다. Boggis 씨는 너무 충격을 받아서 아무 말도 할 수 없었다.
|해설| ⓒ 탁자의 다리를 자르는 내용이 이어지는 것으로 보아 탁자 다

리를 자르자고 제안하는 내용이 들어가는 것이 자연스럽다.

11 |해설| '~에게 …을 묻다'라는 의미의 4형식 문장으로 「ask+간접목적어(him)+직접목적어(간접의문문)」의 형태로 쓴다. 물은 것은 과거시제 asked로 쓰고, 가구를 구한 것은 더 이전에 일어난 일이므로 과거완료 had got〔gotten〕으로 쓴다.

12 |해설| Boggis 씨는 골동품 가구를 사고파는 판매상이었다. 그는 작은 마을에 사는 사람들이 그들의 물건이 얼마나 값진지 몰랐기 때문에 좋은 물건을 아주 싸게 살 수 있었다.
|해설| Boggis 씨는 골동품 가구 판매상이었고, 자신들의 물건이 얼마나 값진 것인지 모르는 작은 마을 사람들을 이용하여 좋은 물건을 매우 싸게 구입할 수 있었다고 했다.

13 |해석| ⓐ Boggis 씨는 무엇으로 유명했는가?
ⓑ Boggis 씨는 언제부터 작은 마을들을 방문하기 시작했는가?
ⓒ Boggis 씨는 작은 마을들에서 얼마나 많은 가구를 샀는가?
|해설| ⓐ 첫 번째 단락을 통해 Boggis 씨가 좋은 물건을 낮은 가격에 사서 높은 가격에 파는 것으로 유명했다는 것을 알 수 있다.

14 |해설| 밑줄 친 an idea는 뒤에 나오는 내용으로, Boggis 씨의 차에 들어갈 수 있도록 탁자의 다리를 자르는 것을 가리킨다.

15 |해설| Boggis 씨는 매우 충격을 받아서 아무 말도 할 수 없었다.
|해설| '매우〔너무〕 ~해서 (그 결과) …하다'는 「so+형용사/부사+that+주어+동사」 표현을 사용해서 나타낼 수 있다.

16 |해설| (1) Bert는 Boggis 씨가 탁자 값을 지불하지 않을 것을 걱정했다.
(2) Rummins는 Boggis 씨에게 탁자 다리를 자른 것에 대해 비용을 청구하고 싶지 않았다.
|해설| (1) Bert는 탁자가 차에 들어가지 않게 되어 Boggis 씨가 탁자 값을 지불하지 않을 것을 걱정했다.
(2) Rummins는 탁자 다리를 잘라 준 것이 호의라고 말하며 그것에 대해 Boggis 씨에게 비용을 청구하지 않겠다고 했다.

서술형 100% Test

pp. 136~139

01 (1) worth (2) favor (3) offer (4) charge
02 (1) advantage of (2) on her way (3) fell over
03 (A) for (B) with (C) laughing　**04** (A) I'm so〔really/very〕 excited. (B) Congratulations!　**05** I'm really happy to have a chance to work for my class.　**06** (1) the matter (2) too bad (3) feel better soon
07 ⓒ → |모범 답| I'm so happy for you.　**08** ⓒ call → text message　**09** Romeo, excited, Congratulations, get the role she wanted, too bad, disappointed　**10** (1) called, had gone (2) felt, had been busy　**11** (1) What he gave me (2) What she wanted to do (3) What, was known for
12 his car had been stolen　**13** (1) ⓑ → What he bought for her was a scarf. / The thing that〔which〕 he bought for her was a scarf. (2) ⓒ → Junsu had never ridden a bike before he was 15.　**14** People didn't know how valuable

their things were   **15** He was so excited that he almost fell over.   **16** (1) a table which(that) was a priceless piece of eighteenth-century English furniture (2) the (their) table was a reproduction   **17** (A) to bring (B) smiling (C) began   **18** what(What)   **19** When Mr. Boggis came back, the legs (of the table) had been cut off.   **20** cutting off the legs / cutting the legs off   **21** excited → |모범 답| shocked / surprised

01 |해석| (1) 가치가 있는: 특정한 가치를 가지고 있는
  (2) 호의, 친절: 누군가를 돕기 위해 하는 일
  (3) 제안, 제의: 누군가에게 무언가를 원하는지 묻는 행동
  (4) (요금·값을) 청구하다: 사람들에게 어떤 것에 대해 특정 금액의 돈을 지불하라고 요구하다

02 |해설| (1) take advantage of: ~을 이용하다
  (2) on one's way (to): (~로) 가는 길에
  (3) fall over: 넘어지다, 넘어지며 구르다

03 |해석| Charlie는 웃긴 것으로 유명하다. 그가 정색하며 농담을 할 때마다 우리는 웃지 않을 수 없다.
  |해설| (A) be known for: ~로 알려져 있다, 유명하다
  (B) with a straight face: 정색하며, 시치미를 떼고
  (C) can't help -ing: ~하지 않을 수 없다

04 |해설| (A) 자신의 감정을 표현할 때 「I'm+감정 형용사」로 말한다. 신난 감정은 excited로 나타낸다.
  (B) 축하의 말을 할 때는 Congratulations (on ~)!으로 나타낸다.

05 |해석| 우리 반을 위해 일할 기회가 생겨서 나는 정말 기뻐.
  |해설| 감정 형용사(happy) 뒤에 그 감정의 원인을 나타내는 부사적 용법의 to부정사(to have)를, 명사 a chance 뒤에 명사를 수식하는 형용사적 용법의 to부정사(to work)를 써서 자신의 감정을 표현하는 말을 완성한다.

06 |해석| 인호는 독감에 걸려서 몸이 좋지 않다. 그는 병원에 갔고, 현재 약을 먹고 있다. 수미는 그가 곧 낫기를 바란다.
  A: 너 몸이 안 좋아 보인다. 인호야. 무슨 일 있어?
  B: 나는 독감에 걸렸어.
  A: 안됐구나. 병원은 가 봤어?
  B: 응. 약을 먹고 있어.
  A: 음, 네가 곧 낫기를 바라.
  B: 고마워, 수미야.
  |해설| (1) 안 좋은 일이 있어 보이는 상대방에게 무슨 일이 있는지 묻는 표현인 What's the matter?가 알맞다.
  (2) 안 좋은 일이 있는 상대방에게 유감을 표현하는 That's too bad.가 알맞다.
  (3) 곧 낫기를 희망한다는 말은 I hope you feel better soon.으로 할 수 있다.

07 |해설| 상대방의 좋은 일에 대해 축하를 하고 있는 상황이므로 I'm so happy for you. / I'm proud of you. / You did a good job. 등이 와야 자연스럽다.

08 |해설| ⓒ 지호는 첫 연극 연습에 관한 안내를 문자 메시지로 받을 것이다.

09 |해석| 지호: 엄마, 제가 '로미오와 줄리엣'에서 로미오가 될 거예요. 정말 신나요.
  엄마: 멋지구나. 축하해!
  지호: 고마워요, 엄마.
  엄마: 수미는 어때?
  지호: 그녀는 원했던 역할을 맡지 못했어요.
  엄마: 안됐구나.
  지호: 네, Carter 선생님이 수미가 매우 실망했다고 말씀하셨어요.

10 |해석| (1) 내가 어젯밤에 Sue에게 전화했을 때, 그녀는 잠자리에 든 상태였다.
  (2) Jackson은 일주일 동안 바빴었기 때문에 어제 피곤함을 느꼈다.
  |해설| 과거의 특정 시점에 일어난 일보다 먼저 일어난 일이나 상태를 나타낼 때 「had+과거분사」 형태의 과거완료를 쓴다.

11 |해석| (1) 그는 나에게 자신의 신작 소설을 주었다.
  → 그가 내게 준 것은 자신의 신작 소설이었다.
  (2) 그녀는 집에서 쉬고 싶었다.
  → 그녀가 하고 싶어 한 것은 집에서 쉬는 것이었다.
  (3) Wilson 씨는 재미있는 연설로 유명했다.
  → Wilson 씨가 유명한 것은 그의 재미있는 연설이었다.
  |해설| '~하는 것'이라는 의미로 선행사를 포함하는 관계대명사 what이 이끄는 절이 주어 역할을 하도록 바꿔 쓴다.

12 |해설| 차를 도난당한 것은 경찰에 신고한(reported) 과거 시점보다 더 이전에 발생한 일이므로 과거완료 수동태인 「had been+과거분사」 형태로 써야 한다.

13 |해석| ⓐ 그녀는 일주일간 아팠다고 말했다.
  ⓑ 그가 그녀에게 사 준 것은 스카프였다.
  ⓒ 준수는 15살이 되기 전에는 자전거를 타 본 적이 없었다.
  ⓓ 우리는 부모님이 우리를 위해 해 주시는 것에 감사해야 한다.
  |해설| ⓑ The thing이 선행사이므로 what을 목적격 관계대명사 which 또는 that으로 바꾸거나, The thing 없이 선행사를 포함하는 관계대명사 What으로 써야 한다.
  ⓒ 과거의 특정 시점 이전(before he was 15)의 경험을 나타내므로 과거완료(had+과거분사)로 써야 한다.

14 |해설| '자신들의 물건이 얼마나 값진지'라는 의미로 know의 목적어 역할을 하는 간접의문문의 어순(의문사+주어+동사)으로 써야 한다.

15 |해설| '매우(너무) ~해서 …하다'는 「so+형용사/부사+that+주어+동사」 형태로 나타낸다. 과거의 일이므로 과거시제로 쓰는 것과 부사 almost를 동사 fell 앞에 쓰는 것에 주의한다.

16 |해석| (1) Boggis 씨는 Rummins의 집 거실에서 무엇을 발견했는가?
  → 그는 그곳에서 매우 귀중한 18세기 영국 가구인 탁자를 발견했다.
  (2) Boggis 씨는 Rummins와 Bert에게 무엇에 대해 거짓말을 했는가?
  → 그는 그들에게 그 탁자가 복제품이라고 거짓말을 했다.
  |해설| (1) Boggis 씨는 매우 귀중한 18세기 영국 가구인 탁자를 발견했다.
  (2) Boggis 씨는 그 탁자가 복제품이라고 거짓말을 했다.

17 |해설| (A) 목적을 나타내는 부사적 용법의 to부정사가 알맞다.
  (B) '~하지 않을 수 없다'는 can't help -ing로 나타낸다.

(C) 등위접속사 and로 took out과 연결된 병렬 구조이므로 과거형인 began이 알맞다.

18 |해설| '~하는 것'이라고 해석하며 각각 보어와 주어 역할을 하는 명사절을 이끄는 관계대명사 what이 들어가는 것이 알맞다.

19 |해설| 돌아온(came back) 과거 시점 이전에 탁자의 다리가 이미 잘려져 있었던 것이므로 과거완료 수동태(had been+과거분사)를 사용한다.

20 |해설| Rummins는 탁자의 다리를 자르는 것이 Boggis 씨를 위한 호의라고 생각했다.

21 |해설| 모든 판매상이 꿈꾸는 귀중한 가구의 다리가 잘린 것을 본 Boggis 씨는 놀라고 충격을 받아서 아무 말도 하지 못했다는 내용이 되어야 자연스럽다.

모의고사

01 ④	02 ②	03 ⑤	04 couldn't help feeling nervous
05 ⑤	06 (D)-(A)-(C)-(B)	07 ②	08 ②	09 didn't get the role she wanted
10 ⑤	11 ④	12 had	13 ⑤
14 ③, ④	15 ⓑ → selling	16 ⑤	17 ④	18 ⑤
19 ⑤	20 priceless	21 ③	22 thirty pounds	23 ③
24 ④	25 What he wants is only the legs.		

01 |해석| 어떤 것을 다른 것에 고정시키거나 결합하다
① (선거로) 선출하다 ② 움직이다 ③ 두드리다
⑤ (요금을) 청구하다
|해설| attach(붙이다)의 영영풀이이다.

02 |해석| ① 이 스카프는 50달러의 값어치가 있다.
② 이 고대 화병들은 대단히 귀중하다.
③ 아빠는 나무에서 나뭇가지 몇 개를 잘라 내셨다.
④ 나는 풀밭에서 뱀을 발견하고 깜짝 놀랐다.
⑤ 이 그림은 Klimt가 그린 'The Kiss'의 복제품이다.
|해설| ② priceless는 '(값을 매길 수 없을 만큼) 대단히 귀중한'이라는 의미이다.

03 |해석| • 나는 공항으로 가는 길에 Jim을 만났다.
• 너는 이 기회를 이용해야 한다.
• 저 작은 식당은 뛰어난 음식으로 유명하다.
|해설| • on one's way (to): (~로) 가는 길에
• take advantage of: ~을 이용하다
• be known for: ~으로 알려져 있다, 유명하다

04 |해설| can't help -ing: ~하지 않을 수 없다

05 |해석| A: Sue, 너 신나 보인다. 무슨 일이야?
B: 내가 학급 회장으로 당선되었어. 정말 신나.
A: _____

①, ④ 잘됐다. ② 축하해! ③ 멋지다.
⑤ 그 말을 들으니 유감이야.
|해설| 좋은 일이 생겨 신이 난 사람에게 축하의 말을 하는 것이 자연스러우므로 유감을 표현하는 말인 ⑤는 어색하다.

06 |해석| (D) 너 몸이 안 좋아 보인다, 인호야. 무슨 일 있어?
(A) 나는 독감에 걸렸어.
(C) 안됐구나. 병원은 가 봤어?
(B) 응. 약을 먹고 있어.
A: 음, 네가 곧 낫기를 바라.
|해설| 안 좋아 보이는 사람에게 무슨 일이 있는지 묻자(D) 독감에 걸렸다고 답하고(A), 그에 대해 유감을 표현하며 진료를 받았는지 묻는 말에(C) 진료를 받았으며 약을 먹는 중이라고 답하고(B), 곧 낫기를 바란다는 말을 하는 흐름이 자연스럽다.

07 |해석| A: 미나야, 안 좋은 일 있니?
B: 음, 내 스마트폰을 잃어버렸어. 정말 신나(→ 속상해).
A: 아, 그 말을 들으니 정말 유감이야. 마지막으로 언제 사용했는지 기억나니?
B: 음, 매점에서 그것을 가방에서 꺼낸 것은 기억나.
A: 그럼 그것을 찾으러 매점에 다시 가 보자.
|해설| ② 스마트폰을 잃어버린 상황이므로 신난다고 이어서 말하는 것은 어색하다.

08 |해석| ① 다음번에는 더 열심히 노력하렴.
② 정말 기쁘구나.
③ 그 말을 들으니 정말 유감이야.
④ 나는 내 자신이 정말 자랑스러워.
⑤ 다음번에는 네가 그 역할을 맡기를 바라.
|해설| 연극에서 주인공 역할을 맡게 된 지호를 축하해 주는 상황이며, 이어서 그 역할을 얼마나 맡고 싶어 했는지 알고 있다는 말을 하는 것으로 보아 상대방의 좋은 일에 대해 기쁨을 표현하는 말인 ②가 들어가는 것이 알맞다.

09 |해석| 수미는 그녀가 원했던 역할을 맡지 못했다.
|해설| ⓑ는 수미가 원했던 역할을 맡지 못해 실망했다는 말을 듣고 유감을 표현하는 말이다.

10 |해석| ① 지호는 자신이 원했던 역할을 맡아서 매우 신났다.
② 지호는 학교 연극에서 로미오가 정말 되고 싶었다.
③ Carter 선생님은 수미가 실망했다고 말한다.
④ 지호는 '로미오와 줄리엣'의 첫 연습에 참여할 것이다.
⑤ 지호는 첫 연습에 관한 이메일을 곧 받을 것이다.
|해설| ⑤ 첫 연극 연습에 관한 문자 메시지(a text message)를 곧 받게 될 것이라고 했다.

11 |해석| 작은 운동장은 내가 우리 학교에서 좋아하지 않는 것이다.
|해설| '~하는 것'이라는 의미로 선행사를 포함하는 관계대명사 what이 알맞다.

12 |해설| 주어진 단어들을 배열하여 문장을 완성하면 He told me that he had seen the movie.이므로 6번째로 올 단어는 had이다.

13 |해석| ① Susan은 내가 숨겨 놓은 것을 찾았다.
② 그녀는 내가 그녀에게 크리스마스에 준 것을 좋아했다.
③ 나는 내가 너를 위해 만든 것을 가져오는 것을 잊었다.
④ 나는 지난주에 주문한 것을 아직 못 받았다.

⑤ 당신이 추천한 식당은 오늘 문을 닫았다.

|해설| ⑤에는 선행사 The restaurant를 수식하는 목적격 관계대명사 which나 that이 알맞고, 나머지에는 모두 선행사를 포함하는 관계대명사로 '~하는 것'이라고 해석하는 what이 알맞다.

14 **|해석|** ⓐ 그는 전에 곤충을 먹어 본 적이 있었다고 말했다.
ⓑ 산타는 내가 받고 싶었던 것을 주지 않았다.
ⓒ 그 티셔츠는 모든 학생들이 입고 싶어 하는 것이다.
ⓓ Mike가 교실에 돌아왔을 때, 모두 이미 집에 가고 없었다.
ⓔ 나는 누군가가 밤중에 내 자전거를 훔쳐갔다는 것에 깜짝 놀랐다.

|해설| ⓐ 말한(said) 과거 시점보다 더 이전에 곤충을 먹어 본 적이 있다는 내용이므로 과거완료(had+과거분사)로 쓰는 것이 알맞다. (had ate → had eaten)
ⓑ give의 직접목적어인 명사절을 이끄는 관계대명사 what이 쓰이는 것이 알맞다. (which → what)
ⓔ 놀란(was shocked) 과거 시점보다 누군가가 자전거를 훔쳐간 것이 더 이전에 일어난 일이므로 과거완료(had+과거분사)로 써야 한다. (had steal → had stolen)

15 **|해설|** ⓑ 전치사 for의 목적어이며 and then으로 buying과 연결된 병렬 구조이므로 동명사 형태로 써야 한다.

16 **|해석|** ① 가구 판매상이 누구였는지
② Boggis 씨의 가구가 얼마였는지
③ Boggis 씨가 어디에서 가구를 팔았는지
④ Boggis 씨의 가구가 왜 비쌌는지
⑤ Boggis 씨가 가구를 어디에서 샀는지

|해설| 밑줄 친 It은 사람들이 Boggis 씨에게 묻는 내용을 가리키며, 그것은 '그가 가구를 어디에서 구했는가'이다.

17 **|해석|** Boggis 씨에 대한 설명으로 틀린 것은?
① 그는 오래된 가구를 사고팔았다.
② 그는 좋은 물건을 싸게 사는 것을 잘했다.
③ 그는 오래된 가구를 사기 위해 일요일마다 작은 마을로 갔다.
④ 그는 자신들의 가구의 값어치를 아는 사람들에게서 물건을 샀다.
⑤ 그는 작은 마을의 사람들을 이용했다.

|해설| ④ 그는 자신들이 가진 가구가 얼마나 값어치가 있는지 모르는 사람들에게서 가구를 싸게 샀다.

18 **|해설|** 주어진 문장은 '그리고 그곳에 그것이 있었다!'라는 의미이므로, it을 부연 설명하는 말 앞인 ⑤에 들어가는 것이 알맞다.

19 **|해설|** ⓔ '너무 ~해서 …했다'의 의미가 되어야 하므로 「so+형용사+that+주어+동사」 구문의 so가 알맞다.

20 **|해설|** '대단히 귀중한'은 priceless(대단히 귀중한)의 영영풀이이다.

21 **|해설|** ⓒ는 Boggis 씨의 탁자를 가리키고, 나머지는 모두 Rummins의 탁자를 가리킨다.

22 **|해설|** 밑줄 친 This는 Boggis 씨가 Rummins에게 제안한 금액으로 앞 문장의 thirty를 가리키는데, 뒤에 pounds가 생략되었으므로 thirty pounds가 알맞다.

23 **|해석|** ① Boggis 씨는 왜 Rummins와 Bert에게 탁자가 복제품이라고 말했는가?
② Boggis 씨는 처음에 탁자 가격으로 얼마를 지불하고 싶어 했는가?
③ Rummins는 그의 탁자에 얼마를 지불했는가?

④ Boggis 씨는 왜 Rummins의 집에서 나갔는가?
⑤ Boggis 씨는 왜 자신이 운이 좋다고 생각했는가?

|해설| ③ Rummins가 얼마를 주고 자신의 탁자를 구입했는지는 언급되지 않았다.

24 **|해석|** ① 톱 ② 지불하다 ③ 호의 ④ ~에 대한 ⑤ 깜짝 놀란

|해설| ⓐ에는 if, ⓑ에는 pay, ⓒ에는 saw, ⓓ에는 favor, ⓔ에는 shocked가 들어가는 것이 알맞다. ⓐ에는 '~면 어쩌지?'라는 의미의 what if가 알맞으므로 about은 어디에도 들어갈 수 없다.

25 **|해설|** 주어인 '그가 원하는 것'은 선행사를 포함하는 관계대명사 What으로 시작하는 명사절로 나타낸다. that은 이 문장에 필요하지 않다.

제2회 대표 기출로 내신 적중 모의고사 pp. 144~147

01 ② 02 ③ 03 (a)ntique 04 ⑤ 05 ④ 06 ①
07 ③, ④ 08 ④ 09 ⑤ 10 what you suggest 11 ⑤
12 we had finished cooking 13 ④ 14 ③ 15 ④
16 ③ 17 didn't know how valuable their things were
18 ④ 19 ④ 20 reproduction 21 ④ 22 the thing
what → what 또는 the thing which(that) 23 what if this
thing doesn't go in his car 24 (A) What (B) had (C) that
25 ⑤

01 **|해석|** [보기] 싼 – 비싼
① 틀다 – 재생하다, 다시 듣다/보다 ② 낮은 – 높은
③ 흥미진진한 – 신이 난 ④ 화가 난 ⑤ 귀중한

|해설| [보기]와 ②는 반의어 관계이다.

02 **|해석|** • 나는 도서관에 가는 길에 같은 반 친구 Jeff를 만났다.
• 그녀는 자신의 이웃집에 가서 문을 두드렸다.

|해설| 첫 번째 문장에는 '~로 가는 길에'라는 의미의 on one's way to가 알맞고, 두 번째 문장에는 '~을 두드리다'라는 의미의 knock on이 알맞다.

03 **|해석|** 오래되고 종종 귀중하거나 아름다운
→ 그 박물관에는 골동품 피아노들이 소장되어 있다.

|해설| antique(골동품인)의 영영풀이이다.

04 **|해석|** 누구도 당신의 약점을 이용하게 두지 마세요.
① 잘라 내다 ② 넘어지다 ③ 한번 보다 ④ ~으로 유명하다

|해설| take advantage of(~을 이용하다)가 들어가는 것이 알맞다.

05 **|해석|** A: _____
B: 아, 그 말을 들으니 유감이야.
① 새로 산 내 카메라가 고장 났어.
② 나는 지난주 토요일에 내 강아지를 잃어버렸어.
③ 나는 기말시험에 떨어졌어. 속상해.
④ 내가 학교 마라톤에서 1등을 했어.
⑤ 나의 가장 친한 친구가 다른 도시로 이사갈 거야. 나는 슬퍼.

|해설| 유감을 표현하는 말이 이어지는 것으로 보아 빈칸에는 자신에게 일어난 안 좋은 일을 나타내는 말이 알맞으므로, ④는 적절하지 않다.

06 |해설| A: Sally, 너 신나 보인다. <u>무슨 일 있어?</u>

B: 나는 Dream 콘서트에 갈 거야. 드디어 표를 구했어.

A: 축하해! 네가 얼마나 가고 싶어 했는지 알아.

② 확실하니? – 나는 최선을 다했어.

③ 안됐다. – 잘됐다.

④ 축하해! – 천만에.

⑤ 안 좋은 일 있니? – 정말 고마워.

|해설| (A)에는 신이 나 보이는 이유를 묻는 What's up?(무슨 일 있니?)이 알맞고, (B)에는 콘서트에 갈 거라는 말을 듣고 축하를 전하는 Congratulations!나 Good for you.가 알맞다.

07 |해석| 작년 여름에 나는 내 강아지 보미를 잃어버렸어. 내가 공원에서 물을 마시는 사이에 그녀가 사라졌어. 다행히, 이틀 뒤에 그녀를 찾을 수 있었어. 나는 너무 <u>기뻐서</u> 그녀를 품에 꼭 안았어.

① 초조한 ② 지루해하는 ⑤ 실망한

|해설| 잃어버렸던 개를 찾은 후에 기뻐서 꼭 안았다는 내용이 되는 것이 자연스럽다.

08 |해석| ① 무슨 일 있나요?

② 무슨 문제라도 있나요?

③ 학교 연극을 보셨나요?

④ 연극에서 제가 주인공 역할을 맡게 됐나요?

⑤ 학교 연극을 위해 우리는 무엇을 할 건가요?

|해설| 대답으로 Yes, you did.(그렇단다.)라고 했고 연극에서 주인공 역할인 Romeo를 맡게 된 것을 전하며 축하하는 내용이 이어지고 있으므로, 빈칸에 들어갈 말로 ④가 알맞다.

09 |해설| ⓔ 수미가 원했던 배역을 얻지 못해 실망했다는 말에 대한 응답으로 그 말을 들어서 기쁘다고 하는 것은 어색하다.

10 |해석| 우리는 <u>당신이 제안하는 것을</u> 고려할 것입니다.

|해설| the thing that you suggest는 '당신이 제안하는 것'이라는 의미이므로, the thing that은 선행사를 포함하는 관계대명사 what으로 바꿔 쓸 수 있다.

11 |해석| ① Ted는 그 책을 읽어 봤다고 말했다.

② 나는 네가 전화하기 전에 설거지를 했다.

③ Sue는 그곳에 여러 번 가 봤다고 말했다.

④ 나는 내 자전거가 고장 나서 탈 수 없었다.

⑤ 아빠가 집에 오셨을 때, 나는 이미 저녁을 먹은 뒤였다.

|해설| ⑤ 아빠가 집에 온 것은 내가 저녁을 이미 먹은 것(had already eaten dinner)보다 나중에 일어난 일이므로 과거시제(got home)로 써야 한다. 따라서 빈칸에 had가 들어갈 수 없다. 나머지는 모두 과거의 특정 시점보다 앞서 일어난 일을 나타내는 과거완료로 써야 하므로 빈칸에 had가 들어가야 한다.

12 |해설| 할머니가 집에 오신(came home) 것보다 요리를 끝낸 것이 먼저 일어난 일이므로 과거완료인 「had+과거분사」의 형태로 쓰는 것이 알맞다. '~하는 것을 끝내다'는 「finish+동명사」의 형태로 쓴다.

13 |해석| Sue는 여동생이 그녀에게 만들어 준 것을 정말 마음에 들어 했다.

|해설| 첫 번째 빈칸에는 '~하는 것'이라는 뜻으로 선행사를 포함하는 관계대명사 what이 알맞다. 두 번째 빈칸에는 마음에 든(liked) 과거 시점보다 여동생이 만든 것이 더 이전에 일어난 일이므로 과거완료(had+과거분사)가 알맞다.

14 |해석| ① 그는 자신이 가진 것을 다른 사람들과 나누었다.

② Eric은 전에 알래스카에 가 본 적이 있다고 말했다.

③ 조깅은 Susan이 아침에 하기 좋아하는 것이다.

④ 내가 부엌에 갔을 때 내 여동생은 피자 한 판을 막 다 먹은 상태였다.

⑤ 김 선생님이 돌아왔을 때 학생들은 이미 교실을 청소한 상태였다.

|해설| ③ 선행사를 포함하며 보어 역할을 하는 명사절을 이끄는 관계대명사 what이 쓰이는 것이 알맞다. (→ what)

15 |해설| ⓐ 전치사(for)의 목적어이므로 동명사 형태가 알맞다.

ⓑ 사람들이 물어본(asked) 과거 시점보다 Boggis 씨가 가구를 구한 것이 더 이전에 일어난 일이므로 과거완료(had+과거분사)가 알맞다.

16 |해석| ① 사람들은 그것들을 팔고 싶어 하지 않았다

② 사람들은 그것들을 높은 가격으로 팔았다

③ Boggis 씨는 그들을 이용했다

④ Boggis 씨는 그들에게 충분한 돈을 주었다

⑤ 그들은 Boggis 씨가 그들의 물건을 사기를 원하지 않았다

|해설| ③ 사람들은 자신들의 물건이 얼마나 값진 것인지 몰랐다고 했고, Boggis 씨는 물건들을 매우 싸게 살 수 있었다고 했으므로, 그가 사람들을 이용했다(took advantage of them)는 내용이 들어가는 것이 자연스럽다.

17 |해설| Q: 물건들을 싸게 구입하는 Boggis 씨의 비밀은 무엇이었는가?

A: 그는 <u>자신들의 물건이 얼마나 값진 것인지 모르는</u> 사람들에게서 물건들을 구입했다.

18 |해설| ⓓ 「so+형용사+that+주어+동사」(너무 ~해서 …하다)의 형태가 되어야 하므로 so excited that이 알맞다. exciting은 '흥미진진한, 신나는', excited는 '신이 난, 흥분한'의 의미이고, so that은 '~하기 위해서'라는 목적의 의미를 나타낸다.

19 |해설| ① Rummins와 Bert는 작은 마을에 산다.

② Rummins는 Boggis 씨에게 자신은 고가구가 전혀 없다고 말했다.

③ Rummins는 Boggis 씨에게 자신의 집을 둘러보게 했다.

④ Rummins는 자신의 탁자가 대단히 귀중하다는 것을 알고 놀랐다.

⑤ Boggis 씨는 Rummins와 Bert에게 진실을 말하지 않았다.

|해설| ④ Boggis 씨가 복제품이라고 거짓말을 했기 때문에 Rummins는 자신의 탁자가 귀중한 것인지 알지 못했다.

20 |해설| '그림과 같은 물건의 복제본'은 reproduction(복제품)의 영영풀이이다.

21 |해설| ④ Boggis 씨는 탁자가 차에 들어가지 않을 것 같다는 Rummins의 말에 한번 보겠다고 하며 차를 가지러 집 밖으로 나갔다.

22 |해설| 관계대명사 what은 선행사를 포함하므로 선행사 the thing을 삭제하거나, what을 목적격 관계대명사 which나 that으로 고쳐야 한다.

23 |해석| 아빠, 만약 이게 그의 차에 안 들어가면 어쩌죠?

|해설| '만약 이게 그의 차에 안 들어가면 어쩌죠?'라는 의미가 되도록 「What if+주어+동사 ~?」로 문장을 완성한다.

24 |해설| (A) '~하는 것'이라는 의미로 주어인 명사절을 이끄는 관계대명사 What이 알맞다.

(B) Boggis 씨가 돌아온(came back) 과거 시점보다 더 이전에 일어난 일이므로 과거완료(had+과거분사)가 알맞다.

(C) 「so+형용사+that+주어+동사」(너무 ~해서 …하다)의 형태가 되는 것이 알맞다.

25 |해설| ⑤ 문맥상 Rummins와 Bert가 Boggis 씨에게 탁자를 파는 상황이므로 탁자 다리를 자른 것은 호의였고, 탁자 다리를 잘라 준 것에 대해 비용을 청구하지(charge) 않겠다고 말하는 것이 자연스럽다.

제 **3**회 대표 기출로 내신 **적중** 모의고사   pp. 148~151

01 ⑤   02 ③   03 ③   04 ①   05 so sorry to hear that
06 ④   07 ②   08 ④   09 ④   10 what   11 ③
12 ④   13 arrived, had started   14 ⑤   15 (A) for
(B) on (C) of   16 cheaply   17 ①, ③   18 One, the other
19 ④   20 ⑤   21 ⑤   22 what every dealer dreamed
of   23 reproduction, low, thirty   24 ②   25 ⓓ → had
been cut off

01 |해석| • 배송은 요금 없이 무료입니다.
• 그들은 당신에게 배송비를 청구하지 않을 것이다.
① 운, 행운   ② 제안, 제의   ③ 사다   ④ 가격
|해설| 명사로 '요금', 동사로 '(요금을) 청구하다'라는 의미를 모두 지닌 단어는 charge이다.

02 |해석| • 남자는 정색하며 거짓말을 했다.
• 나는 내 낡은 청바지의 아랫부분을 잘라 냈다.
• 버스가 갑자기 출발해서 나는 넘어졌다.
|해설| • with a straight face: 정색하며, 시치미를 떼고
• cut off: ~을 잘라 내다
• fall over: 넘어지다

03 |해석| ① 부주의한 운전자는 사고를 유발할 수 있다.
② Davis 씨는 자동차 판매상으로부터 트럭을 샀다.
③ 유감스럽게도, 나는 댄스 경연 대회에서 1등을 했다. (×)
④ 사람들은 그가 그 음악을 너무 많이 재생했기 때문에 지루해했다.
⑤ 이 그림은 싸다. 반 고흐가 그린 '해바라기'의 복제품이다.
|해설| ③ 이어지는 내용이 좋은 일이므로 '유감스럽게도, 불행하게도'를 의미하는 Unfortunately가 쓰이는 것은 어색하다.

04 |해석| • 상자에 메모를 붙여 주십시오.
• 그 골동품 의자는 500달러 이상의 값어치가 있다.
• 나는 내 방에 있는 가구 몇 개를 옮겨야 한다.
• 우리는 박물관에서 대단히 귀중한 그림들을 많이 보았다.
|해설| ⓐ attach(붙이다) ⓑ worth(~의 값어치가 있는)
ⓒ furniture(가구) ⓓ priceless(대단히 귀중한)

05 |해석| A: 미나야, 안 좋은 일 있니?
B: 음, 내 스마트폰을 잃어버렸어. 속상해.
A: 아, 그 말을 들으니 정말 유감이야.
|해설| 상대방이 스마트폰을 잃어버려서 속상해하는 상황이므로 I'm so sorry to hear that.을 사용하여 유감을 표현할 수 있다.

06 |해석| ① A: Min, 무슨 문제 있니?
B: 음, 나는 경기에서 졌어. 속상해.
② A: Sue, 너 신나 보인다. 무슨 일 있어?
B: 내가 학급 회장으로 당선되었어.

③ A: 내 스마트폰이 고장 났어.
B: 안됐어.
④ A: 학교 마라톤에서 금메달 딴 것을 축하해.
B: 멋지다! 너는 잘했어.
⑤ A: 내가 말하기 대회에서 1등을 했어. 정말 기뻐.
B: 멋지다. 축하해!
|해설| ④ 자신을 축하해 주는 말에 대한 응답으로 멋지다며 상대방에게 잘했다고 하는 것은 어색하다.

07 |해석| A: 너 몸이 안 좋아 보인다, 인호야. 무슨 일 있어?
B: 나는 독감에 걸렸어.
A: 안됐구나. 병원은 가 봤어?
B: 응, 약을 먹고 있어.
A: 음, 네가 곧 낫기를 바라.
B: 고마워.
|해설| 주어진 문장은 '안됐구나.'라는 의미로 좋지 않은 일이 있는 상대방에게 유감을 표현하며 위로하는 말이다. 따라서 독감에 걸렸다는 말을 듣고 하는 말인 ②에 들어가야 알맞다.

08 |해석| ① 질문 하나 해도 될까요?
② 정말 신나요.
③ 나도 정말 기쁘구나.
④ 그녀는 분명 스스로가 자랑스러울 거야.
⑤ 너는 그것에 관한 문자 메시지를 곧 받을 거야.
|해설| ④ 수미가 원했던 역할을 맡지 못했다고(Unfortunately, no.) 답한 후에 그녀는 스스로가 자랑스러울 것이라고 말하는 것은 어색하다.

09 |해석| ① Carter 선생님은 왜 지호를 축하하고 있는가?
② 학교 연극에서 누가 로미오를 연기할 것인가?
③ 지호는 어떤 역할을 맡기를 원했는가?
④ 수미는 어떤 역할을 맡기를 원했는가?
⑤ 첫 연습은 언제 어디서 하는가?
|해설| ④ 수미가 원했던 역할을 맡지 못했다는 언급은 있으나 어떤 역할을 원했는지에 대한 언급은 없다.

10 |해석| A: 그 가게에서 무엇을 샀니?
B: 아무것도 안 샀어. 그 가게에는 내가 사고 싶었던 것이 없었어.
|해설| '내가 사고 싶었던 것'이라는 의미가 되도록 선행사를 포함하는 관계대명사 what이 have의 목적어인 명사절을 이끄는 것이 알맞다.

11 |해석| 내가 돌아왔을 때 거실은 이미 형에 의해 청소된 상태였다.
|해설| 내가 돌아온(came back) 과거 시점보다 더 이전에 거실이 '청소된' 것이므로 과거완료 수동태(had been+과거분사)로 나타내는 것이 알맞다.

12 |해석| A: 내 여동생에게 무엇을 사 줘야 할지 모르겠어.
B: 그녀에게 가장 필요한 것을 사는 게 어때?
|해설| 첫 번째 빈칸에는 「의문사+to부정사」로 '무엇을 사 줘야 할지'를 나타내도록 의문사 what이, 두 번째 빈칸에는 buy의 목적어로 '그녀에게 가장 필요한 것'이라는 의미의 명사절을 이끄는 관계대명사 what이 알맞다.

13 |해석| 우리는 영화관에 도착했다. 그 전에 영화가 시작했다.
→ 우리가 영화관에 도착했을 때, 영화는 이미 시작한 상태였다.
|해설| 영화관에 도착한(arrived) 과거 시점보다 앞서 이미 영화가 시작한 것이므로 과거완료를 사용하여 「had+과거분사」의 형태인 had

started로 쓴다.

14 |해석| ① 이것이 내가 찾고 있던 것이다.

② 우리가 그곳에 도착했을 때 그들은 떠나고 없었다.

③ 나는 네가 이미 잠자리에 들었는 줄 알았다.

④ 아빠가 우리에게 요리해 주신 것은 맛있었다.

⑤ 엄마는 우리가 그녀의 생일 선물로 산 선글라스를 좋아하셨다.

|해설| ⑤ what은 선행사를 포함하는 관계대명사이므로 선행사 the sunglasses 뒤에 쓸 수 없다. 목적격 관계대명사 which나 that을 쓰는 것이 알맞다.

15 |해설| (A) be known for: ~으로 알려져 있다, 유명하다

(B) knock on: ~을 두드리다

(C) take advantage of: ~을 이용하다

16 |해설| at a low price는 '낮은 가격으로'라는 의미이므로 부사 cheaply (싸게)와 바꿔 쓸 수 있다.

17 |해석| ① 그가 몇 살이었는지

② 그의 직업이 무엇이었는지

③ 그가 어디서 물건을 팔았는지

④ 그가 무엇으로 유명했는지

⑤ 그가 좋은 물건을 어떻게 낮은 가격에 샀는지

|해설| Cyril Boggis의 나이와 그가 물건을 판 곳에 대한 언급은 없다.

② 골동품 가구 판매상이었다.

④ 좋은 물건을 싸게 사서 비싸게 파는 것으로 유명했다.

⑤ 자신들의 물건이 얼마나 값진 것인지 모르는 사람들로부터 물건을 싸게 샀다.

18 |해설| 둘 중 하나는 one, 나머지 하나는 the other로 나타낸다.

19 |해석| ① 무언가 있으신가요?

② 한번 둘러봐도 될까요?

③ 무슨 일인가요?

④ 당신의 탁자는 정말 귀중한 것 같아요

⑤ 그것은 몇 파운드의 가치밖에 안 돼요.

|해설| ⓓ Boggis 씨가 귀중한 Rummins의 탁자를 복제품이라고 거짓말했다는 내용이 이어지므로 '당신의 탁자는 정말 귀중한 것 같다'라고 말하는 것은 알맞지 않다.

20 |해석| ① Boggis 씨는 자신의 오래된 가구를 팔러 작은 마을에 갔다.

② Rummins는 Boggis 씨를 자신의 집에 들여보내고 싶지 않았다.

③ Boggis 씨는 먼저 거실로 갔다.

④ Rummins는 골동품 가구를 많이 가지고 있었다.

⑤ Boggis 씨는 사고 싶은 것을 발견해서 매우 흥분했다.

|해설| ⑤ 고가구를 사러 간 Boggis 씨는 Rummins의 거실에서 매우 귀중한 탁자를 발견하고 몹시 흥분해서 넘어질 뻔했다.

21 |해설| ⓔ Boggis 씨는 모든 판매상이 꿈꾸는 탁자를 운 좋게 사게 되었으므로 '걱정하지 않을 수 없었다'라는 내용은 어색하다.

22 |해석| Boggis 씨는 모든 판매상이 꿈꾸는 것을 살 수 있었기 때문에 운이 좋다고 느꼈다.

|해설| Boggis 씨는 모든 판매상이 꿈꾸는 탁자를 사게 되어서 자신의 행운을 믿을 수 없었다는 내용이다.

23 |해석| Boggis 씨는 탁자를 낮은 가격에 사고 싶어서 Rummins에게 탁자가 복제품이라고 말했다. 마침내 Rummins는 탁자를 30파운드에 팔기로 결정했다.

24 |해설| 문맥상 '~면 어쩌지?'라는 의미의 「What if+주어+동사 ~?」 형태가 알맞다.

25 |해설| ⓓ 탁자 다리를 자른 것은 Boggis 씨가 돌아온(came back) 과거 시점보다 앞서 일어난 일이며, 탁자 다리는 '잘린' 것이므로 과거완료 수동태(had been+과거분사)로 써야 한다.

제 4 회 고난도로 내신 적중 모의고사 pp. 152~155

01 replay, recycle **02** ⑤ **03** ③ **04** ③ **05** so happy to get a chance to see **06** (A) ⓑ (B) ⓐ (C) ⓒ
07 ② **08** ④ **09** sorry to hear that **10** ①, ②
11 what we saw **12** ② **13** ④ **14** had already finished solving, the bell rang **15** ④ **16** that **17** ⑤
18 ⓐ worth ⓑ attach **19** ③ **20** ③, ⑤ **21** ②
22 ② **23** priceless(valuable), a reproduction, cheaply
24 ⓐ The thing what → What / The thing which(that)
ⓑ had come back → came back ⓒ such → so **25** ④

01 |해석| 다시- + 생산하다 → 복제하다

쉬다 / 재생하다 / 도달하다 / 재활용하다 / 깨닫다

|해설| [보기]처럼 '다시'의 의미를 가진 접두사 re-가 동사 앞에 붙어 만들어진 단어는 replay(재생하다, 다시 듣다/보다)와 recycle(재활용하다)이다.

02 |해석| ① 그녀는 새 가구를 만들었다.

② Bob 삼촌은 그 빵가게의 주인이다.

③ 그들은 아직 최종 결정을 하지 않았다.

④ Ben은 고대 그리스에 관심이 많다.

⑤ 이 책은 수백 달러의 가치가 있다.

|해설| '특정한 가치를 지니고 있는'은 worth(가치가 있는)의 영영풀이이다.

03 |해석| • 제 부탁 좀 들어 주실래요?

• 나는 그의 농담을 들었을 때 웃지 않을 수 없었다.

• 어떤 사람들은 다른 사람의 약점을 이용한다.

|해설| 첫 번째 문장은 '호의, 친절'을 뜻하는 favor를 써서 '부탁 좀 들어 주실래요?'라는 의미를 나타내며, 두 번째 문장에는 '~하지 않을 수 없다'를 뜻하는 can't help -ing가 쓰이는 것이 알맞다. 세 번째 문장에는 '~을 이용하다'를 뜻하는 take advantage of가 쓰이는 것이 알맞다.

04 |해석| ① 피곤한 ② 속상한 ③ 신난 ④ 걱정하는 ⑤ 실망한

|해설| Sally가 가고 싶어 했던 콘서트에 가게 되었다는 내용이므로 '신나' 보이는 것이 자연스럽다.

05 |해설| 감정(happy)의 원인을 나타내는 부사적 용법의 to부정사(to get)와 a chance를 수식하는 형용사적 용법의 to부정사(to see)를 써서 문장을 완성한다.

06 |해석| A: 너 몸이 안 좋아 보인다, 인호야. 무슨 일 있어?

B: 나는 독감에 걸렸어.

A: 안됐구나. 병원은 가 봤어?

B: 응. 약을 먹고 있어.

A: 음, 네가 곧 낫기를 바라.

B: 고마워.

l해설l (A) 몸이 안 좋아 보인다고 했으므로 무슨 일이 있는지 묻는 What's the matter?가 알맞다.

(B) 독감에 걸렸다고 했으므로 유감을 표현하는 That's too bad.가 알맞다.

(C) 곧 낫기를 바란다는 위로의 말인 Well, I hope you feel better soon.이 알맞다.

07 **l해설l** ⓐ 고마워. 다음번에는 더 열심히 노력할 거야.

ⓑ 나는 기말고사에 합격했어.

ⓒ 음, 나는 학교 연극에서 역할을 맡지 못했어.

ⓓ 너 기분이 안 좋아 보인다. 무슨 일 있니?

ⓔ 아, 그 말을 들으니 정말 유감이야. 그렇지만 너는 분명히 다음번에는 역할을 맡을 수 있을 거야.

l해설l 상대방의 좋지 않은 일에 대해 유감을 표현하고 격려하는 대화로, ⓓ-ⓒ-ⓔ-ⓐ의 순서가 되어야 알맞다. 좋은 일을 나타내는 ⓑ는 이 대화의 흐름상 필요하지 않은 말이다.

08 **l해설l** 우리말을 영어로 옮기면 I know how much you wanted the role.이므로 5번째로 올 단어는 you이다.

09 **l해석l** 아, 그 말을 들으니 유감이에요.

l해설l 수미가 원했던 역할을 맡지 못해 실망했다는 말 다음에 이어지는 말이므로 안 좋은 소식에 대한 유감을 표현하는 말이 들어가는 것이 알맞다.

10 **l해석l** Tom이 집에 왔을 때, 그의 여동생은 _____.

① 잠이 들어 있었다

② 책을 읽고 있었다

③ 시끄러운 음악을 듣는다

④ 그의 노트북을 사용해 오고 있다

⑤ 그녀의 숙제를 끝냈다

l해설l Tom이 집에 온(came home) 것이 과거의 일이므로 여동생은 그 시점 이전에 잠들었거나(과거완료), 그 당시 책을 읽고 있던 중(과거진행형)일 수 있다.

11 **l해설l** '~하는 것'이라는 의미로 선행사를 포함하는 관계대명사 what을 사용하고, 과거의 일이므로 과거시제로 쓴다.

12 **l해석l** 그녀가 내게 준 것은 작은 상자였다.

l해설l 주어가 '~하는 것'이라는 의미의 명사절이 되어야 하므로 빈칸에는 선행사를 포함하는 관계대명사 What 또는 The thing which(that)이 들어가는 것이 알맞다. be동사의 단수형인 was가 쓰였으므로 The things that은 들어갈 수 없다.

13 **l해석l** ⓐ 그곳에서 우리가 들은 것은 놀라웠다.

ⓑ Emma는 선생님이 말한 것을 이해했다.

ⓒ 내가 그곳에 도착했을 때 그들은 저녁을 다 먹은 상태였다.

ⓓ 그 집은 내가 태어나기 전에 지어졌다.

l해설l ⓑ 관계대명사 what은 계속적 용법으로 쓰이지 않는다. (→ 콤마(,) 삭제)

ⓓ 집이 지어진 것이 태어난(was born) 시점 이전의 일이므로 과거완료 수동태(had been+과거분사)로 쓴다. (has → had)

14 **l해석l** Ted는 자신이 어제 과학 시험을 잘 본 것 같다고 생각한다. 종이 쳤을 때 그는 문제를 이미 다 푼 상태였다.

l해설l 종이 친(the bell rang) 과거 시점보다 문제를 이미 다 푼(had already finished solving) 것이 더 이전에 일어난 일이므로 과거완료(had+과거분사)로 쓴다. finish는 동명사를 목적어로 취하는 동사임에 유의한다.

15 **l해설l** ⓓ priceless는 '매우 귀중한'이라는 의미로 valuable과 바꿔 쓸 수 있다.

16 **l해설l** (A)에는 told의 직접목적어로 쓰인 명사절을 이끄는 접속사 that, (B)에는 선행사 a house를 수식하는 관계대명사절을 이끄는 목적격 관계대명사 which나 that이 알맞으므로, 공통으로 알맞은 것은 that이다.

17 **l해석l** ⓐ 그는 생계 수단으로 오래된 가구를 사고팔았다.

ⓑ 그가 어디서 가구를 샀는지는 비밀이었다.

ⓒ 그는 그에게 가구를 어디서 구했느냐고 묻는 사람들을 이용했다.

ⓓ 그는 골동품 가구를 팔러 가기 위해 Rummins와 Bert의 집으로 갔다.

l해설l ⓒ Boggis 씨는 자신들의 물건이 얼마나 값진 것인지 모르는 사람들을 이용하여 물건을 싸게 살 수 있었다.

ⓓ Boggis 씨는 고가구를 팔기 위해서가 아니라 사기 위해 Rummins와 Bert의 집에 갔다.

18 **l해설l** ⓐ '특정한 가치를 가지고 있는'의 의미로 가격 앞에 쓰여 '~의 값어치가 있는'의 의미를 나타내는 worth가 알맞다.

ⓑ '어떤 것을 다른 것에 고정시키거나 결합하다'는 attach(붙이다)의 영영풀이이다.

19 **l해석l** 그는 몹시 흥분해서 거의 넘어질 뻔했다.

l해설l 주어진 문장은 몹시 흥분해서 거의 넘어질 뻔했다는 내용이므로 Boggis 씨가 매우 귀중한 골동품 가구를 발견한 후이며, 그에게 괜찮냐고 묻는(What's wrong?) 말 앞인 ③에 들어가는 것이 자연스럽다.

20 **l해석l** ① Andy는 사진 찍는 것을 잘한다.

② 그는 톱을 사용해서 나무를 베었다.

③ 그들은 컴퓨터 게임을 하고 있다.

④ 그녀는 낚시하러 가기를 고대하고 있다.

⑤ 나는 삼촌이 방에서 코 고는 소리를 들을 수 있었다.

l해설l can't help -ing는 '~하지 않을 수 없다'라는 뜻으로 이때 -ing는 동명사이고 ③, ⑤는 현재분사이다. (①, ② 전치사의 목적어로 쓰이는 동명사 ④ go+동명사: ~하러 가다)

21 **l해석l** 윗글에 따르면, Boggis 씨의 성격으로 알맞은 것은?

① 정직하고 친절한   ② 영리하지만 정직하지 않은

③ 친절하고 너그러운   ④ 유머러스하고 정직한

⑤ 똑똑하지만 게으른

l해설l Boggis 씨는 영리하지만 자신이 필요한 것을 얻어내기 위해 상황에 맞게 거짓말을 하는 사람이므로 Boggis 씨의 성격으로 ② '영리하지만 정직하지 않은'이 알맞다.

22 **l해석l** ⓐ Rummins와 Bert는 Boggis 씨를 초대했다.

ⓑ Rummins는 자신의 집에 비싼 무언가가 있다는 것을 알고 있었다.

ⓒ Boggis 씨는 Rummins의 거실에서 귀중한 탁자를 발견했다.

ⓓ Rummins의 탁자는 18세기 영국 가구였다.

ⓔ Boggis 씨는 Rummins의 탁자가 대단히 귀중한 것이라고 Rummins에게 거짓말을 했다.

|해설| 윗글의 내용과 일치하는 문장은 ⓒ와 ⓓ이다.
ⓐ Boggis 씨가 찾아간 것이지, 초대받은 것이 아니다.
ⓑ Rummins는 자신에게 값비싼 골동품 가구가 있다는 것을 몰랐다.
ⓔ Boggis 씨는 탁자가 복제품이라고 거짓말을 했다.

23 |해석| 왜! 이 탁자는 매우 <u>귀중한</u> 가구야. 나는 Rummins와 Bert에게 그것이 단지 <u>복제품</u>일 뿐이라고 말해서 내가 그것을 <u>싸게</u> 살 수 있게 해야겠어.

24 |해설| ⓐ 주어가 '그가 원하는 것'이므로 선행사를 포함하는 관계대명사 What으로 시작하거나 선행사 The thing 뒤에 목적격 관계대명사 which 또는 that이 이어지는 것이 알맞다.
ⓑ 돌아온 시점보다 탁자의 다리가 잘린 시점이 더 이전이므로 돌아온 것은 과거시제(came back), 잘린 것은 과거완료 수동태(had been cut off)로 나타내는 것이 알맞다.
ⓒ '너무 ~해서 …하다'는 「so+형용사/부사+that+주어+동사」로 나타낸다.

25 |해석| ① 탁자를 팔지 않는 것
② 탁자를 Boggis 씨의 차에 넣는 것
③ Boggis 씨의 부서진 탁자에 다리를 붙이는 것
④ Boggis 씨를 위해 탁자 다리를 자르는 것
⑤ Boggis 씨가 그 탁자를 샀다는 것을 아무에게도 말하지 않는 것
|해설| 밑줄 친 this는 Rummins와 그의 아들 Bert가 Boggis 씨를 위해 탁자 다리를 자른 것을 가리키는 말이다.

Lesson 7
Technology in Our Lives

STEP A

W Words 연습 문제 — p. 159

A
01 질병, 병
02 규칙적으로
03 의미 있는
04 예측(하다), 예보(하다)
05 알아보다, 확인하다, 식별하다
06 교통수단, 탈것; 운송, 수송
07 산업
08 증상
09 흔적, 자취, 발자국
10 방법, 방식
11 양, 액수
12 개선하다, 향상하다
13 (잠긴 것을) 열다
14 예측하다
15 분석하다
16 복잡한
17 추가의, 더 이상의
18 구입(하다), 구매(하다)
19 포함하다
20 확산, 전파; 퍼지다, 퍼뜨리다

B
01 national
02 draw
03 avoid
04 communication
05 crime
06 place
07 collect
08 technology
09 influence
10 performance
11 prevention
12 leave
13 appreciate
14 insert
15 database
16 rent
17 develop
18 flu
19 press
20 analysis

C
01 역할을 하다
02 이제부터
03 ~에 근거하여
04 ~할 것 같다
05 ~에 집중하다
06 A를 B에게 추천하다
07 ~ 덕분에
08 ~을 벗다

D
01 focus on
02 take off
03 play a role
04 based on
05 thanks to
06 from now on
07 be likely to
08 recommend A for B

W Words Plus 연습 문제 — p. 161

A 1 method, 방법, 방식   2 include, 포함하다   3 avoid, 피하다   4 improve, 개선하다, 향상하다   5 symptom, 증상

6 flu, 독감   7 database, 데이터베이스   8 purchase, 구입(품), 구매(품)

B 1 identify   2 trace   3 crime   4 analyze   5 spread

C 1 based on   2 Take off   3 focus on   4 play an, role
5 are, likely to

D 1 complex   2 meaningful   3 wisely   4 disease
5 generally

A |해석| 1 어떤 것을 하는 방법
2 무언가를 전체 중 일부로 가지고 있다
3 누군가 또는 무언가를 멀리하다
4 더 나아지다 또는 어떤 것을 더 나아지게 만들다
5 특정한 병에 걸렸을지도 모른다는 것을 보여 주는 것
6 심한 감기 같지만 매우 심각할 수 있는 병
7 컴퓨터 시스템에 저장된 대량의 정보
8 어떤 것을 사는 행위; 구입된 물건

B |해석| 1 아기들은 자신의 엄마를 쉽게 알아볼 수 있다.
2 그 여자는 흔적도 없이 사라졌다.
3 경찰은 범죄를 예방하기 위해 열심히 일했다.
4 이 소프트웨어는 마케팅 데이터를 분석하는 데 사용된다.
5 손을 씻음으로써 이 질병의 확산을 막을 수 있다.

D |해석| 1 잠그다 : 열다 = 간단한 : 복잡한
2 도움 : 도움이 되는 = 의미 : 의미 있는
3 규칙적인 : 규칙적으로 = 현명한 : 현명하게
4 예측하다 : 예측하다 = 병 : 병
5 가능한 : 아마 = 일반적인 : 일반적으로

W Words 실전 TEST
p. 162

01 ⑤   02 ④   03 ⑤   04 ③   05 possibly   06 ②
07 played an, role   08 Take, off

01 |해석| 어떤 것을 바꾸거나 어떤 것에 영향을 주다
① (사용료를 내고) 빌리다   ② 예측하다   ③ 피하다   ④ 알아보다
|해설| influence(영향을 미치다)의 영영풀이이다.

02 |해석| 예측하다 : 예측하다
① 잠그다 : 열다   ② 국가 : 국가의   ③ 간단한 : 복잡한
④ 병 : 병   ⑤ 일반적인 : 일반적으로
|해설| [보기]와 ④는 유의어 관계이다. ①과 ③은 반의어, ②는 「명사 – 형용사」, ⑤는 「형용사 – 부사」의 관계이다.

03 |해석| • Jim은 자신의 프로젝트에 집중하려고 노력했다.
• 나는 이제부터 모바일 게임을 그만둘 것이다.
|해설| focus on: ~에 집중하다 / from now on: 이제부터

04 |해석| • 그 도둑은 범죄 현장에 아무 흔적도 남기지 않았다.
• 그들은 이번 주말에 여수로 떠날 것이다.
① 피하다   ② (결과를) 이끌어 내다   ④ 수집하다   ⑤ 성장하다
|해설| leave는 동사로 '남기다'와 '떠나다'라는 두 가지 의미를 모두 갖

는다.

05 |해석| 규칙적인 : 규칙적으로 = 가능한 : 아마
|해설| 「형용사 – 부사」의 관계이다. possible의 부사형은 possibly이다.

06 |해석| • 나는 매일 내 블로그에 사진을 많이 업로드한다.
• 일기 방식(→ 예보)에 의하면 내일 비가 올 것이다.
• 나에게 런던에서 방문하기 좋은 장소를 추천해 주겠니?
• 그들은 역에 12시 정도에 도착할 것 같다.
• 그 병의 첫 증상은 기침이다.
|해설| ⓑ '일기 예보(weather forecast)에 의하면 내일 비가 올 것이다.'라는 의미가 되는 것이 알맞다. (→ forecast)

07 |해설| '역할을 하다'는 play a role로 표현한다. important가 모음으로 시작하므로 an을 쓰는 것에 유의한다.

08 |해설| '~을 벗다'는 take off로 표현한다.

L&T Listen and Talk 만점 노트
pp. 164~165

Q1 교통 카드에 돈을 충전하는 방법   Q2 T   Q3 F
Q4 choose the snack he wants   Q5 ⓑ   Q6 ⓐ   Q7 T
Q8 컵에 뜨거운 물 붓기   Q9 ⓑ

L&T Listen and Talk 빈칸 채우기
pp. 166~167

Listen and Talk A-1 Can you tell me, First, Second, the amount of money, Last, insert, into, simple
Listen and Talk A-2 how to use, First, next, take, out, Got
Listen and Talk A-3 rent a bike, tell me how to use, log in to, Then, what, to unlock, appreciate your help
Listen and Talk C robot for, you tell me how, place, screen, Second, type, looking for, that all, take, to, isn't it, Yes, amazing
Talk and Play Do you know, put a tea bag, pour hot water, then, Last, I got it, appreciate
Review - 1 how to plant a potato, First, cut, into small pieces, Second, Then, cover the holes, sounds simple

L&T Listen and Talk 대화 순서 배열하기
pp. 168~169

1 ⓔ - ⓑ, ⓐ - ⓓ   2 ⓑ - ⓐ - ⓓ - ⓒ - ⓔ
3 ⓒ - ⓑ - ⓐ - ⓓ - ⓔ   4 ⓗ - ⓑ - ⓔ, ①, ⓒ - ⓐ
5 ⓓ - ⓐ, ⑨, ① - ⓔ   6 ⓔ - ⓐ - ⓒ - ⓓ

01 ⑤   **02** ④   **03** ②   **04** ⑤   **05** ③   **06** ④   **07** ①

08 ①, ④   **09** ②, ④

[서술형]

10 (1) Do you know how to make tea (2) I really appreciate your help   **11** (1) put water and the eggs in a pot (2) boil the water and the eggs for 10 to 12 minutes (3) Last (Then)   **12** (3)-(1)-(2)

---

01 |해석| A: 저는 과자를 사고 싶어요. 이 과자 자판기를 어떻게 사용하는지 아세요?

B: 네. 원하는 과자를 고르고 돈을 넣으세요. 그런 다음 과자를 꺼내세요.

① 저에게 간식 좀 사 주실래요?

② 매점에 가려면 어떻게 가야 하나요?

③ 과자 자판기는 어디에 있나요?

④ 간식을 살 수 있는 곳이 있나요?

|해설| 대답으로 과자 자판기에서 과자를 구입하는 방법을 설명하고 있으므로 빈칸에는 방법이나 절차를 묻는 표현이 알맞다.

02 |해석| A: 복사기를 어떻게 사용하는지 알려 주시겠어요?

B: 그럼요. 먼저, 복사기에 종이를 놓으세요. 그런 다음 종이 크기와 복사할 매수를 선택하세요. 마지막으로, START 버튼을 누르세요.

A: 알겠습니다. 도와주셔서 정말 고맙습니다.

① 괜찮아요.

② 별말씀을요.

③ 도움이 필요하신가요?

⑤ 그것을 복사해 주셔서 고맙습니다.

|해설| 복사기를 사용하는 방법을 설명해 준 사람에게 도와줘서 고맙다는 말을 하는 것이 자연스럽다.

03 |해석| A: 실례합니다. 교통 카드에 돈을 충전하는 방법을 알려 주시겠어요?

B: 유감이지만 그럴 수 없습니다(→ 그럼요). 먼저, 기계에 카드를 넣으세요. 두 번째로, 충전하고 싶은 금액을 선택하세요.

A: 알겠어요.

B: 마지막으로, 기계에 돈을 넣으세요.

A: 간단한 것 같네요. 고맙습니다.

|해설| 교통 카드 충전 방법을 이어서 설명하고 있으므로, ②는 Sure. 나 Of course. 등 충전 방법을 묻는 말에 대한 긍정의 응답이 되는 것이 알맞다.

04 |해석| A: 공원에 어떻게 가는지 아세요?

B: 네. 두 블록을 쭉 걸어가서 왼쪽으로 도세요.

A: 도와주셔서 감사합니다.

① 실례합니다. ② 참 안됐군요. ③ 찾을 수 있을 거예요.

④ 별말씀을요.

|해설| 밑줄 친 문장은 길을 알려 준 것에 대해 감사하는 표현이므로 ⑤와 바꿔 쓸 수 있다.

05 |해석| A: 실례합니다. 자전거를 빌리고 싶은데요. 이 앱을 어떻게 사용하는지 알려 주시겠어요?

(B) 그럼요. 먼저, 앱에 로그인하세요. 그런 다음 RENT 버튼을 찾아서 터치하세요.

(A) 그다음에는 뭘 하죠?

(D) 그러면 앱이 자전거 잠금을 해제할 수 있는 번호를 알려 줄 거예요.

(C) 고맙습니다. 도와주셔서 정말 감사해요.

|해설| 자전거를 빌리고 싶어서 앱 사용법을 묻는 말에 첫 번째와 두 번째 절차를 설명하고(B), 그다음에는 무엇을 해야 하는지 묻는 말(A)에 앱이 자전거 잠금을 해제하는 번호를 알려 줄 것이라고 설명하자(D) 고마움을 표현하는(C) 대화의 흐름이 자연스럽다.

06 |해석| A: 감자 심는 방법을 알려 주겠니?

B: 그럼. 첫 번째로, 감자를 작은 조각으로 잘라.

A: 알았어.

B: 그 다음, 땅에 구멍을 파.

A: 그다음에는?

B: 두 번째로(→ 세 번째로/그런 다음), 구멍에 감자 조각들을 넣어.

A: 그게 다야?

B: 아니. 마지막으로, 흙으로 구멍을 덮어.

A: 간단한 것 같네. 고마워.

|해설| ④ 설명의 흐름상 세 번째 절차에 해당하므로 Third나 Then을 쓰는 것이 알맞다.

[07~09] |해석|

A: 실례합니다만, 이 로봇은 용도가 뭔가요?

B: 아, 그것은 책을 찾아 주는 로봇이에요.

A: 정말요? 어떻게 사용하는지 알려 주시겠어요?

B: 그럼요. 먼저, 도서 대출 카드를 로봇 화면 위에 대세요.

A: 알겠어요.

B: 두 번째로, 당신이 찾고 있는 책의 제목을 입력한 다음 ENTER를 누르세요.

A: 그게 다인가요?

B: 네. 그러면, 로봇이 그 책을 찾아서 안내 데스크로 가져다줄 거예요.

A: 그러면 저는 그냥 안내 데스크로 가서 책을 받을 수 있네요?

B: 그렇습니다. 아주 쉬워요, 그렇지 않아요?

A: 네, 정말 놀랍네요. 고마워요.

07 |해설| 주어진 문장은 로봇의 사용법을 묻는 말이므로 첫 번째 사용 절차를 설명하는 말 앞인 ①에 들어가는 것이 알맞다.

08 |해설| 로봇은 책을 찾는 용도로 사용되고, 로봇의 사용법은 대화에서 순서대로 설명하고 있다.

09 |해석| ① 괜찮습니다.   ② 고맙습니다.

③ 천만에요.   ④ 도와주셔서 고맙습니다.

⑤ 그 말을 들으니 유감이야.

|해설| 사용법을 알려 줘서 고맙다는 감사의 표현이 들어가는 것이 알맞다.

10 |해설| A: 너는 차 만드는 방법을 아니?

B: 그럼. 먼저, 컵에 티백을 넣어. 그런 다음, 그 컵에 뜨거운 물을 부어.

A: 그다음에는?

B: 마지막으로, 3분 뒤에 티백을 꺼내.

A: 알겠어. 도와줘서 정말 고마워.

|해설| (1) 상대방에게 방법이나 절차를 물을 때 「Do you know how to+동사원형 ~?」으로 말할 수 있다.

(2) 도와줘서 고맙다고 할 때는 I (really) appreciate your help.라고 말할 수 있다.

11 |해설| 달걀 삶는 방법

1. 냄비에 물과 달걀을 넣는다.

2. 10~12분간 물과 달걀을 끓인다.

3. 달걀을 꺼내서 식힌다.

A: 너는 달걀 삶는 방법을 아니?

B: 그럼. 먼저, 냄비에 물과 달걀을 넣어. 그런 다음, 10~12분간 물과 달걀을 끓여.

A: 그다음에는?

B: 마지막으로(그런 다음), 달걀을 꺼내서 식혀.

|해설| (1), (2)에는 각각 주어진 메모의 첫 번째, 두 번째 절차를 쓰고, (3)에는 마지막 절차를 나타내는 말인 Last나 Then을 쓴다.

12 |해석| 음료수 자판기를 어떻게 사용하는지 알려 줄게요. 먼저, 자판기에 돈을 넣으세요. 두 번째로, 원하는 음료를 고르세요. 그럼 다음 음료수를 자판기에서 꺼내세요.

|해설| First, Second, Then의 순서대로 알맞은 내용을 나타내는 그림에 번호를 쓴다.

G ▶ Grammar 핵심 노트 1 QUICK CHECK p. 172

1 (1) Doing (2) Hearing (3) Dancing
2 (1) Waiting for the bus (2) Not feeling well
  (3) Calling my name

1 |해석| (1) 숙제를 하면서 그는 졸음을 느꼈다.
  (2) 그 소식을 들었을 때 그녀는 울기 시작했다.
  (3) 아빠와 춤을 추면서 그녀는 환하게 웃었다.

2 |해석| (1) 나는 버스를 기다리다가 Tom을 만났다.
  (2) 나는 몸이 좋지 않아서 집에 있었다.
  (3) Anne은 내 이름을 부르면서 우리를 향해 걸어왔다.

G ▶ Grammar 핵심 노트 2 QUICK CHECK p. 173

1 (1) as (2) As (3) As
2 (1) ⓑ (2) ⓐ (3) ⓒ

1 |해석| (1) 내가 그곳에 도착했을 때, 회의가 시작되었다.
  (2) 이전에 내가 말했듯이 우리는 6시에 만날 것이다.
  (3) 밖에 비가 오기 때문에, 우리는 오늘 외출하지 않을 것이다.

2 |해석| (1) 산꼭대기에 서 있을 때, 그는 기분이 무척 좋았다.
  (2) 우리는 나이가 들어감에 따라 더 현명해진다.
  (3) 나는 해야 할 숙제가 많았기 때문에 오늘 체육관에 가지 않았다.

G ▶ Grammar 연습 문제 1 p. 174

A 1 ⓑ 2 ⓒ 3 ⓓ 4 ⓐ
B 1 While she waited(was waiting) for the train

---

2 Because they were too busy
  3 If you solve this problem
C 1 Seen → Seeing
  2 When use → (When) Using
  3 Knowing not → Not knowing
  4 heard → hearing
D 1 Listening to, watered the plants
  2 Arriving home, opened all the windows
  3 Not having friends, was always lonely

A |해석| 1 그녀는 너무 아파서 병원에 일주일 동안 있어야 했다.
  2 이 버스를 타면 시청에 10분 안에 도착할 수 있다.
  3 우리는 극장에 들어가면서 휴대전화를 껐다.
  4 나는 전혀 졸리지 않아서 밤새 책을 읽었다.
  |해설| 각각 이유(1, 4), 조건(2), 동시동작(3)의 의미로 쓰인 분사구문과 의미상 자연스럽게 연결되는 주절을 찾아 문장을 완성한다.

B |해석| 1 기차를 기다리면서, 그녀는 샌드위치를 먹었다.
     = 그녀는 기차를 기다리는 동안 샌드위치를 먹었다.
  2 너무 바빠서, 그들은 우리와 함께 캠핑을 갈 수 없었다.
     = 그들은 너무 바빴기 때문에 우리와 함께 캠핑을 갈 수 없었다.
  3 이 문제를 해결하면, 너는 상을 받을 것이다.
     = 너는 이 문제를 해결하면 상을 받을 것이다.
  |해설| 1 동시동작(~하면서)을 나타내는 분사구문이므로 접속사 while을 사용한 부사절로 바꿔 쓰며, 주절의 시제에 맞게 과거시제나 과거진행형으로 쓴다.
  2 이유(~ 때문에)를 나타내는 분사구문이므로 접속사 because를 사용한 부사절로 바꿔 쓰며, 주절의 시제에 맞게 과거시제로 쓴다.
  3 조건(~하면)을 나타내는 분사구문이므로 접속사 if를 사용한 부사절로 바꿔 쓴다. 조건절에서는 미래의 일도 현재시제로 쓴다.

C |해석| 1 길에서 나를 보자마자, 그는 도망쳤다.
  2 이 칼을 사용할 때, 너는 매우 조심해야 한다.
  3 무엇을 해야 할지 몰라서, 그는 나에게 도움을 청했다.
  4 전화 소리를 못 들어서, 나는 전화를 받지 못했다.
  |해설| 1 주어 he가 나를 '보고' 도망갔다는 능동의 의미를 나타내야 하므로 분사구문은 현재분사 Seeing으로 시작하는 것이 알맞다.
  2 '이 칼을 사용할 때'라는 의미를 나타내는 분사구문으로, use를 현재분사(using)로 써야 알맞다. 분사구문의 의미를 명확하게 하기 위해 분사구문 앞에 접속사를 쓰기도 한다.
  3 분사구문의 부정은 분사 앞에 부정어 not을 써서 나타낸다.
  4 '전화 소리를 못 들어서'라는 의미를 나타내는 분사구문이므로, 부정어 Not 뒤에 현재분사(hearing)를 쓰는 것이 알맞다.

D |해설| 분사구문이 쓰인 문장을 완성한다.
  3 분사구문의 부정은 분사 앞에 부정어 not을 써서 나타낸다.

G ▶ Grammar 연습 문제 2 p. 175

A 1 the leaves will turn yellow and red
  2 as I walked out of the café

A |해석| **1** 시간이 지남에 따라, <u>나뭇잎은 노랗고 빨갛게 변할 것이다.</u>

2 나는 카페에서 걸어 나오다가 커피를 쏟았다.

3 날씨가 추워지고 있어서 <u>우리는 불을 피웠다.</u>

4 <u>눈이 많이 와서 소풍은 취소되었다.</u>

|해설| **1** '~함에 따라'를 뜻하는 접속사 as가 쓰인 부사절과 어울리는 말을 골라 문장을 완성한다.

2 '카페에서 걸어 나오다'라는 의미의 부사절이 이어지는 것이 자연스럽다.

3 '~ 때문에'를 뜻하는 접속사 as가 쓰인 부사절과 어울리는 말을 골라 문장을 완성한다.

4 '눈이 많이 와서'라는 의미의 부사절이 이어지는 것이 자연스럽다.

B |해석| **1** 그 방에 들어갔을 때, 나는 내 스마트폰을 떨어뜨렸다.

2 나는 <u>아침부터 아무것도 먹지 않았기 때문에</u> 정말 배가 고프다.

3 어떤 사람들은 <u>공부할 때</u> 음악을 듣는다.

|해설| **1, 3** 접속사 as가 때를 나타내므로 when과 바꿔 쓸 수 있다.

2 접속사 as가 이유를 나타내므로 because와 바꿔 쓸 수 있다.

C |해설| 각각 '~하듯이', '~ 때문에', '~함에 따라'를 뜻하는 접속사 as를 사용하여 부사절을 완성한다.

D |해설| **1** '~하는 대로'의 의미를 나타내는 접속사 as가 쓰인 문장을 완성한다.

2 '~함에 따라'의 의미를 나타내는 접속사 as가 쓰인 문장을 완성한다.

3 '~ 때문에'의 의미를 나타내는 접속사 as가 쓰인 문장을 완성한다.

ⒼGrammar 실전 TEST　　　pp. 176~179

01 ②	**02** ⑤	**03** ③	**04** ②	**05** ③	**06** ③
07 ③, ⑤	**08** ①	**09** ⑤	**10** ③	**11** ②	**12** ③
13 ②	**14** ③	**15** ④	**16** ④	**17** ④	

[서술형]

18 As(as)　**19** (1) Eating ice cream　(2) Playing the guitar (3) Talking on the phone　(4) Drinking water　**20** Feeling hungry after shopping, we went to the food court to eat something.　**21** (1) As he grew old(older)　(2) As I said before　(3) As we predicted　**22** (1) Finishing her

homework　(2) Not having enough money　(3) Walking on the beach　**23** (1) As he got off the bus, he said hello to me.　(2) Getting off the bus, he said hello to me.

24 (1) As I wasn't(was not) that hungry, I didn't(did not) eat anything.　(2) Not being that hungry, I didn't(did not) eat anything.　**25** (1) As I arrived late, I missed the beginning of the movie.　(2) As I entered the kitchen, I could smell Mom's cookies.　(3) As the doctor told me, I will take this medicine every day.

01 |해석| 그녀는 손을 흔들면서 열차에 올라탔다.

|해설| '~하면서'라는 의미로 동시동작을 나타내는 분사구문이 되어야 하므로 현재분사 Waving이 알맞다.

02 |해석| 나는 요리에 관심이 있었기 때문에 요리 동아리에 가입했다.

|해설| '~ 때문에'의 의미로 쓰인 as이므로 이유를 나타내는 접속사 because와 바꿔 쓸 수 있다.

03 |해석| <u>커피를 너무 많이 마셔서,</u> 나는 쉽게 잠들지 못한다.

|해설| 분사구문은 부사절의 접속사를 생략하고, 주절의 주어와 부사절의 주어가 같을 때 부사절의 주어를 생략한 뒤, 마지막으로 부사절의 동사를 「동사원형＋-ing」로 바꿔 만든다.

04 |해석| ① 그는 독감에 걸렸기 때문에 외출하지 않았다.

② 어두워짐에 따라 더 추워졌다.

③ 그들은 내가 해 달라고 요청한 대로 하지 않았다.

④ 나이가 듦에 따라 나는 독서를 더 즐긴다.

⑤ 모두가 알고 있듯이, 수진이는 최고의 선수다.

|해설| ② 접속사 As가 '~함에 따라'의 의미로 쓰였다.

05 |해석| 나는 샤워를 하고 있는 동안 누군가가 문을 두드리는 것을 들었다.

① 만약 내가 샤워를 한다면

② 내가 샤워를 하지 않으면

④ 비록 나는 샤워를 하지 않았지만

⑤ 내가 샤워를 하지 않고 있었기 때문에

|해설| '나는 샤워를 하고 있는 동안 누군가가 문을 두드리는 것을 들었다.'라는 의미가 자연스러우므로 '~하는 동안'이라는 의미의 접속사 While을 사용하는 것이 알맞다.

06 |해석| 비가 많이 왔기 때문에, _____.

① 지나는 운전을 할 수 없었다

② 나는 우비를 입었다

③ 땅이 더 건조해졌다

④ 소풍이 취소되었다

⑤ 그들은 테니스를 치지 못했다

|해설| 접속사 As가 '~ 때문에'라는 의미로 쓰인 문장이므로 비가 몹시 내린 결과 ③ '땅이 더 건조해졌다'는 것은 의미상 어색하다.

07 |해설| 이유를 나타내는 접속사 as를 사용하거나 분사구문을 사용하여 표현할 수 있다. 분사구문의 부정은 분사 앞에 not을 써서 나타낸다.

08 |해석| 강을 따라 걸으면서, 나는 개 다섯 마리와 함께 있는 한 남자를 보았다.

|해설| While I was walking along the river, I saw a man with five dogs.와 같은 의미가 되도록 부사절을 분사구문으로 바꿔 쓰면 Walking along the river, I saw a man with five dogs.이다.

09 |해석| 그녀는 피곤했기 때문에, 일찍 잠자리에 들었다.
① 나는 네가 바라는 대로 하겠다.
② 내가 저녁을 요리하고 있을 때, 전화벨이 울렸다.
③ 너도 알듯이, 이것은 좋은 질문이 아니다.
④ 그녀는 자랄수록 더욱 아름다워졌다.
⑤ 눈이 많이 와서 캠핑이 취소되었다.
|해설| [보기]와 ⑤의 접속사 As는 '~ 때문에'라는 의미이다.

10 |해석| ① 그는 음악을 들으면서 자전거를 탔다.
② 나는 저녁을 먹으면서 TV 프로그램을 보았다.
③ 배가 너무 고파서, 나는 피자를 전부 먹었다.
④ 왼쪽으로 돌면 은행이 보일 것이다.
⑤ Tim은 책을 읽으면서 쿠키를 먹었다.
|해설| '배가 너무 고파서'라는 의미를 나타내는 부사절(As I was too hungry)을 분사구문으로 바꿔 쓰면 Being too hungry, I ate a whole pizza.가 된다. (Was → Being)

11 |해석| ① 그가 내 전화를 받지 않았기 때문에, 나는 그에게 문자를 보냈다.
② 비록 그들은 쌍둥이지만, 전혀 다르게 생겼다.
③ 날씨가 추워짐에 따라, 사람들은 더 두툼한 옷을 입는다.
④ 내가 방을 청소하고 있었을 때, 엄마가 집에 오셨다.
⑤ 아빠가 너에게 말하셨듯이, 너는 패스트푸드를 너무 많이 먹지 말아야 한다.
|해설| ②에는 '비록 ~이지만'이라는 의미의 Though(Although)가 알맞다.

12 |해석| ① 그녀는 사과를 먹으면서 TV를 봤다.
② 그는 혼잣말을 하면서 운전했다.
③ 온라인 게임을 하는 것은 매우 흥미진진하다.
④ 그는 문자를 보내면서 아침을 먹었다.
⑤ 나는 창밖을 보면서 차를 마셨다.
|해설| ③은 주어로 쓰인 동명사이고, 니머지는 모두 분사구문에 사용된 현재분사이다.

13 |해석| ⓐ 그는 축구를 하다가 다리를 다쳤다.
ⓑ 너도 볼 수 있듯이, 나는 노래를 잘하지 못한다.
ⓒ 그는 라디오를 들으면서 저녁을 준비했다.
ⓓ 나는 너무 피곤해서 시험에 집중할 수 없었다.
ⓔ 그녀는 돈이 많았기 때문에 신발을 살 수 없었다. (×)
|해설| ⓐ 축구를 하다가 다리를 다친 것이므로 Played는 현재분사 Playing이 되어야 한다.
ⓔ 문맥상 이유를 나타내는 접속사 As가 아니라 '(비록) ~이지만'을 뜻하는 Though나 Although가 사용되어야 한다.

14 |해석| ① 두 블록을 곧장 가. 그러면 공원이 보일 거야.
→ 두 블록을 곧장 가면 공원이 보일 거야.
② Kevin은 모바일 게임을 했다. 그는 동시에 샌드위치를 먹었다.
→ Kevin은 모바일 게임을 하면서 샌드위치를 먹었다.
③ 미나는 그녀의 친구들을 기다렸다. 그녀는 전화 통화도 하고 있었다.
→ 미나는 전화 통화를 하면서 친구들을 기다렸다.
④ 나는 그 사고에 대해 몰랐다. 그래서 나는 할 말이 없었다.
→ 그 사고에 대해 몰랐기 때문에, 나는 할 말이 없었다.
⑤ Jessica는 끔찍한 두통이 있었다. 그래서 그녀는 하루 종일 침대에 누워 있었다.
→ Jessica는 끔찍한 두통이 있어서 하루 종일 침대에 누워 있었다.
|해설| ③ 분사구문을 사용하여 '미나는 전화 통화를 하면서 친구들을 기다렸다.'라는 의미가 되도록 Mina waited for her friends, talking on the phone.으로 써야 한다.

15 |해설| '풀밭에 앉아'를 분사구문으로 나타내면 Sitting on the grass이므로 sat은 필요 없는 단어이다.

16 |해석| ① 나는 그 사고를 봤을 때 거의 넘어질 뻔했다.
② 지금 떠나면 너는 마지막 기차를 탈 수 있다.
③ 그는 늦잠을 자서 항상 학교에 지각한다.
④ 불난 집을 봤을 때 나는 119에 전화해서 도움을 요청했다.
⑤ 그는 부상을 당해서 마라톤을 끝마치지 못했다.
|해설| ④ 불난 집을 보고 119에 전화했다는 과거의 내용이므로 부사절의 시제가 주절과 같은 과거시제여야 한다. (see → saw)

17 |해석| (A) 조금 늦었기 때문에, 우리는 택시를 탔다.
(B) 제주도에 도착해서, 나는 친구 Tim에게 전화를 했다.
(C) 겨울이 옴에 따라, 점점 더 추워진다.
|해설| ④ (B)의 분사구문을 부사절로 바꾸면 When(After) I arrived in Jeju-do이므로, 접속사(When/After)를 생략하고, 주절의 주어와 일치하는 부사절의 주어(I)를 생략한 뒤, 동사원형에 -ing를 붙인 Arriving으로 시작하는 것이 알맞다.

18 |해석| • 시간이 지남에 따라 상황은 더 좋아졌다.
• 그녀는 매우 화가 나서 말없이 집에 갔다.
• 의사가 네게 말했듯이, 너는 이 약을 먹어야 해.
|해설| 첫 번째 문장은 '~함에 따라, 할수록', 두 번째 문장은 '~ 때문에', 세 번째 문장은 '~하듯이'라는 뜻의 접속사가 적절하므로 공통으로 알맞은 접속사는 as이다.

19 |해석| (1) 아이스크림을 먹으면서, Eric은 책을 읽었다.
(2) 기타를 연주하면서, 유미는 노래를 불렀다.
(3) 전화 통화를 하면서, Amy는 그녀의 개를 신책시켰다.
(4) 물을 마시면서, 지호는 버스를 기다렸다.
|해설| 모두 두 가지 일을 동시에 하고 있는 상황이므로, '~하면서'라는 의미로 동시동작을 나타내는 분사구문으로 쓸 수 있다.

20 |해석| 언니와 나는 엄마 생신 선물을 사기 위해 쇼핑몰을 돌아다녔다. 쇼핑을 한 후에 배가 고파서, 우리는 무언가를 먹기 위해 푸드코트에 갔다.
|해설| 부사절에서 접속사를 생략하고, 주어가 주절의 주어와 일치하므로 주어도 생략한 후, 동사원형에 -ing를 붙여 분사구문으로 쓴다.

21 |해설| '~함에 따라', '~하듯이', '~하는 대로'는 모두 접속사 as를 사용하여 나타낼 수 있다.

22 |해석| (1) 그녀는 숙제를 끝낸 후에 잠자리에 들었다.
→ 숙제를 끝낸 후에, 그녀는 잠자리에 들었다.
(2) 그는 충분한 돈이 없기 때문에 지금 그 차를 살 수 없다.
→ 충분한 돈이 없어서, 그는 지금 그 차를 살 수 없다.
(3) 나는 해변을 걸을 때 바다에서 수영하는 사람들을 보았다.
→ 해변을 걸을 때, 나는 바다에서 수영하는 사람들을 보았다.
|해설| 분사구문은 부사절의 접속사를 생략하고, 주어가 주절의 주어와 일치하면 주어도 생략한 뒤, 동사원형에 -ing를 붙이는 형태로 만든다. 분사구문의 부정은 분사 앞에 not을 써서 나타낸다.

23 |해설| '~하면서'의 의미를 나타내는 접속사 as로 시작하는 부사절을 포함한 문장을 쓴다. 부사절 As he got off the bus를 분사구문으로 나타낼 때, 접속사(As)를 생략하고, 주절과 같은 주어(he)를 생략하고, 동사는 현재분사(Getting)로 쓴다.

24 |해설| '~ 때문에'의 의미를 나타내는 접속사 as로 시작하는 부사절을 포함한 문장을 쓴다. 부사절 As I wasn't that hungry를 분사구문으로 나타낼 때, 접속사(As)를 생략하고, 주절과 같은 주어(I)를 생략하고, be동사의 현재분사형(being) 앞에 Not을 쓴다.

25 |해석| (1) 나는 늦게 도착했기 때문에 영화의 시작 부분을 놓쳤다.
(2) 부엌에 들어갔을 때, 나는 엄마의 쿠키 냄새를 맡을 수 있었다.
(3) 의사가 내게 말한 대로, 나는 이 약을 매일 먹을 것이다.
|해설| 각각 '~ 때문에', '~할 때, ~하면서', '~하는 대로'라는 의미를 나타내는 접속사 as를 사용하여 문장을 연결한다.

Ⓡ Reading 빈칸 채우기   pp. 182~183

01 been surprised by, recommended for   **02** looked interesting   **03** what you liked   **04** because of   **05** data sets, complex   **06** As, much   **07** because, leaves a trace   **08** For example, records, purchases   **09** collecting, not enough   **10** be analyzed, is done   **11** Using, analyze, draw   **12** be used to   **13** is influencing   **14** understand, needs   **15** helps people avoid   **16** uses, endless   **17** disease, as, forecast the weather   **18** thanks to   **19** comes, will buy, flu   **20** symptoms   **21** is analyzed, be predicted   **22** Are you   **23** performance, making, exciting   **24** example, national   **25** by collecting, analyzing   **26** how much, how long   **27** With the help of, was able to   **28** predict crime   **29** Through the analysis of, hot spots   **30** is most likely to   **31** prevent, by focusing on   **32** has, changed   **33** from here   **34** for sure, important role

Ⓡ Reading 바른 어휘 · 어법 고르기   pp. 184~185

01 been surprised   **02** interesting   **03** what   **04** because of   **05** that   **06** much   **07** leaves   **08** For example   **09** is   **10** by   **11** Using   **12** used   **13** influencing   **14** sell   **15** avoid   **16** are   **17** as   **18** to   **19** comes   **20** more   **21** If   **22** fan   **23** making   **24** national   **25** by   **26** he had   **27** win   **28** before   **29** Through   **30** likely   **31** focusing   **32** changed   **33** from   **34** knows

Ⓡ Reading 틀린 문장 고치기   pp. 186~187

01 ×, been surprised by   **02** ×, interesting   **03** ○   **04** ○   **05** ×, are   **06** ×, greater   **07** ○   **08** ×, are   **09** ○   **10** ○   **11** ○   **12** ×, be used to make   **13** ○   **14** ○   **15** ×, avoid   **16** ○   **17** ○   **18** ○   **19** ×, when   **20** ○   **21** ×, be predicted   **22** ○   **23** ×, more exciting   **24** ○   **25** ×, collecting   **26** ○   **27** ×, to improve   **28** ○   **29** ×, analysis   **30** ○   **31** ×, on   **32** ×, has   **33** ○   **34** ○

Ⓡ Reading 실전 TEST   pp. 190~193

01 ④   **02** ④   **03** ⑤   **04** ②   **05** ①   **06** predict   **07** ②   **08** ⑤   **09** ③   **10** ④   **11** ④   **12** ④   **13** ②   **14** ②   **15** ④   **16** ③

[서술형]

17 Big data is data sets that are very big and complex.
18 (1) ⓒ → because of (2) big data는 명사구이므로 앞에 because of가 와야 한다. because 뒤에는 절이 온다.   **19** (정보 통신 기술이 발달함에 따라) 우리가 갖고 있는 데이터의 양이 이전보다 훨씬 더 많아지고 있는 것   **20** ⓐ be analyzed ⓑ to make
21 They analyze big data and draw meaningful results from it.   **22** ⓐ that ⓑ as ⓒ If   **23** treat → forecast
24 making sports more exciting   **25** players, improve, win

01 |해석| 당신은 온라인 서점을 방문해서 그 서점이 당신에게 추천한 책들을 보고 놀란 적이 있는가? 그 책들 중 다수가 당신에게 흥미로워 보였다. 그러면 그 서점은 당신이 무엇을 좋아하는지 어떻게 알았을까? 이것은 모두 빅데이터 때문에 가능하다.
① ~와 같은 ② ~에 대한 감사 ③ ~ 대신에 ⑤ ~에 더하여
|해설| 문맥상 '빅데이터 때문에'라는 뜻이 되는 것이 자연스러우므로, '~ 때문에'를 의미하는 because of가 알맞다.

[02~06] |해석|
빅데이터는 매우 크고 복잡한 데이터의 집합이다. 정보 통신 기술이 발달함에 따라 우리가 갖고 있는 데이터의 양이 이전보다 훨씬 더 많아지고 있다. 이것의 주된 이유는 우리가 온라인상에서 하는 거의 모든 것들이 흔적을 남기기 때문이다. 예를 들어, 당신이 블로그에 올린 사진들과 온라인 상점에서의 구매 기록들이 모두 빅데이터의 일부이다.
하지만 단순히 데이터를 수집하는 것만으로는 충분하지 않다. 빅데이터는 분석되어야 하는데, 이것은 빅데이터 전문가들에 의해서 이루어진다. 전문가들은 다양한 방법들을 사용하여 빅데이터를 분석하고, 그것으로부터 의미 있는 결과들을 도출한다. 그런 다음, 이런 결과들은 의사결정을 하거나 미래를 예측하는 데 사용될 수 있다.

02 |해석| ① 그녀는 그곳에서 의사로 일한다.
② 내가 어제 부탁한 대로 일을 해 줘.
③ 나는 늦게 도착했기 때문에 수업을 들을 수 없었다.

④ 나이가 들어감에 따라, 그는 훨씬 더 조용해졌다.

⑤ 내가 게임을 하고 있을 때, 엄마가 집에 오셨다.

|해설| ⓐ와 ④의 As는 '~함에 따라'라는 뜻으로 쓰인 접속사이다.

03 |해석| ① 그러나 ② 게다가 ③ 마침내 ④ 그에 반해

|해설| 우리가 온라인상에서 하는 거의 모든 것들이 흔적을 남긴다는 내용에 이어 그에 대한 예시가 빈칸 뒤에 이어지고 있으므로, '예를 들면'이라는 의미의 연결어 For example이 알맞다.

04 |해설| (A) '훨씬'이라는 의미로 비교급을 강조하여 수식하는 부사는 much이다. very는 비교급을 수식할 수 없다.

(B) 데이터 분석이 전문가들에 의해 '되어진다'는 의미의 수동태(be동사+과거분사)가 되어야 하므로 과거분사 done이 알맞다.

(C) '다양한 방법들을 사용하여'라는 의미의 분사구문이 되어야 하므로 현재분사 Using이 알맞다.

05 |해석| ① 우리는 지금보다 과거에 데이터가 더 많았다.

② 우리가 온라인에서 하는 것은 빅데이터의 일부가 될 수 있다.

③ 빅데이터 전문가들이 하는 일은 빅데이터를 분석하는 것이다.

④ 빅데이터 전문가들은 빅데이터로부터 결과를 도출한다.

⑤ 빅데이터로부터 도출해낸 의미 있는 결과는 사람들이 의사결정을 하는 것을 도울 수 있다.

|해설| ① 정보 통신 기술이 발달함에 따라 이전보다 우리가 갖고 있는 데이터의 양이 훨씬 더 많아지고 있다고 했다.

06 |해설| '어떤 일이 일어날 것이라고 말하다'는 predict(예측하다)의 영영풀이이다.

[07~10] |해석|

빅데이터는 우리 삶의 거의 모든 부분에 영향을 미치고 있다. 그것은 회사들이 소비자들이 필요로 하는 것을 더 잘 이해하고 더 많은 상품을 팔도록 도와준다. 그것은 사람들이 교통 체증을 피하도록 도와준다. 그것의 쓰임은 끝이 없는데, 여기 몇 가지 흥미로운 예들이 있다.

(B) 당신은 날씨 선문가들이 날씨를 예측하는 것과 같이 현재 건강 전문가들이 질병을 예측할 수 있다는 것을 알고 있었는가?

(A) 이것은 빅데이터 덕분에 가능하다. 예를 들어, 독감의 계절이 오면 사람들은 독감 약을 더 많이 구입할 것이다. 그들은 또한 온라인상에서 독감 증상에 대해 더 많이 검색해 볼 것이다.

(C) 이런 종류의 데이터가 현명하게 분석된다면, 독감의 확산은 예측될 수 있다.

07 |해설| 빅데이터가 우리의 삶에 영향을 미친다는 내용에 이어, 빅데이터 쓰임의 예시로 건강 전문가들이 현재 질병을 예측할 수 있다는 것을 알고 있는지 묻는 질문(B)과 함께 그것이 빅데이터 덕분이라는 내용과 그 예시(A)로 독감 관련 내용이 나오고, 질병과 관련한 데이터의 분석이 질병의 확산을 예측할 수 있다는 내용(C)으로 이어지는 것이 자연스럽다.

08 |해설| ⑤ 독감의 확산이 '예측될' 수 있다는 내용이므로 수동태(be동사+과거분사)로 쓰이는 것이 알맞다.

09 |해설| ⓐ는 문장 앞부분에 있는 companies를 가리키고, ⓑ는 앞 문장의 It과 마찬가지로 첫 문장의 Big data를 가리킨다.

10 |해석| ① 빅데이터는 기업에 어떤 도움이 되는가?

② 빅데이터의 쓰임에 한계가 있는가?

③ 건강 전문가들은 현재 무엇을 예측할 수 있는가?

④ 날씨 전문가들은 빅데이터를 어떻게 분석하는가?

⑤ 독감의 계절이 오면 사람들은 무엇을 할 것인가?

|해설| ④ 날씨 전문가들이 빅데이터를 분석한다는 내용은 언급되지 않았다.

[11~13] |해석|

당신은 스포츠 팬인가? 빅데이터는 스포츠를 더 흥미진진하게 만들면서 선수들의 경기력을 향상하고 있다. 한 유명한 사례가 독일 국가 대표 축구팀이다. 그 팀은 선수들에 관한 엄청난 양의 데이터를 모으고 분석함으로써 데이터베이스를 구축했다. 예를 들어, 그 데이터는 각각의 선수들이 얼마나 많이 달렸고, 얼마나 오랫동안 공을 갖고 있었는지를 포함했다. 이 데이터베이스의 도움으로, 독일 국가 대표 축구팀은 경기력을 향상할 수 있었고, 2014년 월드컵에서 우승할 수 있었다.

11 |해설| 주어진 문장은 (독일 국가 대표 축구팀이 구축한) 데이터에 어떤 정보가 포함되어 있었는지에 대한 예시이므로, 독일 국가 대표 축구팀이 선수들에 관한 데이터베이스를 구축했다는 문장 뒤인 ④에 들어가는 것이 알맞다.

12 |해설| '~하면서'라는 의미의 동시동작을 나타내는 분사구문을 이끄는 현재분사 making이 알맞다.

13 |해설| ⓑ by+동명사: ~함으로써

ⓒ with the help of: ~의 도움으로

[14~16] |해석|

빅데이터 덕분에 경찰은 이제 범죄가 발생하기 전에 그 범죄를 예측할 수 있다. 범죄의 유형, 시간 및 장소에 관한 빅데이터 분석을 통해, 경찰은 범죄 다발 지역의 지도를 만들 수 있다. 이 지도는 범죄가 언제, 어디에서 가장 발생할 것 같은지 알려 준다. 경찰은 이 지도가 예측하는 지역과 시간대에 집중함으로써 추가 범죄를 예방할 수 있다.

빅데이터는 이미 세계를 크게 변화시켰다. 그러면 빅데이터 산업은 여기에서부터 어디로 가게 될까? 누구도 확실히 알지는 못하지만, 전문가들은 빅데이터가 우리 삶에서 더욱 더 중요한 역할을 할 것이라는 데에는 동의한다.

14 |해설| ⓑ be likely to: ~할 것 같다

15 |해설| (A)에는 범죄가 일어나기 전에 '예측할(predict)' 수 있다는 내용이 되는 것이 알맞고, (B)에는 추가 범죄를 '예방할(prevent)' 수 있다는 내용이 되는 것이 알맞다.

16 |해설| • 지민 → 범죄 다발 지역 지도로 범죄가 일어날 수 있는 때와 장소를 알 수 있다.

• 소미 → 빅데이터로 범죄를 미리 예측할 수 있다는 내용은 있지만, 빅데이터가 발생한 범죄를 처리하는 데 주로 쓰인다는 내용은 없다.

[17~19] |해설|

당신은 온라인 서점을 방문해서 그 서점이 당신에게 추천한 책들을 보고 놀란 적이 있는가? 그 책들 중 다수가 당신에게 흥미로워 보였다. 그러면 그 서점은 당신이 무엇을 좋아하는지 어떻게 알았을까? 이것은 모두 빅데이터 때문에 가능하다.

빅데이터는 매우 크고 복잡한 데이터의 집합이다. 정보 통신 기술이 발달함에 따라 우리가 갖고 있는 데이터의 양이 이전보다 훨씬 더 많아지고 있다. 이것의 주된 이유는 우리가 온라인상에서 하는 거의 모든 것들이 흔적을 남기기 때문이다. 예를 들어, 당신이 블로그에 올린 사진들과 온라인 상점에서의 구매 기록들이 모두 빅데이터의 일부이다.

17 |해설| 보어로 쓰인 선행사 data sets를 주격 관계대명사 that이 이끄는 관계대명사절이 수식하는 형태로 쓴다.

18 |해설| 뒤에 이유를 나타내는 명사(구)가 올 경우 because of를 쓰고, 「주어+동사」로 이루어진 절이 올 경우에는 because를 쓴다.

19 |해설| This는 앞 문장(As information ~ than before.)의 내용을 의미한다.

[20~21] |해석|

하지만 단순히 데이터를 수집하는 것만으로는 충분하지 않다. 빅데이터는 분석되어야 하는데, 이것은 빅데이터 전문가들에 의해서 이루어진다. 전문가들은 다양한 방법들을 사용하여 빅데이터를 분석하고, 그것으로부터 의미 있는 결과들을 도출한다. 그런 다음, 이런 결과들은 의사결정을 하거나 미래를 예측하는 데 사용될 수 있다.

20 |해설| ⓐ '분석되어야 한다'는 의미가 적절하므로 수동태(be동사+과거분사)로 쓴다.

ⓑ '결정하는 데 사용되다'라는 의미가 되어야 하며 등위접속사 or 뒤의 to predict와 병렬 구조를 이루므로 「be used to+동사원형」(~하는 데 사용되다) 형태가 되도록 to make로 쓴다.

21 |해설| Q: 빅데이터 전문가들이 하는 일은 무엇인가?

A: 그들은 빅데이터를 분석하고 그것으로부터 의미 있는 결과를 도출한다.

|해설| 빅데이터 전문가들이 하는 일은 빅데이터를 분석하고 그것으로부터 의미 있는 결과들을 도출하는 것이다.

[22~23] |해석|

당신은 날씨 전문가들이 날씨를 예측하는 것과 같이 현재 건강 전문가들이 질병을 예측할 수 있다는 것을 알고 있었는가? 이것은 빅데이터 덕분에 가능하다. 예를 들어, 독감의 계절이 오면 사람들은 독감 약을 더 많이 구입할 것이다. 그들은 또한 온라인상에서 독감 증상에 대해 더 많이 검색해 볼 것이다. 이런 종류의 데이터가 현명하게 분석된다면, 독감의 확산은 예측될 수 있다.

22 |해설| ⓐ 명사절을 이끄는 접속사 that이 알맞다.

ⓑ '~하듯이'를 의미하는 접속사 as가 알맞다.

ⓒ '(만약) ~하면'을 의미하는 접속사 If가 알맞다.

23 |해설| 빅데이터는 건강 전문가들이 질병을 치료하는(→ 예측하는) 것을 도울 수 있다.

|해설| 빅데이터는 건강 전문가들이 질병을 예측하는 데 도움을 준다고 윗글에 언급되어 있다.

[24~25] |해석|

당신은 스포츠 팬인가? 빅데이터는 스포츠를 더 흥미진진하게 만들면서 선수들의 경기력을 향상하고 있다. 한 유명한 사례가 독일 국가 대표 축구팀이다. 그 팀은 선수들에 관한 엄청난 양의 데이터를 모으고 분석함으로써 데이터베이스를 구축했다. 예를 들어, 그 데이터는 각각의 선수들이 얼마나 많이 달렸고, 얼마나 오랫동안 공을 갖고 있었는지를 포함했다. 이 데이터베이스의 도움으로, 독일 국가 대표 축구팀은 경기력을 향상할 수 있었고, 2014년 월드컵에서 우승할 수 있었다.

24 |해설| 빅데이터는 스포츠를 더 흥미진진하게 만들면서 선수들의 경기력을 향상하고 있다.

|해설| 「make+목적어+형용사(목적격보어)」(~을 …하게 만들다)의 형태를 사용하여, 현재분사 making으로 시작하는 분사구문을 완성한다. exciting의 비교급은 more exciting으로 쓰는 것에 유의한다.

25 |해설| 선수들에 대한 빅데이터 덕분에 독일 국가 대표 축구팀은 경기력을 향상시키고 2014년 월드컵에서 우승할 수 있었다.

 기타 지문 **실전 TEST**   p. 195

01 Let me tell you how to use a drink machine.   **02** ③

03 ②   **04** Looking at the results   **05** free time activities, traveling, watching TV   **06** ④   **07** ③

[01~02] |해석|

음료 자판기 사용하는 법을 알려 드리겠습니다. 먼저, 기계에 돈을 넣으세요. 그런 다음, 원하는 음료를 고르세요. 마지막으로, 기계에서 음료를 꺼내세요. 간단하죠.

01 |해설| '제가 ~하겠습니다'는 「Let me+동사원형 ~.」 형태로 쓰고, 수여동사 tell 뒤에 간접목적어 you와 직접목적어 how to use a drink machine을 이어서 쓴다.

02 |해설| 순서나 절차를 설명할 때 first, second, then, last 등의 순서를 나타내는 말을 사용하면 순서나 절차를 더 명확하게 나타낼 수 있다. 순서를 나타낼 때는 서수로 쓴다.

[03~05] |해석|

우리는 100명의 청소년들에게 그들의 여가 시간 활동에 대해 질문했습니다. 그 결과 청소년들이 가장 하고 싶어 하는 여가 시간 활동은 여행인 것으로 보입니다. 34%가 여가 시간에 여행을 하고 싶다고 말했습니다. 하지만, 그들이 실제로 가장 많이 하는 여가 시간 활동은 TV 시청입니다. 39%가 여가 시간에 TV를 시청한다고 말했습니다. 이 결과를 보면, 우리는 청소년들이 여가 시간에 하고 싶어 하는 것과 여가 시간에 실제로 하는 것 사이에 큰 차이가 있다는 것을 알 수 있습니다.

03 |해석| ① 그러므로 ③ 결과적으로 ④ 무엇보다도 ⑤ 예를 들어

|해설| 설문 조사에서 여가 활동으로 가장 하고 싶다고 답한 것과 실제로 가장 많이 하는 여가 활동이 다르다는 상반된 내용이 이어지므로 연결어로 However(그러나, 하지만)가 알맞다.

04 |해설| 부사절을 분사구문으로 나타낼 때 부사절의 접속사를 생략하고, 부사절의 주어가 주절과 같은 경우 주어를 생략한 뒤, 동사를 「동사원형+-ing」로 바꾼다.

05 |해석| 그들의 여가 시간 활동에 대한 청소년들의 응답에 따르면, 그들이 가장 하고 싶어 하는 것은 여행이지만, 그들이 실제로 가장 많이 하는 것은 TV 시청이다.

|해설| 본문은 청소년들의 여가 시간 활동(free time activities)에 관한 조사 결과를 설명한 것으로, 청소년들이 가장 하고 싶어 하는 것은 여행(traveling)이지만, 실제로 가장 많이 하는 것은 TV 시청(watching TV)이라고 언급되어 있다.

[06~07] |해석|

설문 조사를 바탕으로, 우리는 경주를 골랐습니다. 10명의 학급 친구들이 졸업 여행지를 고를 때 활동이 가장 중요하다고 생각합니다. 온라인으로 자료를 찾아본 후, 우리는 경주에 볼 것과 할 것이 많이 있다는 것을 알게 되었습니다.

06 |해설| ④ 온라인으로 자료를 '찾았다'는 의미가 되어야 하므로, 빈칸에는 searched가 알맞다.

07 |해설| '볼' 것이라는 의미로 many things를 뒤에서 수식해야 하므로, 형용사적 용법의 to부정사가 되는 것이 알맞다.

STEP B

01 ③	02 ②	03 ⑤	04 ②	05 ④	06 ④
07 symptom	08 ⑤	09 ④	10 From now on		11 ④
12 ⑤	13 ①	14 ②	15 ③		

01 |해석| • 법이 허용하지 않는 행위
• 어떤 사람이 누구인지 또는 어떤 것이 무엇인지를 알아차리다
① 흔적 – (결과를) 이끌어 내다 ② 구입, 구매 – 넣다
④ 거리 – 예측하다 ⑤ 산업 – 업로드하다
|해설| 첫 번째 영영풀이는 crime(범죄), 두 번째 영영풀이는 identify (알아보다)에 해당한다.

02 |해석| 의료용 마스크를 착용하는 것이 독감의 확산을 방지하는 데 도움이 될 수 있다.
① 방법, 방식 ③ 사회 ④ 예측 ⑤ 양, 액수
|해설| '확산'을 의미하는 spread가 들어가는 것이 알맞다.

03 |해석| • 그들은 직장에서 자신들의 수행력을 향상시킬 방법을 찾고 있다.
• 공연 중에는 휴대전화 사용이 금지되어 있습니다.
① 차이, 격차 ② 분석 ③ 증상 ④ 영향 ⑤ 수행(력); 공연
|해설| '수행(력)', '공연'이라는 뜻을 모두 갖는 명사 performance가 알맞다.

04 |해석| • 어떤 일이 일어날 것 같다.
• John과 그의 팀 덕분에, 우리는 프로젝트를 제시간에 끝낼 수 있었다.
|해설| be likely to: ~할 것 같다 / thanks to: ~ 덕분에

05 |해석| ① 잠그다 : 열다 = 간단한 : 복잡한
② 도움 : 도움이 되는 = 국가 : 국가의
③ 현명한 : 현명하게 = 가능한 : 아마
④ 규칙적인 : 규칙적으로 = 의미 : 의미 있는
⑤ 병 : 병 = 복잡한 : 복잡한
|해설| ④ regular와 regularly는 「형용사 – 부사」의 관계이고, meaning과 meaningful은 「명사 – 형용사」의 관계이다.

06 |해석| ① 예방이 언제나 치료보다 낫다.
② 5월은 한국에서 매우 의미 있는 달이다.
③ Mike는 자신의 감정에 근거하여 결정을 내린다.
④ 나는 Jane 덕분에 영어 발음을 향상시켰다.
⑤ 지하철은 안전하고 편리한 교통수단이다.
|해설| ④ thanks to는 '~ 덕분에'라는 뜻이고, '~에 대한 감사'는 thanks for로 표현한다.

07 |해석| 명 특정한 병에 걸렸을지도 모른다는 것을 보여 주는 것
내 생각에 너는 감기 초기 증상이 있는 것 같아.
|해설| symptom(증상)의 영영풀이이다.

08 |해석| 다음 문장의 밑줄 친 부분과 바꿔 쓸 수 있는 것은?
당신은 다가올 지진을 예측하는 것이 가능하다고 생각하는가?
① (결과를) 이끌어 내다 ② 떠나다, 남기다 ③ 성장하다, 발달하다
④ 분석하다 ⑤ 예측하다

|해설| predict는 '예측하다'라는 뜻으로 forecast와 바꿔 쓸 수 있다.

09 |해석| ① 버튼을 누르고 네 카드를 여기에 삽입해라.
② 서울에는 국립박물관이 몇 군데 있다.
③ 만약 더 자세한 정보가 필요하면, 이 센터에 전화하면 됩니다.
④ 그 사안은 너무 복잡해서 모두가 이해할 수 있다. (×)
⑤ 과학이 발달할수록 세상은 더욱 편리해진다.
|해설| ④ '그 사안은 너무 복잡해서(complex) 모두가 이해할 수 있다'라는 의미는 어색하다.

10 |해설| from now on: 이제부터

11 |해석| ① 그들은 실수를 방지하기 위해 최선을 다했다.
② 이것은 당신의 뼈에 해를 끼치는 병이다.
③ 그는 몇몇 가구를 매우 싸게 샀다.
④ 아마 그는 내일까지 그 프로젝트를 끝낼 수 있을 것이다.
⑤ 모든 정보를 수집하는 데에는 시간이 걸린다.
|해설| ④ '아마'라는 뜻을 나타내는 possibly는 mainly(주로)와 바꿔 쓸 수 없고, perhaps, maybe 등과 바꿔 쓸 수 있다.

12 |해석| 매일 연습하면 요리 실력이 빠르게 향상될 것이다.
① 행동을 취하다
② 어떤 것을 바꾸거나 어떤 것에 영향을 주다
③ 어떤 것을 주의 깊게 검토하다
④ 어떤 일이 일어날 것이라고 말하다
⑤ 더 나아지다 또는 어떤 것을 더 나아지게 만들다
|해설| 매일 연습하면 요리 실력이 빠르게 향상될 것이라는 의미가 되는 것이 자연스러우므로 빈칸에는 improve(개선하다, 향상하다)가 들어가는 것이 적절하며, improve의 영영풀이로 ⑤가 알맞다.

13 |해석| ① 분석(→ 방법): 어떤 일을 하는 방법
② 피하다: 누군가 또는 무언가를 멀리하다
③ 포함하다: 무언가를 전체의 일부로 가지고 있다
④ 독감: 심한 감기 같지만 매우 심각할 수 있는 병
⑤ 데이터베이스: 컴퓨터 시스템에 저장된 대량의 정보
|해설| ① '어떤 일을 하는 방법'을 뜻하는 단어는 method(방법, 방식)이다. analysis는 '분석'이라는 뜻이다.

14 |해석| ⓐ 그녀는 8시에 집을 떠날 것이다.
ⓑ 그 도둑은 발자국 하나 남기지 않았다.
ⓒ 메시지를 좀 더 남기는 게 어때?
ⓓ 나는 첫 버스를 타기 위해 아침 일찍 출발할 것이다.
ⓔ 이름과 전화번호를 남기면 자전거를 빌릴 수 있습니다.
|해설| ⓐ, ⓓ의 leave는 '떠나다'라는 뜻으로 쓰였고, ⓑ, ⓒ, ⓔ는 '남기다'라는 뜻으로 쓰였다.

15 |해석| • 음악은 사람들의 감정에 영향을 미칠 수 있다.
• 그 이야기 후에 어떤 일이 일어날 것 같은가?
• 너는 주어진 데이터에서 결과를 이끌어 낼 수 있다.
• 야외 활동은 산악 자전거 타기와 카누 타기를 포함한다.
|해설| ⓐ에는 influence(영향을 미치다), ⓑ에는 be likely to(~할 것 같다)를 이루는 likely, ⓒ에는 draw(이끌어 내다), ⓓ에는 include (포함하다)가 알맞으며, avoid(피하다)는 어느 곳에도 들어갈 수 없다.

01 ③　　02 ②, ③　　03 ③　　04 ③　　05 ③　　06 ②, ④

[서술형]

07 I appreciate your help.　　08 your(the) library card, Type the title, press ENTER, the front desk
09 (1) library　(2) to the front desk　　10 Do you know how to plant a potato?　　11 ⓑ First ⓒ Third(Then)　　12 dig holes in the ground　　13 ⓑ → The fourth step of planting a potato is to cover the holes with dirt.

---

01 |해석| A: 차 만드는 방법을 아니?
　B: 그럼. 먼저, 컵에 티백을 넣어. 그런 다음, 그 컵에 뜨거운 물을 부어. 그리고 3분 뒤에 티백을 꺼내.
　① 차 좀 마실래?
　② 차 좀 마시는 게 어때?
　④ 차 만드는 방법을 배우고 싶니?
　⑤ 차 마실 수 있는 곳을 알려 주세요.
　|해설| 대답으로 차 만드는 방법을 설명하고 있으므로 빈칸에는 차 만드는 방법이나 절차를 묻는 말이 와야 한다. 방법이나 절차를 물을 때 Do you know how to ~? 또는 Can you tell me how to ~? 등으로 말할 수 있다.

02 |해석| A: 이 과자 자판기를 어떻게 사용하는지 알려 줄래?
　B: 응. 먼저, 원하는 과자를 골라. 그런 다음, 돈을 넣어. 마지막으로, 과자를 꺼내.
　A: 알겠어. _____
　①, ⑤ 정말 고마워.　　② 별말씀을.
　③ 별일 아니야.　　④ 도와줘서 고마워.
　|해설| B가 과자 자판기 사용법을 설명해 주었고 A는 알겠다고 답했으므로, 빈칸에는 감사의 말이 들어가는 것이 자연스럽다. It's my pleasure.와 Don't mention it.은 감사의 말에 대한 응답이다.

03 |해석| A: 실례합니다. 이 기계를 어떻게 사용하는지 알려 주시겠어요?
　B: 그럼요. 먼저, 복사기에 종이를 놓으세요.
　A: 알겠어요.
　B: 마지막으로(→ 두 번째로/그런 다음), 종이 크기와 복사할 매수를 선택하세요.
　A: 그 다음에는요?
　B: 마지막으로, START 버튼을 누르세요.
　A: 감사합니다. 도와주셔서 정말 고마워요.
　|해설| ⓒ는 첫 번째 순서와 마지막 순서 사이에 있는 순서이므로, 마지막 순서를 뜻하는 Last(마지막으로)가 쓰이는 것은 적절하지 않다. Second, Then 등의 표현이 쓰이는 것이 알맞다.

04 |해석| 자연스러운 대화가 되도록 (A)~(E)를 순서대로 바르게 배열한 것은?
　(B) 실례합니다. 이 책들을 반납하고 싶어요. 어떻게 하는지 아세요?
　(E) 그럼요. 간단합니다. 먼저, 기계에 도서 대출 카드를 넣으세요. 두 번째로, 이 상자 안에 책들을 넣으세요.
　(C) 그 다음에는요?
　(A) 그런 다음 그냥 카드를 꺼내세요.
　(D) 도와주셔서 정말 고맙습니다.

|해설| 책을 반납하고 싶다고 말하며 방법을 묻는 말(B)에 첫 번째 절차와 두 번째 절차를 설명하자(E) 그 다음 절차를 묻고(C), 답한(A) 후 감사를 표현하는(D) 흐름이 자연스럽다.

05 |해석| ① 자전거를 어떻게 사는지
　② 자전거를 어디서 타야 할지
　③ 이 앱을 어떻게 사용하는지
　④ 앱을 어떻게 만드는지
　⑤ 자전거 대여점에 어떻게 가는지
　|해설| 소녀의 물음에 대한 답으로 남자가 앱 사용법을 설명하고 있으므로, 빈칸에는 앱 사용법을 묻는 말이 알맞다.

06 |해석| ① 소녀는 자전거를 빌리고 싶어 한다.
　② 남자는 소녀에게 자전거 잘 타는 법을 알려 준다.
　③ 그 앱은 자전거를 빌리는 데 사용된다.
　④ 남자는 소녀를 위해 자전거의 잠금을 해제해 준다.
　⑤ 소녀는 그 남자의 도움에 고마워한다.
　|해설| ② 남자는 소녀에게 자전거를 잘 타는 방법이 아니라 자전거 대여를 하기 위한 앱 사용법을 알려 주었다.
　④ 남자는 앱을 사용하여 자전거 잠금을 해제하는 방법을 알려 주었다.

07 |해설| appreciate(감사하다)를 사용하여 감사의 표현을 완성한다.

08 |해설| 1. 로봇 화면 위에 도서 대출 카드를 댄다.
　2. 원하는 책의 제목을 입력하고 ENTER를 누른다.
　3. 안내 데스크로 가서 책을 받는다.
　|해설| 세호의 설명에 따르면, 먼저 로봇의 화면 위에 도서 대출 카드를 대고, 원하는 책의 제목을 입력하고 ENTER를 누른 후, 안내 데스크에서 로봇이 가져다준 책을 받으면 된다.

09 |해석| (1) Lucy와 세호는 지금 어디에 있는가?
　→ 그들은 도서관에 있다.
　(2) 로봇이 찾은 책을 어디로 가져가는가?
　→ 그것은 책을 안내 데스크로 가져간다.
　|해설| (1) Lucy와 세호가 도서관의 책을 찾아 주는 로봇을 보며 그것을 사용하는 방법에 대해 대화하고 있으므로 도서관에 있음을 알 수 있다.
　(2) 로봇은 찾은 책을 안내 데스크로 가져다줄 것이라고 했다.

10 |해설| 소년이 감자 심는 방법을 설명하고 있는 것으로 보아, 소녀는 감자 심는 방법을 아는지 질문하는 것이 자연스럽다. 방법이나 절차를 물을 때는 「Do you know how to+동사원형 ~?」으로 말할 수 있다.

11 |해설| ⓑ 첫 번째 절차에 해당하므로 First가 들어가는 것이 알맞다.
　ⓒ 세 번째 절차이므로 Third 또는 '그다음에'를 뜻하는 Then이 들어가는 것이 알맞다.

12 |해석| 위 대화에 따르면, 소녀는 첫 번째 단계 이후에 무엇을 해야 하는가?
　→ 그녀는 땅에 구멍을 파야 한다.
　|해설| Then, dig holes in the ground.가 첫 번째 단계(감자를 작은 조각으로 자르기) 다음 단계인 두 번째 단계에 해당한다.

13 |해석| ⓐ 소녀는 감자를 심기 위해 감자를 작은 조각으로 잘라야 한다.
　ⓑ 감자를 심는 네 번째 단계는 구멍에 물을 주는 것이다(→ 구멍을 흙으로 덮는 것이다).
　ⓒ 소녀는 자신을 도와준 소년에게 고마워한다.
　|해설| ⓑ 감자를 심는 마지막이자 네 번째 단계는 구멍을 흙으로 덮는 것이다.

G **Grammar 고득점 맞기** pp. 202~204

01 ④ 02 ② 03 ⑤ 04 ③, ④ 05 ②, ④ 06 ④
07 ⑤ 08 ③, ④ 09 ② 10 ② 11 ③

[서술형]

12 (1) Hearing a dog bark (2) Not feeling well 13 (1) As time passed, Jack felt weaker and weaker. (2) As the bread is very delicious, Jenny buys it every morning.
14 He holding → Holding / As(While) he held(was holding)
15 (1) Drinking a cup of coffee, she surfed the Internet. / Surfing the Internet, she drank(was drinking) a cup of coffee. (2) Not wearing glasses, he can't read books.
16 (1) ⓑ Knowing not → Not knowing (2) ⓔ Ran → Running 17 As I told you, you have to use your smartphone less. 18 (1) As(While) he sang(was singing) a song, he cleaned his car. (2) Singing a song, he cleaned his car. 19 (1) Riding a bike in the park, she fell down. (2) Seeing a mouse in the kitchen, she screamed. (3) Playing the piano, she sang a song. / Singing a song, she played the piano. (4) Waiting for the bus, she talked on the phone. / Talking on the phone, she waited for the bus. 20 (1) As everyone knows → 모든 사람이 알듯이, 해는 동쪽에서 뜬다. (2) As you exercise more → 운동을 더 많이 할수록 너는 더 건강해질 것이다.

01 |해석| • 음악을 들으면서 그는 설거지를 하고 있다.
• 숲속을 걷다가 그녀는 다람쥐를 보았다.
|해설| 각각 '음악을 들으면서'라는 뜻의 분사구문 Listening to music과 '숲속을 걷다가'라는 뜻의 분사구문 Walking in the forest가 되는 것이 알맞다.

02 |해석| • 그는 보조 요리사로 일한다.
• Tim은 너무 바빴기 때문에 오지 않았다.
• 어두워짐에 따라 더욱 조용해졌다.
|해설| '~로서'라는 뜻의 전치사와 '~ 때문에', '~함에 따라'라는 뜻의 접속사로 모두 쓰일 수 있는 것은 as이다.

03 |해석| 그녀는 전혀 배가 고프지 않아서 점심을 먹지 않았다.
|해설| 분사구문은 부사절의 접속사를 생략하고, 주절의 주어와 같을 때 부사절의 주어를 생략한 뒤, 동사를 현재분사 형태로 바꿔서 만든다. 분사구문의 부정은 부정어 not을 분사 앞에 써서 나타낸다.

04 |해석| 그녀는 할 일이 많았기 때문에 나갈 수가 없었다.
|해설| As는 이 문장에서 부사절을 이끄는 접속사로 쓰였고, '~ 때문에'라는 의미로 이유를 나타내므로 접속사 Since나 Because로 바꿔 쓸 수 있다.

05 |해설| When I saw my old friend, I shouted with joy.라는 부사절을 쓴 문장과 부사절을 분사구문으로 바꾼 Seeing my old friend, ~.로 쓸 수 있다.

06 |해석| 그녀는 너무 피곤했기 때문에, _____.
① 일찍 잠자리에 들었다 ② 수영하러 가지 않았다
③ 그 일을 끝낼 수 없었다 ④ 쉽게 밤을 샐 수 있었다

⑤ 친구와의 약속을 취소했다.
|해설| 주어진 부사절이 '그녀는 너무 피곤했기 때문에'라는 의미이므로 그와 관련된 결과가 들어가는 것이 알맞다.

07 |해석| ① 팝콘을 먹으면서 그들은 영화를 보았다.
② 몸이 좋지 않아서 나는 일찍 집으로 돌아왔다.
③ Peter는 석양을 바라보면서 천천히 걸었다.
④ 너무 졸려서 나는 바로 잠자리에 들었다.
⑤ 그녀는 친구들에게 작별인사도 하지 않고 교실을 떠났다.
|해설| ⑤는 전치사(without)의 목적어로 쓰인 동명사이고, 나머지는 모두 분사구문에 쓰인 현재분사이다.

08 |해석| ① 그가 거짓말을 했기 때문에 그녀는 그를 믿었다. (×)
② 아들들을 기다리며 그는 저녁 식사를 준비했다.
③ 외투를 입지 않으면 너는 감기에 걸릴 것이다.
④ 뮤지컬이 시작되자 모든 불이 꺼졌다.
⑤ 샤워를 하고 있어서 그는 전화를 받지 않았다.
|해설| ① 문맥상 부사절이 '비록 ~이지만, ~임에도 불구하고'의 의미가 되어야 하므로 접속사로 As는 알맞지 않다. (As → Though/ Although/Even though)
② '기다리면서'라는 능동의 의미가 되어야 하므로 분사구문은 현재분사 Waiting으로 시작해야 한다. (Waited → Waiting)
⑤ 문맥상 이유를 나타내는 분사구문이나 부사절이 쓰여야 한다. (Been taking → Taking/As he was taking)

09 |해석| [보기] 시간이 지남에 따라 그녀의 영어는 향상되었다.
① 나는 도서관에 가다가 Jane을 만났다.
② 그는 나이가 들수록 더 건강해지고 있다.
③ 그가 걸어 나오자, 모두가 그를 쳐다봤다.
④ 그는 버스를 놓쳐서 학교에 늦었다.
⑤ 그 남자는 바라던 대로 그 대학교에 입학했다.
|해설| [보기]와 ②의 As는 '~함에 따라, ~할수록'의 뜻으로 쓰였다.

10 |해석| ① 나는 차에서 내릴 때 Kate를 보았다.
② 네가 원하는 대로 이야기를 바꿀 수는 없다.
③ 나는 신발이 너무 커서 반품하고 싶다.
④ 양치질할 때는 물을 잠궈라.
⑤ 나는 영화가 마음에 들지 않았기 때문에 바로 극장 밖으로 나왔다.
|해설| ② as가 '~하는 대로'라는 의미로 쓰였으므로 이유를 나타내는 접속사 because(~ 때문에)와 바꿔 쓸 수 없다.

11 |해석| ⓐ 나는 핫도그를 먹으면서 영화를 보았다.
ⓑ 너무 놀라서 나는 한마디도 할 수 없었다.
ⓒ 밤이 늦었기 때문에 우리는 집으로 돌아갔다.
ⓓ 온도가 올라감에 따라 얼음은 녹는다.
ⓔ 역에서 기다리는 동안 나는 Tommy를 만났다.
|해설| ⓑ 분사구문이므로 현재분사 Being으로 시작하거나 또는 Being을 생략할 수 있다. (Was → (Being))
ⓔ 분사구문의 의미를 강조하기 위해 접속사를 함께 쓰는 경우 접속사는 현재분사 앞에 쓰며, 생략 가능하다. (Waiting while → (While) Waiting)

12 |해석| (1) 개가 짖는 소리를 듣고 그녀는 밖을 내다보았다.
(2) 몸이 좋지 않아서 나는 학교에 갈 수 없었다.
|해설| 부사절의 접속사를 생략하고, 주절의 주어와 같은 부사절의 주어를 생략한 뒤, 동사를 현재분사 형태로 바꿔서 분사구문을 만든다. 분

사구문의 부정은 분사 앞에 not을 써서 나타낸다.

13 |해석| (1) 시간이 지나갔다. Jack은 점점 더 약해졌다.
(2) 그 빵은 매우 맛있다. Jenny는 매일 아침 그것을 산다.
|해설| (1) '~함에 따라'라는 의미의 접속사 as를 사용하여 '시간이 지남에 따라 Jack은 점점 더 약해졌다.'라는 뜻이 되도록 문장을 쓴다.
(2) '~ 때문에'라는 의미의 접속사 as를 사용하여 '그 빵이 매우 맛있어서, Jenny는 매일 아침 그것을 산다.'라는 뜻이 되도록 문장을 쓴다.

14 |해설| 분사구문의 주어가 주절의 주어와 같을 때는 분사구문의 주어를 생략한다. 또는 '~하면서'를 뜻하는 접속사 as나 while을 사용한 부사절로 쓸 수도 있다.

15 |해석| (1) 그녀는 커피를 마시는 동안 인터넷 서핑을 했다.
(2) 그는 안경을 쓰지 않을 때는 책을 읽을 수 없다.
|해설| (1) 동시동작을 나타내는 분사구문을 포함한 문장을 쓴다.
(2) 분사구문의 부정은 분사 앞에 not을 써서 나타낸다.

16 |해석| ⓐ 뉴욕에 머물면서, 나는 이모를 방문했다.
ⓑ 무슨 말을 해야 할지 몰라서, 그녀는 잠자코 있었다.
ⓒ 나는 그녀를 생각하면서 거리를 걸었다.
ⓓ 몸이 안 좋으면(안 좋을 때) 너는 이 약을 먹어야 한다.
ⓔ 계단을 달려 내려가다가, 나는 넘어져서 무릎을 다쳤다.
|해설| ⓑ 분사구문의 부정은 분사 앞에 not을 써서 나타낸다.
ⓔ '계단을 달려 내려가다'라는 의미의 분사구문이 되도록 현재분사 Running으로 시작해야 한다.

17 |해설| '~하듯이'라는 뜻으로 부사절을 이끄는 접속사 as를 사용하여 쓴다.

18 |해설| '~하면서'라는 뜻의 접속사 as 또는 while이 이끄는 부사절을 포함한 문장을 쓰고, 그와 같은 의미의 분사구문을 쓴다.

19 |해석| (1) 공원에서 자전거를 타다가 그녀는 넘어졌다.
(2) 부엌에서 쥐를 보고 그녀는 비명을 질렀다.
(3) 피아노를 치면서 그녀는 노래를 불렀다. / 노래를 부르며 그녀는 피아노를 쳤다.
(4) 버스를 기다리면서 그녀는 전화 통화를 했다. / 전화 통화를 하면서 그녀는 버스를 기다렸다.
|해설| 시간((1), (2))이나 동시동작((3), (4))을 나타내는 분사구문이 포함된 문장을 쓴다. 분사구문은 「동사원형＋-ing」 형태의 현재분사가 이끈다.

20 |해석| (1) 모든 사람들이 알듯이, 해는 동쪽에서 뜬다.
(2) 운동을 더 많이 할수록 너는 더 건강해질 것이다.
|해설| 접속사로 쓰인 as는 문장에서 '~하듯이,' '~할수록, ~함에 따라' 등의 다양한 의미를 나타낸다.

R Reading 고득점 맞기 pp. 207~209

01 ④   02 ④   03 ①   04 ④   05 ②   06 ①   07 ④
08 ②   09 ③   10 ②   11 ①
[서술형]
12 (1) ⓑ → that(which) (2) ⓔ → make   13 블로그에 올린

사진들과 온라인 상점에서의 구매 기록들   **14** big, complex, big data experts, make decisions, predict the future
15 ⓑ → It included information about how much each player ran and how long he had the ball.   **16** (1) a map of crime hot spots (2) by focusing on the areas and the times a map of crime hot spots predicts

01 |해설| 「Have you ever＋과거분사 ~?」 형태로 경험 여부를 묻는 현재완료 문장이며, 과거분사 visited와 등위접속사 and로 연결되었으므로 과거분사를 사용한 been surprised가 알맞다.

02 |해설| This는 앞부분에서 언급한 내용, 즉 '온라인 서점이 당신이 무엇을 좋아하는지 알고 흥미로워 보이는 책들을 추천하는 것'을 가리킨다.

03 |해석| ① 빅데이터란 무엇인가?
② 빅데이터는 얼마나 큰가?
③ 빅데이터는 어디서 찾을 수 있는가?
④ 우리는 미래를 어떻게 예측할 수 있는가?
⑤ 정보 통신 기술은 얼마나 빨리 발전하고 있는가?
|해설| 빅데이터의 정의와 설명으로 이루어진 글이므로 글의 주제로 ①이 가장 적절하다.

04 |해석| ① 어떤 것을 하는 방법
② 어떤 것을 사는 행위
③ 어떤 것을 주의 깊게 검토하다
④ 누군가 또는 무언가를 멀리하다
⑤ 어떤 일이 일어날 것이라고 말하다
|해설| ①은 method, ②는 purchase, ③은 analyze, ⑤는 predict에 관한 영영풀이이다. ④는 avoid(피하다)에 해당하는 영영풀이로, 윗글에 없는 단어이다.

05 |해설| ⓑ 주어가 everything이므로 단수 취급하여 동사를 leaves로 써야 한다.
ⓔ '다양한 방법을 사용하여'라는 의미를 나타내는 분사구문이 되어야 하므로 현재분사 Using으로 써야 한다.
ⓕ 주어인 '결과들'이 의사결정이나 미래 예측에 '사용되는' 것이므로 수동태인 can be used로 써야 한다.

06 |해석| ② 필요로 하다 ③ 원하다 ④ 예상하다 ⑤ 영향을 미치다
|해설| '~가 …하도록 돕다'의 의미가 되는 것이 자연스러우며 목적격보어가 모두 동사원형(understand, sell, avoid)이므로, 「help＋목적어＋목적격보어(동사원형)」 형태로 쓰이는 동사 helps가 알맞다.

07 |해설| 그들은 또한 온라인상에서 독감 증상에 대해 더 많이 검색해 볼 것이다.
|해설| 주어진 문장의 주어가 they이고 also가 사용된 것으로 보아 독감의 계절이 되면 사람들이 할 행동으로 제시된 문장 뒤인 ④에 들어가는 것이 자연스럽다.

08 |해설| (A) make의 목적격보어 자리이므로 형용사가 알맞다.
(B) 전치사 by의 목적어이므로 동명사가 알맞다.
(C) was able to에 연결되어 improve와 병렬 관계를 이루므로 동사원형이 알맞다.

09 |해석| ⓐ 그것은 스포츠 선수들의 경기력에 영향을 미칠 수 있다.
ⓑ 독일 국가 대표 축구팀은 선수들에게 그것을 분석하게 했다.
ⓒ 그것 덕분에 독일은 2014년 월드컵을 개최하였다.

ⓓ 그것은 독일 국가 대표 축구팀이 2014년 월드컵에서 우승하는 것에 도움을 주었다.

|해설| ⓑ 독일 국가 대표 축구팀이 선수들에 대한 엄청난 양의 데이터를 모으고 분석했다는 언급은 있지만, 선수들에게 데이터 분석을 시켰다는 언급은 없다.

ⓒ 독일이 2014년 월드컵에서 우승했다는 내용은 있지만 월드컵을 개최했다는 내용은 없다.

10 |해석| 윗글의 빈칸 (A)에 들어갈 말로 알맞은 것은?
① 그것이 발생한 후에
② 그것이 발생하기 전에
③ 그들이 그것을 예방한 후에
④ 그들이 빅데이터를 분석하지만
⑤ 그들이 빅데이터를 분석하기 전에

|해설| ② 빈칸 앞에 범죄를 예측할 수 있다는 내용이 있으므로 문맥상 '범죄가 발생하기 전에'가 알맞다.

11 |해설| ⓐ be likely to+동사원형: ~할 것 같다 (→ to happen)

12 |해설| ⓑ the amount of data가 선행사이고 이어지는 절에서 have 의 목적어가 없으므로 목적격 관계대명사 that 또는 which가 쓰이는 것이 알맞다.
ⓔ 문맥상 '결정하는 데 사용되다'가 되어야 하므로 동사원형인 make 가 알맞다. 「be used to+동사원형」은 '~하는 데 사용되다'라는 의미이고, 「be used to+동명사」는 '~하는 데 익숙하다'라는 의미이다.

13 |해설| 윗글에서 trace(흔적)는 우리가 온라인상에서 하는 거의 모든 활동에서 생긴 것을 의미하며, 그 예시가 바로 뒤에 이어진다.

14 |해석| 빅데이터는 매우 크고 복잡한 데이터의 집합이며, 그것의 양은 이전보다 더 많아지고 있다. 그것은 빅데이터 전문가들에 의해 분석되며, 사람들은 그것의 결과를 의사결정을 하거나 미래를 예측하는 데 사용할 수 있다.

15 |해석| ⓐ 독일 축구팀은 데이터베이스를 구축하기 위해 얼마나 많은 데이터를 수집했는가?
ⓑ 독일 국가 대표 축구팀이 수집한 데이터는 무엇을 포함했는가?
ⓒ 독일은 2014년 월드컵 결승에서 어느 팀과 경기를 했는가?

|해설| 독일 국가 대표 축구팀이 수집한 데이터는 각 선수들이 얼마나 많이 달렸고, 얼마나 오랫동안 공을 갖고 있었는지에 관한 정보를 포함했다.

16 |해설| (1) 경찰은 빅데이터 분석을 통해 무엇을 만들 수 있는가?
→ 경찰은 범죄 다발 지역의 지도를 만들 수 있다.
(2) 경찰은 어떻게 추가 범죄를 예방할 수 있는가?
→ 경찰은 범죄 다발 지역의 지도가 예측하는 지역과 시간대에 집중함으로써 그것을 예방할 수 있다.

서술형 100% Test
pp. 210~213

01 (1) analyze (2) symptom (3) develop (4) spread
02 (1) is likely to (2) play a, role (3) focus on **03** (1) Can

〔Could〕 you tell me how to use this application? (2) I really appreciate your help. **04** ⓐ Finally → |모범 답| First ⓑ Don't mention it. → |모범 답| Thank you. **05** Do you know how to use it? **06** ⓑ Is that〔it〕 all? ⓒ It's so〔very〕 easy, isn't it? **07** (1) ⓑ → Place your library card on the screen. (2) ⓓ → Press ENTER. (3) ⓔ → Go to the front desk and get the book. **08** (1) while she sat〔was sitting〕 on the grass (2) If you turn left (3) Because she was too busy **09** (1) The boy soon fell asleep as he was very tired. (2) As we went up the mountain, it became colder. (3) As the teacher announced yesterday, the sports day will be canceled. **10** (1) Talking with me, he kept looking at his cell phone. (2) Not feeling comfortable, she left the party early. **11** (1) listening to music (2) Not having enough money **12** (1) Not knowing what to do, he asked for my help. (2) As he didn't know what to do, he asked for my help. / He asked for my help as he didn't know what to do. **13** (1) ⓑ → much〔even/far/still/a lot〕 (2) ⓓ → is done **14** Using various methods **15** (1) the photos you upload on your blog (2) the records of your purchases at online stores **16** It helps people avoid heavy traffic. **17** ⓒ → The spread of the flu can be predicted thanks to big data. **18** collecting and analyzing a huge amount of data, how much each player ran and how long he had the ball **19** big data will play a more and more important role in our lives **20** (1) the analysis of big data about the type, time and place of crime (2) identifies when and where crime is most likely to happen (3) prevent further crime (by focusing on the areas and the times the map predicts) 또는 predict crime before it happens

01 |해석| (1) 분석하다: 어떤 것을 주의 깊게 검토하다
(2) 증상: 특정한 병에 걸렸을지도 모른다는 것을 보여 주는 것
(3) 성장하다, 발달하다: 더 크고, 더 좋거나 더 중요한 것으로 성장하고 변화하다
(4) 확산, 전파: 어떤 것의 성장이나 발달로 인해 더 큰 지역이나 더 많은 수의 사람들에게 영향을 미치는 것

02 |해설| (1) be likely to: ~할 것 같다
(2) play a role: 역할을 하다
(3) focus on: ~에 집중하다

03 |해석| A: 실례합니다. 자전거를 빌리고 싶은데요. 이 앱을 어떻게 사용하는지 알려 주시겠어요?
B: 그럼요. 먼저, 앱에 로그인하세요. 그런 다음 RENT 버튼을 찾아서 터치하세요.
A: 그다음에는 뭘 하죠?
B: 그러면 앱이 자전거 잠금을 해제할 수 있는 번호를 알려 줄 거예요.
A: 고맙습니다. 도와주셔서 정말 감사해요.
|해설| (1) 어떤 일의 절차나 방법을 묻는 표현인 「Can you tell me how to+동사원형 ~?」을 사용한다.

⑵ Thank you for helping me.와 같은 의미로 I (really) appreciate your help.를 써서 감사를 표현할 수 있다.

04 |해석| A: 실례합니다. 교통 카드에 돈을 충전하는 방법을 알려 주시겠어요?
　　B: 그럼요. 마지막으로(→ 먼저), 기계에 카드를 넣으세요. 두 번째로, 충전하고 싶은 금액을 선택하세요.
　　A: 알겠어요.
　　B: 마지막으로, 기계에 돈을 넣으세요.
　　A: 간단한 것 같네요. 별말씀을요(→ 고맙습니다).
　|해설| ⓐ 첫 번째 절차를 설명하고 있으므로 Finally(마지막으로, 마침내)는 알맞지 않고, First를 쓰는 것이 알맞다.
　ⓑ 감사의 말에 응답하는 표현이 아니라 Thank you. 등 감사의 표현을 쓰는 것이 알맞다.

05 |해설| 로봇의 사용법을 알려 주는 말이 이어지므로 빈칸에는 로봇을 사용하는 방법을 묻는 표현이 알맞다. 단어 수로 보아 Do you know how to ~?를 사용해야 한다.

06 |해설| ⓑ 상대방이 말한 것이 전부인지 묻는 표현을 쓴다.
　ⓒ 앞의 문장에 대해 확인이나 동의를 구하는 부가의문문을 사용하여 문장을 쓴다. be동사가 사용된 평서문이므로 끝에 「, be동사+not의 축약형+주어?」의 형태로 부가의문문을 쓴다.

07 |해석| 당신을 위해 책을 찾아 주는 로봇
　이 로봇을 사용하는 방법
　1. 화면 위에 당신의 도서 대출 카드를 고른다(→ 댄다).
　2. 찾고 있는 책의 제목을 입력한다.
　3. FINISH(→ ENTER)를 누른다.
　4. 로봇으로(→ 안내 데스크로) 가서 책을 받는다.
　|해설| ⓑ 첫 번째로 화면에 도서 대출 카드를 대라고 했다.
　ⓓ 책 제목을 입력한 후에 ENTER를 누르라고 했다.
　ⓔ 안내 데스크로 가서 책을 받으라고 했다.

08 |해석| ⑴ 소녀는 잔디에 앉아서 일몰을 보았다.
　⑵ 왼쪽으로 돌면 그 서점을 볼 수 있다.
　⑶ 너무 바빠서 그녀는 파티에 갈 수 없었다.
　|해설| ⑴ 접속사 while과 주절의 주어와 같은 주어(she)를 쓰고, 동사를 주절에 맞게 과거시제 또는 과거진행형으로 쓴다.
　⑵ 접속사 if와 주절의 주어와 같은 주어(you)를 쓰고, 조건을 나타내는 부사절이므로 동사는 현재시제로 쓴다.
　⑶ 접속사 because와 주절의 주어와 같은 주어(she)를 쓴 후, 동사를 주절에 맞게 과거시제로 쓴다.

09 |해석| ⑴ 소년은 매우 피곤해서 곧 잠들었다.
　⑵ 우리가 산을 오를수록 더 추워졌다.
　⑶ 어제 선생님이 공지하셨듯이, 운동회는 취소될 것이다.
　|해설| ⑴은 '~ 때문에'를 뜻하는 접속사 as, ⑵는 '~함에 따라, 할수록'을 뜻하는 접속사 as, ⑶은 '~하듯이'를 뜻하는 접속사 as를 사용하여 부사절을 쓰고, 의미상 자연스럽게 어울리는 주절과 연결해 문장을 완성한다.

10 |해설| ⑴ 그는 나와 이야기하고 있었다. 그는 계속 휴대전화를 보았다.
　　→ 그는 나와 이야기하면서 계속 휴대전화를 보았다.
　⑵ 그녀는 마음이 편하지 않았다. 그녀는 파티를 일찍 떠났다.
　　→ 그녀는 마음이 편하지 않아서 파티를 일찍 떠났다.

|해설| ⑴ 첫 번째 문장을 동시동작을 나타내는 분사구문으로 쓴다.
　⑵ 첫 번째 문장을 이유를 나타내는 분사구문으로 쓴다. 분사구문의 부정은 분사 앞에 not을 써서 나타낸다.

11 |해석| ⑴ A: Peter, 뭐 하고 있니?
　　B: 내 블로그에 사진 몇 장을 올리고 있어. 지금 음악도 듣고 있어.
　　→ Peter는 음악을 들으면서 자신의 블로그에 사진 몇 장을 올리고 있다.
　⑵ A: 민지야, 왜 코트를 안 샀니?
　　B: 나는 충분한 돈이 없었어.
　　→ 충분한 돈이 없어서 민지는 코트를 살 수 없었다.
　|해설| ⑴ '음악을 들으면서'라는 의미로 동시동작을 나타내는 분사구문으로 쓴다.
　⑵ '충분한 돈이 없어서'라는 의미의 분사구문으로 쓴다. 분사구문의 부정은 분사 앞에 not을 써서 나타낸다.

12 |해설| ⑴ 동사원형에 -ing를 붙이고 앞에 not을 쓴 형태로 분사구문의 부정을 나타낸다.
　⑵ 이유를 나타내는 접속사 as를 사용하여 부사절을 쓴다.

13 |해설| ⓑ '훨씬'이라는 의미로 비교급을 강조하는 수식어는 much, a lot 등이며, very는 비교급을 수식할 수 없다.
　ⓓ 빅데이터 분석이 전문가들에 의해 '이루어지는' 것이므로 수동태(be동사+과거분사)로 쓰여야 한다.

14 |해설| 현재분사 Using으로 시작하는 분사구문을 쓴다.

15 |해설| For example로 시작하는 문장에 빅데이터의 구체적인 예시가 나와 있다.

16 |해설| '~가 …하도록 돕다'의 의미가 되도록 「help+목적어+목적격보어(동사원형)」의 형태로 문장을 완성한다.

17 |해설| ⓐ 빅데이터의 쓰임은 특정 산업에만 국한되지 않는다.
　ⓑ 빅데이터는 건강 전문가들이 질병을 예측하는 데 도움을 줄 수 있다.
　ⓒ 빅데이터 덕분에 독감의 증상(→ 확산)이 예측될 수 있다.
　|해설| ⓒ 독감의 증상(symptoms)이 아니라 확산(spread)이 예측될 수 있다고 하였다.

18 |해석| **기자**: 당신의 팀은 2014년 월드컵에서 우승했습니다. 그 비밀은 무엇이었나요?
　감독: 선수들에 대한 엄청난 양의 데이터를 수집하고 분석함으로써, 우리 팀은 경기력을 향상시킬 수 있었습니다.
　기자: 그것은 어떤 종류의 데이터였나요?
　감독: 그 데이터는 각 선수가 얼마나 뛰었는지, 얼마나 오랫동안 공을 가지고 있었는지에 대한 정보를 포함했습니다.
　기자: 와, 빅데이터는 정말로 스포츠를 더 흥미진진하게 만드네요.

19 |해설| '역할을 하다'라는 의미의 play a role를 사용하며, role을 수식하는 '점점 더 중요한'은 「비교급+and+비교급」(점점 더 ~한)을 사용하여 more and more important로 나타낸다.

20 |해석| ⑴ 경찰은 어떻게 범죄 다발 지역의 지도를 만들 수 있는가?
　　→ 그들은 범죄의 유형, 시간 및 장소에 관한 빅데이터 분석을 통해 그것을 만들 수 있다.
　⑵ 범죄 다발 지역의 지도가 하는 일은 무엇인가?
　　→ 그것은 범죄가 언제, 어디에서 가장 발생할 것 같은지를 알려 준다.
　⑶ 경찰은 범죄 다발 지역의 지도를 사용함으로써 무엇을 할 수 있는가?
　　→ 경찰은 (지도가 예측하는 지역과 시간대에 집중함으로써) 추가

범죄를 예방할 수 있다 / 범죄가 발생하기 전에 예측할 수 있다.

|해설| (1) 범죄의 유형과 시간 및 장소에 관한 빅데이터 분석을 통해 범죄 다발 지역의 지도를 만들 수 있다고 했다.

(2) 범죄 다발 지역의 지도는 언제, 어디에서 범죄가 가장 발생할 것 같은지를 알려 준다고 했다.

(3) 경찰은 범죄 다발 지역의 지도가 예측하는 장소와 시간대에 집중함으로써 추가 범죄를 예방할 수 있다고 했다. 또한 단락의 첫 부분에서 범죄가 일어나기 전에 범죄를 예측할 수 있다고도 했다.

모의고사

제 **1** 회   대표 기출로 내신 **적중** 모의고사   pp. 214~217

01 ②　02 ③　03 ②　04 ②　05 ④　06 (A) ⓒ (B) ⓐ (C) ⓑ　07 (D)-(A)-(C)-(B)　08 Can(Could) you tell me how to use it?　09 ②　10 find　11 ③　12 ①
13 entering the room　14 ④　15 ②　16 big data
17 ②　18 ④　19 ⑤　20 ③　21 (1) ⓑ → making
(2) '만들면서'라는 뜻으로 동시동작을 나타내는 분사구문이 되어야 하므로 현재분사인 making으로 써야 한다.　22 ③　23 ④
24 ①　25 (1) analyzing (2) crime hot spots (3) prevent

01 |해석| 잠그다 – (잠긴 것을) 열다
① 현명한 – 현명하게 ② 간단한 – 복잡한 ③ 국가 – 국가의
④ 가능한 – 아마 ⑤ 예측하다 – 예측하다
|해설| [보기]와 ②는 반의어 관계이다. (①, ④ 형용사 – 부사, ③ 명사 – 형용사, ⑤ 유의어)

02 |해석| 누군가 또는 무언가를 멀리하다
① 모으다, 수집하다 ② 분석하다 ④ 알아보다 ⑤ 예측하다
|해설| avoid(피하다)의 영영풀이이다.

03 |해석| • 교사들은 우리 사회에서 중요한 역할을 한다.
• 밖이 너무 시끄럽다. 나는 공부에 집중할 수 없다.
|해설| play a role: 역할을 하다 / focus on: ~에 집중하다

04 |해석| ① 그 개는 흔적도 없이 사라졌다.
② 부모님은 내 인생에 가장 많은 영향을 주신다.
③ 한국의 영화 산업은 빠르게 성장하고 있다.
④ 당신은 다음 구매에 할인을 받을 수 있습니다.
⑤ 우리의 목표는 질병의 확산을 막는 것이다.
|해설| ② influence는 '영향을 미치다'라는 뜻이다.

05 |해석| A: 감자 심는 방법을 알려 주겠니?
B: 그럼. 먼저, 감자를 작은 조각으로 잘라.
① 너는 감자를 심고 싶니?
② 너는 어디에 감자를 심었니?
③ 너는 감자를 언제 심어야 하는지 아니?
⑤ 너는 감자를 몇 개 심을 예정이니?
|해설| 이어지는 대답으로 보아 감자를 심는 방법을 알려 달라는 말이

알맞다.

06 |해석| A: 저는 과자를 사고 싶어요. 이 과자 자판기를 어떻게 사용하는지 아세요?
B: 네. 먼저, 원하는 과자를 고르세요.
A: 이미 했어요. 그다음은 뭔가요?
B: 돈을 넣으세요. 그런 다음 과자를 꺼내세요.
A: 알겠어요. 고마워요.
|해설| (A)에는 과자 자판기 사용 방법을 묻는 말, (B)에는 다음 단계를 묻는 말, (C)에는 감사를 표현하는 말이 알맞다.

07 |해석| (D) 너는 차 만드는 방법을 아니?
(A) 그럼. 먼저, 컵에 티백을 넣어. 그런 다음, 그 컵에 뜨거운 물을 부어.
(C) 알겠어.
(B) 마지막으로, 3분 뒤에 티백을 꺼내.
A: 알겠어. 도와줘서 정말 고마워.
|해설| 차 만드는 방법을 아는지 묻자(D) 그에 대한 첫 번째와 두 번째 절차를 알려 준(A) 다음 알겠다는 대답(C)을 듣고 마지막 절차를 설명하는(B) 흐름이 자연스럽다.

08 |해설| 로봇 사용 방법을 설명하는 말이 이어지는 것으로 보아, 빈칸에는 방법이나 절차를 물을 때 사용하는 표현인 「Can you tell me how to+동사원형 ~?」으로 로봇 사용 방법을 묻는 말을 쓰는 것이 알맞다.

09 |해석| ① 당신은 로봇을 도와야 한다
② 로봇이 그 책을 찾을 것이다
③ 당신은 책값을 지불해야 한다
④ 로봇이 그 책을 읽을 것이다
⑤ 로봇이 당신에게 도서 대출 카드를 줄 것이다
|해설| 로봇의 용도가 책을 찾아 주는 것이라고 했으므로 로봇이 책을 찾아서 안내 데스크로 가져다줄 것이라는 내용이 알맞다.

10 |해석| 사람들은 도서관에서 책을 찾고 싶을 때 로봇을 사용할 수 있다.
|해설| 로봇이 사람들이 찾고 있는 책을 찾아서 안내 데스크로 가져다준다는 내용의 대화이므로, 사람들이 도서관에서 책을 찾을(find) 때 로봇을 사용할 수 있다고 하는 것이 알맞다.

11 |해석| 나는 길을 따라 걷다가 옛 친구를 만났다.
|해설| ③ '길을 따라 걷다가'라는 뜻의 시간을 나타내는 분사구문이 되는 것이 알맞으므로, 현재분사 형태가 알맞다.

12 |해석| ① 내가 전에 말했듯이, 나는 약속을 지킨다.
② 지나는 긴장했기 때문에 실수를 했다.
③ 그 영화가 지루해서 Jason은 잠들었다.
④ 우리는 회의에 늦었기 때문에 서둘렀다.
⑤ Jenny가 학교에 오지 않아서 나는 그녀에게 전화를 했다.
|해설| ①의 As는 '~하듯이'라는 뜻의 접속사로 쓰였고, 나머지는 모두 '~ 때문에'라는 뜻으로 쓰였다.

13 |해석| Cathy는 방에 들어서면서 우리를 향해 웃었다.
|해설| 접속사 As를 생략하고, 주절의 주어(she)와 같은 대상을 가리키므로 부사절의 주어(Cathy)를 생략한 뒤, 동사 entered를 현재분사 형태로 바꾸어 동시동작을 나타내는 분사구문을 쓴다.

14 |해석| ⓐ 그는 내가 요청했던 대로 했다.
ⓑ 우리는 샌드위치를 먹으며 TV를 시청했다.
ⓒ 그녀는 나이가 들수록 더 현명해졌다.

ⓓ 나는 추워서 난방기구를 틀었다.

ⓔ 열심히 노력하면 분명히 시험에 통과할 것이다.

|해설| ⓑ '먹으면서'라는 능동의 뜻을 나타내도록 현재분사를 써서 분사구문으로 나타낸다. (eaten → eating)

ⓓ 분사구문의 주어와 주절의 주어가 같은 경우 분사구문의 주어는 생략한다. (I feeling → Feeling)

15 |해설| 주어진 문장은 '이것은 우리가 온라인상에서 하는 거의 모든 것들이 흔적을 남기기 때문이다'라는 내용으로, 주어 This가 가리키는 내용(정보 통신 기술이 발달함에 따라 우리가 가진 데이터의 양이 훨씬 더 많아지고 있다) 뒤이면서 온라인상에 남기는 흔적들의 예시(블로그에 올린 사진과 온라인 상점에서의 구입 기록)를 다룬 문장 앞인 ②에 들어가는 것이 자연스럽다.

16 |해설| 빅데이터에 대해 설명하면서 빅데이터가 될 수 있는 것들의 예를 들고 있으므로, 빈칸에는 big data가 알맞다.

17 |해석| ① 빅데이터를 수집하는 것

② 빅데이터를 분석하는 것

③ 빅데이터를 구매하는 것

④ 다양한 방법들을 사용하는 것

⑤ 의사결정을 하거나 미래를 예측하는 것

|해설| this는 문장 앞 부분의 Big data has to be analyzed를 가리킨다.

18 |해설| 이어서 빅데이터가 우리 생활에서 활용되는 예들을 설명하고 있으므로, 우리 삶의 거의 모든 부분에 '영향을 미치고(influencing)' 있다는 내용이 되어야 자연스럽다.

19 |해설| 마지막 문장에서 '빅데이터의 쓰임은 끝이 없고 여기 그 흥미로운 예들이 몇 가지 있다'라고 했으므로, 다양하게 쓰이는 빅데이터의 예시를 다루는 내용이 이어질 것임을 유추할 수 있다.

20 |해석| 빅데이터를 활용한 질병 예측

① 시장 조사 ② 온라인 검색 ④ 날씨 예측 ⑤ 사고 예방

|해설| 빅데이터 덕분에 질병 예측(disease forecast)이 가능해졌다는 내용의 글이다.

21 |해설| ⓑ '스포츠를 더 흥미진진하게 만들면서'라는 의미의 분사구문이 되도록 현재분사 making을 써야 한다.

22 |해설| this database는 독일 국가 대표 축구팀이 선수들에 대한 자료를 모아 분석하여 만든 것으로, ③ 독일 국가 대표 축구 선수들이 얼마나 오랫동안 공을 갖고 있었는지도 포함했다고 언급되었다.

23 |해석| ① 빅데이터는 무엇인가

② 경찰의 역할

③ 빅데이터의 정의

④ 우리 생활에서의 빅데이터의 영향(력)

⑤ 일상 생활에서 빅데이터를 수집하는 방법

|해설| 범죄를 예방하는 빅데이터의 활용 예시를 들며 빅데이터가 우리의 일상생활에서 점점 더 중요한 역할을 하게 될 것이라는 내용의 글이므로, 글의 주제로 ④ '우리 생활에서의 빅데이터의 영향(력)'이 알맞다.

24 |해설| ⓐ '~ 덕분에'라는 뜻의 thanks to가 되는 것이 알맞다. thanks for는 '~에 대한 감사'라는 뜻이다.

25 |해설| 빅데이터를 <u>분석함으로써</u> 경찰은 <u>범죄 다발</u> 지역의 지도를 만들고, 그것을 추가 범죄를 <u>예방하는</u> 데 사용할 수 있다.

제2회 대표 기출로 내신 **적중** 모의고사　pp. 218~221

01 ③　02 ⑤　03 to　04 ④　05 ③　06 Can you tell me how to add money to my transportation card?

07 ⑤　08 ②　09 **|모범 답|** I really appreciate your help.

10 (C)-(B)-(A)　11 ④　12 ③, ④　13 As Tony grew older, he became braver.　14 ⑤　15 ③　16 ⑤

17 ④　18 ③　19 ①, ③　20 (1) influence (2) disease

21 making sports more exciting　22 ⑤　23 ④　24 ①

25 police can predict crime before it happens 또는 police can prevent further crime

01 |해석| ① 현명하게 ② 주로 ④ 규칙적으로 ⑤ 일반적으로

|해설| ③은 '친절한, 상냥한'의 의미로 「명사+-ly」 형태의 형용사이고, 나머지는 모두 「형용사+-ly」 형태의 부사이다.

02 |해석| ① 영향을 미치다: 어떤 것을 바꾸거나 어떤 것에 영향을 주다

② 범죄: 법이 허용하지 않는 행위

③ 피하다: 누군가 또는 무언가를 멀리하다

④ 포함하다: 무언가를 전체의 일부로 가지고 있다

⑤ 증상(→ 데이터베이스): 컴퓨터 시스템에 저장된 대량의 정보

|해설| ⑤의 영영풀이에 해당하는 단어는 database(데이터베이스)이다. symptom은 '증상'이라는 뜻으로, 알맞은 영영풀이는 something that shows you may have a particular illness이다.

03 |해석| • 그는 여기에 정시에 도착할 것 같지 않다.

• 인터넷 덕분에 우리의 삶은 더 편리해졌다.

|해설| be likely to: ~할 것 같다 / thanks to: ~ 덕분에

04 |해석| ① 열은 감기 증상이다.

② 우리가 알고 있듯이, 캐나다는 거대한 나라이다.

③ 미국에는 많은 국립공원이 있다.

④ 나는 그 차를 구매해서 돈을 많이 벌었다. (×)

⑤ 오늘의 일기 예보에 대해 들었니?

|해설| ④ 문맥상 '차를 팔고 돈을 벌었다'라는 뜻이 자연스러우므로 purchase(구입, 구매)는 어색하다.

05 |해석| A: 저는 과자를 사고 싶어요. 이 과자 자판기를 어떻게 사용하는지 아세요?

B: 네. 먼저, 원하는 과자를 고르세요.

A: 이미 했어요. <u>그다음은 뭔가요?</u>

B: 돈을 넣으세요. 그런 다음 과자를 꺼내세요.

A: 알겠어요. 고마워요.

|해설| 주어진 문장은 그다음 절차가 무엇인지를 묻는 말이므로 B가 알려 준 첫 번째 절차를 이미 했다고 말한 다음인 ③에 들어가는 것이 자연스럽다.

06 |해석| A: 실례합니다. 교통 카드에 돈을 충전하는 방법을 알려 주시겠어요?

B: 그럼요. 먼저, 기계에 카드를 넣으세요.

|해설| 상대방에게 어떤 일을 하는 방법이나 절차를 물을 때 「Can you tell me how to+동사원형 ~?」으로 말한다.

07 |해석| A: 실례합니다. 자전거를 빌리고 싶은데요. 이 앱을 어떻게 사용하는지 알려 주시겠어요?

B: 그럼요. 먼저, 앱에 로그인하세요. 그런 다음 RENT 버튼을 찾아서 터치하세요.

A: 그다음에는 뭘 하죠?

B: 그러면 앱이 자전거 잠금을 해제할 수 있는 번호를 알려 줄 거예요.

A: 고맙습니다. 천만에요. (×)

|해설| ⑤ Don't mention it.은 상대방의 고맙다는 말에 대한 응답이므로, 고맙다는 말에 덧붙이는 말로 적절하지 않다.

08 |해설| ① 실례합니다　　　② 책 좀 찾아 주실래요?

③ 그게 다인가요?　　　④ 그러면

⑤ 아주 쉬워요, 그렇지 않아요?

|해설| ⑥ 뒤에 이어지는 내용이 책을 찾아 주는 로봇을 사용하는 방법에 대한 설명이므로, 빈칸에는 로봇 사용법을 묻는 말이 들어가는 것이 알맞다.

09 |해설| I appreciate ~.으로 상대방에게 감사를 표현할 수 있다.

10 |해설| 로봇 화면에 도서 대출 카드를 대고(C) 책의 제목을 입력한(B) 후 안내 데스크에서 책을 받는(A) 순서가 알맞다.

11 |해석| 그는 친절하기 때문에 모두가 그를 좋아한다.

|해설| As가 '~ 때문에'라는 뜻의 이유를 나타내는 접속사로 쓰였으므로 Because와 바꿔 쓸 수 있다.

12 |해석| 그녀는 음악을 크게 틀어 놓고/노래를 부르며 스파게티를 요리했다.

|해설| 빈칸에는 현재분사로 시작하는 분사구문이 올 수 있는데, 분사구문의 의미를 명확하게 하기 위해 현재분사 앞에 접속사를 쓸 수도 있다.

13 |해석| Tony는 더 나이가 들었다. 그는 더 용감해졌다.

→ Tony는 나이가 들수록 더 용감해졌다.

|해설| '~함에 따라, ~할수록'이라는 뜻을 나타내는 접속사 as를 사용하여 부사절을 쓴다.

14 |해석| ① 나는 노래를 부를 때 초인종 소리를 들었다.

② 내가 집에 도착했을 때, 아무도 집에 없었다.

③ 아기는 밝게 웃으며 엄마에게로 걸어갔다.

④ 나는 계단을 내려가다가 동전을 발견했다.

⑤ 그녀는 한국어를 몰라서 그 책을 읽을 수가 없었다.

|해설| ⑤ 첫 번째 문장은 '그녀는 한국어를 몰라서 그 책을 읽을 수 없었다.'라는 뜻이고, 두 번째 문장은 '그녀는 한국어를 알지만 그 책을 읽을 수 없었다.'라는 뜻이다.

15 |해설| ⑥ that은 목적격 관계대명사로 선행사 the books를 수식하는 관계대명사절을 이끈다.

ⓐ 경험 여부를 묻는 현재완료 표현이므로 과거분사 visited가 알맞다.

ⓒ 책들이 흥미롭게 보이는 것이므로 현재분사형 형용사 interesting이 알맞다.

ⓓ 뒤에 명사(구)가 이어지므로 because of가 알맞다.

16 |해석| ① 내가 말하는 대로 해 주세요.

② 나는 졸려서 서둘러 잠자리에 들었다.

③ 나갈 때 불을 꺼 줄래?

④ 내 차가 고장 났기 때문에 나는 직장에 늦었다.

⑤ 인구가 증가함에 따라 사람들은 더 많은 집이 필요하다.

|해설| (A)와 ⑤의 As는 '~함에 따라'라는 의미로 쓰였다.

17 |해석| 전문가들에 의해 분석된 빅데이터로부터의 의미 있는 결과들은 미래를 예측하는 데 사용될 수 있다.

18 |해설| ⓒ 문맥상 빅데이터 덕분에 질병 예측이 가능하다(possible)라고 하는 것이 알맞다.

19 |해설| '독감의 계절이 올 때'라는 의미가 되어야 자연스러우므로 빈칸에는 때를 나타내는 접속사인 as나 when이 알맞다.

20 |해설| 빅데이터가 우리 생활에 미치는 영향과 그것이 질병 예측에 쓰일 수 있는 방법

|해설| 빅데이터가 우리의 생활에 주는 영향과 그 한 가지 예로 빅데이터가 질병 예측에 쓰이는 것을 설명하는 글이다.

21 |해설| '~하면서'라는 의미를 나타내는 분사구문으로 쓴다. 분사구문은 현재분사(동사원형+-ing)로 시작하며, '(목적어가) ~하게 하다'는 「make+목적어+목적격보어(형용사)」의 어순으로 쓴다.

22 |해설| ① ~ 대신에　② ~에 대한 감사　③ ~에 덧붙여

④ ~와 대조를 이루어

|해설| 독일 국가 대표 축구팀이 구축한 데이터베이스의 도움으로(with the help of) 독일 국가 대표 축구팀은 경기력을 향상시키고 2014년 월드컵에서 우승할 수 있었다는 내용이 되는 것이 자연스럽다.

23 |해석| ① 빅데이터는 스포츠에서 사용될 수 있다.

② 독일 국가 대표 축구팀은 빅데이터 사용의 좋은 예이다.

③ 독일의 국가 대표 축구팀은 데이터베이스를 구축하기 위해 선수들에 관한 많은 데이터를 모았다.

④ 독일 국가 대표 축구팀이 수집한 데이터는 팀에서 누가 가장 빨리 달리는지 보여 주었다.

⑤ 선수들에 관한 데이터베이스는 독일 국가 대표 축구팀이 2014년 월드컵에서 우승하는 데 도움이 되었다.

|해설| ④ 독일 국가 대표 축구팀이 수집한 데이터에 선수들 중 누가 가장 빠른지에 대한 정보가 있는지는 본문에 언급되어 있지 않다.

24 |해설| (A) be likely to+동사원형: ~할 것 같다

(B) 전치사 by의 목적어이므로 동명사인 focusing이 알맞다.

(C) 동사 agree의 목적어 역할을 하는 명사절을 이끄는 접속사 that이 알맞다.

25 |해석| 빅데이터를 사용함으로써 이제 경찰은 범죄가 일어나기 전에 예측할 수 있다 / 경찰은 추가 범죄를 예방할 수 있다.

|해설| 빅데이터가 우리 생활에서 점점 더 중요한 역할을 하게 된 것의 예시로 본문에는 빅데이터를 활용하여 범죄를 예측하고 예방할 수 있다는 내용이 언급되었다.

제3회 대표 기출로 내신 **적중** 모의고사　**pp. 222~225**

01 ②　02 ④　03 ②　04 ③, ④　05 how to use a drink machine　06 ④　07 ①　08 (A)-(C)-(B)　09 ⑤
10 as　11 Arrived → Arriving　12 ②　13 ④　14 ⑤
15 우리가 온라인상에서 하는 거의 모든 것들이 흔적을 남기기 때문에　16 ④　17 ②　18 ⓔ → comes　19 ④　20 ③
21 information about how much each player ran
22 (1) helped　(2) performance　(3) win　23 ①　24 ②
25 ⑤

01 |해석| • 나는 그 질문에 쉽게 답할 수 있었다.
• 건강하기 위해서 우리는 규칙적인 식사를 해야 한다.
|해설| 첫 번째 빈칸에는 동사 answer를 수식하는 부사 easily가, 두 번째 빈칸에는 명사 meals를 수식하는 형용사 regular가 알맞다.

02 |해석| ① 나는 배의 윤곽선을 그리고 있다.
② 페이지 하단에 선을 그리시오.
③ 너희 가족 그림을 그리는 게 어때?
④ 너는 회의에서 결론을 이끌어 냈니?
⑤ 내 남동생은 여가 시간에 그림 그리는 것을 좋아한다.
|해설| ④의 draw는 '(결과를) 이끌어 내다, 도출하다'라는 뜻으로 쓰였고, 나머지는 모두 '그리다'라는 뜻으로 쓰였다.

03 |해석| • Jessica 덕분에 나는 내 손목시계를 찾을 수 있었다.
• 그는 대화에 집중하려고 노력했다.
• 이 팀이 경기에서 승리할 가능성이 가장 높다.
• 우리는 재활용을 통해 엄청난 양의 에너지를 절약할 수 있다.
• 스마트폰은 우리 생활에서 중요한 역할을 하고 있다.
|해설| ⓑ '~에 집중하다'라는 뜻의 focus on이 되는 것이 알맞다.

04 |해석| A: 초대해 주셔서 감사해요.
B: 천만에요.
① 죄송하지만 당신을 초대할 수 없을 것 같아요.
② 당신을 저녁 식사에 초대하고 싶어요.
③ 초대해 주셔서 정말 감사해요.
④ 초대해 주셔서 진심으로 감사드려요.
⑤ 당신이 초대받지 못하다니 유감이네요.
|해설| 밑줄 친 문장과 ③, ④는 모두 초대해 줘서 고맙다고 감사를 표현하는 말이다.

05 |해석| A: 음료 자판기 사용하는 방법을 아니?
B: 물론이야. 먼저 기계에 돈을 넣어. 그런 다음, 원하는 음료를 고르고 기계에서 음료를 꺼내.
A: 와, 쉽구나.
→ 화자들은 음료 자판기를 사용하는 방법에 대해 이야기를 나누고 있다.
|해설| '~하는 방법'은 「how to+동사원형」으로 나타낸다.

06 |해석| ① A: 그다음은 뭐니?
B: 그런 다음, 돈을 넣어.
② A: 그게 다야?
B: 아니. 마지막으로, 네 카드를 빼.
③ A: 도와줘서 고마워.
B: 내가 좋아서 한 거야.
④ A: 너는 차를 만드는 방법을 아니?
B: 물론이지. 알겠어. (×)
⑤ A: 이 앱을 사용하는 방법을 알려 주시겠어요?
B: 물론이죠. 먼저, 앱에 로그인하세요.
|해설| ④ I got it.은 '알겠어.' 또는 '이해했다.'라는 의미로, 방법을 알려 주는 말을 듣고 나서 할 수 있는 말이므로, 차 만드는 방법을 아는지 묻는 말에 대한 응답으로 어색하다.

07 |해설| 로봇이 사람들이 찾고 있는 책을 찾아서 안내 데스크로 가져다준다고 했으므로, 책을 찾아 주는(finds) 로봇이라고 용도를 설명하는 것이 알맞다.

08 |해설| 첫 번째 절차를 듣고 나서 알겠다고 답을 한 후, 두 번째 절차를

듣고(A) 그것이 전부인지 묻자(C) 그렇다고 답하고 나서 부연 설명을 해 주는(B) 대화의 흐름이 자연스럽다.

09 |해석| ① 누가 로봇의 사용법을 아는가?
② 사람들은 어디에서 그 로봇을 사용할 수 있는가?
③ 로봇을 사용하기 위해서는 무엇이 필요한가?
④ 로봇을 사용하기 위한 마지막 절차는 무엇인가?
⑤ 로봇을 사용하는 데 비용은 얼마나 드는가?
|해설| ⑤ 로봇을 사용하는 비용은 대화에 언급되어 있지 않다.

10 |해석| • 날이 어두워지고 있어서 우리는 집에 가기로 결정했다.
• Sam은 도서관에서 사서로 일하고 있다.
|해설| 첫 번째 빈칸에는 '~ 때문에'의 의미로 쓰이는 접속사 as, 두 번째 빈칸에는 '~로서'의 의미로 쓰이는 전치사 as가 알맞다.

11 |해석| A: 호수로 갔던 주말 여행은 어땠니?
B: 너도 알다시피, 날씨가 좋았어. 우리는 그곳에 도착하자마자 텐트를 치고 호수로 낚시하러 갔어.
|해설| 때를 나타내는 분사구문으로, 주어(we)가 '도착해서, 도착하자마자'라는 능동의 의미가 되어야 하므로, 현재분사 Arriving이 쓰여야 한다.

12 |해석| [보기] 네가 좋을 대로 해라.
① 날이 갈수록 더 추워진다.
② 너는 왜 그가 네게 말한 대로 하지 않았니?
③ 일요일이기 때문에 나는 일찍 일어날 필요가 없다.
④ 나는 창문을 열었을 때 Tom이 뛰고 있는 것을 보았다.
⑤ 그가 내 집 근처에 살기 때문에 그는 종종 나를 본다.
|해설| [보기]와 ②의 as는 '~하는 대로'라는 뜻의 접속사로 쓰였다.

13 |해석| ⓐ 나는 바빠서 그녀에게 전화하지 않았다.
ⓑ 우리는 악수를 하면서 서로 인사했다.
ⓒ 왼쪽으로 돌면 그 건물을 발견할 것이다.
ⓓ 그녀는 버스에서 내리기 전에 Jake를 만났다.
ⓔ 내가 밖으로 나가려고 할 때 누군가가 문을 두드렸다.
|해설| ⓒ 조건을 나타내는 분사구문이 되는 것이 알맞다. 주어(you)가 '왼쪽으로 돌면'이라는 능동의 의미가 되어야 하므로 현재분사 Turning을 써야 한다. (Turned → Turning)

14 |해석| Tom은 축구를 하다가 팔이 부러졌다.
|해설| 밑줄 친 분사구문을 의미상 '~하는 동안'을 뜻하는 접속사 while이 쓰인 부사절로 바꾸는 것이 알맞다. 부사절의 주어는 주절의 주어(Tom)와 같은 he로 쓰며, 동사는 주절과 같도록 과거시제나 과거진행형으로 쓴다.

15 |해설| 뒤 문장(This is mainly because ~.)에 우리가 갖고 있는 데이터의 양이 이전보다 훨씬 더 많아지고 있는 이유가 언급되어 있다.

16 |해설| ⓑ '다양한 방법들을 사용하여'라는 의미를 나타내는 분사구문이 되어야 하므로 현재분사 형태인 Using이 알맞다.
ⓒ 결과들(These results)이 결정을 하거나 미래를 예측하는 데 '사용될' 수 있다는 내용이 되도록 수동태(be동사+과거분사)로 써야 한다.

17 |해설| ② 온라인 상점에서 구매한 기록도 빅데이터의 일부라고 했다.

18 |해설| ⓔ 시간을 나타내는 부사절에서는 미래의 일도 현재시제로 쓴다.

19 |해석| ① 독감이 빠르게 확산될 수 있다
② 독감 약이 효과가 있다
③ 독감이 더 자주 생길 것이다

④ 독감의 확산이 예측될 수 있다

⑤ 다양한 독감 증상들이 사라지지 않을 것이다

|해설| 빅데이터 덕분에 건강 전문가들의 질병 예측이 가능하다고 했으므로, 독감 관련 데이터가 현명하게 분석되면 ④ '독감의 확산이 예측될 수 있다'고 하는 것이 알맞다.

20 |해석| 그 팀은 선수들에 관한 엄청난 양의 데이터를 모으고 분석함으로써 데이터베이스를 구축했다.

|해설| 주어진 문장은 독일 국가 대표 축구팀이 선수들에 대한 데이터베이스를 구축했다는 내용으로, 주어 The team은 ③ 앞에 언급된 Germany's national soccer team을 가리킨다. 또한, ③ 뒤의 문장에 있는 the data가 주어진 문장의 a huge amount of data on players를 가리키므로 ③에 들어가는 것이 자연스럽다.

21 |해설| information about 뒤에 전치사의 목적어 역할을 하는 간접의문문(의문사＋주어＋동사)을 쓴다. '얼마나 많이'를 how much로 쓰는 것에 유의한다.

22 |해석| 독일 국가 대표 축구팀에 의해 구축된 데이터베이스는 팀이 경기력을 향상하고 2014년 월드컵에서 우승하게 도왔다.

23 |해설| ⓐ thanks to: ~ 덕분에

ⓒ by -ing: ~함으로써

24 |해석| ⓐ 그것은 범죄 다발 지역을 보여 준다.

ⓑ 그것은 추가 범죄를 예방하는 데 도움이 될 수 있다.

ⓒ 그것은 범죄에 관한 빅데이터 분석을 통해 만들어진다.

ⓓ 그것은 범죄가 일어날 것 같은 이유를 예측한다.

|해설| ⓓ This map은 바로 앞에 언급된 a map of crime hot spots를 가리키며, 이 지도는 범죄가 일어날 것 같은 이유가 아니라 지역과 시간대를 예측한다고 했다.

25 |해설| 마지막 문장에서 전문가들이 빅데이터에 관해 동의하는 바를 알 수 있다.

제 4 회 고난도로 내신 **적중** 모의고사   pp. 226~229

01 ③   **02** influence   **03** ⑤   **04** ⑤   **05** ②   **06** Can you tell me how to use this(the) printer
07 ⓔ → |모범 답| Thank you. / I (really) appreciate your help.
08 what is this robot for   **09** ③   **10** (1) How to (2) Place your(the) library card (3) Type the title of the book (you're looking for) (4) Press ENTER (5) Go to the front desk
11 ①, ④   **12** ⑤   **13** ③   **14** ②   **15** ①, ③, ④   **16** ④
17 ③   **18** making → make   **19** ②   **20** ⓒ → They can (now) forecast a disease (using big data).   **21** ③   **22** (A) how much each player ran   (B) how long he had the ball
23 ②   **24** ⑤   **25** ②

01 |해석| 방법 : 방법 = 병 : 병

① 독감 ② 흔적, 자취 ④ 확산, 전파 ⑤ 예방, 방지

|해설| method(방법)와 way(방법)는 유의어 관계이므로 빈칸에는 illness(병, 질병)의 유의어인 disease가 알맞다.

---

02 |해석| ⑧ 어떤 것을 바꾸거나 어떤 것에 영향을 주다

⑩ 사람들이나 사물에 영향을 미치는 힘

|해설| 두 의미를 모두 나타내는 단어는 influence(영향을 미치다; 영향)이다.

03 |해석| ① 나는 축구 광팬이다.

그 화재의 원인은 선풍기였다.

② 그녀는 내게 매우 친절했다.

너는 어떤 종류의 음악을 좋아하니?

③ 그는 버스에 무엇을 두고 내렸나요?

부산으로 떠나는 기차는 얼마나 자주 있나요?

④ 종이에 직선을 그리시오.

너는 그 보고서에서 어떤 결과를 도출했니?

⑤ Jackson은 자신의 경기력을 향상하기 위해 매일 훈련했다.

그는 그의 축구팀 팀원들의 경기력을 칭찬했다.

|해설| ⑤ 두 문장의 performance는 '경기력, 수행(력)'이라는 뜻으로 쓰였다.

04 |해석| ① 도와주셔서 감사합니다.

② 정말 고맙습니다.

③ 당신에게 감사를 표현하고 싶어요.

④ 도와주셔서 고마워요.

⑤ 도와주시면 감사하겠습니다.

|해설| ⑤는 '도와주시면 감사하겠습니다.'라는 부탁의 의미이고, 나머지는 모두 (도움에) 감사하는 표현이다.

05 |해석| A: 감자 심는 방법을 알려 주겠니?

B: 그럼. 먼저, 감자를 작은 조각으로 잘라. 둘째로, 땅에 구멍을 파.

A: 그다음에는?

B: 그런 다음 구멍에 감자 조각들을 넣고 흙으로 구멍을 덮어.

A: 간단한 것 같네. 고마워.

① 알겠어. ② 무슨 일 있니? ③, ④, ⑤ 그 다음에는?

|해설| 빈칸에는 알겠다는 응답이나 다음 순서를 묻는 말이 알맞다. ②는 무슨 일이 있는지 묻는 표현이다.

06 |해석| Ryan은 과학 보고서를 인쇄하기 위해 도서관에 갔지만 그는 프린터를 사용할 줄 몰랐다. 그때, 그는 반 친구인 Jane을 보았다. 그녀는 다른 컴퓨터에서 무언가를 출력하고 있었다.

Ryan: 안녕, Jane. 이 프린터를 어떻게 사용하는지 알려 주겠니?

|해설| 프린터를 사용할 줄 아는 Jane에게 「Can you tell me how to＋동사원형 ~?」을 사용하여 프린터 사용 방법을 알려 달라고 요청하는 것이 알맞다.

07 |해석| A: 실례합니다. 자전거를 빌리고 싶은데요. 이 앱을 어떻게 사용하는지 알려 주시겠어요?

B: 그럼요. 먼저, 앱에 로그인하세요. 그런 다음 RENT 버튼을 찾아서 터치하세요.

A: 그다음에는 뭘 하죠?

B: 그러면 앱이 자전거 잠금을 해제할 수 있는 번호를 알려 줄 거예요.

A: 알겠어요. 그 말을 들으니 정말 유감이에요.(→ 도와주셔서 정말 감사해요.)

|해설| ⓔ 절차를 설명해 준 상대방에게 유감을 표현하는 것은 어색하다. 감사하다는 말을 하는 것이 알맞다.

08 |해설| What is(are) ~ for?는 물건의 용도를 묻는 표현이다.

09 **|해석|** ① 도서관에는 사람들을 도울 수 있는 로봇이 있다.

② 세호가 Lucy에게 로봇 사용법을 알려 준다.

③ 로봇을 사용하기 위해서는 학생증이 있어야 한다.

④ 찾고 있는 책의 제목을 로봇에 입력하면 로봇이 그것을 찾아 줄 것이다.

⑤ Lucy는 이 로봇이 사용하기 쉽다고 생각한다.

|해설| ③ 도서 대출 카드를 화면에 대야 하므로, 학생증이 아니라 도서 대출 카드가 필요하다.

10 **|해석|** 이 로봇을 사용하는 방법

STEP 1. 화면 위에 당신의 도서 대출 카드를 댄다.

STEP 2. (찾고 있는) 책의 제목을 입력한다.

STEP 3. ENTER를 누른다.

STEP 4. 안내 데스크로 가서 책을 받는다.

|해설| 로봇 화면에 도서 대출 카드를 대고, 책의 제목을 입력한 뒤 ENTER를 누른 후, 로봇이 찾아온 책을 안내 데스크에 가서 받으면 된다고 세호가 로봇 사용법을 알려 주었다.

11 **|해석|** 그녀와 이야기를 하면 너는 그녀를 잘 이해할 수 있다.

|해설| 조건을 나타내는 분사구문이므로 접속사 if를 쓴 부사절로 바꿔 쓸 수 있다. 분사구문의 주어가 생략되어 있는 것으로 보아 부사절의 주어는 주절의 주어(you)와 같고, 조건을 나타내는 부사절이므로 동사는 현재시제로 써서 If you talk with her로 바꿔 쓸 수 있다.

12 **|해석|** ① 도둑은 경찰관을 보자마자 도망쳤다.

② 나는 그의 전화번호를 몰라서 그에게 전화를 할 수 없었다.

③ 오른쪽으로 돌면 그 가게를 쉽게 찾을 수 있다.

④ 그는 음악을 들으면서 공원에서 달렸다.

⑤ Melanie는 너무 놀라서 거의 울 뻔했다.

|해설| ⑤ 부사절의 접속사를 생략하고, 주절의 주어와 부사절의 주어가 일치하므로 부사절의 주어를 생략하고, 동사를 현재분사(Being)로 바꿔 분사구문을 만든다. 분사구문에서 Being은 생략 가능하므로 Too surprised로 쓸 수 있다.

(① Saw → Seeing ② Didn't know → Not knowing ③ Turn → Turning ④ Being listened → Listening)

13 **|해석|** ① Tom은 나이가 들수록 수줍음이 많아졌다.

② Lisa는 경주를 마쳤을 때 기분이 무척 좋았다.

③ 엄마는 그곳에서 영어 선생님으로 일하신다.

④ 내가 이전에 말했듯이 연습은 완벽을 만든다.

⑤ 우리 모두가 알듯이, Andrew는 농구를 정말 잘한다.

|해설| ③의 as는 '~로서'라는 의미의 전치사로 쓰였고, 나머지는 모두 접속사로 쓰였다.

14 **|해석|** ⓐ 그는 아들을 생각하며 편지를 썼다.

ⓑ 그들은 내가 그들의 개를 찾아 준 것에 대해 고마워했다.

ⓒ 독감에 걸려서 나는 파티에 갈 수 없었다.

ⓓ 피곤하지 않아서 그는 계속 운동을 했다.

ⓔ 그 일을 하는 것은 쉽지 않았지만, 나는 그것을 즐겼다.

|해설| ⓐ, ⓒ, ⓓ는 분사구문에 쓰인 현재분사이고, ⓑ, ⓔ는 각각 전치사의 목적어와 주어로 쓰인 동명사이다.

15 **|해설|** '빅데이터 때문에 가능하다'라는 의미가 되어야 자연스러우므로 because of(~ 때문에)나 thanks to(~ 덕분에), with the help of(~의 도움으로)가 들어가는 것이 자연스럽다.

16 **|해설|** ⓐ complex(복잡한), ⓑ amount(양, 액수), ⓒ methods(방법들), ⓓ meaningful(의미 있는)이 들어가는 것이 알맞다.

17 **|해설|** 주어진 문장은 '하지만 단순히 데이터를 수집하는 것만으로는 충분하지 않다'라는 내용으로, 우리가 온라인에 남기는 모든 흔적이 빅데이터로 수집된다는 내용 뒤이자 '빅데이터는 분석되어야 한다'라는 내용 앞인 ③에 들어가는 것이 자연스럽다.

18 **|해설|** '~하기 위해 사용되다'의 의미가 되어야 하며, 뒤의 to predict와도 병렬 구조가 되어야 하므로 「be used to+동사원형」의 형태가 되는 것이 알맞다. 「be used to+동명사」는 '~하는 데 익숙하다'라는 의미이다.

19 **|해설|** (A) '~가 …하는 것을 돕다'는 「help+목적어+목적격보어(동사원형)」의 형태로 나타내므로 동사원형을 쓰는 것이 알맞다.

(B) '~하듯이'를 뜻하는 접속사 as가 알맞다.

(C) 독감의 확산이 '예측되어질' 수 있는 것이므로 수동태(be동사+과거분사)로 쓰는 것이 알맞다.

20 **|해석|** ⓐ 빅데이터는 소비자들을 어떻게 돕는가?

ⓑ 날씨 전문가들은 언제 빅데이터를 사용하기 시작했는가?

ⓒ 건강 전문가들은 빅데이터를 사용하여 현재 무엇을 예측할 수 있는가?

|해설| ⓒ 건강 전문가들은 빅데이터를 사용해서 질병을 예측할 수 있다.

21 **|해설|** ⓒ 빅데이터가 선수들의 경기력에 영향을 끼치는 한 예로 독일 국가 대표 축구팀의 경우를 설명하고 있으므로, 빈칸에는 example (예, 예시)이 알맞다.

22 **|해설|** 의문사가 사용된 간접의문문(의문사+주어+동사 ~)을 쓴다. (A)에는 '얼마나 많이'를 뜻하는 how much, (B)에는 '얼마나 오랫동안'을 뜻하는 how long을 사용한다.

23 **|해설|** ⓐ 주어(it)가 '일어나는' 것이므로 능동태인 happens가 알맞다.

ⓓ 동사 has changed를 수식하는 부사 greatly가 알맞다.

ⓔ '점점 더 ~한'은 「비교급+and+비교급」의 형태로 나타낸다.

24 **|해설|** '누구도 ~하지 않다'는 주어로 nobody를 사용하여 나타낼 수 있으며, nobody에 부정의 의미가 있으므로 동사를 부정의 표현으로 쓰지 않는다. '확실히 알다'는 know for sure로 나타낸다.

25 **|해설|** • 빅데이터 덕분에 경찰은 범죄 다발 지역의 지도를 만들 수 있다.

• 범죄 다발 지역의 지도는 범죄가 왜 일어날 것 같은지 알려 준다.

• 범죄 다발 지역의 지도가 제공하는 정보로 경찰은 범죄를 예방할 수 있다.

|해설| ⓑ 범죄 다발 지역의 지도가 범죄가 왜 일어날 것 같은지 알려 준다는 말은 본문에 언급되지 않았다.

memo

기출예상문제집

중학 영어 3-2 중간고사 윤정미

정답 및 해설

영역	브랜드	초1~2	초3~4	초5~6	중1	중2	중3	고1	고2	고3
독해	[중등] 기본서 READING CLEAR				READING CLEAR 1	READING CLEAR 2	READING CLEAR 3			
	[중등] 수능 대비서 **수작 중학 비문학 영어 독해**				수작 비문학 영어 독해	수작 비문학 영어 독해	수작 비문학 영어 독해			
	[고등] 기본서 **Supreme 구문독해 / 유형독해**							Supreme 구문독해 / Supreme 유형독해		
	[중·고등] 문장독해 **공식으로 통하는 문장독해** 기본 완성							공통문 / 공통문		
듣기	[중등] 듣기모의고사 **LISTENING CLEAR 중학영어 듣기모의고사**				LISTENING CLEAR 1	LISTENING CLEAR 2	LISTENING CLEAR 3			
	[고등] 듣기모의고사 **Supreme 수능 영어 듣기 모의고사** 기본 실전							Supreme / Supreme		
어휘	[초·중·고등] 영단어, 영숙어 **뜯어먹는 시리즈**	뜯어먹는 필수 영단어 1 / 뜯어먹는 필수 영단어 2			뜯어먹는 중학 기본 영단어 1200	뜯어먹는 1800	뜯어먹는 중학 영숙어 1000	뜯어먹는 수능 1등급 1800	뜯어먹는 수능 1등급 1800	뜯어먹는 1200
	[중·고등] 영단어 **보카클리어**				보카클리어	보카클리어	보카클리어	보카클리어 고등입문편	보카클리어 수능편